Global transformation

US paid for Viet by using "inflation tax" on others   176
loss of nat'l control over economy, 176

hoffmann, 70

Note to the reader from the UNU

In 1990 the United Nations University initiated the Programme on Multilateralism and the United Nations System (MUNS) to study the interaction between the changing structure of the world order and the process of international organization. The underlying assumption of the programme is that the world order sets the framework that conditions the kind of multilateralism that is possible; multilateralism, in turn, can influence the emerging shape of the world order. Multilateralism is given a broad meaning to encompass all those entities that may be or may become relevant to negotiation concerning general issues or issues in specific sectors of policy, whether at the world level or at the level of a more limited grouping.

This volume, representing the outcome of research on global structural change, examines the political, economic, and social implications of the post-Cold War transformation as perceived from various perspectives and regions. It addresses in particular the tension between globalization and democratization as it is manifested in different regions and cultures.

Global transformation: Challenges to the state system

Edited by Yoshikazu Sakamoto

**United Nations
University Press**

TOKYO • NEW YORK • PARIS

United Nations University Press
The United Nations University, 53-70, Jingumae 5-chome, Shibuya-ku, Tokyo 150, Japan
Tel: (03) 3499-2811   Fax: (03) 3406-7345
Telex: J25442   Cable: UNATUNIV TOKYO

Typeset by Asco Trade Typesetting Limited, Hong Kong
Printed by Permanent Typesetting and Printing Co., Ltd., Hong Kong
Cover design by Apex Production, Hong Kong

UNUP-855
ISBN 92-808-0855-9
04500 P

Contents

Foreword   ix
Acknowledgements   xiii

Editor's introduction   1

1   A perspective on the changing world order:
A conceptual prelude   15
Yoshikazu Sakamoto

Part I The Internationalization of the State

2   Globalization and the liberal democratic
state   57
David Held and Anthony McGrew

3   The internationalization of the state in the
Middle East   85
Nassif Hitti

v

Contents

4   The internationalization of the state: The case of Japan   107
Takehiko Kamo

5   The regional factor in the formation of a new world order   134
Björn Hettne

Part II   The globalization of political economy

6   Structural change and global political economy: Globalizing élites and the emerging world order   169
Stephen Gill

7   The cadre class and public multilateralism   200
Kees van der Pijl

8   The structure of finance in the world system   228
Susan Strange

9   Changing global finance structures: The impact on the Philippines   250
Leonor M. Briones and Aileen An. R. Zosa

10   The global restructuring of production and migration   276
James H. Mittelman

Part III   Transnational social movements

11   Citizens and the UN system in a changing world   301
Chadwick F. Alger

12   The democratization movement in Latin America: The case of Chile   330
Rodrigo Baño

vi

13 The transnational indigenous movement in a
    changing world order   356
    Bice Maiguashca

Part IV Change, violence, and normative order

14 Violence, resistance, and order in international
    relations   385
    Raimo Väyrynen

15 The United Nations and non-violence   412
    Toshiki Mogami

16 The changing world order and the international
    legal order: The structural evolution of
    international law beyond the state-centric
    model   439
    Georges Abi-Saab

17 The role of the United Nations in the context of
    the changing world order   462
    Maurice Bertrand

18 Democratizing, internationalizing, and
    globalizing   475
    Richard A. Falk

    Contributors and their main publications   503

385 – 402
475 – 99

Foreword

Multilateralism has become a growth industry among scholars. The reasons are readily apparent. The United Nations has once again become a centre of global diplomacy after having been marginalized in the foreign policies of the most powerful states during the Cold War years. The international economic agencies have never been more powerful than now in propagating a set of doctrines and policies. Power and influence attract attention, not least among scholars.

When the United Nations University launched a five-year study on multilateralism to run from 1991 through 1995 it was necessary to define an approach that would be at once distinctive in relation to many other studies and consistent with the basic aims of the UNU. Few social scientists nowadays will maintain that research can be or should pretend to be value free. It is thus of the first importance to make explicit the purposes and values of the Programme on Multilateralism and the United Nations System (MUNS).

There is a "mainstream" school of international organization studies that has privileged the analysis of "regimes." Regimes are the ways in which multilateral processes in specific issue areas are conventionally organized, whether through formal organization and regulation or through informal expectations of international behaviour. Despite the considerable work accomplished through this approach, one should bear in mind that the study of regimes in practice views multilateralism from the top down. It takes on the perspective of those forces with the most influence on outcomes – the Group of Seven (G7), the principal trading powers in the GATT, and the agencies of the world economy dominated by the richer countries. It tends to be policy driven in the short and medium term. It is centred upon states as the actors in multilateral relations. Regimes analysis is status quo oriented and aims at problem-solving in this context.

The MUNS programme, by contrast, has focused on long-term structural change, is critical rather than problem-solving in its approach,[1] and takes a bottom–up view, privileging the concerns and interests of the less powerful, while not ignoring the constraints imposed by the more powerful. Because these concerns are often more clearly apparent at the level of people than at the level of the state, MUNS has looked into the transformations of civil society and the democratization of political authority as component elements in a future multilateralism.

The MUNS programme has made its value preferences explicit: greater social equity, greater diffusion of power among countries and social groups, protection of the biosphere, moderation and non-violence in dealing with conflict, and mutual recognition of the equality of civilizations.

The programme's method has been to examine two dynamics: the dynamic of global structural change, and the dynamic of multilateralism. Global structural change defines the limits of the possible for a future multilateralism. Existing multilateralism can influence the direction of structural change within those limits. The programme has been designed and developed to explore the interrelationship of these two dynamics.

A number of projects exploring different aspects of these dynamics have resulted in the books that will form this series. One project reviews the study of multilateralism outside of the "mainstream" literature that is already easily accessible, mostly published in English and in the United States. The project looks particularly at work other than in the English language and that reflects perspectives from different cultures and regions. Another project took up and expanded a study initiated earlier by the Canadian Institute for International Peace and Security and the Academic Council of the United Nations System on the relationship between various countries and the UN system, giving emphasis to society as well as to the state in this relationship.[2]

The question of global structural change was taken up in a project that provided the basis for this first book in the series, *Global Transformation*, edited by Professor Yoshikazu Sakamoto. This project enquired into the changing character of the state and international relations, social forces and movements, and movements for democratization and human rights. The work of this project was extended through a symposium focusing more particularly on the global political economy.

The problematic of multilateralism in the context of the changing foundations of the world order and the perspectives of different cultures and civilizations is the theme of another project and book. Finally, projects envisage sources of innovation in multilateralism, and the salient tasks and political foundations for a new multilateralism.

Apart from the production of books, the MUNS programme has built up a network of scholars committed to the study of multilateralism and the world order who have contributed in some manner to MUNS. This network may prove to be its main legacy. The network embraces senior and junior scholars, people from South and North, women and men. The programme has aimed at comprehensiveness and diversity among its participants. A particular point has been to encourage younger scholars, amongst whom lies the promise of continuing development of the intellectual process initiated through MUNS. Young academics and graduate students who have undertaken research on aspects of multilateralism have been invited as participants to the various symposia convened under the auspices of MUNS. A special event was organized by the international relations department of the University of Amsterdam with presentations by a dozen graduate students about their research before a panel of senior scholars (October 1993). MUNS will encourage emulation of this model by other university centres. The network will continue the initiative of MUNS beyond the termination of its formal existence as a UNU-financed programme.

Robert W. Cox
Programme Coordinator

Notes

1. I use the term "critical" to describe an enquiry into how an institution or practice came into being and what forces may be changing the framework within which it operates, whereas "problem-solving" takes that framework as given and examines only how the institution or practice operates within the given framework.
2. This earlier study is being published by UNU Press as a companion volume to the MUNS study.

Acknowledgements

This book is a product of the intensive discussion among the contributors who participated in the first phase of the United Nations University Programme on Multilateralism and the United Nations System, directed by Robert W. Cox. We are indebted to him for his intellectual insights and thoughtful coordination.

Our gratitude also goes to the United Nations University, particularly to Dr. Takeo Uchida, for the continued support and concern for this project; to Governor Kazuji Nagasu and his staff of Kanagawa Prefecture for hosting a conference in Yokohama, without which direct dialogue among the contributors would not have been possible; and to the staff of the International Peace Research Institute of Meiji Gakuin University for the administrative assistance offered for the conduct of the project. Further, we are grateful to the Peace Research Institute of the International Christian University, Tokyo, for its support, which made it possible for me to complete the editorial work.

Yoshikazu Sakamoto

Editor's introduction

I

Underlying the present global transformation, there seem to be forces that are generating fundamental changes on two dimensions – change toward internationalization and change toward democratization. The former, an evolving process of extension, cuts across the boundaries of the state, society, and region; the latter, a process of deepening, cuts across the boundaries of class, race, religion, ethnicity, gender, age, etc., in a society. Each trend gives rise to a variety of conflicts – for instance, internationalization to trade frictions, and democratization to populist unrest. More fundamental, however, seems to be the contradiction between internationalization and democratization.

In theory, there is nothing intrinsically contradictory about internationalization and democratization. The ideal harmony between the two was emphasized in the Wilsonian ideology. In practice, however, contradictions are inevitable because internationalization proceeds unequally and unevenly. Let us examine how internationalization develops.

1

II

Today, internationalization is under way on two closely interrelated levels – internationalization of the state and globalization of the capitalist market economy.

It goes without saying that, in the contemporary world, no "sovereign" state can act in isolation from or in disregard of other states without inflicting considerable damage on itself. The "impermeability" that characterized the classical model of the sovereign state is being widely challenged.

Obviously, the internationalization of the state is closely related to the globalization of the capitalist economy; but the former is not determined only by the latter. First, the internationalization of the state has been under way as a result of those strategic factors in the age of nuclear and high-tech weapons systems, those informational factors in the age of the global communication village, and those ecological factors that made the sovereign state permeable. Secondly, globalization of the economy does not of necessity lead to internationalization of the state; on the contrary, the political response may take the opposite form of nationalist protectionism.

What is perhaps more important is the fact that the general trend toward interpenetration and interdependence develops, first and foremost, on the level of the advantaged in the system of the world – the advantaged who have the informational, human and material resources at their disposal that make it possible for them to utilize the potential of internationalization for their interests. Internationalization, therefore, proceeds in the North, among big powers, among big business, and among the governing élites, such as international bureaucrats, much ahead of, and often at the expense of, the South, smaller nations, labour and smaller business, and the people.

It must always be questioned who promotes internationalization, for whom and how. Differentiation is inevitable between those who are advantaged and disadvantaged by a particular process of internationalization. Hence the suspicion, reluctance, or even opposition on the part of the disadvantaged in regard to internationalization; and correspondingly, the need for the advantaged to legitimize the internationalization process in the eyes of the public at home and abroad by creating the image that internationalization is going hand in hand with democratization, benefiting the population at large.

To illustrate this intricate relationship between the two trends, the

policy pursued by the United States in the first post-Cold War international crisis (i.e. the Gulf War) may be cited.

As a result of the demise of the Soviet Union, the strategic bipolar
system turned into a unipolar system, with the United States holding
unrivalled military hegemony. This was quite visible at the time of the
Gulf War. Yet, internationalization of the state showed a dual development.

On the one hand, the United States dominated or "hijacked" the
United Nations and the multinational coalition forces. Internationalization of the state in this respect took the form of incorporating other
states into the hierarchical system of US military hegemony in the
interests of the United States. Thus, the UN authorization of war became almost coterminous with the legitimation of the United States'
hegemonic internationalization of member states.

On the other hand, it may also be noted that it is precisely at this
juncture that the United States acted in the name of international organization (UN). In international relations, to act within the multilateral framework of international organization implies the admission
that the democratic consent of other member states be secured.
Even if the United States had the military capability, if not sufficient
financial capability, to enforce its policy, it could not provide by itself
the legitimation of its action. Further, legitimation of internationalization in terms of democracy, not hegemony, is called for particularly when, as a result of the demise of authoritarian state socialism,
the very democracy for which the United States stands has conceivably demonstrated and reinforced its legitimacy in terms of international universality.

Thus, the United States had to rely on the United Nations as a
source not only of the internationalization of power (and "burden")
but also of the internationalization of legitimacy, which implies the
internationalization of the democratic source of legitimacy.

This is in sharp contrast with the Cold War period when, as dramatized by the Cuban missile crisis in 1962, the United States was almost
ready to go to nuclear war alone, without calling for a UN resolution
to legitimize nuclear war or even the prior consent of its Western
allies. The same is true of the war in Viet Nam.

It has now become increasingly difficult and undesirable for even a
hegemonic military power to engage in a relatively large-scale military operation without creating the impression that legitimacy based
on democratic consent has been accorded by the international com-

munity. This requirement has become unmistakably clear during the initial phase of the US deployment of force in Somalia for apparent humanitarian considerations. At the same time, this universal democratic commitment soon revealed its conflict with the hegemonic power considerations of the United States. This indicates the duality of the action of a power that calls for internationalized legitimacy in today's world.

Thus, in comparison with the exercise of the sovereignty of a single power, *internationalized Realpolitik* of the advantaged is bound to be more vulnerable to criticism of the disadvantaged (e.g. the Palestinians) on the grounds of inequitable "double-standards." The more universalized a legitimation is, the more conspicuous the inegalitarian, discriminatory practices become. This is nothing but a manifestation of the potential contradiction between the internationalization of the state, on the one hand, and democratization, on the other.

A similar contradiction is observable in connection with the globalization of the market economy.

III

As a result of the collapse of state socialism, the world has acquired essential homogeneity as a single capitalist market. The globalization of the capitalist economy, while making the world economy more interpenetrating and interdependent than before, involves world society in intensified competition.

As in the case of the internationalization of the state, the globalization of capitalist marketization is led, first and foremost, by the advantaged, such as competitive capitalist and high-tech élites and, in the words of Robert Reich (*The Work of Nations*, New York, 1991), "high-value, symbolic-analytic services," at the expense of high-volume businesses and low-skilled labour.

In the former socialist bloc, the introduction of a competitive market economy has widened the socio-economic gap between the advantaged and disadvantaged. On the level of the North–South divide, with the exception of the newly industrializing economies (NIEs), the disparity has gone from bad to worse. Even within the North, the gap between the rich and poor is growing, while the position of the middle class is downgraded.

In fact, the globalization of the capitalist economy is best demonstrated by the globalization of the widening gap and increasing inequality between the North and the South, within the South, and within the North. There is an undeniable contradiction between the globalization of the market economy and that of democracy.

This contradiction can be seen in the emergence of a counter-trend in response to the trend of inequitable development. In opposition to the internationalization promoted by capital, protectionist tendencies are likely to experience a resurgence among the disadvantaged, particularly those sectors that are adversely affected by internationalization owing to their lack of competitiveness. Further, internationalization of labour, particularly the rapidly growing international migration from the South to the North, has aggravated ethnic tension and even evoked a violent protectionist response in the North. Thus, protectionism in relation to trade, investment, and migration reinforces ethno-nationalism, and vice versa.

It is said that the end of the Cold War gave rise to the eruption of ethno-nationalist conflict. Since ethno-nationalist conflicts in various parts of the world predate the Cold War, a critical examination is needed in order to determine whether and in what respects the conflict is a consequence of the end of the Cold War.

It is true that the world has been characterized by the universalization of nationalism as a result of the disintegration of the multi-ethnic Soviet bloc. It would therefore appear that the universalization of nationalism has culminated in the resurgence of nationalism in the Soviet Union and Eastern Europe as well as the earlier reinstatement of ethnic identity in the United States, Western Europe, and practically every region of the world.

IV

Nevertheless, we do not in this book attach as much importance to the universalization of nationalism as we do to internationalization and democratization because we consider that the latter two have much greater *long-term* implications than do the former for the future development of world order.

In our view, there is a paradox in the universalization of nationalism in the sense that it will foreshadow the end of the age of traditional nationalism. By traditional nationalism we mean the policy and movement aimed at establishing a sovereign state in which the unit is identical with the underlying national cultural community.

It seems that, precisely as a result of the universalization of nationalism, two things have become clear to the people. First, what has long been perceived as a "nation-state" is nothing more than a state of the dominant national or ethnic group, characterized by discrimination against national/ethnic minorities. Secondly, building a nation-state in accordance with the traditional principle of the self-determination of every national/ethnic group is impossible and, if enforced, is likely to lead to violence and bloodshed to the detriment of the national/ethnic groups themselves. This hold true particularly in an age when the universalization of nationalism coincides with rapidly growing international migration, including relocation of refugees.

Thus, the search for national/ethnic identity will have to opt either for political self-government of one form or another, or for equal, non-discriminatory social status, both within the larger framework of a state that will assume the character of a *multicultural political federation*. Separation of the political unit and the cultural unit is necessary and even inevitable. In other words, it is no longer on the basis of individual national self-determination but on the basis of *multicultural collective self-determination* that the political framework called the state will retain its resilience and legitimacy.

Thus, precisely as a result of the universalization of nationalism, we are witnessing the beginning of the end of traditional nationalism. And, in its relation to other national/ethnic groups, the new identity has to be defined on the basis of *egalitarian association*, which is the synthesis of "inter-nationalization" and "democratization," or inter-nationalized democracy (with "nations" referring to ethnic groups as well). This will of course be a thorny path; but the experience of West European peoples who have undergone critical phases of nationalism much ahead of other nations indicates what is likely to come next. There is an element of *déjà vu* in the ethno-national conflict of the present world.

Further, with respect to the internal structure of a national/ethnic group, nationalism could become oppressive unless it is coupled with democracy. Nationalism will contradict itself if it alienates or antagonizes the people of the nation.

It may be noted that this alienation of the people could be the function not only of an oppressive nationalist state but also of populist nationalism, which brings about a monolithic state ostensibly "from below."

Nationalism can continue to perform a liberating function provided that it joins hands with democracy in its resistance to oppression. This point has become abundantly clear precisely to those peoples in the South, and now those in the former "East" as well, who have undergone the phase of post-independence disenchantment with "national liberation" that did not lead to the liberation of the people. It is also in this sense that the age of traditional nationalism is coming to an end.

V

We have observed so far that internationalization of the state will reinforce the hierarchical structure of the world unless it is coupled with the establishment of the democratic rights of the disadvantaged people, and that globalization of the capitalist market economy will aggravate global disparity and inequality unless it is coupled with national and international policy and popular movements for equitable, sustainable development. In other words, it is with reference only to the dynamic of democratization that the question has to be answered whether or not the trend toward internationalization will provide opportunities and positive implications for the present and future of the people of the world.

In fact, in the light of recent developments in the "East" and the South, including South Africa, it seems that we are witnessing, for the first time in history, the beginning of the age of the globalization of democracy and democratic values – democracy that is recognized as the most fundamental principle of universal validity. Obviously there is a gap, even an enormous gap, between the globalization of democratic values and the globalization of democratic practice. A long process of democratic struggle is called for in order to fill the gap. This is natural because democracy is not a static institution but is essentially a perpetual process of activation and reactivation of people's commitment to democratic values.

In dealing with the globalization of democracy, we must take note of the following point.

A clear distinction must be made between inter-nation democracy and global democracy, because the former, as illustrated by the "democratization of the United Nations," will not in itself bring about positive consequences. It may or it may not, depending on whether democratization does or does not stop at the inter-nation level, failing to deepen itself further to the level of the democracy of citizens.

In the context of the relative decline of US hegemony and the development of multipolarization, the demand for inter-nation equalization of power could lead to a world that is highly egalitarian in terms of the distribution of military capability. This might be a world where every nation has acquired a most sophisticated modern weap-

7

ons system; this might be a world where nuclear weapons have proliferated equally to all nations. This is a Hobbesian state of nature that is universally nuclearized. This might be a highly egalitarian world; but it would be a horrible disutopia, and its occurrence cannot be totally dismissed. For instance, what else does the poor and powerless South have, as some leaders in the South ask, as leverage to force the North to take North–South issues seriously?

This could conceivably be an egalitarian world on the inter-nation level. The heavily armed and highly militarized states, however, would be very inegalitarian in their domestic structure. These states would be quite oppressive, marginalizing deprived peasants, the urban poor, and ethnic minorities; they would be likely to be patriarchal, discriminating against women. This is egalitarian "democracy" of the state, not of the people. This is a democratic rhetoric of the state, not the principle of citizen's democracy that we refer to in terms of the "globalization of democracy."

VI

In the context of the dialectic between internationalization and democratization discussed above, this book consists of four parts: I, The Internationalization of the State; II, The Globalization of Political Economy; III, Transnational Social Movements; and IV, Change, Violence, and Normative Order.

We begin with the internationalization of the state, since our main focus is on the structural change of the state system – the system that is the foundation of modern international order. Then parts II and III shed light on the global political–economic forces and the transnational socio-political forces that have brought about the changes occurring in the state system in terms of internationalization and democratization. Part IV deals with the implications of the changing state system for the issues of violence, international legal norms, international organization represented by the United Nations, and the dialectic between the resilient state system and the growing democratic challenges to the Westphalian normative order.

The introductory chapter 1 (Sakamoto) presents a conceptual framework for a macro-historical interpretation of the changing world order, and its implications for theories of "international relations." By focusing on the complex historical dialectic of capitalism vs. socialism, nationalism vs. internationalism, and democracy vs. authoritarianism, this chapter is also intended to provide a comprehensive conceptual framework for this volume. It will encompass the diverse perspectives that characterize the following multifaceted analysis – for example, the specifically political-economy perspective developed mainly in part II and the socio-political and institutional perspectives shown in other chapters.

In part I, which deals with *The Internationalization of the State*, chapter 2 (Held and McGrew) discusses the implications of globalization processes, which are promoted by Europe itself, for the European liberal democratic state, with special reference to the disjunctures (in the areas of security, economy, government, and law) between the state in its national setting and the dynamics of the global order, and also the implications of these changes for political theory and international relations theory as well as democratic politics, all based on the nation-state system model.

In the Middle East, in contrast, which is dealt with in chapter 3 (Hitti), the internationalization of the state is taking place as a result of the external impact of the United States and the European Union (EU) and of the penetration of the triumphant model of a liberal, utilitarian market economy, both on a scale that transcends individual states. Further, the state in this region, again unlike in Europe, has never firmly established its legitimacy in the face of the internal impact of Arab nationalists and Islamists, both of whom activate trans-state, regional loyalties. The overall effect seems to be the construction of regional and subregional orders.

Standing in-between these two models is a variation, Japan, which is the subject of chapter 4 (Kamo). In the context of its modern history since the end of the last century, what we today term "internationalization" amounted to a nationalist, or even imperialist, ideology in defence of the "Westernization," industrialization, militarization, and de-Asianization of Japan aimed at catching up with Western empires. In the post-World War II period, internationalization was largely equated with Americanization. In the post-Cold War phase, the discrepancy between its economic internationalization and its politico-cultural particularism, which alienates its regional partners, is creating critical uncertainties.

Chapter 5 (Hettne) presents a comparative overview of the regionalization that is going on throughout the world, though with a high degree of complexity and diversity. This change is taking place at three interacting levels: the structure of the world system, e.g. the demise of the bipolar hegemonic regionalism; interregional relations, with European regionalism acting as the trigger for global regionalization; and the internal pattern of each region, where tendencies toward economic and political homogeneity, toward a "regional civil society" based on a common cultural identity, and toward a shared security order for intraregional conflict management emerge.

Part II, *The Globalization of Political Economy*, begins with chapter 6 (Gill), which analyses the current process of global restructuring led by globalizing élites consisting of the capitalist class and the "cadres." Beneath the cadre stratum are located the segmented labour force and still more marginalized people, such as indigenous peoples. Despite the conflict in the debate among the élites between "trilateralism" and "three blocism," the prevailing neo-liberal perspectives stress economic efficiency, competition, and global factor mobility in favour of the "new constitutionalism," which generates increasing hierarchies of power and deepening social inequality, which contradict democracy.

Shedding light on the process of global restructuring by specifically focusing on the change that took place in the cadre stratum in advanced capitalism and public multilateralism, chapter 7 (Van der Pijl) examines the reformist role played by the radicalized cadre class in the early 1970s in support of regulation, and its defeat in the face of the neo-liberal transnational counter-offensive in the 1980s, which achieved the deregulation and globalization of capital on the level of the world economy, particularly global finance, and also on the level of the United Nations system.

Chapter 8 (Strange) analyses changes in world finance in terms of its enormous growth in size, its rapid change in technology, its increasing penetration of national financial markets, the increased competition with reduced regulation, and the changed relation of demand and supply. In the context of this structural change in global finance, the power to control finance shifted from governments to markets, debtors suffered so much that the reverse flow of funds from South to North increased, the old and the uneducated were adversely affected, and the negative effects on democracy were hardly avoidable, resulting in a derogation of popular power as well as of the bargaining power of organized labour.

Complementing the previous chapter, chapter 9 (Briones and Zosa) reports from a Southern perspective on the impact of changing global finance structures on the Philippines, one of the highly marginalized debtor countries. Adversely affected by the shift in priorities of global finance from the South to the former "East" and by the structural adjustment programmes, the debtors have been afflicted by negative resource transfers in favour of the North, exacer-bated economic and social inequalities, and export promotion at the expense of basic social services. External debt is the source as well as the consequence of the unequal global economic power structure. To help the poor of indebted countries survive and develop themselves, greater roles have to be played by non-governmental organizations (NGOs), social movements, and UN agencies.

Besides the financial flow, migratory flows have been restructured, as examined in chapter 10 (Mittelman), in accordance with the global restructuring of production. Further, the global restructuring of power has stimulated migration from the "East," generating competi-tion with the South. In the North–South setting, the benefits of migration have been distributed unequally; and the feminization of labour generally reinforces gender discrimination. Multiculturalism in the workforce tends to make culture play a role in labour segmen-tation. Multilateralism, if it is based on the sovereignty of the nation-state, embodies fundamental human dilemmas that globalized pro-duction and migration have thrust into sharp relief.

While the two preceding parts deal with the challenge of interna-tionalization, some cases of democratic response are treated in part III, *Transnational Social Movements*. Chapter 11 (Alger) provides an analytical framework in which the transnational citizens' move-ments and the United Nations system in their dynamic interaction – an area of marginal interest for traditional international relations the-ory – are identified as critical agents of global transformation. The dynamics can be observed in the UN system's conduct of its relations with non-governmental organizations, NGO participation in UN glo-bal conferences, and citizens' positive role of great diversity focused on human rights and development issues.

The democratization movement that developed transnationally in Latin America through complex politico-economic processes is ana-lysed in chapter 12 (Baño) with specific reference to the case of Chile. While generating pressures against human rights violation, the West, particularly the United States (and the International Mone-tary Fund and the World Bank), gave determined support to the regime's neo-liberal economic policy, which altered the social struc-ture. The extreme left failed to adapt to the new structure, and the moderate centre–left coalition gave the democratic transition its def-initive push. But a mass of urban poor, the product of the structural change, have been de-activated and left unrepresented, posing a problem yet to be resolved under the new democracy.

11

Of a variety of new critical social movements (environment, equitable development, human rights, women, peace, etc.), the international indigenous movement is taken up in chapter 13 (Maiguashca) as one of the fundamental challenges to the normative foundations of today's international system. It emerged in the context of the global expansion of capitalism, which posed the threat of displacement, the expansion of the nation-state, which generated the threat of assimilation, and the development of international law, which provides a potential resource for indigenous peoples. Their counter-hegemonic project has developed the indigenous cosmocentric view of economy and culture, the collective egalitarian view of peoples and rights, and the non-Eurocentric concept of "internal self-determination."

It may be noted in this connection that part III was originally intended to include one chapter each on the democratization movement in Africa, the feminist movement, and the environmental movement. To our regret, we had not been able to ensure the participation of the authors on these topics by the time the conference of contributors was held. Fortunately, articles on the global women's movement will be included in another book to be published later on this programme of the United Nations University.

In the era of global transformation, reflections on the visions of global normative order and its institutionalization are called for. Equally crucial is a critical examination of the changing role of the violence and non-violence involved in the transformative process.

Part IV, *Change, Violence, and Normative Order*, begins with chapter 14 (Väyrynen), which presents a theoretical overview of the contemporary discourse on violence and order in international relations. The focus of analysis is on the issues of democracy and war, centred on the Kantian thesis; on the taxonomy of violence in terms of instrumental vs. expressive, rational vs. legitimate, actor-specific vs. structural; and on the relations between violence, power, competence, and non-violence, with special reference to the emancipatory "power of the powerless" demonstrated in Eastern European revolutions. In the light of this conceptual analysis, the prospective order of Europe can be envisaged as a non-Clausewitzian regional "concert."

Chapter 15 (Mogami) points to the contradiction that the United Nations, labelled as a peace organization, takes it for granted that unit violence of the sovereign state should be countervailed by the collective superviolence of the United Nations, not by non-violence. Since this dialectic suggests the transitory nature of the United Nations with regard to violence, the relevance of non-violence to the United Nations has to be enhanced by giving substance to the prevention and peaceful settlement of disputes, by making peace-keeping forces maximally non-violent and peace-enforcement units non-combatively enforcive, not non-enforcively combative as in the Congo, and by acting as a guardian of the right to peaceful existence, paying greater attention to the elimination of structural violence.

Reflecting on the changing international legal order, chapter 16 (Abi-Saab) elucidates that, in the post-World War II period, the human hold on nature (nuclear energy, seabed, space), the communications revolution, the growing awareness of ecological limits, and the advent of new states with heterogeneous civilizational and colonial backgrounds brought about contradictory legal responses and consequences. Whereas the unilateral approach, which led to the extension of the state's jurisdiction (e.g. high seas), contributed to the intensification of jurisdictional conflict and the growing recognition of the limits of state control, the multilateral collaborative approach, which led to the proliferation of international organizations, gave rise to renewed awareness of the limits of solidarity and the resistance of states.

The role to be played by the United Nations in coping with these dilemmas is critically examined in chapter 17 (Bertrand). The apparent renaissance of the United Nations is due to the US hegemony in the United Nations, which, while refusing to activate the North–South dialogue, led to its selective use of the United Nations' "collective security" mechanisms. As the sources of global insecurity will increasingly be located in the North–South divide and intra-state conflict, the present collective security system would transform the United Nations into a specialized agency legitimizing repressive roles in the South. Instead, a new United Nations should be devoted to the preventive eradication of the causes of world insecurity through the globalization of the "working peace system" (European Union) and the "cooperative security" approach (Conference on Security and Cooperation in Europe), which requires a radical change in the attitude of the North.

Finally, chapter 18 (Falk) presents an interpretation of the dynamic of contemporary global transformation from three complementary perspectives: the structure of global apartheid that underlies the world political economy; the heated race between environmental degradation and environmentalism; and growing democratizing challenges to the Westphalian normative order. The resilience of the

13

state system is tested (1) by internationalizing market forces, (2) by the environmental agenda, (3) by corporate and even geopolitical pressures for global governance, and (4) by the globalization of information/popular culture. The state will show its resilience by aligning with these globalizing tendencies, which, however, reveal a contradictory potential by promoting the emergence of global civil society and forces of global democratization.

As part of the programme on Multilateralism and the United Nations System, all the chapters in this volume are devoted to critical reflections on the structural transformation that the world is undergoing.

1

A perspective on the changing world order: A conceptual prelude

Yoshikazu Sakamoto

In the light of developments since the late 1980s, it is clear to everyone that a global change is under way. It is, however, not clear exactly what is changing, how, and into what. Why?

One obvious reason is that, although it can be determined that an era has come to an end, it cannot of necessity be determined what will come next. More specifically, the way the next era will be created depends on how the political and economic forces that constitute this process of change interpret the change and act accordingly. In the process of change is involved an element of subjective interpretation and action, i.e. "reflexivity" (Giddens, 1990), without which no historical change develops. We must, then, ask what is the appropriate way to interpret and conceptualize the contemporary global change.

One can, of course, take the view that this global change was a consequence of the ending of the Cold War. Thus the present can be defined as the "post-Cold War" phase, with the end of the Cold War serving as the point of origin of the present. It is true that the end of the Cold War marked a dramatic turn in post-World War II history. But does it mean that the change the world is undergoing is a consequence of the end of the Cold War?

For instance, is the eruption of ethnic conflict almost all over the world a result of the end of the Cold War? Or is ethno-nationalism one of the forces that brought about the collapse of the Soviet empire in Eastern Europe? Similarly, is democratization in the Soviet Union and Eastern Europe a result of the end of the Cold War? Or is it one of the engines that brought about the collapse of the Soviet empire and the regimes of its satellites?

In brief, are the end of the Cold War itself and the subsequent developments not manifestations or consequences of a much deeper change that the world has been undergoing? To appreciate the meaning of a fundamental transformation like the one we are witnessing today, is it not imperative for us to conceptualize the contemporary phase of history not merely as the "post-Cold War" period but as a manifestation of a deeper and longer-term historical change that has generated shorter-term changes such as the Cold War and the subsequent change called the post-Cold War era?

This is the question this essay addresses. To answer this question, one must first of all ascertain what the Cold War was. Then, one may be able to determine whether the end of the Cold War can be considered to be the cause of the subsequent changes or whether both the Cold War and its end should be treated as a manifestation of a more fundamental historical development.

Conceptualization of the Cold War

The Cold War was generally conceived as consisting of two dimensions. On the one hand, it was a conflict of two ideologies, defined either in terms of the socio-economic system ("capitalism vs. socialism") or in terms of the political system ("liberal democracy vs. communist totalitarianism").[1] Ideology refers to the principle of the system of society; and, although the ideological conflict had two aspects (i.e. economic and political), it was generally assumed that capitalism and liberal democracy are characterized by affinity, as are socialism and communist totalitarianism. In fact, one of the salient features of the Cold War was the tendency to dismiss the fact that these equations are not always tenable in the light of modern historical developments.

On the other hand, the Cold War was defined as a conflict between two big powers or "superpowers," particularly with reference to their nuclear capacity to annihilate humankind. It was argued that it did

16

not matter whether Russia was communist or tsarist; as long as it was a superpower with its own geopolitical interests, conflict with another superpower, the United States, was inevitable (Morgenthau, 1951). It was this bipolar power-political structure that gave rise to the precarious balance of power (or terror) situation called the Cold War.

Although views diverged as to which dimension, ideological or geopolitical, should be considered to be of primary importance, a general conception emerged that the Cold War was a complex superimposition of the two.[2]

This twofold conception of the Cold War or the East–West conflict provided a cognitive framework for those who were involved in the conflict and acted in accordance with the way the conflict was defined by the parties. The policy makers and opinion leaders during the Cold War period generally formulated their views on the conflict within the framework of the variations of the twofold conception. For them the task was to assess how the ideological conflict evolved, how the power-political or geopolitical rivalry unfolded, and how the combination of the two gave rise to the vicissitudes of the power relations between the East and the West, in the context of which decisions had to be made to gain as much advantage as possible.

In other words, for them the East–West conflict was a *given* and the main issue was essentially "strategic" – i.e. how to maximize payoffs under the conditions of the Cold War. They did not, and they thought they did not have to, think about what would occur *after* the Cold War was over and what the long-term, macro-historical meaning of the Cold War would be. In fact, the views and actions geared to the idea that the Cold War could be brought to an end were often regarded as "unrealistic." The lack of consciousness of the terminability of the Cold War was so deep-seated that the lack itself remained unconscious (Gaddis, 1992, preface).

In this respect, the twofold conception of the Cold War was *ahistorical* – namely, bipolar geopolitical conflict is perennial, and the ideological conflict is a matter of timeless principle, right or wrong. Both defy historicity. The Cold War discourse was based on the implicit, if not explicit, premise that the Cold War would *conceptually* continue indefinitely. This conceptual ahistoricity is best illustrated by the widespread acceptance of ahistorical game theory as the model of decision-making and decision-making analysis with "scientific" credibility (Schelling, 1963). The general failure of the mainstream political leaders and strategists to foresee and envisage the ending of the

Cold War points to an unmistakable conceptual deficiency in their thinking.

Furthermore, the following two features of the US–USSR conflict contributed to reinforcing this ahistorical conceptualization. First, on the level of power politics, the conflict centred on nuclear rivalry, which was the race of "ultimate" or "absolute" weapons. This gave rise to a military eschatology that the emergence of nuclear weapons would foreshadow "the end of history." If there were to be no further changes, there was no point in historical thinking. Second, on the level of ideological conflict, whereas the United States was convinced that American democracy and the American way of life were the best in the world, the USSR presented communism as the final, highest stage of historical development. Each took the position that the challenge to its own ideology, whether it was "the world revolution" or "the imperialist counter-revolution," stemmed from outside, as if there could be no source of self-transformation from within. This was another form of "the end of history." All these features aggravated the ahistoricity of the concept of the Cold War held on both sides.

Nowadays everybody would agree that it is unrealistic to insist that the Cold War has not ended. The present focus of public debate is on the post-Cold War world. To identify the main features of the post-Cold War world, however, it is not adequate to define the "post-Cold War" period as merely "*post* Cold War," using the Cold War as the point of reference. To understand the implications of the historic change under way, we should not conceptualize the present only as "post Cold War" as distinct from the Cold War but should consider both the Cold War and the post-Cold War as the manifestation of a more profound change. This is not to suggest that we dismiss the significance of the change that took place between the Cold War phase and the post-Cold War; it is to interpret this change as a continuation of the change that, at a certain phase of its development, took the form of the Cold War.[3]

Three dimensions of modern global conflict

To place the Cold War in the context of relative historicity does not diminish its historical importance. On the contrary, what constituted the dual conflict that characterized the Cold War can be considered to be of great significance since it was a particular manifestation of a deeper contradiction that underlies modern historical developments. It refers to a fundamental contradiction on the following three dimensions, in terms of which major conflicts and changes in modern history can be accounted for: capitalism (C) vs. socialism (S); state nationalism (N) vs. internationalism (I); and democracy (D) vs. authoritarianism (A). What is termed here an "ism" refers not merely to an ideology but to a driving force that generates historical changes with a particular orientation toward "structuration." To understand modern historical changes, this conceptual framework is adopted for two reasons.

First, it is true that historical change cannot be appreciated without identifying who the agents of change are. And, obviously, the agents who constitute a historical driving force of a particular orientation toward "structuration" vary depending on the historical and social contexts. It is, therefore, of crucial importance for decision makers and scientific observers to identify the agents in the context of historical and regional diversity. Despite their immense diversity, however, the historical roles played by a variety of agents can be categorized with reference to these three fundamental macro-historical contradictions. The threefold conceptual basket is used by us because the primary purpose of this essay concerns the interpretation of the *meaning* of historical changes rather than the identification of the agents of change.

Secondly, it would appear that, since the industrial revolution that initially took place in Europe, these three contradictions have engendered fundamental conflicts and the evolution of these conflicts either within a society or a state, or between societies or states, or both. These conflicts are fundamental because they stem from the dialectic of three sets of structures (C vs. S; N vs. I; and A vs. D) that are fundamentally contradictory. Of course, conflict among capitalisms, and particularly among nationalisms, has also been a source of significant change. It is, however, precisely the conflict among nationalisms that has recurrently given rise to the counter-actions on the part of governments, firms, and citizens aimed at establishing international norms and rules of conduct; and the contradiction between nationalism and internationalism is of a more fundamental nature, particularly from a long-term historical perspective. And these three fundamental contradictions have generated "world conflict" and consequent changes in the sense that no society or state can be immune from the structural constraints of these contradictions. For this reason, the basket is used in this essay as a conceptual framework for the understanding of fundamental changes in modern history.

It may be noted in this connection that we make a distinction between "early starter" and "latecomer" in terms of the uneven industrialization of nations. This distinction is important because industrialization brings about a qualitative change in the structure of production as well as the productivity of a capitalist society or the world as a whole. For this reason, this essay focuses on the age of "industrial capitalism," taking both the Weberian and the Durkheimian perspectives into consideration.

It may also be mentioned that we adopt a *complex* model consisting of three dimensions, such as economic system, international system, and internal political system, because it is imperative to treat these dimensions holistically, without taking a reductionist approach either from the inside to the outside, or the other way round.

Of these three sets of concepts, "nationalism" is most elusive. It can be "imperialist"; it can be "anti-imperialist." Here it refers to the primary political orientation to the self-identified "sovereign nation-state," which may include an empire. The term "state nationalism" is used because the so-called "nation-state," which in reality comprises without exception more than one nationality, embodies the nationalism of the dominant national or ethnic group in the state who claim that it is they, not subordinate or marginalized minorities, who constitute the "state." If we borrow the remark of Louis XIV, who said, "L'État, c'est moi," it is this *state-nation* that asserts, "L'État, c'est *nous*." In this respect, every "nation-state" is an empire.[4]

"Internationalism" refers both to the driving force that enhances international or inter-state cooperation and organization and to that which promotes transnational "cobweb" building. "Authoritarianism" includes the force that buttresses exclusionary state power, limiting the political participation of citizens, and also that which supports the state power of totalitarian mobilization.

It goes without saying that one of the fundamental features of modern history is "uneven development," which manifests itself in a variety of complex nexus. First, each component of the contradictions mentioned above develops unevenly. This is not confined to capitalist economic development. It also applies to the development of nationalism and that of democracy (and also to their respective antitheses). Uneven capitalist economic development gives rise to structural disparity, such as the metropole's domination and the periphery's dependence; the uneven development of nationalism engenders the system of political/military imperialism and colonized society, including internal imperialism imposed on national minorities; and the uneven development of democracy leads to international conflict between political ideologies in terms of civil liberties and human rights.

Secondly, uneven development manifests itself cross-dimensionally. For instance, a certain mode of capitalist development is likely to be coupled with a certain mode of nationalism and a certain mode of democracy or authoritarianism. The historical implications of these various modes of composite uneven development will be examined below. It must be noted in this connection that this composite development does not mean that the development of nationalism or democracy can be considered as a direct function of the development of capitalism. No simple causal relations can be posited among the three categories of development.

Thirdly, uneven development gives rise to political and social counter-moves and counter-movements opposed to the inequality and inequity resulting from uneven development, and they too develop unevenly.

In sum, all these constitute the complex dialectical processes and structures of modern world development.

Capitalism–nationalism–democracy model

The engine of what Polanyi termed the "great transformation" (Polanyi, 1957) and concomitant uneven development in modern history included the leading "advanced countries" in the nineteenth-century West, i.e. Great Britain, the United States, and, to a lesser extent, France, which acquired the mode of development characterized by the composite formation of three forces of change: *capitalism–nationalism–democracy* (C–N–D). Naturally, there were variations in the mode of development in these three countries.

While the capitalist–democratic development underwent a series of revolutions and counter-revolutions in France and the Civil War in the United States, it grew in Great Britain within the framework of parliamentary reform. Whereas nationalism was articulate, politicized (even revolutionized), and "formal" in France and relatively diffuse and distinctively isolationist (from Europe) in the United States, it remained inarticulate and "informal" in Great Britain because of the economic, industrial, and naval comparative advantage it enjoyed in pursuing its policy, not of isolationism as in the case of the United States, but of "liberal" overseas expansionism. There was not much need to resort to an articulate ideology of nationalism. Thus, it was possible for Great Britain to achieve capitalist development with an open economy, without much intervention from a strong state, and therefore with the incremental reformist development of parliamentary democracy. It was considerably less so in the United States, and definitely less so in the case of France, as illustrated by state "dirigisme" in economic development.

Despite these variations in the capitalism–nationalism–democracy complex, by the end of the nineteenth century the three countries had attained the position of early-starter, highly competitive, capitalist democratic empires.

Capitalism–nationalism–authoritarianism model

The growth and consolidation of these core (C–N–D) countries in turn evoked the dialectical response of *less* developed empires – among others Germany, Japan, and Italy – which were *capitalist–nationalist–authoritarian* (C–N–A). These countries presented the first model of those less developed societies that, in the face of the capitalist predominance of the core and in a nationalist attempt to catch up with the core, would seek capitalist–nationalist economic development at the expense of political democracy.

To attain the goal of rapid economic and industrial development as the foundation of national independence and imperialist competitiveness, the state in these countries played a crucial role in determining the mode of the political as well as the economic system. This led to exclusivity, both political and economic, and also both external and internal – externally in the form of protectionism and militarism, internally in the form of state capitalism and antidemocratic oppressive exclusion (or ultranationalist pseudo-inclusion) of labour and the masses.

The conflict between the early-developed core empires and the late-developed industrial empires provided the arena of World War I and World War II – the two *non*-cold world wars. World War II, in particular, represented a sharp conflict between the capitalist–nationalist–democratic system and the capitalist–nationalist–authoritarian system.

A deeper and longer-term implication of the C–N–A system concerns the contradiction between capitalism and democracy, on the one hand, and between nationalism and democracy, on the other, both of which are of great historical and theoretical importance. (To a lesser extent, it involves a contradiction between capitalism and nationalism, as illustrated by the conflictual symbiosis of big business and the fascist regime; Milward, 1976.) It is a complex contradiction that is necessitated, first and foremost, by the uneven capitalist development of the world. This is a problem very much on the agenda of today's world, particularly in connection with the South. We shall return to this point later.

As the late-developed Axis (C–N–A) empires were defeated by the "United Nations," whose core coalition predominantly consisted of the early-developed (C–N–D) empires, the former Axis powers were incorporated into the world order of liberal capitalist economy and liberal democracy under the hegemonic rule of the Western powers. In 1945 the two hot world wars were to be taken over by a cold world war.

Socialism–nationalism–authoritarianism model

Another antithesis to the capitalist–nationalist–democracy core, which is *socialist–nationalist–authoritarian* (S–N–A), came to the fore on the global level in the wake of World War II, as illustrated by the Soviet Union and, later, China. It led to the intensification of the East–West Cold War, which, in effect, had been under way since the time of the Russian Revolution, or even since much earlier times. In fact, it emerged as an antithesis to the capitalist–democratic empires (C–N–D), which were later coupled with capitalist–authoritarian empires (C–N–A).

Socialism in modern times is a child of capitalism and is an ideology of the marginalized class of capitalist society. It has been pointed out that the socialist revolution, which, contrary to the Marxist prognosis, did not occur in advanced Western capitalist societies, took place in non-advanced, less developed capitalist countries. It is true that, in this respect, the Marxist prediction proved untrue. But the prediction was true in the sense that the marginalized periphery, whether within or outside the advanced capitalist societies, would provide the source of revolutionary change.

The international spread of the marginalized and politicized periphery from inside the advanced capitalist societies to the overseas less developed capitalist societies was a consequence of the international expansion and penetration of the capitalist imperialist powers.

23

The penetration of capitalist–imperialist democracy from the nineteenth century up to the early part of the twentieth primarily took the form of economic and financial expansion frequently buttressed by military invasion; and the penetration of capitalist–imperialist authoritarianism in the twentieth century – i.e. fascism and militarism – primarily took the form of military invasion coupled with economic expansion.

In this connection, it is noteworthy that the latter form of penetration, which brought about a decisive turn in history toward the outbreak of socialist revolution and the building of socialist states, was exemplified by Imperial Germany, which invaded Russia during World War I, and by Imperial Japan, which invaded China in the 1930s and 1940s. These invasions dealt a heavy blow to the old regime and unleashed the forces for socialist revolution (Skocpol, 1976). In other words, the most crucial, *direct* impact leading to the emergence of state socialism was generated, not by the early-developed Western (C–N–D) empires, but by late-developed capitalist–authoritarian (C–N–A) empires in their struggle to catch up with the West.

Obviously, this was in part due to geopolitical factors, such as geographical proximity. But this factor does not account for why Germany or Japan embarked on military aggression. This was also due to the fact that these late-developed empires, having insufficient military capability to defeat Western early-developed empires directly and having insufficient economic and financial capability to outrun the West in the race to penetrate Russia and/or China economically, resorted to *military* invasion of these peripheral old empires with a view to catching up with the early-developed hegemonic empires in the struggle to build empires. It illustrated the constraints of the hierarchical world order under which the late-developed empires took the course of anti-democratic militarism.

Thus, the international spread of socialist forces was a consequence of the international penetration of the capitalist mode of production, of the subsequent international proliferation of the newly marginalized classes, and of the corresponding international dissemination of socialist revolutionary ideologies and movements.

The state and socialism

The spread of socialist forces was characterized by the following contradictions.

24

First, this process was a manifestation of the historical phase in which, in the words of E. H. Carr, "nationalization of socialism and socialization of nationalism" took place simultaneously (Carr, 1945). One may recall that, in the West, workers' parties began to participate in national government in the inter-war period, and socialist movements were co-opted by the nation-state, which was essentially capitalist. In the East, socialism took over the state, and the socialist state in turn co-opted socialist movements, leading to "socialism in one country." In Central Europe, the force of despair called "national socialism" seized state power, which, as mentioned above, embodied the capitalist–nationalist–authoritarian complex.

So far, Carr's thesis is valid. But, although it helps to highlight the similarity of the three models – namely, C–N–D, C–N–A, and S–N–A, all containing N in common – it tends to underrate the difference. In the West, capitalism held state power, co-opting socialist movements; thus, through its restructuring, the West retained the capitalist–nationalist–democratic complex. In the East, socialism held state power, co-opting socialist movements; thus it established the socialist–nationalist–authoritarian complex. The contradiction of international socialist movements in relation to the state was more profound in the East than in the West. In the West, socialist movements were co-opted by the capitalist state by having publicly ceased to be revolutionary socialist. In the East, socialist movements were co-opted by the *socialist* state through ostensibly attaining the goal of revolutionary socialist movements. State socialism was a self-defeating self-fulfilment of socialist movements.

Secondly, just as the socialist movements within capitalist states were the manifestation of the aspiration for socio-economic democracy on the part of the deprived classes, the socialist revolution outside capitalist states was also the manifestation of the aspiration for equality and equity on the part of the marginalized classes in an internationally marginalized society. In this respect, the Russian Revolution was an extension of the democratization movement that originated in the West.[5]

The crucial point is that, whereas socialist movements in the West were based on the prior and continuing development of civil society, which is both the societal precondition and the product of the democratization process, socialist movements in Russia with a potential orientation to anti-tsarist, anti-autocratic democracy had to be unfolded in the near-absence of civil society. As a result, whereas socialist movements in the West contributed to a *deepening* of democracy, socialist movements in the East led to the *perversion* of democracy in the name of "democratic centralism" and "mass mobilization," which replaced popular participation. This was socialism without democracy. Again, there was a self-denying self-fulfilment of the revolutionary movements for mass democracy.

In sum, it is true that the conflict between the West and the East contained a twofold antithesis: capitalism vs. socialism and democracy vs. authoritarianism. And it must be noted that the antithesis on both of these two dimensions centred on the nature of the state, which began to override both socialism and democracy. The state in the East was far removed not only from "democracy" but even from "socialism" as originally defined in the Western context with reference to the idea of civil "society" that is autonomous *vis-à-vis* the state. In many respects, Marxian socialism was originally an heir to bourgeois civil society.

The peripherized empires in the East with a weak state and a weak economy – i.e. Russia and China – had to be restructured by relying primarily on the revolutionary strong state to counteract the impact of the capitalist world, i.e. C–N–D plus C–N–A. This was a world-systemic constraint. Further, in the late-starter empires, civil society was so weak that it failed to counteract the power of the state. This was a historical internal constraint. There was thus a twofold primacy of the state. As a result, in the socialism–nationalism–democracy nexus, which was what a socialist state was expected to be, the state assumed such an overriding role that both socialism and democracy underwent structural distortion. The disproportionate importance attached to the strong state was also illustrated by the overriding priority given to the combination of heavy industries and defence industries as the nucleus of massive industrialization after 1929, which laid the groundwork for the Soviet military–bureaucratic–industrial complex, and by the attainment of parity *vis-à-vis* the United States in terms of the state's nuclear capability (Holloway, 1983).

The national/international nexus

The problematic of the nature of the state in the East became all the more pronounced on the international level when it was matched by its counterpart in the West as World War II came to an end. In the process of international bipolarization, a curious combination of the "international" and the "national" emerged. While the "international" socialist ideology and movement were "nationalized" by the Soviet state, the national states of the East were internationalized and incorporated into the Eastern bloc. Similarly, while the internationalist or universalist ideology of liberal capitalism was "nationalized" by the United States (not so much by post-war social democratic Western Europe), the national states of the West were internationalized and incorporated into the Western bloc. Both East and West formed a bloc under the hegemony of the respective superpowers.

There was a significant difference between the two types of bloc, however. On the Eastern side, it was the state that dominated both the economy and society; and it was the state (including the state Party) that served as the mainstay of the bloc. In parallel with the monolithic Soviet state, the Eastern bloc was consolidated into a monolithic international bloc headed by a superstate at the expense of the indigenous economy–nation–society of the satellite countries. The bloc was the extension of the Soviet state to the Eastern bloc as a whole.

On the Western side, the capitalist economy and civil society retained relative autonomy from the state, as far as the United States and Western Europe were concerned. It is true that the overwhelming American nuclear superiority provided the military mainstay of the bloc on the state level. Further, at times, as illustrated by McCarthyism, the United States fell victim to monolithic anti-communism, a reversal of Soviet monolithic communism. In general, however, the state did not dominate the economy and civil society (although the economy of the allies was considerably internationalized under the United States hegemony). This pluralistic political structure was even more pronounced in Western Europe, where political parties and social forces of significant ideological difference were recognized as a legitimate component of the state. These conditions for internal and international pluralism are the legacy and privilege of early-developed capitalist societies of the West.

A monolithic international structure was observable on the Western side, however, as far as the anti-communist United States allies in the South were concerned. The state, mostly operated by a militarized regime, retained a relatively dominant position *vis-à-vis* the local economy and society; and it was through this state that the United States consolidated a monolithic bloc at the expense of the endogenous development of the economy–nation–society of satellite countries. The medium of this structured intervention consisted of the strategic "aid" programme, the counter-insurgency/low-intensity warfare strategy, and so forth. The bloc of the Southern "free world" was, in effect, a replica of the pre-World War II Western empire.

In short, these are the major differences that characterized the conflict between the two blocs. The crucial point is the differing role played by the state.

At the same time, one development seems to have intriguing positive implications. It must be noted that the East–West antithesis stemmed not only from the *difference* in the "internal" structure of the state on each side. It also derived from the *similarity* of the "international" bloc formation. This similarity can be appreciated if the two blocs are compared with the Nazi state. The latter, by the nature of its racist–ethnocentric ideology and practice, could hardly provide the foundation of an "international–universalist" bloc. For instance, Hitler's well-known contempt for yellow Asians was an unsettling element in Japan's alliance with Nazi Germany. Both the East and the West, in contrast, were equipped with an "internationalism" that facilitated the legitimation of a bloc formation based on hegemonic internationalization.

It is true that this hegemonic internationalization contains contradictory tendencies of an "international state" – one toward internationalism, the other toward "hegemonic statism." It is noteworthy, however, that, out of the ordeal of World War II, only the West and the East, both characterized by this contradictory national/international nexus, emerged as viable models. This should be interpreted as an indication of the profound transformation of the classical state system that had been under way. It was clear that, under the technological and industrial conditions of Fordist mass production and mass consumption, as well as Fordist mass destruction (dramatized by the strategic bombings in Europe and the atomic bombings in Japan), the days of the classical sovereign state system were numbered.[6] It is probably no accident that, while states with ethnocentric particularist ideologies failed to retain their hegemonic empires, only states with international/universalist ideologies demonstrated their compatibility with the scale of political economy and military technology that transcends classical national boundaries.

Obviously, a question must be raised as to whether and in what sense the East and the West were "international." The collapse of the Eastern bloc testifies to its failure to sustain viability. But the point is that, when World War II came to an end, a new era began when the beginning of the end of the classical sovereign state system was made unmistakably perceptible and basically irreversible. It is true that one particular bloc formed at that time later proved incompatible with the further internationalization of political economy and technology. But this is precisely a manifestation of the underlying process of the erosion of the state system, which began even to repudiate the boundaries of the two "sovereign" blocs.

It is therefore natural that the "ethno-nationalist disputes" that have erupted in the wake of the end of the East–West conflict should largely assume a regressive character, politically if not culturally.

In its formative years in the nineteenth-century West, nationalism was generally recognized, particularly in the eyes of its protagonists, as a positive principle of a new international order. This was clearly true of Wilsonianism at the time of World War I. Even fascist nationalism of the 1930s presented itself as the force of political renovation and even cultural revitalization overcoming the "decline of the West." Nationalism in the post-World War II setting was committed to the liberation and solidarity of the colonized peoples in the Third World. In contrast, what is referred to as "nationalism" or "ethno-nationalism" in the post-Cold War context mostly points to ethno-nationalist *conflict*, with little positive vision of a new international *order*. If it is divorced from universal principles such as democracy and human rights, it is bound to be an atavistic regression to unreason inherited from the past.

The state and uneven development

We have observed that, by the end of World War II, three models of states had emerged and played a dominant role in the world history of the previous nearly two centuries.

What makes the crucial distinction among the three – capitalism –nationalism–democracy, capitalism–nationalism–authoritarianism, and socialism–nationalism–authoritarianism – is the nature and role of the state as a function of global uneven development.

In the early-developed capitalist–nationalist–democratic countries, the state played a relatively secondary role, with the market and civil society acquiring an autonomous dynamic of development. Since these countries, particularly Great Britain, had no even earlier developed dominant capitalist states ahead of them, they did not have to rely on continued strong state intervention in order to protect their respective non-interventionary capitalist free markets.

In contrast, practically all late-developed countries had to resort to structured strong state intervention and protection, whether capitalist or socialist. In fact, the early-developed empires are the exceptions in

29

history. Nevertheless, they exerted a preponderant influence on world development by setting the general rule for the development of latecomers. Sometimes it has been said that a "weak state" is the main feature of the early-developed countries. Their "state" was weak in relation to their own economy and civil society, which were strong and autonomous; but it was quite strong and hegemonic, militarily and economically, in its relations with other states, particularly the late-developed ones. Put more precisely, it was this external hegemonic strength of early-developed empires that made it possible for the state to be "weak" *internally*.

Under the world-systemic constraints imposed by the early-developed countries, the late-developed capitalist powers sought to build a strong, imperialist state in order to make up for the weakness of their economy and civil society. And the building of a strong state in turn made the economy and society dependent on and subservient to the state. External exigencies prevailed over the endogenous development of civil society; and the weakness of civil society led to the weakness of democracy, as in Germany and Japan.

The same is true of late-developed empires that turned into socialist states. The main difference is that the old states, tsarist Russia and Kuomintang China, when they were subject to foreign invasion, had not attained a degree of consolidation comparable to the authoritarian state capitalism (C–N–A) of the late nineteenth century. And the foreign invasion in turn made their respective states even weaker. Thus, the old regimes had to be replaced by state socialism in which civil society and democratic forces autonomous from the state were virtually absent. The ideology of the "dictatorship of the proletariat" reveals the paradoxical dynamic through which potentially democratic forces, when not embedded in autonomous civil society, turned into the guardian of a dictatorial state.

The history of the development, or maldevelopment, of the Third World countries in the post-World War II period is not much different. The need for a strong state for developing countries was reflected in the formation of a near-consensus in the international community, particularly in the Third World, in support of political decolonization and the building of an independent state. But the defence of a "strong state" generally ran counter to the formation of autonomous civil society and democratic forces. Where the state controlled its capitalist economy and achieved considerable export-led growth, this took the form of state capitalism. These countries were called the newly industrializing economies (NIEs), which referred particularly to the "successful" NIEs in East Asia.

Thus a capitalism–nationalism–authoritarianism complex emerged in the *post-colonial* context, as distinct from the *imperialist* context of Germany, Japan, and so forth. The "success" of Asian NIEs, such as South Korea and Taiwan, was in part due to the enormous amount of strategic aid given by the United States for Cold War considerations. In this respect, they were dependent strong states. At the same time, land reform undertaken in these societies was a first step to the modernization of their economic system. These two conditions contributed to the establishment of an efficient, militarized authoritarian state. Just as in the case of late-developed empires, the post-colonial state of the NIEs achieved capitalist growth at the expense of democracy.

Obviously, most Third World countries have a weak state, particularly after the demise of state socialism. These "weak" capitalist states in the South are in disarray and ineffective in terms of equitable and democratic development. The economy is not under state control, not because it is autonomous but, on the contrary, because it is dependent on and incorporated into the world capitalist economy. The state is not autonomous, not because it is restrained by autonomous civil society but, on the contrary, because the state, under international constraints, fails to provide a political framework for the autonomous civil society that should lay the groundwork for an autonomous democratic nation-state.

In sum, one may draw a picture of the hierarchy of world capitalist uneven development in the context of which three types of response emerged. First, at the top, early-developed empires adopted liberal and internationalized economic policy as long as it conformed with the interests of the élites. Secondly, a variety of countries in the middle adopted statist policy, whether state capitalism or state socialism, as long as it was necessitated by the interests of the élites. Thirdly, a number of Third World countries at the bottom have no alternative but to adopt neo-liberal, internationalized policy, as illustrated by structural adjustment enforced under the pressure of IMF and the World Bank, as long as it serves the interests of transnationals and the transnationalized local élites. This is how the structure of uneven development has manifested itself.

Challenges and consequences

The challenge to this structure was first posed by late-developed capitalist–nationalist–authoritarian empires. The revolt took the form of the two world wars, particularly World War II. This challenge did not change the system of the world; on the contrary, it changed the challenger's own system. From 1945, the main struggle against the dominant system, which took the form of the Cold War, was waged by state socialism – socialist–nationalist authoritarianism. This did not change the dominant system of the world; on the contrary, it changed the challenger's own system.

The consequences of World War II and the Cold War reveal differences and similarities.

There are two major differences. First, World War II came to an end through the military defeat of the Axis powers. The military defeat was more than a mere military defeat because, in militarist states like the Axis powers, military invincibility was an integral part of the political legitimacy of the regime. Military defeat, therefore, was a political and ideological defeat.

The Cold War came to an end through the economic defeat of the socialist states. Here economic defeat was more than an economic defeat because, in socialist states that had been based on the promise of a high level of people's well-being unattainable under capitalism, economic victory was an integral part of the political and ideological legitimacy of the regime. Economic defeat, therefore, was a political and ideological defeat.

Secondly, whereas the militarist states of the Axis powers had to be dismantled by such a violent means as total war, the transformation of the socialist states and the ending of the Cold War were brought about largely by non-violent means. This was, of course, in part due to the fact that, for the West, it did not make sense to try to change the state-socialist system by military means, particularly in the nuclear age. More significantly, it was due to the fact that, on the Eastern side, in accordance with the professed goals of socialism, the élite such as Gorbachev were committed to the principle of democracy and took the initiative for political democratization from above. This would have been inconceivable under the Nazi regime or the old Japanese Emperor system.

From these two differences one may conclude that, whereas the fascist challenge was essentially of a negative nature, containing an element of political nihilism with no long-term vision of the future (Neumann, 1942), the socialist challenge, despite all its drawbacks and distortions, had within itself a long-term utopia and a corresponding positive ideological potential for long-term *self*-transformation that could be accelerated by external impact (Gorbachev, 1987).

Besides differences, there are important similarities. First, the end of World War II and that of the Cold War, while bringing about the dismantling of the old state and the national humiliation of the old élites, led to the political liberation of the people and the promotion of democratization. The "defeated" people became the beneficiaries of the defeat and the subsequent reform. The state's loss could be the people's long-term gain even if the people had to endure "post-war" – post-World War II or post-Cold War – political disorder, economic austerity, and social anomie.

Secondly, the transformation had much to do with external impact. World War II had to be brought to an end by external forces, and the post-Cold War, post-perestroika changes had to proceed in connection with external responses. More specifically, in both cases, the growth of the capitalist market economy in the former anti-West countries was boosted by the West through the introduction of large-scale aid programmes. Reform of the state was encouraged and inspired by the West. Democratization and the establishment of human rights were pressed for by the West. The reform was a combination of endogenous and exogenous dynamics.

Thirdly, these two similarities, which are interrelated, point to the reality of the contemporary world that the traditional distinction between internal and international has considerably lost its validity. There has long been an argument in favour of indigenous revolution or reform as against foreign-inspired change and the "export of revolution" on the grounds that indigenousness means spontaneity, which is the primary source of legitimacy for democratization. Although this argument has been generally tenable, it is a product of the age when the myth of the impermeability of the sovereign nation-state was taken for granted. This myth of state sovereignty would not make sense if a large majority of the people, as distinct from a small group of privileged ruling élite, would benefit from democratization resulting from intervention from outside. The idea of the identity of interest of the entire "imagined community" (Anderson, 1983) does not hold, since, in these circumstances, the line of division within a nation carries greater weight than that between states. In fact, for the élites of the old regime, even an endogenous revolution is an *external* intervention from below. No significant political transformation can take place without this "externality" of the source of change.[7]

More generally, it has become more questionable than before why "interference in domestic affairs" should be considered intrinsically impermissible at a time when no major developments in one country can be immune from external interactions, and vice versa, and why external support or pressure for the democratization of a country should be abstained from in favour of the persistence of indigenous anti-democratic practices. It is natural that today these fundamental questions should be addressed to the logic of the classical sovereign state system. The discourse on "humanitarian intervention" by the United Nations is a case in point. Of course, there seems to be an international consensus that the cultural autonomy and diversity of nations should be respected and that no crusading military intervention to impose a particular ideology should be allowed. Yet, "interference" through the free flow of ideas and information is not only unavoidable but considered permissible.

Today, on the one hand, the sharp distinction between the internal and the international has become highly questionable, both empirically and normatively. On the other hand, a clearer distinction between indigenity and spontaneity has become necessary. The end of the two wars and their aftermath demonstrated that the boundary between the internal and the international had become very blurred and that there was a need for a new way of conceptualizing democratization in a time of internationalization.

In short, democracy has been globalized in today's world in two respects. First, for the first time in history practically every state recognizes democracy as the foundation of the legitimacy of its regime. Even if its practice is removed from what democracy should be like, the undemocratic practice is generally rationalized as only a transition step toward ultimate democratization. Secondly, not only is democratization under way individually in every state; democratization in one country also reinforces democratization in other countries, and vice versa. These resonance effects are creating a world situation where, despite inevitable occasional setbacks, democracy and human rights are assuming the character of international/global norms that may transcend a state's sovereignty and go beyond the sum total of the norm of individual states.

Global capitalism vs. global democratization

Examination of the historical development of capitalism–nationalism–democracy shows that, while the state has played the determinant role as stated above, each of the three components stands in a dual and even contradictory relationship to the state. Depending on the historical-structural context, capitalism may identify itself with or resist the state. Similarly, nationalism may identify itself with or resist a particular state, and democracy many identify itself with or resist the state.

What we see as a manifestation of contradictions with the state in the post-Cold War world is a twofold development: on the one hand, the globalization of the capitalist economy; on the other, the globalization of democracy. The combination of the two strands of change apparently amounts to the globalization of the capitalist–nationalist–democratic (C–N–D) model. Since it is globalized, it may be called capitalist–internationalist–democratic (C–I–D). This led to the "triumphalism" represented by the notion of the "end of history" that emerged in the hegemonic (C–N–D) country (Fukuyama, 1989).

This cannot be the end of history, however, because there is a contradiction involved. Capitalist economic development, which is essentially uneven, gives rise to widening disparity and inequity, which contradict democracy. For instance, as a result of the universalization of the liberal competitive market economy represented by the United States, disparity is widening on a world scale; and, ironically, the competitive market economy, at the very moment of its "triumph" over the socialist command economy, is universalized so thoroughly and ruthlessly that it affects not only the outside world, particularly the South, but American society itself. Thus it is inflicted with chronic relative economic decline and widening domestic disparity. At the moment the external Soviet threat disappeared, the American people found themselves threatened internally by the increasing fear of unemployment, the widening structural gap between rich and poor, and the decline of the middle class – in other words, the end of the American dream. All these aggravate crime, drug abuse, ethnic conflict, and other forms of violence in everyday life.

This took place at a time when the globalization of democracy and human rights was under way. Even under undemocratic regimes, the presence of popular demands and movements for the democratization of the state and society is unmistakable. The contradiction is felt by a growing number of the disadvantaged. It is therefore natural that, for instance, the American people in 1992 opted for the Presidential candidate who stood for "time for change." This is a reflection of the awareness of the contradiction, although whether "change" is feasible within the present capitalist framework remains to be seen.

Obviously, there is a contradiction between capitalism, which seeks growth and profit accompanied by disparity and inequity, on the one hand, and democracy, which seeks equal rights and equity, on the other. But the two are similar in the sense that both are being trans-nationalized and globalized. Two problems must be noted in this connection.

First, the two strands of change are unfolding unevenly, in that the globalization of the capitalist economy is surpassing the globalization of democracy. Secondly, between these two trends stands the state, which remains national. It still tends to confine democracy within its national borders. The state is therefore being exposed to the impact of globalizing capitalism and globalizing democracy, both of which transcend the framework of the nation-state. Thus, even the state's response to globalizing capitalism and democracy at times has to be transnationalized, as illustrated by the search for various forms of regional integration.

The underlying question is how to put the globalizing economy under democratic control, which will also have to be transnationalized. In other words, how to ensure *transnational democratic socio-economic development* in a world of globalization is the crucial question confronting us today.

Democracy: National and international

One model aimed at coping with the contradiction between capitalism and democracy is the *socialist–nationalist–democratic* (S–N–D) complex, as represented by the social democracy of Scandinavian countries, particularly in post-war Sweden.

It is noteworthy that the state in Sweden, while taking a liberal policy in the area of international economy, adopted a domestic compensation policy to ensure an equitable distribution of wealth (Katzenstein, 1983). Socialism in this case is an extension and a reinforcement of democracy in the area of economy and society. The role played by the state was to achieve economic development by acting as the guarantor of both liberal trade policy abroad and social democracy at home. Although this is a model of great importance to our theme, it has been adopted by only a small number of small countries in the North (i.e. Europe); and its *national* social democracy faces difficulties in the age of internationalization, as illustrated by the Swedish dilemma arising from its prospective admission to the European Union.

Further, the relevance of this model as a development alternative

36

mutatis mutandis for today's Southern countries remains to be seen. In fact, a number of social movements, which came to question the viability of the state-socialist "delinking" strategy, are in search of an alternative similar to this social democratic development model, though defined in the context of the South. Instead of focusing on the transformation of the world system, as exemplified by the New International Economic Order (NIEO) of the 1970s, the primary emphasis is on bottom–up development through the democratization of the internal system of the countries of the South.[8] Though innovative and legitimate, this approach cannot avoid the question of internationalization.

It is therefore clear that a dimension that is pertinent to alternative models concerns *internationalism* rather than nationalism. At a time of internationalization, this is the area that deserves special consideration.

In fact, the end of World War I ushered in a new era of internationalization, which manifested itself in the two models of internationalism. First, the *capitalism–internationalism–democracy* (C–I–D) complex was advanced by Woodrow Wilson as a model of a new world order, exemplified by the League of Nations. Although the Covenant of the League of Nations predominantly dealt with interstate war/peace issues, it was premised on the universality of the civilizational standards of Western capitalist democracy. The concomitant establishment of the International Labour Organization as a bulwark against bolshevism is a case in point.

Because of the inclusion of socialist states, its heir, the United Nations, as far as its Charter is concerned, was not explicitly modelled on a capitalist world order. In practice, however, the main pillars of the "functional" (economic/financial) structure of the United Nations system, such as the Bretton Woods institutions (International Monetary Fund, International Bank for Reconstruction and Development, and the General Agreement on Tariffs and Trade), are essentially "capitalist."

Another important example of this category (C–I–D), though at the regional level, is the European Union. There is no doubt that the EU, which emerged in the region where the sovereign state system had come into being ahead of other regions of the world, has significant implications for the future of the state system worldwide.

The importance of the capitalism–internationalism–democracy model does not necessarily lie in the fact that it has provided the institutional framework for "international organization." What is more fundamental is the global process through which both capitalism and democracy are transnationalized and the sovereignty of states eroded. In the internationalizing process of capitalism and democracy is enmeshed international organization, which is a reflection of this deeper process of global transformation.

The second model of internationalism, which emerged almost at the same time as the first, is the *socialism–internationalism–authoritarianism* (S–I–A) complex. This other form of transnationalization was represented by the Communist International (Comintern), which was Lenin's counter-model to Wilson's League of Nations, both founded in 1919 (Carr, 1953; Mayer, 1959). It was an organizational framework through which both socialism and authoritarianism were internationalized and the autonomy of national communist parties and movements was eroded. The Comintern, which was dismantled in 1943 for the sake of the Allied wartime collaboration, was resuscitated in 1947 under the name of the Cominform and served to expel Tito's Yugoslavian party in 1948 in support of internationalized Soviet Stalinism.

It may be noted that, as in the case of socialist–nationalist authoritarianism as against capitalist–nationalist democracy, socialist–internationalist authoritarianism stood in an asymmetric relationship to capitalist–internationalist democracy and assumed a much stronger hegemonic Soviet statist character than did the international organization of C–I–D. The irony of history is that, as a result of the hegemonic internationalization of socialism and authoritarianism, democratic resistance in the late 1980s to socialist authoritarianism was also internationally synchronized, leading to the interlinked disintegration of the Eastern bloc and the Soviet empire.

On the international level as on the national level, the capitalist–democratic complex survived. So did its contradiction.

First, the capitalist–internationalist (C–I) complex is far ahead of the democratic–internationalist (D–I) complex in the consolidation of its institutional framework. On the governmental level, the Economic Summit and the Group of Seven leading industrial nations (G7) have established themselves as the core of the global economic/financial and even political oligarchy. On the non-governmental level, multinational corporations have seized a similar dominant power in the global economy. On the level of the more formal United Nations institutions, the International Monetary Fund, the World Bank, and regional banks are run on the basis of unequal weighted voting that favours the Northern rich countries. The five permanent members

(P5) of the Security Council, which hold a privileged position, used to constitute the cardinal arena of the East–West conflict; but since the end of the Cold War even the decisions of P5 tend to be virtually predetermined by the United States, the United Kingdom, and France, with Russia (and increasingly China) incorporated into the capitalist–internationalist complex. All this amply demonstrates that the capitalist–internationalist complex constitutes an unegalitarian, oligarchical structure. In contrast, the egalitarian institutions of democratic internationalism have acquired much less binding power and visibility, as illustrated by the UN General Assembly. Even the *concept* of the "democratization of the United Nations" remains undefined.

These discriminatory tendencies have been further aggravated by the fact that the world, in particular the people of the South, has been adversely affected by the impact of another model – the *capitalism–internationalism–authoritarianism* (C–I–A) complex. This provides the familiar structural background against which internationalized capital (the multinationals) often forms alliances with the authoritarian regimes of Third World countries (Evans, 1979). Even if, as in the 1980s, "formal" political authoritarian regimes underwent institutional change involving "civilian government" and a "multi-party system," the underlying hierarchical socio-economic structures were often left intact. As long as this capitalist–internationalist authoritarianism continues to prevail transnationally through penetration of the South, it is natural that socialist–nationalist–democratic forces and/or socialist–internationalist–democratic movements should emerge and proliferate at the bottom of global society despite their occasional setbacks. But it is difficult for socialist–nationalist–democratic forces to prevail in a time of internationalization, as is illustrated by the Soviet or Maoist model adopted by several developing countries, which gave priority to socialist nationalism at the expense of democracy in the course of resisting the penetration of capitalist internationalism. To avoid these pitfalls, both socialism and nationalism have to be redefined. Thus, we shall examine the prospects of *international* socio-economic democracy.

International social democracy

The combination of *socialism–democracy* and *internationalism* developed as an international extension of the socialism–nationalism–democracy complex. More specifically, the socialism–internationalism–democracy model has been promoted in the form of social movements for which the initiatives have been taken by social democratic forces in the North. The best-known examples are the recommendations of the Brandt Commission (Independent Commission on International Development Issues, 1980), and the Socialist International Committee on Economic Policy (1985).[9] A number of transnational social movements and NGO activities, in both the North and the South, seeking to overcome the North–South disparity, are also a case in point. Authoritarian state socialism is on its way out; but there seems to be a structural need, inherent in the inequitable development of the world economy, for democratic international socialism as a development alternative.

The contradiction between capitalist development, on the one hand, and political and social democracy, on the other, used to be perceived as a conflict within the nation-state in the North. The national response to this challenge was the welfare state. The conflict was also identified in terms of international inequality and disparity, especially disparity embedded in the colonial structure. In this case the dialectic unfolded in the form of the struggle for national liberation and the dismantling of the formal empires, with the narrowing of the North–South gap yet to be achieved. Now, particularly in the post-Cold War world, the contradiction has been globalized – globalized, not in the form of globalized conflict between the two superpowers but in the form of cutting across *all* national boundaries, in the North, in the former East, and in the South. Accordingly, the dialectical response of social movements is bound to be generated transnationally.

This concept of a global dialectic may appear to resemble the Leninist notion of "world revolution." There are, however, crucial differences. First, Lenin assumed that, as a result of uneven capitalist development, socialist revolution would break out in one or more countries where revolutionary conditions were ripe and, with these states serving as the base for revolutionary struggles, world revolution would be achieved. Contemporary transnational social movements, in contrast, do not presuppose that global change should begin with the creation of a revolutionary state. The primary emphasis is not on state power but on the emerging global civil society, which should transcend the framework of nation-state. Furthermore, transnational democratization is defined not in terms of governance structure but in terms of continual *processes*.

Secondly, in the light of our experiences in the twentieth century, social movements are likely to turn out to be self-defeating not only when they seek to seize state power but also when they pursue that goal by resorting to force and violence. Violence runs counter to democratic processes.

In post-World War II history, the main forces of change have been socialist and/or nationalist. And neither socialists nor nationalists ruled out violence as a legitimate means of social change. Nowadays, in a time of globalized democratization, the efficacy and legitimacy of both state socialism and state nationalism (as well as state capitalism and even national democracy) are questioned. With the decline of statism – "state" referring to the "monopoly of the legitimate use of violence" – violence is subject to critical re-examination. And it is this change that is enhancing the positive role that non-violence can play in bringing about *democratic* social transformation – locally, nationally, regionally, and globally.

The theory of history and the history of theories

We have spelt out that, in the modern world since the industrial revolution, three complex models acted as engines of change: (1) the capitalist–nationalist–democratic (C–N–D) model represented by the early-starter developed empires such as Great Britain and the United States; (2) the capitalist–nationalist–authoritarian (C–N–A) model, exemplified by late-starter developed empires such as Germany, Japan, and Italy, and by early-starter less developed countries such as the newly industrializing economies (NIEs) in Latin America and Asia (and the irregular case of oil-producing countries); and (3) the socialist–nationalist–authoritarian (S–N–A) model, illustrated by another late-comer empire, Russia, and another type of newly industrializing country (NIC), China. It goes without saying that these models are not exhaustive, intended to interpret the macro-historical meaning of world uneven development. Those societies or countries in the South that are not included in these models were peripherized in the course of world development, serving up to the present mainly as the object, rather than the subject, of contemporary global change.

It must be noted that these three complex models have constituted not only the actual process of historical change but also the process of conceptualizing the process of historical change. Hence the formation of three models of theory for the interpretation of actual historical change. Further, the fact that all three models have one component in common, namely, the sovereign nation-state and the state system, implies that the theory that corresponded to each of the three models centred on the locus of the nation-state in the context of world order – namely, "international relations." The three corresponding theories of international relations are: liberalism, realism, and Marxism. These three have been representative perspectives on international relations in modern times even up to the present. We must then ask how these three perspectives evolved in modern history, and how they are related to and constrained by the actual process of change generated by the three complex models. By relating these theories to actual historical development, we will be able to appreciate the implications of these theories for the past, present, and future of the world.

Changing perspectives of liberalism

In the seventeenth and eighteenth centuries, when the sovereign state system based on absolute monarchy came into being in Europe, there were broadly two strands of thought on international relations. One was the view that defined the sovereign state system as anarchy, which resulted from the disintegration of the medieval universal order, and conceptualized international relations in terms of the "reason of state." The other was the view that envisaged, in the wake of the disintegration of the medieval universal order, a potential international order based on universal "human reason." The former included, as pointed out by Meinecke (1957), Richelieu and his contemporary publicists, Hobbes, Spinoza, Frederick the Great, and so forth. The latter included Crucé, Grotius, Abbé de Saint-Pierre, and so forth (Knutsen, 1992). Since this is not the main topic of this essay, however, we shall not dwell upon the perspectives on international relations at that time.

The theme of this essay directly concerns the ethos of the early-developed capitalist empires in the age of industrial revolution, as best exemplified by the ideas of Jeremy Bentham. His idea that the maximization of the pleasure of the individual would lead to the maximization of the utility of society seems to be akin to the ideas of Adam Smith, which provided a rationale for the capitalist initial high growth. What is more noteworthy is the following.

According to Bentham, a maximum degree of rational calculation and pursuit of interests by the individual calls for a minimum degree of intervention by the state. Peace as the collective, international interest can be attained by public opinion, which is the sum total of the rational calculations of citizens, and this calls for open diplomacy on the part of government. The greatest world interest can be achieved through the pursuit of economic interest by the individual, which implies that uneconomical means of political power such as the colony and armaments are useless (Bentham, 1962; Hinsley, 1963).

It is clear that the autonomy of the individual and of the market coupled with a "weak state," as advocated by Bentham, presaged the stand to be articulated more publicly later by the "strong capitalism–weak nationalism–liberal democracy" model of early-developed empires. The Benthamite liberal–utilitarian, economistic perspective on international relations exerted considerable influence in mid-nineteenth-century England, particularly as it was reinforced by the free trade movement. Bentham's idea can be considered the prototype of the liberal perspective on international relations in which an autonomous civil society and market as well as the state constitute "transnational" relations that are "pluralistic and universal."

In contrast, the position of late-developed Germany was defended by Friedrich List, who challenged the free trade policy by formulating a theory of protectionism aimed at consolidating the German customs union. Further, a wide range of intellectual forces, which included Romantic nationalists such as Herder, conservative nationalists such as Clausewitz, the founding historicist Ranke, and a number of national liberals, while retaining a diversity of ideas, all converged, especially after 1848, as far as the defence of a strong, unified nation-state is concerned. The diversity refers to different ways of legitimizing the unified German nation-state. These currents crystallized into the Bismarckian authoritarian state of "blood and iron," of which the external dimension was "Realpolitik," which was widely accepted in Germany at that time. It is clear that this realism was an heir to the traditional idea of "reason of state."

Thus two strands of thought on international relations emerged – the liberalism of the early-developed empires and the realism of the late-developed empires; and these two stood in severe tension originating in the historical process of uneven development. In the face of the challenge of the state-nationalist realism of late-developed empires closing in on the early-starter empires, the latter responded by transforming themselves from liberalism to realism.

Great Britain, however, responded to German nationalism, not by evoking a British version of nationalism but by resorting to racism with social Darwinist overtones. This ideology performed the following functions.

First, an admittedly significant shift took place from the positive non-zero-sum concept that international free competition and trade would bring about gains to society or the world as a whole to the zero-sum notion that international competition must be conducted on the principle of the survival of the fittest. Nevertheless, the same underlying concept of *competition* served to ensure the continuity of the bourgeois world-view and thereby maintain the legitimacy of the bourgeois regime, thus avoiding its legitimacy crisis.

Secondly, while legitimation of the early-starter empires on the basis of nationalism was hardly possible, the racism of white supremacists was ideally suited to legitimate an empire. In fact, the rivalry between the two empires was not presented in terms of a conflict between two "nation-states" or nationalisms. Rather, as a corollary to the legitimation of the British empire on the basis of white man's racism against non-whites, it undertook legitimation of its superiority to the Germans on the basis of racism within the white race.

Thirdly, if superiority can be demonstrated only through strength, strength may be regarded as the only source of superiority and excellence, which amounts to the logic "might is right." In fact, this is not far from the logic of "reason of state," albeit it refers not to a state but to an empire. Thus "reason of state" is in effect "reason of empire," which is the rationale for the vested interests of an empire.

It may be noted that this is the first instance of an early-developed empire transfigured from liberalism to realism in response to the challenge of realism advanced by late-starter empires. We shall return to this point later.

Through World War I, however, early-developed empires consisting, among others, of Great Britain, France, and the United States, emerged as victors; and the United States, where, thanks to isolationism, the liberal perspective was untouched by realism, began to exert great influence on the international scene. As a result, the liberal perspective, which was "pluralist and universal" with multi-layer transnationalism based on civil society, the nation-state, and international organization, regained conceptual hegemony. Wilsonianism is a case in point and is akin to Bentham's ideas on international relations. As is well known, it was in the 1920s that the academic field called "international relations" mushroomed in the West, particularly the United States, with a predominantly liberal imprint.

Against this hegemonic liberal trend emerged two strands of an ideological counter-trend challenging the legitimacy of the international order founded at Versailles – bolshevism (S–N–A) and fascism (C–N–A). Of the two, the challenge on the level of power politics was first staged by fascism, particularly Nazism. In the face of it, the Wilsonian response turned out to be ineffective, and its embodiments, such as the Versailles settlement and the League of Nations, collapsed in the 1930s. As a consequence, early-starter empires had to undergo a re-transformation from liberalism to realism. Along with wartime strategic and geopolitical studies on policy issues, the foundation was laid in the United States for the more theoretical "classical realism" of Hans Morgenthau, George Kennan, and Reinhold Niebuhr. In their theories, realism was equated with the emphasis on the primacy of power politics in international relations.

American realism

Realism in America was essentially an adaptation of the idea of "reason of state" that had been part of political common sense in Europe. Its novelty lay not so much in its substance as in its systematization (best exemplified by Morgenthau's work) and its peculiarly American context. In the intellectual milieu of the United States, realism was either defended, with a sometimes excessive leaning toward power politics, or rejected because it was perceived as an excessive defence of power politics. There are a couple of reasons for this peculiarity. First, since the power politics of the Nazis, unlike Bismarck's sophisticated and limited Realpolitik, was unlimited, naked violence, its reverse, i.e. the counter-realism of America, was bound to stress the power-political dimension of international relations. Second, since the Wilsonian tradition was so deep-seated in American thinking, American realism tended deliberately to stress specifically the counter-Wilsonian, power-political dimension of international relations.

Underlying these features of American realism was one common element. This was the assertion that, in order to counteract an evil, power politics must be approved as a necessary evil. In this respect, although realism was a critique of Wilsonian moralism, the critique itself was often an inculcation with moralistic overtones.

What is more important is the fact that both Wilsonianism and realism tended to neglect historicity. Just as Wilsonian liberalism was ahistorical, American realism, which was its reverse, tended to assert the presence of immutable "laws" (classical realists) or struc-

45

ture (neo-realists). Herein lies a significant difference from historical realism represented, for instance, by E. H. Carr (Carr, 1946).

This problematic is illustrated by the failure of realism to appreciate the crucial historical difference between the realism of early-starters and that of latecomers.[10]

First, the realism of early-starter empires was designed to preserve their superiority and vested interests in the existing international order. The realism of late-developed empires, in contrast, was oriented to changing the existing international order, with a view to closing in on the early-starter empires. Further, the superiority of early-starter empires was not confined to superiority in power-political terms; it also referred to superiority in terms of the early establishment of political democracy and a capitalist market economy. Although the avowed objective of realism was to counterbalance or contain the power of the adversary on the power-political level, it was in effect intended to preserve superiority in all these respects. In contrast, the realism of late-starters aimed to counteract uneven international development through political mobilization based on the establishment of an authoritarian regime and state intervention in the economy. And it was in reaction to this late-developed empires' realism that the realism of early-starter empires had been articulated. Between these two types of realism, there is clearly a *difference that is historically correlated*; in particular, the realism of early-starter empires tended to fail to take cognizance of the historically defined asymmetry between the two.

Secondly, the realism of originally liberal early-starter empires was historically defined as a response to the realism of late-starters. In this respect, there is a similarity between Great Britain of the late nineteenth century and the United States in the Cold War period. Yet the realism of post-World War II America differed in its faint awareness of the historical asymmetric correlation and in its sole preoccupation with difference and antagonism *vis-à-vis* the "other," to the extent that the response often fell victim to inflexibility in conception. This seems to be due to the following reasons:

(1) Although it is true that there was an ideological conflict between English parliamentary democracy and "German militarism," the King of England and the German Kaiser belonged to the club of monarchs who retained international kinship and affinity. In contrast, the ideological conflict between the United States and the Soviet Union was considered to be a total confrontation. The conflict was, therefore, represented as antagonism between parties that were *intrinsically different and heterogeneous*, with

46

no historical correlation, which made the power-political conflict even deeper.

(2) In the nineteenth century, the international system was multi-polar – France and Russia as well as Great Britain were key actors in the alliance to contain Germany. In this multipolar configuration, there was a high degree of uncertainty in the conduct of diplomacy; but there was also room for flexibility and manoeuvrability. In the Cold War period, the United States was one of the two key actors in a bipolar system and the role of counterbalancing the Soviet Union had to be almost totally assumed by it. This created a situation where rigid black-and-white thinking prevailed, according to which those who were not friends were automatically regarded as foes.

(3) This rigidity was further aggravated by the following fact. In England at the turn of the century, where people had not experienced a "world war" for nearly a century since the Napoleonic War, "war drew visibly nearer ... and yet its outbreak was not really *expected*" (Hobsbawm, 1987, p. 304). In contrast, in the United States at the time the Cold War was intensified, people had just witnessed the horror of a "world war" and began to act in preparation for the next world war. Consequently, ahistorical *military realism* based on the strategy of nuclear hardware tended to overshadow the finesse of political realism.

In sum, what characterizes American realism is the tendency on the one hand to *dismiss the historical correlation* between early-starter empires and Russia by treating the Soviet Union or communism as alien or "other," and, on the other hand, to *dismiss the historical difference and asymmetry* in the world-systemic context of the two by stressing their homogeneity in power-political terms as the "two superpowers." Generally, whereas late-starters are compelled to be aware of their historical distance from early-starters and are accordingly forced to be conscious of "historicity," early-starters have the historical tendency to regard their superiority as "natural." This "ahistoricity" of conception is in itself a manifestation of historicity. Realism is no exception.

Thus, in early-developed empires, the liberal perspective was dominant, regarding the capitalist free market economy and free trade as well as liberal democracy as an integral part of the "natural order." Realism in these empires was *reactive realism* evoked by the power-political realism of late-starter empires. The same is true of American realism in the Cold War period. It has the following two features.

First, American realism had to stress the sharp distinction between the logic of domestic politics and that of international politics. Any analogy between the two was emphatically rejected. In other words, strong emphasis was put on the difference between the logic of the domestic politics of liberal democracy, where the consent of citizens would prevail, and the logic of international power politics, where the power of the nation would count. Here is a distinctive awareness of the incongruence between internal consent and external coercion. Hence the emphasis on the peculiar feature of power politics – peculiar, because it was supposedly absent in domestic politics. But in late-starter empires, whether fascist or communist, the preponderant logic of authoritarian domestic politics was coercion and a high degree of congruence was observable between internal and external power politics. Such is the prototype of "reason of state" originated in the regime of absolute monarchy. It is therefore not going too far to say that late-starter empires are the model state of realism, whereas early-starter empires are bound to be the state of reactive and derivative realism.

Secondly, it is small wonder that, in opposition to the largely derivative realism, the liberal counter-perspective of early-starter empires on international relations, based on "pluralist and universal" interactions, has repeatedly re-emerged *from within*. In the days of mounting Cold War tension, it took the form of a critical exposition of "totalitarianism," i.e. total power politics, both internal and external, which was perceived as the antithesis of pluralist universalism.[11] Its objective function was to provide ideological weapons for a total confrontation with monolithic communism, and thereby it often transformed itself into a monolithic anti-communist ideology. Subjectively interpreted, however, it was a reactive uniformity of pluralism itself in its response to "totalitarian" uniformity.

As detente brought about a relaxation of rigid tension and monolithic uniformity in the 1970s, the liberal perspective came to the surface in the form of the theory of "interdependence," which shed light on transnational interactions, transactions, networks, and organizations, and the theory of the "international regime," which refers to the institutionalization of transnational interactions conceptualized mainly on the level of inter-state relations (Keohane and Nye, 1971, 1977).

It is no accident that these theories of interdependence and regime were put forward in early-starter developed countries. They are a reflection and projection of the perspective of advanced empires, which is flawed by its failure to be explicit about its bias in favour of the

North. The same failure was observable in the doctrine of free trade and Wilsonianism. All these liberal theories largely took the hegemony of advanced empires for granted. It is precisely for this reason that, as people became explicitly aware of the relative decline of US hegemony, hegemony began to be theorized. Hence the emergence of the theory of "hegemony" or "hegemonic stability." This is a theoretical testimony to the inherent orientation of the capitalist–liberal democratic state (C–N–D) toward international and transnational penetration.

Marxist perspectives

The transnational liberal penetration of early-starter empires gave rise to two forms of counter-orientation. One was, as we have seen above, realism based on the nationalist orientation of late-starter empires. The other was Marxism, which was another form of transnational orientation. It goes without saying that Marxism did not neglect the nation-state; its strategy was designed, as the initial stage of socialist revolution, to seize political power within the framework of the nation-state. But the strategy was premised on the idea that the proletarian states thus founded would acquire transnational class homogeneity. In reality, Marxist socialist movements were to be coopted by strong authoritarian states such as the Soviet Union and China (S–N–A). It is precisely against this background that a counter-perspective has been repeatedly presented *from within* Marxism.

The "betrayed revolution" of the Soviet authoritarian bureaucratic state, the failure of the world revolutionary movements led by Trotsky and other anti-Stalinists, and the bitter disputes between socialist states – Sino-Soviet, Sino-Viet Nam, and so forth – all contributed to renewed efforts to reinterpret Marxist theory. The "dependency" theory and the "world-system" theory are cases in point. Their perspective is no longer that of the proletarian class peripherized within a single country, or that of a socialist state peripherized in the arena of international politics, but that of a transnational or global periphery. Perhaps it is no accident that this Marxist transnational perspective came to the fore in the 1970s when the capitalist transnational perspective in the advanced countries manifested itself in the form of "interdependence" theory. This could be one instance of the Marxist dialectic that the development of capitalism gives birth to socialist antitheses.

History and theory

We have examined the three perspectives on international relations – liberalism, realism, and Marxism – not for the purpose of testing their "scientific" validity but in order to interpret their meaning in the light of changing macro-historical realities. Then, by relating these perspectives and theories on international relations to the historical development of the three complex models discussed in this essay, we must ask what the implications are of the macro-history of the three models for the perspective on international relations.

The first thing we can identify in the dialectical macro-history of the three complex models is the historical resilience of democracy. Not only did democracy survive the confrontation with the two political systems antithetical to democracy, namely fascism (C–N–A) and communism (S–N–A); but both of these systems collapsed and took the course of democratization. These changes imply that the perspectives of "state realism" and "state socialism" cannot be of effective use as a theoretical response to the contemporary challenge of changing world order – "model state realism" and "state socialism" for their reliance on the authoritarian regime, and "reactive state realism" for its failure adequately to recognize the relevance of "internal" democracy to the theory of international politics (Doyle, 1986).

Obviously, to say that democracy is resilient does not mean that democratization is and will be a process of linear "progress." The process is dialectic, giving rise to anti-democratic forces as seen, for instance, in Germany or Russia in the post-Cold War phase. Anti-democratic moves are the shadow of democratization. And what instigates and encourages regressive moves is, among other things, the inequitable maldevelopment of the capitalist economy. Where capitalism does not ensure equitable development, people who are alienated and marginalized are likely to be won over by an authoritarianism based either on the myth of imagined national community, or on the myth of imagined class community, or on a tactical combination of the two.

In similar vein, liberalism, if its capitalist component fails to ensure democratic equality and equity, cannot be of effective use as a theoretical response to the challenge of a contemporary changing world order. In other words, whether capitalism is preferable to socialism, or vice versa, cannot be theoretically assessed in general terms; this has to be done in terms of whether capitalism or socialism *in its concrete form* is compatible with democratic values and conducive to democratization. The fact that Marxism is no longer opting for a perspective of state power, but seeks a perspective of marginalized global peripheries suggests that this would be the only way for Marxism to be of effective use in the contemporary changing world.

Another conclusion that can be drawn from our observation of the dialectic of three complex models concerns the resilience of the internationalist or globalist perspective, or, more precisely, the resilience of the contradiction between nationalism and internationalism. As mentioned above, the presence of nationalism in all three models indicates how resilient the statist orientation is. At the same time, it must be noted that, by definition, capitalism, socialism, and democracy are not confined to state boundaries but are embedded in civil society, which, by its nature, can be transnational.[12]

Accordingly, in a world where the transnationalization of interactions and organizations is under way and the globalization of the crucial problématique is also under way, transition from state nationalism to internationalism or globalism is inevitable, regardless of the difference in the composition of the model. The same is true of theoretical perspectives on international relations.

In fact, in the liberal perspective today, interdependence, international regime, and international organization are carrying greater weight than before. For the revitalization of Marxist theory, state socialism is being superseded by a world-systemic perspective. In contrast, realism, by its nature, is embedded in the state; and a framework that transcends the state will be tolerated only as long as it coincides with the "national interest." Nevertheless, the realism of the liberal state composed of capitalism and liberal democracy is subject to internationalization since the market and civil society are being transnationalized. Hence the coupling of the maintenance of the hegemonic state of the early-starter empire, on the one hand, and the need for internationalization, on the other – namely, the theory of "hegemonic stability" in defence of a hierarchical world order.

Thus far can liberal realism go. But this cannot be "the end of history." First, precisely because capitalism, which is an integral part of liberalism, is globalized under the American influence, the United States itself must be exposed to the challenge of less developed countries that are becoming increasingly competitive and undermining the hegemonic superiority of the United States. Secondly, precisely because liberal democracy, which is another integral part of liberalism, is globalized under the American influence, resistance to the disparity and inequality between the United States and other countries will

grow with an increasingly credible legitimacy, making it more difficult for the advanced West to retain the monopoly on the privileges
of early-starter democracies. These are the fundamental contradictions of "liberal realism."

If the advanced trilateral West seeks to retain its hegemony in
world capitalism and world politics at the expense of global democratization, the global Marxist perspective will be recurrently resuscitated as a source of effective critical theory, particularly in the area
of political economy.

What is crucial is whether liberalism will accord priority to a deepening of democracy and whether that democracy will give priority to
its own internationalization.

Notes

1. "Soviet Communism starts with an atheistic, Godless premise. Everything else follows from
   that premise ... Also, since there is no God, individuals have no God-given rights" (Dulles,
   1950, p. 8).
2. It is interesting to note that a debate on the dual character of the Cold War seems to have
   been resumed by non-American observers at the time not of the beginning of the Cold
   War, as with Americans, but of its ending (Banks and Shaw, 1991).
3. Most of the studies published so far on the end of the Cold War undertake an analysis by
   placing the Cold War as the primary point of reference. For instance, on the implications of
   the Cold War as contemporary history, see Hogan (1992); on its theoretical implications,
   see Bowker and Brown (1993).
4. The term "state-nation" used in this essay is not identical with Meinecke's "*Staatsvolk*,"
   which refers to a political or politicized nation as distinct from a cultural nation (*Kultur-
   volk*) (Meinecke, 1907, ch. 1).
5. One of the most stimulating historical accounts of democracy and socialism in Europe is
   Rosenberg (1939). For a comparative study of the crucial role played by the working
   class, if not always socialist movements, as the driving force behind democracy, see
   Rueschemeyer et al. (1992).
6. On the importance of war-making for modern state-building, see Tilly (1992). War-making
   has now generally ceased to be conducive to state-building.
7. It is quite noteworthy that Abbé Sieyès, one of the revolutionary pamphleteers at the time
   of the French Revolution, eloquently stated that the nobilities are aliens and cannot be a
   part of the nation (E. J. Sieyès, *Qu'est-ce que le tiers État?* 1789).
8. One of the most remarkable achievements in this category is the Grameen Bank in Bangladesh (Huq and Sultan, 1991).
9. For a useful critique of these reports, see Ekins (1992).
10. Thus American realism is characterized by the near-absence of the historical perspective
    under which fascism and communism can be related to the West and the historical proble-
    matic of fascism and communism as mass movements from below, as well as regimentation
    from above, can be adequately understood.
11. Obviously, there was a natural conceptual analogy, implicit or explicit, applied to Nazism
    and communism. One of the early, serious discussions was the conference held in 1953 by
    the American Academy of Art and Sciences. For the proceedings, see Friedrich (1964).
12. Authoritarianism, which does not allow the autonomy of civil society, is coterminous with

the state. Of course, the authoritarian state often goes beyond its boundaries to dominate other states. But that is simply an expansion of the scale of the state without causing any qualitative change in the statehood itself.

References

Anderson, Benedict (1983) *Imagined Communities*. London: Verso.

Banks, Michael, and Martin Shaw (1991) *State and Society in International Relations*. New York: St. Martin's Press.

Bentham, Jeremy (1962) "Principles of International Law" [1786 to 1789]. In: *The Works of Jeremy Bentham*. New York: Russell & Russell, Vol. 2, pp. 535–560.

Bowker, Mike, and Robin Brown, eds. (1993) *From Cold War to Collapse: Theory and World Politics in the 1980s*. Cambridge: Cambridge University Press.

Carr, E. H. (1945) *Nationalism and After*. London: Macmillan.

―――― (1946) *The Twenty Years' Crisis, 1919–1939*, rev. edn. London: Macmillan.

―――― (1953) *The Bolshevik Revolution, 1917–1923*, Vol. 3. London: Macmillan.

Doyle, Michael W. (1986) "Liberalism and World Politics." *American Political Science Review* 80, no. 4.

Dulles, John F. (1950) *War or Peace*. New York: Macmillan.

Ekins, Paul (1992) *A New World Order*. London: Routledge.

Evans, Peter (1979) *Dependent Development: The Alliance of Multinational, State, and Local Capital in Brazil*. Princeton, NJ: Princeton University Press.

Friedrich, Carl J., ed. (1964) *Totalitarianism*. New York: The University Library.

Fukuyama, Francis (1989) "The End of History?" *National Interest*, Summer.

Gaddis, John L. (1992) *The United States and the End of the Cold War*. New York: Oxford University Press.

Giddens, Anthony (1990) *The Consequences of Modernity*. Stanford, Calif.: Stanford University Press.

Gorbachev, Mikhail (1987) *Perestroika: New Thinking for Our Country and the World*. New York: Harper & Row.

Hinsley, F. H. (1963) *Power and the Pursuit of Peace*. Cambridge: Cambridge University Press.

Hobsbawm, E. J. (1987) *The Age of Empire, 1875–1914*. London: Weidenfeld & Nicolson.

Hogan, Michael J., ed. (1992) *The End of the Cold War: Its Meaning and Implications*. Cambridge: Cambridge University Press.

Holloway, David (1983) *The Soviet Union and the Arms Race*. New Haven, Conn.: Yale University Press.

Huq, Muzammel, and Maheen Sultan (1991) "'Informality' in Development: The Poor as Entrepreneurs in Bangladesh." In: A. Lawrence Chickering and Mohamed Salahdine, eds. *The Silent Revolution*. San Francisco: ICS Press.

Independent Commission on International Development Issues (1980) *North–South: A Programme for Survival*. London: Pan Books.

Katzenstein, Peter J. (1983) "The Small European States in the International Economy: Economic Dependence and Corporatist Politics." In: John G. Ruggie, ed. *The Antinomies of Interdependence*. New York: Columbia University Press.

Keohane, Robert O., and Joseph S. Nye Jr., eds. (1971) *Transnational Relations and World Politics*. Cambridge, Mass.: Harvard University Press.

———— (1977) *Power and Interdependence: World Politics in Transition*. Boston: Little, Brown.

Knutsen, Torbjorn L. (1992) *A History of International Relations Theory*. Manchester: Manchester University Press.

Mayer, Arno J. (1959) *Wilson vs. Lenin: Political Origins of the New Diplomacy, 1918–1919*. New Haven, Conn.: Yale University Press.

Meinecke, Friedrich (1907) *Weltbürgertum und Nationalstaat*. Munich: R. Oldenbourg Verlag, 1963.

———— (1957) *Machiavellism*. London: Routledge & Kegan Paul.

Milward, Alan S. (1976) "Fascism and the Economy." In: Walter Laqueur, ed. *Fascism*. Berkeley, Calif: University of California Press.

Morgenthau, Hans J. (1951) *In Defense of the National Interest*. New York: Alfred A. Knopf.

Neumann, Sigmund (1942) *Permanent Revolution: The Total State in a World at War*. New York: Harper.

Polanyi, Karl (1957) *The Great Transformation*. Boston: Beacon Press.

Rosenberg, Arthur (1939) *Democracy and Socialism*. New York: Alfred A. Knopf.

Rueschemeyer, Dietrich, E. H. Stephens, and J. D. Stephens (1992) *Capitalist Development and Democracy*. Oxford: Polity Press.

Socialist International Committee on Economic Policy (1985) *Global Challenge: From Crisis to Cooperation: Breaking the North–South Stalemate*. London: Pan Books.

Schelling, Thomas C. (1963) *The Strategy of Conflict*. New York: Oxford University Press.

Skocpol, Theda (1976) "States and Revolutions: France, Russia and China." In: David Held et al., eds. *States and Societies*. Oxford: The Open University, 1983.

Tilly, Charles (1992) *Coercion, Capital and European States, AD 990–1992*. Cambridge, Mass.: Blackwell.

Part I
The internationalization of the state

2

Globalization and the liberal democratic state

David Held and Anthony McGrew

Introduction

On first appearance it might seem somewhat curious to be studying the efficacy of the liberal democratic state just at the historic moment when liberal democracy seems to have triumphed on a global scale. Yet, within contemporary Europe, the nature of political community and sovereign power has been thrown into question by the resurgence of ethnic nationalism, the intensification of regional integration, and global turbulence. Taken together, these forces appear to deliver a fundamental challenge to the democratic ideals that underpin liberal democratic states. This chapter seeks to evaluate the nature of this challenge. It invites specific consideration of the consequences of these "threats from above" and "threats from below" for the character of the modern state.

The chapter comprises four parts. The first section discusses the nature of globalization and its implications for the nation-state. Drawing upon recent European experience, section two maps the major disjunctures between liberal democracy in its national setting and the dynamics of the contemporary global order. It describes how the contours of sovereign political authority and the national political community are shifting in response to the complex interplay of regional and global forces. This is followed by a brief examination of the significant limitations of existing political and international theory in providing a satisfactory account of the predicament of the liberal democratic state in an increasingly interconnected world and of how these limitations might be overcome. In the final section, some concluding reflections are offered on the future of liberal democracy in the global order of the twenty-first century.

Globalization and the liberal democratic state

In his analysis of the resurgence of European nationalism, Hobsbawm identifies a somewhat curious situation in that today's nationalist revival, associated as it is with the clamour for national autonomy, coincides with the intensification of patterns of global interdependence that are eroding the very capacity of liberal democratic states to carry out some of their most important traditional functions, such as the management of their own domestic economies (Hobsbawm, 1990, p. 175). In a similar vein, Rosenau considers that the intensification of globalization in the post-war era has contributed simultaneously to an expansion of the liberal democratic state's functional responsibilities and to an erosion of its capacity to deal effectively with the new demands placed upon it (Rosenau, 1990, pp. 127–132). In effect, globalization has become associated with a "crisis of the territorial nation-state."

Nowadays, goods, capital, people, knowledge, images, and communications, as well as crime, culture, pollutants, drugs, fashions, and beliefs, readily flow across territorial boundaries. Transnational networks, social movements, and relationships are extensive in virtually all areas of human activity. The existence of global systems of trade, finance, and production binds together the prosperity and fate of households, communities, and nations across the world. Territorial boundaries are therefore arguably increasingly insignificant in so far as social activity and relations no longer stop – if they ever did – at the water's edge.

Globalization can be conceived as having two interrelated dimensions: scope (or "stretching") and intensity (or "deepening"). On the one hand, the concept of globalization defines a universal process or set of processes that generate a multiplicity of linkages and interconnections that transcend the states and societies that make up the modern world system; the concept therefore has a spatial connotation. Social, political, and economic activities are becoming "stretched" across the globe, such that events, decisions, and activities in one part of the world can come to have immediate significance for individuals and communities in quite distant parts of the global system. On the other hand, globalization also implies an intensification in the levels of interaction, interconnectedness, or interdependence between the states and societies that constitute the modern world community. Accordingly, alongside this "stretching" goes a "deepening" such that, even though "everyone has a local life, phenomenal worlds for the most part are truly global" (Giddens, 1991, p. 187). Thus, globalization involves a growing interpenetration of the "global human condition" with the particularities of place and individuality (Robertson, 1991).

A discussion of the causal logics and dynamics of globalization is beyond the brief of this chapter but several points are worth noting in passing. First, whereas theoretical accounts of globalization stress either a single causal logic (e.g. Wallerstein's world systems theory) or a multi-causal logic (e.g. Giddens' emphasis upon the industrial, military, political, and capitalist origins of globalizing tendencies), the analysis here is sympathetic to the view that globalization is best conceived as a multidimensional process (cf. Wallerstein, 1979, 1983, 1991; Giddens, 1990, 1991). Globalization is evident within a number of key institutional domains – the economic, political, military, cultural, legal, etc. – and is best understood as being driven by a set of discrete but intersecting logics. Secondly, globalization is essentially concerned with the reordering of time and space in social life. Technology and capitalism have "shrunk the globe," annihilating distance and social time as the dominant constraints upon social interaction and relations. Thirdly, the consequences of globalization are not experienced uniformly across the globe or even within the same state or community. Globalization has a differential reach and impact reflecting existing asymmetries in the geometry of global power relations. It should be conceived more as a dialectical than as a linear process, since it stimulates the "mutually opposing tendencies" of global integration versus fragmentation, universalism versus particularism, and cultural homogenization versus differentiation (Giddens, 1990, p. 64; McGrew, 1992b, p. 74). Finally, it is important to draw a distinction between globalization and regionalization as distinct processes. If globalization is understood as global interconnectedness, then regionalization can be conceived as the intensification of patterns of inter-connectedness between geographically contiguous states that define the contours of a regional subsystem.[1] Thus within Europe it is possible to identify the European Union with the political and economic boundaries of an emerging regional community of states and societies; while in South Asia, the Association of South East Asian Nations defines the boundaries of a developing regional economic complex. Regionalization and globalization are interrelated processes but it is important to ensure that the former is not conceptually elided with the latter.

Globalization is a complex multidimensional process that operates simultaneously across several institutional domains. Its consequences are profound in both practical and intellectual terms since the modern theory of the liberal democratic state presupposes the idea of a "national community of fate" – a community that rightly governs itself and determines its own future. This premiss is challenged fundamentally by the scope and intensity of global interconnections, since it is evident that "national communities by no means exclusively 'programme' the actions, decisions and policies of their governments and the latter by no means simply determine what is right or appropriate for their citizens alone" (Held, 1991, p. 202). The result is that globalization is stimulating a "re-articulation of international political space" (Ruggie, 1991, p. 37) in which the notions of sovereignty and democracy are being prised away from their traditional rootedness in the national community and the territorially bounded nation-state (Beitz, 1991).

The liberal democratic state: Powers and disjunctures

Although there is much fragmentary evidence to suggest that the "sovereign structure" of the liberal democratic state is being recast and reconstituted by global forces, there has been no systematic mapping of this "re-articulation of international political space." Such a mapping can be attempted, in the first instance, by identifying the "internal" and "external" disjunctures between, on the one hand, the formal domain of political authority that liberal democratic states claim for themselves and, on the other, the ways in which international, regional, and global power structures condition the actual practices of states. This will provide an overview of how globalization is redefining the scope and nature of the sovereign authority of the liberal democratic state.

   The power of political parties, bureaucratic organizations, corporations, and networks of corporatist power are among a variety of forces putting pressure on the range and scope of decisions that can be made within the liberal democratic state. At the international level, there are disjunctures between the idea of the state as in principle capable of determining its own future and the existence of a global hierarchy of power, a world economy, international regimes and organizations, international law, and treaty commitments that together operate to condition and constrain the actions of individual liberal democratic states. In the discussion that follows the focus will be upon "external" disjunctures; the question of "internal" disjunctures opens up a plethora of issues that cannot be addressed within the confines of this chapter (see Held, forthcoming). But even the enumeration of these "external" disjunctures, it should be stressed, is simply illustrative; it is not assumed to be exhaustive. It is intended simply to indicate the extent to which globalization, in several key domains of state power, can be said to constitute constraints or limits on political agency; and to what extent state sovereignty and democracy are thereby challenged.

   When assessing the impact of "external" disjunctures, it is important to bear in mind that sovereignty is eroded only when it is displaced by forms of "higher" and/or independent authority that curtail the rightful basis of decision-making within a national polity. For sovereignty is understood here to mean the political authority within a community that has the undisputed right to determine the framework of rules, regulations, and policies within a given territory and to govern accordingly (Held, 1989, p. 215). Sovereignty should be distinguished from state "autonomy," or the state's capacity to act independently, within circumscribed parameters, in the articulation and pursuit of domestic and international policy objectives. State autonomy can be further differentiated with respect to both its "scope" and the "domains" within which it can be exercised. By "scope" is meant the level or intensity of constraints on state action, while "domains" refers to the policy spaces or issue areas over which such constraints operate. Bearing these distinctions in mind, it can be shown that external disjunctures map a series of processes that define the contours and effective limits to state action within a delimited territory. But the central question to pose is: has sovereignty remained intact while the autonomy of the liberal democratic state has diminished, or has the liberal democratic state actually experienced a diminution of its sovereignty? In addressing this question the analysis of external disjunctures will draw heavily upon the contemporary European experience.

Disjuncture one: International security structures and power politics

One of the essential functions of the state is to ensure the security of its citizens and its own territorial integrity. As Elias observed, the nation-state is the primary "survival unit" of the modern era (Mennel, 1990). However, there is an obvious disjuncture between the notion of the state as an autonomous actor with an independent military capability and ultimate responsibility for its own survival, and its insertion into a global power hierarchy of states and security structures that impose significant constraints upon the kinds of defence and foreign policies (or actions) that democratically elected governments may pursue.

Until fairly recently the security of all states was shaped decisively by the "Great Contest" between the United States and the Soviet Union. In a system dominated by two great powers and two rival power blocs, the scope for states to initiate an "independent" foreign and defence policy was considerably limited. In the post-Cold War world of the 1990s such external constraints have not been eradicated but have merely been re-configured. Instead of bipolarity, the global system now exhibits the characteristics of a more multipolar distribution of political and economic power (cf. Waltz, 1979). Within this more complex structure, the strategic and foreign policy options confronting an individual state are defined by its location in the global power hierarchy. Despite the ending of the Cold War, it is still the case that the structure of global power relations continues to exert a profound constraint upon individual state action.

For much of the post-war period, European security was guaranteed through the operation of the two respective alliance organizations, the North Atlantic Treaty Organization (NATO) and the Warsaw Treaty Organization (WTO). These alliance systems provided collective security, although they were radically different in respect of their decision-making structures and levels of military integration. NATO established an integrated military command and its own political and administrative structures both to assist in the co-ordination of national military efforts, as well as to ensure that in a military crisis national armed forces would operate according to collectively agreed plans and strategies. NATO provided the main forum within which West European defence strategies were formulated and pursued. Moreover, it facilitated the creation of strong transgovernmental networks amongst national defence bureaucracies. Even the ending of the Cold War has not undermined the primary functions of NATO, and it continues to operate as the main international forum within which Western security matters are debated and defence policies coordinated. Indeed, following the collapse of the WTO, NATO established the North Atlantic Cooperation Council (NACC). NACC brings together the governing bodies of the Alliance and military and diplomatic representatives from the newly established East European and Soviet states to discuss European-wide security and military matters. Both in the routine conduct of its affairs and in times of international crisis (such as the 1991 Gulf War), NATO can be seen to impose significant constraints upon national military autonomy while also qualifying the sovereignty of member states in distinctive ways.

NATO articulates in a quite dramatic manner the "internationalization of security." But the ending of the Cold War, combined with instabilities in Europe, has encouraged further this internationalization or, more accurately, regionalization of security affairs (Mearsheimer, 1990; Rosecrance, 1992). Existing institutions such as the Western European Union (WEU) and the Conference on Security and Cooperation in Europe (CSCE)[2] have been given new responsibilities and functions, which have involved the creation of distinctive mechanisms of multilateral consultation and coordination. Europe, in effect, is witnessing the emergence of new structures of collective security – a new "Concert of Europe" – which invite a stronger international integration of military and security affairs. Moreover, given increasing budgetary constraints and the escalating costs of defence hardware, "in the not too distant future, no European country will be able to mount a unilateral conventional military campaign that can defeat any adversary able to conduct modern military operations" (Zelikow, 1992). One implication of this, as Zelikow acknowledges, is to intensify the pressures for stronger collective organization of defence functions. As the "New Concert of Europe" evolves, aspects of state autonomy and sovereignty are being renegotiated for nearly all states.

Disjuncture two: The world economy

There is a disjuncture between the formal authority of the state and the spatial reach of contemporary systems of production, distribution, and exchange, which often function to limit the competence and ef-

63

fectiveness of national economic policies (Frieden, 1991; Garrett and Lange, 1991; Gourevitch, 1986; O'Brien, 1992; Webb, 1991).

Two aspects of international economic processes are central: the internationalization of production and the globalization of financial transactions, organized in part by a relatively small number of powerful transnational corporations. Most transnational companies organize production, marketing, and distribution on a regional or global basis. Even though all transnational corporations have a national base, their activities are predominantly geared to maximizing their international competitive position and profitability such that individual (national) subsidiaries operate in the context of an overall corporate strategy. Investment and production decisions therefore may not always reflect local or national conditions. With the internationalization of production has come too the globalization of banking and financial services (Frieden, 1986; O'Brien, 1992). Information technology has transformed the finance sector such that a single global financial market now exists with almost round the clock trading. O'Brien refers to this financial revolution as defining the "end of geography" as currencies, stocks and shares, futures, bonds, etc., are traded electronically within a single global market-place (O'Brien, 1992).

Advances in transport and communication technology are rapidly eroding the boundaries between hitherto separate national markets – boundaries that were a necessary requirement for national economic management (Garrett and Lange, 1991; Keohane and Nye, 1972, pp. 392–395). Markets, and thus societies, are becoming more sensitive to one another. The Stock Market crash of October 1987 is one obvious illustration of this. Another example is the way in which violent movements in international financial markets impinge directly upon the monetary and fiscal policies of individual national governments and thus individual households and citizens. The existence of transnational networks of production, investment, and exchange ensures that few national markets or sectors of national economies can insulate themselves entirely from international conditions or external competitive pressures.

This globalization of economic forces has transformed the parameters within which national economic management is pursued. Although distinctive national styles of economic management exist, Gourevitch observes a general policy convergence amongst the advanced capitalist states specifically in respect of broad macro-economic measures (Gourevitch, 1986, p. 33). Thus, in the 1980s, the demise of the Keynesian strategy of "managed capitalism" – within the advanced capitalist countries – can be traced, in part, to an intensification of "interdependence," which undercut the effectiveness of the fiscal and interventionist policies necessary to sustain it (Cox, 1987; Gourevitch, 1986). Keynesianism functioned well in the context of "embedded liberalism," which provided the political and economic foundations for both national and international economic management in the post-war years (Keohane, 1984a). But the oil crisis of 1973 contributed to the demise of "embedded liberalism," which in turn undermined the whole basis of "managed capitalism." In a highly competitive but interconnected global economy, state economic strategies, together with the domestic political coalitions that underpin them, have become increasingly sensitive to world economic conditions. Frieden observes that "in April 1989, foreign exchange trading in the world's financial centres averaged about $650 billion a day, equivalent to nearly $500 million a minute and to forty times the amount of world trade a day" (Frieden, 1991, p. 428). This, as Webb indicates, was twice the amount of the total foreign reserve holdings of the US, Japanese, and UK central banks combined for the entire month (Webb, 1991, p. 320n). Accordingly, a very convincing argument can be made that the "implications of interdependence ... are clear: governments no longer possess the autonomy to pursue independent macroeconomic strategies effectively, even if they were to seek to do so" (Garrett and Lange, 1991, p. 543). This is simply because it is exceedingly difficult to "buck" global markets. However, although national economic policies are severely constrained, this does not mean that governments are completely immobilized.

The erosion of national economic autonomy is, of course, not uniformly experienced across countries or economic sectors; some countries and some markets can insulate themselves from transnational economic forces by, among other things, attempts to restore the boundaries or "separateness" of markets and/or to extend national laws to regulate internationally mobile factors and/or to adopt cooperative policies with other states for the coordination of economic and industrial policies (Cooper, 1986, pp. 1–22; Gilpin, 1987, pp. 397ff; Webb, 1991). According to Gordon, "the role of the state has grown substantially since the early 1970's; state policies have become increasingly decisive on the international front, not more futile ... And small consolation though it may be everyone including transnational corporations has become increasingly dependent upon coordinated state intervention" (Gordon, 1988, p. 63). In addition, the growing regionalization of the world economy is fuelled in part by the opportunities it affords for states to combat the more damaging consequences of global competitive forces. Economic activity appears increasingly to be clustered around several poles, amongst them the European Union, North America, Asia, and the Pacific rim (cf. Hine, 1992, p. 119).

It cannot, therefore, simply be concluded that the very idea of a national economy and national economic management is wholly superseded. As Frieden notes, "hampered as national governments may be or appear to be in the face of an internationally integrated financial system, they continue to have weapons in their policy arsenal" (Frieden, 1991, p. 451). Scharpf, too, convincingly argues that states matter by demonstrating that, despite global constraints, national economic policies and economic performance in Europe have not converged as much as is often assumed (Scharpf, 1991). However, the internationalization of production, finance, and exchange is unquestionably eroding the capacity of the individual liberal democratic state to control its own economic future. At the very least, there appears to be a diminution of state autonomy, and a disjuncture between the notion of a sovereign state directing its own future and the dynamics of the contemporary world economy.

Disjuncture three: Internationalization of the state

A third major disjuncture issues from the internationalization of the liberal democratic state itself. In the post-war period, states have found themselves increasingly engaged in multilateral forms of international governance. Governments now participate in an expanding array of international regimes and organizations that have been established to manage specific global issue areas (trade, the oceans, space, telecommunications, and so on). The growth in the number of these new forms of multilateral association reflects the rapid expansion of transnational activities, the growing interpenetration of foreign and domestic policy, and the corresponding desire by most states for some form of international governance and regulation to deal with collective policy problems (Cox 1992; Krasner 1983; Luard 1977).

The development of international regimes and international organizations has led to important changes in the structure of decision-making in world politics. New forms of multilateral and multinational politics have been created and with them distinctive styles of collective decision-making involving governments, intergovernmental organizations (IGOs), and a whole variety of transnational pressure groups and non-governmental organizations (INGOs). For example, the deliberations of the Earth Summit in Rio de Janeiro in June 1992 were attended by delegates from over 120 governments and scores of transnational and national environmental pressure groups and other transnational organizations.[3]

Among the spectrum of international governmental organizations are those UN specialized agencies whose primary responsibilities have been technical: the Universal Postal Union, the International Telecommunications Union, the World Meteorological Organization, and a host of others. These agencies have tended to function effectively and uncontroversially – providing, in most cases, extensions to the services offered by individual nation-states (Burnheim, 1986, p. 222; Luard, 1977). To the extent that their tasks have been highly delimited, they have been for the most part politically uncontroversial. At the opposite pole lie organizations like the World Bank, the International Monetary Fund, the General Agreement on Tariffs and Trade, and the United Nations itself. Preoccupied with the fundamental issues of rule making and resource allocation, these bodies have been highly politicized. Unlike the smaller, technically based agencies, these organizations are at the centre of a continual conflict over the control and direction of global policy (Burnheim, 1986, pp. 220ff; Soroos, 1986). Although the mode of operation of these organizations varies, they tend to function on the basis of consensual decision-making and so have benefited over the years from a certain "entrenchment of authority," which has bestowed on them some decisive interventionary powers. In addition to these organizations, there also exist a range of more informal global institutional structures and networks of political coordination that have considerable influence on global affairs. The Group of Seven (G7), for instance, brings together the world's advanced capitalist states and operates as a kind of "global directorate" (Lewis, 1991).

Despite its unique characteristics, the European Union (EU) provides a dramatic illustration of the issues posed by international organizations. The EU's authority reaches further than that of any other kind of international organization owing to its right to make laws that can be imposed on member states; more than any other international agency, it justifies the label "supranational" (Keohane and Hoffmann, 1990). Amongst EU institutions, the Council of Ministers has a unique position; for it has at its disposal powerful legal instruments (above all regulations and directives) that allow it to formulate and enact policy with a minimum of national democratic accountability. Of all these instruments, "regulations" are the most notable because they have the status of law independently of any further negotiation or action on the part of member states. Accordingly, the member states of the EU are no longer the sole centres of power within their own borders (Hoffmann, 1982; Keohane and Hoffmann, 1990). As the EU's Court of Justice has noted, "by creating a Community of unlimited duration, having its own institutions, its own personality ... and, more particularly, real powers stemming from a limitation of sovereignty or a transfer of powers from the States to the Community, the member States have limited their sovereign rights" (Mancini, 1990, p. 180). On the other hand, it is important to bear in mind that the EU's powers were gained by the "willing surrender" of aspects of sovereignty by member states. It is also worth recalling that the total EU budget amounts to no more than 2–3 per cent of member states' total public expenditure. This underlines the fact that national governments retain almost exclusive control over the public purse and so indicates where effective power still frequently lies (Wallace, 1991, p. 652).

Like many other international organizations, the EU provides distinctive opportunities and restraints. The member states of the EU retain the ultimate and most general power over many areas of their domestic and foreign affairs – and through the notion of "subsidiarity" the EU itself appears to have reinforced their options in some of these domains. However, within the EU, sovereignty is now also clearly divided: any conception of sovereignty that assumes that it is an indivisible, illimitable, exclusive, and perpetual form of public power – embodied within an individual state – is defunct.

Disjuncture four: International law

The development of international law has subjected individuals, governments and non-governmental organizations to new systems of legal regulation. Powers and constraints, and rights and duties, have been recognized in international law that transcend the claims of nation-states and that, while they may not be backed by institutions with coercive powers of enforcement, none the less have far-reaching consequences.

There are two legal rules that, since the formation of the international community, have been taken to uphold national sovereignty:

"immunity from jurisdiction" and "immunity from state agencies." The former prescribes that "no state can be sued in the courts of another state for acts performed in its sovereign capacity"; and the latter stipulates that "should an individual break the law of another state while acting as an agent for his country of origin and be brought before that state's courts, he is not held 'guilty' because he did not act as a private individual but as the representative of the state" (Cassese, 1988, pp. 150ff). The underlying purpose of these rules is to protect a government's autonomy in all matters of foreign policy and to prevent domestic courts from ruling on the behaviour of foreign states (on the understanding that all domestic courts everywhere will be so prevented). The upshot has traditionally been that governments have been left free to pursue their interests subject only to the constraints of the "art of politics." It is notable, however, that these internationally recognized legal mainstays of sovereignty have been progressively questioned by Western courts. And although it is the case that national sovereignty has most often been the victor when put to the test, the tension between national sovereignty and international law is now marked, and it is by no means clear how it will be resolved. Within the framework of EU law, this tension has developed into a "crisis"; with the passing of the Single European Act, which replaces unanimity by "qualified majority voting" within the Council of Ministers for a significant number of issue areas, the place of national sovereignty is no longer ensured (Noel, 1989).

Of all the international declarations of rights that were made in the post-war years, the European Convention of the Protection of Human Rights and Fundamental Freedoms (1950) is especially noteworthy. In marked contrast to the United Nations' Universal Declaration of Human Rights (1947) and subsequent UN charters of rights, the European Convention was concerned, as its preamble indicates, "to take the first steps for the *collective enforcement* of certain of the Rights of the UN Declaration" (emphasis added). The European initiative was committed to a most remarkable and radical legal innovation: an innovation that in principle would allow individual citizens to initiate proceedings against their own governments. European countries have now accepted an (optional) clause of the Convention that permits citizens to petition directly the European Commission on Human Rights, which can take cases to the Committee of Ministers of the Council of Europe and then (given a two-thirds majority on the Council) to the European Court of Human

Rights. Although the system is far from straightforward and is problematic in many respects, it has been claimed that, alongside the legal changes introduced by the EU, it no longer leaves the state "free to treat its own citizens as it thinks fit" (Capororti, 1983).[4] It is interesting to note too that the Maastricht Treaty (1992) makes provision for the establishment of European Union citizenship and an Ombudsman to which citizens may appeal directly.

The gap between the idea of membership of a national community, i.e. citizenship, which traditionally bestows upon individuals both rights and duties, and the creation in international law of novel forms of liberties and obligations is exemplified further by the judgments of the International Tribunal at Nuremberg. The Tribunal laid down, for the first time in history, that when international rules that protect basic humanitarian values are in conflict with state laws, every individual must transgress the state laws (except where there is no room for "moral choice") (Cassese, 1988, p. 132). The legal framework of the Nuremberg Tribunal marked a highly significant change in the legal direction of the modern state; for the new rules challenged the principle of military discipline and subverted national sovereignty at one of its most sensitive points – the hierarchical relations within the military.

International law is a "vast and changing corpus of rules and quasi-rules" that set out the basis of coexistence and cooperation in the international order. Traditionally, international law has identified and upheld without qualification the idea of a society of sovereign states as "the supreme normative principle" of the political organization of humankind (Bull, 1977, pp. 140ff). In recent decades, the subject, scope, and source of international law have all been contested; and opinion has shifted against the doctrine that international law is and should be a "law between states only and exclusively" (Oppenheim, 1905). At the heart of this shift lies a conflict between claims made on behalf of the states system and those made on behalf of an alternative organizing principle of world order – ultimately, a cosmopolitan community. This conflict is, however, far from concluded, and the renewed intensity of nationalism suggests that claims mobilized on behalf of a cosmopolitan community look, at the very least, hastily made.

Taken together, the four major disjunctures discussed above – security, economy, polity, and law – identify shifting patterns of powers and constraints that are redefining the architecture of sovereign political power associated with the liberal democratic state. They identify a set of forces that blur the boundaries of domestic and international politics, alter the institutional, organizational, and legal context of national polities, and obscure the lines of responsibility and accountability of national states themselves (Held, 1991, p. 222). In combination, they articulate the complex interaction of national and international processes that are reconstituting sovereign political structures. But how are we to interpret this new constellation of political power? What are its political meaning and implications? These questions can be addressed, in the first instance, by exploring the existing literatures of political theory and international relations for potential insights into the contemporary predicament of the liberal democratic state.

The limits of political theory and international relations theory

Ideas such as sovereignty and democracy still carry with them the marks of their earliest formulation during the epoch in which the nation-state – the liberal democratic nation-state – was being forged. It is evident that nineteenth- and twentieth-century social and political theories generally regarded the world beyond the liberal democratic state as a given – subject to a *ceteris paribus* clause. The "sovereignty" of the liberal democratic state was rarely questioned (see Held, 1989). It was generally assumed that the state had control over its own fate, subject only to compromises it must make and limits imposed upon it by groups and forces operating within its territorial boundaries, and by agencies and representatives of other nation-states. The concept of the liberal democratic state was regarded as unproblematic. The leading perspectives on societal change assumed that the origins of social transformation were to be found in processes internal to society (see Dunn, 1990; Giddens, 1985; Mann, 1986). Change was assumed to occur via mechanisms "built in," as it were, to the very structure of a given society, and governing its development. The world beyond the nation-state – the dynamics of the world economy, the intensification of transnational links, international law and institutions, for example – was barely theorized.

It is intriguing to note that conceptions of the state were not always like this. Early theorists of "international society" – such as Grotius and Kant – sought to develop an understanding of the state in the context of the "society of states" (Bull, 1977; Held, forthcoming;

Hinsley, 1967). They explored the conditions and requirements of co-existence and cooperation among states, focusing in particular on the nature and extent of law-governed relations. These thinkers provided a crucial stimulus to the development of international law and to international political theory. Although elements of their work survived in international law and international relations theory, they were all too often lost to political and social theory as a whole, as can be seen in the literature on the theory of modern democratic government as it developed in the nineteenth century.

Among the dominant figures here was John Stuart Mill. Mill, as is well known, sought to defend a conception of political life marked by individual liberty, accountable government, and an efficient governmental administration unhindered by corrupt practices and excessively complex regulations (see Mill, 1951). Yet, while admirable in a number of respects, Mill's analysis remained essentially inattentive to the restructuring of the national polity brought about by an emerging global division of labour and the demands of empire. Mill produced one of the most eloquent accounts of democratic government but, along with nearly all subsequent democratic theorists, failed to examine the extent to which the very idea of a national system of accountability and control was compromised in an increasingly complex and interconnected global system. While this failure is quite understandable in Mill, since Britain was the world's hegemonic power in the nineteenth century, it is less and less understandable in contemporary political thinking.

Responding to the rapid and disorienting processes of nineteenth-century industrial development in Europe, Marx and Weber provided some of the most enduring analyses of state–society relations by focusing on class, power, and the nature of democratic organization (see Beetham, 1984; Giddens, 1985; Held, 1989, chs. 1 and 2; Mommsen, 1974; Perez-Diaz, 1978; Wright, 1978). But the views of these classical thinkers cannot simply be accepted. Marx left a thoroughly ambiguous heritage, never fully reconciling his understanding of the state as an instrument of class domination with his acknowledgement that the state might be a system of power *sui generis*. Weber, in contrast, resisted all suggestions that forms of state organization were directly determined by class relations. He stressed the internally homologous nature of private and public administration as well as their independent dynamics. However, although Marx sought to relate his conception of the state to the nature of international capital, and Weber sought to understand national politics in the context of the European states system, neither of these figures appreciated fully that the attempt to understand the interconnections between the national and the international must involve a process of mapping their mutual interpenetration.

Twentieth-century social and political science has, to a large degree, been preoccupied with an examination and assessment of the contribution of these thinkers. A variety of diverse and competing traditions has been spawned. A central tradition in Anglo-American political science elaborated a pluralist conception of society and posed a set of claims about the state that contrasts strongly with Marxist positions – rejecting all claims that state power has a class basis (see the *locus classicus*, Dahl, 1956, 1971; Truman, 1951; and cf., for example, Lindblom, 1977). In opposition to pluralists, contemporary Marxists attempted to revise the interpretation of the state as a class state in the light of the complex practices of Western post-war governments (see Miliband, 1969; Offe, 1984; and Jessop, 1990). While modifying Marx's original analysis, they preserved some of the essential links he drew between political power and class power and adopted some of Weber's insights into the workings of state administration. A third school, which emerged forcefully in the 1970s, found the claims of neither pluralist theory nor Marxist theory fully satisfactory. Theorists of "corporatism" challenged the validity of these other theories, focusing particularly on an explanation of state policies and institutional arrangements that seek to harmonize conflicting social interests (see, for example, Panitch, 1977; Schmitter, 1979; Winkler, 1976; cf. Cerny, 1990). But none of these theories, like their predecessors, systematically confronted the issue of the growing permeability of state and society to external forces. Given these deficiencies, it is natural that any social scientist seeking to understand the predicament of the liberal democratic state in the context of a global system of action would turn to the well-established frameworks of international relations theory.

For much of this century the study of international relations has been dominated by the realist tradition (see Smith, 1989). This tradition has often been referred to as "statist," because it is almost exclusively concerned with how the global states system conditions the behaviour of liberal democratic states (Morgenthau, 1967; Waltz, 1979). Within realist thinking, the complex interplay of internal and external forces remains largely unexplored in accounts of state action. For, in the context of a global states system, the liberal democratic state is conceived principally as a sovereign, monolithic, and organic entity whose primary purpose is to promote and defend the national interest in a world in which there is no recourse to a higher authority. At its crudest, the realist tradition views the state as a vehicle for securing national and international order through the exercise of national power. In some respects the state is regarded almost as an epiphenomenon. Moreover, the categories "state," "nation-state," and "nation" are used interchangeably, even though these terms refer to distinct conceptual entities (Tilly, 1990). Similarly, there is a strong tendency in realist literature to conflate "state" and "society," illustrating a remarkable failure to conceptualize this critical relationship.

However, realism has not failed totally to acknowledge the significance of processes of globalization (see, for example, Gilpin 1981, 1987). On the contrary, sophisticated treatments of the emergence of international regimes and intergovernmental cooperation have been developed (Keohane, 1984a; Young, 1989). Behind this theorizing is a strong sense of the continued primacy of the liberal democratic state in world politics combined with an explicit rejection of those accounts that interpret the intensification of global interconnectedness as portending a "crisis of the territorial nation-state." But although "neo-realism" has revived intellectual interest amongst international relations scholars in the "state," this has so far not been expressed in any systematic theoretical enquiry. Only in more sophisticated neo-realist analyses has the notion of the "state" come to be explored with any rigour (Krasner, 1978, 1988; Mastanduno et al., 1989). Yet, even here, the state is conceived as little more than a sovereign, rational, egoistic actor on the global stage (Keohane, 1986; Waltz, 1979). Accordingly, there is much evidence to suggest that realism and neo-realism do not possess a systematically articulated or convincing theory of the liberal democratic state despite the fact that realism itself retains a powerful grip on the international relations community and diplomats the world over.

Some attempt to theorize the modern liberal democratic state within its web of global interconnectedness is to be found in the rather eclectic literature that has its philosophical roots in the "liberal–idealist" tradition in international relations (Howard, 1981). Despite its eclecticism, the common thread uniting this particular school of thought is the assumption that increasing global interconnectedness is transforming the nature and role of the state in the global system (see Brown, 1988; Morse, 1976; Rosenau, 1988, 1990). In essence, this "transformationalist" literature portrays the modern state as trapped within an extensive web of global interdependence, heavily permeated by transnational forces, and increasingly unable to fulfil its core functions without recourse to international cooperation (Keohane and Nye, 1972; Mansbach et al., 1976; Rosenau, 1990; Soroos, 1986). There is considerable emphasis in this work on the decline or the crisis of the territorial nation-state brought about by the tempo and diffusion of modernizing processes. A world of "complex interdependence," it is argued, has dramatic implications for the autonomy and sovereignty of the liberal democratic state. Interdependence involves a sensitivity and vulnerability to external developments, compromising the autonomy of states, and crucially eroding the boundaries between the internal and external domains (Keohane and Nye, 1989). Moreover, the growth of regional and global institutions is interpreted as further evidence of the limited capacity of the liberal democratic state to resolve independently the key policy problems that confront it.

At the heart of this "transformationalist" conception of the state is an essentially pluralist set of assumptions (Brown, 1988). This involves a conceptualization of the state as a fragmented institutional ensemble overseeing multiple policy-making arenas that are increasingly permeated by both domestic and transnational forces. Significant emphasis is also placed upon the conceptual differentiation between the state and civil society (Luard, 1990). This encourages a particular focus on the mechanisms by which the extensive penetration of civil society by transnational activity transforms the relationship between state and society, as well as the conventional distinction between domestic and international politics (Morse, 1976). As a consequence, the realist notion of the monolithic, unitary, sovereign state is viewed with considerable scepticism. But although such observations may be valid, the transformationalist literature has so far failed to provide a convincing or coherent account of the modern liberal democratic state itself. In particular, it tends to exaggerate the erosion of state power in the face of globalizing pressures and fails to recognize the enduring capacity of the modern state apparatus, especially in regional contexts, to control the direction of domestic and international politics. The degree to which the state enjoys "autonomy" under various conditions is underestimated and, therefore, a key basis for a systematic and rigorous account of the modern state is too hastily neglected.

Many of the same developments that gave rise to the "transformationalist" critique of realism have also injected renewed vigour into more radical approaches to international relations. The apparent intensification of economic interdependence between advanced capitalist states, combined with the emergence of the newly industrializing countries on the world's so-called "periphery," has challenged classical Marxist explanations of world politics (see Warren, 1973). Imperialism and theories of monopoly capitalism no longer seem convincing approaches to understanding the complexities of a new global division of labour and the associated transnationalization of capital (Kitching, 1982). Like realism, Marxism has advanced new conceptions of the state in its global setting. World systems theory, and associated neo-Marxist projects, have attempted to engage with the globalization of capitalism (see Amin, 1972, 1990; Cox, 1987; Sunkel and Fuenzelida, 1979; Wallerstein 1974, 1979, 1983, 1990, 1991). At the intellectual core of these approaches is an account of the modern state that stresses its limited autonomy from the dictates of transnational capital or the structural requirements of the global capitalist order. States are thus conceived as partially autonomous political entities (Cox, 1987; Gill and Law, 1989).

Although neo-Marxist attempts to confront the ramifications of economic globalization for the modern state have led to a more sophisticated conceptualization of the state's relation to global economic forces, significant issues remain largely unaddressed. In particular, the emphasis given to the relative autonomy of the state from transnational and national capital arises out of a recognition that the global states system, as opposed to the world capitalist system, has its own internal logic and imperatives. Yet the formation and operation of states tend to be explained primarily in terms of the global expansion of capitalism or Western-led modernization, i.e. the state is conceived as an epiphenomenon (see Skocpol, 1977; Tilly, 1990; Zolberg, 1981). This apparent failure to reconcile the independent dynamics of a global states system with the functioning of the world capitalist system is a profound weakness in many neo-Marxist analyses. World systems theory, along with associated Marxisant theories of the global political economy, has not delivered a satisfactory theory of the modern state in its global context.

Within the post-Marxist and post-structuralist literatures on international relations there is a serious attempt to address the nature of the state in the face of globalizing pressures and forces (Walker, 1988, 1990). Indeed, this "dissident" strand of contemporary theorizing starts from the assumption that "any theory of the state that takes the distinction between insider/outsider [internal/external] as unproblematic, or worse, as simply given, must be questioned" (Walker, 1988, pp. 26–27). However, as Ferguson and Mansbach acknowledge, "dissident" accounts, largely because of their critical aspirations, have engaged more fully with the deconstruction of existing approaches to international relations than with the task of constructing alternative paradigms that might offer a coherent and convincing analysis of the contemporary predicament of the state (Ferguson and Mansbach, 1991).

The traditional literature of state theory and the existing frameworks of international relations theory have complementary limitations. One cannot go to either literature to make good the defects in the other. The theory of the modern liberal democratic state is without a conception of the state in the global arena, and theories of the global system are without a conception of the modern liberal democratic state. As the discussion of disjunctures suggests, these limitations must be overcome if a sophisticated understanding of the reconstitution of sovereign political power is to be achieved. Simply stated, there cannot be an account of the liberal democratic state any longer without an examination of the global system, and there cannot be an examination of the global system without an account of the liberal democratic state. The way forward is to transcend the endogenous and exogenous frameworks of, respectively, the theory of the state and international relations.[5]

The liberal democratic state in the global order

It could be objected that there is nothing particularly new about global interconnections, and that the significance of globalization for politics has, in principle, been evident for some time. Such an objection could be elaborated by emphasizing that a dense pattern of global interconnections began to emerge with the initial expansion of the world economy and the rise of the modern state from the late sixteenth century. Further, it could be suggested that domestic and international politics have been interwoven throughout the modern era: domestic politics has always to be understood against the background of international politics; and the former is often the source of the latter. However, it is one thing to claim that there are elements of continuity in the formation and structure of modern states, economies, and societies; quite another to claim that there is nothing new about aspects of their form and dynamics. For there is a fundamental difference between, on the one hand, the development of particular trade routes and the global reach of nineteenth century empires, and, on the other hand, an international order involving the conjuncture of: a global system of production and exchange that is beyond the control of any single nation-state (even of the most powerful); extensive networks of transnational interaction and communication that transcend national societies and evade most forms of national regulation; the power and activities of a vast array of international regimes and organizations, many of which reduce the scope for action of even leading states; and the internationalization of security structures that limit the scope for the independent use of military force by states. Whereas in the eighteenth and nineteenth centuries trade routes and empires linked distant populations together through quite simple networks of interaction, the contemporary global order is defined by multiple systems of transactions and coordination that link people, communities, and societies in highly complex ways and that, given the nature of modern communications, virtually annihilate territorial boundaries as barriers to socio-economic activity and relations.

What is distinctive about the contemporary global system is the degree to which globalization and regionalization have become inscribed in the dynamics of modernity and modern social existence. In comparison with previous epochs, a globalizing imperative is evident in each of the key institutional domains – the political, the legal, the economic, and the military – that help define the characteristic form of modern societies. Within each of these domains, globalization is driven by a discrete dynamic of change; and the chronic intensification of patterns of interconnectedness to which it gives rise is mediated by a global communications infrastructure and new information technology. Politics unfolds today, with all its customary uncertainty and indeterminateness, against the background of a world shaped and permeated by the movement of capital, the flow of communication, and the passage of people (Kegley and Wittkopf, 1989, p. 511).

This is not to argue that processes of globalization and regionalization are necessarily leading to greater integration; that is, to a political order marked by the progressive development of a unified society and institutionalized polity. For, as noted earlier, these processes generate both fragmentation and unification. Fragmentation or disintegrative trends are evident for several reasons. The growth of dense patterns of interconnectedness among states and societies increases the range and impact of developments affecting people or communities in particular locations. By creating new patterns of transformation and change, globalization and regionalization can weaken established political and economic structures without necessarily creating new systems of regulation. Further, the impact of global and regional processes is likely to vary under different international and national conditions – for instance, a nation's location in the world economy, its place in particular power blocs, its position with respect to particular international regimes and organizations. In addition, globalization and regionalization engender an awareness of political difference as much as an awareness of common identity; enhanced international communications highlight conflicts of interest and ideology, and not merely remove obstacles to mutual understanding (Bull, 1977).

In this context, the meaning and place of democratic politics have to be rethought in relation to a series of overlapping local, regional, and global processes and structures. At least three elements of change are essential to recognize: first, the way processes of economic, legal, political, and military interconnectedness are altering the nature, scope, and capacity of the sovereign state from above, as its "regulatory" ability is challenged and reduced in some spheres; secondly, the way local and regional groups, movements, and ethnic communities are questioning the liberal democratic state from below as a representative and accountable power system; and, thirdly, the way global interconnectedness creates chains of interlocking political decisions and outcomes among states and their citizens, reconstituting in the process the relationship between sovereignty, democracy, and the territorial political community. Democratic politics has to come to terms with all of these developments. If it fails to do so, it is likely to become ever less effective in determining the shape and limits of political activity. The globalization of politics and civil society has, accordingly, to be built into the foundations of democratic thought and practice – a task barely begun today (see Held, 1992).

Notes

1. For a good discussion of regionalization and regionalism, see Buzan (1991) and Cantori and Spiegel (1970).
2. The WEU is a collective defence organization of nine West European states formed in 1948. It is developing a significant military and political role, linking the EU and NATO structures. The CSCE is a grouping of 50 states (all European states in addition to the United States and Canada) whose main function is to foster political stability and military security in Europe.

3. In 1909 there were 37 IGOs and 176 INGOs. In 1989 there were nearly 300 IGOs and 4624 INGOs.
4. In Britain alone, for example, telephone tapping laws have been altered after intervention by the European Commission, and the findings of the European Court of Justice have led to changes in British law on issues as far-reaching as sexual discrimination and equal pay.
5. Significant steps have been taken in this direction recently by Skocpol (1979), Gourevitch (1986), Giddens (1985, 1990), Hall and Ikenberry (1989), Mann (1986), and Tilly (1990), amongst others. They share in common a stress on integrating international conditions and processes into an analysis of the modern state. Their research and writings stand as a major advance on the traditional state literature. However, while their contribution is highly significant, it can be taken only as a starting point, for it does not fully engage international relations with political science or political sociology.

Bibliography

Amin, S. (1972) *Accumulation on a World Scale*. New York: Monthly Review Press.
——— (1990) *Delinking*, 2nd edn. London: Zed Books.
Beetham, D. (1984) "The Future of the Nation-State." In: G. McLennan et al., eds. *The Idea of the Modern State*. Milton Keynes: Open University Press.
Beitz, C. (1991) "Sovereignty and Morality in International Affairs." In: D. Held, ed. *Political Theory Today*. Cambridge: Polity Press.
Brown, S. (1988) *New Forces, Old Forces and the Future of World Politics*. Boston: Scott/Foreman.
Bull, H. (1977) *The Anarchical Society*. London: Macmillan.
Burnheim, J. (1986) "Democracy, the Nation State and the World System." In: D. Held and D. Pollitt, eds. *New Forms of Democracy*. London: Sage.
Buzan, B. (1991) *People, States and Fear*. Brighton: Harvester Press.
Cantori, L. J., and S. Spiegel (1970) *The International Politics of Regions: A Comparative Approach*. Englewood Cliffs, NJ: Prentice-Hall.
Capororti, F. (1983) "Human Rights: The Hard Road towards Universality." In: R. St. J. Macdonald and D. M. Johnson, eds. *The Structure and Process of International Law*. The Hague: Martinus Nijhoff.
Carr, E. H. (1946) *The Twenty Years Crisis 1919–1939*. London: Macmillan.
Cassese, A. (1988) "Violence, War and the Rule of Law in the International Community." In: *Violence and Law in the Modern Age*. Cambridge: Polity Press.
Cerny, P. G. (1990) *The Changing Architecture of Politics*. London: Sage.
Cooper, R. N. (1986) *Economic Policy in an Interdependent World*. Cambridge, Mass.: MIT Press.
Cox, R. W. (1987) *Production, Power and World Order*. New York: Columbia University Press.
——— (1992) "Multilateralism and World Order." *Review of International Studies* 18, no. 2: 161–180.
Dahl, R. (1956) *A Preface to Democratic Theory*. Chicago: University of Chicago Press.
——— (1971) *Polyarchy: Participation and Opposition*. New Haven, Conn.: Yale University Press.
Dunn, J. (1990) "Responsibility without Power." In: *Interpreting Political Responsibility*. Cambridge: Polity Press.

Falk, R. A. (1970) *Status of Law in International Society*. Princeton, NJ: Princeton University Press.

Ferguson, Y., and R. Mansbach (1991) "Between Celebration and Despair." *International Studies Quarterly* 35: 303–386.

Frieden, J. (1986) *Banking on the World*. New York: Basic Books.

────── (1991) "Invested Interests: The Politics of National Economic Policies in a World of Global Finance." *International Organization* 45, no. 4: 425–453.

Garrett, G., and P. Lange (1991) "Political Responses to Interdependence: What's Left for the Left?" *International Organization* 45, no. 4: 539–565.

Giddens, A. (1985) *The Nation-State and Violence*. Cambridge: Polity Press.

────── (1990) *The Consequences of Modernity*. Cambridge: Polity Press.

────── (1991) *Modernity and Self Identity*. Cambridge: Polity Press.

Gill, S., and D. Law (1989) "Global Hegemony and the Structural Power of Capital." *International Studies Quarterly* 33, no. 4: 475–500.

Gilpin R. (1981) *War and Change in World Politics*. Cambridge: Cambridge University Press.

────── (1987) *The Political Economy of International Relations*. Princeton, NJ: Princeton University Press.

Girvan, N. (1980) "Swallowing the IMF Medicine in the Seventies." *Development Dialogue* 2.

Gordon, D. (1988) "The Global Economy." *New Left Review* no. 168: 24–65.

Gourevitch, P. (1978) "The Second Image Reversed: The International Sources of Domestic Politics." *International Organization* 32, no. 4.

────── (1986) *Politics in Hard Times*. New York: Cornell University Press.

Hall, J., and P. Ikenberry (1989) *The State*. Milton Keynes: Open University Press.

Harvey, D. (1989) *The Condition of Postmodernity*. Oxford: Basil Blackwell.

Held, D. (1989) *Political Theory and the Modern State*. Cambridge: Polity Press.

────── (1991) "Democracy, the Nation-state and the Global System." In: D. Held, ed. *Political Theory Today*. Cambridge: Polity Press.

────── (1992) "Democracy: From City-states to a Cosmopolitan Order?" *Political Studies* September (special issue).

────── (forthcoming) *The Foundations of Democracy*. Cambridge: Polity Press.

Held, D., and A. G. McGrew (1989) "Globalization and the Advanced Industrial State." Unpublished research paper.

Hertz, J. H. (1976) *The Nation-State and the Crisis of World Politics*. New York: McKay.

Hine, R. (1992) "Regionalism and the Integration of the World Economy." *Journal of Common Market Studies* 30, no. 2: 115–123.

Hinsley, F. (1967) *Power and the Pursuit of Peace*. Cambridge: Cambridge University Press.

Hobsbawm, E. (1990) *Nations and Nationalism since 1780*. Cambridge: Cambridge University Press.

Hoffmann, S. (1982) "Reflections on the Nation-state in Western Europe Today." *Journal of Common Market Studies* XXI, nos. 1 and 2.

Howard, M. (1981) *War and the Liberal Conscience*. Oxford: Oxford University Press.

Jessop, B. (1990) *State Theory*. Cambridge: Polity Press.

Kegley, C. W., and E. R. Wittkopf (1989) *World Politics*. London: Macmillan.

Keohane, R. (1984a) *After Hegemony*. Princeton, NJ: Princeton University Press.

81

────── (1984b) "The World Political Economy and the Crisis of Embedded Liberalism." In J. H. Goldthorpe, ed. *Order and Conflict in Contemporary Capitalism*. Oxford: Oxford University Press.

────── (1986) *Neo-Realism and its Critics*. New York: Columbia University Press.

Keohane, R., and S. Hoffmann, eds. (1990) *The New European Community*. Oxford: Westview Press.

Keohane, R., and J. Nye, eds. (1972) *Transnational Relations and World Politics*. Boston: Harvard University Press.

────── (1989) *Power and Interdependence*, 2nd edn. Boston: Little Brown.

King, A., ed. (1991) *Culture, Globalization and the World System*. London: Macmillan.

Kitching, G. (1982) *Development and Underdevelopment in Historical Perspective*. London: Methuen.

Kolko, J. (1988) *Restructuring the World Economy*. New York: Pantheon.

Krasner, S. (1978) *Defending the National Interest*. Princeton, NJ: Princeton University Press.

────── (1983) *International Regimes*. Ithaca, NY: Cornell University Press.

────── (1988) "Sovereignty: An Institutional Perspective." *Comparative Political Studies* 21, no. 1: 66–94.

Lewis, R. (1991) "The G7$\frac{1}{2}$ Directorate." *Foreign Policy* no. 85: 25–40.

Lindblom, C. E. (1977) *Politics and Markets*. New York: Basic Books.

Luard, E. (1977) *International Agencies: The Framework of Interdependence*. London: Macmillan.

────── (1990) *Globalization of Politics*. London: Macmillan.

McGrew, A. G. (1992a) "Conceptualizing Global Politics." In: A. G. McGrew, P. Lewis et al. *Global Politics*. Cambridge: Polity Press, pp. 1–28.

────── (1992b) "A Global Society?" In: S. Hall, D. Held, and A. McGrew, eds. *Modernity and its Futures*. Cambridge: Polity Press.

Mancini, G. (1990) "The Making of a Constitution for Europe." In: R. Keohane and S. Hoffmann, eds. *The New European Community*. Oxford: Westview Press.

Mann, M. (1986) *The Sources of Social Power*, vol. 1. Cambridge: Cambridge University Press.

Mansbach, R. et al. (1976) *The Web of World Politics*. New York: Prentice Hall.

Mastanduno, M. et al. (1989) "Towards a Realist Theory of State Action." *International Studies Quarterly* 33, no. 4: 457–474.

Mearsheimer, J. (1990) "Back to the Future." *International Security* 15, no. 1: 5–56.

Mennel, S. (1990) "The Globalization of Human Society as a Very Long Term Process: Elias's Theory." In: M. Featherstone, ed. *Global Culture*. London: Sage.

Miliband, R. (1969) *The State in Capitalist Society*. London: Weidenfeld & Nicolson.

Mill, J. S. (1951) "Considerations on Representative Government." In: H. B. Acton, ed. *Utilitarianism, Liberty and Representative Government*. London: Dent.

Mommsen, W. (1974) *The Age of Bureaucracy*. Oxford: Basil Blackwell.

Morgenthau, H. (1967) *Politics Among Nations*. New York: A. Knopf.

Morse, E. (1976) *Modernization and the Transformation of International Relations*. New York: Free Press.

Noel, J. (1989) "The Single European Act." *Government in Opposition* 24.

Nordlinger, E. (1983) *On the Autonomy of the Democratic State*. Boston: Harvard University Press.

O'Brien, R. (1992) *The End of Geography*. London: Routledge/RIIA.

Offe, C. (1984) *Contradictions of the Welfare State*. London: Hutchinson.

Oppenheim, L. (1905) *International Law*, vol. 1. London: Longman.

Panitch, L. (1977) "The Development of Corporatism in Liberal Democracies." *Comparative Political Studies* 10, no. 1.

Perez-Diaz, M. (1978) *State, Bureaucracy and Civil Society*. London: Macmillan.

Richelson, J., and D. Ball (1986) *The Ties That Bind*. London: Allen & Unwin.

Robertson, R. (1991) "Social Theory, Cultural Relativity and the Problem of Globality." In: A. King, ed. *Culture, Globalization and the World System*. London: Macmillan.

Rosecrance, R. (1992) "A New Concert of Powers." *Foreign Affairs* 71, no. 2: 64–82.

Rosenau, J. (1980) *The Study of Global Interdependence*. London: Frances Pinter.

―――― (1988) "The State in an Era of Cascading Politics." *Comparative Political Studies* 21, no. 1: 13–45.

―――― (1990) *Turbulence in World Politics*. London: Harvester.

Ruggie, J. G. (1982) "International Regimes, Transactions and Change: Embedded Liberalism in the Post War Economic Order." *International Organization* no. 36.

―――― (1991) "Finding Our Feet in Territoriality," mimeo.

Scharpf, F. (1991) *Crisis and Choice in European Social Democracy*. Ithaca, NY: Cornell University Press.

Schmitter, P. (1979) "Models of Interest Intermediation and Models of Societal Change in Western Europe." *Comparative Political Studies* 10, no. 1.

Skocpol, T. (1977) "Wallerstein's World Capitalist System: A Theoretical and Historical Critique." *American Journal of Sociology* 82, no. 5: 1977–1990.

―――― (1979) *States and Social Revolutions*. Cambridge: Cambridge University Press.

Smith, R. (1987) "Political Economy and Britain's External Position." In: *Britain in the World*. London: ESRC.

Smith, S. (1989) "The Fall and Rise of the State in International Politics." In: G. Duncan, *Democracy and the Capitalist State*. Cambridge: Cambridge University Press.

Soroos, M. (1986) *Beyond Sovereignty*. Columbia, S.C.: University of South Carolina Press.

Staniland, M. (1985) *What Is Political Economy?* New Haven, Conn.: Yale University Press.

Sunkel, O., and E. Fuenzelida (1979) "Transnationalization and Its National Consequences." In: J. Villamil, *Transnational Capitalism and National Development*. Brighton: Wheatsheaf.

Tilly, C. (1990) *Coercion, Capital and European States, AD 990–1990*. Oxford: Blackwell.

Truman, D. B. (1951) *The Governmental Process*. New York: Knopf.

Walker, R. (1988) *State Sovereignty, Global Civilization and the Rearticulation of Political Space*. Princeton University Center for International Studies.

―――― (1990) "Sovereignty, Identity, Community: Reflections on the Horizons of Contemporary Political Practice." In R. Walker and S. H. Mendlovitz, eds. *Contending Sovereignties*. London: Lynne Reiner.

Wallace, H. (1991) "The Europe That Came in from the Cold." *International Affairs* 67, no. 4: 647–663.

Wallerstein, I. (1974) "The Rise and Future Demise of the World Capitalist System." *Comparative Studies in Society and History* XVI, no. 4: 381–415.

—— (1979) *The Capitalist World Economy*. Cambridge: Cambridge University Press.

—— (1983) *Historical Capitalism*. London: Verso.

—— (1990) *Antisystemic Movements*. London: Verso.

—— (1991) *Geopolitics and Geoculture*. Cambridge: Cambridge University Press.

Waltz, K. (1979) *Theory of International Politics*. New York: Addison-Wesley.

Warren, B. (1973) "Imperialism and Capitalist Industrialization." *New Left Review* no. 81 (Sept/Oct).

Webb, C. (1991) "International Economic Structures, Government Interests, and International Co-ordination of Macro-economic Adjustment Policies." *International Organization* 45, no. 3: 309–343.

Winkler, E. (1976) "Corporatism." *Archives européennes de sociologie* 17, no. 1.

Wright, E. (1978) *Class, Crisis and the State*. London: New Left Books.

Young, O. (1989) *International Cooperation*. Ithaca, NY: Cornell University Press.

Zelikow, P. (1992) "The New Concert of Europe." *Survival* 34, no. 2: 12–30.

Zolberg, A. (1981) "Origins of the Modern World System: A Missing Link." *World Politics* 33, no. 2: 253–281.

3

The internationalization of the state in the Middle East

Nassif Hitti

The changing world order, which is not to be confused with the politico-messianic slogan of the New World Order, embodies certain traits, the interaction of which with different regional systems depends by and large on two factors: first, how well entrenched these traits already are in the post-Cold War order; and, secondly, the nature of the regional dynamics and particularities of each system. In this context, internationalization is best defined as the responsiveness of the state at both the formal and societal levels to these systemic changes.

The second Gulf crisis, provoked by Iraq's invasion of Kuwait, constitutes a fundamental intervening variable in these interactions, for it came amidst a period of transition. The crisis was acclaimed by the victors as the "First real test," to quote President Bush, of the "New World Order."[1]

In the case of the Middle East, which was both the geographical and the psychological epicentre of the crisis, the tremor of the crisis acted as a catalyst, a facilitator, and sometimes the channel of change and thus responsiveness to the changing world order.

A Pax Americana or a tricontinental order?

The US victory in the Gulf War reinforced the perception of a Pax Americana order or a unipolar structure. The proponents of this pyramidal power structure base their argument solely on the factor of military capabilities. Yet this view suffers from two shortcomings: a unicausality in assessing the hierarchy of power and a self-imposed temporal limitation in generalizing about a process of system building that should go beyond the illusion of the moment.

In the Gulf crisis the aggrandizement of the US role was not due particularly to the element of military power. By the nature of things, the balance of power was disproportionately tilted against Iraq. It was rather the nature of the conflict and Iraq's management of the conflict that created the opportunity for the US victory.

Indeed, the United States would not have been able to conduct the war against Iraq without substantial financial backing from allies and friends. As stated by the chairman of the UN Study Group on Nuclear Deterrence, "A nation that requires billions from other nations to finance a war with a developing country cannot expect to impose its own order on the globe."[2]

Thus, the Gulf crisis is likely to be of more interest to historians because of its uniqueness than to political scientists who are looking for new patterns of conflict diplomacy in the post-Cold War era. With the rise of the logic of geo-economics at the expense of the logic of geopolitics, the world order appears to be moving toward a tricontinental model evolving around three core continental powers:

- the United States and the American continent, starting with the North American Free Trade Area and gradually moving south;
- the European Union (EU), with its eco-magnetic power attracting a Europe that extends from the Atlantic to the Urals. Within the EU, the French–German couple stands as the moving force;
- the Asian Pacific region evolving around Japan, which is trying to assert itself politically by searching for a status appropriate to its economic capabilities.

The competition over regional influence has been shaping up among the three. For instance, during the multilateral talks in the Arab–Israeli peace process held on 28 and 29 January 1992 in Moscow, the European Community accused the United States, which had tried to keep the EC outside the Committee on Disarmament and Arms control, of wanting to run with the ball alone.

Because of its vast economic resources and the high absorption capacities of its markets, the Middle East is the most suitable arena for such competition. Two aspects of the Gulf crisis could be considered to be an American attempt to score against its fellows in the "North." Perhaps this explains the degree of reticence that characterized the behaviour of the two leading economic powers, Japan and Germany.

The first instance is the competition over oil; the US image as the prime security guarantor and balance holder in the Gulf is a precious dividend in the new competition over resources. The United States has since become a strong influencer of OPEC policies. Thus, the international oil regime has been deeply penetrated by the United States through the Middle East.

The second post-crisis dividend was the gigantic financial opportunity for reconstruction in the Gulf. Around US$79 billion will be spent on oil infrastructure in the Gulf in the years to come.[3] The announcement was made by the Deputy Secretary of Energy in the United States, which enjoys preferential status in the competition over the Gulf market. The perception of the United States not only as the sole guarantor of stability but also as a conflict manager with the ability to settle the Arab–Israeli conflict increased its regional clout and made the Middle East more receptive and vulnerable to American demands and interests. States that are surrounded by a high-level threat environment are turning to the United States for security arrangements and arms transfer. This is the case of the Gulf Cooperation Council states. Others, which need to change an unsustainable status quo, are seeking US help in this respect. The parties to the Arab–Israeli conflict fall into this category. While the US presence is strongly felt from the Suez to the Persian Gulf, specifically on its Arabian shores, the periphery of the Middle East was cultivating relations with the two other major powers. Iran's economic relations are developing steadily with Japan, with which there exist no psychological barriers like those that are erected between Iran and the United States and to a lesser degree between Iran and Europe. This cooperation structure is reinforced by Iran's perception of Japan as a culturally authentic non-Western model of development.

On the other hand, the EU, particularly its Mediterranean members, is diversifying its links with the Maghreb countries, namely Tunisia, Algeria, and Morocco. Because of the dependence of the latter countries on the export of goods and labour to the EU and the importance of stabilizing these countries as a vital European goal, a network of both multilateral and bilateral links is being reinforced.

While the Anglo-Saxons are in the Arab East and the continental

Europeans in North Africa, it seems the old history of tension and confrontation between the great powers and the Middle East is being replaced by strong economic and security dependence. Thus, the two sides in each equation are still imprisoned in their long relationship, although turning a page of history for a new chapter. As long as the Middle East environment embodies sources of threat at the regional level, there will be both an opportunity for and a constraint on the US role. Although the United States should succeed in trading off its security guarantees for economic goodies, it could also run the risk of becoming entangled in a regional or local conflict. As far as Japan and the EU are concerned, they could promote their interests through economic aid diplomacy. Theoretically, the formation of a tricontinental order should increase the margin of profitability of Middle Eastern actors by allowing them to manoeuvre among the Big Three. But again, unless there is a free or low-risk environment, the regional actors' economic choices will remain politicized and thus less apt for bargaining, and more conducive to linkage between security and economic goods. Thus, the end of the geostrategic competition over the Middle East paved the way for geo-economic competition. Though the actors are different in the two cases, the goals could bear a certain resemblance in some aspects of the competition. Whereas the United States acted to contain the Soviet Union and keep it outside the region as part of the geostrategic competition, it is now working toward the same end *vis-à-vis* Japan and the EU as part of the geo-economic competition.

A triumphant model

The emerging North–South axis does not have anything in common with the North–South dialogue of the 1970s. The latter was an ideology advocated by third worldists, then a popular constituency in the developed world calling for the redress of the injustices done to a South still toying with different forms of eclectic ideologies of state interventionism in the economy. On moral grounds, there was a sense of guilt among the Northern advocates of the dialogue and a sense of injured pride and transfer of responsibility on the part of the people of the South. Yet that "ideology" was short-lived and overshadowed by the East–West divide.

Whereas the dialogue was heavily concentrated in the economic field, the North–South encounter nowadays is more encompassing. The North is not apologetic. It is indeed defiant, parading a triumphant model (remember Fukuyama's "The End of History?"[4]) of Western liberal democracy. It is a model that scored a dual victory over the "East" and also over a Western model that prided itself on being the "middle model" of "social democracy," or "grey ideology" in the words of film-maker Ingmar Bergman. The welfare state is retreating in the West. Sweden, the Mecca of social democracy, was won over to the triumphant model.

The market economy and participatory democracy, the twin pillars of the model, assume the prevalence of a utilitarian culture for their success. The moral superiority of the model is best illustrated by the messianic statement of one of its advocates, Jean François Revel, who said, "the Democracies have signed a contract with history." They made the implicit commitment that in the future everything that was right would be strong.[5] In opposition to a strong and triumphant North stands a fragmented, heavily indebted, ideologically demoralized, and impoverished South, where 1 billion people live in absolute poverty.[6]

Jean Christophe Ruffin compared the axis that is pitting the North against the terrae incognitae in these terms: "The East–West opposition was a war ideology which established an equilibrium of peace. The North–South divide looks like a peaceful new order: It contains disequilibrium and confrontation."[7]

The North is pursuing an aggressive policy on the economic front, promoting the market economy and privatization, which will tremendously increase regional dependencies on the tricontinental centres. The International Monetary Fund (IMF), the World Bank, and the Paris Club are the key instruments of that policy. The urgent need for aid and debt rescheduling in a global market suffering from financial investment shortages has increased the pressure on these states of the "South." They are responding to the demands of the institutions of the "North," sometimes disregarding the social price of the strongly applied medicine.

The Middle East is no exception to this, namely heavily indebted states with a large or relatively large population where there appears to be a broad response to economic reforms. In the Arab world, the acute demographic problems represented by an average population increase of 3 per cent per year and the indebtedness of certain Arab countries, which amounted to US$142 billion in 1989 with a yearly debt service of US$14.1 billion, or 33.2 per cent of the export earnings of these countries,[8] have increased the pressure on the one hand and added to the incentives on the other hand for economic reforms. Within the Arab world, the gap remains wide between the "north," which groups the nine oil-producing countries with small populations (except for Algeria and Iraq), and the "south," which groups the remaining 12 Arab countries. The gross domestic product of the former group reached US$300 billion in 1990 compared with a GDP of only US$119 billion in the latter group.[9] Moreover, the structural problems from which many Arab economies suffer, and which worsened owing to certain international developments such as the Gulf crisis and the European Economic and Monetary Union, have added to the incentives to adopt market economies and privatization.

In addition, the failure of the socialist model in the "East" increased the pressure on Arab states that had adopted an eclectic socialism based on a heavy-handed interventionist policy to break with socialist policies. Egypt, which started the process earlier and accelerated it recently, Tunisia, and Algeria are good examples. So is Iraq, which started to liberalize its economy before the war, and Syria, which is moving timidly along the same path.

The calls for structural economic reforms, along the lines of privatization, at the Economic and Social Council meeting of the Arab League in February 1992, as well as certain resolutions adopted by the Council,[10] indicate the degree and the extent of the support that reforms are gaining at the regional level.

Indeed, both the market economy and privatization represent the future in the Arab world,[11] but the phenomenon is not limited to the Arab part of the Middle East, although it is at work now from Morocco to Oman. Iran is liberalizing its economy gradually. One might notice in this respect the increasing role of the bazaar again. Israel is under pressure at home and from the United States to start the desocialization of certain sectors of the economy to make them more effective and to become less dependent on foreign aid. As an example of such advice, in 1992 the American ambassador in Tel Aviv urged the newly formed government to speed up its reforms, "particularly trade liberalization and privatization."[12]

Turkey, a Middle East newcomer, has taken giant steps in this respect, acting both as a Western model to emulate and as a promoter of the market economy in the former Soviet republics. Yet privatization is still facing some resistance from well-entrenched politico-bureaucratic interests. It is frustrated sometimes by the fact that it has to be preceded by the establishment of the market mechanism, the liberalization of foreign trade and prices, before it can be implemented effectively, which is not yet the case in certain instances.

Participatory democracy, the other pillar of the triumphant model,

90

is not pursued as forcefully as the first pillar despite the democratic fever in the world. The fact that no state can threaten any longer to move to the "Eastern" bloc has lent more credibility to external pressure, when applied, for democratic reforms. Progress has been achieved in Europe, Africa, Asia, and Latin America. The democratic revolution sweeping across the world has had modest results in the Middle East in terms of the acceptance of the democratic principle of the alternation of power, which remains an anathema to the mostly predominant authoritarian regimes. However, greater political liberalization is being witnessed in the Middle East, mainly in the increasing level of tolerance of the media, the growing activities of political groupings and civic associations, the establishment of "Shura" (consultation) councils, and the organization of parliamentary elections. It has been argued that political participation could be the most appropriate procedure for some Arab states as a transitional phase between undemocratic government and a democratic one, particularly when the elites in power still reject the principle of the alternation of power.[13]

Political participation in a controlled democracy functions as follows. It allows for criticism and even a change of government but not for invoking the same rights *vis-à-vis* the higher authority, i.e. the head of the state, though the latter is responsible for goal formulation, the allocation of resources, and the setting of priorities. Although the function of the government is to act as a shock absorber in many instances, its rotation allows for both elite circulation and recruitment, thus providing support for the regime in power.

Two paradoxes have emerged in this respect. The first is concerned with the relationship between economic liberalization and democracy. Some apologetics argue that democracy does not lead to economic prosperity. Indeed they argue that it is more important to start with restructuring before adopting any "glasnost" policies, which could otherwise frustrate reforms. They look to South Korea's example as an illustration of this argument. Yet the issue remains how much you can open up economically and thus respond to the new international environment while keeping the lid on political participation. Would not economic liberalization create irreversible conditions for political participation? As Albert Wohlsletter once observed, "the fax shall make you free." It has been argued that the pattern of democratization in the Middle East today suggests that the state has moved tactically toward political liberalization in the face of "economic necessity."[14]

The second paradox addresses itself to the nature of the opposition. Whereas in the former Soviet Union and Eastern Europe the opposition, which might carry the seeds of future authoritarianism, dismantled the totalitarian regimes, in the Arab world the most organized groups and the strongest, because of either the absence or the weakening of the civil society, are the Islamist populist groups. These groups carry the seeds of replacing authoritarian and semi-open regimes with totalitarian ones. Such a fear, which is sometimes exaggerated or displaced, is complicating the democratization process by creating a tight bipolarization between the Islamists and the state. This situation is derailing or delaying the democratic process by neutralizing the non-Islamic opposition groups.

Tunisia and Algeria are good illustrations of this point. Whereas in the case of the former Soviet Union and Eastern Europe the major powers were supportive of the change, this is not the case in the Middle East, where at best these powers remained neutral while the Arab state system actively protected and defended one of its components against the threat of drastic change (the case of Algeria). Faced with making a choice between the Iranian model (the success of the revolution) and the Algerian model (a last-minute intervention to prevent the Islamist takeover), a wide schism developed in the Middle East along the lines spelled out in the second paradox mentioned above.[15] The Arab world is engaged in debate on this paradox. At the centre of the debate are questions of the sort: Should we accept a "one man, one vote, one time" formula, as covertly espoused by some Islamists? Will electoral politics temper and moderate absolutist tendencies?[16] What are the implications of an Islamist electoral victory in a bi-religious or bi-ethnic state? Would "pactism" work? In other words, can the Islamists be committed *a priori* to a pact contracted by the state and the different political groupings that stipulates the parameters of the democratic game? The debate is also shaped by what the Egyptian philosopher Fouad Zakaria calls the double alienation of the Arab intelligentsia[17] – a spatial alienation, which certain Westernized intellectuals suffer from, and a temporal alienation, which certain Islamist intellectuals suffer from. The first group advocates the imposition of Western democracy in a mechanistic fashion on a traditional Muslim society; the second group, the larger one, with a fixation on the past, seeks to emulate the "democracy" of the righteous caliphates. This group makes a total abstraction of the complex set of elements that are the product of 14 centuries, which constitute the distance between the model and the call for its implementation.

The debate is further compounded by the cultural element. Islam as a religion and a state allows for a variety of interpretations, particularly in its second pillar, thus creating another debate within the Islamist constituency. Modernist interpretations of political Islam accommodate the Western concepts of democracy, party politics, and pluralism. Whereas modernists reconcile the "Shura" with democracy, fundamentalists consider that the "Shura" system does not necessarily imply pandering to the views of the majority. Indeed the "Shura" system calls for only an ad hoc, non-binding, and limited form of political participation. It does not imply an institutionalized and permanent structure of consultation. Nor does it necessitate consultation that reaches all the body politic. Fundamentalists reject democracy as an alien concept on theological grounds. Democracy is based on the sovereignty of the people, whereas Islamic rule is based on the governance of God, in the case of Sunni fundamentalism, or the Wilayat al Fakih (the rule of the highest jurisprudence), in the case of Shi'a fundamentalism.[18] This denotes the moral superiority of the fundamentalists *vis-à-vis* others. It raises doubts about their acceptance, without relaxing this basic precept of their doctrine, to deal with secular groups on an equal footing within a democratic framework, particularly if they achieve power. Adel Hussein, the editor-in-chief of the Egyptian newspaper *Al Sha'ab*, presented the fundamentalist version of democracy *à la carte*. He stated that "some friends tell me that our position on the multi-party experiment in Sudan contradicts our position on this experiment in Algeria and Egypt. I would like to tell them that the multi-party experiment is not an idol that should be worshipped. It is the road to stability and reform in some countries but may harm and sabotage under other conditions."[19]

Other than the two aforementioned paradoxes, the following elements will influence and shape the democratization process in the Middle East:

(1) The weakness and sometimes the absence of civil society's institutions, particularly non-primordial ones, owing to the invasion by the state of the socio-political and economic domains in the society. Whether it is a "progressive nationalist" state or a conservative monarchical state, the traditional state, according to Burhan Ghalioun, defined itself as responsible not for the future and destiny of citizens but rather for the nation in its entirety against external aggression and internal subversion. It placed itself above and outside society.[20] None the less, the delegit-

imation of the "progressive" state, the failure of economic interventionism, and the decreasing capabilities of the rentier state are together making for the retreat of the state and the freeing of society, thus opening the way for society's internationalization.

(2) The lack of a politico-socialization process that favours the values of reconciliation, compromise, and diversity.

(3) The crisis of credibility of many of the political groupings that raised the slogan of democracy either because they were associated at one time in their history with "undemocratic" governments or because their internal structure and practices lack democracy. This is the case of the ideological secular opposition that groups Arab nationalists, Baathists, and leftists. The second Gulf crisis is revealing in this case. The conversion process that led Arab nationalists to espouse ideas of democracy and pluralism in the 1980s did not stand the test of the crisis. Soon the nature of the government in Iraq and of its actions was ignored, for its slogan of unity struck a very sensitive cord.

(4) The acute socio-economic problems, compounded by a culture that puts special emphasis on primordial identity and the constant fear that this identity is being threatened or invaded, devalued the importance of democracy on the agenda of the elites.

The double revolution, or the paradox of the unleashed forces

The two vehicles of change that together brought the downfall of the last geopolitical empire appear to be coming from two different places and heading for different ends: nationalism as the revival of primordial loyalties; and Westernism as the appeal to adopt utilitarian values. Each has a frame of reference with different sets of priorities and goals. They are not contradictory by definition. Yet they might collide in the transitional phase that most of the developing countries and the freed societies are undergoing.

Fukuyama saw the "End of History" after the triumph of the Western mode of thought. But what has emerged victorious is one Western mode of thought over another; they are both Western in terms of belonging to the same cultural heritage and tradition. This was a competition within the same frame of reference of utilitarian values, whereas Marxism–Leninism was ousted by liberalism and capitalism. But liberalism and capitalism did not dismantle another frame of reference, which embodies ethnicity, religion, and nationalism. The outcome of the competition between the two remains to be seen wherever there exists such an encounter. Indeed, American triumphalism reflects a deeply embedded tradition of optimism that sees the evolution of the world in linear terms. "Americans look upon their differences from the rest of the world as progressive and normative – at the leading edge of a development in liberty, where others must follow." William Pfaff goes on to describe American civilization as one "for which optimism has been a historical necessity."[21]

Against this optimism, after the page had been turned on communism, André Glucksman warns against the "forces of darkness." Communism was one face of a totalitarian mentality that is rising and might rise under different names[22] but with the same power of disruption. Jack A. Goldstone observed that any ideology that features a strong tension between good and evil, emphasizes the importance of combating evil in this world through active remaking of the world, and sees politics as simply one more battlefield between good and evil may serve as the foundation for a revolutionary ideology.[23] Integral nationalism and religious fundamentalism are two faces of this phenomenon.

The Middle East, being imbued with a culture of symbolism that is religious or national or an amalgamation of the two, is very receptive and sensitive to these trends. Western values, which had already permeated Middle East societies, got another shot in the arm with the triumph of their value system against its deadly enemy. They are now well entrenched (as indicated before), particularly in their socio-cultural and economic dimensions, in the minds of the elites in power and in a large modernizing constituency in Middle East societies. Nevertheless, revisionist Zionism preaching the realization of Greater Israel and Islamic fundamentalism operating within the "Dar al-Islam" as a theatre of legitimate action have been encouraged by the demonstration effect of the triumph of mass movements with revisionist goals. Fundamentalism has also been exacerbated by the growing invasion of Western values, which are permeating all walks of life in a "provocative" manner as regards the socially conservative and economically deprived segments of the society.

The frontier as a "spearhead of civilization" is perceived as a zone of contact with another civilization.[24] That these frontiers might cut across states, or encompass many states, or be within a state, does not change the nature of the tense encounter that helps revive the self-consciousness of one group *vis-à-vis* another. This is the case of Islamism in the frontier zone with Israel and in the Maghreb in the frontier zone with Europe. This is also the case of Islamism feeling invaded at home by an alien international, i.e. Western, culture. One might argue about an Islamic theory of dependencia: the Westernized core of the peripheral societies transmits its value system to the social periphery of the peripheral societies.

Thus, by espousing revisionist goals and believing in radical means of actions, primordial ideologies provoked by contact with increasing Westernization constitute a threat to the emergence of a civil society and endanger the establishment of an "ordered" regional system should they gain power. The more the transitional period undergone by the Middle East societies is delayed or faces bottlenecks, the greater the chance that fundamentalism will gain momentum as the only alternative to the triumphant ideology espoused by the Arab establishment.

The end of the nation-state taboo

The sanctity of the nation-state was a major taboo that fell victim to the end of the Cold War. Protected by a bipolar nuclear system and conceived of as conventional wisdom in the rules that govern interstate relations, the taboo was a cornerstone in the stability of the Cold War order. Regional organizations endorsed this principle, most visibly in the case of the Organization of African Unity (OAU) because of Africa's fragile tribal structure. This code of honour was suitable for almost everybody. Newly independent states in the 1950s and 1960s found in this principle a systemic source of support to guarantee, among other things, their control over their societies. Moreover, both the Western and Eastern schools of thought considered that they succeeded in achieving the building of the nation-state through a legitimizing process based on their respective sets of utilitarian values.

The Soviet earthquake shattered this taboo. The post-Cold War period has witnessed an explosion in the number of new states reminiscent of the 1960s at the end of colonialism in Africa. While self-determination was considered only in the framework of colonialism in the Cold War era, secessionist self-determination is becoming more and more acceptable nowadays.[25] The demonstration effect of the opening of "Pandora's box," compounded by the strong revival of primordial loyalties and the perception of a new permissiveness to that end in the changing world order, has encouraged that kind of revisionism.

In the Middle East, revisionism was always a latent phenomenon that was curbed by the Cold War. Indeed, the Arab states evolved in a milieu that always questioned the legitimacy of the nation-state. Whether for the Islamists or the Arab nationalists, the frame of reference, in terms of loyalty and aspirations, is always larger than the existing territorial state. This frame lies in the "Dar al-Islam" in the case of the Islamists or the Arab "umma" (nation) in the case of Arab nationalists. The parameters of the political domain are drawn around each constituency's *umma*. Thus, trans-state or anti-state actions or loyalties are no longer considered to be an aberration but rather are seen as legitimate and normal behaviour. According to Abdallah Laroui, Arab thinkers are not concerned about the existing state. Having a different utopia since the early Islamic ages, the territorial state was delegitimized.[26]

The concept of the nation-state is alien to the Islamic Middle East, particularly to its Arab part, with the exception of Egypt, which shares with Iran and Turkey, the two non-Arab Islamic states, a socio-historical evolution that reinforced their territorial nationalisms. Indeed, both the Arab nationalist and Islamist discourses would use the concept of "a-dawla al-wataniyya" (the homeland state) to refer to the existing state. By doing so, both discourses admit the existence of diversity within the unity of the *umma*. Yet, on a theoretical as well as on a practical basis, most of the time diversity remains subordinated if not suppressed by the utopia of unity.

Perhaps what illustrates best the legitimacy problem of the state is the descriptive label of *al-qutr* used to refer to it, which carries the connotation of an interim or transitional state, thus rejecting the finality of *a-dawla al-wataniyya*. In the case of the Islamists, the erosion of faith consolidated these "components" of the *umma* at the expense of the central and legitimate Islamic authority. Both Islamists and Arab nationalists lay the blame for the fragmentation of their respective *ummas* on Western colonialism. For the Islamists, the introduction of the concept of territorial nationalism was held responsible for the process of implosion carried out partly by Westernized Arabs. For the Arab nationalists, it was the partition policies advocated by the colonialist powers that created the many Arab states. In their extreme forms, both discourses uphold the view of the artificiality of the Arab state, a view that suffers from generalization and a total insensitivity to the sociocultural and economic elements in the making of the Arab state.

Hence, in the Arabo-Islamic collective consciousness the umbilical cord was never severed between the state and the utopia of a certain *umma*. The Arab discourse supportive of Iraq in the wake of its invasion of Kuwait is the most recent example that the utopia, though destructive, is still alive and well.

Today, another form of revisionism is on the ascendancy in the Middle East. It is encouraged by the worldwide revisionism of the post-Cold War era. It emanates from sub-state identities that tend to define ethnic or sectarian nationalism. In some cases, sub-state revisionism is basically a reaction to the rising tide of Islamism. Nowadays, the consolidation of the "us versus them" identity can be observed at the level of Sunnis versus Shiites, Christians versus Muslims, or even Sunni Arabs versus Sunni non-Arabs. Sub-state revisionism is also a reaction to the inherent failure of the Arab state to establish structural legitimacy; in other words, to integrate marginalized or suppressed minorities.

It is one thing for the emerging world order not to allow, for the time being, a secession to occur in a particular region or state because its effect would upset a delicate balance of power, as in the case of the Kurds in Iraq or the Afars in Djibouti. It is another thing for those revisionist movements now to define their goals to include self-determination, though they might proceed in a gradual and realist manner in order not to provoke potential supporters or alarm opponents. They are encouraged on this path by the reputation effect of what has been achieved elsewhere in the world. The opposition to the dismantling of Iraq, which appears to be Saddam Hussein's insurance card at present, does not preclude the restructuring of Iraq along federal lines – an issue that is on the table today and might create a Yugoslavia formula of regions with ethnic or sectarian majorities. This appears to be an odd recipe for stabilization bearing in mind what has happened to Yugoslavia. Iran's potential for successful revisionism is still alive, checked only by American power. So is an Israeli revisionism with the Likud's espousal of the Jordan as Palestine formula.

In Arab Africa, the situation is more fragile and thus lends itself to successful revisionism. The tribal–racial tension in Mauritania, the same axis of tension in Sudan exacerbated by religion, the unsettled Polisario case, and the Arabo-Islamic assimilation discourse of the Islamic Front for Salvation in Algeria, which is provoking the strengthening of ethnic identity in the collective consciousness of the Berbers, are all examples of potential sources of successful revisionism. But the case for fragmentation is strongest in the Horn of Africa.

The devaluation of the strategic importance of the region with the ending of bipolarity has eroded a basic stabilizing element. The most plausible cases for statehood are in this part of the Middle East. With two declarations of independence in hand (Somaliland and Erythrea) and an active retribalization of politics, one might wonder how effective the OAU charter will be in keeping the lid on such centrifugal forces. In the post-Cold War order, the balkanization of the Middle East is looming on the horizon. Its success will depend on the ability of other traits that tend to act as centripetal forces and as a counterweight to the centrifugal forces. Democratization and development are important elements in this respect.

Conflicts: Old wine in new bottles

The end of communism revived one basic rule of the old form of the classical balance of power in international relations, i.e. the end of the "alliance handicap," in the words of George Liska. The domain of alliance politics has been opened up with the end of the ideological divide. The dis-ideologization of inter-state relations prevails, even where communism has remained.

In the Middle East, the new trend, compounded by the second Gulf crisis, has transformed the pattern of politics in the region and across the region. It is also having a great impact on the balances of power in the Middle East, especially the Arab–Israeli one:

- The Arab-instigated diplomatic containment of Israel has been shattered.
- Cooperation between Arab states and the United States is no longer considered a liability by the United Sates in its Arab environment and so cooperation is becoming more transparent.
- What was taboo in terms of the Arab states' "behaviour" *vis-à-vis* Israel has changed. The psychological and political constraints have been either lifted or weakened.

Another major change has occurred concerning the nature of conflict management. Conflicts, such as that in Angola, that thrived on and were perpetrated by the bipolar order have been settled. Others, such as that in Afghanistan, have been freed of this bipolar dimension and thus have been reduced and localized. However, a different type of ethno-national or religious-based conflict is spreading. These escape the logic of the Cold War. Yugoslavia is a case *par excellence* of this sort of conflict; the Palestinian issue is another. Regardless of the attempts to find a solution, such conflicts carry a resistance capability that derives from their being imbued with cultural symbolism rather than being the mere product of politico-strategic considerations. Both Palestinian and Kurdish nationalisms, the ethno-religious conflict in Sudan, and the ethnic tension in Algeria, Mauritania, Djibouti, and Somalia are of this sort.

Unachieved nationalisms of the ethnic or religious type, in the new era of national revolution in the Middle East and elsewhere, are a key source of disorder. The management of such conflicts needs more than a particular balance of military power. It has to be based on a balance of fulfilled legitimate demands. Otherwise the conflict will be contained but not resolved.

Meanwhile, what adds to the threats of the new tension spots is the proliferation of weapons of mass destruction to different regional systems, which could upset regional stability and encourage an arms race. South Asia, the Korean peninsula, the Commonwealth of Independent States, and the Middle East are important candidates here. Yet the United States' potential for success in curbing this new trend appears to be higher in the Middle East than elsewhere. President Bush's Arms Control Initiative for the Middle East of 29 May 1991 is a good illustration of this US potential. The United States is trying to shape the structure of power distribution and the level of capabilities too. Yet this is complicated by the existence of many semi-independent balances of power in the Middle East. Such efforts by the United States are exacerbating the feeling that it is an American attempt to disfavour the Arabs in the equation of power with Israel rather than a genuine attempt at arms control. In this context, Egypt has presented a more comprehensive plan, more in line with a call for a Middle East free of non-conventional weapons, which has gained wide support among the Arab countries.

This brings us to the role of the reactivated, rather than rejuvenated, United Nations. It appears that, in conflicts where the UN role could open the door to solutions that the United States might not prefer or that would give a partnership status to other great powers, thus allowing them to split the cake with the United States, the UN is called upon to assume a legitimizing role for a US-led action. This was the case in the second Gulf crisis and it is the case in the Arab–Israeli conflict diplomacy – a role that the UN Secretary General has rejected by not attending the Moscow multilateral talks. This has been undermining the credibility in the Middle East of the new UN as a conflict-manager, for the active internationalization of its role has been perceived in the Arab world as the Americanization of that role.

The construction site

The world resembles a construction site where political architects are engaged in the process of restructuring relations in different regions. Whether these regions gain sovereignty, become dominated by the United States, or become controlled by a concert of powers remains to be seen.[27] Thus, two observations appear to be relevant to this construction process:

(1) The concept of regional arrangements as a framework for collective security and cooperation is becoming more popular among the great powers and is welcomed at the regional level; the United States is leading, not without some uneasiness, the great powers in the Middle East construction site.

(2) Regional arrangements are construed not as closed systems connected hierarchically to a great power in the Cold War tradition, but rather as interconnected horizontally. Indeed they would look like a complex construct of geographical and functional layers. Membership is based not on geography, but rather on the goals of the framework of cooperation.

The Middle East has not escaped the fever of this organizational revolution. Internationalization is increasing through regionalization. Thus, the Arab Maghreb Union (AMU) was formed in 1989 to cope with the fundamental problems that link its members to southern Mediterranean Europe. The Gulf Cooperation Council (GCC) is trying to become a third pillar of a regional tripolar order in the Gulf through more coordinative and integrative measures. Reflecting this sweeping trend, the arithmetics of organizations in the Middle East include, as examples, the following established or ad hoc cooperative and consultative frameworks: the "5 + 5," which brings together the AMU and the European Mediterranean countries; the "5 + 12," which brings together the AMU and the EU countries; the "6 + 2," or the Damascus Declaration, which includes the GCC countries with Syria and Egypt. The same GCC countries are conducting consultations with Iran in what might be labelled the "6 + 1" formula; and the "6 + 12" witnesses the dialogue between the GCC and the EU.

Meanwhile, Iran, Turkey, and Pakistan have reactivated the once dormant Organization of Economic Cooperation, opening it up to the newly established Central Asian Muslim countries as, among other things, a forum for competition between Iran and Turkey. Moreover, Turkey announced the formation of the Black Sea Economic Cooperation Pact, while Iran followed with the formation of the Caspian Sea Organization. The Arab Cooperation Council became obsolete after the Gulf crisis and thus faded away, although officially it is considered to be suspended. On the other hand, the League of Arab States is facing the urgent challenge of task expansion, particularly in the areas of conflict management and preventive diplomacy. This is what the Charter reform project is trying to address.[28]

The internationalization of the state is also occurring at a systemic level, that is, a Middle East order is being built on the basis of a network of functional regimes, which will be the culmination of the multilateral negotiations in the Arab–Israeli conflict. The success of this venture necessitates the fulfilment of two conditions: the normalization of inter-state relations and regional integration, for no order can be established unless it is based on a common set of values and norms in the conduct of relations among its members and also on a community of interests widely defined.

In the Cold War period, plans for a Middle East order, particularly in the 1950s, were always defined by extraregional powers in terms of an outward-oriented strategic identity serving the global interests of these powers, particularly the United States. In the post-Cold War era, the Middle East is being defined from an intraregional perspective in terms of an inward-looking identity based on security and economic cooperation. Turkey and Israel strongly support this idea. The vast majority of Arab states are also receptive to this idea. The participation of many Arab countries, particularly representatives of the Gulf Cooperation Council and the Arab Maghreb Union, in the multilateral talks of the Arab–Israeli peace process is an important illustration of the new trend toward the establishment of the Middle East order. The only condition attached to the building of the new Middle East order by Arab countries lies in a successful outcome to the peace process. Equally important is the fact that the same idea is being debated in the Arab media and advocated by many Arab intellectuals.[29] But the challenges to this new Middle East remain enormous. Arab nationalist groups still reject the idea on the grounds that it threatens Arab identity. Islamist groups also stand against it for being another attempt at Western domination of part of the Islamic world. It is important to note that the concept of the Middle East is abstract and artificial and does not obey any sociological definition, like Arabism or Islam. Nor does it obey any geocultural one, like Europeanism or Africanism.

The post-Cold War order is encouraging the emergence of a Middle East order as follows:

- States that constituted a frontier between two geocultural areas, such as Turkey, are reorienting their strategies to become a bridge between the two areas. Turkey will be integrated in a Middle East order because of still persistent opposition to its integration in the EU on implicit religio-cultural grounds. The Middle East is a natural environment for Turkey to rediscover the nostalgia of a glorious past.
- Turkey is already perceiving its role and acting accordingly, not only as a bridge between Europe and the Middle East, but also as a bridge between Europe and the Islamic republics in Central Asia.
- The end of the East–West confrontation greatly devalued the strategic roles of Turkey and Israel and encouraged the regionalization of their role, which in the case of Israel could alleviate the financial burdens of its dependency on the United States when it is successfully integrated in a Middle East order based on economic co-operation. Moreover, both states will function as stabilizers in this new order.
- In a world environment of growing cooperation, Iran's decade of struggle between the logic of revolution and the logic of state is ending in favour of the latter, encouraged and accompanied by systemic changes as a *sine qua non* condition for Iran's integration in this order.
- The many values shattered in the Arab world by the second Gulf crisis have greatly influenced the rethinking in the Arab world, thus lessening the opposition to integration in a world order based on utilitarian values, particularly if normalization and conflict settlement conclude the Arab–Israeli conflict. The post-Cold War period in the Arab world is witnessing the setting of a new agenda with different priorities.
- Like the fall of the ideological and concrete Berlin Wall, which paved the way for the emerging European order, so will a successful settlement of the Arab–Israeli conflict dismantle the wall of hatred of religio-nationalism, thus paving the way for regional normalization.
- Once this occurs, utilitarian values of cooperation will act as a centripetal force for regional integration in the Middle East.
- The establishment of a Middle East order is facilitated by the mere

fact that it does not threaten the vital interests of any global power that might try to obstruct its emergence. Indeed, no global power is excluded from being a member or partner in this order.

Conclusion

Such an order, once established, will resemble a building with geographical and functional layers, as indicated before. Each layer will act as a multilateral forum, or perhaps as an actor, or as both in representing and addressing the relevant regional, subregional, or transregional identities or issues. Thus, the emergence of a Middle East order necessitates the formation of a community of values, among them stability, collective security, peaceful settlements of disputes, and the optimization of benefits through cooperation. For this reason, the successful settlement of primordial conflicts will boost the process of regional order building and bring with it a greater internationalization of the state in the Middle East.

Notes and references

1. See President Bush's speech delivered at March Airforce Base on 13 April 1991 in *Document*, US Embassy, Cairo, Egypt.
2. Cited in Robin Wright, "Old Ways Falling but New World Order is still Murky," *Los Angeles Times*, 25 June 1991, p. H–I.
3. *Al-Hayat*, 26 January 1992, p. 9.
4. Francis Fukuyama, "The End of History?" *National Interest* (Summer 1989).
5. *Le Point*, 11 March 1991, p. 22.
6. Robert McNamara cited in Strobe Talbott, "How Bush Has Wimped Out," *Time*, 16 December 1991, p. 22.
7. Jean Christophe Ruffin, *L'Empire et les Nouveaux Barbares*, Paris: Editions J. C. Lattes, 1991, p. 22.
8. The Secretariat General of the Arab League, *The Arab Unified Economic Report 1991*, Cairo: The Arab League, 1992, pp. 5 and 13.
9. Ibid., pp. 39, 40, 164, and 169.
10. The Secretariat General of the Arab League, The Directorate of Economic Affairs, *The Economic and Social Council, The 50th Session, February 2–5, 1992: Report and Resolutions*, Cairo: The Arab League, 1992.
11. Ibid., pp. 168 and 169.
12. Cited in Patrice Claude, "Israel: La Clé de la Relance Economique est à Washington," *Le Monde*, 8 July 1992, p. 8.
13. Saad Eddine Ibrahim, "Fi al Musharka fi al Sulta" [On Participation in Government], *Civil Society*, 4 April 1992, p. 2.
14. Louis Cantori, "Democratization in the Middle East," *American Arab Affairs*, no. 36 (Spring 1991), p. 2.
15. See, for example, the criticism levelled by an Islamic intellectual at Arab intellectuals who supported the military's intervention in Algeria, in Ismail al Shatti, "The Victory of the Islamic Front in Algeria: Scary Joy," *al-Hayat*, 19 January 1992, p. 13.

16. See, for example, Graham E. Fuller, "Let's See How Islamic Politicians Cope and Learn," *IHT*, 14 January 1992, p. 6.
17. *Le Point*, 25 March 1991, p. 60.
18. See, for example, the opposing views of Ibrahim Dessouki Shatta, "Hazza a Talil a Dimocrat'i an al Islam was Nazariuatitihi fi al Siyasa" [This Democratic Distortion of Islam and its Theory of Politics], *al-Hayat*, 20 July 1992, p. 14. See also Fahmi Howaydi, "Hakkuna Fian Nakhtalif" [Our Right to Differ], *al-Majalla*, 1–7 July 1992, pp. 42, 43.
19. *Al-Ahram Weekly*, 13–19 August 1992, p. 6.
20. Burhan Ghalioun, *Le Malaise Arabe: L'Etat Contre la Nation*, Paris: Editions la Découverte, 1991, p. 67.
21. William Pfaff, *Barbarian Sentiments: How the American Century Ends*, New York: Hill and Wang, 1989, pp. 50 and 52.
22. André Glucksman, *Le Onzième Commandement*, Paris: Flammarion, 1991.
23. Jack A. Goldstone, "The Comparative and Historical Study of Revolutions," *Annual Review of Sociology* 8 (1982), p. 203.
24. Peter Taylor, *Political Geography: World Economy, Nation State and Locality*, New York: Longman Inc., 1985, p. 105.
25. Alexis Heraclides, "Sessionist Minorities and External Involvement," *International Organization* 44, no. 3 (Summer 1990), pp. 351 and 352.
26. Abdallah Laroui, *Mafhoum a-dawla* [The Concept of the State], Beirut: Arab Cultural Centre, 1984, pp. 169–170.
27. Richard Rosecrance, "Regionalism in the post-Cold War," *International Journal* XLVI (Summer 1990), p. 379.
28. The actual Charter reform proposals were initiated in 1979. Committees of experts representing the Arab League and the member states worked toward that goal. The reform proposals include, among other things, the establishment of an Arab Court of Justice and the strengthening of the crisis management role of the League.
29. See, for example, Lutfi al-Khuli, "'Arab? Na'am, Wa Lakin Shark Awsatiyyun Aydan!" [Arabs? Yes, but Middle Easterners too], *al-Hayat*, 20 May 1992, p. 13; also Mustafa 'Alwi, "Nahwa Ta'awun Ma Jiranuna fi Itar Iqlim Jadid" [Towards Cooperation with our Neighbours in a New Regional Framework], *'Alam al Yom*, 1 March 1992, p. 13.

Bibliography

Avineri, Schlomo. "Beyond Saddam: The Arab Trauma." *Dissent* 38 (Spring 1991), no. 1.

Bennis, Phyllis, and Michael Moushabeck, eds. *Beyond the Storm: A Gulf Crisis Reader*. New York: Olive Branch Press, 1991.

Esposito, John, and James Piscatori. "Democratization and Islam." *Middle East Journal* 45 (Summer 1991), no. 3.

Fukuyama, Francis. *The End of History and the Last Man*. New York: Free Press, 1992.

Halliday, Fred. "The Gulf War and Its Aftermath: First Reflections." *International Affairs* 67 (1991), no. 2.

Lellouche, Pierre. *Le nouveau Monde: De l'Ordre de Yalta au Désordre des Nations*. Paris: Grasset, 1992.

Rabie, Mohamed. "Arab–Israeli Peace: A New Vision for a Transformed Middle East." *America–Arab Affairs*, no. 36 (1991).

Salame, Ghassan, and Giocomo Luciane. *The Politics of Arab Integration*. New York: Croom Helm, 1988.

Sharabi, Hisham, ed. *Theory, Politics and the Arab World: Critical Responses*. New York: Routledge, 1991.

────── *Neopatriarchy: A Theory of Distorted Change in Arab Society*. New York: Oxford University Press, 1988.

Tomadonfar, Mechran. *The Islamic Polity and Political Leadership: Fundamentalism, Sectarianism, and Pragmatism*. Boulder, Colo.: Westview Press, 1989.

4

The internationalization of the state: The case of Japan

Takehiko Kamo

Introduction

The internationalization of Japan is a complex and multilayered phenomenon that involves not only political and strategic, but also economic and cultural aspects of Japanese society. It encompasses the relationship of each of these aspects to the changing structures of the world order. Although Japanese economic influence has grown internationally, there has not been a corresponding shift in Japanese international political influence. Indeed, despite very significant changes in Japan's economic and military capabilities and in the world order, the basic stance of Japanese foreign policy is still configured by ideas and associations that have deep historical roots. Of course, there are many reasons for this, two of which are often ignored but are of the first importance: first, the lack of democratization of Japanese civil society and the state, and, secondly, continued feelings of vulnerability to outside pressures and threats, a feeling that is especially central to the political consciousness of politicians. This partly explains the prioritization of economic growth and security as well as the dependence on, and deference to, the United States in matters of international security. However, it is now generally appreciated in Japan that the 1990s may well be a turning-point in Japan's place in the changing world order, as the frozen certainties of the Cold War system begin to melt.

This essay, then, advances a number of factors to help explain the process of the internationalization of the state in Japan, and then outlines, through research based on a small survey, the various conceptualizations of world order changes, world order problems, and foreign policy views for Japan to be found among Japanese politicians, public officials, and citizens. My focus is mainly on strategic and international political issues, and less on broader economic issues. The surveys indicate that there is quite a wide divergence of views, both between politicians and bureaucrats and between politicians and citizens. Many politicians seem to be keen on enhancing the status of Japan as a great power, and are drawn to different forms of Japanese nationalism (or "Japanism"). Many officials and citizens, on the other hand, prefer policies that would seek to insert Japan into a more multilateral world order, and to move away from great power politics towards world order politics.

The changing world order and Japan

The changing world order has always influenced the ways in which Japan would commit itself to international society. There is no doubt that the internationalization of Japan (*Nihon no Kokusai-ka*) has been substantially affected by the changing world order for almost 130 years since the Meiji Restoration. Today, in the 1990s, international politics is experiencing a revolutionary change that seems to be unparalleled since the end of World War II.

Obviously Japan faces new problems and challenges caused by the changing world order. What might be the implications of these developments for Japanese internationalization (or transnationalization) at both governmental and societal levels? For example, will we witness a more creative and moral orientation in changing the world order toward global security and interdependence where power politics would lose its traditional legitimacy?[1]

Since the end of the 1980s, we have witnessed a fundamental international structural change that has brought to an end the bipolar system symbolized by the Pax Russo Americana. This is not an example of a cyclical change, in which the thawing in East–West tensions will eventually lead to a new round of strain on different fronts, but rather one in which the very rules of the game of international relations have shifted.[2] The end of the Cold War is not merely a termination of East–West ideological tensions. The collapse of the Soviet Union means the end of a socialist empire or a socialist hegemonic power. Likewise, the United States is now experiencing a loss of hegemony, although much of its capacity for dominance remains. The erosion of American hegemony is not necessarily caused by US "strategic over-extension" or "imperial overstretch," as Paul Kennedy argues.[3]

The main reason is that the hegemonic order itself is inadequate for legitimately and ethically reconstructing global common security. Indeed, a key change is not so much that the United States is in decline, but rather that there has been a shift in its political economy towards greater internationalization and, consequently, greater centrality in the global political economy. Nevertheless, the policies of the US government have become less amenable to the interests of the rest of the world economy and more nationalistic (e.g. Nixon shocks in 1971; Reaganomics in the 1980s).

Secondly, whilst one might hope that the end of the Cold War would encourage further progress in arms control and disarmament between the United States and the Commonwealth of Independent States (CIS), and between other nuclear powers, in order to enhance a confidence-building system (and to move away from the so-called "prisoners' dilemma"), it is worth remembering that disarmament efforts are still incomplete between the two former superpowers. However, these efforts at restructuring global security need to be supplemented by other efforts, for example grass-roots movements for peace and for ecology to enhance transnational security.

Thirdly, the demise of the Cold War indicates that relations between nation-states are moving towards greater polycentrism, with global expansion into a new brand of power dynamics also taking place. A hegemonic order, however, if one uses a Gramscian definition, must have substantial procedural and substantive legitimacy. Nevertheless, it is doubtful if an order founded on the dominance of one state (i.e. the term "hegemony" as normally used in the international relations literature) could in fact be widely perceived to be legitimate. Precisely owing to the fact of greater polycentrism, however, there is more interdependence at the strategic and economic levels. This strengthened interdependence has actually led to increased economic friction between the industrialized countries, and to much more serious conflicts between developed and developing countries precisely because of imbalance or asymmetry in the interdependent structure. An apt symbol of this reality is the difficulty in reaching consensus on the Uruguay Round of the General Agreement on Tariffs and Trade (GATT), making the management of this interdependence a vital issue.

Furthermore, despite increased mutual dependency, a move towards ethnic nationalism (observed in the recent case of Yugoslavia's internal turmoil) and other forms of "democratization" in international politics is taking place. In regard to the process of greater democratization, it seems true that, whereas there appears to be an increase in the number of people in liberal democratic regimes, the growing social and economic inequality that has simultaneously occurred is narrowing the substantive basis and capacity of the mass of people for democratic participation. Also, as the case of Yugoslavia illustrates, democratization can go hand in hand with ethnic rivalries and with increased violence. Quite interestingly, the processes of democratization do not appear to be synonymous with the processes of nationalism in the changing world order. This is because, while democratization tends to mean a normative concept of sharing values and decisions within and among countries in changing the centre–periphery type of international structure, nationalism suggests a self-assertive strategic concept that does not consider the distribution of values and powers in the international system.

Japan and the internationalization of the state

If the internationalization of the state is defined as the global process whereby national policies and practices have been adjusted not only to the exigencies of the world economy but to the necessary transformation of the world system or order,[4] how will Japan, as a society, respond to the currently changing world system and order?

The internationalization of the state is an analytical concept that is used to show how nation-states have responded, or do or can respond to changes in the world political economy. The concept may imply a normative orientation in policy or behaviour. For example, it might imply a global process whereby nation-states would or could make attempts to reconstruct the world system not only for national interests, but for transnational (common) interests in international society.

Professor Robert Cox has elaborated the meaning given to the term "internationalizing of the state": (1) there is a process of inter-state consensus-formation regarding the needs or requirements of the world economy within a common ideological framework; (2) participation in this consensus-formation is hierarchically structured; (3) the internal structures of states are adjusted so that each can best transform the global consensus into national policy and practice.[5]

An important question has been how Japan has actually adjusted its policies and practices to the world political economy. Quite interestingly, for more than a century the internationalization of Japan has been quite different or has deviated from Cox's concept of internationalizing the state. Why is this so? Japanese policies and practices have always been related to the consolidation of an integral state in Japan, one that would be secure from foreign challenges and economically powerful.[6] Simply stated, Japan's foreign policy behaviour has been substantially based on nationalist, imperialist, and mercantilist ideology, which should be distinguished from the processes of consensus-formation regarding the needs or requirements of the world political economy.

Yet Japan's foreign policy behaviour has been characterized by a lack of normative orientation towards improvement of the world system. The important historical fact seems to be that Japan's internal commitment has been closely associated with policy efforts and attitudes on the part of Japanese élites demonstrating Japan's national determination to increase its power and status in the world political economy. In this sense, it is not incorrect to argue that the internationalization of the state has occurred in quite a different way in the case of Japan. Thus, the internationalization of the state has been almost identical with the nationalization of Japan (*Nihon-no-Kokkaka*). If we borrow from E. H. Carr's conceptualization of nationalism, the Japanese case appears to have been analogous to *the first period of nationalism* (a combination of argumentation of the power of the state with the ideology of mercantilism), particularly from the Meiji Restoration of 1868 up to the end of World War II.[7] It is interesting to note that neither the democratization of nationalism nor the socialization of the nation has occurred in the case of the internationalization of Japan.

We can assume that the internationalization of Japan has been, in actuality, *a false internationalization* in the sense that Japan has made serious efforts to catch up with the European nation-state model in terms of Westernization symbols. There have always been less co-operative policies and practices in regard to the exigencies of the world economy and of the necessary transformation of the world system or order.

First, it is not the internationalization but rather the nationalization of Japan that has been synonymous with the national policies of Westernization. Why Westernization? This provided a model whereby Japan has attempted to build a nation-state in order to be recognized as a member of the international system.

Secondly, nationalization meant industrialization to Japan. For industrialization has been an effective means of adjusting to the global economy as a powerful nation.

Thirdly, nationalization has been closely associated with the formation and militarization of the nation-state. The reason was that Japanese political leaders and élites considered military might or strength as a kind of passport to great power status. At the same time, it was viewed as a major means of exerting political influence over weaker nations, as well as *vis-à-vis* imperial powers such as the United Kingdom, Germany, France, Russia (the Soviet Union), and the United States. As a matter of fact, Westernization, industrialization, and militarization have been almost synonymous in style with the formation and development – or modernization – of the Western type of nation-state in Japan since the Meiji Restoration. In the processes of modernization of the nation-state, Japan pursued a national policy of *Fukoku-Kyohei* (a combination of military strength with economic prosperity) for more than 60 years.

Fourthly, the nationalization of Japan gave the momentum to pursue centrality, not only in world politics but also in Asia.[8] In particular, Japan's propensity for regional centrality is important in understanding why pre-war Japan became an aggressor country in Asia, where almost all nations were on the periphery of the international subsystem. Therefore, Japan used Asian nations only to maximize its strategic and economic interests. In other words, the false internationalization of Japan meant, as an underlying assumption for national policy, the processes of non-Asianization and anti-Asianization, regardless of its geographical location and of its close cultural ties with Asian countries.

Fifthly, though not finally, the nationalization of Japan always widened the gaps in attitudes and policies between the intensification (or internalization) of Japanese political culture and the expansion (or externalization) of global commitment. By intensification I mean strengthening attitudes and policies that rejected assimilation into foreign political cultures, whether Western or Asian. Japan made serious efforts to introduce its own variant of a Western type of political and economic system and to introduce into society a Western educational system. A key goal was, of course, to catch up with advanced

112

countries in Europe. However, as a national policy as well as a social tendency, Japan has retained its own unique political culture, that is, a socially hierarchical regime with the emperor system at the apex, and a very homogeneous (as a national race) family type in distinguishing "in" people from "out" people.

By expansion I mean incessant efforts both by governments and by other elements in the private sector to increase national economic capability (innovations and applications of technology were emphasized because of the scarcity of important raw materials such as crude oil) and to strengthen national physical forces (especially military force as a naval power).

Here, some explanations are necessary to demonstrate how unique and idiosyncratic the emperor system was as a means of legitimizing and symbolizing the cultural, political, and social modernization of Japan. It was a means of both internalizing *and* internationalizing the state: the emperor system had long been considered to be the most important symbol of integrity and continuity for the Japanese people. The Japanese "community" was, then, identified as the *family of the nation (Kazoku-Kokka)*, whose ultimate source of authority lay in the emperor system. In other words, the Emperor was seen as the authentic "Father" of the Japanese family. Through the emperor system, the image of Japan as a nation-state was reproduced as something identical to the *family of the nation* because of its ethnic homogeneity. In this sense, the processes of the internationalization of Japan have been closely associated with the continuity of the emperor system itself. More to the point, the emperor system has worked as the most effective political ideology in distinguishing the Japanese community (*Mura-Kyodotai*) from foreign communities, whether they are Westerners or Asians. Of course, it is true that the emperor system was changed after World War II to become a symbol of the integration of the Japanese people, rather than the ruler of the state. However, the emperor system still seems to be a powerful political cultural mechanism for maintaining the idea of the homogeneity of the Japanese community. The internationalization of the state is, therefore, unique simply because the modernization process (which involved the bureaucratization of the state and modernist principles of nation-building) was accompanied by a national consciousness of the *family of the nation* through the maintenance of the emperor system, elements that produced a unique form of political identity.[9]

Why is there such a discrepancy between intensification and expansion? The reasons are not difficult to identify. First, Japan embarked on global processes of internationalizing the state without trying to harmonize its own political culture with those of foreign countries. Secondly, expansion had often been successful in enhancing Japan's strategic position and in producing a relatively prosperous nation. Some of the consequences of these policies have been devastating: Japan's aggression in Asia, and Japan's attack on Pearl Harbor and defeat in the war.[10]

Post-war internationalization: What has changed?

What has changed in the substance and ways of internationalization in Japan since the end of World War II? Many characteristics appear to be unchanged: policies of Westernization have basically continued, with an emphasis on Americanization; industrialization has also been encouraged further; centrality in world politics has been replaced by the quest for centrality in world economics. What has changed is, in theory, both militarization and non-Asianization (and anti-Asianization) in the policy efforts of Japan since the war. The major reason for this change lay in the new reality that Japan was not allowed to become a military great power because of self-restraint in its national security policy (i.e. Article 9 of the Peace Constitution). In other words, there was no political room for Japan to become an imperialistic or hegemonic power.

However, it seems very doubtful whether Japan has essentially transformed the substance of the nation-state towards humility in external behaviour and non-militarization in national security policies. My argument is that the gaps in attitudes and policies between the internalization of Japanese political culture and the externalization of global commitment have been further widened, so that the problem of internalizing Japan continues to be full of contradictions and paradox. There has always been *inconsistency* in the national security policy between the idea of peace orientation espoused in writing and the reality of expansionism in actual behaviour. As is widely known, Japan maintained and nourished its military force, the Self-Defence Forces (SDF), despite the constitution. A good example is found, for instance, in an episode in the late 1960s, which demonstrates how such inconsistency is absorbed in Japanese politics. That was the case in which the famous "three non-nuclear principles" were eventually adopted as a new national security policy by the cabinet. The Sato cabinet initially announced four nuclear policies, which were as follows: (1) a set of non-nuclear principles (not to develop

114

nuclear weapons, not to allow the introduction of nuclear weapons to Japan, not to possess nuclear weapons); (2) to endeavour to eliminate nuclear weapons in order to achieve nuclear disarmament; (3) to depend upon the US nuclear deterrent force in confronting international nuclear threats; and (4) to make efforts to develop nuclear energy for peaceful purposes. It is noteworthy then that the "three non-nuclear principles" were originally linked to the role of nuclear weapons – that is, with Japan's security policy of depending upon the American nuclear deterrent force against the Soviet Union. Later, the Sato cabinet's nuclear policies were changed to declare simply the "three non-nuclear principles" following debates in the Diet.[11]

Let us next discuss how Japan is adjusting its national policies and practices in the light of the historic change in world politics.

Although the end of the Cold War system is in fact exerting important influences upon the internationalization of Japan in policy and practice, the gaps between internalization and externalization in transforming Japan pose a serious, unresolved problem.

First, the end of the Cold War has contributed to changing political leaders' and élites' perceptions of the world order. In their eyes, the collapse of the Soviet Union is clear, and Soviet threats have almost vanished as a result of much more than *détente* between the former two superpowers. However, particularly encouraged by the Gulf crisis, Japanese political leaders and élites tend to see that the post-Cold War era is most likely to be quite conflictual in terms of international security. Therefore, the Liberal Democratic political leaders are beginning to be very concerned with the idea of internationalizing Japan, among others through an "international contribution" (*Kokusai Koken*), for example in committing itself to the United Nations peace-keeping operations (PKO). Leaders are making efforts to *legitimize* the SDF within the international context and, if possible, to send military personnel to troubled areas to demonstrate how useful Japan is as a politically great power, like member countries, for instance, of the Coalition Forces at the time of the Gulf War. On 15 June 1992, the United Nations Peace Cooperation Bill was finally passed in the Japanese Diet. As a consequence of this, the Japanese government could send the SDF to troubled areas for the purpose of peace-keeping activities as well as for international humanitarian and relief activities. The Miyazawa government attempted to grope towards a new policy option by sending the SDF to Cambodia to help in the peace-keeping activities under the leadership of the United Nations Transitional Authority for Cambodia, if some conditions were satisfactorily met.[12] Japan seems, therefore, to be embarking on a significant change in its post-war foreign and national security policy (that is, the policy of not sending any military personnel abroad for any reason).

More to the point, Japan appears to be adjusting itself to other advanced countries' pressures or requests in regard to the "international contribution." In so far as the United Nations Peace Cooperation Bill is concerned, the Kaifu government had originally proposed that Bill with the aim of opening the way for Japan to participate in international military activities in the Gulf. The Prime Minister, Toshiki Kaifu, said before the Diet, on 12 October 1991: "We must never forget that Japan is one of the nations that has most benefited from international peace. Japan, a resource-poor trading nation, will be able to continue to enjoy its prosperity only if world peace is maintained." Therefore, he added: "Contributing to efforts to keep world peace is a natural and inevitable cost arising from Japan's international position."

However, we should not dismiss the true point of why such a Bill was proposed. The main reason, as I see it, is that the Japanese government had perceived mounting pressure from the Americans to play a very positive role in the multilateral effort to contain Iraq. Therefore, one important reason for such an "international contribution" was reflected in the so-called Americanization in the post-war internationalizing pattern of Japan. Americanization is here symbolic in adjusting Japan's national policies and practices to the transformation of the world political economy. As Professor Robert Cox argues, this is also the case when Japan wants to participate in consensus-formation among the major advanced capitalist countries. According to Professor Cox, this is the top level of the internationalization of the state structure.[13]

An example is where Japan is determined to play a part in the making of international regimes for post-war security matters. However, it is doubtful whether Japan has actually been involved in the evolution of policy harmonization for the "international contribution." Unlike the European Community (EC), Japan does not seem to have decided to participate in the collective decision-making processes for the "sharing of sovereignty." At the top level of internationalization, Japan does not seem prepared to accept the *collective identity* in the making of international regimes. Instead, Japan has made attempts to adjust itself for its own sake without showing the grand design for "international contribution" (e.g. how to rebuild the United Nations forces under the leadership of the Secretary General).

In contrast to the Japanese case, the member countries of the European Community have rather successfully pursued consensus-formation through the international regime of European Political Cooperation, for instance with regard to international assistance to the former Soviet Union, the CIS. It is also noteworthy that German unification (1989–1990) would not have been successfully accomplished without progressive diplomatic and strategic congruence in interests and policies between the then Gorbachev government and the member countries of the EC (particularly initiated by President Mitterrand of France). Consensus-formation at the top level of internationalizing the state structure seems by and large to have been effective in the EC member countries' foreign policy behaviour since the end of the 1980s. However, this sort of internationalizing mechanism does not seem to be working effectively in Japan. Despite the end of the Cold War, Japan has to continue to negotiate with the CIS to resolve northern territorial issues. It is rather doubtful whether both the Japanese government and the Japanese public could have a shared opinion on the necessity of protecting the CIS from the danger of disintegration, which may occur before the conclusion of an agreement on the return of four islands to Japan.

President Yeltsin's sudden cancellation of a visit to Tokyo at the beginning of September 1992 may have caused negative responses to the Russo-Japanese relationship. However, Japan has not yet decided to encourage consensus-formation processes with other advanced capitalist nations in regard to the issue of international assistance to Russia. In this context, it is very important that the member countries of the EC have agreed on a common foreign and security policy as the rule of the game in international security and, in the strategic field, in the Maastricht Treaty on European Union.[14]

In so far as an "international contribution" is concerned, it can be argued that changed perceptions of the world order on the part of political leaders and élites are closely linked with a heightened feeling of nationalism – Japanization or "Japanism" in the era of global political economy – in which to legitimize the SDF within the international context is a necessary condition for great power status. In this sense, the internationalization of Japan means maximization of its power status in the global political economy. There is ample evidence for this new trend. Let us take another case to demonstrate

the "nationalism" hypothesis: the Liberal Democratic Party's internationalization policy after the Gulf crisis, which has emerged despite the rather cautious or ambiguous attitudes in Japanese public
opinion (described later).

The special study committee for consideration of "Japan's role in
international community" (Ozawa Committee) made public its report to the LDP on 20 January 1992. The committee first insisted
that Japan should and could assume greater responsibility and roles
in international security after the Cold War. Secondly, it proposed
that Japan should embark on an active peace orientation, instead of
a passive one, in order to contribute to world security and prosperity.
Furthermore, the committee suggested that Japan should and could
send the SDF to the United Nations Forces stipulated in Article 43
of the UN Charter if such military force were established in the future, and that this contribution by the SDF would not be in conflict
at all with any interpretation of the Japanese constitution (e.g. Article 9: prohibition of the use of physical force to resolve international
conflicts). The main point in this report is apparently that the LDP's
previous national security policies could be, and ought to be, changed
in the newly transformed international environment.[15]

It is obvious, however, that there has been a lack of popular support for Japan's greater role, particularly in the international security field, even if this were to be circumscribed by means of Japan's
long-sustained security policy after World War II. One might argue
that, should Japan seriously attempt to change its security policy, the
government also needs international public opinion for full support in
doing so. Otherwise, what the present Japanese government is seeking is indeed a *unilateral* decision on the new global commitment.

Why is nationalism increasing among political leaders and policy
élites? One reason is, as noted earlier, a reflection of an externalization of the global commitment. It is also manifested in attitudes of
great power orientation in the élites' consciousness. The other reason is no doubt linked with securing access to foreign markets and
with reducing vulnerability stemming from dependence upon raw
materials and resources. The second point is related to the psychology of Japanese leaders and their sense of the economic vulnerability of Japan in the world economy networks. Despite Japan's
remarkable economic and technological success over many years,
and in spite of the growing interdependence of the world economy,
Japanese leaders and élites still appear to be obsessed with the vulnerability concept in formulating and executing their foreign eco-

nomic policies. It is almost a cliché to say that Japan has long enjoyed a success story in achieving a record of recovery and growth in post-war international relations. Japan's economic success is well documented and needs little elaboration here.

However, Japanese leaders and élites are often afraid of being isolated from foreign countries as a perceived consequence of Japan's economic victory in international competitiveness. Today, in the 1990s, a close relationship with the United States may be called into question, particularly because of economic rivalries between the United States and Japan, and because of mutual criticism with regard to managing strategic as well as economic interdependence.

In this new international environment, Japanese feelings of vulnerability are clearly linked to a positive re-evaluation of nationalism on the part of political leaders and policy élites. Moreover, in so far as such nationalistically oriented psychology is concerned, the combination of feelings of vulnerability and status enhancement has often encouraged Japanese political leaders (especially in the conservative LDP) and policy élites (in the strategic establishment) in the direction of Japanese militarization, regardless of changes in world politics.

Militarization in Japan has always been closely related to military efforts in the economic and technological sense. Militarization is not necessarily linked with an assertive defence policy (e.g. a policy of extending its military bases and committing its collective defence networks) or with global strategy beyond "defensive defence." Put differently, militarization in Japan has manifested itself in military efforts *in parallel with* economic growth and strength.

Related to the issue of militarization, we should note the important fact that Japan has been embedded in the Pax Americana regional system in North-east Asia since World War II. Slowly, Pax Americana has given way to the *Nichi-bei* (Japan–United States) bi-hegemony system, particularly since the mid-1980s. According to Mitchell Bernard's incisive analysis of the political economy of North-east Asia, Pax Americana (American predominance to construct an open world economy excluding the Soviet sphere) has been the most important systemic factor in maintaining the hegemonic order in this region. Under Pax Americana, Japan served as "a model; it incorporated American production techniques and became a major exporter of manufactured goods... The structure of the hegemonic order was also conducive to the revival of the links between producers in Japan and its two former colonies (Taiwan and Korea), this time not in an

119

autarkic division of labour, but in one linked to the world order."[16] Simultaneously, Pax Americana led to the internationalization of production. Again, an important fact is that, since the mid-1980s, especially since the Plaza Accord (which was related to *endaka*: a drastic appreciation of the yen against the dollar), "Japan's political economy, the dynamics of Northeast Asia and the Japanese role in the world order, are on the verge of profound changes."[17] Despite *endaka*, East Asian exports to the United States have not fallen. Instead, it has resulted in a surge in imports from Taiwan and South Korea. And yet Japan has experienced substantial economic growth in this period, and capital outflows have doubled and direct investment overseas has trebled since the Plaza Accord. However, Bernard notes the consequences of these changes in the Japanese economy:[18]

Japanese companies have set up shop overseas in unprecedented numbers, predominantly in neighbouring East Asia and in the financial markets of North America and Europe. The multinationalization of Japanese business has brought an interminable stream of foreign politicians and business leaders to Tokyo, cap in hand, seeking direct Japanese investment for their constituencies. These changes in world trade and investment patterns, along with increasingly desirable Japanese technology and the enormous sums of money at Japan's disposal, have made it untenable for Japan to maintain its position as the financier of American political–military hegemony. A new nationalist movement has emerged in Japan which views changes in the international political economy as related to Japan's preeminence in microelectronics.

As a consequence of the transnationalization of Japan in the economic field, it seems important to note the fact that Japan has embarked on the assertion of its own political stance, for instance in acting as a political broker in Asia. This change has been related to Japan's aid policy. Japan has become the largest donor of Official Development Assistance (ODA) to third world countries since the end of the 1980s. Foreign direct investment from Japan also increased during the 1980s. The increase in foreign direct investment (FDI) by Japan is illustrated in table 4.1, which shows Japan's FDI to newly industrializing economies (NIEs) and Association of South East Asian Nations countries for the period 1972–1990. The share of Japan's and the United States' FDI in those countries has been high, so that the *Nichi-bei* (bi-hegemony) system has been clearly embedded in the Asian regional (north-east and south-east) interna-

Table 4.1 **Japan's annual foreign direct investment in Asia (NIEs & ASEAN), 1972–1990 (US$ million)**

	1972	1973	1974	1975	1976	1977	1978	1979	1980	1981
South Korea	146	211	77	93	102	95	222	95	35	73
Taiwan	10	34	33	24	28	18	40	39	47	54
Hong Kong	29	123	51	105	69	109	158	225	156	329
Philippines	10	43	59	149	15	27	53	102	78	72
Thailand	30	34	31	14	19	49	32	55	33	31
Malaysia	13	126	48	52	52	69	48	33	146	31
Singapore	42	81	51	55	27	66	174	255	140	266
Indonesia	119	341	375	585	931	425	610	150	529	2,434
Total	2,338	3,494	2,395	3,280	3,462	2,806	4,598	4,995	4,693	8,931

	1982	1983	1984	1985	1986	1987	1988	1989	1990
South Korea	103	129	106	135	435	647	483	606	284
Taiwan	55	103	65	114	291	367	372	494	446
Hong Kong	400	563	412	132	502	1,072	1,662	1,899	1,784
Philippines	34	65	46	60	21	73	134	202	258
Thailand	94	72	118	49	124	249	859	1,276	1,154
Malaysia	83	140	153	69	158	163	387	674	724
Singapore	180	322	225	339	302	494	747	1,903	840
Indonesia	410	374	374	408	250	545	586	631	1,105
Total	7,703	8,145	10,153	12,220	22,321	33,364	47,022	67,540	56,912

Source: *Annual Report of the International Finance Bureau*, Ministry of Finance, 1985–1991.

tional economy. In particular, through the internationalization of production, Japan has developed its international competitiveness not only in relation to advanced countries but in relation to developing countries. And yet production patterns are moving increasingly beyond the ambit of state control and state objectives. Therefore, regardless of the Japanese government's political and economic strategy, Japanese companies may try to solidify the system for trade and investment in North-east and South-east Asia. It should be noted that, if we again borrow Robert Cox's conceptualization, Japan's internationalizing of the state structure at the third level (i.e. in the third world) has not required developing nations to cooperate with Japan on an equal footing. Japan has tended to fix the parameters of the developmental options of late-industrializing countries.[19] Unilateralism has been a consistent pattern on the part of Japan at the third level of internationalization.

121

Japan in a post-hegemonic era: Elite attitudes and expectations

What is a possible new world order in the post-Cold War era? Or, more to the point, how could a new world order be established for global society as a whole? Let us put particular emphasis on élite perceptions in dealing with the matter of the internationalization of the state. For there is a serious question with respect to the internationalization of the state in the case of Japan. There is a clear lack of creative thinking on the part of policy élites concerning a normative world order as well as of penetrative understanding of the meaning of the changing world order in the 1990s. Roughly stated, despite increased friction and conflict in the attitudes and policies between the United States and Japan in regard to economic (and, simultaneously, technological) competitiveness and political culture, the internationalization of Japan still seems chained to the idea of adjusting Japanese global policies to what the United States, particularly its public officials, tells Japan about assuming its international role. However, I would like to emphasize the fact that the former Bush administration did show what a new world order ought to be, if cooperation and coordination were available among nation-states.

The meaning of a new world order is not necessarily clear in President Bush's description of policies and attitudes.[20] But what President Bush did indicate more clearly was America's determination to keep political leadership in securing freedom after the demise of the Cold War structure. Quite interestingly, there was no mention of a new world order in Bush's 1992 State of the Union Message. Bush repeatedly mentioned the theme that "America won the Cold War" in his address. Instead of efforts to clarify what a new world order must be in the early 1990s, Bush referred to the idea of increasing "his nation's good," stating that "America continues as the economic leader of the world."[21] It is not incorrect to argue that a paradox appears in the United States' policies for maintaining its political and economic leadership, precisely because the United States is moving towards more aggressive defence of American economy and security. The United States appears to be inward looking in terms of national attitudes. I am not saying that the United States has already returned to a new isolationism. However, it is clearly having trouble in maintaining its political and economic leadership as a superpower.

If my understanding of the essence of the changing world order is correct, and not only the CIS but also the United States are in trouble in terms of sustaining their power and interests, then I suggest that

Japan should think more independently about prescriptions for a new world order. It is of great importance that the Japanese public as well as Japanese leaders and élites should consider in depth how a new world order ought to be created, and argue at different levels of society for desirable and sustainable forms of the internationalization of the Japanese state. Desirable and sustainable means that the Japanese new type of internationalization could be accepted and welcomed by the world society; this would require resolving the problem of narrowing the gap in attitudes and policies between the internalization of Japanese political culture and the externalization of global commitment to international affairs, and demonstrating in the processes of international commitments a universal model for contributing to the democratization of decision-making among nation-states. This might allow for the establishment of common security through dialogue and negotiation, which would cover the protection of human rights and global ecology.

How do Japanese policy élites see the end of the Cold War in terms of the internationalization of Japan? First, Ministry of Foreign Affairs people do not seem to be changing the major policy of maintaining Japan's alliance relationship with the United States in the post-Cold War era. However, when we look, for instance, at the 1991 Foreign Ministry *Blue Book*, it is noteworthy that the foreign policy people are beginning to search for a new role in the world political economy. The 1992 *Blue Book* suggests that Japan should make clear what international role it must play in the third stage of Japanese diplomacy since the end of World War II. The first stage of diplomacy was from 1945 to the early 1970s when Japan tried to return to the world community, with the aim of restoring the Japanese economy. The second stage, from the 1970s to the 1980s, was the period in which Japan attempted to increase its international role and responsibility as a "member of the western democratic advanced nations." According to the *Blue Book,* Japanese diplomacy is now entering the third stage of commitment to building a new world order. The *Blue Book* emphasizes the increased importance of Japan–USA and Japan–Europe relationships and the necessity of cooperation among countries in the Asia–Pacific region. The *Blue Book* also refers to issues of assistance for the former Soviet Union, commitment to the management of regional conflicts, support for arms control and disarmament, and strengthening the security functions of the United Nations. However, there is a lack of a clear grand design to demonstrate how Japan, as a society *in toto*, should and could contribute to

the improvement of the international environment, towards the institutionalization of a non-war community or a security community at
the global level, towards the democratization of the distribution of
economic and ecological values in the North–South problem, and towards multilateralism in the transnationalization of nation-states in
terms of political culture as well as economic interdependence. The
Blue Book says that the idea of diplomacy on which Japan stands is
that of the Japanese Peace Constitution. But a critical point is that
the Book has not shown how to carry out this idea of diplomacy as a
new grand design.[22]

It can be said that the foreign policy élite's perceptions reflected in
the *Blue Book* are those of increased influence and role expansion in
the world political economy without an accompanying clear and universal grand design for creating a new world order for mankind.
Thus, at the level of governmental foreign policy, the internationalization of Japan does not seem to have basically changed since the end
of the Cold War.

How then would other policy élites see the demise of the Cold War
in the changing world order? It is difficult to identify changes of
perceptions in the formation and execution of external and internal
policies at the present time. However, let me introduce into the discussion the results of my own survey of a small group of the policy
élite in different bureaucracies.[23]

The survey was conducted in June 1991 among public officials coordinated by the National Personnel Agency (Centre for Training
Executive Officers). In this survey, 15 public officials (almost all of
director status at each bureaucracy) and 7 private companies' executive officers responded in writing to my questions. The number of respondents is very small, so that we cannot make generalizations
about policy élites' perceptions concerning the changing world order. However, I assume that the results of their perceptions might
be useful in discussing Japanese policy élites' ideas or images of national roles and problems in relation to transformation in the international system. It is interesting to note that the perceptions of a small
number of policy élite members seem to be different from those of
the conservative LDP politicians and those of the foreign policy
élite, in that they reveal rather cautious ideas about the internationalization of Japan at this critical time.

It became clear from my survey that perceptions of the changing
world order were split into two sets of ideas, that is, *significant, structural changes* or *significant, but not structural in terms of the essence of*

the dynamics. Six executive officers (Economic Planning Agency, Agency for Public Accounting, Ministry of Finance, Prime Minister's Office, Ministry of Health and Welfare, Secretariat for the House of Councillors) saw the changes as significant and structural, being quite different from changes in the past. And nine executive officers (National Personnel Agency, Ministry of Transport, Secretariat for the Supreme Court, Imperial Household Agency, Ministry of Justice, Defence Agency, Ministry of Construction, Ministry of Home Affairs, Self-Defence Forces) saw the changes as significant but not structural. Those who saw the changes as significant and structural tended to expect that changes would have implications for the transformation of power politics caused by the end of the Cold War. Those who saw the changes as significant but not structural, on the other hand, tended to raise the following issues: (1) true disarmament would be less likely to be achieved, (2) American hegemony would not easily vanish, (3) there would be a lack of a legal international framework for resolving nations' conflicts, (4) there would also be a lack of initiatives on the part of nation-states in Asia to change the regional international system, (5) there was uncertainty about the changes observed in the CIS, China, and other socialist nations, etc.

Secondly, there were interestingly different views over the questions of what international roles and responsibility Japan should and could play in the changing world order. Unlike some political leaders in the LDP, the policy élite people, in so far as this survey is concerned, tended to be cautious about sending military personnel to troubled areas for United Nations peace-keeping operations. Even those who supported the passage of the Peace Cooperation Bill suggested that sending military personnel would need a clear attempt to change the Japanese Peace Constitution as a democratic measure. Rather, respondents seemed to be much more concerned with economic and ecological issues than with military-related issues. Even when they were interested in the PKO issues in order to play a greater role in international security fields, executive officials put emphasis upon international public support, particularly from Asian countries. Why did they turn policy attention to economic and ecological issues rather than military and strategic issues? The reason appears to be obvious. It stems from the policy élites' feelings or concerns that Japan should think of not being isolated from the international community.

However, so far as this very small survey is concerned, the policy élites did not try to argue in depth the ways and means by which

Japanese trustworthiness and confidence could be enhanced in the process of internationalizing Japan. Unless a specific way of producing trust and confidence on the part of Japanese society is discussed, there appears to be risk as well as ambiguity in containing resurgent nationalism in Japanese society. Why do I think so? Even my small survey shows that Japanese bureaucrats have not paid much attention to narrowing the gap in internationalization between the internalization of Japanese political culture and the externalization of the global commitment to the international community.

Concerning the issue of the United Nations Peace Cooperation Bill in particular, therefore, let me introduce the results of a public opinion poll conducted in June 1992 by *Mainichi Shimbun* for further discussion. According to this survey, 31 per cent of respondents supported the UN Peace Cooperation Law, whereas 37 per cent of people were against it; 30 per cent did not give clear "Yes" or "No" answers (2 per cent gave no response). If the results of this opinion poll are compared with those of an earlier survey conducted by *Mainichi Shimbun* (September 1991), those who supported the Bill dropped slightly, from 35 per cent to 31 per cent, while those who were against increased from 15 per cent to 37 per cent. Those who abstained dropped from 46 per cent to 30 per cent. As far as the Mainichi survey is concerned, Japanese public opinion seems to be split in regard to the new law concerning Japan's commitment to the UN peace-keeping operations. We should note that the majority of Japanese people appear to be quite cautious about the way in which Japan should try to change its traditional policy towards the SDF's participation in the United Nations peace-keeping operations.

The split in public opinion seems to be the present trend in Japan in regard to the UN PKO issues. According to a public opinion poll conducted by *Asahi Shimbun* on 4 July 1992, 42.8 per cent supported the United Nations Peace Cooperation Bill (17.2 per cent strong support, and 24.6 per cent weak support). On the other hand, 54.3 per cent were against the Bill (24.3 per cent disapproved strongly and 30.0 per cent disapproved weakly). Concerning the status of the SDF military personnel if they were dispatched to troubled areas in the future, the Japanese public appears to be split again. According to the *Mainichi Shimbun* survey, 35 per cent supported the present status of the SDF military personnel without change; 19 per cent expressed the opinion that a new status was needed if the SDF participated in the UN PKO; 11 per cent maintained that, if the SDF military personnel were dispatched, their status should be suspended; 18 per cent were against any idea of dispatching the SDF personnel. The results of the public opinion poll are given in part in the Appendix.

It appears from these surveys that the majority of people have not demonstrated resurgent nationalism related to matters of the changing world order. This sort of internationalism or transnationalism is observed much more clearly in the attitudes of the general public than in previously surveyed policy élites' attitudes. However, the question is whether or not, and how much, internationalism or transnationalism would be likely to exert an influence upon policy élites' preferences for the endorsement of *Japanism*? Whenever external pressures (criticism) from foreign countries increase in strength, there is always a tendency for the general public to withdraw into a Japanese type of insular mentality.

Concluding reflections

Karel G. van Wolferen once wrote in a famous article:[24]

What makes conflict between Japan and the United States so menacing is that the two countries do not know how to cope with each other. The United States does not understand the nature of the Japanese political economy and thus cannot accept the way it behaves. Americans can hardly be blamed for this, as the Japanese themselves present their country as simply another member of the community of democratic nations committed to the free market. Japan is largely unaware of the threat posed by America's unwillingness to accept it for what it is.

Of course, Wolferen's view of the Japan problem is part of the complex picture of problems related to the internationalization of Japan. However, as Wolferen analyses sharply, Japan, as a whole society, has not attempted to change the "priority of unlimited industrial expansion" in terms of its external behaviour. And yet Japan has not been willing to transform its political culture towards a more or less universal type where individualism and democracy form a set of ethical values. Without changing the substance of the internationalization of its political culture, Japan seems to be embarking on the internationalization of the nation-state.

In the post-Cold War era, the Japanese are increasingly aware of Japan's big power status, particularly in economic and technological terms. Accordingly, national pride seems to be heightened and widened at different levels of society. What is needed is to bridge the gap between the internationalization of the political culture and the externalization of the global commitment. I would like to argue that Japan, among other things, should make greater efforts to promote its network of transnational organizations at such levels as political parties, local autonomies, enterprises, and the media. The fact that Japan's political institutions, culture, and political leadership are regarded as rather "inward looking" by foreigners is by no means surprising. One of the reasons for the argument that Japan is unique repeatedly boils down, in my view, to the "closure" of its society against certain forms of foreign advances. Japanese society must work hard to improve its value system *vis-à-vis* different countries through increased frequency of exchange. Furthermore, it seems that, in order to explore and create a new order, the open political idea of "shared sovereignty" is increasingly essential.

Although this essay has focused mainly on issues of security with reference to élite attitudes, perceptions, and expectations, there is still evidence here to substantiate the claim that the process of internationalization of the nation-state is quite insufficient, if we take this to mean the development of a more deep-seated form of internationalization that involves both the deepening of democracy and accountability within Japanese political life, and a foreign policy orientation that accepts and appreciates differences in culture, society, and economy. For a form of internationalization of Japan to emerge that was premised on forms of identity other than exclusive ones, it would presuppose a shift in the form of the state in Japan. As was noted earlier, a crucial dimension of the internationalization of Japan was the way it was bound up with the consolidation and centralization of power within Japan itself. Thus for a form of internationalization to emerge that diverged from policies designed to promote the twin goals of economic power and great power status would imply a loss in the power of the conservatives in the LDP, in the bureaucracies, and in the corporate sector. Only then would it be possible to redefine not only Japan's international but also its domestic political identity and culture. Further, it is my view that the recent re-emergence of nationalist forms of identity and interest, with their associated instrumentalist policies of internationalization, is not consistent, in the long run, with a secure place for Japan in an interdependent, multilateral world, where, of course, "security" is a multifaceted problem. Equating security with economic strength and military might, as is articulated in the nationalist ideologies in Japan, is likely to cause more problems than it solves in the contemporary period of world history. In this sense, when we speak of the "internationalization of Japan," we are discussing an ongoing historical process, and we have focused on selected aspects of the current phase.

Postscript

The internationalization (or transnationalization) of Japan as a nation-state requires substantive changes in Japan's political culture. In the 1990s, Japan seems to be at a critical stage with respect to the problem of change and continuity in internal as well as external policies. Japan must consider in depth a new set of alternatives for its international commitment to the changing world order.

In the general election in July 1993, the Liberal Democratic Party (LDP) lost its parliamentary majority and was replaced by a coalition government. A crucial dimension of the internationalization of Japan was, as noted earlier, the way it was bound up with the consolidation and centralization of power within Japan itself. Therefore, a loss in the power of the conservatives in the LDP may indicate good opportunities for a new form of internationalization. Moreover, the change of government could lead to new opportunities for improving Japan's commitment to world affairs.

Put simply, one of the important alternatives for Japan is whether it can choose multilaterally oriented civilian policies for the betterment of the regional and global international system, instead of being a unilaterally oriented great power. Unilateralism (being a "normal great power" and possessing military might) would seem to be the worst alternative for Japan. Unilateralism is associated with the emergence of a new nationalism in Japan as a result of being an economic power. It would encourage Japan to move towards an isolationist position, probably with an associated policy of military build-up (the nuclearization of Japan might not be inhibited under this alternative).

The coalition government in Japan has not yet made clear its grand design of internationalizing the nation-state because of differences in policy attitude among the political parties within the coalition. The Hosokawa government seems to be oscillating in its policy response to so-called international contributions (for instance, the question of whether Japan should apply for permanent membership of the United Nations Security Council). Despite the ambiguity in policy choices, Japan cannot but choose multilateralism, and it should expand its policy commitment to a variety of important international organizations (e.g. the United Nations, the G7 Economic Summits, GATT) through economic (financial) as well as technological and humanitarian assistance.

Multilateralism is also the new alternative for democratization and peace-building under the regional and global international system. This should not be confined to the narrow idea of collective defence (an "us versus them" confrontation) that was often observed in the Cold War era. Japan should choose flexibly these liberal approaches to international relations. What is needed from Japan is both the vision and the effort to contribute to the improvement of an international society that is still based on an anarchic world image.

Acknowledgements

I am very grateful to Professors Yoshikazu Sakamoto, Robert Cox, and Stephen Gill for their comments and criticism on my earlier draft. In particular, I would like to thank Professor Gill for his extensive suggestions and advice for the revision of the paper.

Notes and references

1. By power politics I mean an implicitly authorized international rule of conduct by which the threat or use of military force is legitimized as an effective diplomatic and strategic tool.
2. On the paradox and contradictions of the "new world order" at the present time, see Yoshikazu Sakamoto, "Paradox of 'World Order'" [*Sekai Chitsujo no Gyakusetsu*], *Sekai*, January 1992.
3. Paul Kennedy, *The Rise and Fall of the Great Powers: Economic Change and Military Conflict from 1500 to 2000*, London and Sydney: Unwin Hyman, 1988, pp. 514–535. The United States has certainly expended too much economic energy and investment on the military strategic sectors in order to maintain its hegemonic status. However, this is just one part of the reason why American hegemony is eroded. What Professor Kennedy does not look at in the political dynamics of the rise and fall of the great powers is the change of power and influence in operation.
4. The definition here of the internationalization of the state is different from what Professor Robert W. Cox originally proposed in *Production, Power, and World Order: Social Forces in the Making of History*, New York: Columbia University Press, 1987, p. 253.
5. Ibid., p. 254.
6. There are many studies on the theme of internationalizing the state focusing on the example of Japan. For instance, Toru Yano, *Kokusai-ka no Imi* [The Meaning of Internationalization], Tokyo: Nihon Broadcasting Publishers, 1986; Ryuhei Hatsuse, ed., *Uchinaru Kokusai-ka* [Internationalization at Home], Tokyo: Sanrei Shobo, 1985.
7. E. H. Carr, *Nationalism and After*, London: Macmillan, 1945, esp. pp. 1–37.
8. Indeed the strategy of nationalization was also linked to the centralization of power within Japan and the internal aspects of state formation.

130

9. See particularly, on this point, Masao Maruyama, *Nihon no Shiso* [Japanese Thought], Tokyo: Iwanami Publishers, 1961, pp. 37–52.

10. However, in regard to the periodization of the internationalization, it seems important to make a historical distinction between the 1930s and the 1940s in terms of Japanese foreign policy behaviour. The latter was not a mere continuation of Japan's internationalization characterized by the five features mentioned above. The 1930s saw the peak or completion of the internationalization of Japan. Japan was able to exert its diplomatic and political influence over Asia, particularly *vis-à-vis* China, through military means. But in the 1940s, when Japan was determined to wage war against the United States and against the United Kingdom, Japan was not capable, unlike in the 1930s, of executing aggressive behaviour. Therefore, there was discontinuity between the 1930s and the 1940s in terms of the development of the internationalization of the nation-state in so far as this is equated with its international dominance. I am very grateful to Professor Junji Banno for this comment.

11. Prime Minister Eisaku Sato is reported to have opposed the idea of selecting only the "three non-nuclear principles" from the four nuclear policies. The reason for this was probably that Sato may have feared the possibility of conflicts with the substance of the Japan–US Security Treaty. I assume that, in his opinion, the US extended deterrence must have been much more important than Japan's non-nuclear policy (Susumu Takahashi and Takehiko Kamo, "The Significance of Giving Legal Status to Japan's 'Three Non-Nuclear Principles' in an Era of Global Structural Change in International Politics," Paper prepared for the 56th Pugwash Symposium on "Peace and Security in the Asian-Pacific Region," 16–19 September 1989, Tokyo).

12. The conditions are: (1) there is a cease-fire agreement among parties in conflicts; (2) there is an agreement among the parties concerned in regard to the dispatch of Japanese military personnel for peace enforcement activities; (3) the peace-keeping forces should maintain neutrality; (4) if conditions are not met, the Japanese commitment can be withdrawn; and (5) weapons can be based on the part of the SDF only on the necessary minimum, that is, for self-defence. The formal name of the law is "Law Concerning Cooperation for United Nations Peace-Keeping Operations and Other Operations."

13. Cox, op. cit., p. 259.

14. *Treaty on European Union*, Office for Official Publication of the European Communities, 1992, Title V, esp. Article J. 4, p. 126. It seems important to note that the Maastricht Treaty has not yet been ratified, that many of its provisions are unpopular and controversial, and that the least publicly debated aspects relate to common security and foreign policy.

15. The Ozawa Committee says that previous government interpretation of the constitution (i.e. prohibition of collective self-defence) has lost relevance in policy-making. See committee report, *Yomiuri Shimbun*, 21 February 1992.

16. Mitchell Bernard, *Northeast Asia: The Political Economy of a Postwar Regional System*, Asia Papers No. 2, Toronto: Joint Centre for Asia Pacific Studies, 1989, pp. 4–5.

17. Ibid., pp. 33–34.

18. Ibid., pp. 38–39.

19. Cox, op. cit., pp. 250–261. Here, in these situations, "Third World élites do not participate in the same effective status as top-level élites in the formation of the consensus."

20. The State of the Union Address by President George Bush before Congress, 29 January 1991. Official Text, Press Office, USIS, American Embassy, Tokyo, 30 January 1991.

21. Bush's State of the Union Message, 28 January 1992. Official Text, USIS, American Embassy, Tokyo, 29 January 1992.

22. *The Diplomatic Blue Book*, Foreign Ministry, 1992, esp. pp. 22–36.

23. In this survey, no public officials were invited from the Ministry of Foreign Affairs. Before conducting a survey of them, I had been requested to speak on the changing world order as a guest instructor.

24. Karel G. van Wolferen, "The Japan Problem," *Foreign Affairs* 65 (Winter 1986/87), no. 2, p. 288.

Appendix: Public opinion poll on diplomatic and strategic issues (*Mainichi Shimbun*, June 1992; figures in brackets refer to 1991 poll)

1. The United Nations Peace Cooperation Bill was passed in the Japanese Diet. The Law stipulates that the SDF could be dispatched for the purpose of the UN peace-keeping operations with prior recognition by the Diet, and that the SDF's participation in peace-keeping forces would be frozen for the time being. Would you approve or disapprove of the Bill?
A. Approve: 31% (35)
Supporting party:* LDP 49%, JSP 9%, KP 59%, JCP 4%, DSP 35%, SDA 22%, Other parties 24%, Independents 19%
Male 39% (43)
Female 23% (27)
Profession: Business management, professionals, free (medical doctors, engineers, teachers, artists) 45%, Office workers 26%, Skilled workers 31%, Labour 28%, Wholesalers 26%, Self-employed 42%, Agriculture & fishery 42%, Housewives 23%, Students 27%, Others 31%
B. Disapprove: 37% (15)
Supporting party: LDP 20%, JSP 66%, KP 21%, JCP 80%, DSP 42%, SDA 53%, Other parties 45%, Independents 41%
Male 36% (17)
Female 37% (13)
Profession: Business management, professionals, free 36%, Office workers 41%, Skilled workers 36%, Labour 36%, Wholesalers 41%, Self-employed 33%, Agriculture & fishery 28%, Housewives 37%, Students 61%, Others 34%
C. Neither Approve nor Disapprove: 30% (46)
Supporting party: LDP 29%, JSP 22%, KP 20%, JCP 16%, DSP 23%, SDA 24%, Other parties 28%, Independents 38%
Male 23% (37)
Female 36% (55)
Profession: Business management, professionals, free 16%, Office workers 31%, Skilled workers 31%, Labour 34%, Wholesalers 30%, Self-employed 24%, Agriculture & fishery 30%, Housewives 38%, Students 12%, Others 31%
2. The Bill stipulates that the status of SDF personnel would remain the same as it is if they were dispatched to a conflict area. How would you think of their status?
A. The present status would be the best without being changed: 35%(41)
Supporting party: LDP 48%, JSP 23%, KP 36%, JCP 23%, DSP 48%, SDA 27%, Other parties 41%, Independents 28%
Male 36% (43)
Female 35% (22)

* LDP, Liberal Democratic Party; JSP, Japan Socialist Party; KP, Clean (Komei) Party; JCP, Japan Communist Party; DSP, Democratic Socialist Party; SDA, Socialist Democratic Association.

Profession: Business management, professionals, free 30%, Office workers 31%, Skilled workers 37%, Labour 38%, Wholesalers 31%, Self-employed 42%, Agriculture & fishery 46%, Housewives 36%, Students 27%, Others 39%

B. Additional status should be given to the SDF personnel: 19% (22)

Supporting party: LDP 24%, JSP 14%, KP 38%, JCP 7%, DSP 17%, SDA 22%, Other parties 7%, Independents 17%

Male 22% (23)

Female 17% (21)

Profession: Business management, professionals, free 25%, Office workers 22%, Skilled workers 19%, Labour 22%, Wholesalers 19%, Self-employed 28%, Agriculture & fishery 15%, Housewives 15%, Students 23%, Others 13%

C. The existing status of SDF personnel should be suspended if they were dispatched: 11% (8)

Supporting party: LDP 8%, JSP 14%, KP 7%, JCP 14%, DSP 8%, SDA 20%, Other parties 10%, Independents 15%

Male 12% (10)

Female 11% (7)

Profession: Business management, professionals, free 12%, Office workers 15%, Skilled workers 12%, Labour 12%, Wholesalers 10%, Self-employed 7%, Agriculture & fishery 8%, Housewives 11%, Students 8%, Others 10%

D. Retired personnel (SDF) should be sent: 4% (3)

Supporting party: LDP 4%, JSP 7%, KP 4%, JCP 2%, DSP 4%, SDA 2%, Other parties 3%, Independents 4%

Male 4% (4)

Female 4% (2)

Profession: Business management, professionals, free 5%, Office workers 4%, Skilled workers 4%, Labour 3%, Wholesalers 4%, Self-employed 4%, Agriculture & fishery 1%, Housewives 3%, Students 4%, Others 7%

E. No SDF personnel should be dispatched: 18% (14)

Supporting party: LDP 9%, JSP 32%, KP 10%, JCP 48%, DSP 15%, SDA 31%, Other parties 31%, Independents 22%

Male 17% (14)

Female 19% (14)

Profession: Business management, professionals, free 19%, Office workers 21%, Skilled workers 18%, Labour 14%, Wholesalers 23%, Self-employed 14%, Agriculture & fishery 13%, Housewives 18%, Students 35%, Others 15%

5

The regional factor in the formation of a new world order

Björn Hettne

Micro-states, regionalism, and world order

The states that constitute the basic units of the world system are increasingly challenged both from within and from the outside. Subnational movements question the legitimacy of the state system. We for long believed that the number of states making up this system, until recently roughly 160, had reached a certain stability after the post-colonial explosion of state formations. In the course of a couple of decades it seemed as if the world had arrived at a stable political organization. The existing states were regarded as the given constituents of the world system. Biafra proved the futility of separatism, and the partition of Pakistan, explained by its peculiar geopolitical situation, was the exception that proved the rule.

Today, however, we are facing a flood of new states, or "micro-states." Paradoxically, the micro-state phenomenon seems to be related to the process of transnationalization and the turbulent creation of a new world order. Traditional state structures are being shaken, and new identities are emerging or re-emerging as a first line of defence for social groups losing their foothold. The internationalization of what previously were regarded as "national economies" is further eroding the legitimacy of the state and destroying its capacity as an economic actor. Multiple ecological threats are generating new causes of conflict that, sometimes in a very real sense, concern life or death for specific groups. All this raises new and quite serious problems of governance, as well as queries about the optimal levels of governance. It is necessary to rethink concepts like citizen, nation, state, and security in the emerging post-Westphalian world.

The building blocks of the international system, the nation-states, are becoming "black holes" (a metaphor coined by Richard Falk). The reason is that the structure of the world order is changing, thus lifting the "overlay" of stabilizing controls that formed part of the old order, i.e. the Cold War. The peripheral tendencies characterizing a number of state formations containing great regional, socio-economic, and cultural differences will consequently take the upper hand as the geopolitical environment becomes transformed and creates new possible alignments and a direct approach to the world economy.

The domestic and the external processes are interrelated in complex ways, and there is consequently a strong need for innovative and constructive leadership in disintegrating countries. The tendency, however, is rather to resort to ethno-nationalism, which speeds up the process of disintegration. To the extent that there is a regional institutional framework that can be used for the purposes of conflict resolution, the tendency is for the region to intervene in intra-state conflicts. The alternatives are the UN system or unilateral action by the remaining superpower.

For obvious reasons, "black holes" are seen as critical problems within the region concerned, whereas they look less threatening from a great distance. Europeans worry more about Yugoslavia than about Liberia, the Japanese more about Cambodia than about Somalia. Thus one has reason to believe that regional engagement in regional conflict resolution is preferable to global engagement.[1]

Instead of order, there is increasing chaos, celebrated as "the rule of the market" by those who are in a position to benefit from the change. For others, there is little apart from tribalism and fundamentalism (religious or secular) to resort to. In this situation, the current debate about "the end of history" and "the new world order" is highly ironic, and the idea of planetary citizenship extremely utopian.[2] But the issue of global governance is important, and therefore ought to be removed from the contending areas of "realism" and "utopianism" and into the realm of "realistic utopias." We know that the old order is gone and that a new one is emerging. The question is, what kind of order and what can be done to influence the creation process.

The new regionalism should be distinguished from the equally new phenomenon of trading blocs, which seem to be emerging as the world economy becomes increasingly fragmented. What is characteristic about these emerging blocs, compared with the Cold War blocs, is their lack of internationalist legitimation, whether socialist or liberal (Sakamoto, 1992). They are simply defensive trade coalitions, non-permanent and "non-hegemonic." They do, however, express a move towards a political/territorial logic compared with the functionalist liberal/economic logic implied in the market principle and an interdependent world economy.

None the less, regionalization processes from below will also take place within the new regional mega-markets centred on the three capitalist centres. All this contributes to making the regionalization process exceedingly complex and unpredictable.

The "new regionalism" refers to the second wave of regionalism, which started in the 1980s after the decline of neo-functional integration theory and praxis in the 1970s. This decline is associated with both the slow-down in West European integration and the failure of third world free-trade areas. The new regionalism implies a more comprehensive regional cooperation, with stronger emphasis on the political dimensions. It is, furthermore, a worldwide phenomenon, although (as was also the case with the first wave) it started in Europe. It is an expression of a post-hegemonic multipolar world order. It can be defined as a world order concept, since any particular regionalization process has systemic repercussions throughout the world.

It must be emphasized that *world regions* as distinct political actors are evolving through a dialectical historical process, and that they, consequently, differ a lot in their capacity *as actor*. We could perhaps speak of *degrees of regionness*, in analogy with concepts such as "stateness" and "nationness." Five such levels can be distinguished:

The first level is region as a geographical and ecological unit, delimited by natural barriers: "Europe from the Atlantic to the Urals," or the Indian subcontinent.

The second level is region as a social system, which implies translocal relations of a social, political, cultural, and economic nature. These may be positive or negative, but, either way, they constitute some kind of regional complex. For instance, they can form a security complex, in which the constituent units are dependent on each other as well as the overall political stability of the regional system, as far as their own security is concerned. At this level, power balance or some kind of "concert" is the sole security guarantee. From a regionalist perspective this is a primitive security mechanism. A transformation from negative to positive complexes is seen in the density of international regimes covering the region.

The third level is region as organized cooperation in cultural, economic, political, or military fields. In this case region is defined by the membership of the regional organization in question. The creation of a regional organization is a step towards multilateralism in a regional context. Without a formal organization, it is rather pointless to talk of regionalism in any meaningful sense of the word, whether "old" or "new." It is important that the organized cooperation covers the relevant region. It should not be any group of countries in temporary coalitions. Regional cooperation through a formal organization is sometimes rather superficial, but at least a framework for cooperation is created. This is of great value if and when an objective need for cooperation arises.

The fourth level is region as regional civil society, which emerges when the organizational framework promotes social communication and convergence of values throughout the region. Here the role of culture must be emphasized, particularly the pre-existence of a shared civilizational tradition.

The fifth level is region as a historical formation with a distinct identity and actor capability, as well as a certain level of legitimacy. The organizational expression of this is also more complex, as the transformation of the European Community (EC) into a European Union (EU) shows. The ultimate outcome of this could be a region-state. The higher degrees of regionness define what I mean by the New Regionalism.

The regionalization process can be compared with the formation of nation-states, with the important difference that a coercive centre is lacking. The difference between regionalism and the infinite general process of economic integration is that there is a politically defined limit to regionalism. This limitation, however, is a historical outcome of attempts to find a transnational level of governance that includes certain shared values and minimizes certain shared perceptions of danger. Like the formation of ethnic and national identities, the regional identity is dependent on historical context and shaped by conflicts. And, like nations and ethnic groups, regional formations, as here defined, are "imagined communities" (Anderson, 1983).

The comparative framework that is employed has been derived from studying the process of Europeanization – the development of a regional identity in Europe (Hettne, 1991a, 1991b) – and applied to other existing, emerging, or potential world regions, under the assumption that, in spite of many structural and contextual differences, there is an underlying logic behind processes of regionalization. This logic does not refer to a single dimension and is hard to pinpoint, since it is influenced by the overall change in the world order, and also by changes in the relations between as well as in the structures within the regions. However, some key dimensions are *cultural identity*, providing a potential base for a "regional civil society," tendencies towards *economic and political homegeneity* among the countries of the region, and the nature of the *security order*, above all the manner in which "internal" regional conflicts are managed.

The structure of the necessarily rather sketchy essay is based on the emerging trade blocs as core areas around which the process of regionalization from below – the new regionalism – takes shape. In the case of Europe, the two otherwise distinct phenomena coincide. The issue is rather what we mean by "Europe," and where the European frontier will ultimately be drawn.

The European transformation

Recent debates in international political economy have focused on the role of hegemonic stability in the functioning of the international economy, as well as the implications of hegemonic decline. Relative hegemonic decline and multipolarism in the post-Cold War period will result in a more autonomous Europe as a whole. The future security system will reflect this broader integration pattern, often referred to as the "Europeanization" of Europe. The essential meaning of this concept is the process towards increasing homogeneity, the elimination of extremes (Hettne, 1991b).

The process of homogenization in Europe has gone through three recent phases: in the South, the disappearance of fascist regimes in the mid-1970s; in the West, the self-assertion of the Atlantic partners in the early 1980s; and in the East, the downfall of the communist regimes in the late 1980s.

Both fascism and communism can be seen as nationalist "catching-up" ideologies in a historical context of Western technological superiority over Eastern and Southern Europe. The elimination of the

Mediterranean dictatorships removed some anomalies from the European scene and put the continent on the road towards political homogeneity, a basic precondition for substantial economic integration. As far as former Eastern Europe is concerned, the system had simply exhausted its potential, not least as a model of development. The framework of pluralist politics will, however, contain rather different political paths, which is only to be expected in view of the original diversity of the subregion in question.

Homogenization also implies increased similarity as far as economic and even social policies are concerned. The course towards economic union and a common financial structure in Europe is now firmly set, even if the timetable as well as the order of travelling may change.[3] Thus, Europe more and more appears as one single actor in world politics, albeit gradually and not without birth-pangs. Europe is outgrowing the integrative framework of the EU and this makes it necessarily more concerned with "domestic" issues. There are forces that want to make Europe a global power, but these forces are countered by other interests and movements favouring a non-hegemonic world system. There are thus several Europes and, consequently, several possible future scenarios, regarding both internal developments and external policies.

The process of homogenization has led to a state of liberal hegemony in Europe. Democracy and the market will therefore provide the basis for future integration. This political homogenization of Europe is and will be expressed in the enlargement of the EU.

As long as an applicant is a capitalist democracy with a European culture, however defined, it would seem hard to draw a line between the welcome and the unwelcome, between "Europe" and "non-Europe." In the course of the 1990s, the number of members could thus reach perhaps 20 and, beyond that, the EU will coincide with Europe as a whole.

Thus, Europe will grow territorially as well, and as it grows it will also have to turn inwards. The new Europe will be more heterogeneous than the European Economic Community of the Six, on which the original project was based. New levels of economic and political action will appear: subregions, transnational growth zones, and ethno-nationalism. Ethno-nationalism will be legitimized and possibly less destructive in the new Europe. Ethno-national movements, creating tensions in the context of present state structures, will partly achieve their purpose in a Europe without borders.

The external effect of the process of Europeanization will differ depending on alternative "domestic" developments. There are different views on which developments are more likely.

One position, which can be called "Euro-scepticism," denies that "Europe" is a real thing and doubts that it will survive as a homogeneous political actor as the current globalization process continues. This also implies that the federal project will fail. Either it will disappear into the general global interdependence or it will dissolve into "micro-regions." There are, however, degrees of global interdependence, from transatlanticism through trilateralism and triadism, to full interdependence, where the functional logic completely subsumes the territorial.

Another position, "Euro-optimism," maintains that Europe is a distinct historical formation with its own independent life and independent will, although this may go in different directions depending on the relative strength of internal political forces. Either way, the territorial/political principle will be in command.

The fallout of Maastricht was a compromise and can be interpreted in very different ways, depending on what kind of expectations one started out from: a centralized federation or a loose unit of states. It is important not to forget that "Europe" is a historical process, not something that is born on the negotiating table. After Maastricht, the people's verdict has gone against a federal project, or at least an élite-steered process towards federalism. At present, the dearest principle in the integration process seems to be "subsidiarity," i.e. taking decisions at the lowest possible level rather than in Brussels.

Outside Europe, the economic analysts try to guess which way Europe is moving and political leaders search for options. Some regions are getting prepared for a "Fortress Europe" and organize accordingly. Some regions have to make up their minds about whether they are outside or inside Europe. Their actions will define the future frontiers of Europe. It is along these frontiers that tensions and conflicts, if not wars, will develop.

The frontiers of "Europe"

Europe lacks an obvious frontier to the east. Rather, this area has historically been a moving zone of tension between the European paradigm and what in the European intellectual tradition has been known as "oriental despotism," the negative "other," concretized in the Russian and the Ottoman empires. Thus, the historical frontiers

140

of Europe separate it from Islam and the Orthodox church. Both frontiers play their role in the current Balkan crisis as well as in the tensions of the post-Soviet region.

The Balkan imbroglio

"Balkanization" is often understood as the opposite to regionalization as here defined. To discuss the prospects of regional cooperation in this region may therefore sound paradoxical. In the Balkans, the traditional regional power has been Turkey. European identity took shape in relation to an alleged "oriental despotism," for which Turkey stood as the first model. Turkey was consequently not welcomed into the EC, and is now in the process of developing regionalist alternatives in Central Asia, as well as in the Balkans and around the Black Sea.

The Balkan crisis, triggered by the dissolution of Yugoslavia, underlined the power vacuum in a Europe still searching for a viable security order. The major conflict has always been between Serbs and Croats. Ethnically more homogeneous Slovenia is geopolitically in a safer position than Croatia, further away from Serbia, and closer to Italy and Austria. Serbs refused to live in non-Serb countries, and the Croat leaders unwisely failed to guarantee minority rights to the Serbian minority. Thus the cleansing operation started and the road to the only sensible solution – a Balkan federation – was blocked. Croats and Slovenes have now in effect joined Europe.

The other ethnic groups claiming their independence from a Serbianized Yugoslavia are the Albanians of Kosovo (as well as those living in Macedonia and Montenegro) and the Macedonians, who, apart from being the dominant community in Macedonia, constitute minorities in Bulgaria and Greece. The so-called "Macedonian question" illustrates how closely related these conflicts are with history and the interpretation of history. The fledgling nation is surrounded by neighbours equally eager to cut it into pieces.

Bosnia, closer to this fate, has an extremely complex ethnic situation. Bosnian Croats and Serbs would prefer to join their new homelands rather than constituting minorities in a Muslim country. Both Croatia and Serbia are grabbing what they can and, if this succeeds, Europe will have its own "Palestinian problem." There are also restive Muslims in Kosovo (under Serbian rule), in Albania, and in Bulgaria (where they are Turkish speaking).

Peace-keeping in Yugoslavia has proved very frustrating for the new Europe and this is undoubtedly one reason behind the recent Euro-scepticism. Behind "Europe" appeared the familiar old national interests. Austria and Germany were more understanding towards the secessionist republics, whereas other countries, among them France (sharing the Serbian view of Slovenia and Croatia as an extension of the German sphere of influence), were more anxious to retain the Yugoslav federation.

As the crisis deepened, general European opinion turned increasingly against Serbia. The Serbs, on the other hand, failed to see the EC intervention as "European." According to their view, rooted in historical experience, Germany was merely returning to old power ambitions in the Balkan area. Furthermore, the eagerness with which the Vatican recognized Slovenia and Croatia led to a rift between the Orthodox and Catholic churches. It is therefore logical that peace-keeping became increasingly internationalized. The regional approach thus did not succeed, but it should be recognized that, in fact, no easy resolution to the conflict exists. The ineffectiveness of the EC intervention shows that Europe still has far to go before becoming a regional actor. The increasing mess in Yugoslavia coincided with the Maastricht hangover.

The Balkans are thus far from being a regional formation. An internal cleavage is developing between, on the one hand, Turkey, Bulgaria, and Albania and, on the other, Serbia, Romania, and Greece. Its low degree of regionness indicates that it will be an area in which Europe will intervene repeatedly, most likely under growing protests from Turkey and Russia. Serbia is now drawing the frontier between Europe and non-Europe.

The post-Soviet region

The Soviet empire contained "European" as well as "non-European" areas. The Soviet "hegemony" did not assume the Gramscian quality of acquiescence (Cox, 1983). The situation was therefore more akin to an older type of imperial dominance, and in fact there was a striking continuity between the tsarist empire and the now dissolved state. The major factor that could keep the successor, the Commonwealth of Independent States (CIS), together is precisely the very serious conflict pattern.

Homo Sovieticus is, thus, extinct. Instead there are many "black holes," which only in a rather optimistic scenario can be seen as emerging nations. In order to avoid economic fragmentation and political tensions, they will have to sort out their relations within some kind of regional framework. The level of regionness is low. Some countries of the external ex-Soviet empire will "escape" the region by "de-easternization," and consequently join Europe, but for most of them this option is not open.

Economic nationalism on the level of the previous republics does not make sense. Russia is demographically dominant and there are 25 million Russians outside Russia. Russia produces 63 per cent of the region's electricity, 91 per cent of its oil, 75 per cent of its natural gas, 50 per cent of its meat, and 85 per cent of its paper (Tishkov, 1991). Yet the urge for self-determination defies economic logic. Inmates of the "prison of nations" are beginning to fight each other. Even Russia is sinking into general poverty, and in the peripheral areas major hunger catastrophes should not be excluded.

The only CIS country that can to some extent match Russia is the Ukraine, and the tension between the two new European great powers is clearly visible. It is most likely that the Ukraine will go it alone, or perhaps coordinate its external economic policy with the Central European EU candidates.

The Caucasian region will also go its own way, which means many different national paths and many conflicts in the coming decade. This will have an enormous impact on southern Russia, an area already becoming unsafe for Russians.

The Central Asian republics may also want to build a future of their own, if they can. Many external interests are involved, but in any event it will become a non-European area.

Even with all these separatist tendencies, old Russia remains a giant and a geopolitical challenge for Europe as well as for the other blocs when (perhaps even before) the era of economic austerity comes to an end. The crucial issue is whether Russia will become "European" or not. If Russia follows its anti-Europe tradition, as urged by the conservatives, with their deep-rooted scepticism against the West, as well as by the current communist–fascist alliance, the situation in the Europeanized regions with Russian populations will become problematic. If this problem can be solved through enlightened minority policies in the countries concerned, Russia, separated from Europe by Belorussia and the Ukraine, would perhaps rather "go Pacific" (Wilson, 1992). For Russia, Europeanization (i.e. the Western model of modernization) has always been painful, a sort of surrender. The victim of this collective feeling of inferiority is the Jewish population.

North Americanization of the Americas?

The emergence of Europe, regardless of the ultimate outcome of its external policy choices, will have an impact on how the world organizes itself politically. The mere existence of a more autonomous Europe (after having been simply an arena for competition between the superpowers) implies a new political order, since the division of Europe formed the most essential part of the old security order. The reactive impulse from other power centres – established or emerging – will also be to form blocs, while watching the nature of the European regional formation and its impact on the structure of interdependence. Even the hegemon of the post-war order, or the Bretton Woods system, is preparing for an eventual regionalization of the world order.

The emergence of NAFTA

A new free trade area (The North America Free Trade Area – NAFTA), "from the Yukon to the Yukatan," due to take effect in 1994, was recently negotiated between the United States, Canada, and Mexico and was supposed to result in a single market over a period of 15 years. It will be an expansion of the 1989 free trade agreement between the United States and Canada. Little enthusiasm is expressed within the countries concerned, although all of them seem ready to go through with it. As in Europe, however, there is an increasingly critical public debate. Canadians are unhappy even with the current free trade agreement, which is claimed to increase national economic dependence. In the United States there is a fear of losing investments and jobs, and in Mexico the environmentalists are worried about the environmental damage when polluting industries move south of the border (*International Herald Tibune*, 13 August 1992). As in Europe, real (economic) integration goes on even without formal agreements: northern Mexico and Texas are merging into one subregion, while southern Mexico is marginalized. Unlike in Europe, there are no social and regional funds to compensate the disadvantaged.

NAFTA should be seen as a reaction to the threatening fragmentation of the world economy, a "Fortress North America" as a response to the eventual "Fortress Europe." The economic issues, such as the "local contents problem," are dominating the rather technical debate.

There is little to suggest that a genuine regional identity is emerging among the three traditionally not very closely related subregions.

In the United States, the environmentalists are alarmed, and the labour unions are worried about low-cost competition.

In Canada, the bilateral agreement was already highly controversial and criticism grew as the typical consequences of free trade between two asymmetric parties became visible.

In Mexico, the tradition of nationalism, protectionism, and "anti-gringoism" is still alive. However, the economic reforms undertaken by President Salinas will speed up the inevitable integration into the North American economy so much feared by the Mexican left. The position of self-reliance (financed by oil) has now lost credibility. Some even argue for an integration into "Fortress America" as the best future that Latin America can hope for.

Mexico, which earlier had some potential of becoming a regional power (Hettne and Sterner, 1988), is the first to draw the conclusion that joining North America, i.e. NAFTA, is the only possible way out of stagnation. Mexico has abandoned the third world concept, which was so important for the image of some previous Mexican presidents (*Latin American Regional Report [LARR] – Mexico & Central America*, 18 July 1991). Thus Central America is tilting towards the north.

The Caribbean Basin: Threats of marginalization

The smaller Central American states have strong incentives for regional cooperation, and the change of regime in Nicaragua has increased the political homogeneity of the region. The crucial issue is whether the countries can develop a common approach to the emerging USA–Canada–Mexico bloc, or whether they will join this bloc as individual client states.

In the Caribbean, the 13-member regional organization CARICOM (Caribbean Community and Common Market) now contains fewer than 6 million people. The United States traditionally follows a policy of bilateralism, which does not facilitate regional cooperation. On the other hand, the European connection through the Lomé framework is pushing them towards a wider community. The European single market has provided incentives both for a Caribbean deepening towards a more integrated market (1993) and for an enlargement. There are, however, altogether only 32 million people in greater Caribbean. The next step would therefore be to form a

Caribbean Basin region including Central America. There is widespread concern that the Caribbean risks being marginalized in a world of large trading blocs (*Caribbean Insight* [*CI*], vol. 14, no. 1). Consequently, the islands are more or less ready for a degree of regional integration beyond the old colonially based cultural areas.

The disappearance of the Soviet factor will further eliminate artificial Cold War frontiers and increase the political homogeneity of the region. At the same time, changes in the external world are creating new difficulties. The privileged treatment of some countries in a position to play the geopolitical card will disappear. All the countries of the region will now have to cooperate regionally.

The Caribbean countries face, in an extreme form, problems that are common to all exporters that, in an era of changing structures of trade, are dependent on trade preferences (Stevens, 1991). In the emerging world economy the Caribbean prospects are bleak. In fact this region may be one of the main losers from "1992." In no region are the arguments for regionalism stronger, in no region are the obstacles to regionalism greater. Between the many islands there are cleavages resulting from colonial history and language; within the islands there are what have been called "dual societies," characterized by their lack of common civic culture. Thus not only the region but the societies within the region are fragmented and divided. For this reason it is realistic to expect that economic as well as geopolitical factors will push the Caribbean, like Central America, towards NAFTA, either as a group or as single countries. This view has already been expressed in the region (*CI*, vol. 15, no. 6).

The Southern Cone: Protective or offensive regionalism?

Since the mid-1980s Latin American countries have been in a process of restructuring their economies and have opened up their economies to greater international competition, at the same time as different subregional schemes are tested. The traditional groupings are (apart from Mexico and Central America) the Andean Group and the Southern Cone. The convergence of economic policies throughout the continent creates unprecedented possibilities for regional integration (Lahera, 1992).

Also, the disappearance of the socialist alternative in this region means that the countries will become even more dependent on the United States, and the room for manoeuvre is now definitely very limited. Not only the Soviet but also the European counterweight has evaporated (Castaneda, 1990). As shown by the recent US intervention in Panama, the end of the Cold War will not change the pattern of dominance, merely the pretexts for intervention.

The economic and geopolitical changes in the north of Latin America are putting a certain amount of pressure on the Southern Cone, which contains 44 per cent of Latin America's population and 52 per cent of its GNP. The democratization from the mid-1980s paved the way for more solid regional cooperation. A treaty signed by Argentina and Brazil removed some traditional causes of tension between the two countries and put fresh life into the integration process in the region. In March 1991 a free trade agreement (MERCOSUR) was signed between these two countries, and also Uruguay and Paraguay (*LARR – Brazil*, 2 May 1991). This new kind of cooperation, designed to prevent the further marginalization of Latin America in the world economy, is modelled on the EU. Even a subregional parliament is being established and democracy institutionalized in a regional framework.

The fledgling common market will enable the free circulation of goods, services, capital, and manpower by gradually reducing customs tariffs and other barriers in the member countries during the period up to 1995. These countries will also coordinate certain aspects of macroeconomic policy and foreign currency policy, as well as their economic relations with third countries. The treaty is open to other Latin American countries as they restructure their economies.

The Andean subregion will, in the event that MERCOSUR really develops into a viable regional grouping, feel the pull from both the north and the south. For instance, Chile (at present vacillating between north and south) and Bolivia have been invited to join. Chile, which is far in advance of the other Latin American countries as far as structural reform is concerned, prefers bilateral negotiations with the United States (*LARR – Southern Cone*, 4 July 1991). Bolivia is already a member of the Andean Pact.

The comparative strength of the new organization is that it will contain only members committed to the integration project. It is thus to a large extent a case of "regionalism from below," but it can hardly provide a regional system with its own dynamic. Its third worldist posture lacks credibility. The coherence of, in particular, Brazilian society is fragile, as shown by a report from Escola Superior de Guerra warning against street children as a future potential revolutionary army (*LARR – Brazil*, 28 November 1991).

It is more likely that NAFTA will expand to cover the whole of the

Americas, in line with George Bush's Enterprise for the Americas Initiative (EAI). The Latin American regionalist schemes seem to be a preparation for this, a continental drop-out from the "third world." In this perspective it will be of importance to note the fate of the internal peripheries, for instance north-east Brazil.

Regionalism in the Asia–Pacific area

The Pacific area contains three regions: East Asia, South-East Asia, and the European Pacific. Australia and New Zealand, although geographically distant from Europe, have European, and particularly British, origins. Under the impact of successive immigrations, the European heritage is becoming less distinctive. Economically, they are becoming part of Asia and dependent on Japan (Mennell, 1992). Politically they are not quite part of the region.

The Asia–Pacific "region," or rather area, was most affected by the Cold War, and the recent lifting of the superpower overlay has therefore created a kind of vacuum and great uncertainty in the security field. Several powers (great powers and middle powers) have more or less open regional ambitions, which must be related to turbulent and highly unpredictable domestic situations in the countries concerned. At the same time the overall regional framework for conflict resolution is weak, hardly existing in East Asia and confined to one of the two subregions in South-East Asia. East Asia and South-East Asia are hard to separate from each other, and will be even more so in the future as countries in South-East Asia try to apply the newly industrialized country (NIC) strategy strongly associated with East Asia.

East Asia: The Japanese dilemma

East Asia is the most dynamic of the world regions, containing a hegemonic contender (Japan), an enormous "domestic" market (China), three NICs (South Korea, Taiwan, and Hong Kong), and a socialist autarky (North Korea). It is preparing itself for major changes that may alter the pattern of cooperation within the region. A reunification of Korea, a democratization of China, and a more independent Japanese role would release an enormous potential. These changes are admittedly not immediate, but on the other hand quite feasible.

At present the region is a region largely in the geographical and cultural sense of the concept. Previous experiences of "regionalism"

148

have been various imperialistic projects. The degree of "regionness" is thus low, in spite of the fact that unplanned economic integration is now taking place owing to the dominance of the yen (*Far Eastern Economic Review* [*FEER*], October 1990). Regionalism is thus developing without much formal institutionalization (Palmer, 1991, p. 5).

The ending of the Cold War opened up new possibilities for inter-subregional contacts, widening the potential regional cooperation. The Confucian model provides a dominant pattern of social and po-litical organization, which is now frequently hailed as a cultural alter-native to Westernization (*Herald Tribune*, 13 July 1992). Many coun-tries are facing internal basic policy options that will have a crucial impact on further regionalization and future regional configurations.

Korean unification is the key to formal regional cooperation. Con-sidering the economic superiority of South Korea and the political lag in North Korea, it will probably be a spontaneous process of the Ger-man type, an "Anschluss," unless a more organized model can be found through preparatory negotiations. The point in time is deter-mined by the health of Kim Il Sung.

South Korea, together with the other NICs, is facing changes in the objective conditions that originally made them into NICs, and their strategy in the 1990s will probably be to bet on the domestic market, preferably a regional market. The regional framework is still, how-ever, in flux.

China will continue along the long road towards a more open econ-omy in spite of the temporary isolation following in the wake of the Tiananmen Square incident. China's self-reliance-oriented economy, built in the Cold War context, is in need of transformation, which (as in the case of Viet Nam) inplies a change in the regional balance of power away from Beijing and towards the south, where foreign in-vestment flows. Guangdong Province is forging links with Hong Kong, and Fujian with Taiwan, while Japan invests primarily in the Shanghai area, and South Korea in Shangdong Province. China as a centralized empire is doomed, but it is to be hoped that its dissolution will be less turbulent than that of the Soviet empire.

Perhaps the most complex issue in the region is the future role of Japan. Will it remain number two in the Pax Americana or take a more independent global role? The latter, and perhaps more likely, option would imply the accumulation of military strength and a break with the introverted Japanese world-view. It would also imply reversing the process of "de-Asianization" begun in the nineteenth century. The former course presupposes that the United States itself will not turn to isolationism, which would create great confusion as far as Japan is concerned (Tamamoto, 1990). References to "global partnership" cannot hide the fact that the old security order is defunct, owing to the disappearence of the main threat, against which the order was built, and the emergence of new threats.

The pressure on Japan is also increasing as a result of the regionalist and protectionist trend in the world economy. In 1990, Malaysia, in frustration over the General Agreement on Tariffs and Trade (GATT), urged Japan to act as a leader of an East Asian Economic Grouping (EAEG), which would create an East Asian and South-East Asian superbloc with a Sino-Japanese core. EAEG (it has since been modestly renamed East Asia Economic Caucus – EAEC) would be a sort of response to the European and North American "fortresses." A more comprehensive alternative is the forum for Asia Pacific Economic Cooperation (APEC), which has been developed in case GATT fails, and has trade expansion as its main goal (*Asiaweek*, 28 August 1992). However, the idea of any kind of regionalism is very controversial in a region extremely dependent on unhindered world trade, and the debate is carried out largely in terms of an "insurance policy" (*FEER*, 25 July 1991).

Japan, not a great practitioner of but increasingly dependent on free trade, has so far been rather negative to the idea. If regionalization were to be the main trend, Japan would appear as a regional power in more than one sense, which is bound to create suspicions throughout the region. Some countries have vivid memories of the Greater East Asian Co-prosperity Sphere, and even today the Japanese attitude towards Asia is not free from arrogance. As in the case of Germany in the EC/EU, a comprehensive regional framework would help protect Japan against itself. It has a rather weak identity as an *Asian* power, and the prospect of "re-Asianization" does not seem to be very popular. This is the Japanese dilemma. Its future path depends on the development of Japanese–US relations, as well as on the process of regionalization elsewhere (*FEER*, 20 June 1991). At the moment, Japan has "a regional policy for Asia but not a policy of regionalism" (*FEER*, 18 June 1992).

Towards a greater South-East Asia?

South-East Asia, like Europe, has been divided in two economic and political blocs: the Association of South East Asian Nations (Indonesia, Thailand, Singapore, Malaysia, the Philippines, and – since 1984 – Brunei), which has existed since 1967, and the Indo-Chinese area (Viet Nam, Kampuchea, and Laos). The Indo-Chinese subregion has been under communist rule, with Viet Nam exercising subregional hegemony. This role is now being played down at the same time as market-oriented economic policies (*doimoi*) are being tried.

Viet Nam, and behind it the Soviet Union, was earlier seen as a threat by the ASEAN countries. This is the reason why ASEAN has worked rather well as a regional organization. Inter-state conflicts were also instrumental. The source of common cause and identity was thus partly an external threat, and there were few incentives for economic cooperation. Only recently has a free trade agreement within the ASEAN region (AFTA) been achieved. From the very beginning it was a political organization (Yamakage, 1990).

In fact there are strong inter-state as well as intra-state tensions in the two subregions. The latter can be exemplified by ethnic tensions (Malaysia, the Philippines) and the former by old territorial disputes (Indonesia vs. Malaysia) as well as contrasting views on regional security (Singapore vs. Indonesia and Malaysia).

As in Europe, the dismantling of the Cold War system will change the pattern of conflict rather than eliminate the conflicts. We can therefore expect more relaxation between the two subregions but more conflicts within them. The ASEAN framework is possibly now strong enough to deal with them. An ASEAN meeting in Manila, for instance, addressed the tension over the Spratly Islands in the South China Sea, which triggered a wider ASEAN interest in discussing a future security arrangement "in the post Cambodia era" (*The Nation*, Bangkok, 23 July 1992). Ad hoc consultations may no longer be sufficient (Leifer, 1992).

The countries in ASEAN could be described as capitalist in economic terms and conservative in political terms, although, for instance, Singapore and Indonesia differ significantly in their economic policies. The organization assumed importance as a regional organization only after 1975, when there were increasing political uncertainties in the region. The economic integration that has taken place so far is rather modest, and the figure for intra-region trade is only about 20 per cent. The external dependence on Japan is felt to be problematic.

The national economies are outward oriented, and the political systems are formally democratic but in practice more or less authoritarian. The Confucian model has a strong impact on this region too, so authoritarianism in fact constitutes the homogenizing political factor. The ASEAN countries are at various stages along an NIC-type development path. Problems in the international market usually reinforce domestic authoritarianism because of the strong two-way causal relationship between economic growth and political stability: economic growth and redistribution are a precondition for ethnic peace; political stability is a precondition for the economic confidence expressed by international capital towards the region.

The Kampuchean issue has been of major concern for the ASEAN countries. Peace in the larger region, which now seems to be under way, would, however, change the basic parameters for the way ASEAN operates at present. As the superpowers pull out, old rivalries are emerging, at the same time as the objective preconditions for a cooperation encompassing the whole region in the longer run are improving. This trend will be reinforced by great power ambitions in the larger Asia–Pacific area, where South-East Asia is sandwiched between East Asian (China, Japan) and South Asian (India) regional powers (Buszynski, 1990). A strong feeling of encirclement and external penetration in the region coexists with a tradition of reliance on external security support. Somehow this contradiction must be overcome.

Regionalism in the peripheral regions

Regional integration in the "third world," if by that now somewhat contested term we mean the predominantly poor, dominated, and peripheral regions, has not been a great success. Three reasons are evident:

- *The structure of the world economy*, which under hegemonic control has tended towards interdependence, or dependence for the third world countries, rather than regionalization, in the sense of collective self-reliance in the regional context.
- *The structure of the world order*, which has been polarized on the global level, imposing security-motivated regional arrangements with little economic underpinning.
- *The free-trade area concept of regional cooperation*, which in a situation of asymmetry has reintroduced the global hierarchy of dependency relations in the region, and undermined the confidence in regional approaches to solving the problem of underdevelopment.

Today, there seems to be a new wave of a more comprehensive regionalism, albeit with varying preconditions and results. Let us look at some current trends in the poor and peripheral regions of the world. This is not to say that all the regions discussed above can be considered rich. Poverty can no longer be associated with geography. We are here particularly interested in regions that have no immediate link with the three trading blocs, although they will probably in the future have to lean on one or another of them. Thus South Asia will have stronger links with the Pacific bloc, Africa with the European bloc, and the (post-Gulf War) Middle East with the North American bloc.

South Asia: A poor man's club?

The South Asian region, geographically easily identified, is internally dominated by one "regional power," although Pakistan and India had a kind of competitive relationship before the splitting up of Pakistan in 1971. This division further destabilized the region, transforming it into an arena of superpower competition, as a weakened Pakistan received support from both China and the United States, while India entered into a treaty with the Soviet Union.

India is a giant. Size is not always a source of power, however. The process of modernization is creating conflicts that are a great strain on India as a centralized nation-state, in contradistinction to India as a decentralized culture with a special capacity for handling diversities and contradictions. In the former sense, the country may not survive in its present form, since the internal forces of disintegration are tremendous and the predominant political trend is Hindu chauvinism. A nation-state is not the most appropriate political organization for a culturally heterogeneous territory.

The domestic situations in Pakistan and Sri Lanka reveal similar weaknesses in terms of national coherence, while the ethnically more homogeneous Bangladesh has suffered almost since its creation from general economic and political decay. These ominous trends are bound to have security implications both for regional security and for the national political systems concerned (Hettne, 1988; Jørgensen, 1991).

Thus the security situation in South Asia cannot be understood unless the ethnic, regional, and religious conflicts within the states – and the way these affect inter-state relations – are carefully considered. In a situation of geopolitical dominance by India, ethnic strife, secession, and disintegration are the main vehicles for change in the inter-state system (Buzan and Rizvi, 1986).

Inter-state relations have been bad. The traumatic India–Pakistan conflict until recently prevented all efforts towards regionalism. Furthermore, after the assassination of Sheik Mujibur Rahman in 1975, Bangladesh's relationship with India was characterized by distrust and hostility (Rahman, 1985). India and Sri Lanka have had a tense and complicated relationship owing to the Tamil issue. A reversal of this disintegrative trend in the region would essentially be a return to a more integrated Indian subcontinent, as in the times of the British Raj, but in the completely new context of the New Regionalism.

In 1985, after five years of preparations, South Asian cooperation at last got its own organization: the South Asian Association for Regional Cooperation (SAARC). The initiative originated from Bangladesh. India was rather lukewarm, while the smaller countries strongly felt the need for some kind of regional cooperation to balance Indian bilateralism (Muni, 1985). Thus regional cooperation has been initiated as a counterforce to regional hegemonism. The economic rationale for regional cooperation is not overwhelming at present; rather it has to be created (Adiseshiah, 1987).

It is both a strength and a weakness that SAARC contains all the South Asian states (India, Pakistan, Bangladesh, Sri Lanka, Bhutan, Nepal, and the Maldives). It is a weakness because the conflicts in the region will paralyse SAARC for a long time to come, confining its scope to marginal issues like tourism and meteorology. It is a strength precisely because controversial problems can be handled within one organization and because at least a framework for regional conflict resolution has been created. Put differently, the regional organization coincides with the regional security complex and can be seen as an embryo for a security community.

If the internal power structure is becoming more balanced through a weakening of Delhi and greater political autonomy for the regions of India, there is also a trend towards political homogenization in the form of democratic openings in Pakistan, Bangladesh, and Nepal. India will also opt for a more open economy as a result of pressures from the International Monetary Fund (IMF), thus reducing the gap in economic policies between the regional power, with its tradition of import substitution, and the smaller, more externally oriented states.

Many SAARC summits have been haunted by problems, controversies, and delays. The most recent one (Colombo 1991) was no exception. In spite of this, the time for more substantial achievements should be now, let us say in the next five-year period.

Thus objective forces lead to regionalization, while the institutional framework is lagging behind.

Africa: Collapse of the nation-state project

Africa is culturally divided between Arab and African areas. In Sub-Saharan Africa there has been little regional integration, simply because there is little to integrate. Only 5 per cent of the continent's trade is inter-African. The need is rather for "integrated economic development" on the regional level (Thisen, 1989), an element conspicuously lacking in Africa's structural adjustment programmes (*West Africa* [*WA*], 22–28 July 1991). "Developmental regionalism" has thus been the main issue.

Regionalism, however, has been a highly politicized issue, which tends to create suspicion in the national centres of decision-making. Of Nkrumah's pan-Africanism little remains today, but what was then a dream has now, nevertheless, become a necessity, and not only for economic reasons. The ethnic conflicts, for instance, cannot be resolved within the nation-state framework, particularly as the unsuccessful nation-building project is in fact the main cause behind these conflicts. Of importance is the ongoing democratization in Africa, including South Africa, which will increase the political homogeneity of the region and in the longer run provide the foundations for an African security community.[4] Similarly, economic policies are "harmonized" owing to the dramatically increased dependence on the IMF and the World Bank, as well as on the donor countries. The new political conditionalities can be criticized from many points of view, but they undoubtedly harmonize the political cultures.

At the 1991 summit of the Organization of African Unity (OAU) in Abuja it was repeatedly stressed that the ongoing integration of Europe called for a collective response from the member states, in the form of an African Economic Community (AEC). The theme of the summit was the threatened marginalization of Africa, to which regionalism was seen as the remedy. Many previous initiatives had been taken in this direction, for instance the Lagos Plan of Action (1980), but undoubtedly the issue has now assumed a special urgency. The implementation of the AEC will take decades, and the first five-year period will be devoted to the strengthening of existing regional economic communities as building blocks in the creation of a continent-wide unity. Promising efforts are being made in southern, western, and northern Africa. Another significant development is that the OAU has opened a Division of Conflict to deal with tensions between and within member states. The principle of non-interference is thus being reconsidered (*North African*, June 1992, no. 297).

The most important subregional initiative, at least in terms of declared objectives, is SADCC (Southern Africa Development Coordinating Conference), which covers 10 countries. The main function of SADCC was originally to reduce dependence on South Africa, a regional power with very evident designs of regional control through the destabilization of "hostile" regimes. Thus it is a fairly clear example of the New Regionalism, since SADCC is not simply based on the common market concept but has wider political objectives. So far, however, the instruments have been lacking and no supranational powers have been conferred (Tostensen, 1992). Attempts are now being made to upgrade the level of regional integration by establishing a formal treaty. The most recent documents indicate an awareness of the need for political intervention to prevent regional disparities from destabilizing the security situation.

Now that apartheid has been declared a "closed book," the agenda for regional cooperation in southern Africa will change fundamentally – and the incentives will perhaps become positive rather than negative. Much depends on the character of the post-apartheid regime, not only for southern Africa but for the whole of Sub-Saharan Africa. Three possible scenarios can be mentioned (Martin, 1991): (1) "regional restabilization" under South African dominance, (2) regional breakup, peripheralization, and bilateralization of internal and external relations, and (3) a neo-regional alternative implying regional restructuring based on a symmetrical and solidarity-oriented pattern of development.

As with all regional scenarios, it is the domestic politics of the constituent states that will play the decisive role. To this must of course be added the international arena from which southern Africa (including South Africa) has been increasingly marginalized. The way I see it, regional cooperation must include South Africa in order to move from a defensive alliance between "front-states" to a real regional actor. This would necessitate a strong economic base, without which regional cooperation at the most can play the role of a negotiation cartel.

The prospects for regional cooperation, however, are generally beginning to look brighter, partly as a result of the weakening of the previously all-powerful nation-states as the dominant political institutions. This does not mean that a complete disintegration of the states

156

in a region (for instance the Horn of Africa) can be seen as a path towards regionalism.

In West Africa, where the Economic Community of West African States (ECOWAS) has been more or less paralysed, there are signs of economic and political homogenization and a somewhat more active regionalism. National repressive regimes are crumbling, the "socialist" experiments are over, and even old "liberal" autocracies such as Côte d'Ivoire are slowly democratizing. The delinking of the state apparatus from élite interests may lead to a strengthening of the regional as well as the local level – the regional because of the development imperative, the local because this is where the democratic forces are. The regional or rather subregional structures, however weak, will play an increasing role in conflict resolution in real and potential "black holes," of which Africa has its fair share. One example will suffice.

In the shadow of the Kuwait crisis, ECOWAS intervened in a rather improvised way in the Liberian civil war, with the explicit purpose of preventing a general massacre of the population. Although this move was not fully backed by the whole region and, furthermore, was not a highly successful operation in terms of conflict resolution, it was unprecedented in the history of African regional cooperation. Since an agreement between the factions has now been made, the Liberian crisis can be said to have speeded up the process of regional cooperation. A comparison with the Yugoslavian crisis in Europe could be made. The shared view in the region was that "the ECOWAS states cannot stand idly by and watch a member state slide into anarchy" (*WA*, 1–7 July 1991). From now on, the more stable regimes within a particular region may feel obliged to interfere through regional institutions in countries on route toward anarchy. It need not be said that there are dangers in this as well.

In the Maghreb subregion, which forms part of the Arab world, harsh realities in terms of both inter-state conflicts and social and economic problems led to new attempts at stimulating regional integration. In February 1989, the five countries' Arab Maghreb Union was created in order to tackle both peace (the Western Sahara conflict) and development (the debt crisis) issues. There was great fear that the traditional European markets would close after 1992.[5] The aim of the Maghreb Union is to stimulate trade between member states, increase non-traditional exports, and cut imports (*South*, May 1989).

The southern European countries are much concerned about stability in Arab North Africa and have developed the project of creating a Conference on Security and Cooperation in the Mediterranean (CSCM) modelled on the Conference on Security and Cooperation in Europe, but based on an even broader concept of security, including for instance water scarcity as a security risk. This is significantly different from the approach inherent in the US Middle East paradigm (Hadar, 1991), which is now being repeated in the case of Libya.

The Middle East: Search for power balance and identity

The Middle East "region," which is a region mainly in the geographical sense, is in many ways the most complex, and regionalism is therefore bound to emerge and re-emerge in different manifestations and constellations, and has to transcend many contradictions. The region is extremely diverse in ethnic terms, at the same time as it is largely dominated by one religion and one linguistic culture. Great ambitions towards regional unity coexist with constant conflicts beween states and ethnic groups.

Of importance is the frustrated but still enduring idea of an Arab Nation, nurtured not least by Arabic Christian minorities – at least in the initial period of Arab nationalism – and today politically articulated in Syrian and Iraqi Baathism. This idea, badly undermined by the Gulf War, corresponds to a potential "regional civil society," today at best a dormant potentiality. With the rise of political Islamic movements in the 1980s and 1990s, it looks as though Islamism today has gained the upper hand over pan-Arabism.

The present political boundaries were externally imposed by the European colonial powers, and they lack emotional significance, not only because they are so recent but because they have been changed so often in the past. Urban centres such as Cairo, Damascus, Baghdad, and Istanbul thus have all possessed a regional significance far beyond their present national roles. It is the region of "realist thinking" *par préference*. The artificial boundaries, the competing élites, and the lack of a democratic tradition make the power play between heavily armed states as close to Machiavelli's world as one can come. Superpower involvement has followed the same cynical logic. Allies have been sought with little regard for their domestic human rights record. Previous regional arrangements have been dictated by external powers (hegemonic regionalism), and several states (Iran under the Shah, Turkey, and Israel) have played "sub-imperialist" roles.

The problem of regional hegemonism has a long historical tradition. There are several competing major states with a potential for regional leadership or hegemony, but also with decisive handicaps in performing that particular role. Iraq was the strongest candidate before the war that crippled it; Syria and Egypt, the remaining Arab contenders, have become too much involved with the West to be credible. Turkey is an outsider, being a member of NATO and having ambitions to become a European state, but is now finding a new role in the Middle East. Iran, now in a process of rearming while Iraq is forced to rearm, is feared throughout the region as non-Arabic and Shiite.

Despite the difficulties, there are several regional groupings and institutions. The best known is the Arab League, which is based on the idea of Arab unity. Owing to the decline of Arab nationalism and political conflicts between the Arab states, however, it will probably be the many different sub-organizations of the Arab League that will be of importance in the future. Further, subregional cooperative arrangements such as the Gulf Cooperation Council (GCC) and the formation of the Arab Cooperation Council right before the outbreak of the Gulf War may indicate that various *sub-regional* arrangements will be the way in which regionalism in the future expresses itself in the Middle East. A recent cooperative agreement between Turkey, Iran, and Pakistan, in which the post-Soviet Central Asian republics are included, is one example of the many possible (but until now short-lived) regional initiatives in this region of diversity (*FEER*, 5 September 1991). This is a non-Arabic organization containing a quarter of the Muslims of the world, but with an internal Turkish–Persian cleavage. Turkish initiatives for the formation of a Turkic subregion are also seen in the formation of the Black Sea Economic Cooperation Pact in June 1992.

For obvious economic and strategic reasons, superpower involvement in the region has been deep. In the political crisis in the region triggered by Iraq's occupation of Kuwait in August 1990, attempts at finding a regional solution, which were not very realistic anyway, were halted by US intervention, leading to a polarization within the region between conservative and radical currents. As the Soviet Union opted out, the United States, with the help of frustrated potential regional influentials, established itself in the region – nobody knows for how long, since the threatened breakup of Iraq could be the beginning of a long struggle for regional power, in which external interests headed by the United States will play a major role. The Gulf crisis meant a back-seat for Europe (the EC). To restore its image and counter US influence, the strategy now involves a major role for Iran, where anti-US feelings are strongest (*The Middle East*, July 1991). However, the intervention of regional influentials such as Egypt, Turkey, and Syria was not necessarily popular among the people of these regions. This opens the door for unexpected domestic repercussions, which in turn will affect the power game. The regional alliance is already cracking up and the smaller Gulf countries seem to define their security as a US presence, while the major players have their own, usually incompatible, schemes.

It is thus very difficult to foresee what a new security system in the Middle East might look like. The so-called peace process initiated in the summer of 1991 offers few clues. Ironically, Saddam Hussein is still needed for balance of power purposes, since no alternative military government has come forward to guarantee the status quo. What now binds the countries together is their fear of Iraq becoming the regional hegemonic power. The problems to be solved are, however, many: first of all to contain the power and influence of Iran, to find a solution to the Palestine question, and to reduce the gap between the rich Gulf states and the poor Arab masses. Then there is a host of minority and human rights problems, of which the most urgent is the Kurd question. A regional democratization wave, such as the one going on in Africa, would be needed to create a more solid civil society base for regional initiatives.

Regionalization and globalization: Contradictory and complementary processes in the formation of a new world order

What conclusions can be drawn from a comparative overview of regionalization throughout the world, and in particular attempts at regional cooperation from below?

Regionalization is an uneven and complex process of change taking place simultaneously at three levels: the structure of the world system as a whole, the level of interregional relations, and the internal pattern of each single region. It is not possible to state which of these levels comes first, or which one is most important, since changes on the three levels interact, and their relative importance differs from one region to another. In fact regionalization is a process that necessarily involves all three levels.

The structure of the world system must permit the regional actors room to manoeuvre, at the same time as the increase in regional activity in itself constitutes structural change on the world level. True regionalism, or what I call the New Regionalism, would not have been consistent with the hegemonic regionalism of the bipolar Cold War system, since the "quasi-regions" in this system tended to reflect the global ideological divisions. This was evident in Europe, East Asia, South-East Asia, and the Middle East. In South Asia, the dominant power was associated with the Soviet Union, whereas the rest of the countries tended towards the other pole. In Latin America and the Caribbean, there were exceptional cases where countries departed from the dominant geopolitical camp, and also had to face the consequences. In Africa, the Cold War pattern was less ingrained, but it played a part in the development aid game. In contrast with this Cold War pattern of hegemonic regionalism, the dynamics of regionalization is at present more from below.

Moving to the level of interregional relations, I have made the point that European regionalism is the trigger for global regionalization, at least in two different ways: one positive, the other negative.

In the *positive* way, Europe is seen as a success story in regional cooperation, a model to emulate.[6] The EU is, furthermore, actively encouraging regional formations in the third world through its "regional dialogue" or "group-to-group" diplomacy. This is in contrast with the deeply entrenched bilateralism of the United States.

The *negative* aspect is of course the infamous European Fortress – the threat of regional protectionism that will provoke rather than promote other regional bloc formations.

As far as the regional level itself is concerned, we have noted that a process of homogenization in terms of type of political regime and economic development policy is a necessary precondition for a deepening of the regionalization process. The security system in particular strongly influences the pattern of economic relations between the states of the region. In Europe, economic organizations such as the European Economic Community, the European Free Trade Association, and the Council for Mutual Economic Assistance were reflections of the Cold War order. The end of this order characterized by hegemonic regionalism created a new situation as far as economic cooperation was concerned. The same trend can now be discerned in most regions.[7]

The process of regionalization will have many faces: a regionalization of the world economy, the emergence of Europe as the first world region, attempts by other regions to follow suit, the growth of subregionalism within Europe, and (as national borders fade) the development of smaller, multinational economic regions.

The overall result will be a new balance of power system within as well as between the regions – but power may increasingly be more of the economic than of the military kind, "soft" rather than "hard" power. This dimension will distinguish regions that search for a role in the world economy from regions that helplessly turn into war zones because there are no regional institutions strong enough to arrest a process of disintegration. Europe is of the first type, the CIS may turn out to be of the latter. The ASEAN subregion of South Asia may in the coming years establish some kind of regional security structure. East Asia so far lacks an institutional framework, mainly owing to the ambivalence of Japan. In Africa, the situation differs radically from one subregion to another, for instance West Africa and the Horn of Africa.

The actual process of regionalization is triggered by events whose importance can be understood only in retrospect. It seems as if regionalization not only provokes processes of national disintegration, but actually feeds on these crises, whose solution necessitates further regional integration. However, this can involve an element of force and coercion that does not form part of a genuine process of regionalization from below.

The New Regionalism, expressing an advanced level of regional complexity – a regional formation with a distinct identity and a capacity as actor – can be seen as a form of "extended nationalism" (Seers, 1983). It does not preclude a function for the nation-state, which for certain purposes could be a useful level of decision-making. In the case of other issues, however, the nation-state prevents rational solutions, whereas the regional level opens up new and previously untapped possibilities to solve conflicts built in to the state formation. The larger region can absorb conflicts that have become institutionalized in the historical state formations. Under the umbrella of multilateralism, the regional actor can, with less risk of provoking bilateral tensions, intervene in intra-state conflicts that threaten to become destructive. The outcome is by no means uniform. Rather it would be correct to say that incidents of national disintegration can make or break regional organizations.

As an "imagined community," the region perhaps constitutes the limit of human empathy. Is it a new kind of tribalism nurtured by fear and hostility, and provoking more of the same? Is it an obstacle or a road to planetary citizenship? In the present turbulence, regionalism seems to be a stabilizing factor.

The history of regionalism shows that regional institutions become relevant only when there is an objective need for them, and possibly for different purposes than were originally conceived. The EC developed far behind the schedule as laid down in the 1957 treaty, but today one can question its relevance for the dramatic and largely spontaneous process of integration in Europe – the emergence of a European civil society. There are in fact several competing frameworks, particularly in the area of security. Maastricht represents a first step towards a unification and consolidation of several institutional structures into one.

What about the non-European regions? On the "frontiers" of Europe there is hardly anything in terms of institutional structure to fall back on, and these areas may be areas for European intervention, as can already be seen in the Balkans. The CIS was formed as a reaction to the disintegration of the Soviet empire and is patently inadequate in view of the challenges it faces. North American regionalism (including Central America and the Caribbean) is a new departure, so far limited to free trade. The rest of the Americas, the Andean area and the Cone, still have to make a basic choice about how to relate to NAFTA. East Asia is another case lacking an institutional structure with unhappy remembrances of hegemonic regionalism. ASEAN became relevant as a defensive organization in the face of a Vietnamese threat. Only today are its members discovering the economic usefulness of the organization. SAARC was originally an attempt by the smaller states to organize against the regional bully, but now the regional organization is seen as a useful adaptation to world order changes, including the regionalization of other areas. ECOWAS slumbered until complete anarchy enveloped one of its members, and the organization took upon itself a role unprecedented in the history of African regional cooperation. SADCC is tentatively moving from defensive to offensive regionalism. In the Horn of Africa there is disintegration of states (Ethiopia, Somalia) without any transnational organization whatsoever.[8]

The overall picture is one of regionalism as an emergent phenomenon. We cannot tell much about its final shape and its ultimate role in the formation of a new world order, but it is not a step that can be skipped.

It should finally be underlined that the process of regionalization is a combined result of global and domestic changes. The objective need for further steps may appear sooner than the political leaders expect. The actual shape of regions will depend on dynamics not easily foreseen, particularly not in the political vacuums created by the black hole syndrome.

Notes

1. The UN interventions in Yugoslavia and Cambodia will be an indication of whether the immediate neighbours will contribute in accordance with geographical proximity. Under UN rules, Japan's share of the Cambodian mission would be 12.5 per cent, compared with 30 per cent for the United States. But it is most likely that Japan will pay more than this and the United States less.
2. "It would be idealistic and futile to expect that contemporary nation states could now be integrated directly on the global level" (Ervin Laszlo at the conference "Europe into the Third Millennium," Exeter, April 1992).
3. After Maastricht, the euphoria of European integration was replaced by a continental hangover, reflected in the "earthquake" elections in April 1992 and the Danish referendum in June 1992.
4. "A new wind is bringing multi-party democracy" (*New African*, July 1991). The arguments for the one-party state may have been theoretically correct, but in reality they were a cover for authoritarianism.
5. At one stage Morocco even signalled an interest in joining the EC.
6. This was explicitly stated in the 1991 Colombo meeting of the South Asian Association for Regional Cooperation (SAARC). Similarly the Abuja summit of the Organization of African Unity (OAU) in 1991 called for an African Economic Community on the lines of the EC.
7. The external effect of the process of Europeanization differs depending on alternative "domestic" developments. Possible scenarios can be divided into two categories, the first doubting that "Europe" will survive as a homogeneous political actor, the second maintaining that Europe is a distinct historical formation with its own independent life and independent will. The first (Euro-sceptic) position contains three scenarios: (1) the neo-Atlanticist scenario, perceiving Europe as a more open trading system consisting of sovereign nation-states protected by a modified Atlantic security system; (2) the trilateral scenario, underlining the need for collective management of a liberal world economy; (3) the "Greening of Europe" scenario, envisioning Europe as a loose, undefined informal structure of regions and local communities within a world order of similar decentralized structures.
8. I appreciate the help received from Bertil Odén, Helena Lindholm, Marie Thynell, and Joakim Öjendal in the time-consuming job of watching regional developments.

Bibliography

Books and articles

Adiseshiah, M. (1987) "The Economic Rationale of SAARC." *South Asia Journal* 1, no. 1.
Anderson, B. (1983) *Imagined Communities*. London: Verso.
Buszynski, Leszek (1990) "Declining Super Powers: The Impact on ASEAN." *The Pacific Review* 3, no. 3.

Buzan, B., and G. Rizvi, eds. (1986) *South Asian Insecurity and the Great Powers*. London: Macmillan.

Castaneda, J. G. (1990) "Latin America and the End of the Cold War." *World Policy Journal* VII (summer), no. 3.

Cox, Robert W. (1983) "Gramsci, Hegemony and International Relations. An Essay in Method." *Millenium* 12 (summer), no. 2: 162–175.

Edwards, G., and E. Regelsberger, eds. (1990) *Europe's Global Links. The European Community and Inter-Regional Cooperation*. London: Pinter.

Gill, S. (1990) *American Hegemony and the Trilateral Commission*. Cambridge: Cambridge University Press.

Gilpin, R. (1987) *The Political Economy of International Relations*. Princeton, NJ: Princeton University Press.

Haas, E. B. (1970) "The Study of Regional Integration: Reflections on the Joy and Anguish of Pretheorizing." *International Organization* no. 24 (autumn).

Hadar, Leon T. (1991) "The United States, Europe and the Middle East." *World Policy Journal* VIII, no. 3: 421–449.

Hettne, B. (1988) "India." In: J. Carlsson and T. M. Shaw, eds. *Newly Industrializing Countries and the Political Economy of South–South Relations*. London: Macmillan.

—— (1991a) "Europe and the Crisis: The Regionalist Scenario Revisited." In: Marguerite Mendel and Daniel Salée, eds. *The Legacy of Karl Polanyi. Market, State and Society at the End of the Twentieth Century*. London: Macmillan.

—— (1991b) "Security and Peace in Post-Cold War Europe." *Journal of Peace Research* 28, no. 3: 279–294.

Hettne, B., and H. Hveem, eds. (1988) *Regionalism and Interregional Relations*. Gothenburg: Padrigu Papers.

Hettne, B., and T. Sterner (1988) "Mexico as a Regional Power." In: J. Carlsson and T. M. Shaw, eds. *Newly Industrializing Countries and the Political Economy of South–South Relations*. London: Macmillan.

Hormats, R. O. (1991) "The Roots of American Power." *Foreign Affairs* 70, no. 3.

Jørgensen, B. D. (1991) "Ethnic Dimensions of Regional Security: The Case of South Asia." In: L. Ohlsson, ed. *Regional Conflicts and Conflict Resolution – Case Studies II*. Gothenburg: Padrigu Papers.

Lahera, Eugenio (1992) "Hacia un nuevo concepto de integracion?" *Cono Sur* (Flacso, Chile) XI (May–June).

Leifer, Michael (1992) "ASEAN: Now for the Next 25 Years." *International Herald Tribune*, 13 August.

Martin, William G. (1991) "The Future of Southern Africa: What Prospects After Majority Rule." *Review of African Political Economy*, no. 50: 115–134.

Mennell, S. (1992) "The Crisis of Europeanness Overseas. A View from Australasia." Paper for the conference "Europe into the Third Millennium," Exeter, April.

Muni, S. D. (1985) "SARC: Building Regions from Below." *Asian Survey* XXV (April), no. 4.

Palmer, N. D. (1991) *The New Regionalism in Asia and the Pacific*. New York: Lexington Books.

Polanyi, K. (1945) "Universal Capitalism or Regional Planning." *London Quarterly of World Affairs*, January.

Rahman, Atiur (1985) *Political Economy of SARC*. Dhaka: University Press.

Rosecrance, R. (1986) *The Rise of the Trading State*. New York: Basic Books.

Rosenau, J. N., and H. Tromp, eds. (1989) *Interdependence and Conflict in World Politics*. Aldershot: Avebury.

Ruggie, J. G. (1986) "Continuity and Transformation in the World Polity: Toward a Neorealist Synthesis." In: R. O. Keohane, ed. *Neorealism and Its Critics*. New York: Colombia University Press.

Sakamoto, Yoshikazu (1992) "Changing World Order: A Conceptual Prelude to the UNU Project on Global Structural Change." Tokyo: United Nations University.

Seers, D. (1983) *The Political Economy of Nationalism*. Oxford: Oxford University Press.

Stevens, Christopher (1991) "The Caribbean and Europe 1992: Endgame?" *Development Policy Review* 3/91.

Sutton, P. ed. (1991) *Europe and the Caribbean*. London: Macmillan.

Tamamoto, M. (1990) "Japan's Search for a World Role." *World Policy Journal* VII, no. 3.

Thisen, J. K. (1989) "Alternative Approaches to Economic Integration in Africa." *Africa Development* XIV, no. 1.

Thomas, C. Y. (1988) *The Poor and the Powerless. Economic Policy and Change in the Caribbean*. London: Latin American Bureau.

Tishkov, V. A. (1991) *The Soviet Empire Before and After Perestroika*. UNRISD.

Tostensen, Arne (1992) "What Role for SADCC in the Post-Apartheid Era?" Uppsala: Scandinavian Institute of African Studies.

Wilson, D. (1992) "Russia's Pacific Century." *Japan Times*, 23 March, p. 23.

Yamakage, Susumu (1990) "ASEAN from Regional Perspective." *Indonesian Quarterly* XV, no. 3: 430–446.

Regional magazines

Asiaweek
Caribbean Insight
Eastern Europe Newsletter
Economic and Political Weekly
Far Eastern Economic Review
India Today
International Management
Latin American Regional Report
The Middle East
New African
South
West Africa

Part II
The globalization of political economy

6

Structural change and global political economy: Globalizing élites and the emerging world order[1]

Stephen Gill

The contemporary process of global restructuring is generating increasing hierarchies of power and deepening social inequality. Globalizing forces are serving to both integrate and disintegrate key aspects of social life on the planet. Globalizing élites – intellectual and practical apparatuses within transnational capitalism – are at the apex of social hierarchies in the emerging world order.[2]

The dialectic of integration—disintegration—world order may entail the second "Great Transformation" of the politics and economics of the twentieth century, with its own "double movement" (Polanyi, 1957). Tendencies towards global integration and attempts to reconstitute power at the core of the world order are also bound up with tendencies towards social disintegration and chaos. Existing socioeconomic structures and forms of state are mutating, or are driven to collapse, in all three main categories of country. This historical dialectic is being shaped by both élites and social movements, and thus consciousness and action, mobilization and strategy are involved. Thus an initial task is to identify what Braudel (1981) called "the limits of the possible" for different groups, classes, coalitions, nations, within which social reintegration can take place.

Globalization, integration–disintegration, and world order

What is meant by "world order"? In this chapter, "order" is under-stood as how things actually are, not as a normatively desirable or stable condition. It consists of a relatively persistent pattern of events and structures over time, as existed, for example, in the metro-politan core of the global capitalist system in the 1950s and 1960s (the system was less consensual or hegemonic in the third world, and it was countervailed by, on the one hand, Soviet-led and, on the other, Chinese communism).

As noted above, one way to describe the present state is that it is one of disintegration/reintegration in a condition that I call one of "patterned disorder." Old political, economic, and social structures are under stress or breaking down, and social chaos and disorder characterize conditions in much of the world; new structures are only beginning to become perceptible. At the same time, the ideas, institutions, and material capabilities of the vanguard elements of the globalizing élites of contemporary capitalism are seeking to re-construct new patterns of dominance and supremacy at the core of the system. Thus a general restructuring of power is occurring in a less consensual and more conflictual, post-hegemonic world order.

Indeed, the collapse of the USSR has thrown into relief attempts by globalizing élites to reconstitute hegemony, under very different social conditions from those that prevailed following World War II. Here, then, the collapse of the USSR is the most dramatic case of the "descent from production into entropy." What is meant by this phrase is a situation where a functioning economic system begins to self-destruct, partly because of its internal contradictions, and partly because of conscious choices that accelerate its road to collapse. Thus, although Soviet economic performance began to stagnate in the 1970s and 1980s, it was only in the later part of the 1980s follow-ing Gorbachev's policies of *perestroika* (*glasnost*, or political open-ness, was quickly abandoned) that production began to decline and the physical capital and infrastructure of the USSR began to disinte-grate. Recently, the International Monetary Fund (IMF) estimated that since 1989 the GNP of the Soviet Union has declined by over 50 per cent, and further decline and social atomization are to be pre-dicted, particularly since the existing political structures are inchoate and the pauperization of the population is accelerating.

Indeed, the process in the former Soviet Union is an extreme ex-ample of key aspects of global structural change; Robert Cox (1992) has coined the phrase "global perestroika" to describe this process. Thus, rather than being simply explicable in terms of conscious political decisions and the direct use of political power, global perestroika (that is, the process beyond the former USSR) has produced a type of institutionalized chaos that is propelled by the restructuring of global capitalism. Of importance here are accelerating changes in production, finance, and knowledge that have given rise to a relatively coherent, interrelated pattern. In this pattern there has been a cumulative if uneven rise in the structural power of internationally mobile capital (Gill and Law, 1988, 1989), a rise that has brought with it certain limits and contradictions.

This emerging world order, then, can be contrasted with the one that prevailed in the metropolitan nations in the 1950s and 1960s. From the vantage point of the early 1990s, it appears to be characterized by deepening social inequalities, economic depression for most parts of the world, and a reconfiguration of global security structures. These changes are strengthening the strong, often at the expense of the weak. The principle of distributive justice that is increasingly associated with this order is, to paraphrase the Book of Matthew, "to him that hath shall be given, to him that hath not shall be taken away." This is what I mean by the term "patterned disorder."

The restructuring of globalizing capitalism is bound up with the renaissance of the power of money capital in an increasingly economic liberal form of capitalist development (I use the term "economic liberal" since it may go not only with liberal democracy as its political form, but also with authoritarianism). In turn, certain aspects of contemporary development can be understood in terms of their deeper roots, that is, as structures of material life. In the 1980s and 1990s, the commoditization and monetization of social life are extending and deepening. The current phase of transformation can be related to Fernand Braudel's concept of *longue durée*, in so far as the structure and language of social relations are more systematically conditioned such that capitalist norms and practices pervade the *gestes répétés* of everyday life. Tendencies towards the globalization of capitalism thus condition the limits of the possible for different agents and social movements in the emerging world order.

Historically, the form of the state and the nature of economic and social regulation have varied according to the political relations and struggles between labour and capital, and to the state's international position. In the post-1945 period, partly because of the development of socialism and trades unions, the gradual democratization of the liberal state, and the effects of World War II, the scope for capital mobility and unfettered, self-regulating markets was substantially constrained in a system of "embedded liberalism" (Ruggie, 1982). This was premised upon a series of "welfare nationalist" forms of state (Cox, 1987). These forms, in North America and Western Europe, were products of the socio-political response to the austerity and economic depression of the 1930s. The contradictions of the inter-war period were associated with the application of the "pure liberal" orthodoxy of sound money and attempts to extend the logic of the self-regulating market form of civil society at the domestic and international levels.

By contrast, the post-1945 world order was politically constructed so as to give primacy to production over finance, and to consolidate the political centre against right- and especially left-wing forces, a struggle that intensified with the onset of the Cold War. Thus part of the social basis for the post-war hegemonic settlement (which many commentators argued existed in the 1945–1970 period) was a rough balance between the demands and pressures of internationally mobile economic forces and those of domestic social welfare. Vulnerable, geographically immobile domestic groups and productive sectors were given protection that allowed time for social adjustment to the demands of international competition. At the same time, the global security structure was configured primarily by two militarized alliance structures led by the United States and the USSR respectively, and a war of ideology was sustained between them.

Social structures of accumulation in the main capitalist countries rested upon Fordist production and consumption structures, corporatism, Keynesian macroeconomic management, and a regime of very cheap energy (reflecting the subordination of the third world), which assisted the vanguard industries (often associated with the military–industrial complex, such as arms production, oil, vehicle manufacture, aerospace, computing) in a period of unprecedented growth and prosperity in the West and Japan. Fordist production structures, albeit of a different type, also prevailed in the USSR, with heavy emphasis given in plans to military–industrial capacity and mass, assembly-line production, in a Stalinist Leviathan, reflecting one variant of the "Hobbesian" state form (van der Pijl, 1989).

Post-war economic liberalization in the West was partial and politically embedded in a consensus between labour, capital, and the state. In Europe and to a lesser extent the United States this involved varied forms of state capitalism in the "mixed" economy. Nevertheless, there were limits to state engagement in economic life in the "Lockian heartland" (van der Pijl, 1989) of transatlantic capitalism. The term "Lockian" is used here to reflect the fact that the system was premised on the existence of a vigorous and relatively self-regulating civil society. It reflected the formal separation of public and private, of state and civil society, in liberal democratic capitalist "civil governance." This contrasted with the mercantilist, interventionist "Hobbesian" state form in the Soviet Union and China, and, in a different way, in much of the third world.

The international policy-making processes of the West and East differed in ways that partly reflected the two ideal-typical forms of state noted above. In the East, the USSR was dominant (and communism appeared to be unified, at least until the split with China in 1960), and the communist parties of the world tended to follow orders directly from the Communist Party of the Soviet Union. In the countries of the Council for Mutual Economic Assistance (Comecon), all economic and political roads led to Moscow. In the West, although the United States led, it did so through a less centralized process, involving a complex set of inter-state and ideological apparatuses, with ongoing bargaining over economic questions. Thus the United States and its allies built a political process to institutionalize international economic conflict in regimes and international organizations (such as the IMF, the World Bank, the Bank for International Settlements, the Organization for Economic Co-operation and Development, the United Nations) and in forums like the Group of 10. Crucial to this process were private, informal transnational apparatuses, such as the private international relations councils (e.g. Bilderberg, see Gill, 1990, pp. 122–142). This reflected the post-1945 re-emergence of international civil society, after its relative decline in the inter-war years, modelled on the institutional pluralism of liberal democratic capitalism at the domestic level.

The development of such an international civil society had been curtailed in the 1930s with the rise of inter-capitalist and proto-Cold War rivalries, reflecting the near-collapse of international money and trade, and mass unemployment in much of the capitalist world. This was accompanied by the rise of new forms of state – e.g. authoritarian nationalism, fascism, Nazism, Stalinist socialism-in-one-country. The beggar-thy-neighbour economic policies of the 1930s in response to the global economic crisis were inimical to the development and extension of an international civil society of capitalist internationalism, although such an internationalism existed on a regional basis (e.g. the British-dominated sterling preference area, the Empire and Commonwealth; US dominance in the Americas; Japanese ascendancy in Asia), with third world countries revolving politically and economically like satellites around their imperial planets (the republics revolved around Russia in the USSR).

In contrast to the quasi-autonomous financiers of the pre-Renaissance period, and *haute finance* in the nineteenth century (Polanyi, 1957), international civil society in the post-war era was less exclusive (and, in some sense, less capitalist); organized labour, social democrats, and members of the cadre class were included (see chap. 7 in this volume). This was because, from the 1930s onward, productivist forces (both labour and capital in manufacturing and extractive industries) asserted their political power so as to subordinate partly *rentier* or money capital in the making of economic and foreign policy. This process resulted in the emergence of the new forms of state noted above. The post-war settlements reflected the fact that, with variations across countries, statist planners and productivist forces pressed successfully for the creation of a national economic capacity (and policy autonomy), welfarism, and Keynesianism, with specific policies designed to inhibit the pure mobility of short-term speculative capital. The aim, in the words of the US Secretary of Treasury during the New Deal, was to make finance the "servant" rather than the "master" of production. Thus, in the post-1945 period, following European and Japanese reconstruction, the public and private, national and international institutional apparatuses of capitalism sought to reconcile the economic and politico-strategic aspects of the post-war system of the Pax Americana.

Liquidity for the international economy was provided by a seemingly endless supply of US dollars through its balance of payments deficits, themselves partly generated by US military expenditures overseas and by the foreign investments of US corporations. Nevertheless, the international mobility of money capital was more constrained in the Bretton Woods era than it had been in the inter-war years, at least until after 1931. The effects of the Great Depression and World War II were crucial in the (partially successful) attempts at Bretton Woods to make international capital flows serve productive purposes and to finance directly trade and real investment in extractive industries and manufacturing.

Nevertheless, the appearance of stability in the transatlantic social structure of accumulation and the relative coherence of the circuits of trade and investment were deceptive. Powerful forces linked to changes in the state and the internationalization of capital began to unravel the social hegemonies and politically centrist arrangements associated with what, for example, in UK politics was known as the Butskellite consensus, that is, the compromises between the Labour and Conservative parties on the fundamentals of economic and social policy.

The start of the 1970s saw the onset of a period of slower growth, higher inflation, and unemployment, the recurrence and increasing severity of recessions and a growth in fiscal deficits at all levels of government (federal, regional, local). There were periodic crises for the dollar (resulting in President Nixon's decision in 1971 finally to decouple the dollar from gold and to create a global dollar standard, removing some of the external constraints on US policy autonomy). Nixon's manoeuvre shocked the United States' key allies, who interpreted it as a shift towards economic nationalism and a return to "beggar-thy-neighbour" economic policies. However, a key reason for the change in policy – apart from a perception of a decline in the competitiveness of US industries and the fact of rising unemployment – was that financial capital had found ways to evade the capital and exchange controls imposed during the Bretton Woods era, especially after convertibility of currencies was restored in Europe in 1958, when the European Economic Community (EEC) was created. Capital mobility and growing payments imbalances between the major economies undermined the sustainability of the system of fixed exchange rates.

Offshore financial markets began to grow rapidly during the 1960s. By the end of the 1970s these markets already constituted a vast pool of money capital, beyond the direct control of any one state. The Euromarkets were crucial in financing the spread of transnational companies during the 1960s, and in the 1970s, and they supplied funds to all categories of government for payments financing following the oil price "shocks."

The twin processes of globalization and economic liberalization quickened in the 1970s, with the "Volcker shift" in US monetary policy of 1979–1980 a key catalyst for their acceleration. The Chairman of the US Federal Reserve, Paul Volcker, raised real interest rates to unprecedented levels (breaking usury laws in some US states) to prevent a massive depreciation of the dollar. This precipitated the deepest global recession since the 1930s. Soon afterward, the US government combined very tight monetary policy with a Keynesian-style fiscal expansion, producing soaring budget deficits (partly caused by Reagan's military buildup, which was aimed in large part at undermining the Soviet economy by intensifying the superpower arms race).

Reaganomics had the effect of sucking the bulk of the world's surplus savings into the US economy, forcing other countries to deflate; their interest rates rose to high levels to prevent even greater capital outflows to the United States. Part of the reason for this was structural: the integrated financial markets came to constitute a massive disciplinary force-field, not only on firms but also on the policy autonomy of states. Thus international financial constraints forced the United Kingdom to go to the IMF for a loan in 1976 (a move that split the ruling Labour Party and set the economic stage for Thatcherism), and anticipatory capital flight undermined Mitterand's attempt at "Keynesianism-in-one-country" economic expansion in France in the early 1980s.

The monetarist deflations of the early 1980s meant that globalization coincided with slower growth, recession, and growing indebtedness (much of which was caused by fiscal crisis at local, regional, and federal levels of government). Driven by the imperatives of economic competition and inter-state rivalry, this accelerated restructuring in a neo-liberal direction. The debt crisis of the 1980s was a part of a general fiscal crisis, as well as a crisis of development. The mechanisms through which the crisis was transmitted internationally were primarily financial. In the 1970s, because of the glut of petrodollars recycled through the Euromarkets, third world countries were able to borrow at very low real rates of interest (in some cases these were negative). In the early 1980s, as their terms of trade deteriorated and recession lowered demand for their exports, they were faced with much larger interest bills. The costs of repaying their debts went up at the very moment when their capacity to repay had declined. This set the stage for IMF and World Bank policies of "structural adjustment."

Even the United States, as the world's biggest debtor (the federal government's cumulative debt at the start of 1992 was approximately US$4 trillion), came to feel the constraints of the global financial system. For example, in the late 1980s, in the midst of recession, the United States was unable to finance its war effort in the Gulf by the means it had used in the 1960s. To finance the war in Viet Nam, President Johnson decided to print more dollars, forcing others to hold IOUs in a depreciating currency, thus imposing an inflation tax on the rest of the world. In 1991, the United States was forced by its macroeconomic situation to press other countries for contributions to the so-called Defence Co-operation Account at the Treasury to pay its costs in the Gulf War. By raising interest rates to finance a war loan, it would have risked worsening the already deep recession and further weakening the fragile US financial system by tightening credit (the savings and loan bailout is estimated to cost at least US$250 billion of taxpayers' money).

Since the late 1960s we have witnessed global restructuring that has given added weight in the world economy to the OECD nations. The forces of transnational capital have been at the vanguard of this process.[3] Restructuring has involved growing international competitive and disciplinary pressures on states and economic agents (individuals, firms, unions, governments), speeding up the necessary response time for economic survival. The 1980s was associated with a "third wave" of technological innovation, knowledge-intensification, and organizational change. There was an accelerating shift away from Fordism to post-Fordism in the OECD region, and an associated secular decline in the power of traditional forms of organized labour. National systems of financial regulation and control were displaced by an integrated, 24-hour global financial system, which in some ways resembled a casino, beyond the control of any single government. By the late 1980s economic globalization approached levels that approximated those immediately prior to 1914, often considered to be the high-water mark of capitalist economic internationalism.

None the less, trends in the ownership, location, and nature of economic activity suggested that the identity and allegiance of firms have taken on a less and less territorial aspect in the 1990s. This indicates potential contradictions between globalizing and more territorially bounded social forces and institutions, and between economics and politics at the global level. The economic system is one of increasingly planetary reach, whereas political authority is still primarily constituted at the national level, although this situation is mutating since changes in economic conditions have served to reinforce political trends set in motion during the 1970s towards the "redimensioning" or globalization of the state into a more neo-liberal form.[4] States are being recast into a kind of transmission belt for globalizing forces – a transformation that has been developing since the 1970s, and that accelerated in the 1980s, especially in the third world. This process would appear now to be under way in the former communist states, where Poland was the initial laboratory for the social experiment supervised by the IMF. So far this experiment appears to have failed, abysmally, with the situation in the former East Germany (DDR) appearing increasingly catastrophic. Unemployment in the former DDR may have reached 40 per cent in late 1992, and racist violence and Nazism are again on the rise.

Such developments do not suggest a general weakening of state capacities; rather they imply that some aspects of the state will expand in importance (for example to police markets, including labour markets; to sustain law and order; to sustain some of the social and economic conditions for accumulation; and to help legitimate a liberalizing capitalism). Nevertheless, especially in the third world, the state's economic sovereignty is being undermined once again *vis-à-vis* global economic forces, in so far as neo-liberal structural adjustment is forcing the abandonment of the statist mercantilism that developed, for example in Latin America, from the 1930s onward. Not only Group of Seven (G7) governments, but also the IMF and World Bank, and the regional development banks, are demanding reductions in the size and scope of public sector intervention in the economy (which had been established to develop and sustain state capitalist strategic industries and to give protection to "infant industries").

Despite the use of direct political power by G7 institutions, the key difference between this form of external domination and that which prevailed in colonial times is that it is ultimately structural and indirect, exercised primarily through creating new constitutional structures that serve to liberate the power of market forces. At the same time, partly because of growing disparities of income and wealth, the sovereignty of the people is being reduced. Political pluralization and incipient liberal democracy in the third world, then, are not accompanied by an extension of capacities to participate. Social restructuring is accompanied by greater political and economic discipline, largely imposed from above.

In sum, the "international" political economy of the immediate post-war period has evolved towards an "emerging global" political economy. This change has transformed the former balance between finance and production, and the relations between capital, labour, and the state. The current conjuncture, with neo-liberal forces in the ascendant, reflects a shift away from the integral hegemony in the transatlantic heartland and the beginnings of an erosion in the coherence of the "organic" alliances organized under and directed by the United States. These alliances served to "contain" communism within the major capitalist states, and restricted the geographical spread of the Soviet bloc during the Cold War era. Communist and third world mercantilisms are giving way to neo-liberalism and the growing power of capital.

Finally, the role of the United States in the process of global structural change has become more contradictory and ambiguous. Thus, in Robert Cox's view:

the United States, as the apex of this structure of world order and centre of convergence of the military-territorial and economic-interdependence principles, is in a precarious position ... declining rates of productivity, high military costs, and an intractable budgetary deficit. This has been bridged by foreign borrowing ... principally from Japan. The Gulf War underlined the nature of the structure of power – a war decided upon by the United States [which] required that it then be financed by Japan, Germany, Saudi Arabia, and Kuwait ... the war served to restimulate the U.S. economy through its military-industrial component. What was, in the decades following World War II, a hegemonic system in which the United States provided both an emulated model and material resources to Europe, Japan, and to some extent the Third World, became transformed into a tributary system in which others paid to sustain American power. Since the United States has been living beyond its means through foreign subsidies and U.S. military protection may no longer seem either necessary or desirable by Europe and Japan, it becomes problematical how long the foreigners principally concerned will find it in their interests to continue to sustain this system.[5]

Perspectives, classes, and élites

To give order to the remainder of my exposition, two preliminary points are needed. My first point relates to the question of classes. I use the term in a Marxist sense but with a complex model of class stratification (see fig. 6.1 below). The concept of capital implies a social relation of inequality, involving a contrast between those who have a substantial and indeed privileged ownership or control of the means of production, i.e. physical or financial assets, and those who do not (most of society). In this sense, a class corresponds to a certain "objective" reality, constituted primarily by a property relation (class-in-itself). In addition, we can distinguish subjectively and politically between classes, or fractions of classes – in terms of those that are, or are not, self-conscious of their common interests and attempt to unify their forces in a common struggle (class-for-itself).

In this chapter, the term "globalizing élites" refers to a directive, strategic element within globalizing capitalism. It is not used in the

179

reactionary and determinist sense of writers such as Mosca and Pareto, who stressed the inevitability of élite rule because of either their superior organization or their innate ability, relative to the subordinated, inert, or inferior masses.

The distinctions between "class-in-itself" and "class-for-itself" correspond to objective and subjective aspects of the power of capital in the international system. The objective forces of capital are expressed in both the organization and control of production and mechanisms of exchange (e.g. markets). They are expressed subjectively in terms of the awareness of capitalists and political leaders of the general conditions of existence of the system, and more specifically in perceptions of the business climate and investors' confidence in government policy. The direct power of capital is reflected in the capacity and willingness of capitalists to organize political parties and/or lobby governments for preferred courses of action. These dimensions operate simultaneously at domestic and international levels.

In the context of our subsequent discussion, I distinguish between those elements of internationally mobile capital that seek long-term and politically stable conditions for the coordination of global accumulation (generally associated with productive capital and "compensatory" liberals); and those that tend to take a more short-term view, with coordination and discipline indirectly achieved through the liberalization of market forces (often exemplified by financial interests and "pure" liberalism).

Each of these tendencies represents an alternative strategy towards the management of the emerging global political economy. In turn, the interests of transnational capital may be counterpoised to more nationally oriented forces, embodied by the US military–industrial complex or the Japanese bureaucracy and *keiretsu* (business conglomerate), which have been generally associated with a mercantilist or more state capitalist perspective, opposed to domestic liberalization, at least for "strategic industries." There is no concrete "general" class interest of capital. Thus we can speak of the potential for significant intra-class struggles, particularly when conflict concerns the stability of the world economy and/or the question of national sovereignty and autonomy.

The second preliminary point to be made is that perpectives are not merely ideologies, or simply explanations, but are *a part of* the political economy. Perspectives guide the conceptualization of problems and strategies, relative to other definitions and possibilities.

Thus the term "perspective" includes the theoretical and practical outlook, world-view, and identity of a given set or constellation of social forces, movements, and institutions. A perspective exists in political time and space and implies a particular standpoint, be it that of a group, nation, or class. For a perspective to be both coherent and politically effective, it implies not only theoretical plausibility but also an institutional and intellectual apparatus that can help to promote certain interests.

A perspective becomes hegemonic when the theories and arguments it entails, and the social forces it embodies, come to prevail in setting the agenda for debate and policy in a given historical situation. This does not imply a lack of contestation; merely that, for practical purposes, alternatives are not fully considered because they lack weight, plausibility, credibility, or practical effectiveness. Previously hegemonic perspectives may become partly or wholly discredited, such as mercantilism in the United Kingdom in the mid-nineteenth century, and Stalinism in Eastern and Central Europe today.

Under the global leadership of the United Kingdom and the United States, the study of economics in the West (and in much of the third world) has come to be dominated by neo-classical liberalism, originating in the work of Adam Smith and David Ricardo. This perspective is closely associated with the market system and the practical outlook and world-view of capitalists (although individually and collectively capitalists may cooperate, as in monopoly or oligopoly, to prevent competition). Neo-classical liberalism is widely represented in the most prestigious academies of the West. In turn, many economists in government and the private sector in developing countries cut their institutional spurs in organizations like the IMF and the World Bank, which exemplify the international application of this perspective, with its methodological individualism and practical stress on market policies to increase global economic efficiency and welfare. Its basic assumption is that economic efficiency requires a fully functioning market system driven by entrepreneurship, competition, and private capital accumulation.

In the study of international relations, by comparison, the realist paradigm, with its stress on national security, inter-state rivalry, and strategy, still constitutes the orthodoxy. It is noteworthy that the economic doctrine associated with realism, i.e. mercantilism, still informs the outlook and policy stance of important elements within the ranks of state and capital in the West and Japan. As I have noted, it is nor-

181

mally central to the economic policy stance of the security complexes, with their emphasis on relative self-sufficiency and national control over key, strategic industries.

Globalizing élites and social stratification

Capitalist élites are representative of different interests within a globalizing capitalism. Capitalism is, of its nature, pluralistic (van der Pijl, 1989). Indeed, the reproduction of capitalism on national and world scales requires an institutional pluralism that allows one disintegrating form to be challenged and replaced by another, more securely based, newly leading form. This negates the thesis that a crisis of capitalism will necessarily lead to the replacement of capitalism by another socio-economic system.

At present, there is a struggle between at least two broadly defined, leading forms of capitalism: the neo-liberal form associated with the Anglo-Saxon countries and the state capitalist, mercantilist form that seeks to base itself more securely in a corporatist organization of production and a welfare net for the more disadvantaged. The neo-liberal form is most developed in the Anglo-Saxon countries, the state capitalist form in continental Europe and, in a modified variant, in Japan.[6]

Globalizing élites can be defined as a grouping of organic intellectuals and political leaders within what can be called the transnational fraction of the capitalist classes of the world (Gill, 1990). As such they are located at the intersection of the two main ideal types in globalizing capitalism, that is, at the interface between territorial and globalizing aspects of world order, and they seek to reconcile the contradictions of these aspects through a process of political synthesis.

Such élites are in part constituted by their positions in key strategic locations in transnational companies, banks, universities, think tanks, media companies, governments, and international organizations such as the IMF, the World Bank, and OECD, and by the discourse of neo-liberal globalization. Their activities seek to make transnational capital a class "for itself" by theorizing the world order and by synthesizing strategy. Key members are located in organizations at the apex of global knowledge, production, and financial structures, as well as in key political parties and government agencies in the major capitalist states, notably in the members of the Group of Seven (G7). This grouping has a public and a private face. Its members in the private

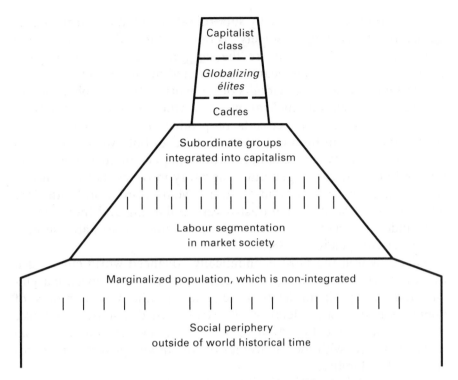

Fig. 6.1 **The structure of global stratification**

realm of civil society are intimately related to "political society" at both "national" and "international" levels (Gill, 1990).

The term "élites" is used in the plural so as to, on the one hand, avoid the implication of homogeneity and, on the other, emphasize the vantage point and privileged perspective that the various members bring to bear. This reflects the plurality that inheres in the leading elements of capitalism, even where globalization takes on the appearance of a totalizing set of social forces. The place of such élites in the social structure is sketched in figure 6.1. Social structure is represented as a hierarchical series of layers in an ever-widening pyramid with a massive base. The upper, narrow cone would correspond to Braudel's (1981) social and spatial concepts of a sphere of "world capitalism." The origins of this part of the social structure can be traced back to the era of merchant capitalism, and to the trade and financial links between "world cities" such as Venice, Florence, Nuremburg, Lyons, Amsterdam, London, Delhi, Nanking, and Osaka in the fifteenth to eighteenth centuries.

The second layer is normally subordinated within and from an urban centre. Thus "market society" is both within and surrounding the world cities. Finally, there are the marginalized zones of material existence. These are significantly articulated neither into the productive system and exchange circuits of the world cities of global capitalism nor into market civilization. Nevertheless, the marginals of society may disrupt the circuits of production and exchange and change the configuration of power relations of both world capitalism and market society. For example, worsening economic conditions in rich and poor countries generate migratory movements to the urban centres of both "North" and "South." Many third world cities are overpopulated, with their infrastructure collapsing and their centres surrounded by shanty towns, all of which threaten to paralyse economic activity (Vieille, 1988).

Indeed, within the most economically advanced world cities, such as New York and London today, there is a process of social marginalization and peripheralization, reflected in the vast numbers of homeless people who sleep on the streets. In this sense, cities like Rio de Janeiro and Los Angeles serve as metaphors for the global social structure, with their extremes of wealth and poverty, their violence and instability.

In this model then, the capitalist class is viewed as not primarily concerned with the question of different trajectories of capitalism. This task is performed by organic intellectuals drawn from the stratum broadly described as the cadres, e.g. as seen in the composition of the Trilateral Commission, in which academics and senior civil servants (cadres), mainly from the OECD countries, participate and prepare the analyses considered by the chieftains of transnational firms and government leaders.

The cadre stratum is divided between an upper layer, integrated with global capitalism, and a broader lower layer less committed by interest and ideology to one or other form of capitalism. Within this lower layer, some stress the need for autonomous, technocratic management of production by cadres, some the potential for decentralization through the application of electronic technologies, some a concern for environmental degradation and the potential for new non-polluting and anti-pollution technologies, etc. Nevertheless, as Kees van der Pijl's contribution to this volume (chap. 7) shows, social democratic cadres favouring not only socialized forms of ownership of the means of production but also more systematic and accountable forms of public multilateralism to regulate important aspects of global activity (reflected in the debates over the New International Economic Order), including public control over international finance, have been marginalized from the upper echelons of the cadre stratum. However, it might still be suggested that, in many respects, the potential for alternative forms of production, different forms of industrial consciousness, and alternative industrial strategies lies primarily within this social stratum.

Beneath the cadres stratum, the labour force is increasingly segmented. Traditional organized labour is declining in strength, notably in the old Fordist mass production industries with their industrial unions. The restructuring of production on a global scale is making "flexible" use of a labour force located in many different places, separated not only geographically but also by nationality, ethnicity, religion, and gender. To achieve a common consciousness, organization, and strategy within this diversity has become very difficult, especially as unemployment has tended to rise in most OECD countries to very high levels during the last decade. In this sense, there has been "peripheralization" within the OECD countries, as previously established and privileged workers lose their security of employment and suffer a decline in their standard of living. The latter phenomenon has been very noticeable in the United States since the late 1960s, with real wages for the vast majority of US workers less now than they were then. This is the case not only for blacks and members of other ethnic minorities, but also for the "white" working class.

There is still a proportion of the world's population only partially linked to global capitalism. Among these populations, traditionally conceived of as outside world-historical time (and often written out of history), the indigenous populations are of particular interest:

They have in recent years achieved a new degree of self-consciousness and articulate political expression and organization on both national and global scales. Indigenous peoples have also perceived the opportunity of access to the United Nations system, e.g. on human rights issues, to press their claims, using transnational networks to press their claims in particular cases, e.g. against hydro-electric developments in northern Quebec and Japan. Indigenous peoples' organization may be a paradigm for marginalized people more generally.[7]

Globalism, territorialism, and the United States

The reproduction of the neo-liberal order depends upon those governments that are the most economically, politically, and militarily

185

powerful. Of these, the most important are the United States, Japan, and Germany. The G7 and other informal, private organizations such as the World Economic Forum and the process of international organization and law can be viewed as serving to constitute a partial internationalization of authority. This is not the same, however, as saying that such authority is legitimate. Part of the reason for this is the role of the United States in the world order; this increasingly takes on the character of a "universal contradiction" (Nicolaus, 1970).

In the United States, transnational liberalism vies for hegemony with territorially bounded sets of interests, identities, and discourses (such as "America first" nationalism). A key element of the United States' contradictory role is that, whereas the US government is the key military enforcer of the functioning rules of the global economy of transnational liberalism, it is not prepared to play by the rules it seeks to set for others, partly because of the structure of the US political system, where key political forces prevent the government from deviating substantially from the logic of existing policy. The United States is a relatively inward-looking, ethnocentric, and, in economic terms, undisciplined and consumerist nation (reflected in high budget deficits and a low savings rate). Economic and political agents in the United States operate with very short time-horizons – in a country with a relatively short history. This inward-looking aspect contrasts with US global primacy, defined in terms of both its capacity for structural dominance, which stems from US economic centrality, and its supremacy in global security. US economic policies can have disruptive consequences for the rest of the world, especially since the United States has become more integrated into global circuits of production and finance in contrast to its previous situation of relative self-sufficiency.

Nevertheless, the US government is attempting to lead, for example through a dominant role in the United Nations and through the reconstruction of an inter-state system and world economy that could become the political basis of the "new world order." Part of this strategy involves initiatives to restructure the relations between "North" and "South," "West" and "East," and between the United States and its major capitalist allies and rivals (the European Union and Japan). In this regard, central to élite debates in the 1980s and 1990s is the question of to what degree the world order is perceived as evolving towards "three blocism" or, conversely, towards a more interdependent "trilateralism" between the three dynamic poles of contemporary capitalism.

186

In these debates there is a cleavage between transnational liberals and the increasingly influential geo-economic strategists. Edward Luttwak summarizes the perspective of the latter grouping as an "admixture of the logic of conflict with the methods of commerce" (cited in Toal, 1992). The strategists tend to interpret history in terms of cycles of rise and decline of great powers and stress inter-state rivalry and the need for state control over economic policy, for example using ideas drawn from the new literature on strategic trade theory. In the "declining" United States, much of the focus of attention has been on the "rising" power of Japan and the "problem" this poses for US policy. Here, key intellectuals include the so-called "gang of four" revisionists on the Japan question, notably Chalmers Johnson (1982), who portrays Japan as a developmental state, with centralized, corporatist, and bureaucratic structures qualitatively different from Anglo-American political economies. Thus, as the major threat to US primacy, Japan must be treated differently from others (other "gang" members are James Fallows, 1989, Clyde Prestowitz, 1989, and Karel van Wolferen, 1989).[8]

More ominous elements in the United States are attempting to replace the "lost enemy" (the USSR) with new "demons" or new forms of "otherness" so as to galvanize US foreign policy. Examples here are the (leaders of) "rogue regimes" (e.g. Saddam Hussein, Moamer Gaddafi) and, increasingly, Japan as "public enemy number one." For example, at a meeting of centrist political leaders from the United States, Canada, and Western Europe, discussing the future of transatlantic relations after the Cold War, there was almost no detailed discussion of the repercussions of a united Germany, but considerable disquiet expressed at the fact that Japan was creating the biggest problems for US foreign policy. No Japanese were present at this meeting.[9]

The salience of territorialist perspectives was reflected in the 1988 Omnibus Trade Act, in the US positions in the Strategic Impediments Talks and in the Yen–Dollar Committee during the 1980s, and in President Bush's decision to take a troop of US corporate chief executives to Japan. This group was intended to influence the Japanese government to show favour towards "American" producers like GM and Chrysler (both of which have joint ventures and co-production agreements with their erstwhile Japanese competitors, reflecting a more general transnationalization of the US economy).[10]

A more centrist variant of the geo-economic argument is that of Michael Porter (1990). This influential work applies business strategy concepts to economic and foreign policy, and advocates more comprehensive state engagement to ensure the competitive success of enterprises operating within and from a given territory. Here it is worth noting that mercantilist thought has a long lineage in the United States, going back to Alexander Hamilton's *Report on Manufactures*. Indeed the great theoretician of German mercantilism, Friedrich List, was an adviser to the US government during the nineteenth century.

Linked to this debate is one concerning the likelihood of a resurgence of quasi-Leninist forms of inter-imperialist rivalry ("capitalism in conflict") after the "glue" of the Cold War had been dissolved, especially between the United States and Japan (Islam, 1990). This involves consideration of the institutional and social differences, or the "many flavours of capitalism" (e.g. world wide: Vernon, 1992; that of Japan: Krause, 1992; the variants in Western Europe: e.g. Woolcock and Hodges, 1992; and the "two faces" of US capitalism: Kogut, 1992). This kind of endeavour is linked to the efforts by transnational liberals to dampen potential frictions between the United States, the EU, and Japan. For example, the New York Council on Foreign Relations, the Trilateral Commission, the Brookings Institution, and many of the Ivy League universities have sought to preserve the integrity of the USA–Japan relationship and to protect Japan from the criticism associated with the geostrategic thinkers.[11] They have sought to demonstrate the importance of foreign investment in the United States, whilst minimizing the strategic threats this might pose.

A parallel current is the concerted critique of the thesis of US relative decline associated, for example, with Paul Kennedy (1987). In particular, Joseph Nye (1990) has argued that the United States has maintained its economic position since the early 1970s, noting the tremendous internationalization of the US economy in the period[12] and that the United States has consolidated its strategic primacy considerably as the USSR weakened. Nye maintains that US power and capabilities are more integral than those of any previous hegemonic power. Thus, the United States is bound (destined) to lead the major capitalist states. Nye was the key author of a recent Trilateral Commission report (Nye et al., 1991) that argued that the 1990s would not see the emergence of "three-blocism," despite the possibility of a growth in centrifugal forces among the trilateral countries. Trends in technology and economics and in security (with Europe and East Asia still needing US support), as well as the nationalism of many "smaller, non-trilateral nations, fearing dominance from a large trilateral neighbour," would serve to sustain many forces in favour of trilateral and global cooperation. For this possibility to be enhanced:

groups favouring cooperation will need to reinforce each other by forming coalitions across national borders. The Trilateral Commission will need to think of itself as helping to *formulate transnational coalitions* that advance the common good ... the wealthy countries ... as the largest players in the world economy, should see themselves as *trustees of the public good* of sustainable economic growth. As trustees, they need to resist domestic veto groups, keep their markets open, and promote sustainable growth in the poorer parts of the world. (Nye et al., 1991; pp. xiii, 41; my emphasis)[13]

This is a quintessential – although somewhat patronizing and paternalistic – statement of the perspective of the transnational liberal, globalizing élites, and the prerogatives that its members feel they ought to possess. The theoreticians of this flank within the United States agree that domestic "problems" in the United States need urgent attention if the United States is to remain strong and confident in its leadership. Of particular concern is the lack of discipline in US fiscal policy and the incapacity of the political system to provide for an adequate infrastructure and education system, both of which are vitally needed in order that the United States can sustain its competitive advantage (understood in the terminology of Porter, 1990).

Moreover, many leading intellectuals in the United States, and even larger numbers of their counterparts within the ranks of globalizing élites in Europe and Japan, would like to see a United States not just "bound to lead" but also, like Ulysses, forgoing the temptations of the Sirens, "bound to the mast." In other words, some of the organic intellectuals from within the ranks of globalizing élites see it as being in their collective interest, as well as in the particular interest of the United States, that it "puts its own house in order."

In other words, from other elements in the globalizing élites comes an argument that "trusteeship" of international public goods is not enough. What is needed is a set of mechanisms that will tie the hands of future politicians in the OECD countries (and elsewhere), lock in neo-liberal constitutional and economic reforms, and thus lengthen the "shadow of the future" for economic agents and provide a predictable politico-economic environment for internationally mobile capital.

These arguments relate to what I call the "new constitutionalism," in so far as many of the debates over neo-liberal restructuring have

189

been framed around the reformulation of concepts of sovereignty and discipline in matters of political economy. Associated political initiatives – like the EEC's 1992 programme and the North American Free Trade Agreement (NAFTA) – are intended to promote the reconfiguration of global political and civil society along Lockian lines. The broad process involved can be related to the ideas of "governance without government" (i.e. there is no government of the world economy but there appears to be a set of governing principles and concepts; see Rosenau and Czempiel, 1992), in so far as this has an inter-subjective and material aspect that conditions the limits of the possible for different groups, classes, and nations.

The "new constitutionalism" and economic austerity in the 1990s

The key concepts of neo-liberal constitutionalism are market efficiency, discipline and confidence, policy credibility and consistency viewed from the standpoint of new theories in neo-classical economics in a world of international capital mobility. One aspect concerns the institutional arrangements designed to insulate key aspects of economic life from the interference of (elected) politicians – to impose binding constraints on democratic authority over the economy in the future. Thus new constitutionalist arguments usually involve a stress on the need to strengthen the GATT and IMF surveillance mechanisms and capabilities to reinforce, respectively, microeconomic and macroeconomic market discipline at the multilateral level, and to help to sustain the legal and political conditions for transnational capital (Gill, 1992).

At the same time, EU initiatives along these lines can be interpreted as a seeking to bring neo-liberal constitutionalist discipline to bear more fully on the United States in the future. For example, the idea of a more fully fledged European economic and monetary union is seen by some member governments (notably the French) as a means of offsetting not only German economic power, but also that of the United States and Japan. Thus EU leaders like Jacques Delors see the liberalization of European financial markets as a step on the way to a single currency, but look forward to the day – perhaps in the twenty-first century – when Europe will be able to countervail US economic, especially monetary, power and thus force the US government to be more cooperative and less unilateral in its dealings with the EU. Similar strategic arguments apply to EU–Japan relations.

190

New constitutionalist thinking is at the heart of the Delors Report of 1989, and in the 1991 Maastricht agreements, which, if ratified by national parliaments, would tie the hands of future governments with regard to their control over macroeconomic (including fiscal) and microeconomic policy (including trade), creating a more centralized collective capacity. This is partly why the EU is creating a transnational legal framework for the deepening of market discipline in ways that reflect the anti-inflationary ideology of the Bundesbank. However, this form of discipline and the constitutional arrangements that it entails have proved to be deeply unpopular as recession ravages the West European economies.

German economic policies have become very controversial since unification of the two Germanies in 1989. German policy is similar to that of Reaganomics in the early 1980s: high budget deficits and very high real interest rates. This has forced up the general level of interest rates in Europe, and deepened and lengthened the very severe recession experienced through most of Europe since 1989, such that a 1930s-style slump has been widely discussed as a possibility. In this sense, German domestic preoccupations are slowing the momentum towards unification.

Moreover, German reluctance to concede to G7 and/or US pressure to reflate its economy in 1992 (the Bundesbank feared inflation might get out of control in Germany) is only one instance of what has come to be known as the "Sinatra Doctrine." This means that the big three countries (the United States, Japan, Germany – G3) have become so preoccupied with domestic economic and political problems since the late 1980s that they have been unable to cooperate to revitalize global economic growth; rather, they try to do it "My Way." So far the Japanese do not look either willing or able to take on the full mantle of economic leadership, despite their surpluses of capital and the initiatives they have taken in the debt and development area. Indeed, the Japanese government is seeking to restore its fragile, scandal-ridden financial system following the excesses of the speculative bubble economy of the late 1980s, and to revive flagging domestic growth. Germany is preoccupied with its unification problems. The US economy has been in recession since 1989, and its growth record under President Bush was the worst since World War II. In this sense, globalization is accompanied by economic divergences and conflicts in the G7.

The situation in the early 1990s was reminiscent in some respects of the debt deflation of the 1930s, although central bank/treasury cooperation to contain financial panics and crises appeared to be more systematic. The parlous state of the global financial system was revealed in 1982 in the Mexican default, which almost caused a collapse of the US and the world financial systems. Similar crisis management managed to contain the global stock market crash in October 1987, with no one jumping out of windows on Wall Street. In September 1992, a currency crisis caused mayhem in the capitals of Western Europe, and the British, Italian, and Spanish governments were forced into humiliating devaluations as the European Exchange Rate Mechanism threatened to split apart, or at a minimum to retrench into a two-tier system of hard and soft currencies.

Thus the "new constitutionalism" is contradictory in its effects, and it applies more forcefully to some than to others. It appears to have the least impact on the reconfiguration of the domestic politico-economic structures of the G3. Its most profound impact is upon weaker states, the least competitive firms, and the most vulnerable social groups, not just in Europe but world wide.

Strategy towards the third world and post-communist states

A second set of élite debates relates to tactics and strategy with regard to the incorporation and subordination of the third world, and more recently towards the restructuring of former communist states. Here, matters of strategy, economics, and politics are intimately connected.

For example, under US influence, debates concerning the World Bank and the IMF structural adjustment policies in the third world have changed to place more emphasis on state-building so as to be better able to "redimension" the state along the lines noted earlier (see note 4). New forms of conditionality involve political and constitutional demands, including control of arms proliferation in the third world. These developments reflect reconsideration of how the dominant institutions of the "North" can better incorporate the "South" in the attempt to reconstitute hegemony, that is, how to extend capitalist, neo-liberal hegemony beyond the core. Here it is worth noting that Antonio Gramsci's (1971) concept of hegemony involves both coercive and consensual aspects of power: that is to say, power relations perceived as legitimate or acceptable are necessarily underpinned by material power and a coercive apparatus. Thus it is noteworthy that many of the "best and brightest" of the third world have been trained by the UN economic institutions and form part of transnational élite cadres that seek to implement and sustain the policies of liberalization and structural adjustment that have characterized the last decade.

In other words, the wider aspect of constitutionalizing neo-liberalism is that it represents the political strategy of attempting to make (where possible or necessary, liberal democratic) capitalism the sole model for future development. Involved here are attempts to re-define "public" and "private" spheres in the economy, for example in ways that guarantee both investment and the entry and exit options for international capital in different nations. The military forces of the major G7 countries are being reconfigured in ways that, in conjunction with the deepening of market forces and the commodification of social life, add a further disciplinary aspect. The economic initiatives concerning the third world are related to new forms of military mobilization by the United States and its NATO allies, in the form of European as well as US Rapid Deployment Forces for swift intervention, especially in the Gulf to control the strategic resource of oil. Western strategy towards the former Soviet republics involves attempts to weaken them militarily.

On the "economic" front, debates can be analysed in terms of "compensatory" and "pure" liberal models of transition. Compensatory liberals range from those who called for substantial aid transfers to the former USSR in the form of a "second Marshall Plan" to those who argued for debt write-offs and more modest levels of transitional and humanitarian aid. Pure liberals are more likely to be "shock therapists," who blooded their Eastern strategy in Poland in 1989–1990, following previous experiments in Latin America earlier in the decade. So far the aid actually offered to Poland and Russia has been meagre, mainly in the form of "advice." This suggests either that the pure liberals have the upper hand, or that the key strategic objective is further to weaken the former USSR and its former allies, perhaps for decades to come, or a combination of the two. Since 1988, all the former Comecon states have been in a spiralling economic depression, involving the physical liquidation of capital and massive falls in output.

The medicine that has been applied in practice by the IMF in Poland (and mooted in Russia) has stressed the need for independent central banks, swift convertibility of currencies in the former USSR (post-war convertibility was restored in the most powerful West European states only in 1958), the creation of markets for labour and capital, with rapid development of a system of private property rights and privatization programmes, and the promotion of an "en-terprise culture" that goes beyond gangsterism and the former black economy.

Finally, it perhaps needs to be emphasized that the politics of the transition from communism to capitalism involves much more than the G7, IMF, OECD, and other public institutions. A wider "trans-national historic bloc" (see Gill, 1990) of public and private neo-liberal forces is leading the restructuring process, in concert with its counterparts within the former Soviet bloc.[14] The key individuals in this process are bound together by a shared framework of thought (economic liberalism) and economic necessity (he who pays the piper calls the tune). In the transition, the "West" has refused to countenance any alternatives to Anglo-Saxon-style liberal capitalist institutions (for example the "third way"). This is despite the fact that a growing number of economists have warned that the structural adjustment/shock therapy was likely to prove more lethal than the original disease. Many have predicted that its implementation would be followed by an even more massive economic collapse, following the political collapse of the Hobbesian state structures of Soviet communism.

Concluding reflections

Class interests are contestable and are linked to the perspectives of different fractions of capital. Intra-class as well as inter-class strug-gles take place at both domestic and international levels, and any set of ideas, institutional proposals, and policy arrangements will favour some interests rather than others. At the present point in time, the prevailing perspectives appear to be those associated with large inter-nationally mobile elements of capital in the metropolitan countries.

These perspectives stress economic efficiency, competition, and global factor mobility, and the need to constrain some of the inter-vention capacity of the state that might impede globalization. Never-theless, in both political and economic terms these policies may prove to be profoundly contradictory. By this I mean that the deflationary thrust of policy, the impoverishment of masses of people in many countries, and the marginalization of labour and the cadres from policy-making circles in the OECD substantially narrow the social basis for hegemony. In this sense, the legitimacy and political durabil-ity of neo-liberal dominance can be seen as sowing the seeds of its own contradictions.

Moreover, if all deflate, global depression ensues, and in the early

1990s one would need to be a Pangloss to be optimistic about the global economic outlook. Economic depression and spiralling decline have become a fact of life in much of Latin America and Africa for at least 10 years, and the situation in Eastern Europe and the former USSR is grim. Economic and political deterioration in many parts of the world is becoming chronic. Moreover, in the context of the restructuring of global production, massive migratory movements are occurring, mainly from South to North. With the collapse of the USSR, there are likely to be more migrants and refugees from East to West, and more political conflict as the privileged countries seek to impose limitations on the movement of these peoples into their economies. All of these developments, along with environmental, security, and other problems, suggest a turbulent period to come.

Nevertheless, the political agenda of globalizing élites – despite political conflicts within the ranks of G7 leaders – is to consolidate the political and geographical core of the system while extending the power and penetration of capital into previously closed territories, such as China, India, and the former USSR. This extension of capital into new territories reflects the fact that an aspect of its structural power is the division of the globe into rival sovereign states. It also explains why the globalizing élites in general do not favour a world state or even a more minimal global institution such as a world central bank; this might prove to be an object of global class struggle, and institutional pluralism and innovation provide greater political flexibility to the powerful.

All in all, then, this is a world that can be described as post-hegemonic in Gramscian terms, in so far as the basis of its political appeal and capacity to include and incorporate subordinate elements is being replaced by a politics of dominance and supremacy. This development is in contradiction to the historical global trend towards the extension of democracy. Counter-hegemonic social movements and associated political organizations must mobilize their capabilities and create the possibility for the democratization of power and production.

There is, of course, no guarantee that this will materialize, especially given the growing power and reach of transnational capital and the increased disciplinary aspect of the emerging world order. Nevertheless, we might witness a 1990s version of Polanyi's "double movement" as social movements are remobilized and new coalitions are formed to protect society from the unfettered logic of disciplinary neo-liberalism and its associated globalizing forces. As in the 1930s, we can anticipate that not all of these new forces will be progressive;

indeed, there are already signs of reaction and authoritarianism in many of the former communist states, especially in the context of a resurgence of inter-communal violence and political chaos, fuelled by the descent into economic entropy. The role of the IMF and the G7 is becoming bitterly controversial in Russia and the consequences of a deepening of resentment at the "shock therapy" need careful reflection. In this sense, the bankers' initiatives in Russia may come to be seen, in retrospect, as the low point of capitalist internationalism in the twentieth century.

Notes and references

1. This chapter is based partly upon preliminary discussions held at Barboleusaz, Switzerland, 14–16 October 1991. Those present were Georges Abi-Saab, Robert Cox, and Kees van der Pijl.
2. "In the analysis of social structural change, structure and agency are to be understood as dialectically interrelated. Structures are conceptual instruments of analysis, representing patterns of actions and expectations shaped by the historical experience of human groups collectively confronting the salient problems posed by their material environment (Braudel's *gestes répétés* of history). The transformation process is marked by a dialectic of events and historical structures (Braudel's *histoire évènementielle* and *longue durée*) wherein the contradictions of existing structures are revealed and transcended. Contradictions arise from the opposed perceptions and interests of distinct social groups confronting the same complex of material circumstances. Contradictions are inherent in the historical process. There is no 'end to history'. Each new structural formation gives rise to new contradictions which push the transformation process forward" (Robert Cox, "Methodological note," Barboleusaz meeting, Switzerland, 14–16 October 1991).
3. Global foreign direct investment (FDI) rose rapidly between 1985 and 1990, growing four times faster than domestic output and two and a half times faster than the growth in exports. Annual flows of FDI in 1990 were US$225 billion, in a total stock of FDI of US $1.7 trillion. In 1990, OECD countries attracted 83 per cent of world FDI, up from 75 per cent in 1985 (the United States, EEC, and Japan attracted 70 per cent of the 1990 world total). The rest was in the third world, although 53 per cent of the third world total was accounted for by East and South Asia (United Nations, 1992).
4. The term "redimensioning of the state" was coined by the Peruvian President, Alberto Fujimori, and his Oxford-educated finance minister, Carlos Bolona, spelled out what this meant at the 1991 meeting of the InterAmerican Development Bank in Nagoya, Japan:

   The reinsertion of Peru in the international scene is not only ... a question of renegotiating with our foreign creditors in order to receive more credit or grants. It implies a transformation of our industries and of the infrastructure that supports them and a change in attitudes: a reform of the state and its institutions; of the obsolete and meaningless character of barriers to trade and capital flows.

   The *Wall Street Journal* noted some of the effects of the liberalization of finance, investment, capital flows, and goods and services, and an end to state monopolies:

   Inflation is down from 40% a month ... to 6%–9% and still falling ... [however, there is] ... an overvalued currency (Lima is much more expensive than Miami in dollar terms) and very high interest rates [of 25% when currency is available]. At the same time, salaries are at an all-time low in inflation-adjusted terms and are bordering on subsistence levels.

Nurses, working overtime at nights to save poor souls from the cholera epidemic, make only $60 a month. (Ortiz de Zevallo, "New Peruvian Finance Minister Preaches Free-Market Gospel," *WSJ*, 29 March 1991)

5. Robert Cox, Note, Barboleusaz meeting, 14–16 October 1991.
6. As Robert Cox points out:

   These two forms of capitalism are ... ideal types ... [but are] not to be represented in a static manner. Each has its own internal contradictions tending towards its transformation. And the interactions between the two forms also have a transformative effect on each. The two ideal types ... [help] ... in a dialectical understanding of a complex process of transformation. In addition, some strategies envisaging a transcendence of capitalism and which part from the logic of capitalism will interact with the rivalry within capitalism in this process. One stage of analysis is to examine which élite perspectives are associated with different projects of capitalism and post-capitalism. (Note, Barboleusaz meeting, 14–16 October 1991)

7. Robert Cox, Note, Barboleusaz meeting, 14–16 October 1991.
8. Toal (1992) notes that populist representations of this perspective by journalists and freelance economic writers begin from assumptions such as "our corporations," "the national" economy, "the industrial base of the country," and move towards a discourse replete with metaphors of warfare and zero-sum reasoning, with references to "Japan's financial empire," its "warrior culture," and a US political system "riddled" with "foreign penetration." For many of the populist writers Toal discusses, a key date is "Black Monday", 19 October 1987, "one of those critical days in history when the shift in power from one empire to another can be marked, precisely and indelibly" (Toal, 1992, p. 22, citing D. Franz and C. Collins, *Selling Out: How we are letting Japan buy our land, our industries, our financial institutions and our future*, Chicago: Contemporary Books, 1989).
9. "A Redefinition of American Foreign Policy Priorities, with Special Reference to Europe," Conference of the Ditchley Foundation and the Chicago Council on Foreign Relations, Wingspread, Racine, Wisconsin, 9–11 May 1991.
10. Clyde Prestowitz's Economic Strategy Institute, created in 1990, gains 95 per cent of its funding from supporters in three industries: apparel, automobiles, and semiconductors. Each of these favours more activist government policies because of threats from foreign, especially Japanese, competition. Automobiles and auto parts accounted for about 75 per cent of the US trade deficit with Japan in 1990. President Bush pressed for concessions on these items during his visit to Japan, apparently with some success.
11. The Association of International Investment, key US foundations, and pro-Japanese intellectuals ("The Chrysanthemum Club") "seek to co-opt, direct and mollify anti-Japanese sentiment" (Toal, 1992).
12. In 1970, US imports were 7.3 per cent of US GNP, exports 8.6 per cent; in 1988 imports were 13.1 per cent and exports 15 per cent of GNP. Between 1980 and 1990 the value of US trade in constant dollars almost doubled. (Cited in Toal, 1992, p. 8, using figures from *The Economist*.) The US and Canadian share of world product in 1970 was 28.8 per cent; in 1989 it was 28.3 per cent (Nye et al., 1991, p. 5, table 1). Figures are based on CIA estimates, with GNP statistics converted to a common unit using OECD purchasing-power-parity exchange rates.
13. Whereas the United States is viewed as being too profligate by trilateralists, Japan is seen as being too large to be a "free rider" or simply a banker. "Japan, with due sensitivity to historical and legal constraints, should be more involved in international financial institutions, decision making in the United Nations and in other informal mechanisms of world order." If Europe's trilateral partners treat Europe as an entity they can encourage the integration process (and retard this process if they seek to play off European states against each other). European integration should be linked to NATO and the United States in light of the No-

vember 1990 Transatlantic Declaration. With regard to European security, "Navigation and a sense of direction will be more important than the details of architecture. We should head in the direction of a greater European capacity to contribute to its own defence without removing the residual insurance policy provided by the American security guarantee" (Nye et al., 1991, p. 45).

14. In Russia, Paul Volcker appears to have become a key figure in supervising the reconstruction of the financial and monetary system. The key academics advising the Russian government on the "shock transition" to a market economy are Professors Jeffrey Sachs of Harvard, Anders Aslund of Stockholm, and Richard Layard of the LSE ("Volcker may be guru to save rouble," *Financial Times*, 11 February 1992). In addition, in June 1992 the formation of the Russian–American Bankers' forum was announced, the initiative coming from the US Federal Reserve, top US bankers, and senior advisers to President Boris Yeltsin. US members include David Rockefeller, former chair of Chase Manhattan and founder of the Trilateral Commission; Cyrus Vance, former US Secretary of State; John Opel, former chair of IBM; John Whitehead, former co-chair of Goldman Sachs; and Richard Debs, ex-president of Morgan Stanley. The Forum is chaired by Gerald Corrigan, president of the Federal Reserve Bank of New York. ("US launches forum to reform Russian banking," *Financial Times*, 20/21 June 1992.)

References

Braudel, F. (1981) [1979] *The Structures of Everyday Life: The Limits of the Possible.* Vol. I of *Civilisation and Capitalism, 15th–18th Centuries.* Translated by Siân Reynolds. New York: Harper & Row.

Cox, R.W. (1987) *Production, Power and World Order.* New York: Columbia University Press.

——— (1992) "Global Perestroika." In: R. Miliband and L. Panitch, eds. *The Socialist Register 1992: The New World Order.* London: Merlin Press, pp. 26–43.

Fallows, J. (1989) *More Like Us.* Boston: Houghton Mifflin.

Gill, S. (1990) *American Hegemony and the Trilateral Commission.* Cambridge: Cambridge University Press.

——— (1991) "Reflections on Global Order and Sociohistorical Time." *Alternatives* 16: 275–314.

——— (1992) "The Emerging World Order and European Change: The Political Economy of European Economic Union." In: R. Miliband and L. Panitch, eds. *The Socialist Register 1992: The New World Order.* London: Merlin Press, pp. 157–196.

Gill, S., and D. Law (1988) *The Global Political Economy.* Baltimore, Md.: Johns Hopkins University Press.

——— (1989) "Global Hegemony and the Structural Power of Capital." *International Studies Quarterly* 33: 475–499.

Gramsci, A. (1971) *Selections from the Prison Notebooks of Antonio Gramsci.* Translated by Q. Hoare and G. Nowell Smith. New York: International Publishers; London: Lawrence & Wishart.

Islam, S. (1990) "Capitalism in Conflict." In: *America and the World: Foreign Affairs, 1990.* New York: Council on Foreign Relations, pp. 172–182.

Johnson, C. (1982) *MITI and the Japanese Miracle.* Stanford, Calif.: Stanford University Press.

Kennedy, P. (1987) *The Rise and Fall of the Great Powers*. New York: Random House.

Kogut, B. (1992) "Two Faces of US Capitalism." *International Economic Insights* 2: 15–16.

Krause, L. B. (1992) "Japanese Capitalism: A Model for Others?" *International Economic Insights* 2: 6–10.

Nicolaus, M. (1970) "The USA: the universal contradiction." *New Left Review* 59: 3–18.

Nye, J. S., Jr. (1990) *Bound to Lead. The Changing Nature of American Power*. New York: Basic Books.

Nye, J. S., Jr., K. Biedenkopf, and M. Shina (1991) *Global Cooperation after the Cold War*. New York: The Trilateral Commission.

Pijl, K. van der (1989) "Ruling Classes, Hegemony, and the State System." *International Journal of Political Economy* 19: 7–35.

Polanyi, K. (1957) [1944] *The Great Transformation*. Boston: Beacon.

Porter, M. (1990) *The Competitive Advantage of Nations*. London: Macmillan.

Prestowitz, C. (1989) *Trading Places: How We Are Giving Our Future to Japan and How to Reclaim It*. New York: Basic Books.

Rosenau, J. N., and E-O. Czempiel (1992) *Governance without Government: Order and Change in World Politics*. Cambridge: Cambridge University Press.

Ruggie, J. G. (1982) "International Regimes, Transactions and Change – Embedded Liberalism in the Post-War Order." *International Organisation* 36: 379–415.

Toal, G. (1992) "Japan as Threat: Geo-Economic Discourses on the U.S.–Japan Relationship in U.S. Civil Society, 1987–1991." Paper presented to Institute of British Geographers conference, 7–10 January, Swansea.

United Nations (1992) *World Investment Report*. New York: UN Publications.

Van Wolferen, K. (1989) *The Enigma of Japanese Power*. London: Macmillan.

Vernon, R. (1992) "The Many Flavors of Capitalism." *International Economic Insights* 2: 2–5.

Vieille, P. (1988) "The World's Chaos and the New Paradigms of the Social Movement." In: Lelio Basso Foundation, eds. *Theory and Practice of Liberation at the End of the Twentieth Century*. Brussels: Bruylant.

Woolcock, S., and M. Hodges (1992) "Euro-Capitalism in Focus." *International Economic Insights* 2: 11–14.

7

The cadre class and public multilateralism

Kees van der Pijl

Prelude to regulation

This chapter is part of a larger project dealing with the global reform movement of the early 1970s and its defeat by a counter-movement of neo-liberal transnational forces in the 1980s. Our purpose is to shed light on the dimension of social class in this process and, more particularly, on what we shall term a *cadre class* of salaried functionaries occupying the intermediate position between the bourgeoisie and the working class in developed capitalism. This cadre stratum, comprising managers, technical cadres, and various bureaucratic personnel, assumed a particular salience in the 1970s, owing to the combined impact of metropolitan student and workers' rebellion and third world revolution. *Regulation*, as favoured by the cadre class, at this point served both to express and to contain the pressures for reform. A neo-liberal drive for *deregulation* in the 1980s disrupted the social prominence and cohesion of the cadre class and also terminated the attempt to install a new global economic regime by means of the United Nations system, to which this class had demonstrated a particular receptivity.

Catalysts of the 1968 student rebellion

The 1960s had been inaugurated under the sign of decolonization and de-Stalinization, to which the West initially responded with a dynamism in the spirit of Woodrow Wilson's reaction to the Bolshevik Revolution. The newly elected US president, J. F. Kennedy, had argued in a seminal article of 1957 for a flexible approach to third world revolt and a more subtle strategy in dealing with the Soviet Union "in order to undercut slowly the foundations of the Soviet order." In Western Europe, Kennedy proposed to cultivate allies among those ascendant politicians who likewise sought to adapt to change, such as Willy Brandt's Social Democratic Party of Germany (Kennedy, 1957, pp. 46–47, 50).

Kennedy's assassination in late 1963 terminated a brief and contradictory attempt to put this programme into practice. By 1965, stagnation and deadlock again prevailed and, in both East and West, a willingness to resort to violence to defend the status quo became apparent. In the USSR, Nikita Khrushchev had been replaced by neo-Stalinist bureaucrats, while Kennedy's successor, Lyndon Johnson, presided over a conservative shift in US foreign policy. The bombing of North Viet Nam, US intervention in the Dominican Republic, and CIA-supported coups in Brazil and Indonesia in 1964 and 1965 brutally shattered illusions concerning third world emancipation by means of reform and negotiation. If, in many respects, the prevailing international atmosphere was reminiscent of the 1950s, this time it was obvious to many that de-Stalinization and non-alignment alone were inadequate to ensure the development of a more democratic socialism and the emancipation of the "wretched of the earth." Under this title, Frantz Fanon had written in 1961, "the question which is looming on the horizon, is the need for a redistribution of wealth. Humanity must reply to this question, or be shaken to pieces by it" (Fanon, 1968, p. 98).

Towards the close of the decade, three seminal events dramatically broke the conservative deadlock. Each of them – the Chinese "Cultural Revolution," Che Guevara's attempt to stir up an insurrection in Bolivia, and the "Tet Offensive" in South Viet Nam – ended in failure, if they were not already self-damaging or even suicidal to begin with. The Cultural Revolution led to internal turmoil and a deepening of China's international isolation; Che's guerrilla unit was discovered by a US space satellite, its location communicated to the Bolivian military, and Che handed over to Cuban exiles; while the

"Tet Offensive," for all its spectacular impact on TV screens across the world, led to the virtual destruction of the South Vietnamese National Liberation Front as an independent fighting force.

Yet the boldness and self-sacrifice that characterized these three instances of revolutionary will-power were to resonate widely among the first post-war generation that was then reaching adulthood in the West. After the call for a better world had been issued with such emphasis at the outset of the decade but subsequently had been silenced again, violent revolt in the third world struck a chord with a youth dissatisfied with the prospect of sullen consumerism. The exhaustion of moderate alternatives for change seemed complete when the advocate of peaceful struggle for racial equality in the United States, Martin Luther King, was assassinated in April 1968.

Students and workers in the 1968 struggles

Not only was the susceptibility of the post-war generation to these instances of self-sacrifice and will-power enhanced by the fact that the dynamic configuration of the beginning of the 1960s congealed into an unimaginative and heavy-handed conservatism. The circumstance that so many university students among this generation had been of "old middle-class" background, that is, children of artisans, shopkeepers, etc. (e.g. Weber, 1973, pp. 27–29), who were swept away by the monopolization of the economy and the parallel growth of the state sector, also contributed to their fervour. An element of *anomie*, being caught up and simultaneously "lost" in a fundamental restructuring of society, perhaps interacted with an inherited small middle-class rebellion against the twin impersonal forces of monopoly capital and the state in shaping their "revolutionary" imagery.

The reference to "the anonymous terrorism of the state-societal machinery" in an article by West German student leader Rudi Dutschke seemed to point in this direction, but otherwise Dutschke's analysis was pertinent to the existing situation. "The ruling class," he wrote, "has undergone a deep transformation. For a long time now it has no longer been identical with the nominal owners of the means of production. Marx had already seen the dawn of a new class of industrial bureaucracy" (Dutschke, 1969, p. 248).

Corporate liberal capitalism as it emerged through the New Deal and Marshall Plan periods was indeed characterized by this rise of a new stratum of managers and technocrats, complemented by the representative structures of the organized working class. The strong (welfare) state role and the macro-regulatory framework of Keynesianism reinforced the social standardization fostered by its Fordist mass production economic base. Although firmly entrenched in a Cold War setting, which, among other things, constrained European colonialism's resistance to the American project for an open world, there was a tendency towards a regulated society from which the more personal forms of enrichment and exploitation seemed to have vanished. But the violence of US intervention in Viet Nam and its daily visibility on TV screens the world over shattered technocratic fantasies about the benevolence of this social order and provoked the 1968 rebellion.

There was also a tentative revolutionary project in production to which the student movement was oriented. This project was grafted on the anticipated convergence of interests and outlook of the radicalized students being educated for management, scientific, or administrative cadre functions and the new type of worker emerging in industry in this period – the creative engineer–worker concerned with job autonomy, described in contemporary labour sociology such as Serge Mallet's *Nouvelle classe ouvrière* (Mallet, 1969). As the dissident communist leader Roger Garaudy, who analysed the movement for productive autonomy and radical democracy in Paris and Prague, wrote at the time, "This demand for active participation in the determination of the ends and the meaning of production is ... the common denominator of the students' aspirations and the conscious objectives of the working class" (Garaudy, 1978, p. 160).

However, the established parties of the left, including the communists, as well as the socialist states of Eastern Europe, were by nature not capable of abandoning their "vanguard" or cadre role relative to the "masses," who were supposed to be helpless without them. Accordingly, the socialist/communist parties and states objectively reinforced the defence line of the established capitalist order against the "May" movement. This left the movement to its confused self and allowed the revolutionary component in production to be defeated, while the counter-culture as such became absorbed by capital. As David Caute wrote, "The hippy–rock–drugs culture disturbed the Puritan ethic but it also served as an experimental space station for the new, dynamic capitalism. Thousands of artisan workshops emerged to pioneer products and pleasures which big business would later mop up" (Caute, 1988, p. 49).

Third world revolt and the UN system

While the above instances of third world revolution influenced the 1968 social movement in the developed capitalist world (and in the more advanced Soviet bloc states), they also had an impact on the multilateral superstructure of the international system. Here, too, the effect was in the nature of a catalyst. China was not a member of the UN system, which symbolized the absence of the revolutionary third world from the forum of states. The enlargement of UN membership as a consequence of decolonization had had its effects, most notably in the setting up of the United Nations Conference on Trade and Development (UNCTAD) and in the formation of the "Group of 77" in 1964. The enlargement of the Security Council in January 1966 (from 11 to 15 member states) constrained American control of the Security Council.

Otherwise, the UN was seen by many observers to be part of the sterile and ineffective configuration of the mid-1960s. Thus the political scientist Hans Morgenthau thought in 1965 that "the Security Council [was] powerless, the General Assembly [was] powerless, and the Secretary-General [was] powerless. The United Nations has ceased to be an effective international organization" (quoted in Stoessinger, 1970, p. 174). Still, in 1971, a typical judgement on the UN (on the occasion of Secretary-General U Thant's departure) read, "a mandate marked by the continuous decline of the Organisation" (*Le Monde Diplomatique*, December 1971, p. 5).

In 1967, however, the Group of 77, preparing for the second UNCTAD conference, adopted the Algiers Charter to press its economic sovereignty. At the actual New Delhi conference in 1968, a General Preference System was agreed upon, envisaging increased third world exports to the West. This project accelerated when the oil price hike by the Organization of Petroleum-Exporting Countries (OPEC) in 1973 seemed to tip the scales between raw material producing third world states and the West. In 1974, the Sixth Special Session of the General Assembly and the regular session in December adopted the documents generally regarded as the outline of the third world's New International Economic Order (NIEO) project (Overbeek, 1982, p. 147).

Meanwhile, the third world thrust had clearly abandoned the arenas where, in 1966–1968, its most spectacular manifestations had occurred. Partly this was a consequence of the defensive restructuring of the US world role. In 1971, the Nixon administration's overture towards

204

China terminated that country's isolation and paved the way for its admission to the UN in the same year. In January 1973, the Paris peace accords inaugurated the process of US withdrawal from Indo-China. The practical advantages held out by the NIEO project simultaneously defused the abstract radicalism of states like Mexico, which moved from support for the Cuban revolution to prominence in the NIEO drive under President Echeverría (1970–1976).

The overall tendency of the NIEO was to extend to the international level the subordination of society to state control that to varying degrees was a characteristic of the underdeveloped countries. As Krasner notes, the third world challenged Western dominance of the global political economy by trying to reorient existing inter-governmental institutions towards political regulation of processes previously left to market mechanisms. It also sought to create a parallel structure of new international organizations confronting the existing liberal ones, such as UNCTAD against the General Agreement on Tariffs and Trade (GATT), and to use the principle of state sovereignty to the advantage of raw material producers, coastal states, etc. Thus, "The South has been able to take two legacies of the North – the organization of political units into sovereign states and the structure of international organizations – and use them to disrupt, if not replace market-oriented regimes over a wide range of issues" (Krasner, 1985, p. 124).

Eventually, the reaction to this was to consist of the acceleration of the internationalization of capital and the reinforcement of centres of power outside (single) state jurisdiction and of international centres of decision-making outside the established international organizations. Thus the anticipated constraints on capital accumulation by the NIEO drive were able to be evaded. But this process, which ultimately resulted in a neo-liberal capitalism in which social compromise was replaced by market discipline, was not a straight transition. For at least five years after 1973, a transitional configuration crystallized that displayed the potential to extend global regulation beyond a capitalist format.

State classes and cadres in the struggle over world order

Markets and social protection

"To allow the market mechanism to be sole director of the fate of human beings and their environment ... would result in the demolition of society," Karl Polanyi wrote in 1944.

For the alleged commodity "labor power" cannot be shoved about, used indiscriminately, or even left unused, without affecting also the human individual who happens to be the bearer of this particular commodity.... Nature would be reduced to its elements, neighborhoods and landscapes defiled, rivers polluted, ... the power to produce food and raw materials destroyed. (Polanyi, 1957, p. 73)

Protecting the integrity of society from the detrimental effects of the market was historically a state task. But the nature of a state's action depends on the given state/society complex (Cox, 1986, p. 205). Those countries for which the capitalist world market is a given, but which are strong enough to maintain a minimal degree of independence, have traditionally produced a state in the Hobbesian sense, or what Gramsci calls the *ethical* or *interventionist* state. Such a state is "connected on the one hand with tendencies to support protection and economic nationalism, and on the other with the attempt to force a particular state personnel ... to take on the protection of the working classes against the excesses of capitalism" (Gramsci, 1971, p. 262). In such settings, state enterprise becomes the vehicle of the attempt simultaneously to resist the superior forces of capital (which are superior only to the degree they are *foreign*) and to mobilize resources to enter into competition with it. In this sense, there is a historical continuity from France in the era of the Cardinals and Louis XIV to the third world states of the NIEO coalition.

If we call the actual personnel of such states (in addition to the bureaucrats proper, the state equivalent of entrepreneurs, managers, and even trade union leaders) a comprehensive "state class," it is clear that such a state class by itself signifies the relative backwardness of the state(s) involved. It will dissolve into the state bureaucracy in the narrow sense, and an actual bourgeoisie emancipated from state tutelage. The process of class formation in a country like France may serve as the prototype (Granou, 1977).

In those countries where this process has been completed (of which England was the first), the state is relegated to a "Lockian" role in the background, "progressively reduc[ing] its own authoritarian and forcible interventions," and interacting with a substratum of local self-government (Gramsci, 1971, pp. 263, 186). Here, capital accumulation develops largely on its own account, and very soon assumes an international dimension.

Sovereignty in the Hobbesian configuration resides clearly with the state and, hence, with the state class. In the Lockian setting, on the other hand, sovereignty tends to shift to a plane superior to the state, and comes to reside in the sphere of *capital*. The continuously widening sphere of capital as the comprehensive set of social forces sustaining capital accumulation goes hand in hand with conflicts with the strongest of the Hobbesian states, and so far has always ended with their absorption into the sphere of capital. The resistance of these states to such integration has to be interpreted as a struggle to improve the conditions of integration, because, ultimately, the state class and, especially, the aspiring bourgeoisie operating under its wings have set their sights on the world market and are drawn into it by various mechanisms, including ideological ones associated with consumerism. The socially protective role of the state classes therefore is necessarily limited and transitory.

A fundamentally different situation prevails where the state itself is subordinated to capital and the market becomes the *ultima ratio* of society. Capital accumulation engenders a scale of operations and a mutual dependence of highly specialized social functions that require that markets are regulated if the destruction of human beings and their natural environment is to be averted. This process of enlarging the scale of operations and increasing specialization/integration is called socialization ("Vergesellschaftung"). It produces a distinct social category in the form of the modern cadres, the managers and technocrats, who may be state-employed but are not to be equated with the state classes referred to earlier. Whereas the state class represents the state/society configuration that precedes a fully developed capitalist pattern, the cadre stratum represents a social constellation that already contains elements of a post-capitalist order.

The concept of a cadre class

The phenomenon of a managerial stratum produced in the process of capitalist socialization was first analysed by Marx in *Capital*, volume III, in the perspective of a transformation to socialism (*MEW* 25, p. 454). In the American New Deal period, the "managerial revolution" was again discovered by A. A. Berle, Jr. and G. C. Means (*The Modern Corporation and Private Property*, 1932) and, of course, James Burnham (*The Managerial Revolution*, 1941). This time, regulation was seen as compatible with capitalist property relations. As Berle (1954, p. 35) put it later, "mid-twentieth-century capitalism has been given the power and the means of more or less planned economy, in which decisions are or at least can be taken in the light of their probable effect on the whole community."

In France, the term used to describe the managers of large-scale production and regulated society was *technocracy*. The technocrats were imbued with the spirit of Ford and Keynes and adopted positions reflecting the technical imperatives of production rather than finance. The technocratic tradition here dated back to Saint-Simon, and prescribed economic expansion, science-based modernization, and a transfer of power from the politicians to "experts." Since the technocrats – men like Mercier, Tardieu, and Laval – were élitist and anti-socialist, there was a strong authoritarian tendency in their politics (Kuisel, 1967, pp. vii–ix; Granou, 1977, pp. 36–37). But then French technocracy in the 1930s was a hybrid between a state class catching up and a modern, managerial sector.

In the socialist movement, Marx's idea of a new stratum of technicians and administrators was reformulated in this managerial–technocratic sense. The Belgian socialist-turned-fascist De Man declared the new middle class "the articulators of the general interest," who by means of planning and ideological hegemony would lead the way to socialism (Wijmans, 1987, pp. 121, 133). From a more critical point of view, the French worker–philosopher Simone Weil argued in 1934 that, between the passive workers and the declining capitalist class, a layer of administrators was emerging that advanced with the growth of new techniques of production and social control. The essence of bureaucratic control lay in the enterprise and consisted of the centralization of the knowledge ("including the secrets") formerly possessed by the workers (Weil, 1978, p. 123). The expropriation of the capitalists in her view would not lead to working-class power, but would turn the administrative (managerial–technocratic) element into a dictatorial bureaucratic caste. This had happened in the Soviet Union, but the "three bureacracies" (in the trades unions, the enterprises, and the state) were developing everywhere (van der Linden, 1992, pp. 68–69).

The 1968 rebellion went directly against the central tenets of the managerial–technocratic ideology. In opposition to the division between manual and intellectual labour, it clamoured for the constitution of the "integral worker" combining the two categories in autonomous productive units; against the positivism of experts monopolizing social knowledge, the students argued for practical, dialectical, and democratic applications of knowledge; against the large-scale organization, the slogan "small is beautiful" was raised; against the antiseptic technofuture desecrated by defoliation and mass bombing in Viet Nam, flower power and psychedelic experiments.

As indicated above, the movement by and large was absorbed by the existing social order. Although labour processes and consumption patterns were changed apparently in favour of workers, the money and commodity forms enveloping them instead reinforced the subordination of labour to capital. A bastard form of this was applied in Central Europe where, following the repression of the Prague Spring, "Gulash communism" served to compensate for other aspirations.

But the students, too, were absorbed into the very structures of socialization and bureaucratization that they had previously combated. The "Long March through the institutions," helped along by the popularization of positivist and anti-voluntaristic versions of Marxism such as Althusser's, led the post-war generation into the ranks (sometimes via the traditional left parties) of the managerial–technocratic stratum. Against the background of a sustained "tertiarization" of advanced capitalist society (Hagelstange, 1988, p. 155; Morioka, 1989, pp. 144–145, table 6.1), the 1970s witnessed a radicalization of the thus expanded managerial–technocratic cadre stratum, indeed its formation into a *class* aspiring for power. In this sense Alain Bihr has coined the notion of a *cadre class* ("l'encadrement capitaliste").

To Bihr, the cadre class is the class that emerges on the terrain of the capitalist socialization of production and reproduction. The division of labour in all its aspects, the organization and integration of labour processes, and also the role of the media in sustaining urban lifestyles conducive to intensive consumption, all these require the special class of functionaries that Bihr designates as the cadre class. The three elements of its class consciousness discussed by Bihr (1989, p. 255f) in our view apply specifically to the situation of the 1970s when newly recruited cadres joined the existing managerial–technocratic stratum in force and radicalized the prior ideological propensities of that class.

The cadres have all along stood for *modernity*. They view themselves as managing the most developed forms of production and social organization, such as the giant corporation and the state apparatus, where the anarchic "robber baron" quality of the capitalist mode of production has been left behind. Contemporary society is seen as having already developed beyond capitalism.

The second characteristic of the cadre outlook is the preference for the *rationalization* of economic development. This, too, had already been pronounced in the 1930s. It was expressed in a preference for planning and regulation, a "social ethic" as Whyte calls it (1963, p. 11), and in the application, by experts, of science. It may be noted in passing here that, as far as the cadre outlook is concerned, "scientific management" and "scientific socialism" are branches of the same line of thought, namely the view that society develops according to laws known to specialists, a vanguard, etc.

The third characteristic of the cadre class is its preference for the *democratization* of society. This is not mere humanitarianism; it is necessary for the cadres to combat prejudice against the *parvenu* on the part of the ruling class, to gain access to education (where its "capital" – knowledge – is obtained), and to be able to negotiate what Bihr calls its "knowledge rent" (1989, p. 203).

Clearly, this third aspect was specific to the 1970s cadre experience. In contrast to the 1930s, when the technocrats in Europe organized "social protection" in a balance of forces unfavourable to the working class, in the late 1960s and early 1970s the working class occupied a strong position. This was reflected in the salience of social democracy in this period.

Cadre class and social democracy in the NIEO struggle

As capital expands by leaps and bounds, every cycle, from short business cycle to the "long waves" associated with the restructuring of control and production, begins in a crisis in which the old configuration of social forces has to make way for a new one. At such junctures, the bourgeoisie may paradoxically be unable to transcend its short-term interests, which by definition are tied to the old situation. This was the case for instance when, in the New Deal, American capitalism was restructured at the national level around a new mode of accumulation (Fordism) under a new (corporate liberal) concept of control, and again in the Marshall Plan period, when the corporate liberal concept was extrapolated to Europe.

In the twentieth century, the representation of the general capitalist interest in such transitions has gravitated to the cadre stratum, and its development into a conscious class was typically tied to these episodes. In the 1930s, the cadres assisted in the "Great Transformation" to state monopolism in this sense. Immediately after the war, one aspect of the Cold War was to reaffirm the dividing lines between New Deal capitalism and Soviet state socialism (which had become blurred during the wartime Grand Alliance), and this entailed restoring cadre discipline in a capitalist context.

In Western Europe, the Marshall Plan and its Cold War setting reinforced the managerialist and technocratic orientation in social democracy (Carew, 1987, pp. 240–241). In the 1950s and early 1960s, programmatic reformulations replaced the anti-capitalist orientation of social democracy with a platform of social reform (the *Godesberg* Programme and its equivalents in other countries). The challenge of 1968 and the restructuring of capital that it inaugurated, which co-incided with rivalry with the United States over Viet Nam and Cold War strategy, were critical factors in again propelling social democracy to the forefront. Social democracy in 1969 was the (co-)governing party in 14 countries, mainly in Europe (Autorenkollektiv, 1977, p. 133).

The prominence of social democratic parties was supported by the rapprochement of the managerial–technocratic element in the economy and the bureaucratic–administrative element in the state apparatus on a common platform of reform. As Bahro writes,

Social Democracy in power is the party of the compromise between the layer of specialists susceptible to "transcendence of the system" and the part of management oriented to "system reform", especially in the public sector, although always respecting the limits imposed by the long-term interests of the monopoly bourgeoisie. But these two tendencies of course only find their common language when they enter into confrontation with the conservative fraction of the bourgeoisie. (Bahro, 1980, p. 157)

The confrontation with the conservative bourgeoisie occurred in events like the demotion of President Nixon and the eclipse of 1950s-style Cold Warriors in several countries in the wake of the Lockheed scandal. In all social democratic parties and even in the Italian Communist Party (PCI), the cadre element meanwhile had gained prominence relative to the working class. This is illustrated in table 7.1. Although the data on which this table is based are heterogeneous, and a category "cadre stratum" can be constructed only tentatively owing to the different definitions used in sources, the trend away from the working class and towards the new middle strata, of which the cadre class represents the directive element, is clear and could be documented at greater length.

The process of class formation of the cadres expressed the political leftward drift as well as the need to guide the restructuring of capital from its post-war Atlantic format to a global format, temporarily disregarding the short-term interests of the actual bourgeoisie. But the salience of social democracy also brought out the need to contain the forces of change within a flexible framework. So, while *expressing* the reform drive, social democracy (and the PCI in Italy in key

Table 7.1 **Cadres and workers in social democratic parties and in the Italian Communist Party (%)**

	Party members	MPs			Congress delegates	
	FRG 1977	Sweden 1968	GB 1977	Den. 1975	France 1973	Italy 1975
Working class	28	12	28	1.5	3.2	36
(previous)	(45)[a]	(38)[b]	(35)[c]			
Cadre stratum[d]	34	58	32	76	63.9	58.2
(previous)	(22)[a]	(5)[b]	(20)[c]			

Sources: France – Granou (1977), p. 218; other countries – calculated from data in Raschke (1981), country tables.
a. 1952
b. 1945
c. 1959
d. Managers, civil servants/state bourgeoisie/bureaucrats, scientific–technical intelligentsia, teachers.

respects conformed to this trend) at the same time operated to *repress* the forces further to the left (here the PCI position was perhaps different). This was brought out most clearly in the German *Berufsverbote* campaign launched by the Brandt government. At the same time, socialist governments reacted positively to cadres' demands for social privilege. Thus in West Germany, under Brandt's successor Schmidt, a new co-determination law was enacted in 1976 that prescribed the mandatory representation of "managing employees" ("leitende Angestellte") in companies. This measure enhanced the special status of 2–2.5 per cent of all employees, a group of approximately half a million people (Briefs, 1979, pp. 1353–1354). In the Netherlands, another country with a socialist-led government, the organization of higher employees (which had seen its membership double between 1972 and 1975) was formally admitted into the collective bargaining framework in 1976 too.

The cadre element in the private economy – "management oriented to 'system reform'," to use Bahro's phrase – also organized outside actual social democratic parties. The formation of the Club of Rome has to be seen in this light. The Club likewise sought to contribute to the development of a comprehensive concept to assist in the transition to a global format of capital accumulation. If what was called "the world problématique" was not tackled on the global level, founder-member and OECD planner Alexander King declared in an interview, governments would continue to stumble from crisis to crisis, from incident to incident (*De Volkskrant*, 21 November 1987).

The first Club of Rome report, the MIT Meadows/Forrester report *The Limits to Growth* of 1971, reflected both the positivistic scientism of the cadre class and its propensity to look for technocratic solutions to the limits of the capitalist pattern (Braillard, 1982). Almost simultaneously, a *Blueprint for Survival*, published by a group of British natural scientists (Julian Huxley and others), added to the growing consensus that a linear continuation of population and economic growth would lead to disaster. It also emphasized the specific role of capitalist development in fostering a destructive pattern of growth. The *Blueprint*'s conclusions were even more pessimistic than the Meadows/Forrester report as it predicted "the breakdown of society and of the life support systems on this planet possibly by the end of this century and certainly within the lifetime of our children" (quoted in *Time*, 24 January 1972).

The NIEO demand arising on the part of the third world countries, and coming on top of metropolitan student and working-class revolt and third world revolution, amplified the cadre position on these issues. The Dutch economist Jan Tinbergen, who in 1972 had been appointed chairman of the Council for World Development Policy of the Socialist International, was commissioned to coordinate a subsequent report for the Club of Rome in 1974. This report, *Reshaping the International Order* (RIO), the English edition of which was published in 1976, was financed by the Dutch social democratic Minister for Development Cooperation, Pronk. It stressed the need for an overhaul, not just of the world economic chaos "created by the relentless operation of market forces," but of the entire normative structure created by post-war capitalism. Hence, the report preferred to speak of a comprehensive New International Order and not just of its economic component (Tinbergen, 1977, pp. 5, 15).

The principle of social protection at this point seemed to overtake the role of guiding the restructuring of capital and to assume a logic incompatible with capitalist relations of production. In the RIO report's technical appendix dealing with the environment, it was stated that "the allocation of resources cannot be left entirely to a market mechanism to which no corrections can be applied and on the one-sidedly profit-oriented foundation of the enterprise. There is need for an adequate institutional instrument that can reinforce the criteria of a *broadened social rationality*" (Tinbergen, 1977, p. 314; emphasis added). There was also talk of curbing advertising to avoid the propagation of wasteful and excessive lifestyles. Even if Tinbergen explained that what he meant by "planning" should not be taken too literally as "detailed global planning," but rather should be seen as a loose planning framework curbing unstable markets (interview in *Wirtschaftswoche*, 31 March 1978), it was clear that the discussion itself at least enhanced the legitimacy of alternatives to capitalism.

The same position was adopted by Willy Brandt, the former Chancellor who was asked in 1977 by then World Bank President McNamara to head a Commission to investigate the persistence of the North–South gap. In frequent meetings with German corporate leaders apprehensive about his intentions, Brandt all along had argued that capitalism should not be overthrown, but should be stabilized by extensive infrastructural supports and regulation ("Ordnungspolitik" – Brandt, 1971, p. 271). This perspective also informed the eventual Brandt Commission reports.

The cadre preference for regulation likewise transpired in the desire for closer cooperation with the statistical and planning infrastructure of the capitalist world economy, such as the OECD, expressed in the discussions between Brandt, Palme, and Kreisky that led to the reorganization of the Socialist International in 1976 (Günsche and Lantermann, 1977, p. 143). The basic idea was always that modern/rational/democratic social relations ultimately reflected a *technical imperative* to which the entire world would eventually have to conform. Convergence theory (Tinbergen was among its advocates), but, more concretely, Brandt's *Ostpolitik* of "change through rapprochement," rested on this premise (Braunmühl, 1973).

In international organizations, the same orientation towards rational solutions, preferably pursued by "experts" outside the established political arenas, has traditionally been part of the organizational ethic. This has been reflected in functionalist integration theory from Mitrany on.

The functional logic relies heavily on the use of dispassionate inquiries, based on value-free modes of research, to expose problems and lay the groundwork for eventual policy compromises. Experts, not politicians, are singled out as the agents for defining the limits for accommodation, preferably along lines of pure computation and problem-solving. (Haas, 1964, p. 153)

The recommendations of the MIT *Limits to Growth* report fell on fertile ground in the UN. In June 1972, the UN environmental conference in Stockholm established the United Nations Environment

Programme (UNEP) as an "embryonal machinery" for monitoring global ecological development. Likewise, the regulationist impulses of the cadre stratum and their concern to contain the social shocks produced by capitalist markets were expressed in various proposals for regulating the operations of multinational corporations by the UN. In this area, the preference for "expert" solutions in the cadres' proposals (including those of social democratic parties and trade unions) occupied a middle ground between the third world state classes' ambition to industrialize and trade without the giant corporations and corporate strategies intended to deflect the demand for regulation to conform to traditional anti-trust and property law (see van der Pijl, 1993).

Compared with the bourgeoisie, and notwithstanding a degree of transnationalization in the form of the Club of Rome and the Socialist International, the cadre classes (partly also on account of their closeness to the state apparatus) tend to be largely *national*. The framework of international organization here serves mutually to adjust standards and outlooks among national and international cadres. The maintenance of *esprit de corps* with professionals at the national level is essential to uphold the prestige of UN specialized agencies and to prevent them from becoming lethargic bureaucracies (Symonds, 1971, p. 118). Managerial ideologies like corporatism in labour relations also largely shape the organizational ideology of an agency like the International Labour Organization (ILO) (Cox, 1977, pp. 407–408).

Although this "expert" ideology has in practice served mainly to allow the bourgeoisie to work out their international arrangements "privately" (Picciotto, 1989), in the context of the 1970s "expertise" began to distance itself from the capitalist order. Qualified support for the third world NIEO project "arose mainly among international officials concerned with aid and specialists associated with them" (Cox, 1979, p. 274).

The cadre class in the process of deregulation

Reducing class cohesion and restoring cadre discipline

In the 1930s, the restructuring of liberal internationalist capitalism to a framework more closely geared to the requirements of national productive structures and domestic class compromise involved what Keynes had called "the euthanasia of the rentier, of the functionless

Table 7.2 **The cash flow of financial corporations as a percentage of the cash flow of non-financial corporations, 1972–1988 (cash flow defined as "total current receipts")**

	USA	Japan	FRG	France	UK
1972	81	63	34	73	46
1975	93	102	44	113	112
1980	118	107	55	150	146
1985	126	137	49	171	113
1988	128	138	49[a]	145	122[a]

Sources: *National Accounts of OECD Countries 1972–1984* (Paris, 1986), vol. II, country tables; *National Accounts of OECD Countries 1976–1988* (Paris, 1990).
a. 1987

investor" (Keynes, 1970, p. 376). Bank capital was placed under state surveillance in most advanced capitalist countries, and technocracy seemed to take the place of bankers and stock exchanges in arbitrating productive investments. By the late 1960s, pressures mounted to rescind Keynesian legislation and allow the banks to function in the restructuring of capital towards a global productive grid. The uncoupling of the US dollar from gold, inflation, and the oil price hike of 1973 combined to flood world capital markets with dollars and inaugurated a period of financial pre-eminence in the world economy. The 1980s in particular witnessed an unprecedented hypertrophy of the financial sector in the profit distribution process in most countries, and a corresponding "relevance" of that sector's world-view in public affairs. This is illustrated in table 7.2.

The consequences of the breakdown of Keynesian controls and the resurgence of international financial markets as the pivot of the world economy were momentous. The principle of social protection that had been inscribed in the corporate liberal post-war order was sacrificed to a pervasive quest for enrichment pioneered by new types of financiers. Competitive deregulation by one country after another (Germany's lagging behind has to be related to the exceptional capacity of industrial capital to control the greater part of profit flows even after 1980) set in motion a dynamic of dismantling obstacles to liberalization such as public enterprise, trade union rights, and even concepts of human dignity.

If we confine ourselves to the consequences of the neo-liberal restructuring for the cadre class, the financial drift and the internationalization of the economy clearly undermined the environment in which the cadre class had functioned to maintain what Bihr (1989, p. 283) calls the "equilibrium of compromises." Industry geared itself to more "craft"-oriented production processes made possible by advances in electronics (Piore and Sabel, 1984), making products directly aimed at world markets. In due course, the entire configuration of management and collective bargaining practices built into the giant corporation, which was linked to national Keynesian protective structures, came under fire. This took various forms. Corporate raiders operating with borrowed money made inroads into large corporations; in Europe, privatization, especially following the stock market crash of September 1987, allowed these raiders to penetrate the former state sector (S. Federbusch in *Le Monde Diplomatique*, November 1987, p. 36).

The fact that the cadres, both on the management and on the organized labour side, had been relatively exempt from the labour market effects of the business cycle (Hagelstange, 1988, p. 176) now became the topic of politically explicit attacks. Thus computer tycoon and short-lived US presidential candidate H. Ross Perot motivated his attempt to gain a foothold in General Motors by the need to terminate the privileged and costly position of "tens of thousands, maybe hundreds of thousands of people at General Motors who are quite insulated from the harsh realities of the competitive marketplace" (quoted in *Newsweek*, 17 June 1985). Both in the United States and (with a delay) in Europe, corporate managers lost power relative to owners (both established corporate heirs and newcomers of the "raider" variety) in the 1980s. "Many ownership turnovers," Useem concludes his research on US data (1989, p. 14), "are justified as disciplinary initiatives. Incumbent management is viewed as having failed to serve effectively and solely as agents of shareholder interests." Middle-level cadres also came under fire. Useem comments on his findings here that, "While the impact of ownership takeovers on managerial employment varies considerably from firm to firm, a study of establishment-level ownership change between 1977 and 1982 reveals that central-office employees are, on average, disproportionately shed" (Useem, 1989, p. 16).

The remaining management and other cadre personnel were won over to neo-liberal positions by various means. In addition to consequences of the neo-liberal reorganization of society such as the spread of possessive individualism, post-modernism, and the disciplinary effect of redundancies, the consultative and planning bodies of the international bourgeoisie such as the International Chamber of Commerce in Paris worked out explicit strategies to enhance these effects.

At its 25th World Congress in 1976, Ian McGregor and Rupert Murdoch acted as committee chairman and rapporteur, respectively, on the issue of how the ideological balance could be tilted in favour of business. They recommended that private enterprise should be propagated more forcefully, by educating the public, through the free press, about "the true role of profit." Company staff ("the internal public") were specifically singled out as a target of the envisaged information offensive (Winqwist, 1976, p. 31). It may be noted in passing that Messrs. McGregor and Murdoch, as chairman of British Coal and president of World News Corporation, respectively, were directly involved in the struggles to break the power of the trades unions in Britain after Mrs. Thatcher's coming to power on a neo-liberal platform.

The second way of mobilizing cadres behind the neo-liberal drive developed parallel to their being offered separate representation in bargaining structures. While the introduction of new technologies in production and office work allowed the standardization and routinization of the work of middle-level personnel hitherto enjoying a degree of job autonomy, the technical and administrative stratum above it was cajoled into identifying with company goals by material incentives, training opportunities, and job autonomy – called "management by seduction" (Doorewaard, 1988). In the US computer industry, a comparable trend has been observed (Greenbaum, 1976).

Finally, a vital but often neglected aspect of the drive to discipline the radicalized cadre class concerned the removal of social democratic leaders in the course of the 1970s and early 1980s. From 1974 onwards, a series of oustings of prime ministers began that involved Willy Brandt in Germany, Gough Whitlam in Australia, and Harold Wilson in Britain. Brandt was removed by the incriminating exposure by the intelligence services of an East German spy on his staff. Whitlam was dismissed by the Governor-General after he ordered an inquiry into the Australian intelligence service's role in assisting the destabilization of the government of Salvador Allende of Chile and threatened not to renew the CIA's Australian satellite base at Pine Gap. Wilson stepped down when conflict over sharing satellite intelligence with the United States became entangled with criticism of his attitude towards *détente* and regional conflicts (Leigh, 1989, pp. 226–233).

Much has still to be clarified about the subsequent unexplained deaths or assassinations of Pope John Paul I, Italian Premier Aldo Moro, and his Swedish colleague, Olof Palme. But these dramatic incidents, too, objectively allowed the further dismantling of the "equilibrium of compromises," national and international, in which the cadre class in the 1970s had obtained its position of power. In all the cases mentioned, personalities embodying this equilibrium and the principle of social protection were removed from the scene.

Restructuring public multilateralism

The transformation from corporate liberal to neo-liberal capitalism, which was achieved partly by first containing and then defeating the drive for an NIEO, also involved the restructuring of public multilateralism. The UN system had served as an indispensable relay and sounding board for the third world demands and as a meeting ground between the third world and Soviet bloc state classes and the cadre element in advanced capitalist society willing to accommodate these demands.

By its own workings, the shift from undisciplined international lending for development, on which the NIEO project had floated into the 1970s, to monetarism enhanced the salience of the Bretton Woods institutions and GATT. Monetarism aimed at controlling inflation and, more particularly, at cutting back socially protective expenditure in the world economy. It synchronized economic policies on a neo-liberal format world wide. André Drainville writes,

Monetary regulation in the Bretton Woods world economy had treated national currencies as simple commodities. [But] the monetarist agenda proposed to regulate not the exchange of national currencies but their production ... [It] sought to fix the terms under which social relations in national social formations were to be subjugated to a path of money growth defined in the world economy. (Drainville, 1992, pp. 13–14)

Deflation forced on the rest of the world (and, until mid-1983, on the US economy itself) ushered in the deregulation and globalization of capital. Via the debt crisis it turned the third world (and Eastern Europe) into a net tributary of the developed capitalist West, indefinitely postponing their ambition to achieve a more equitable position in the global productive grid and balance of wealth. While short-lived strictly speaking, the disciplinary effect of monetarism enhanced the role of the IMF and the World Bank, and even disciplined these institutions themselves. Within two years after the adoption of monetarist strategy by the American monetary authorities, the Reagan administration declared its intention (as of September 1981) "to

219

push the IMF's conditionality back to where it was" (quoted in Krasner, 1985, p. 137).

In addition to the effects of monetarism, a Western strategy was executed actively to reshape the multilateral skyline. The UN system in the NIEO episode constituted the terrain for an attempt to invest the quasi-state structures of public multilateralism with the orientation of the ethical or interventionist state of the periphery, indeed a Hobbesian "Leviathan" on a world scale, committed to equitable growth and social protection. The counter-offensive developing in the later 1970s accordingly involved the reduction of this type of state to the "Lockian" night-watch profile, leaving the economy to its own workings (monitored at best by the IMF, the Bank for International Settlements, the OECD, etc.).

One by one, those parts of the UN system in which the NIEO demands had obtained institutional representation were struck by boycotts. From the conservative point of view, of which the United States made itself the spokesperson, the ILO's World Employment Programme of 1969, which sought to eliminate the exploitation of marginal third world labour, unduly restrained opportunities for profitable production. It led to the US announcement of withdrawal, and the conclusion that "United States policy is tending to limit commitment to existing universal international organizations, and to move selectively towards the use of agencies ... more effectively under US control" (Cox, 1977, p. 422) became the motto for the Reagan administration's attitude towards the UN system. By reducing the funding laid down in the Kassebaum Amendment, by withdrawal, as in the case of the ILO and Unesco, or by obstructing unwelcome appointments, such as that of the Swiss Red Cross veteran Hocke as High Commissioner for Refugees, or that of Saouama as chief of the Food and Agriculture Organization, the United States and its allies (notably Britain under Mrs. Thatcher) pursued a strategy of "leaving globalism to the dispossessed" (Pentland, 1981, p. 347).

The informal control of the state by private groups representing civil society and working through semi-public secretariats setting the state's agenda, which characterizes the Lockian state/society complex, was also applied to the UN system. Instead of the public and largely transparent power structure of the Hobbesian configuration, the Lockian pattern in international affairs has always favoured private élite consultation first. The British Commonwealth at the beginning of the twentieth century provided the outline for a system that has since accompanied the development of public multilateralism.

The Trilateral Commission formed in 1973 (Gill, 1991) was only the latest instance of such a private consultative body prompting the actors on the political stage. One of its recommendations concerned the summit meetings of heads of state and government of the most important capitalist states, established in 1974–1975. These summits not only became a key channel for mutual consultation at the executive level but also were turned into a forum (replacing the UN General Assembly in this respect) from which universal norms and principles could be propagated (M. Bertrand in *Le Monde Diplomatique*, April 1987, p. 16).

Once the neo-liberal restructuring was under way and disrupting the previous unity among the third world countries, proposals were developed formally to subordinate the United Nations to such prior private and diplomatic consultation. In a Ford Foundation report commissioned by the American UN Association, *A Successor Vision: The UN Tomorrow*, it was proposed that the UN be reformed roughly in line with the structure of the European Community, with a Commission functioning as a secretariat preparing decisions for a Council of Ministers (*Le Monde Diplomatique*, November 1987). The demise of the USSR and the fighting of the Gulf War under UN auspices made such constitutional restructuring less urgent. Direct control of the Security Council by the United States could now be obtained by various means of pressure, and when, in January 1992, Cuba and Yemen ended their turn in the Security Council and their places were taken by Venezuela and Morocco (both more amenable to the American agenda), the Bush administration took the unprecedented initiative for a summit meeting of the heads of state of the 15 Security Council members to discuss the future of the UN (Bennis, 1992, p. 30).

Investing the UN with a punitive police authority was also part of the redefinition of public multilateralism from a Hobbesian, socially protective profile, to a Lockian night-watch profile. The threat posed to the established order by the students' and workers' movement of the late 1960s had provoked, parallel to its being channelled into progressive regulation, a response on the part of the security infrastructure of the advanced capitalist world. It would take us too far to develop this here, but the previously mentioned removal of left-of-centre political leaders was one aspect of the heightened vigilance of the security services.

In July 1979, at an international conference in Jerusalem attended by high-level US, British, and Israeli delegations, the theme of terrorism/counter-terrorism, which had helped to reinforce national police authority in the previous five years, was first discussed in terms of its international potential. At the conference, Israeli Prime Minister Begin attacked the Carter administration's criticism of Israeli human rights abuses in the occupied territories. One of the several US delegations, led by the then presidential candidate George Bush and including Ray Cline and Richard Pipes as spokesmen, developed the thesis that violence around the world was orchestrated by the Soviet Union. In the same year, "international terrorism" became the alarm cry in the Western media (Callahan, 1990, p. 6).

The "Evil Empire" rhetoric of the Reagan administration reflected this interpretation of a Soviet orchestration of revolutionary violence. It was aimed at rallying the world behind the American position in the New Cold War, and the terrorism theme was a subsidiary element to deny autonomous status to progressive regimes such as the Sandinistas' in Nicaragua. At this point, the United States still kept aloof from the UN system and ignored such instances of multilateral constraints on its counter-revolutionary foreign activity as the International Court's decision condemning US mining of Nicaraguan harbours.

At the outset of Reagan's second term, however, when American policy abandoned the unilateral strategy of confrontation for one of trilateral consultation, and the rise to power of Mikhail Gorbachev unhinged the "Evil Empire" posture, "terrorism" was given a more central role in US and Western foreign policy. Following the formation of the Vice President's Task Force on Combatting Terrorism in 1985 (on which Oliver North served as the coordinator directly under Vice President Bush), the issue became embroiled in drugs and arms trafficking, ultimately exposed as the Iran–Contra scandal. Yet, under the subsequent Bush administration, the terrorism theme continued to figure prominently in policy and even became part of the West's renewed allegiance to public multilateralism. The use of the UN as a forum to condemn radical third world states by accusing them of terrorist and other criminal acts has proved to be an effective means of isolating such states and destabilizing undesirable leaderships. Reflecting perhaps its origins in the Jerusalem conference, Arab states in particular have been the target of this approach. Although US interventionism also follows a path of its own (Panama), the Gulf War has shown the potential for upgrading the UN as the framework for intervention. Its effectiveness has been most dramatically illustrated in the case of supposed Libyan complicity in the bomb attack on PanAm flight 103 over Lockerbie, which, in spite of detailed evidence to the contrary (notably in *Time*, 27 April 1992), has led to a worldwide boycott of that country.

The contradictions of deregulation

Two aspects of the neo-liberal configuration of forces that has defeated the drive for reform, and for an NIEO in particular, may contain the seeds of a reversal of fortune that affects the cadre stratum in advanced capitalism and public multilateralism. Of course, present developments in the sphere of population growth, environmental degradation, and violence may accelerate to the point where other contradictions of the neo-liberal project assume the status of academic after-thought. The collapse of state authority in parts of the former Soviet Union, in former Yugoslavia, and in many areas of the third world opens up a spectre of random violence assuming uncontrollable proportions. Although such violence may confirm ideological currents in neo-liberalism pitting the civilized West against the "barbarian" outer world (Rufin, 1991), its effects will very soon react back on the advanced states, fostering authoritarianism and racism.

With this in mind, let us note that, first, particular trends in production are converging on a pattern reminiscent of the late 1960s. The most important of these have to do with autonomy in production and the need for planning. This was a theme in the 1968 students' and workers' movement, but, as we saw, it was subordinated to capital again with the aid of new technologies, notably in electronics. But, as the handling, storage, and application of information have become the central axis of the capitalist labour process, a strategy of breaking up large-scale, bureaucratic enterprise and state support, with the aim of destroying the corporate liberal pattern of labour relations grafted on a prior generation of technology, cannot endure.

As Costello writes,

When the micro-computer was first being introduced, the typical form of innovation, promoted by the media and right-wing ideologists, was the small-scale isolated start-up company ... Now the emphasis of technical advance is shifting back towards global efficiency, integration of systems, networks, compatibility and standardisation ... As production becomes increasingly advanced, and the development of new production techniques, products and services requires more use of science and high-level skills, success is less and less a matter of chance and more and more a product of conscious policy. (Costello, 1989, pp. 3, 5)

223

According to the same author, re-regulation along the lines of the social democratic 1970s would merely provoke another owners' revolt. "Tackling red tape and interference in business can only be dealt with *by moving on from regulation to direct control, through public ownership*" (Costello, 1989, p. 6). The workforce that has an interest in such autonomy (whether the technical and administrative élite for which it has been reserved, or the groups from which it has been taken away in the recent past, or newcomers on the labour market and students) will no longer want to delegate its aspirations to a cadre stratum superior to it, because it has itself merged the characteristics of worker and cadre into the "integral worker" celebrated in the 1968 movement. Apart from that, neither social democracy, nor Eurocommunism, nor compromising Christian Democracy for that matter, are any longer available, as they were in the 1970s, to absorb a movement for direct democracy. Neo-liberalism has fostered pervasive notions of individualism and independence, which cannot as easily be subordinated to a cadre-led regulation process.

The second contradiction in the neo-liberal configuration concerns deregulated global finance. The imbalances created by financial flows across the globe, as well as the techniques used to operate in them for personal enrichment, have reached proportions to which even the organizations supposedly belonging to the multilateral infrastructure of world capital cannot remain indifferent. In the second half of the 1980s, US financiers such as junk bond operators Michael Milken, Ivan Boesky, and Dennis Levine were dealt jail sentences for fraud, but, meanwhile, new forms of financing have been developed that have heightened the fragility of the financial system the world over. They have also become a burden to productive enterprise, which, in addition to debt service, has to maintain immense cash funds to repel take-overs by raiders. New forms of financing such as "swaps" have assumed a size dwarfing the value traded on the major stock exchanges. Traded in unregulated offshore markets, according to recent estimates swaps involve some US$ 5 trillion in capital, and, when Milken's firm, Drexel Burnham Lambert, failed, US$ 30 billion worth of swaps were found on its books alone. According to the general manager of the Bank for International Settlements in Basle, the Drexel failure "almost upset the whole [global] payments system" as a consequence (*Business Week*, 1 June 1992). Regulation in this area seems inevitable and will have to go beyond marginal correction such as in the case of the junk bond dealers. If that happens, the hub of neo-liberal capitalism will be affected and the multilateral institutions entrusted with monitoring international finance will become the trustees of more than finance itself.

Obviously, regulation of global finance, as well as being a response to pressures for democracy and planning arising from advanced productive processes, may also assume an authoritarian form, grafted on to attitudes reared in the New Cold War and the counter-attack against the NIEO. Yet it may be that autonomy and democratic social protection, in the face of the disruptive effects of the market idolized by neo-liberalism, will succeed in halting the slide into disintegration and violence, which links Mogadishu to Los Angeles and Sarajevo. It may also be that the disasters threatening human survival are already upon us, setting the pace of events.

Acknowledgements

This chapter is based on discussions with Robert Cox and Stephen Gill in Gryon, Switzerland, in October 1991. It profited from comments by the participants in the Yokohama session of the UNU/MUNS project in March 1992, especially by Dr. N. Hitti and Professor T. Kamo. Additional comments, likewise gratefully acknowledged by the author, were made by Professor Y. Sakamoto and by colleagues in the Department of International Relations of the University of Amsterdam.

References

Autorenkollektiv (W. Kowalski, J. Glasneck, et al.) (1977) *Die Sozialistische Internationale. Ihre Geschichte und Politik*. Berlin: DVW.

Bahro, R. (1980) [1977] *Die Alternative. Zur Kritik des real existierenden Sozialismus*. Reinbek: Rowohlt.

Bennis, Ph. (1992) "The U.N.: Washington's Captive Tool." *Covert Action Information Bulletin* 41 (summer).

Berle, A. A., Jr. (1954) *The 20th Century Capitalist Revolution*. New York: Harcourt, Brace and World.

Bihr, A. (1989) *Entre bourgeoisie et proletariat. L'encadrement capitaliste*. Paris: L'Harmattan.

Braillard, Ph. (1982) *L'imposture du Club de Rome*. Paris: PUF.

Brandt, W. (1971) *Bundeskanzler Brandt. Reden und Interviews*. Hamburg: Hoffmann & Campe.

Braunmühl, C. von (1973) *Kalter Krieg und Friedliche Koexistenz. Die Aussenpolitik der SPD in der Grossen Koalition*. Frankfurt: Suhrkamp.

Briefs, U. (1979) "Leitende Angestellte als Potential für eine neoautoritäre Politik." *Blätter für deutsche und internationale Politik* 24, no. 11.

Callahan, B. (1990) "The 1980 Campaign: Agents for Bush." *Covert Action Information Bulletin* 33 (winter).

Carew, A. (1987) *Labour under the Marshall Plan. The Politics of Productivity and the Marketing of Management Science.* Manchester: Manchester University Press.

Caute, D. (1988) *Sixty-Eight. The Year of the Barricades.* London: Hamish Hamilton.

Costello, N. (1989) "Planning the Digital Economy." Paper, Kaldor Memorial Lectures, Budapest, September.

Cox, R. W. (1977) "Labor and Hegemony," *International Organization* 31, no 3.

—— (1979) "Ideologies and the New International Economic Order." *International Organization* 33 (spring), no. 2.

—— (1986) "Social Forces, States and World Orders: Beyond International Relations Theory." In: R. O. Keohane, ed. *Neorealism and Its Critics.* New York: Columbia University Press.

Doorewaard, H. (1988) "Kantoorautomatisering in Nederland: Management by seduction," *Te elfder ure* 29, no. 3.

Drainville, A. (1992) "International Political Economy in the Age of Open Marxism." *Amsterdam International Studies,* Working Paper no. 27.

Dutschke, R. (1969) [1968] "On Anti-authoritarianism." In: C. Oglesby, ed. *The New Left Reader.* New York: Grove Press.

Fanon, F. (1968) [1961] *The Wretched of the Earth.* New York: Grove Press.

Garaudy, R. (1978) [1968] "Revolt and Revolution." In: V. Fisera, ed. *Writing on the Wall. France, May 1968: A Documentary Anthology.* London: Allison & Busby.

Gill, S. (1991) *American Hegemony and the Trilateral Commission.* Cambridge: Cambridge University Press.

Gramsci, A. (1971) *Selections from the "Prison Notebooks".* Translated and edited by Q. Hoare and G. N. Smith. New York: International Publishers.

Granou, A. (1977) *La bourgeoisie financière au pouvoir et les luttes de classes en France.* Paris: Maspero.

Greenbaum, J. (1976) "Division of Labor in the Computer Field." *Monthly Review* 28 (July/August), no. 2.

Günsche, K-L., and K. Lantermann (1977) *Kleine Geschichte der Sozialistischen Internationale.* Bonn: Neue Gesellschaft.

Haas, E. B. (1964) *Beyond the Nation-State. Functionalism and International Organization.* Stanford, Calif.: Stanford University Press.

Hagelstange, Th. (1988) *Die Entwicklung von Klassenstrukturen in der EG und in Nordamerika.* Frankfurt and New York: Campus.

Kennedy, J. F. (1957) "A Democrat Looks at Foreign Policy." *Foreign Affairs* 36, no. 1.

Keynes, J. M. (1970) [1936] *The General Theory of Employment, Interest, and Money.* London and Basingstoke: Macmillan.

Krasner, S. D. (1985) *Structural Conflict. The Third World Against Global Liberalism.* Berkeley, Los Angeles and London: University of California Press.

Kuisel, R. F. (1967) *Ernest Mercier. French Technocrat.* Berkeley and Los Angeles: University of California Press.

Leigh, D. (1989) *The Wilson Plot. The Intelligence Services and the Discrediting of a Prime Minister.* London: Heinemann–Mandarin.

Linden, M. van der (1992) *Von der Oktoberrevolution zur Perestroika. Der westliche Marxismus und die Sowjetunion.* Frankfurt: Dipa.

Mallet, S. (1969) [1958] *La nouvelle classe ouvrière*. Paris: Le Seuil.

MEW (1956–) *Marx–Engels Werke*. Berlin: Dietz.

Morioka, K. (1989) "Japan." In: T. Bottomore and R. J. Brym, eds. *The Capitalist Class. An International Study*. New York: Harvester Wheatsheaf.

Overbeek, H. W. (1982) "Internationale ontwikkelingshulp en de nieuwe internationale economische orde." *Tijdschrift voor Diplomatie* 9, no. 3.

Pentland, C. (1981) "Building Global Institutions." In: G. Boyd and C. Pentland, eds. *Issues in Global Politics*. New York: The Free Press; London: Collier Macmillan.

Picciotto, S. (1989) "Slicing a Shadow. Business Taxation in an International Framework." In: L. Hancher and M. Moran, eds. *Capitalism, Culture, and Economic Regulation*. Oxford: Clarendon Press.

Pijl, K. van der (1993) "The Sovereignty of Capital Impaired. Social Forces and Codes of Conduct for Multinational Corporations." In: H. W. Overbeek, ed. *Restructuring Hegemony in the International Political Economy*. London: Routledge.

Piore, M., and C. F. Sabel (1984) *The Second Industrial Divide*. New York: Basic Books.

Polanyi, K. (1957) [1944] *The Great Transformation. The Political and Economic Origins of Our Time*. Boston: Beacon.

Raschke, J., ed. (1981) *Die politischen Parteien in Westeuropa*. Reinbek: Rowohlt.

Rufin, J-Ch. (1991) *L'empire et les nouveaux barbares*. Paris: Lattès.

Stoessinger, J. G. (1970) *The United Nations and the Superpowers*. 2nd edn. New York: Random House.

Symonds, R. (1971) "Functional Agencies and International Administration." In: R. S. Jordan, ed. *International Administration*. New York: Oxford University Press.

Tinbergen, J., Coordinator (1977) *Naar een Rechtvaardiger Internationale Orde*. Amsterdam and Brussels: Elsevier.

Useem, M. (1989) "Revolt of the Corporate Owners and the Demobilization of Business Political Action." *Critical Sociology* 16 (summer–fall), no. 2/3.

Weber, S. (1973) *Privilegien durch Bildung*. Frankfurt/M.: Suhrkamp.

Weil, S. (1978) [1951] *Fabriktagebuch und andere Schriften zum Industriesystem*. Frankfurt: Suhrkamp.

Whyte, W. H. (1963) [1956] *The Organization Man*. Harmondsworth: Penguin.

Wijmans, L. (1987) *Beeld en betekenis van het maatschappelijke midden. Oude en nieuwe middengroepen 1850 tot heden*. Amsterdam: Van Gennep.

Winqwist, C-H. (1976) "Corporate Responsibility – Highlights of the 25th ICC World Congress." In: E. C. Bursk and G. E. Bradley, eds. *Corporate Citizenship in the Global Community*. Washington, DC: International Management and Development Institute.

8

The structure of finance in the world system

Susan Strange

Finance – the provision of money in the form of credit – is the life-blood of any capitalist economy. None of the capitalist countries could have grown in wealth as they have done without making use of money. Not only was money needed as a medium of exchange for current transactions; it was also necessary to have it as a store of value, enabling purchasing power to be borrowed, for money to be used as credit. By this means, the savings made in one part of the economy or by one group of people could be temporarily "bought" by other people who wanted to invest it in other parts of the economy. Only thus could essentially risky but potentially productive enterprises be started up so that the wealth and total product of the system could grow.

A market economy of any kind, including the new worldwide one, cannot exist without a competitive market for capital and credit. Such a market will call into existence enterprises devoted to the competitive marketing of credit – borrowed money in all its forms. Some of this credit will result from the intermediation by such enterprises between the savers and the would-be borrowers. But it will result from their power to *create* credit – something Marxists who use the term "capital accumulation" (as though they were talking about squirrels storing up nuts) find it hard to conceptualize. Credit is created when-

228

ever the ratio between the savers' deposits and the borrowers' loans exceeds 1:1; that is, when the banks lend more than they have taken as deposits on the usually safe assumption that not all their depositors will want their money back on the same day. From the very beginnings of banking in the Middle Ages, this was the essence of banking, that more was lent than was deposited.

This point is important in order to establish the basic fact, central to the argument of this paper, that a capitalist economy cannot function effectively without the aid of banks to create, as well as to allocate, credit. It simply cannot function any other way, even though the governments of market economies may decide not to supplant but to supplement the market for credit with state banks, or with state-financed international organizations that will exist side-by-side with commercial competitive banks.

The essential difference, therefore, between a capitalist economy (in the generally accepted meaning of the word) and a socialist economy is that, although in the socialist economy credit is available, it is available *only* on the say-so of the state (or party) and *only* from state-run institutions, whereas in the capitalist economy it is made available through a market. Thus, it is possible to have industrialization and economic growth through state capitalism; but we have seen the results in the former socialist economies of the former Soviet bloc. The experience suggests that, by comparison with the market system, it is infinitely more wasteful and less flexible and has failed to satisfy the material demands of the people.

In the Introduction and chapter 1, Professor Sakamoto has correctly identified the globalization of capitalism as a key element in the changing world order. The present essay seeks to explain in simple terms why and how the structure of finance plays such a crucial role in this globalization of capitalism. In order to do so, it was necessary from the first to explain in a rather basic way what is meant by a structure of finance; to explain, in short, that we are talking about a market-based mechanism for the creation of credit *and* a set of institutions and enterprises set up by governments to monitor and regulate the price relations between national monies, i.e. currencies.

That it has been necessary to do so is the result of some widespread confusion about the close relationship between the *international monetary regime* and *international financial markets*. Together, they may be said to form the international financial structure. The international monetary system – if system it must be called – consists in the arrangements between states for the management of relations between their respective national currencies, in other words, of exchange rates and related matters. Yet even these are not solely within the command of governments; international markets can upset the decisions and agreements of governments. Conversely, international financial markets could not exist without governments, and are subject to whatever rules and restrictions that states may impose upon them. The financial structure, therefore, may be defined as the sum of all the arrangements and institutions governing the availability of credit *plus* all the arrangements and factors determining the terms on which currencies – units of account – are exchanged for one another.

On the whole, it is the latter that has dominated the literature of international political economy. Because there was set up after World War II an institution, the International Monetary Fund (IMF), backed by articles of agreement (usually referred to as the Bretton Woods "regime"), which aspired to lay down rules about these monetary relations and the management of exchange rates, much more attention has been paid by scholars to this development than to the financial markets. Economists in particular have produced a large literature on the Bretton Woods system and the IMF. And since the early 1970s, when the United States decided it no longer liked the fixed exchange rate rules, they have produced another large set of writings about the pros and cons of fixed and floating exchange rates. In the 1980s, yet another large body of literature has existed on the problems, and the experience, of governments in coordinating their monetary policies so as to stabilize (as far as they can) the movement of exchange rates. In Europe especially, where since the early 1970s there have been repeated attempts to negotiate arrangements among the member states of the European Community (EC) that would bring them closer to a monetary union and permanently fixed rates, the debate about monetary union has engaged a lot of academic work as well as the pages of newspapers and journals.

Clearly, this international monetary system, which is dominated by the major national currencies such as the dollar, D-mark and yen and watched over by the finance ministers of the Group of Seven (G7) major industrialized market economies, cannot be separated from, and is intimately related to, developments in the international financial markets. Obviously, if one of the seven governments decides to borrow – or itself to create – a lot of credit in order to go to war or in other ways to expand its money supply, this will have some impact on the global financial structure. It will also affect its relations with other governments in the G7 and thus may have an effect on the international monetary system. And if market operators (banks, for example) decide to cease lending to an indebted government, then that government's relations with the governments of its creditors, and with international organizations like the International Monetary Fund or the World Bank, are suddenly transformed into relations of greater dependency.

The financial structure in the world economy can thus be visualized as a hybrid of states and markets, a halfway house between, on the one hand, the realist conception of separate national societies, surviving on more or less discrete national economies and governed by the political institutions of nation-states, and, on the other, the financiers' and bankers' perception of a single global market for monies and credit instruments and for financial services. In the former, it is state frontiers that matter. In the latter, the most significant divisions in the market are set by the different times that the sun rises and people start work, and that the sun sets and they go home. Between the international monetary system, where it seems as though national governments are the chief actors, and the financial markets, where the decisions of debtors and creditors and their intermediaries seem more decisive, there is a significant difference in the democratic dimension. National governments may be directly subject to popular interests and pressures, whereas in financial markets democratic principles take second place to supply and demand and the vagaries of the markets. And whereas the monetary system is largely a matter for negotiation between governments – of state–state diplomacy – the financial structure is largely a matter of political authority over markets and market operators – of state–firm relationships and bargaining.

This may be one reason why many scholars in international political economy have found international finance difficult to analyse. Most of them were trained in international (i.e. inter-state) relations. They were brought up to think – and for some it is almost an article of faith – that the state is the basic unit of the international system. Political economy in the world system, for many of them, was therefore taken to mean the study of relations between states with reference to matters of money, trade, and (less often) investment. Only a few scholars for one reason or another have shown much interest in the political economy of international finance (Frieden, 1987; Kindleberger, 1978). Though their number is growing, it has to be admitted that most of the contributions to the literature on the subject have come from journalists (or ex-journalists like Fred Hirsch and Andrew Shonfield) or from expert advisers to banks, governments, or

231

international organizations (most notably Robert Triffin but also Jacques Polak, Robert Solomon, etc.). It is paradoxical that international trade, which has proved extraordinarily vulnerable to the self-defensive policies of states, should have been so exhaustively studied by international political economists, whereas international finance, which is rather exceptionally vulnerable to the decisions, or non-decisions, of national monetary authorities, has been comparatively neglected.

That vulnerability makes all the more necessary an examination of the changes in the international financial structure that have taken place since about 1960. This, together with a brief summary of changes in the international monetary system, will form the main part of this essay. However, I will conclude by considering, from an international political economy point of view, the consequences and implications of these changes, first, for the world system as a whole, rather than for individual nation-states, and for the basic values expressed through that system; and, secondly, for people, for the various social and economic groups in world society. In this way, I hope to have something relevant to say concerning Professor Sakamoto's concern for the democratic aspects of world order.

Changes in world finance

Changes in the global financial structure in recent decades can be considered under five main headings:
(1) the system has *grown* enormously in size, in the number and value of transactions conducted in it, in the number and economic importance of the markets and the market operators;
(2) the *technology* of finance has changed as fast as the technology in any manufacturing or productive sector in the world economy;
(3) the global system has *penetrated* national systems more deeply and effectively than ever before – though some people are apt to retort that there is nothing new in international banking or international debt, the degree to which both have played a growing part in national economies and societies is quite new;
(4) the provision and marketing of credit have become overall a much less regulated and a much *more competitive* business than it used to be when national systems were less integrated in the global system; and, not least,
(5) the *relation of demand for and supply of credit* has changed rather radically, with very large implications for the world political economy and for the material prospects of many social groups and social institutions in the future.

232

Size

No one who knows anything about international finance is in any doubt that it has grown rather phenomenally in the last quarter century. There is, however, the problem of measurement and, connected with it, the problem of definition. The numbers that are available are only rough indicators, not precise indices. Here are a few of them:

- Transactions in the Eurocurrency markets had risen to over US$1,000 billion – 1 trillion – in the year 1984, compared with US$75 billion in 1970 and only US$3 billion in the early 1960s.
- Trading in the foreign exchange markets world wide in the late 1980s amounted to over US$600 billion *a day*, no less than 32 times the volume of international commercial transactions world wide.
- Between the mid-1960s and the mid-1980s, international banking grew at a compound rate of 26 per cent a year on average, compared with an average growth rate in international trade of 12.5 per cent and an average growth in output of a little over 10 per cent.
- The issue of bonds is a credit instrument traditionally associated with international finance since the last century. Equal in value to 2 per cent of world exports in 1980, their total value had risen to 9 per cent of world exports by 1985 and they have continued to grow in popularity since. ECU-dominated bond issues, which totalled ECU 1.9 billion in 1982, totalled nearly ECU 17 billion in 1988.
- Transnational trading in shares was comparatively rare even by 1980. Most national stock exchanges dealt only in the shares of nationally registered companies within the state. By 1989, more than 18 per cent of all share trading was in the shares of foreign corporations – only the major multinationals.

Among the significant numbers, we should also note the growth of trading in futures and options in some of the main international financial centres like London, Paris, and Frankfurt. For they reflect not only the growing transnational nature of international finance but also the rise in the perceived risks involved in it. Futures and options are the hedging devices that allow traders and investors to offset the risks inseparable from one financial transaction by buying/selling options or futures contracts on the opposite price movement. The London International Financial Futures Exchange (LIFFE), for example, was started only in 1982. Its turnover by 1991 reached over 38 million contracts. Its French rival, MATIF (Marché à Terme Internationale de France), in the same year traded 37 million contracts, and the German Terminborse (DTB), which opened only in 1990, already traded 15.4 million contracts the next year.

These are only rather rough indicators of both change and growth in international finance. To anyone in the business of banking and finance, it is obvious that the international (or global) financial structure coexists with a lot of national financial structures, some parts of which remain more or less unchanged and are affected only indirectly by developments in international finance. Each overlaps to some extent – for example, when commercial "High Street" banks also engage in international transactions. Thus, there is no clear dividing line between the two, and some national systems remain much more insulated than others (see below).

So much for measurement. As for the definition of what is meant by international financial structure, that, too, is not easy. We cannot identify some institutions as belonging to it while others are outside. Nor can we define some markets as being purely national, while others are integrated in the global structure. So long as people or companies place deposits in foreign banks, or pension fund managers buy shares in foreign companies, the dividing line between the two is blurred. The fact is that the international financial structure is a sort of hybrid, a halfway house between a completely integrated worldwide structure and a totally unintegrated collection of national structures.

What we are analysing though is clear enough. It is the part of the credit-creating mechanism, and the part of the market for financial assets, that is integrated with others across national frontiers. In that structure, market forces are beyond the total control of any single national government. Indeed, with the notable exception of the United States, most governments have very little influence over it. Their vulnerability to its changing character, its volatilities, and the new risks it brings, however, is only too acutely felt.

By way of illustration, we may say that the market for foreign exchange is globally integrated. The price of dollars in yen – and indeed in gold – is virtually uniform everywhere at any given moment. Only where exchange controls have created pockets of black, or illegal, markets for foreign exchange are there local differences. Similarly, the acknowledgement of the London Inter-Bank Offer Rate (LIBOR) for Eurocurrency loans as a standard benchmark for prices world wide – just as Brent Crude or the Middle East posted price for Saudi Arabian light are benchmarks for oil prices – shows that this part of the mechanism belongs in the global structure. The same is true for the international bond market and for some but not all equities, or shares. The big multinationals' shares are traded on all the major stock markets. The shares in other small firms may be traded only on their local bourses. (The fact that, on most local stock exchanges, the shares of national enterprises are more numerous than those of the multinationals explains why daily movements in the index of share prices are often larger in some centres than in others, or even move in opposite directions.)

By and large, the numbers seem to indicate that transactions in the global financial structure are growing faster than are those in local, national structures. They have also tended to be the least regulated ever since the early days of the Eurodollar market back in the 1960s. If trends are extrapolated, this suggests that the unregulated, or underregulated, part of the market will eventually overtake the regulated part.

Technology

The technology of international finance has changed very rapidly in the last two or three decades in two ways: mechanically, and in the nature of the goods and services traded.[1] Banking used to employ hundreds of clerks, entering figures in ledgers by hand. Now, the transactions are registered automatically, through integrated computer systems, communicating with each other by satellites. They are also executed mechanically, by automatic monetary transfer systems (AMTS). One central clearing system in New York – CHIPS – handles all dollar and Eurodollar transfers between banks in the USA. And whereas markets used to operate by personal contact and negotiation, most deals nowadays are concluded by telephone or telefax or through computers. The London Stock Exchange is being revolutionized by the introduction of TAURUS, an automatic system of share transfers that does away with the need for buyers and sellers to meet face-to-face. By these means, financial transactions are concluded in real time. The pace of change in market moods and trends is accordingly accelerated out of all recognition. October 1987 demonstrated how panic, or near-panic, could spread around the globe in a matter of hours.

Some of this mechanical innovation has had important consequences for the efficacy of national bank regulation. But it has probably been less important than the less visible and less tangible innovations of new credit instruments, new ways in which funds can be deposited with banks, new ways in which funds can be borrowed, or new services provided by financial institutions. All these are the result of looser regulation by authorities over financial operators, and of increased competition between them for profits from banking.[2] The first significant step in deregulation, it is generally agreed, was the permission accorded to US banks to deal in Eurodollars – that is, funds denominated in dollars but held in bank branches outside the territorial United States. The story is well known and need not be repeated here. Although the Eurodollar market looked like – and was – an innovative device thought up by inventive bankers, it could have come into being only with the permission of the US and British governments; the one allowed offshore dealings to go on free of US bank rules, and the other allowed dollar dealings to go on free of British rules and regulations.[3]

The same is true of many of the other innovations in financial practice in recent years. In the 1930s, US banks in the Federal Reserve System were not allowed to pay more than nominal interest on short-term deposits. By the 1970s, these rules had been relaxed and customers could put their spare cash on the money market, earning high interest rates for short periods. Similarly in Britain, the old system of a strict separation of function between stockbrokers and stockjobbers, between commercial banks and investment or merchant banks and discount houses, reinforced self-administered rules on banks' behaviour. In the 1970s, from NOW (negotiable order of withdrawal) accounts and Money Market Funds, banks progressed to the creation of "junk bonds" to finance corporate mergers and take-overs. The practice became well known when one of the US banks that had pioneered the issue of junk bonds, Drexel Lambert, got into trouble with the authorities and was the subject of criminal investigations. After that came the growing practice of "securitization," which in plain terms really meant the issue by banks of "commercial paper," i.e. loans to corporations on fixed terms, usually better than those given to shareholders. According to a recent survey of banking, the practice is now spreading to Europe and Japan.[4] As Enkyo (1990) had observed earlier, it is hard for either not to follow a lead in financial innovation in the United States. And the next step in the United States was the creation of a secondary market in what are called C and I (commercial and industrial) loans. Sales of these increased tenfold between 1983 and 1989, when no less than US$290 billion were sold in the third quarter of that year. No wonder a Brookings study observed, "the mass production of credit ... has become the Trojan horse of the American banking system."[5]

Penetration

The signs of the increasing penetration of national financial markets by the global ones are visible in the financial districts of any large city. The passerby can see the nameplates of foreign banks side-by-side with local ones. No major international bank fails to have its offices in at least half a dozen of the biggest financial centres like New York, Tokyo, London, Frankfurt, Toronto, Sydney, Hong Kong, Paris, or São Paolo, not to mention the tax havens in Luxembourg and the Caribbean. Although some countries, especially developing ones, limit the business of foreign banks to foreign trade and investment, the barriers to entry of foreign competitors are gradually crumbling. American banks deal in London in British government securities. Some European banks do business in the United States. More important, perhaps, than this visible sign of penetration is the evidence that local financial markets all around the world market economy are shaken or encouraged by the same world events. This could be seen in their response to such news as the 19 August 1991 coup in Moscow or the start and finish of the Gulf War. The events in themselves may have little direct effect on market conditions, but there is no doubt about their power to affect the mood of market operators. It is proof enough that national financial markets are being invaded, or submerged, by global markets.

Competition

As noted earlier, financial innovation has loosened the grip of national regulatory systems; and interpenetration has brought newcomers in to join local competitors. The point is important because of the difference between financial firms and manufacturing ones. In the latter, more competition generally leads to a shrinking of profit margins, to efforts to cut costs, and eventually to lower prices to the customers. In banking, though, the shrinking of profit margins has historically been followed not only by lower prices so much as by higher risks. The crude fact is that the costs of production for a bank are no greater to organize and service a risky loan than to do the same for a sound one. And if the risky loan is not repaid and has to be written off as a loss, this will happen some time after the profit has been received.

It is true that increased competition from foreign banks will, in many cases, break down the comfortable cartel-like arrangements that have featherbedded local banks in many countries and have

237

kept the price of their services up to consumers. But more competition is not costless. As Toyoo Gyohten, formerly a senior official in the Japanese Foreign Ministry and now adviser to the Bank of Tokyo, observed, the most important question raised by the experience of world finance in the 1980s was "how do you reconcile the pursuit of security with the efficiency of the market?"[6]

Demand and supply

The fifth change to be noted is the changed relation of demand and supply in these integrated transnational markets for credit. Recall that banks not only intermediate between savers and borrowers but also create credit in the process.

If they are tempted to create much more credit in relation to total savings, the result is likely to be an increase in money supply and therefore in inflation – higher prices all round. To the extent that they resist increased demands for credit, thus failing to match supply with demand, the result is likely to be a high price, i.e. higher rates of interest as the price for borrowing. In fact, in recent years, both consequences can be observed: some increase in the rate of inflation in most of the G7 countries; and a real interest rate that, even in the cheapest markets, has been substantially above the rates ruling in the 1930s or 20 years after World War II. To observe this change is not to blame the banks alone. Their actions are only the end of a chain of factors that begins with an almost philosophical, or even psychological, change in the way people and collectivities of people think about spending and saving, how they choose between the two. The distinguished economist Al Hirschman once speculated that capitalism may have benefited from a mental or philosophical carry-over from pre-capitalist societies in which social and economic behaviour was ruled by such non-materialistic notions as honour (in standing by inconvenient contracts) and prudence, parsimony and self-restraint (in eschewing overindulgence in material consumption and the display of wealth). Whether this is right or not, it is historically demonstrable that well-off people in the rich countries – poor people do not have the choice – have tended in this century to spend more and save less than their grandparents. Their governments, which used to consume a rather small proportion of the gross national product, now spend 40–50 per cent or more of the GNP. And what they cannot finance by raising taxes, they finance by borrowing. Firms, large and small, and smaller entrepreneurs like farmers and shopkeepers, which used to finance their new investments by the accumulated prof-its of the past, now go to the banks for credit or raise borrowed money on the financial markets. The oil companies are a striking ex-ample of enterprises that never used to borrow to finance exploration for new oil wells and now regularly do so. Moreover, the thirst for new corporate capital has led to more and more resort to interna-tional financial markets instead of national ones. The latest example of this trend is the decision of Toshiba Corporation to seek additional – and significantly more expensive – finance abroad instead of from the Japanese stock market.[7]

The consequences of structural change in finance

If itemizing the major changes in the international financial and monetary system gives the broad impression of change for the worse, to a more unstable, risky, and volatile system of creating and allocating credit, that is perhaps unavoidable. But these changes should never obscure the salient fact that developed monetary and financial systems *are* engines of economic growth. The creation of credit in a competitive market does enable investment to be made in new products and new, more cost-effective processes, and this raises living standards, if not universally or equally, nevertheless enough to make national economies as units larger and more prosperous. Some economists have been tempted by liberal theories of economic trade to attribute the growing wealth of the world market economy since the 1950s to the reduction of barriers to imports and to more efficient allocation of resources through the exchange of goods and services. Since growth continued, even more in the volume of trade than in output, in the last 10 or 15 years when non-tariff barriers to trade were visibly on the increase, this explanation seems insufficient if not actually wrong. Much more likely, and more consistent with the pattern of economic growth from year to year, is an explanation that finds the cause of growth in the capacity of the financial institutions to create credit and to move it about more freely than ever before. Growth in developing countries was fastest when credit was avail-able to them; and it flagged most dramatically and seriously only in 1983, the year after the onset of the debt crisis – beginning with Mex-ico and Poland and spreading to other indebted countries in Latin America and Central Europe.[8]

In short, the development of a more sophisticated and integrated world market for finance added to the efficiency of the world market. But, in doing so, it also frustrated the "pursuit of security" – which, translated into more oldfashioned language, means the stability of money, the value of the currency in which exchanges take place. This certainly is much more vulnerable in the 1990s than it was in the 1960s. It is the Achilles' heel of global capitalism: the one thing that, if confidence in it failed for any reason, would destroy all that the market economy had achieved in this century. Just as the inability of the socialist system to satisfy the aspirations of the people both for a better material life and for a more effective voice in government eventually destroyed the whole economic system – with what long-term political and social consequences we cannot tell – so financial instability, the precariousness of a banking system that sometimes looks as poorly balanced as a house of cards, could do the same for capitalism.[9]

Change in international money

So much for the changes in international banking and finance. The accompanying changes in the international monetary system are much better known and so can be referred to quite briefly.[10] To make an assessment of the consequences of both, we shall have to look first at the outstanding political and social issues that changes in both the monetary and financial systems have raised and that remain – and look to remain for the foreseeable future – unresolved. Identifying these issues will allow us to make some broader comments on the impact of both on the nature of world society and the basic values expressed therein.

Recall that the arrangements agreed upon between the major Western allied governments at Bretton Woods in New Hampshire, USA, before the end of World War II had to wait 15 years or more before they became effective as a system of rules governing the management of exchange rates between the signatory states. These rules provided for stable rates between their currencies by binding governments first to make their currencies freely convertible into others, and then to maintain the par value of their currencies within narrow limits. (Par value, in effect, meant value in terms of the US dollar. Although, formally, a par value was expressed in terms of gold, in practice the gold price was fixed in US dollars at US$35 an ounce of gold – and had been since the mid-1930s – and, because the US Treasury stood ready to convert on request any dollars presented to it into gold at that price, the system of fixed par values therefore constituted a dollar–gold exchange system.)

Once a member state had made its currency convertible and fixed the par value of its currency, it was entitled to draw on the resources of the International Monetary Fund for short-term help in financing any deficits arising on its current account balance of payments.[11] These drawing rights varied according to its IMF "quota" – fixed rather roughly by the size of the national economy. This quota also determined the amount of its contribution in local currency and gold or dollars to the IMF's resources, and its weighted vote in the IMF Executive Board. Only in 1959, when for the first time the European governments in concert made their currencies convertible, did the Bretton Woods "regime" begin to function. Its reign as a system of clear rules for exchange rate management lasted barely more than a decade, until 1971 when President Nixon declared the dollar inconvertible into gold and allowed the market, rather than the US government, to determine the dollar's exchange rate with other currencies.

Thus, although the IMF as an organization had been set up already in 1947 (11 years before the fixed exchange rate regime came into operation), and although it continued to function as an intergovernmental forum and as overseer, or monitor, of the macroeconomic management policies of states – more particularly, of financially weak, indebted states – it cannot be said that in the last two decades it has really fulfilled its original role and purpose in the management of exchange rates.

It is a paradox of this whole story that the dollar's central role as a reserve currency and as the preferred medium of exchange in the private sector of international trade and finance was built up in the four decades or so between 1934 and 1971 when the gold value of the dollar was fixed and stable, but that the dollar continued to enjoy the benefits and privileges of being the world's top currency – the national currency most used in world business[12] – long after it had ceased to have a stable value in terms of gold, or oil, or any basket of goods and services. Although they knew that the real value of dollars accumulated in national or corporate reserves was variable and that some risk attached therefore to holding dollars, or to fixing prices in terms of dollars, its pre-eminence over its rivals in the system has so far never been seriously in doubt (see Parboni, 1980).

The result for the international monetary system has not just been that the United States has enjoyed the "exorbitant privileges" (to quote General de Gaulle) of its pivotal role in the Bretton Woods gold exchange standard. But since 1973, when the dollar was finally floated, the United States has enjoyed even greater asymmetrical – "super-exorbitant" – privileges. For it has been able to borrow through the international financial system large amounts of money *denominated in its own currency*. With the aid of such credit, it has been able to finance a growing fiscal and balance of payments deficit. No other debtor country has enjoyed this privilege, or the power over the system, for good or evil, that went with such a privilege.

Instead of a fixed system of rules governing foreign exchange rates, therefore, the international financial system has had to live with an international monetary system in which the United States sometimes was content to let the markets decide the value of the dollar, but at other times was inclined to put all sorts of pressure on its affluent allies – to intervene in these markets, or to change their policies, in order to stop the dollar rising too high or falling too low to the perceived detriment of US national interests (see Destler and Henning, 1989; Funabashi, 1988; Marris, 1985). The United States has also been inclined unilaterally to put pressure on some of the newly industrializing countries (NICs) like South Korea or Taiwan to revalue their currencies as a check on the competitive attractions of the exports to the US market.

Although the institution of the Group of Seven summits and regular meetings of finance ministers have seemed to the press and the public like a ruling oligarchy presiding over the international monetary system, the reality behind the bland communiqués issued after every summit reveals much less consensus. America's affluent allies are becoming less compliant. The Europeans, led by the then President of the EC Commission, Delors, agreed to set up their own fixed-rate regime – a European Monetary Union (EMU), making irreversible the commitments under the 1978 European Monetary System – within the undisciplined global monetary system. And the Japanese government, shaken by the political and financial reverberations from its close involvement with the United States, is becoming much less inclined now than in the past to go along so tamely wherever Washington leads.

Yet all is not quite anarchy in the system. Beginning in 1974, when the failures of Bankhaus Herstatt in Germany and the Franklin National Bank in New York brought nightmare visions of the possible consequences of giving too much freedom to operators in financial markets, the governments of the affluent countries, led by the United States, began using the network of central banks organized since 1930 through the Bank for International Settlements in Basle, Switzerland, to tighten the rules on bank supervision. An agreement called the Basle Concordat,[13] supplemented in 1973 by another one, progressively clarified the division of responsibility between national central banks, so that it was clearer who was supposed to see prudential rules observed. The Basle Concordats also sought progressively to harmonize the standards governing the limits on bank lending, as for instance by setting a target ratio between a bank's capital and its outstanding loans. But although progress towards these ends was made, the next collapse of a big international bank, the Pakistani-owned Bank for Credit and Commerce International (BCCI), in 1990 showed clearly that loopholes still existed in the central banks' network of supervision over market operators (see De Cecco, 1987).

To sum up, I might quote from an earlier survey of the state of international money and finance written some six years ago.

An orderly, developed monetary system would thus be characterized by steady (and not too jerky) growth, by increasing controls over the credit structure, its markets and its operators; by increasing allocation of financial resources to the welfare system and further provision of public goods.

A disorderly system, contrari-wise, could be characterized by growth, interrupted by periods of failing confidence and unused, idle productive resources; by the threat of inflation due to the creation of credit-money by governments or banks or by both; by the threat of financial crisis and collapse; and by exploitation of the system by political authority for its own particular ends rather than for the general welfare. (Strange, 1988)

The conclusion was that the global financial structure displayed all the characteristics of a developed monetary and financial system, but that it was less stable and orderly than it might be and ought to be if it was not to put the rest of the world economy at risk. In national economies, ways had been found to compensate for the tendency of bankers to overbank (in Hirsch's words). In a politically divided world, this was more difficult. While the development of sophisticated monetary and financial mechanisms within capitalist economies had led to the rich getting richer and the poor staying poor, national governments, in order to survive and stave off revolution, had used countervailing political power to build welfare systems that compensated for the inherent inequity, but this was more difficult when the financial structures had become globalized. Not only was the political incentive for redistributive welfare lacking, but such foreign aid as there was did not always help the poor. The political system made it too easy for the ruling élites to highjack foreign aid for their own benefit.

Conclusions

Today, it is more vital than ever before to use a political economy approach to global finance and international money. That means to start by asking about *power* in the system: who has it and how do they use it? The main difference between economists and political economists is that most of the economists leave power out of their calculations.

Secondly, it means asking who benefits – "Cui bono?" as the philosophers asked in ancient Rome – and also who suffers, who has greater risks imposed on them, and who has the new opportunities, material or otherwise, opened for them? These allocative questions, moreover, should be asked concerning social groups and not just states.

Thirdly, it means asking questions about the basic social values reflected by the working of the system. Does it value the creation of wealth more than the achievement of social justice? Does the maintenance of order come before the assurance of freedom?[14]

The answers to the first set of questions concerning power are already implicit in the outline of recent changes in the financial and monetary structure. In the financial system, the influence of global markets for money and for credit instruments has grown as the power of governments to influence or control these markets has diminished. Within the markets, the power to move the market up or down has gone more and more to the innovative specialists with their sophisticated information system, and less to their customers, whether depositors or borrowers. The banks, for instance, were able to decide that they would extract profit from their operations by "front-loading" loans with management fees, and the customers could not stop them. They also decide which borrowers must pay so many percentage points above LIBOR for their loans.

In the monetary system, too, the answer is clear enough. For the time being at least, the asymmetric power of the United States to act in monetary affairs unilaterally, and without the constraints imposed on others, is unchanged, whatever weaknesses there may be in the American manufacturing sector.

Answers to the second question have also been addressed from a Filipino point of view in chapter 9 in this volume. Professor Briones makes the valid point that, in the handling of international debt, the debtors have been weak bargainers and have suffered accordingly. Their interests came second to those of creditor banks and creditor governments. Both these were fearful of the consequences of unpaid debts on the stability of the whole financial structure. Banks were therefore told to rebuild their capital base and to be more prudent in lending in the future, and the result, predictably, was to check the outflow of new capital. As debt servicing costs mounted, the reverse flow of funds from South to North increased. This was the reason Professor Robert Triffin (1991), the veteran critic of the International Monetary System (IMS), observed that the letters stood for International Monetary Scandal.

One consequence, relevant to the power questions, is also correctly observed by Professor Briones: that the power that the IMF had lost as a result of the end of the fixed exchange rate regime, it had regained through its key role in the rescheduling of foreign debt. All debtor governments found it harder to resist or reject IMF advice on economic management when IMF approval was a necessary condition for new lending – even though the new loans did not always reduce the total debt burden. The contrast with the last century, when indebted states were able to default on bonds bought by foreign creditors without, in most cases, having to change their internal policies, is worth remarking.

As to the allocation of costs and benefits, risks and opportunities, among other social groups, the mobility of capital created through global finance has certainly weakened the bargaining power of organized labour in the face of the corporate managers of multinational corporations. But while some employees "at home" may have done less well in wage bargaining than in the past, others in the plants located in developing countries have, in fact, enjoyed higher incomes than they would have done if production had not become international.

We may also observe that the development of this integrated financial structure has benefited big businesses over small ones – but, again, not uniformly so. Some big names have disappeared through bankruptcy or take-over from the lists of top companies – and in part as a result of financial changes. And new names have risen and new fortunes have been made by people and firms that were unknown only a few years ago. There are plenty of new Indian, Chinese, and Latin American "multinationals" soon to join these prestigious lists.

Changes in the financial structures have also affected two other categories of society not often considered in the literature of international political economy – the old and the young, and the educated (or smart) and the uneducated and unskilled. Whereas the availability of capital has given new opportunities to younger generations, there is a sense in which their parents and grandparents have paid heavily for post-war economic growth. They worked hard. They saved voluntarily or through state pension funds for their old age. And now, in many cases, they find inflation has eroded the real value of their savings or pension rights, or that the fiscal problems of the state may cause governments to alter the rules to their disadvantage. Worst hit of all are the pensioners of the ex-socialist states.

As for the *cui bono* between educated/unskilled social groups, some might see this as a widening gap between office workers and factory workers (white collars and blue collars); or between peasants still toiling in the fields to produce food and computer programmers or foreign exchange dealers producing only "services" of doubtful value. Both are simplifications. But there is little doubt that financial changes have played a large part in what is referred to as the "information revolution" and that financial resources have flowed more readily to Wall Street "yuppies" and those with new skills and knowledge than to the more traditional occupations. Never has it been more true that, in terms of life chances or entitlements, there is a core in the periphery and a periphery in the core.

These allocative consequences suggest that, in answer to the last set of questions concerning the mix of values reflected by the financial and monetary structure, we should not – and cannot – generalize about the results of change for states or nations. As between the four basic social values of wealth, security, justice, and freedom, we have to ask both *how much* of each the system produces and *for whom* – security for whom, wealth for whom, justice for whom, and the freedom to choose for whom.

How much? unfortunately is unquantifiable. Comparison with past periods suggests only that the world political economy today produces more wealth than it did in the past, but while security of some kinds and for some groups is greater, it is not clear how we balance one kind of security (e.g. from nuclear holocaust) against another kind of insecurity (e.g. from financial crisis).

Most difficult of all, perhaps, is the question posed by Professor Sakamoto concerning democracy: what chances does the system give, or not give, to people to decide their own destiny, through the ballot box or through the political rights associated with the concept of democracy, such as freedom of association, freedom of speech, freedom of religion and belief, freedom from official intimidation and coercion? (Do we all also have the freedom to own property, the freedom to choose life or death for unborn children or for ourselves? As the philosophers have always said, the debate over when freedom becomes licence, over the balance between collective welfare and individual freedom, is an endless one.) Absolute, objective answers are impossible, as well as unwise. I can offer only some subjective observations on the consequential impact of the globalization of capital and capitalism on the global preference for democracy.

The financial structures inseparable from capitalism on a world scale are not democratic. Central banks, for example, are secret, élitist, and authoritarian institutions – but necessary for the safe functioning of financial markets and transactions. The shift of power from governments (democratic or not) to markets is a derogation of popular power. The fact that among governments the most powerful in matters of money and finance is the United States, and the United States counts politically as a democracy, does not alter this derogation of popular power over the economy. Not only is the US Congress unconcerned over financial issues, as it is over trade or employment, even when it is concerned, its decisions are taken in response to the perceived interests of the United States, and its short-term interests at that. The impotence of the developing countries, through the United Nations or any other multilateral organization, to reform or to moderate in any substantial way the arrangements made by the United States and its affluent allies concerning money and finance can only suggest to us the very strict limits on the expression of world opinion on matters central to the capitalist system. History, unfortunately, suggests that the power of bankers and financial markets is seldom checked until *after* a financial crash.

Notes

1. I am indebted to Soichi Enkyo of the Bank of Tokyo for this important distinction. See Enkyo (1990).
2. A key move by the US authorities in 1975, for instance, was the deregulation of fixed commissions for stockbrokers buying or selling shares for their clients.
3. It was indeed some time before expert observers – notably Paul Einzig, Jacques Polak, and Ed Bernstein – even took note of its existence. See Strange (1976).
4. *The Economist* World Banking Survey, 2 May 1992, pp. 10–11.
5. Ibid. The pessimistic remark quoted was by Robert Litan.
6. Quoted by *The Economist*, op. cit.
7. On this point, see also Aglietta (1990).
8. See successive issues of the GATT *Annual Report on International Trade* for the statistical evidence for this statement. The rather large literature on third world debt also tells the same story (e.g. Nunnenkamp, 1985; Moffitt, 1983; Congdon, 1988, and many others).

9. The basic argument about the reasons why the system is rather more vulnerable than most people realize is set out in Strange (1986).
10. There is an ample literature on the subject. Shorter and more accessible titles are Tew (1988), Cohen (1977), Walter (1991), Holm (1991).
11. In the 1950s, in fact, the IMF's Executive Board changed this rule to allow drawings to be made in respect of deficits on *capital* account as well. This was done on the initiative of the United States to help Britain.
12. See Strange (1970). The term was first used then in a discussion of the declining role of sterling in world finance.
13. A Concordat was the name usually given to agreements between a state and a non-state institution, like the 1929 agreement between Mussolini and the Catholic Church in Italy.
14. For an exposition of why political economists should address these questions, and how such an approach differs from that of conventional international relations, which emphasize the importance of international order, while conventional liberal economics emphasizes the importance of wealth and the efficient allocation of resources to produce it, see *States and Markets* (1988), chaps. 1 and 2.

Bibliography

Aglietta, M. (1990) "Savings, Financial Innovations and Growth." Brussels: Centre for European Policy Studies.

Cohen, B. (1977) *Organizing the World's Money: The Political Economy of International Monetary Relations*. New York: Basic Books.

Congdon, T. (1988) *The Debt Threat: The Dangers of High Interest Rates for the World Economy*. Oxford: Blackwell.

De Cecco, M., ed. (1987) *Changing Money: Financial Innovation in Developed Countries*. Oxford: Blackwell.

Destler, I. M., and C. R. Henning (1989) *Dollar Politics: Exchange Rate Policymaking in the United States*. Washington, D.C.: Institute for International Economics.

Enkyo, S. (1990) "Financial Innovation in the US, UK and Japan." Unpublished thesis, University of London.

Frieden, J. (1987) *Banking on the World: The Politics of American International Finance*. New York: Harper & Row.

Funabashi, Y. (1988) *Managing the Dollar from the Plaza to the Louvre*. Washington, D.C.: Institute of Economics.

Holm, E. (1991) *Money and International Politics*. Copenhagen: Academic Press.

Kindleberger, C. (1978) *Manias, Panics and Crashes: A History of Financial Crises*. New York: Basic Books.

Marris, S. (1985) *Deficits and the Dollar: The World Economy at Risk*. Washington, D.C.: Institute for International Economics.

Moffitt, M. (1983) *The World's Money: International Banking from Bretton Woods to the Brink of Insolvency*. London: M. Joseph.

Nunnenkamp, P. (1985) *The International Debt Crisis of the Third World: Causes and Consequences*. Brighton: Wheatsheaf.

Parboni, R. (1980) *The Dollar and its Rivals*. Translated from Italian. London: Verso.

Strange, S. (1970) *Sterling and British Policy: A Political Study of an International Currency in Decline*. Oxford: Oxford University Press.

—— (1976) *International Monetary Relations*. Vol. 2 of *International Economic Relations in the Western World, 1959–1971*, ed. Andrew Shonfield. London: University of London Press for the Royal Institute of International Affairs.

—— (1986) *Casino Capitalism*. Oxford: Blackwell.

—— (1988) *States and Markets: An Introduction to International Political Economy*. London: Pinter.

Tew, B. (1988) *The Evolution of the International Monetary System 1945–1986*. 4th edn. London: Hutchinson.

Triffin, Robert (1991) *IMS – International Monetary System – or Scandal?* Jean Monnet Chair Lecture, 1991. Florence, Italy: European University Institute.

Volcker, P., and T. Gyoten (1992) *Changing Fortunes: The World's Money and the Threat to American Leadership*. New York: Times Books.

Walter, A. (1991) *World Power and World Money: The Role of Hegemony and International Monetary Order*. London: Wheatsheaf.

9

Changing global finance structures: The impact on the Philippines

Leonor M. Briones and Aileen An. R. Zosa

Introduction

About a decade after the debt crisis exploded in 1982, the international finance community has already weathered its most crucial period. The commercial banks have effectively reduced their massive exposure to third world debt. Debt reduction schemes, supported by resources from multilateral and bilateral institutions, have been continuously applied to commercial bank debt. Debt restructuring and rescheduling of official and private debts were negotiated under the Paris Club and Bank Advisory Committees. New money packages were hammered out after sometimes long-drawn-out negotiations. Stabilization and adjustment programmes overseen by the International Monetary Fund (IMF) and the World Bank served as the economic framework towards resolving the economic and financial crises that hit the international community in 1982.

From the point of view of the creditors and donors – the banks, foreign donor governments, and multilateral institutions – the worst of the financial and debt crises are over. Global finance has already adjusted; the banks' profit and loss statements refurbished; their books insulated from further risks. Third world debt jitters have ceased to hog the limelight in global finance. Interest and attention

250

have shifted to development assistance to Russia and the new democracies in Europe like Poland and Germany. The end of the Cold War signalled a policy shift from propping up democratic governments in strategic areas in Asia and Latin America as a countervailing force against communism/socialism to nurturing the growth of the new democracies in Russia and Europe.

Correspondingly, global finance is refocused towards trade initiatives, investment opportunities, and other forms of economic cooperation with Russia and Europe. The opening up of new trade and investment frontiers and the trade implications of a one-Europe movement are the current concerns of Western finance.

Underlying United States–Japan relations are these three basic issues in global finance: development assistance, trade, and investments. In the race to gain or strengthen footholds in new and promising areas, global finance has channelled its efforts towards these areas.

This shift, as seen from the vantage point of a third world debtor like the Philippines, does not offer a solution to its development problem. In the first place, the debt crisis may have been eased from the viewpoint of the creditors but it remains as real and burdensome for third world debtors as it was in 1982. The debt burden constricts growth in developing countries, more so now when debt service continues to exert competing claims on resources while foreign financing for development projects has slowed down. Furthermore, adjustment and stabilization programmes have adversely affected economic development and caused more poverty in debtor nations.

Thus, after the Baker Plan and the Brady Initiative, the debt crisis is far from over for the third world debtors. Starting in 1984, net transfers on long-term lending (i.e. net availments/amortization on long-term debt less actual interest payments) have been negative for indebted countries. During the late 1980s, negative resource transfers reached US$50 billion annually – the debtors paying more than they received in terms of loans and development assistance.

The outcome of these trends in global finance is the widening of the gap between the North and the South in terms of growth, incomes, and overall levels of development. The growth in size, the innovations in technology in international finance, and its greater reach to national markets have not worked to the benefit of struggling/developing economies. The vulnerability of these economies to external factors has even been heightened. The dependency relationship has remained, if it has not been exacerbated.

Moreover, the drive towards increasing assistance to and trade with Russia, Poland, and other budding democracies in Europe reduces the resources and opportunities available to heavily indebted third world countries. With commercial banks wary of providing more new money, the sphere for official development assistance from the United States, Japan, and other developed nations has widened, spreading available resources thinly among the long-suffering debtor nations as new democracies compete for these scarce resources. The political influence and motives in diverting resources to these new democracies are more compelling than the development needs of third world debtor nations like the Philippines. This significant shift in global finance needs to be recognized and its implications faced in the emerging international order and finance structure. Although the creation of credit enables certain national markets to grow and be more prosperous, such availability of credit has so far failed to reach or has so far made less impact on those debt-ridden economies, primarily because either credit is not made available to them in sufficient amounts or credit is available at intolerably high costs. Thus, the creation of credit cannot be identified as an engine of growth in these economies.

Coverage of the paper

This paper dwells on the social and economic implications for the Philippines of global finance structure and its shifts. Since the most pervasive effects of global finance on the Philippines are on its external debt, the focus will be on the changing structure and effects of the Philippine external debt. Shifts in global finance are reflected almost immediately in the structure of and approaches to the external debt.

As one of the many third world debtors, Philippine debt strategies faithfully follow directions set by trends in global finance. Although it is most affected by changes in global finance structure, the Philippines is not significant enough to influence the course of events in the world financial environment. Like many small, open and highly indebted economies, the Philippines is vulnerable to external forces but cannot, on its own, chart or influence policies and directions set by international financial institutions, foreign governments, and other players in the financial, banking, and monetary system. In fact, it is subject to changing directions in global finance to the extent that its growth and economic development depend on whether world conditions are conducive or responsive to its needs and problems.

Other variables in global finance like trade and investment also impact on Philippine trade and investment. It must, however, be stressed that trade and investment conditions in the Philippines cannot be detached from their relationship with the external debt. Trends in trade, for example, mirror trends in the external debt primarily because the external debt or foreign financing are used to close the country's financing gap brought about by import-dependence and a large debt service burden.

Likewise, investments in the Philippines – both foreign and local – depend to a great extent on the external debt. Foreign resources coming into the country in the form of foreign loans and assistance partly determine whether investments will be forthcoming or not. Under a debt–equity conversion programme, investments are linked to the external debt. Also, investments in the Philippines have to be induced by closing the external financing gap through compensatory or balance-of-payments loans with the International Monetary Fund and bilateral creditors.

Thus, the impact of the global finance structure on the Philippines can best be illustrated by an analysis of the Philippine external debt. The effect of the external debt pervades every aspect of economic activity in the Philippines. Monetary and fiscal policies hinge on the external debt strategy adopted by the country's economic and financial managers. The resulting monetary and fiscal policies affect various sectors in the Philippines in varying degrees. Whereas some sectors or segments benefit from the debt strategies so far implemented by the government, other sectors, larger but less able to influence decisions, bear the burden. The external debt thus remains a limiting factor on growth and development in the Philippines, particularly growth that is equitable and of the kind that reduces the gap between the rich and the poor, between the urban and the rural sectors, between management and labour, between the upper 10 per cent of the income ladder and the rest of the population.

Trends in the Philippine external debt

Growth trends

For more than two decades, external debt accumulation in the Philippines has been characterized by an accelerating trend. These are monetary and non-monetary liabilities incurred by both the public and the private sector from foreign entities such as commercial

Table 9.1 **The Philippine external debt, 1970–1991**

Year	Level ($M)	Growth
1970	2,297	282.83
1971	2,393	4.18
1972	2,732	14.17
1973	2,886	5.64
1974	3,755	30.11
1975	4,939	31.53
1976	6,768	37.03
1977	8,069	19.22
1978	10,694	32.53
1979	13,352	24.86
1980	17,252	29.21
1981	20,893	21.10
1982	24,677	18.11
1983	24,816	0.56
1984	25,418	2.43
1985	26,252	3.28
1986	28,256	7.63
1987	28,649	1.39
1988	27,915	−2.56
1989	27,616	−1.07
1990	28,535	3.33
1991[a]	28,799	0.93

Source: Basic data provided by the central bank of the Philippines.
a. As of end July 1991.

banks, multilateral organizations, the International Monetary Fund, the private bond market, foreign government and bilateral agencies, and other foreign institutions.

The Philippine external debt increased almost ninefold between 1972 and 1982 (see table 9.1). This illustrates the policy of development financing during the period – a policy where development projects were financed by borrowings from external sources, particularly from the international financial system, which was awash with recycled petrodollars.

It is important to point out that massive development financing in developing countries was facilitated by the trend in global finance during that period. Transnational banking and the transnationalization of debt through export credits and loan packages enabled developing countries to gain access to world credit markets. Investment and international financial resources flowed into their economies. Unfortunately, global finance innovations also facilitated the outflow of these resources in larger amounts through capital flight, which resulted from the unsettling political and social events prevailing at the time. The outcome was the 1983 debt crisis where debtor economies like the Philippines had to declare a series of moratoria on debt service payments starting in 1983.

Even after the debt crisis, the Philippine external debt continued to rise. This was accounted for mainly by net availment of foreign loans, foreign exchange fluctuations, and capitalized interest on debt service payments after the debt reschedulings following the moratoria (see table 9.2).

Again, shifts in the international financial and monetary systems played a major role in the structure of the Philippine external debt. With the capitalization of unpaid interest after the moratoria, debt stocks rose and correspondingly bloated debt service payments. This necessitated the need for more loans and financial assistance, which the international financial community provided at increasingly higher costs – financially, economically, and politically. The access enjoyed by developing countries to Eurocurrency credit markets in the 1970s and early 1980s made these debtor nations more vulnerable to foreign exchange fluctuations. The volatile currency system and the unstable financial markets following the international debt crisis exerted upward pressure on developing country debt through revaluation adjustments that had to be undertaken on foreign obligations denominated in currencies other than the US dollar. Appreciation of these currencies against the dollar increased the dollar values of outstanding external debts and the corresponding debt service payments.

In the second half of the 1980s, debt reduction schemes were initiated. These were offset, however, by larger net availments as more foreign loans were needed to fuel development and to raise resources, primarily for debt buy-backs and other debt reduction schemes. Current projections show that Philippine debt stocks will continue to rise with no relief in sight.

Debtor trends

The Philippine external debt consists mainly of two types of debtors: the public and the private sector. The public sector includes mainly the national government, the government-owned or controlled corporations, and the central bank.

Private sector external debt was traditionally larger than the public sector debt before 1972. However, the public sector share steadily in-

Table 9.2 **Changes in the Philippine external debt, 28 February 1986 to 30 September 1990 (M$ million)**

	28 Feb 1986	31 December			
		1986	1987	1988	1989
Opening balance	26,342	28,256	28,649	27,915	27,616
Add/deduct transactions for the year:					
1. Regular transactions – Net availment (Net repayment)	941	(124)	411	986	1,729
2. Audit adjustments OA/DA credits	(625)		(194)		
3. Debt reductions – through:	(3)	(316)	(931)	(487)	(1,658)
a. Debt equity conversions	(3)	(259)	(648)	(91)	(92)
b. Debt for debt swap				(76)	(65)
c. Debt for asset swap			(108)	(70)	(112)
d. Debt for note swap				(132)	(2)
e. Debt buy-back					(1,325)
f. Peso prepayment		(57)	(175)	(118)	(51)
g. Offset against placement					(11)
4. Assignment of credits to FCDU		(61)	(53)	(46)	(93)
5. Capitalized interest of restructured debt	208	195	127		510
6. Adjustment for foreign exchange rate fluctuations	1,393	699	(94)	(752)	594
Total additions/ (deductions)	1,914	393	(734)	(299)	1,082
Closing balance	28,256	28,649	27,915	27,616	28,698
	31/12/86	31/12/87	31/12/88	31/12/89	30/09/90

Source: Central bank of the Philippines.

creased such that it started to account for the majority of the Philippine external debt (see table 9.3). This reflected the prevailing policy during the Marcos years whereby the government appropriated for itself resources tapped from foreign sources in the name of economic development. In the course of the public sector borrowing binge, public sector bureaucrats shared in its benefits. As more financial re-

Table 9.3 **External debt outstanding of the public sector, 1965–1991 (as of year-end)**

Year	Amount (US$ bn)	% of total external debt
1965	0.36	59.8
1970	1.07	49.9
1975	1.98	52.1
1980	6.77	53.3
1983	16.73	67.4
1984	17.55	69.0
1985	19.12	69.0
1986	21.83	77.2
1987	22.75	79.4
1988	22.67	81.2
1989	22.22	80.5
1991[a]	23.07	80.2

Source: Central bank of the Philippines.
a. as of July.

sources were placed in the hands of government officials, economic and political power were consolidated in this new bloc in the national spectrum. Furthermore, this new bloc collaborated with the private sector, traditional as well as the new financial élites, in conduiting or re-lending the proceeds of external debt to these specific segments of the private sector.

The public sector share continued to accelerate in the 1980s and 1990s. The national government increasingly accounted for public sector obligations as the external liabilities of the Philippine National Bank (PNB), the Development Bank of the Philippines (DBP), and the Philippine Nuclear Power Plant (PNPP) were assumed by the national government. These external liabilities consisted of publicly guaranteed private loans, the majority of which were behest loans or loans granted by government financial institutions to the private sector that did not follow or comply with the appropriate banking or financial criteria or procedures. These loans offered meagre benefits to the people as they were vehicles of transferring public resources to private hands.

Thus, the Philippine external debt is the source as well as the consequence of the unequal structure of economic power in the country. Using resources made available by international finance, the local governing élite spawned underdevelopment and maintained its dominant relationship over other sectors of society. As the public sector

257

continues to service the debt from the national budget, the inequitable relationship between the haves and have-nots in the country is sustained. The benefits of the debt have long been enjoyed by the governing and favoured élite, and they are still reaping the benefits of the current debt management strategy. The masses, on the other hand, bear the burden of debt service through expenditure cuts in economic and social welfare services in the national budget.

Creditor trends

The Philippines' major creditors include private commercial banks and financial institutions and official creditors, consisting of multilateral and bilateral (including export credit) agencies and foreign governments.

Foreign commercial creditors have played a major role in the Philippine external debt through their lending policies since the 1970s (see table 9.4). In 1983, when the debt crisis exploded, the Philippine external debt was largely sourced from private financial institutions, primarily the commercial banks. The terms of the debt were then commercial in nature; hence its effects and implications were viewed as commercial transactions.

Official creditors were mostly multilateral institutions like the World Bank (WB), the Asian Development Bank (ADB), and the International Monetary Fund (IMF). The remaining creditors were bilateral sources, the biggest of which were Japan, the United States, and export credit agencies.

At the height of debt-financed development in developing countries, the availability of international credit created a bias towards massive infrastructure and development projects. Investments powered growth in these countries. In the middle of this growth were the international contractors and private suppliers who benefited hugely from overseas contracts and infrastructure projects. With the financing facilities provided by the export credit agencies and the commercial banks, large transnational companies and contractors increasingly focused their efforts on lucrative contracts in third world countries like the Philippines.

The share of private/commercial creditors was gradually reduced as a response to the international financial crisis. The commercial banks, in particular, sought to reduce their exposure to the Philippines as part of a general strategy and reaction to the world debt crisis. Throughout the period of instability and high risk in the inter-

Table 9.4 **The Philippine external debt by type of creditors, 1983–1988 (as of end-December 1988, in US\$ million)**

Creditors	1983	1984	1985	1986	1987	1988
A. Official						
1. Multilateral	3,996	4,090	4,486	4,688	5,033	5,069
a. WB	2,041	2,215	2,256	2,297	2,454	2,526
b. IMF	1,166	973	1,232	1,336	1,342	1,171
c. ADB	693	799	885	943	1,097	1,228
d. Others	96	103	113	112	140	144
% of total	(16.10)	(16.09)	(17.09)	(16.59)	(17.57)	(18.16)
2. Bilateral	2,138	2,276	2,860	3,925	5,203	6,509
a. Japan	841	914	1,273	1,769	2,487	3,049
b. USA	415	454	561	574	579	669
c. Export credit agencies	605	656	786	1,332	1,828	2,398
d. Others	277	252	240	250	309	393
% of total	(8.61)	(8.95)	(10.89)	(13.89)	(18.16)	(23.32)
B. Private						
1. Banks	14,671	14,721	14,474	15,356	14,824	13,245
% of total	(59.12)	(57.92)	(55.13)	(54.35)	(51.74)	(47.45)
2. Suppliers' credit	2,855	3,103	3,264	3,085	2,355	2,111
% of total	(11.51)	(12.21)	(12.43)	(10.92)	(8.22)	(7.56)
3. Financial institutions	1,015	1,089	795	828	390	396
% of total	(4.09)	(4.28)	(3.03)	(2.93)	(1.36)	(1.42)
4. Others	141	139	373	374	844	585
% of total	(0.57)	(0.55)	(1.42)	(1.32)	(2.95)	(2.10)
Total	24,816	25,418	26,252	28,256	28,649	27,915

Source: Financial Plan Data Centre, the central bank of the Philippines.

national financial markets, the global objective was to preserve the system through continuous debt service and restructuring. In effect, the income streams of private commercial creditors have been protected and all efforts were taken to assure continuity of debt service to these creditors.

Consequently, the multilateral and bilateral creditors increased their lending to the Philippines, expanding their share to a majority. This brought about a changing facet in the structure and character of the Philippine external debt. Rather than debt transactions being of a commercial nature, the debtor is now faced with a different set of conditionalities. Economic and structural adjustments in trade and monetary matters are made conditions for multilateral lending, while political and strategic factors determine bilateral assistance. The meagre commercial bank exposure to the Philippine debt was limited to short-term trade facilities and lending in the form of non-restructurable new money bonds. This shift reflected the prevailing trend in global finance. Although the result of these events led to the greater integration of national economies in the global economy, it is doubtful whether the debtor nations were able to capture the benefits of this international order.

Debt service trends

Philippine debt service – interest plus principal repayments – exhibited an accelerating trend, especially in the 1980s. Interest payments constituted a major share of debt service. It is important to stress that debt service payments accelerated because interest and principal payments rose steeply. However, interest payments increased faster than principal payments during the period. This was largely the result of the high interest rates prevailing during that period, which affected loans carrying floating interest rates. LIBOR (London Inter-bank Offered Rates) averaged 7.5 per cent between 1970 and 1975 and 9.3 per cent between 1976 and 1980. Largely owing to the Mexican default in 1982, the LIBOR average rose to 11.8 per cent from 1981 to 1985 as global finance sought to cope with the prevailing instability and uncertainty.

In 1986, as the international financial system began to recover and LIBOR fell to 6 per cent, interest payments correspondingly fell as a proportion of debt service. This is not to say that interest payments were reduced. On the contrary, interest payments still increased. But then principal repayments increased faster after 1986 as commercial banks sought to reduce their exposure to third world debt through various debt reduction and refinancing schemes.

As a percentage of Philippine exports of goods and services, debt service ranged from over 20 per cent to almost 40 per cent. This illustrates the constraining effects of debt service on growth. Philippine exports and the country's productive capacity cannot keep pace with a heavy debt service burden.

As the international financial system struggled to ensure continuous debt service, the overall effect was the emphasis by debtor nations on activities that promote the generation of foreign exchange. Export promotion and trade reforms were given high priority.

In the Philippines, various tax and import incentives were accorded to exporters. Labour-intensive exports were also supported as wages were depressed or frozen under a series of stabilization programmes. Labour export was even encouraged, as remittances by overseas contract workers helped ease the need for foreign exchange to pay debt obligations. Every effort was made to sustain, if not enhance, the country's comparative advantage in various export products. While new tax measures primarily hit fixed-income earners, taxes on exports as well as taxes and tariffs on imports used for export production were lifted. Aside from the foreign exchange windfall on account of the series of currency devaluations succeeding the debt crisis, the export sector enjoyed the benefits of the government's thrust to enhance potentials for foreign exchange earnings.

Net resource transfer

Net resource transfer measures the net flow of resources in a debtor–creditor relationship. This indicator consists of net availment/amortization made by the debtor to creditors plus the interest payments on outstanding loans and credits. Thus, net resource transfer determines who benefits more from a relationship and by how much.

From 1986 to 1990, the Philippines' net resource transfer with its creditors was negative (see table 9.5). In other words, the Philippines paid more in interest and principal payments than it received in loan availments. It must be noted that, even when net principal availments were positive, this was more than offset by interest payments.

The negative net resource transfer to the Philippines is largely accounted for by the banks and financial institutions and, to a lesser degree, the multilateral institutions. The bilateral creditors, mostly official development assistance (ODA) donors, showed positive net transfers. It is clear that the debt management strategy adopted by the international financial community favoured the banks at the expense of socio-economic and political stability in debtor countries.

The impact of the global finance structure on the Philippine external debt

The shift to official development assistance from commercial bank lending

The spate of commercial bank lending and suppliers' credits in the 1970s induced third world governments to undertake development

Table 9.5   **Net resource transfers, 1986 – September 1991ᵃ (US$ million)**

Particulars	1986	1987	1988	1989	1990	Jan.–Sep. 1991ᵇ
Total	−1,341	−1,836	−1,923	−1,396	−1,036	−324
Principal, net	747	271	236	1,015	1,118	1,232
Interest	−2,088	−2,107	−2,159	−2,411	−2,154	−1,556
Banks and FIs	−826	−1,222	−1,079	−1,448	−1,129	−495
Principal, net	525	−37	−9	−65	−105	110
Interest	−1,351	−1,185	−1,070	−1,383	−1,024	−605
Multilateral	−248	−476	−542	−48	−290	−47
Principal, net	127	−10	−13	443	273	425
Interest	−375	−466	−529	−491	−563	−472
Bilateral	93	263	91	229	378	229
Principal, net	325	570	566	710	878	633
Interest	−232	−307	−475	−481	−500	−404
Others	−360	−401	−393	−129	5	−11
Principal, net	−230	−252	−308	−73	72	64
Interest	−130	−149	−85	−56	−67	−75
% Distribution						
Total	100.00	100.00	100.00	100.00	100.00	100.00
Banks and FIs	61.60	66.56	56.11	103.72	108.98	152.78
Multilateral	18.49	25.93	28.19	3.44	27.99	14.51
Bilateral	−6.94	−14.32	−4.73	−16.40	−36.49	−70.68
Others	26.85	21.84	20.44	9.24	−0.48	3.40

Memo item:	
Average %	1986–Sep. 1991
Banks and FIs	91.62
Multilateral	19.76
Bilateral	−24.93
Others	13.55

Source: Central bank of the Philippines.
a. After rescheduling of principal payments.
b. Preliminary.

projects through these financing schemes. The result was an acceleration of public sector debt sourced from private financial institutions under commercial terms.

The 1982 world debt and financial crises saw a literal drying up of voluntary lending from the commercial banks. As the commercial banks sought to reduce their exposure to developing country debt, debtor governments assumed private sector liabilities, converting them to public sector debts. Moreover, official creditors – the multilateral institutions, foreign governments, and bilateral agencies – took over the role of providing development funds.

This is borne out by the fact that, since 1980, the long-term debt of developing countries to official creditors more than tripled. In the first half of the 1980s, official lending grew *pari passu* with private lending. After end-1984, the share of official creditors in total debt rose to 46 per cent of the total in 1990 (from 32 per cent in 1984).

This was exactly the trend in the Philippine external debt during the period. The impact was adverse. The bunching up of maturities on commercial loans led to a series of moratoria on debt service. Principal and interest payments grew intolerable even as their magnitudes continued to rise.

In response to the perceived need for stabilization and adjustment, the multilateral and bilateral creditors imposed a set of conditionalities and policy programmes in exchange for official development assistance (ODA), financing facilities, and rescheduling packages. The impact of these developments is the expanded role of multilaterals and bilaterals in the economic and political underpinnings of the debtor countries.

Furthermore, the availability of ODA became more and more subject to political conditions and expediency as perceived by the donor governments. In effect, obtaining foreign funds depends largely on maintaining close alliances and political/strategic alignments with foreign donor governments. Compelling political developments take precedence over the real need of debtors for foreign assistance.

As in the cancellation of 50 per cent of Poland's US$33 billion external debt, debt relief is largely anchored on political and strategic considerations. With no significant bargaining leverage, the Philippines does not stand to be granted substantial debt relief. With the shift in global priorities from third world debtors to the new democracies in Russia and Europe, the Philippines will stand to lose much-needed development assistance. Competition for official loans and grants will grow stiffer and the remaining scarce resources cannot adequately meet the economic needs of third world debtors. Especially since the end of the Cold War, the Philippines does not command the strategicness that would afford it the opportunity for special treatment or an innovative approach to its debt problem.

Increasing debt stocks

As seen in the Philippine case, the debt stock has not really decreased. In fact, it has increased. The increase can be traced to for-

263

eign exchange revaluation. Even with little new money and new loans coming into the economy, the debt continues to rise. This trend is true for all developing country debtors precisely because of the effect of the global finance structure on external debt. In 1990, total developing country debt was estimated at US$1,341 billion, up from US$1,260 billion in 1987, 1988, and 1989. This was brought about by the dollar's depreciation against other major currencies, which increased the debt stock by 10 per cent, or the equivalent of US$46 billion.

Global finance is structured such that movements in the exchange rates literally dictate trends in debt stocks. Between end-1984 and end-1987, debt rose by US$309 billion (about 11 per cent annually), while between end-1987 and end-1989, debt actually declined slightly. The difference mainly lies in movements of the dollar *vis-à-vis* other major currencies.

The need for more loans to finance development in the third world

The sustained increase in the debt stock of developing countries from US$639 billion in 1980 to US$1,341 billion in 1990 indicates the addiction of developing nations to debt financing. Although funds from foreign sources have been reduced, demand is still strong in the face of large debt service requirements and global recession. This is seen in the net flows of debt for the different periods. From 1985 to 1987, debt flows to third world countries totalled US$77.9 billion; from 1988 to 1989, US$53.5 billion; and, in 1990, US$38.1 billion. Although it has been proved that debt creates problems in servicing and economic growth, the need to borrow again and in large amounts is more compelling as debtor nations struggle to survive.

The Philippines is no exception. To finance development, to service its huge external debt, and to close its financing gap due to a large import requirement, the Philippines' only recourse was to borrow. It had to seek IMF financing, in exchange for which it had to submit to a stringent economic stabilization programme. The policy conditionalities therein were also made the bases for official and commercial bank creditors to lend fresh funds to the Philippines. The economic and social costs of the stabilization programme will be discussed in the following sections.

264

Debt service and the elimination of arrears

The primary concern of global finance since the debt crisis started was (and still is) to ensure that debtor countries continue to service their debts. A necessary condition for the IMF's seal of good house-keeping and the inflow of fresh lending is the elimination of interest and principal arrears. This is to protect the creditors, mostly the commercial banks, from undue losses resulting from arrears on outstanding maturities. The purpose of the Baker Plan was the provision of fresh money so as to ensure continued debt service. The Baker Plan also provided a breathing space for commercial banks to strengthen themselves through higher reserves and capital increases. It did not, however, increase commercial banks' desire to resume lending on a significant scale.

Global finance's policy of favouring creditors and donor govern-ments and of reducing the risk to the international financial sys-tem had an adverse impact on debtors. The figures on net resource transfers are proof enough. The main beneficiaries of the present debt strategy so far have been the creditor banks and institutions. Abetted by the multilateral institutions, notably the IMF through adjustment and stabilization programmes, the central concern of bal-ancing the external accounts of the debtors, i.e. ensuring resources for the payment of debt service and imports, has been achieved at tremendous social and human costs in the debtor countries.

This global phenomenon is replicated in the Philippine case. As long as the Philippines persists in honouring and religiously servicing all its debts, net resource transfers with the commercial banks will be chronically negative. Furthermore, the beneficiaries of this debt man-agement strategy are those who have already benefited from the debt-financed development of the past. Those who bear the debt bur-den are the middle and lower classes of Philippine society – those least able to bear the burden.

The socio-economic impact of debt, debt service, and debt-induced adjustment programmes

Even as indebted countries persevered in faithful compliance with IMF and loan covenants, it is now conceded that they are no better off than in 1982 at the start of the global debt crisis.

The Philippine experience is a case in point. The national budget for fiscal year 1990 was virtually designed to adjust Philippine priorities to the requirements of global finance. It set debt service as a primary concern. The debt service burden was guaranteed by automatic appropriations. Thus, from a low 5.2 per cent average share of debt service in the national budget in 1972–1979, it rose to 17.1 per cent in 1980–1985, to a high of 42 per cent in 1986–1989. In the 1990s, it declined to about 30 per cent.

It may be argued that less than half of total debt service in the national budget goes to servicing the external debt, the greater share being that of domestic debt service. But an inextricable relationship exists between domestic and external debt in the Philippines. The government has resorted to domestic borrowings to compensate for foreign debt service. The flotation of high-yielding Treasury bills was also used as an instrument against foreign exchange speculation owing to low dollar reserves. Low dollar reserves are precisely caused by a burgeoning external financing gap due to heavy debt service and import-dependence.

Diverting expenditures to debt service implies heavy opportunity costs on other competing claims on the national budget, notably social services such as health, housing, and social welfare. Here, we focus on the financing of health programmes. First, it must be stressed that spending on health care has been quite low. National expenditures on health in 1985, for instance, were P14.5 billion, equivalent to 2.4 per cent of gross national product. This is less than half the World Health Organization-recommended 5 per cent of gross national product. In the 1990 budget, the share of health expenditures comprised around 3.3 per cent, as against more than 30 per cent for debt service. It was estimated that transferring just 5 per cent of the 1990 debt service allocation to health would more than double the budget of the Department of Health.

Over the years, the proportion of health expenditures in the national budget exhibited an inverse relationship with that of debt service. From 1972 to 1979, health expenditures accounted for 3.9 per cent of the national budget; from 1980 to 1985, the meagre share declined to 3.4 per cent. By 1986–1989, this had plunged further to 3.2 per cent.

Based on the most conservative estimate of Robin Broad and John Cavanagh in their dramatic study, "Repaying RP Debt Kills a Filipino Child Per Hour" (1992), at least 9,200 children could be saved in a year if the Philippines limited debt service payments to 20 per cent of export earnings. In other words, 25 children a day could be saved, or more than 1 child per hour.

The debt problems faced by third world nations are primarily the reason why resort to IMF facilities has been increasing. Unfortunately, the use of these facilities entails submitting to the IMF stabilization and adjustment "recommendations." As overseers of the creditors' interests in ensuring structural adjustment and stabilization in debtor nations, the IMF and World Bank have proved to be very efficient partners. From the viewpoint of the debtors, however, these programmes and packages mean more suffering and economic hardship.

Since the 1970s, the Philippines has been placed under more than 20 economic stabilization/adjustment programmes. Between 1971 and 1985, poverty rates shot up. Rural poverty climbed from 56 per cent in 1971 to 64 per cent in 1985. Urban poverty registered an even bigger increase, from 38 per cent to 56 per cent.

The impact of adjustment and stabilization programmes is well documented. A case study by Unicef on the Philippines (Cornia et al., 1988, pp. 45–47) documents severe reductions in household incomes and consumption, reductions in government expenditure, and corresponding social consequences such as deteriorating health, nutrition, and housing conditions as results of adjustment programmes. These findings are confirmed by local studies on the impact of debt, adjustment, and stabilization on the population. For example, Filomeno Sta. Ana III (1991) documents the damage inflicted on social services, particularly on health (see table 9.6). Through the debt crisis, the effect of global finance on the developing debtor countries has been to exacerbate economic and social inequities as well as to lower the overall quality of life in these countries.

Table 9.6 **Average percentage share of national government expenditures**

Period	Debt service	Health
1965–1972	6.4	5.2
1972–1979	5.2	3.9
1980–1985	17.1	3.4
1986–1989	42.0	3.2

Source: Sta. Ana (1991).

The changing face of commercial bank and private lending

Hardest hit by the debt crisis in its initial stages were the commercial banks and private lenders. This posed a big danger to global finance. Through a series of restructuring and rescheduling packages and a number of initiatives such as the Baker Plan and the Brady Initiative, the commercial banks have now recovered.

Lending to developing countries has ceased to be profitable as secondary market prices for developing country debt sharply declined. Provisions for loan losses attached to third world debt also discourage commercial bank lending. Moreover, high returns are being offered on other financial transactions. Industrial countries offer attractive interest rates to finance their own government deficits. "Junk" bonds and leveraged buy-outs offered banks high returns for a time. Direct lending is thus avoided by banks as much as possible. They have shifted their portfolio to fee-based activities and the "securitization" of loans.

The Philippines is no exception with respect to this strategy by the commercial banks. The 1989 new money package with the commercial banks consisted of new money bonds, which are non-restructurable and auctioned to participating banks. The 1991 new money package involved the "securitization" of the new money provided in the 1987 debt accord. Securitization also included the debt papers of the nuclear power plant, a loan project that is heavily tainted with fraud. The direct impact of securitization is to give the loans "a fresh start" in the books of the banks, thereby giving them a clean image. For debtor countries, securitization is in effect legitimizing fraud-tainted loans – loans that were entered into by corrupt administrations or governments all over the world, including that of the Philippines during martial law.

The current trend in world finance is for the banks to "get out" of developing country debt. The Brady Initiative, while paving the way for voluntary debt reduction schemes, offered the commercial banks an alternative to direct lending and a vehicle for reducing their exposure to developing country debt. For example, US banks, which have provided a substantial fraction of developing country loans, actually have fewer cross-border claims of all kinds now than they did in 1983. The Philippines, one of the first recipients of the Brady Initiative, undertook a debt buy-back operation on commercial bank debt to the tune of US$1.3 billion.

Voluntary debt reduction schemes

Global finance has come up with a menu of debt reduction schemes, mostly voluntary debt reduction of commercial bank debts. More popular are the debt–equity conversion programme, debt for asset swaps, debt buy-back, and debt-for-note/debt swap. Clearly the debt–equity conversion programme links the debt to investments in developing countries. It offers a high premium to foreign investors – the magnitude of the discount on the debt papers – in third world nations. The debt problems faced by these nations have thus become avenues for foreign investors to avail themselves of the resources and opportunities in these countries. Furthermore, the potential danger posed by this scheme to profit remittances continues to be unresolved.

Debt-for-asset swaps involve a direct swap of debt for assets to be privatized or assets held by the public sector. These privatization swaps dovetail the policy thrusts contained in the adjustment/stabilization packages of the IMF and World Bank.

Debt-for-note/debt swaps allow the purchase of debt papers at a discount in exchange for their face value in local currency in the form of domestic debt or notes. Schemes of this type have a highly inflationary effect, aside from increasing the burden of domestic debt service of the government.

The Philippines has reduced around $3.4 billion of external debt through the above-mentioned schemes, including its debt buy-back of US$1.3 billion. It is important to stress that, although these voluntary debt reduction schemes may ease cashflow payments, they are clearly inadequate to reduce overall debt stocks. Furthermore, these schemes are expensive and require foreign exchange resources to implement. For example, the cash buy-back of US$1.3 billion (which involved purchasing the debt papers at 50 cents in the dollar) had to be supported by an official loan of US$650 million from multilateral and bilateral creditors as the Philippines did not have the reserves to support the buy-back. Thus, what was gained in reduction of commercial bank debt was lost in terms of an increase in offical loans.

Furthermore, debt–equity programmes and other debt schemes also create undue inflationary pressure. These, too, link the debt problem to investments in debtor economies like the Philippines. As scarce capital deters local investors, the premium enjoyed by investors in debt–equity programmes and debt-for-note/debt programmes

favours foreign investors and accords them the opportunity of avail-
ing themselves of the assets/resources in the economy at "sweet-
heart" prices. The hold of transnationals in key industries and
sectors of the Philippine economy remains a burning issue. In the
medium and long term, the pressure on foreign exchange reserves
brought about by profit remittances will also have to be addressed.

The impact of official development assistance on the balance of payments

The shift in the character of the Philippine external debt from commercial and private lending to offical lending reflects the overall
trend with respect to developing country debt. In the Philippines,
official development assistance (ODA) has played an important part
in development finance. The Philippine Assistance Programme
(PAP) primarily consists of ODA loans and grants to finance public
sector projects on power, water, industry, infrastructure, agriculture,
science and technology, etc. The PAP secured a total of US$2.9 bil-
lion of pledges in 1989 and US$3.2 billion in 1991. It is noteworthy
that 40 per cent of ODA pledges came from Japan.

The issue of aid-tying, particularly with ODA loans and grants, has
to be resolved. A National Economic Development Agency study of
ODA loans and grants to the Philippines showed that flowback of
ODA loans and grants to the donor countries ranges from 30 cents
to 90 cents in the dollar depending on the type of assistance (Pante
and Reyes, 1989). This is traced to the practice of tying ODA utilization to the procurement of equipment and consultancy services from
the donor country or from a group of countries. Bidding requirements
and project specifications usually favour the contractors from donor
countries, especially if the projects are undertaken on a turnkey basis.

Thus, ODAs serve as a vehicle by which donor countries' trade and
investment are expanded. The impact on the balance of payments of
the debtor country is large. While the debtor copes with debt service,
it also has to face a large import bill as official debt piles up. Foreign
resources inflow to close the external financing gap goes out by way
of imports arising from ODA loans, over and above debt service on
these loans.

Fraud in international debt

Financing development projects in the third world involved the key
players in global finance – the commercial banks, the suppliers and

contractors, the multilateral and bilateral institutions. Until the 1980s, development finance was a lucrative business. With the support of debtor governments, lending to third world countries led to the transnationalization of capital and finance. Whether by design or not, however, one of the effects of this trend in global finance is also to transnationalize fraud on a massive scale.

In the Philippines, this is illustrated in the case of the nuclear power plant loan. Around US$2.2 billion in debt was incurred for the nuclear plant. Undertaken during the Marcos regime, the nuclear plant project was heavily tainted with fraud right from the start. As a result of its policy of honouring all its debts, the Philippines continues to service the loans of the plant, which was mothballed for technical and safety reasons. It pays US$300,000 a day in interest alone for a non-operational power plant.

Evidence points to collusion between the contractor (Westinghouse), former President Marcos and his cronies, and the commercial banks, particularly Citibank, the lead bank of the syndicated loan. This case represents fraud in the highest places in global finance.

Issues and problems

First, the shift in priorities of global finance from third world debt to budding democracies in Russia and Europe signals sharply reduced lending to other debtor economies. This will have a serious impact on the economic development of debtor countries.

Secondly, in the light of recent developments, new and innovative approaches to the debt problem have to be formulated. The debt crisis, as far as the debtor countries are concerned, remains as real and burdensome as ever. The search for lasting solutions is imperative.

Thirdly, the shift to ODA and official lending necessarily means a more "politicized" approach to the debt problem, in particular, and to global finance, in general. Global finance is structured in such a way that debt cannot be delinked from trade and investments, which, in turn, cannot be detached from compelling political and strategic motivations of developed countries and donor governments.

Fourthly, a new international economic order will have to recognize that the economic, social, and human costs of external debt also have serious implications for global finance. Thus, shifts in global finance will have to take into consideration its impact on the debtor economies in real and financial terms.

Fifthly, there is an as yet undeveloped/dormant yet potent area where developing countries could play a key role in global finance. The transnationalization of the debt also means the effect of different debt strategies adopted by debtor governments will be felt on a global scale.

Efforts at resolving the debt problem in Latin America, Asia, and Africa have generally been guided by policies set by international creditors. Rescheduling and restructuring agreements under the Paris Club and Bank Advisory Committees were undertaken on a case-to-case basis, or rather on a country-to-country basis. This enabled the North to maintain its unequal advantage and superior position over the South.

However, it has been recognized that the economies of highly indebted countries collectively form a substantial part of the world economy. As long as the debt constrains growth in these developing countries – with their vast natural resources and their larger trade/market potentials – developed countries will continue to feel the effects of the debt crisis in terms of limited export markets, unemployment, and unavailability of intermediate inputs to support their manufacturing activities. Thus, the current international debt strategy favours the financial class in developed countries and creates inequities with the production and service sectors in these countries. The negative impacts on peoples of the North may include taxpayers' money bailing out banks, a growth in unemployment, closures of manufacturing lines, an increase in drug abuse, etc.

This scenario should prompt governments of the South to explore the benefits of establishing a collective debt resolution strategy. Better terms could be realized in debt accords through the pooling of resources and negotiating leverages among debtor nations. Greater awareness and efforts could be generated to effect a more comprehensive and equitable resolution of the debt problem. The transnationalization of the adverse effects of debt calls for an integrated approach taking into account the needs of the South as well as those of the North. Furthermore, collective efforts by the developing countries need to be geared towards initiating and presenting to the North a new, sustainable, and equitable model of development that will best address the imbalance between North and South.

Sixthly, in the light of the obvious marginalization of debtor countries like the Philippines in the shifting structure of global finance, it is important to enhance the effective role of international and national non-governmental organizations (NGOs). NGOs play a critical role in helping the poor of many indebted countries survive the brutal onslaught of global finance policies, in particular stabilization programmes. They have gone beyond community development and grassroots organizations and are engaging national and international financial organizations in spirited policy debates. They have expanded their traditional roles to include policy advocacy and action.

The debt crisis should not be viewed only as a financial and technical issue. Rather, it is also a political and moral/social concern in a changing global order. If this approach is integrated into the debt strategy, then it is not only the creditor banks, financial and multilateral institutions, and the debtor country's financial and governing élite who are involved in decision-making. The role of NGOs and local communities in debtor countries comes into play. These forces exert pressure on the state for a more participatory and democratic political process in debt management. They are also instrumental in documenting the social and human costs of the debt in developing countries. Furthermore, they are actively involved in identifying illegal or fraudulent debts and waging campaigns against these debts, which never benefited the people but are still being paid by government through taxes and austerity measures. Social movements in debtor nations are effective mechanisms of expression and action for those who bear the burden of the debt.

At the same time, splits in the North are spearheaded by international NGOs and church-based organizations that reflect the position of social movements in the South. At present, link-ups of national and international NGOs like the European Network on Debt and Development (EURODAD) and the UK Debt Network are actively seeking avenues whereby the tension between debt and development can be resolved. These include, among others:

- the call for structural transformation in the financial, commercial, and technological relations between rich and poor;
- joint campaigns for the elimination of destructive structural adjustment conditionalities through the overall restructuring of multilateral agencies like the IMF and the World Bank;
- pressure on governments of the Group of Seven industrialized countries for greater reduction of the debt burden, cancellation of illegal and fraudulent debts, elimination of net resource transfers from South to North, better terms of trade for countries of the South; and
- the development of global policies that enhance transparency and accountability through freedom of access to information, public audits, and NGO participation and consultations on these policies.

It is therefore important further to strengthen national and international NGOs in order to increase the bargaining power of indebted countries that are marginalized and left out of global decisions.

Lastly, any campaign to strengthen the position of poor indebted countries like the Philippines *vis-à-vis* the colossal powers of the international financial institutions should include the mobilization of United Nations bodies. United Nations bodies like Unesco, Unicef, UNCTAD, and UNHCR have consistently criticized the solutions inflicted by international financial institutions upon hapless indebted countries. These UN bodies have documented in horrifying detail the human costs of these solutions.

Nevertheless, as shown by the experience of the Philippines, the views of these UN bodies are largely ignored. The heads of multilateral financial institutions like the World Bank and the IMF routinely go through the motions of requiring programmes for poverty alleviation and the like. However, in terms of actual stabilization programmes, the story has not changed. The specific programmes required by these institutions have the effect of exacerbating poverty levels.

Steps need to be undertaken to increase the effectiveness of these UN bodies so that they can prevail and put pressure on these imperturbable financial institutions. There is a clear need to go beyond expressions of concern and alarm on a global basis.

An important step in this area is the *Human Development Report* issued by the United Nations Development Programme (UNDP, 1992), which pointed out the limitations of debt service ratios as indices of progress. Instead, it offered alternative instruments for measuring development from those used by the IMF and World Bank. These are:

(1) a set of interrelated factors like income growth, income distribution, efficiency of the fiscal system, trade surplus, and domestic returns on investment; and
(2) the human development index, which combines life expectancy, educational attainment, and income indicators to give a composite measure of the overall quality of life.

Furthermore, the UNDP, in coordination with NGOs, has established the international climate for a "global debt bargain" primarily involving a major write-down of debts by official donors and commercial banks as well as by multilateral institutions.

The movements of UN agencies, international NGOs, and religious organizations, together with social movements waged by their counterparts in debtor countries, serve as a take-off point for governments of the North and South to initiate and develop new, sustainable, and equitable models of development. These will require major reforms in the structure of global finance and the international economic order.

References

Broad, Robin, and John Cavanagh (1992) "Repaying RP Debt Kills a Filipino Child per Hour." In: Emmanuel de Dios and Joel Rocamora, eds. *Of Bonds and Bondage.* Quezon City, Philippines: Transnational Institute, Philippine Centre for Policy Studies and Freedom from Debt Coalition.

Cornia, Giovanni Andrea, Richard Jolly, and Frances Stewart (1988) *Adjustment with a Human Face. Vol. 1: Protecting the Vulnerable and Promoting Growth.* Oxford: Clarendon Press.

Pante, Filologo, Jr., and Romeo Rayes (1989) "Japanese Assistance and U.S. Development Assistance to the Philippines: A Philippine Perspective." PIDS Working Paper No. 89-07, April.

Sta. Ana, Filomeno (1991) "The Philippine Foreign Debt and Its Social Impact." In: *Debt Reader.* Quezon City, Philippines: Freedom from Debt Coalition, pp. 59–70.

UNDP (1992) *Human Development Report.* New York: United Nations Development Programme and Oxford University Press.

10

The global restructuring of production and migration

James H. Mittelman

Large-scale transfers of population are a long historical process common to all regions of the world, but in recent decades the global restructuring of production has accentuated differences between receiving and sending countries, drawing massive imports of labour primarily from Asia, Africa, and Latin America to the advanced capitalist areas. Migratory flows from the South are increasingly diverse, for they include new "birds of passage" such as elements of North Africa's middle strata fearing Islamic resurgence and environmental refugees propelled by natural disasters. Meanwhile, the global restructuring of power has brought an influx of migrants from Eastern Europe and the former Soviet Union to Western Europe, North America, Israel, Australia, and elsewhere. Competition between immigrants from the South and the East reflects the interrelationship of the restructuring of global production and global power relations.

The changes in migration patterns are not merely matters of individual choice, but rather reveal structural factors beyond the control of individuals. The displacement of labour is best understood as a movement that both shapes and is constitutive of a restructuring of the global political economy.

Flows of human capital are linked to a hierarchical system of production and power centring on a global division of labour. While production becomes increasingly specialized and spatially dispersed, global society is creating a unified world economy. A consequence of this specialization within a single world economy is the redistribution of human capital. An area's position in the global division of labour and its forms of specialization establish terms for the exit and entry of migrant labour. Powered by technical change, the more dynamic economies act as magnets attracting mobile resources from their points of origin.[1] These interactions of course have profound implications for distribution, inequality, and social justice on a world scale.

The purposes here are to propose a framework for explaining the global restructuring of production and migration as well as to present a challenge for more exploratory research. I will first examine the concept of the division of labour as an organizing principle and then indicate levels of analysis and cross-cutting themes. The third section of this paper suggests relationships among structural factors and notes major trends. Next is a discussion of whether international regimes regulate migration, and the conclusion points the way toward a reformulation of liberal economic theory.

Divisions and redivisions of labour

Although the extensive movement of peoples from their homelands to other areas of work and settlement has been an enduring feature of world history since the 1500s, the patterns and scope of migration have changed dramatically. With the expansion of European capital from 1500 to 1815, peoples from the developed zones of northern and western Europe emigrated to the Americas and parts of Africa and Asia. Concurrent with colonizing migration was the expulsion of slaves, indentured workers, convicts, and new multiracial and multicultural societies, which formed a basis for global society tethered to the international division of labour.

The industrial revolution extended capital overseas, altering the supply of and demand for resources, including labour. The primary movements of population between 1815 and 1914 included 60 million Europeans leaving for the Americas, Oceania, and East and South Africa; about 10 million Russians settling in Siberia and Central Asia; 1 million southern Europeans going to North Africa; 12 million Chinese moving to East and Southern Asia; and 1.5 million Indians finding homes in South-East Asia, East Africa, and South

Africa. In the inter-war period, the depression and restrictive immigration policies substantially reduced flows of population. After 1945, however, international migration rapidly increased, especially from the South to the North, although movements within the South and within the North have remained significant.[2]

What is more, a large portion of South-to-South migration becomes South-to-North flows. Given both political and economic pressures, migrants (e.g. Salvadorans) leave home because of fear of violence and in search of economic well-being, reach a second country (say Mexico) where short-term jobs are available, and perceive better opportunities elsewhere (the United States). For migrants from countries such as Guyana or the Leeward Islands, locales in the South (e.g. the Virgin Islands) are merely stopovers as the newly arrived leapfrog from island to island along the Caribbean archipelago on the way north. There are also countries in the North (Italy and Austria) that serve as way stations for migrants from the South and the East. With the development of southern Europe, Italy, Spain, and Greece have become both transit areas and receiving countries.

Against this backdrop, a discussion of theoretical approaches to labour supply and the spatial reorganization of production necessarily begins with Smithian assumptions set forth in *An Inquiry into the Nature and Causes of the Wealth of Nations*.[3] Contrasting the isolated producer and modern industry, Adam Smith posited a subrational or non-utilitarian origin for specialization (but not its intensification) in a "propensity to truck and barter" innate in humankind. A novel form of specialization, modern industry separates the production process into compartments, each one performing a different task, with implications for rates of profit. In the market-place, buyers and sellers face each other in competitive relationships as autonomous entities. To the extent that these separated producers and buyers and sellers are identified with nations, the international division of labour refers to the specialization of a country in a particular trade or product – e.g. Portugal in wine and England in textiles. Hence, the international division of labour highlights a set of relationships associated with the exchange of goods produced by individual units, namely nations. As the old international division of labour evolved, a small number of industrial countries provided capital goods and consumer goods to exchange for the third world's primary products.

A different structure, however, emerged in the 1960s. Known as the new international division of labour, this structure involved the relocation of industry from the advanced to the underdeveloped countries as well as a marked growth in manufactured products exported from the third world as a percentage of total world exports of manufactured goods. Along with the closing down of plants in the advanced countries came the installation of subsidiaries abroad. Commodity production became increasingly fragmented so that components could be produced and assembled in the countries offering the most profitable combinations of capital and labour.

What makes this structure distinctive is the introduction of modern technologies in the third world and the incorporation of new groups of workers in the industrial labour market. In addition, investment in economic infrastructure, primarily transportation and communications, makes the site of production increasingly independent of geographical distance.[4] The advanced countries thus export manufacturing capital and import labour from the third world, causing wholesale transformations in the domestic divisions of labour.[5] Low-wage labour simultaneously flows to plants in the newly industrializing countries and, also, to the advanced countries to fill different roles or take unwanted jobs.

The concept of a new international division of labour advances knowledge by moving beyond an oversimplified dichotomy of industrialized countries exchanging their finished products for the third world's primary commodities. This construct provides an important angle for viewing the relations between developed and developing countries. However, it lacks the ability to explain the ways that the global political economy is continuing to change. In other words, it does not offer an interpretation of how that system might be transformed. What is wanting is an enlarged conception of multiple levels of analysis interacting with cross-cutting forces and movements within a globalized division of labour.

Levels of analysis

By globalization, I mean a compression of time–space relations. Transnational networks involving world factories, labour flows, lending facilities, communications, new knowledge and information technologies, and cultural norms bridge the boundedness of territorial states with increasing rapidity. Globalization thus delimits reciprocity among actors, the repercussions among their policies, the interpenetration of social forces, and the consequent redistribution of costs and benefits, usually unequally.[6] In the realm of production, some key indicators of globalization – all implying changing employment opportunities for migrants – are the structure and content of a country's manufacturing sector, its share of gross domestic product (GDP), export/GDP ratios, and the percentage of the labour force involved in specific roles in manufacturing and service industries. To identify points of intersection between globalized production and migration, one must explore the following levels without operationally separating theory from method:

(1) The global political economy may be conceived in a Braudelian manner as a system of interactions on a world scale. In other words, the object of study is not the whole world but those entities (individual and corporate) that interact with global structures. The French economic historian Fernand Braudel suggested that a number of "observation points" be identified for viewing history. Specifically, he posited that four axes be established corresponding to "social orders," hierarchy, time, and space. Along these axes, he proposed imagining divergent positions, such as those pertaining to different regions and spatial hierarchies.[7]

(2) In Braudel's sense, states are mapped with dotted-line borders, partly permeable, partly able to regulate transborder flows – a template superimposed on the global economy. In an era of globalization, states – and, more properly, the inter-state system – are not mere epiphenomena, for policies on migration do set conditions for exit and entry, however imperfectly enforced. Production is organized partly within borders and partly crossing borders in transnational flows. Similarly, migratory movements are partly within borders and partly across national frontiers.

(3) With the increase in demand for service sector employment, major world cities offer new opportunities, especially in "information occupations" and in low-wage jobs. The demand in strategic world cities for service employment attracts large concentrations of ethnic minorities as well as workers from such areas as the Caribbean and Mexico. In addition to the classic elements of economic promise and proximity, long-established West Indian and Hispanic communities in North American cities serve as magnets and facilitators, furnishing family ties, legal aid, and places to hide. With its depressed economies, and subject to the influence of tourism and satellite television from the United States, the Caribbean exports more of its people in percentage terms than does any other region. Such mini-states as St Kitts and Nevis, Grenada, and Belize send 1 or 2 per cent of their nationals

to the United States each year, essentially transferring all of their population growth to North American cities.[8]

(4) Macro-regions – the European Union (EU), the North American Free Trade Area (NAFTA), and Asia–Pacific – coordinate capital flows within a spatial unit but also provide access to the globalization process. The formation of macro-regions involves a vast enlargement in the size of the market, a weakening of extant political units, and a reduction in the full meaning of citizenship. Embedded in the state, citizenship is less meaningful because of the separation of citizenship and work. Labourers who live in their home country and work in another include border-crossers (e.g. residents of France with jobs in Switzerland) and computer-based home-workers linked to transnational production processes through electronic means. Macro-regions may thus be regarded as loose geographical units larger than a state with some political and cultural bonds, however varied, tenuous, and sometimes contentious. Although globalization of production is a homogenizing force, local cultures still provide focal points for identity as well as inspiration and sources of creativity (clothing styles, food, and toys) for the assembly line. Cultural boundaries also reinforce the distinctiveness of political and economic groupings.

(5) Subregional patterns enlarge the concept of proximity to encompass factors other than geographical distance. Indeed, historical legacies and economic forces can provide the propellants for the migration of industries, employment creation, and spillovers to other areas as well as demonstration effects. Hence, within the Association of South East Asian Nations (ASEAN), there is a move to link three nodes – the city-state of Singapore, Johore state in Peninsular Malaysia, and Indonesia's Riau Islands – in a Growth Triangle. This strategy of subregional integration seeks to take advantage of Singapore's highly skilled human capital and well-developed infrastructure, Johore's land and semi-skilled labour, and Riau's land and low-cost labour. The Singapore–Johore–Riau Growth Triangle is partly derived from the experience of the twinning of Hong Kong and Shenzhen. Also aimed at pulling subregional entities into a tighter web are the plans for twinning the city-states of Hong Kong and Singapore.

(6) Micro-regional patterns are evident within the boundedness of sovereign states. For example, Catalonia, Lombardy, and Quebec are relatively autonomous entities within the political juris-

diction of states. In addition, industrial districts form a mosaic of highly interdependent economic and technological forces, themselves embedded in a more encompassing network of transactions. The State Council of China, for example, has decided that micro-regions (i.e. provinces) will be national pace-setters for reform and thus serve as locomotives to power the economic growth of the country. It is deemed necessary to make micro-regional advances so that economic structures will form a "staircase pattern." In Guandong Province, Shenzhen is reputedly China's fastest-growing city and the largest of China's four special economic zones, designated environments driven by overseas capital and participation in the global division of labour. Cheap labour – and hence large-scale internal migration – is a crucial factor of production in Shenzhen's expanding import and export trade.[9]

Returning to Braudel's notion of viewing history simultaneously from a number of "observation points," each of which provides diverse shadings of the total picture, it is necessary to move to another position: themes that intersect the several levels of analysis. An approximation of the totality of globalized production and migration can then be obtained by combining the different levels and cross-cutting themes. To derive insights from this perspective, an outline of these themes must first be presented.

To link levels of analysis, commodity chains trace the physical movement of goods from the end of the production process to the sources. One begins with the final commodity and moves back to the initial stages of production. A number of nodes or operations are pivotal points in the production process: marketing, export, the production network, and the supply of raw materials. Commodity chains may also be understood as the totality of production relations. As an analytical tool, commodity chains direct attention to such variables as ownership of the means of production, firm size, concentration of industrial structures, labour cost and supply.[10] The implications of commodity chains for migration follow from the principle that ascent in the global division of labour correlates with increased value-added. Shifts in labour and capital intensity, different rates of industrialization, and upward or downward mobility among countries all shape changing employment patterns. Further, such shifts affect political stability, a key determinant in transnational firms' decisions about where to locate, invest, and hence create jobs.

Technological innovation is a social process linking knowledge and production. Technology is inextricably connected to all phases of movement up the value chain from labour-intensive to capital- and energy-intensive to technology-intensive processes in advanced countries; it is also integral to the devolution of labour-intensive, energy-intensive, and polluting operations to underdeveloped areas. Each phase of innovation entails job creation and loss, requiring diverse skills, incorporating new workers in the labour force, and driving others to search for different sources of employment.

In the early and mid-twentieth century, industrial organization in the United States and other Western countries centred on mass production and the assembly line staffed by semi-skilled workers who could easily be replaced. In the last decades of the twentieth century, the Fordist system of mass production and mass consumption has tended to give way to another structure. Post-Fordism entails a more flexible, fragmented, and decentralized system of production making use of a segmented and often geographically dispersed labour force. The new model is based on greater specialization – batch production in small firms linked through dense networks and niche marketing. Accompanying the movement from Fordism to post-Fordism is a shift from vertical integration of production to vertical disintegration, especially as enterprises seek to establish distinct niches. Fordism is not defunct but based in different sectors of production, namely in low-skill services such as fast food and in various types of labour-intensive processes, sometimes in the peripheral (or export) zones of industrial systems. Although there is vast organizational diversity and no single post-Fordist model, these two emphases draw varied groups of migrants, primarily unskilled and semi-skilled workers in the sectors dominated by Fordism and more defined skills in the post-Fordist sectors.

An integral part of this restructuring process is the weakening of trade unions based in the old Fordist industries. The strength of organized labour has clearly declined in the West, and workers are docile in some other regions, notably so in East Asia. However, this trend is not a universal phenomenon, as demonstrated by the militancy of trade unions in South Africa. Whereas capital is forming large unregulated markets, labour is less capable of transnational reorganization. Capital is increasingly globalized, but labour unions and the collective rights of workers still primarily delimit their reference point as the nation-state. The changing relations between capital and labour – the one clearly on the ascent and the other markedly defensive – are linked to the tension between the economic globalization trend and the Westphalian territorial mode of political organization. By condensing the time–space aspects of social relations, the globalization process transcends territorial states and redistributes the world's labour force. Yet, the varied immigration policies of states represent attempts by sovereign units to control flows of population, thus affirming the logic of the inter-state system. In specific contexts, the process of globalization and the principle of territory interlink differently, shifting in their impact.

Alternative sources of identity – e.g. gender, ethnicity, and religion – are more prominent among new and the more segmented elements of the labour force. Moreover, low-paid, segmented employment has developed in zones formerly considered as core economies. Inasmuch as the core is where core activities – high value-added operations – are spatially concentrated, the "peripheralization of the core" is evident in "putting out" in Manhattan and elsewhere. Migrant labour is prevalent in the Fordist sectors of the new production systems. The core–periphery concept, formerly used in a geographical sense, now requires rethinking in terms of social relations among groups engaged in the production process.

In response to the liberal economic globalization tendency, the balance of social forces on the ground is rapidly changing. The globalization of new social movements may challenge the evolving divisions of labour. Movements at the base can give impetus to change in state policies regarding population flows, in macro-regional practices concerning labour, and ultimately in the structure of the global workforce. It therefore becomes important to identify potential agents of transformation in diverse contexts. These may include pro-democracy forces, women's and youth associations, peasants' organizations, human rights advocates, environmentalists, and fundamentalists. One ought not to glamorize the emergence of these movements, for they are currently defensive and fragmented, a process reinforced by globalization. Moreover, the accountability of these movements is problematic: To whom are they responsible? Whom do they represent? How is their politically unelected leadership constituted? In short, these forces may be either elitist or populist, atavistic and divisive, or constructive and cohesive elements projecting a vision of an alternative order.

Interactions

In this analytical framework, there are exchanges among the different elements, exchanges that reflect a hierarchical ranking of power.

Some forms of technology flows take place within corporate, not geographical, space; technologies may be transferred within a corporation and are not the property of a "recipient" country. Capital flows to capital-abundant zones of the global economy, and labour follows the flow of capital. With what effect?

The World Bank and some liberal economists contend that labour mobility is a means of reducing income inequality world wide. The Bank argues that emigration helps to relieve population pressure, alleviates unemployment, funnels remittances to the country of origin, and may contribute to the diffusion of new ideas and technologies, either when skilled workers return home or through an exchange of information.[11] Seen from a more critical perspective, however, the benefits of migration have been distributed unequally, to the advantage of the already more fortunate receivers. The emigration of skilled personnel to countries where skilled labour is abundant and where incomes are high increases international inequality. The negative flow of human capital from sending countries saves receiving countries the cost of reproducing a sector of their labour force.[12]

Although the World Bank renders a valuable service by providing data on "net workers' remittances" by migrants' countries of origin,[13] remittances are not a substitute for development. With the most vulnerable groups (the young and elderly) at home, and a sizeable portion of the productive labour force overseas, the system of remitting payments deepens the dependence of some societies.[14] The question of the utilization of remittances turns not only on balance of payments, as the World Bank would have it, but also on whether these funds are invested in directly productive activities. Research on the actual use of remittances in various regions shows substantial savings and investment in housing, land purchase, consumer goods, and repayment of personal debts. Data indicate that the bulk of the spending is on consumer items and luxury imports, causing inflationary pressures. Only a small fraction goes toward productive activities.[15]

Quite clearly, a continuing brain drain from capital-poor zones deprives these zones of a large share of their investment in the social reproduction of labour. This implies the extraction of educational services, as in the movement of Jamaican and Filipina nurses to US and Canadian hospitals. The educated strata of disadvantaged zones can most easily migrate, but often they find only menial jobs in the more advanced zones. These strata can also prove to be better qualified by education and attitude for skilled employment in modern industry than are some of the semi-skilled indigenous workers, a tension that

285

may erupt in zones of immigration. However, when receiving countries shift their policies from favouring particular ethnic groups to emphasizing highly skilled immigrants, as did the United States and Canada, the result is not only a marked increase in the brain drain but also a corresponding upsurge of illegal migration, drawing semi-skilled along with unskilled workers. In this respect, a class analysis of migrants and the immigration policies of different states helps to explain the direction of flows of population. Typically, immigration policies include a system for recognizing professional qualifications, ease entry for groups such as physicians and engineers, and erect barriers to the free flow of unskilled labour.

Apart from the loss of skilled and semi-skilled labour, sending countries have long gained sustenance from the cheap labour of their citizens who are sojourners in receiving countries. Yet, migration can detract from a healthy workforce, an essential ingredient of development, by producing changes in sexual behaviour, often first encountered in the big city and labour camps. Away from their families and lacking female companionship, young men are exposed to homosexual practices as well as easy access to prostitutes and drugs. Migrants who have contracted AIDs return to rural communities and small towns at home and contribute to high infection rates in areas where until recently the virus had been unknown. The link between migration and AIDs, although evident, is clouded by stigma and denial.

All told, emigration accentuates the marginalization of zones primarily in the South: Sub-Saharan Africa, much of the Caribbean, and enclaves in other regions. With a population of over 400 million people and a GDP the size of that of Belgium (a country of 8 million people), Sub-Saharan Africa is hampered by costs of production that are too high in comparison with those of other regions. Sub-Saharan Africa's transportation costs are exorbitant, and its skilled and educated middle-level labour force is relatively small. Although the continent is integrated into global financial markets through debt structures, and notwithstanding the heavy involvement of aid agencies, Africa has not participated fully in the global manufacturing system that emerged in the last few decades and in the related expansion of export activities. Seeking to escape a marginalized existence, migrants are attracted by the growth poles of competitive participation in the global division of labour. Paid jobs in manufacturing or service industries in other parts of the world are preferred to the battle for survival, civil strife, or wars at home.

Added to this, flows of military aid and lending from international financial agencies and transnational banks to the poor countries tie the latter more closely into the economic mechanisms and structures of control of the global financial and productive systems. The obligations of debt service require these countries to impose austerity measures that fall most heavily on the socially vulnerable strata. Export-oriented development and structural adjustment policies deepen this pattern. The implementation of these policies often entails repression, which in turn produces a flow of political refugees. The distinction between political and economic refugees, used by receiving countries as a screening mechanism, obscures the fact that both categories of migrants have as their origin the same globalizing of production relations.

Although there are many types of voluntary and involuntary migrants (political refugees and asylum-seekers, environmental refugees, professionals, legal workers, undocumented workers, etc.), the lines of demarcation are increasingly blurred. The proximate causes of migration – civil unrest, ethnic and racial strife, and economic conflicts accompanied by marked inequality – are often combined. Determining causality requires a long view of the historical process and of a zone's political and economic role in the global division of labour. The key question is, how do local dynamics and globalized production merge and interpenetrate to shape migration patterns?

Although the answer to this question is historically contingent, a pertinent example of the interactions between local dynamics and globalized production is the expulsion of foreign workers from Nigeria in 1983. The history of Africa is replete with movements of population propelled by trade, conquest, slaving, natural disasters, and evangelization. The dispersion of Fulani-speaking peoples throughout the northern rim of West Africa is amply documented, as are the seasonal wanderings of herders.[16] In the post-colonial period, centres of industrial production attracted large-scale in-migration, with a substantial flow into Nigeria's oil fields and construction sites in the 1970s. Flush with foreign exchange earnings derived from the worldwide boom in oil prices, Nigeria sought to join the global manufacturing system by converting its new-found surpluses into export-oriented industrialization. Added to employment opportunities in manufacturing and petroleum industries, construction of the capital city of Abuja and the Kainji Dam served as magnets for both skilled and unskilled workers. Moreover, the establishment of universities and polytechnics in each state within Nigeria precipitated a brain drain of Ghanaian teachers eager to partake in Nigeria's prosperity.

287

When oil production dropped to 400,000 barrels in 1982, down from 2.3 million barrels in 1979, Nigerians felt the pinch of unemployment. Lagos came to regard non-citizens as competitors for jobs as well as a strain on the economy, and decided to retaliate for the 1969 expulsion of Nigerians from Ghana. In 1983, Nigeria ordered an estimated 2 million West Africans to leave the country within 14 days. The repatriation of foreign workers to Ghana, Togo, Burkina Faso, and Chad entailed a massive displacement of labour, enforced by inspections of households in search of defaulting aliens, and emergency reception centres to help stop the loss of life and ease the human suffering.[17]

As evident in West Africa and other parts of the world, regionalization today is not to be considered as a movement toward territorially enclosed autarchies as it was in the 1930s. Rather, it represents concentrations of political and economic power competing in the global political economy, with multiple interregional and intraregional flows of population. Heightened competition among and within regions, mediated by such micro-patterns as ethnic and family networks, accelerates cross-flows of migrants, as again seen in the case of West Africa.

Not only do West African professionals, traders, and unskilled workers seek employment in Europe and North America, but population transfers within a stratified regional division of labour reflect a hierarchy among countries and different rates of industrialization. Major migrant-sending countries in West Africa are Mali, Niger, Chad, and Burkina Faso, all located in the Sahel and characterized by low levels of industrial production, high rates of illiteracy, and weak infrastructure. These countries have experienced deforestation, recurrent drought, substantial population pressure on cultivated land, and agricultural stagnation aggravated by unequal land tenure systems and lack of employment opportunities in the industrial sector.

The main stream of intraregional labour migration is from Sahel West Africa to coastal West Africa, especially to the more prosperous countries of Côte d'Ivoire, Ghana, and Nigeria. Another stream of migration takes place within coastal West Africa, where farmworkers and industrial wage-earners originate in Liberia, Sierra Leone, and Ghana and head for centres of export-oriented production, predominantly Côte d'Ivoire and Nigeria.[18] The case of Ghana shows that some countries serve as areas of both origination and destination, making the distinction between sending and receiving countries an artificial one in the context of globalized production.

On the one hand, both globalization and regionalization weaken the state's ability to regulate the flow of labour across borders. The movement of undocumented workers between the United States and Mexico, for example, is almost unimpeded. On the other hand, the variation in migration policies and their consequences cannot be dismissed. The state's exclusive power to grant citizenship, order repatriation, and delimit the social and political rights of non-citizens in their territories could cause (or prevent) an international crisis.[19] There is marked variation in states' policies on asylum-seekers, family reunification, and access to nationality. The interactions between immigration policies and migration flows demonstrate both the diminution and continuing importance of state capacity.

The various spin-off effects of globalization in the context of migration and the restructuring of production include changing social structures and patterns of conflict, political instability, human rights achievements or abuses, and environmental impact. A marked consequence of globalized production is the feminization of labour in both old and new zones of economic development. From Asia's export-processing zones and Mexico's *maquiladora* programme (assembly plants as subsidiaries or subcontracting firms for the manufacture of export-oriented goods) to US factories, jobs increasingly take on characteristics traditionally used to define and justify female employment: finely tuned, light operations performed by docile labourers. Regardless of their levels of skill, women in the workforce encounter lower wages than those of their male counterparts and limited possibilities for promotion. The growth of precarious employment means repetitive tasks, temporary work, substandard safety, and inadequate health protection. Especially in the newer zones, the feminization of labour entails social dislocation that may be regarded in one sense as liberating for women in a strongly patriarchal context, but that invites exploitation and may leave them marginalized in their own community.

Regarded as important sources of flexible labour, women are becoming international migrants as often as men. The migration experience, while offering potential for mobility, does not necessarily provide women with an escape from subordination. Research shows that migrant enclaves reproduce social controls. It is the successor generation of migrant women – frequently treated as "second-generation foreigners," though many of them are born as citizens of their parents' countries of destination – that has the difficult task of coping with the interaction of different cultural values, norms, and attitudes. The offspring group also encounters barriers in securing

289

education and training. Of second-generation Turkish women in Germany, for example, only 21 per cent have sufficient education and training necessary for skilled work. Most of them follow their mothers into the lower strata of the labour force.[20]

Other women are left behind in the homeland. Many of them are placed in a situation of dependence on in-laws or a male relative, leading to seclusion to guard against improper behaviour and adding to a rash of psychological problems, in India known as the "Dubai syndrome": headaches, sleeplessness, loss of appetite, chest pains, fainting, or mock seizures.[21] In South East and East Asia, women, many of them Thai and Filipina, have been recruited to work in the sex industry, often in other countries and against their will. Primary clients are international businessmen and military personnel. States have taken an active part in promoting the sex industry through tourism, licensing, and international advertising.

The role of states is critical in mediating these processes, either hastening or retarding them. States respond to the pressures of internal social forces. They must also take account of the policies of other states that regulate migratory flows. Given that state boundaries are porous, many "illegal" immigrants may be present and tolerated within a state's political jurisdiction, performing work that some nationals no longer will do. These "illegal" immigrants are subject to rigorous control by internal police procedures and the ever-present threat of expulsion. Hence, EU countries have established a computer information centre in Strasbourg, France, to check if a foreign visitor is "wanted" or has been declared "undesirable" elsewhere. The Union members have approved setting up a law enforcement agency, Europol, to coordinate action between their police forces. The mechanisms of political control and surveillance of vulnerable segments of the labour force are a matter of increasing concern in terms of human rights.

The disposable labour force comprises workers employed on a transitory basis in one country, who can be repatriated when they are no longer required, thereby maintaining a high level of employment for national labour, who are the beneficiaries of the expandable–contractible character of a disposable labour reserve. Switzerland and the Gulf States practise a disposable labour policy. In the Gulf region, the ratio of foreign to total population has been the highest in the world, ranging from 23 per cent in Saudi Arabia to 76 per cent in the United Arab Emirates in 1980. As a percentage of the total labour force rather than of population, the proportion of foreign (i.e. temporary) workers has been even greater, reaching around 90 per cent in Qatar and the United Arab Emirates in the same year.[22] Countries in various regions are increasingly opting for "turnkey" projects: a contractor, sometimes the state (as in the People's Republic of China), recruits workers, sends them to enclaves in locales such as Botswana, and repatriates them on termination. A different type of example is South Africa, where both external and internal migrants are a disposable labour resource. The apartheid state used migration to foster ethnic segregation and labour segmentation.

Regulatory "regimes" versus Braudelian structures

The role of the state includes the formal and informal regulation of migrant labour within national borders as well as international and macro-regional regulation. Posing the question of regulation focuses attention on vital but understudied questions about "regimes": Are there manifest or latent regional and interregional "regimes" for migration? If so, what kinds of norms or regulatory rules do such "regimes" embrace?

If international regimes are understood as a set of interactions, it is useful to identify them. However, there is no reason to assume that they exist in every issue area. Moreover, principles, norms, expectations, and operative rules are frequently more subtle than or differ from what is publicly recorded. Public pronouncements of course do not reveal how regimes were first established, tacit understandings, whether transbureaucratic meanings are shared, and whose interpretations of these meanings really count. Most important is to determine whose interests are served by a regime, the extent to which it deepens or alleviates global inequalities, and how it may be transformed.[23]

One explanatory vehicle for examining regulatory regimes is to study migration-driven conflicts. These include conflicts over refugees (Viet Nam and Hong Kong), expulsion of nationals (Senegal and Mauritania), and undocumented workers (Mexico and the United States).[24] In all of these categories, migration preferences substantially reflect the globalization trend, whereas barriers to entry, including forced repatriation and financial inducements offered by the host state to go home, are expressions of the Westphalian territorial principle.

A starting point for discerning international standards is the ideological impetus for the founding of the International Labour Organization (ILO) and the elaboration of its conventions. The mandate for the ILO is contained in the Treaty of Versailles, and reflects pressures from workers' organizations as well as the impact of the October Revolution, pushing post-war governments to establish an international body for the regulation of labour conditions. At the first session of the International Labour Conference, held in Washington, D.C. in 1919, the French delegate, Arthur Fontaine, was the major proponent of placing regulations concerning the migration of workers – equal wages and conditions of employment for immigrant and national workers – on the agenda. France faced a domestic labour shortage, and a number of sending countries sought to protect their workers abroad. Countries favouring restrictive immigration policies (e.g. Canada and Great Britain) feared the adoption and elaboration of international labour standards, and argued that such standards would undermine state sovereignty. This impasse portended common ground limited to vague principles without concrete meaning.

In 1934, the entry of the United States into the ILO, and its status as a major receiving country, promised to give impetus to standard-setting. Additionally, under a new Director General, David Morse, the ILO sought to adopt an ambitious operational programme, e.g. enabling countries to obtain technical knowledge for social and economic development. In 1951, the United States and other Western countries balked at this bid on the ground that the ILO might allow communists to profit from the organization's funds and projects.[25] Inasmuch as Poland and Czechoslovakia were members of the ILO, the United States would not entrust it to transfer European migrants to Latin America and, hence, sponsored a separate organization, the Intergovernmental Committee for European Migration, for this project, one first proposed by Morse shortly after he became Director General.[26] Subsequent decades witnessed an increase in imports of foreign labour, especially on a temporary basis, clandestine migration, international trafficking in labour sometimes conducted by organized crime, and discrimination and xenophobia targeted at migrants, leading to the adoption of the United Nations Convention on the Protection of the Rights of All Migrant Workers and Members of Their Families in 1990.

Such conventions are buttressed by the activities of the United Nations High Commissioner for Refugees, national groups like the US Committee for Refugees, and a host of research centres that collect data and analyse national and multilateral policies.[27] On balance, however, an international regime for migration has not been consolidated, and its pronouncements are largely hortatory and lacking in enforcement mechanisms.

Two macro-regions – North Amercia and Europe – emphasize regional solutions and coordinate their efforts, but neither has adopted common policies. After a number of violent clashes in the Tijuana–San Diego area, the border patrols of the United States and Mexico began to work together in 1990. Law enforcement agencies on both sides are jointly trying to manage problems along a 2,000-mile border where undocumented migrants are routinely robbed, assaulted, and raped by their escorts, bandits, and smugglers, sometimes with the complicity of police paid as part of the extortion racket. Under the eye of human rights groups, officials of the two governments are now making information available to legal and illegal migrants, advising them of their rights, and aggressively prosecuting abusive patrol agents.

In Europe, pressure is mounting for a common policy on immigration, but the EU lacks judicial authority in this area, and member states guard their prerogatives owing to the sensitivity of the issue and the deeply rooted tradition of dealing bilaterally with immigrants' countries of origin. The Treaty of European Union treats immigration policy as a "matter of common interest." Although the EU subscribes to the principle of free movement of persons, permanent immigration and the right of asylum have been left to national governments. Some countries retain border patrols, but nine – all except Denmark, Britain, and Ireland – signed the 1990 Schengen Accord, which, subject to ratification, ends intra-EU passport checks. Anyone legally in a Schengen country may travel to the eight others, but only citizens of those countries have the right to work and settle there. In other words, a German or an Italian, but not an Angolan citizen residing in Portugal or an Algerian in France, could migrate to Belgium to live and work.

An overarching paradox characterizes immigration in Europe. After heavily relying on workforce immigration in the 1950s and 1960s, the majority of Community member states sought to halt permanent legal migration beginning in the 1970s; it continues, however, even though unemployment rates in the Community have been over 8 per cent for a decade (some observers would add, to depress wages). Not only does a persistent influx of workers contradict policy statements, but there also appears to be a loss of control in the area of immigration. Having closed their gates, the northerners, for example, are wary that illegal migrants might slip into, say, Spain or Portugal, and, given the permeability of borders, are unchecked all the way to the North Sea, where they find ways to stay.[28] Although EU initiatives are concerted through its authority to regulate the labour market, illegal immigration demonstrates the limits of the current approach.

A major limitation is that current regulatory regimes are conceived in terms of exclusivity: employment is restricted to persons of indigenous culture, or receiving countries insist on assimilation to the local culture. Thus, culture is one of the instruments in the regulation of international migration, perforce an encounter of people who speak different languages, practise different religions, and have very different habits. It may be hypothesized that regulatory regimes are evolving in the direction of multiculturalism in the workforce, with culture playing a major role in labour segmentation.

International migration is building multi-ethnic societies beset with severe socio-economic problems. Many immigrants and their offspring maintain residential and cultural enclaves in Europe, and are not integrated into the welfare state. A particularly nettlesome issue stems from the *de facto* conversion of workforce migration into settlement migration, which is strikingly evident in the plight of youth. Now there is a successor generation of young people born in the receiving country, some of whom are citizens of that country and who are less compliant than are their parents. Many of these people are marginalized in the educational system and in access to employment. Thus, Britain's young Blacks and France's young Arabs feel they are treated like outsiders, though they are nationals of the countries in which they reside. (A very different situation with multi-ethnic populations has developed in the Middle East, where governments fear "reverse acculturation": a gradual loss of Arab national identity. Yet, a large number of Arab migrants are perceived as a political risk.)

Muslims represent one-third of all immigrants in Western Europe, and, allowing for intraregional flows, two-thirds of non-EU nationals. In fact, the prospect of Islamic fundamentalism in the southern countries causes serious concern. A perplexing problem is structuring political participation among Muslims in these countries, because the Islamic tradition differs from a secular democratic society with its representative bodies. Furthermore, the EU's 5 million Muslims include different strands of Islam (Shiite, Sunni, etc.) and several nationalities (Algerian, Bangladeshi, Moroccan, Pakistani, Tunisian, Turkish, etc.).[29]

Attacks on immigrants in EU countries are increasingly frequent and accompanied by a swell of xenophobia. Politicians on the far right, such as the leader of France's National Front, Jean-Marie Le Pen, and his counterparts, appeal to nativist sentiment, economic insecurities, and apprehension of Brussels as a threat to national identity. Those who are alarmed about an "invasion" of immigrants argue that the EU is amid two areas of poverty: the disintegrating ex-socialist countries to the east and less developed countries across the Mediterranean. In this juncture, the interactions of culture, economic patterns, and demographic pressures are stark. It is estimated that North Africa's population will double over the next 30–35 years, 40 per cent of Maghrebians currently being under 15 years of age. With income levels no more than one-sixth of those in Europe, they may seek to relocate north of the Mediterranean.[30] Immigration policies in Europe clearly reflect concern that the ascent to power of an Islamic fundamentalist regime in Algeria or other North African countries could spark massive trans-Mediterranean flows of population.

Toward an alternative conceptualization

These interactions all bear upon the manner in which multilateralism can confront the issues of restructuring production and migration. Formulating the problem in this way directs attention to access to multilateral processes. Are regulatory regimes the exclusive prerogative of states and inter-state organizations, or will they become more open to the groups most affected by these processes? Do migrants act as agents who challenge multilateral structures, and, if so, what forms of resistance do they adopt and under what conditions?

In sum, multilateralism has come to embody certain fundamental human dilemmas that globalized production and migration have thrust into sharp relief. As noted, international standards, however desirable, are largely unenforced, and receiving countries have no common immigration policy. It is tacit agreements, cultural patterns, and liberal economic ideology that underpin a weak regulatory regime in the area of international migration – a potentially explosive issue because of growing inequalities. International conventions cannot eradicate global inequalities that fuel migration, nor can they circumvent the norms and structures of sovereign statehood. Whereas economic globalization advances worldwide labour mobility at the end of the twentieth century, political units cling to the seventeenth-century doctrine of sovereignty, thus far relinquishing few prerogatives to inter-state organizations, which, in any event, preserve the state.

The dominant conceptualization of globalization is grounded in liberal economic theory. By delimiting politics and economics as separate spheres, it serves the interests of the beneficiaries of an expanded market. In the conventional manner of thinking, the disruptive and socially polarizing effects of globalization are obscured. It is difficult to join argument with the enthusiasts of economic globalization without being obliged to share their terms of reference.

An alternative conceptualization emphasizes the interactions between themes that intersect different levels of analysis. This approach to restructuring and migration focuses on the interpenetration of the internal dynamics of societies and transnational and global processes. Restructuring must be joined to agency by incorporating the views of migrants themselves and challenging dominant perspectives of economic globalization so that both efficiency and equity are enhanced. The aim of this new conceptualization is not to return to pre-globalization conditions, but rather to transcend the current globalization process, to re-embed in global society the unparalleled productive capacities of economic globalization in order to help achieve social justice.

Acknowledgements

This paper builds on the efforts of a working group which met in Toronto on 17 January 1992. Robert W. Cox, Stephen Gill, Ricardo Grinspun, Hélène Pellerin, and Allan Simmons contributed ideas, but I assume sole responsibility for this chapter. In addition, I owe a special debt of gratitude to Robert W. Cox, Stephen Gill, Yoshikazu Sakamoto, and Linda Yarr for comments on preliminary drafts of my manuscript.

Notes and references

1. Keith Griffin and Azizur Rahman Khan, *Globalization and the Developing World: An Essay on the International Dimensions of Development in the Post-Cold War Era*, Geneva: United Nations Research Institute for Social Development, 1992, pp. 43 and 47.
2. Aaron Segal and Linda Marston, "Maps and Keys – World Voluntary Migration 1500–1980," *Migration World Magazine* 17 (1989), no. 1: 36–41; cited by Shirley Hune, "Migrant Women in the Context of the International Convention on the Protection of the Rights of All Migrant Workers and Members of Their Families," *International Migration Review* 25 (winter 1991), no. 4: 800–801.

3. Adam Smith, *An Inquiry into the Nature and Causes of the Wealth of Nations*, Middlesex, England: Penguin Books, 1970.
4. I am drawing on James H. Mittelman, "Marginalization and the International Division of Labor: Mozambique's Strategy of Opening the Market," *African Studies Review* 34 (December 1991), no. 3: 89–106. The seminal work on the new international division of labour is Folker Fröbel, Jurgen Heinrichs, and Otto Kreye, *The New International Division of Labour: Structural Unemployment in Industrialised Countries and Industrialisation in Developing Countries*, trans. by Pete Burgess, Cambridge: Cambridge University Press, 1980.
5. See Robin Cohen, *The New Helots: Migrants in the International Division of Labour*, Brookfield: Gower, 1987; and Saskia Sassen, *The Mobility of Labor and Capital: A Study in International Investment and Capital Flow*, Cambridge: Cambridge University Press, 1988.
6. On the concept of globalization, I am indebted to David Held, personal conversation with the author, Yokohama, Japan, 25 March 1992.
7. Fernand Braudel, "Unity and Diversity in the Human Sciences," in Fernand Braudel, *On History*, trans. by Sarah Matthews, Chicago: University of Chicago Press, 1980, p. 55; and Eric Helleiner, "Fernand Braudel and International Political Economy," *International Studies Notes* 15 (fall 1990), no. 3: 74.
8. "Caribbean Exodus: U.S. Is Constant Magnet," *New York Times*, 6 May 1992.
9. See James H. Mittelman, "The Dilemmas of Reform in Post-Revolutionary Societies," *International Studies Notes* 15 (spring 1990), no. 2: 66.
10. Terence K. Hopkins and Immanuel Wallerstein, "Commodity Chains in the World-Economy Prior to 1800," *Review* 10 (summer 1986), no. 1: 157–170; and Gary Gereffi and Miguel Korzeniewicz, "Commodity Chains and Footwear Exports in the Semiperiphery," in William Martin, ed., *Semiperipheral States in the World-Economy*, Westport, Conn.: Greenwood Press, 1990, pp. 46–77.
11. International Bank for Reconstruction and Development/World Bank, *World Development Report 1990*, New York: Oxford University Press, pp. 93–94.
12. Griffin and Khan, op. cit., pp. 57 and 65–67.
13. *World Development Report 1990*, op. cit., Table 18, pp. 212–213.
14. Aaron Segal, "International Migration: Conflict and Cooperation," paper presented to the annual meeting of the International Studies Association, Atlanta, Georgia, 31 March–4 April 1992, pp. 11–12.
15. Demetrios Papademetriou, "International Migration in a Changing World," in Charles Stahl, ed., *International Migration Today*, vol. 2, *Emerging Issues*, Paris: UNESCO, 1988, pp. 249–250. Griffin and Khan, op. cit., p. 55, indicate that remittance income may reduce world inequality.
16. John A. Arthur, "International Labor Migration Patterns in West Africa," *African Studies Review* 34 (December 1991), no. 3: 65.
17. Ibid., pp. 72–77.
18. Ibid., pp. 75–77.
19. On the consequences of President Idi Amin's 1972 expulsion of Uganda's Asian community, see James H. Mittelman and Onkar S. Marwah, *Asian Alien Pariahs: A Cross-Regional Perspective*, Studies in Race and Nations 6, 1, Denver: University of Denver Monograph Series, 1975.
20. Czarina Wilpert, "Migrant Women and Their Daughters: Two Generations of Turkish Women in the Federal Republic of Germany," in Stahl, ed., op. cit., vol. 2, pp. 168–186.
21. Prema Kurien, "Sojourner Migration and Gender Roles: A Comparison of Two Ethnic Communities in Kerala, India," in *Continuity and Change: Women at the Close of the Twentieth Century*, Providence, Rhode Island: Thomas J. Watson Institute for International Studies, Brown University, Occasional Paper Number 12, 1992, pp. 43–61.
22. Riad Tabbarah, "Prospects for International Migration," in Stahl, ed., op. cit., vol. 2, pp. 256ff.

23. Some of these points about regime theory were raised by Donald Puchala, personal communication with the author, 9 June 1992.
24. Segal, op. cit., pp. 11–12.
25. Michael Hasenau, "ILO Standards on Migrant Workers: The Fundamentals of the UN Convention and Their Genesis," *International Migration Review* 25 (winter 1991), no. 4: 687–697.
26. Robert W. Cox, personal correspondence with the author, 5 November 1992.
27. Segal, op. cit., p. 9.
28. "Europe's Immigrants: Strangers inside the Gates," *The Economist* (London), 15 February 1992, p. 154.
29. Commission of the European Communities, "Policies on Immigration and the Social Integration of Migrants in the European Community" (Sec (90) 1813), Brussels, 28 September 1990, p. 34; and Commission of the European Communities, "Commission Communication to the Council and the European Parliament on Immigration" (Sec (81) 1855), 23 October 1991, p. 25.
30. "Europe's Immigrants," op. cit., p. 153.

Part III
Transnational social movements

11

Citizens and the UN system in a changing world

Chadwick F. Alger

Introduction

To those who take a more traditional approach to the study of international relations, the subject of "Citizens and the UN system" is a topic of marginal concern.[1] After all, the United Nations is an organization composed of "sovereign" states and it is representatives of these states that participate in the meetings of UN bodies. If citizens are involved, it is indirectly, as citizens of the various states. But even this is not believed to be very important because citizens rarely play a prominent role in foreign policy-making of states, including policies to be implemented in UN organizations. Furthermore, many would also say that most citizens are not qualified to become more directly involved in shaping UN policies.

On the other hand, there are two reasons why a volume assessing a changing world should examine the actual and potential involvement of citizens in the UN system. First is the growing scholarship on the spread of social movements across state borders, with contributions by scholars from many parts of the world. Based on insights from research on peace movements in Western Europe, Zsuzsa Hegedus perceives the "planetarization" of practices formerly identified with new social movements in the West:

that is, by the massive emergence throughout the world of collective actions which are non-violent and pragmatic in their methods, non-integrated and multiple in their structures, anti-hierarchical and networking in their organizations, heterogeneous (cross-class, cross-ideology, cross-age) in their constituencies, non-coercive in people participation and non-exclusive in their adherence.

Especially in the West in the 1980s, these movements (e.g. peace and anti-apartheid) are characterized by direct intervention "in a field traditionally considered as exterior and closed to social movements: the international arena." Hegedus laments the fact that "rarely has the discrepancy between the practices and analysis of new social movements been so acute" (1989, pp. 19–20).

Writing out of experience in India, D. L. Sheth also perceives a new mode of politics arising, across regional, linguistic, cultural, and national boundaries. It encompasses peace and anti-nuclear movements, environmental movements, women's movements, movements for self-determination of cultural groups, minorities and tribes, and a movement championing non-Western cultures, tecno-sciences, and languages (Sheth, 1983, p. 23). This bears striking similarity to the vision of two Swedish economists: Mats Friberg and Bjorn Hettne see a worldwide "Green" movement emerging that offers an alternative to the "Blue" (market, liberal, capitalist) and the "Red" (state, socialism, planning) (1988, p. 352). Both Sheth and Friberg and Hettne tend to see a decentralized array of issue movements that will change the world from below. This is compatible with the vast number of movements that use as their slogan: "Think Globally and Act Locally," which Gerlach sees as "the essence of the emerging folk model of decentered and harmonic globalism" (1991, p. 146).

A second reason why the involvement of citizens in the UN system merits our attention is because of dynamic growth in involvement by non-governmental organizations (NGOs) in the UN system. Based on the right of NGO consultation with the Economic and Social Council (ECOSOC) in the UN Charter, NGOs have now established direct relationships with all of the organizations in the UN system. At the same time, their participation has spread from representation at numerous headquarters to extensive involvement in field activities, especially in development programmes. As a result, scholars identifying key actors in efforts to cope with global problems increasingly recognize the significance of NGOs, e.g. human rights (Forsythe, 1991, p. 72), refugees (Gordenker, 1988, pp. 274–302), and environment (Porter and Welsh Brown, 1991, pp. 56–60). Furthermore, Pei-Heng Chiang's comprehensive assessment of NGOs at the United

Nations concludes: "Who shall shoulder the burden of countering the power of states, organizations, elites and bureaucracies? ... it will have to be the NGOs ... there is no one else to do it" (1981, p. 288).

With respect to the global reach of social movements, Hegedus perceives a difference between those of the 1970s and those of the 1980s in that the latter "directly address planetary issues and challenge the dominant problem-solving process at a global level: they proceed in an autonomous manner to the *democratisation*, to the *civilisation*, and *multioptionalisation* of this *self-creative* – and poly-centric – *world system*" (1989, p. 33). Although she perceives social movements now directly intervening in problem-solving at a "global level," she does not indicate that the UN system might be a target of these movements. This is typical of scholarship on social movements that have ventured into global space. It is puzzling in the light of the fact that one of the most significant social movements in the 1980s was the environmental movement, which has played a significant role in placing environmental issues on agendas throughout the UN system.

Perhaps those studying the global reach of social movements neglect to focus on their involvement in the UN system when it does occur, because these movements are viewed as initiatives in search of new forms of participation, whereas the UN is seen as an extension of the same state system that has traditionally excluded democratic processes. On the other hand, there is no doubt that those who focus on the growing activities of NGOs in the UN system are also witnessing a transformation in the state system. As organizations in the UN system have set up headquarters in more cities, and as field programmes have been established throughout the world, this extension of the state system has become directly exposed to more diverse social environments and has become more permeable by a diversity of citizen initiatives.

From these observations we conclude that traditional assumptions about the pre-eminence of states in world affairs are being challenged both by (1) the spillover of traditionally domestic social movements into world space, and by (2) growing NGO participation in the UN system, particularly as its activities extend beyond headquarters. There is no doubt that for some participants in the first category there is a deliberate attempt to transcend all forms of organized power, including both the states and the UN. At the same time, there is no doubt that for some in the second category there is a deliberate effort to democratize the UN by opening it up to the direct participation of "the grass roots." On the other hand, some in the first category have eventually found the UN system to be useful to their cause, as in the case of world movements promoting ecological balance, human rights, the elimination of apartheid in South Africa, and standards for the marketing of infant formula. And some involved in more traditional NGO activity in the UN system often accused of élitism, have perhaps learned from movements in the first category of the need for more direct linkage to the "grass roots."

In some senses, linkage of "new social movements" to the UN may be obscured by the fact that, in UN settings, the term NGO tends to be applied to all citizen groups. This was the case with that great and diverse panoply of citizens' groups represented in the NGO Global Forum at the UN Conference on Environment and Development (UNCED) in Rio de Janeiro. Nevertheless, the two approaches that we have identified do offer significantly different themes in the struggle of citizens to participate directly in global politics. For the most part this paper will focus on the growing involvement of NGOs in the UN system. At present they offer the most concrete evidence and insight on the potential for greater citizen participation in the UN system. Knowledge about this potential may be of value to some social movements that may not yet perceive the relevance of the UN system to their goals. Although we shall focus on NGOs in the UN system, it is important to bear in mind that there are citizens who seek alternative routes for participation in world affairs – routes that may be complementary to those leading to the UN system as well as routes that may be substitutes. We shall return to consideration of these options in our conclusion.

Compiling a comprehensive overview of the relationships between citizens and the UN system would require a major research project. This modest effort will first examine provisions for citizen participation in the UN Charter, including citizen participation in the drafting of these provisions. Next we will offer an overview of offices in the UN system that conduct relations with non-governmental organizations and of procedures that have been developed for participation by citizens in UN global conferences. We shall then examine citizen participation in two broad UN issues, human rights and development. We will conclude with three alternative futures.

The UN Charter

The foundation for citizen participation in the UN was built at the UN Charter Conference in San Francisco, with the participation of

1,200 representatives of non-governmental organizations (Willetts, 1982, p. 11). Dorothy Robins (1971) has given us an extensive account of the involvement of associations from the United States. Hundreds of private groups asked to be included in the US delegation. As a compromise, the State Department invited 42 private associations to send a consultant and up to two associate consultants, promising them an opportunity for two-way interaction with the delegates, advisers, staff and secretariat of the large US delegation. In addition, four times as many other private US groups were encouraged to attend as unofficial observers. These consultants and observers "had measurable direct impact both on the text of the UN Charter ... and on later UN openness to private organizations" (Killough, 1991, p. 8). In particular, they supported Sol Bloom's insistence that the first sentence of the Charter read: "We the peoples of the United Nations," in dramatic contrast with the League of Nations Covenant, which reads: "The High Contracting Parties." They also fought for the inclusion of individual human rights, the right of non-governmental organizations to consult with UN bodies, and the education of citizens as a peace strategy.

In his report on the Conference to the President, US Secretary of State Stettinius "unequivocally attributes credit" to the consultants for the seven references to individual human rights in the Charter. The second phrase after "We the peoples" affirms "faith in fundamental human rights, in the dignity and worth of the human person, in the equal rights of men and women ..." Dorothy B. Robins reports that efforts to include "provisions on human rights and fundamental freedoms in the United Nations Charter ... had to overcome a policy of brevity, especially in the chapters on non-political matters ... linked to the still-prevailing idea of the Charter as a document dealing fundamentally with security problems" (1971, pp. 129–130).

Voluntary organizations at San Francisco also made significant contributions to the economic and social aspects of the Charter. Here again, wrote Russell Porter of the *New York Times*, they strove to overcome the "opinion of the [US] delegation and the State Department at the outset that the conference would have all it could do, and all it needed to do, if it organized the military security of the world" (Robins, 1971, p. 124). Of particular significance in future relations between the UN system and citizens is the insistence of voluntary organizations on Article 71:

The Economic and Social Council may make suitable arrangements for consultation with non-governmental organizations which are concerned with matters within its competence. Such arrangements may be made with international organizations and, where appropriate, with national organizations after consultation with the Member of the United Nations concerned.

Robins gives James T. Shotwell, President of the Commission to Study the Organization of Peace, credit for initiating the essence of Article 71, out of his earlier experiences with the involvement of labour and management representatives in the International Labour Organization (ILO). One consultant from a private organization expressed enthusiasm for Article 71 this way: "we are now embarking on a hope that possibly we may be able to bring into a world organization the common people of the world. I think this thing, if it could be sold to other nations, will have opened a great door" (Robins, 1971, p. 217).

Another way in which private groups built a foundation for UN ties with citizens was their effort to get the word "education" into the Charter. On the opening day of the conference, the Chinese had put forward three proposals, one of which provided that ECOSOC should promote educational and other forms of cooperation. A number of other countries supporting this effort were Lebanon, Ecuador, Uruguay, Greece, the Philippines, and Haiti. Among the US consultants, William G. Carr of the National Education Association took the lead on this issue. In winning the support of other consultants from agriculture, business, and labour, he expressed interest in "making the United Nations Organization a 'people's organization' ... providing explicitly for educational cooperation in the interest of international peace and security." In reflecting on the discussion that followed the presentation of the education proposal of the full group of consultants, Carr wrote:

I have never seen such evidence of the intense determination to make this a "people's peace" or of faith in education.... We had been privileged to participate in what may have been one of the really "historic" moments in this conference. (Robins, 1971, p. 119)

NGOs at headquarters in the UN system

In fulfilment of Article 71, ECOSOC established procedures for establishing consultative status for NGOs. Category I involves organizations with "marked and sustained contact" and those that represent "major segments of the population in a large number of countries." Category II includes those that are internationally known to have special competence with respect to the work of the Council or other UN bodies. Organizations on the roster are expected to have "occasional and useful contributions" to make to the work of ECO-SOC or other UN bodies. Those in Category I may propose agenda items and may, in certain cases, make oral interventions in ECOSOC meetings. Both Category I and II may submit written statements for circulation to member states. All three categories may send observers to ECOSOC meetings and receive documents. Somewhat similar procedures have been developed by a number of UN programmes and specialized agencies. A significant development has been the creation of consortia of NGO representatives present at specific UN headquarters. The most prominent example is the conference of NGOs in Consultative Status with ECOSOC (CONGO), present in Geneva, New York, and Vienna. These organizations collaborate in acquiring needed access to meetings, documents, etc., and in developing common policies on specific issues.

One way to gain insight into the involvement of NGOs in UN politics is keenly to observe UN public meetings, to visit lounges, and to walk the halls of the headquarters of UN agencies. One quickly becomes aware that it is not only state officials and employees of the UN who are present. Individual citizens and representatives of NGOs may be observed talking to delegates and secretariat in the corridors and offices of UN agencies and in national missions. Sometimes they are seeking information to share with their constituents, but they are also lobbying for specific resolutions and programmes, and even providing delegates with drafts of resolutions and speeches. Some delegates will be pleased to accept credit for these materials when presenting them to their government and to fellow delegates. Also to be observed are private members of a multitude of expert and advisory panels, on subjects such as drugs, insects harmful to people, the ozone layer, AIDS, malnutrition, and unemployment. It is significant that this process takes place in the headquarters of over 30 UN organizations and regional economic commissions located in some 20 countries in all continents. In addition, even more citizens come into contact with the UN system in far-flung UN field activities. In these places citizens are in daily contact with UN officials assigned to peace-keeping forces, observer missions, and agricultural, health, educational, vocational training, communications, transportation, and other projects.

At the same time that NGOs have organized themselves to obtain

Table 11.1 **NGO liaison offices in the UN system**

Group	Total	New York	Geneva	Vienna	Rome	Nairobi	Montreal	London	Washington	Paris	Berne	Bangkok	Santiago	Baghdad	Addis Ababa	Athens	Bahrain	Kingston	Mexico City
General service	8	4	2	2															
Substantive departments	54	25	13	12	2	2													
UNEP regional offices	6								1			1				1	1	1	1
Regional Commissions	5		1									1	1	1	1				
Specialized agencies	19	2	7	1	3		1	1	2	1	1								
Total	92	31	23	15	5	2	1	1	3	1	1	2	1	1	1	1	1	1	1

Source: Prepared from directory issued by UN Office of the Under-Secretary General, 1990, published in *Transnational Associations* no. 5 (1990): 292–302.

access to the UN system, UN agencies have created a vast array of offices facilitating relations with non-governmental organizations. In a document released by the office of the Under-Secretary for Political and General Assembly Affairs and Secretariat Services in June 1990, 86 offices were listed. These offices are classified into five groups: (1) 8 NGO general service offices at three main centres of the UN system – New York (4), Geneva (2), and Vienna (2); (2) 54 liaison offices within the substantive departments of the UN Secretariat, in Rome, Geneva, Vienna, and Nairobi; (3) 6 regional offices of UNEP – Washington, Bangkok, Athens, Bahrain, Kingston, and Mexico City; (4) offices in the five Regional Economic and Social Commissions in Geneva, Bangkok, Santiago, Baghdad, and Addis Ababa; (5) 19 specialized agency liaison offices in New York, Geneva, Vienna, Rome, Montreal, London, Washington, Paris, and Berne. Table 11.1 has been developed out of the listings in the UN document. Although this list is probably incomplete, these 92 offices, in 19 cities, reflect the remarkable geographical scope of NGO access to the UN system.

Another perspective on NGO access to the UN system can be developed by a list of the 26 issues on which these offices are focused.

These issues range from ageing and disarmament to migrant workers and social welfare policy (see table 11.2).

What do UN agencies perceive to be the functions of their NGO relations offices? The same UN document provides a phrase describing the activities of each office. In excerpting the relevant words from each, we identified 20 functions, which we have condensed into seven clusters. To facilitate comprehension of what these offices say they are doing, we have arranged the seven functions in an order that proceeds from lesser to greater collaboration with NGOs and from head-quarters to field emphasis:

(1) Provides information on UN issues/activities to NGOs.
(2) Collects/provides information/serves as clearing house on NGO activity.
(3) Supports/assists/advises NGO information activity.
(4) Involves NGOs in UN meetings/seminars/symposia.
(5) Promotes cooperation/consultation/coordination with NGO programmes.
(6) Stimulates/supports NGO field activities.
(7) Promotes community-based/grass-roots approaches.

The list begins with the expected effort by UN offices to inform NGOs about UN activities. But they also collect and disseminate information about NGOs and support NGO information activity. Some NGOs do participate in meetings of UN organs, but many more are involved in seminars and symposia. As called for by Article 71, NGOs consult with ECOSOC and other UN bodies and offices, but this has extended to include the coordination of UN and NGO programmes with each other. In ways probably not foreseen by those drafting Article 71, some UN offices stimulate and support NGO field activities. Finally, in the promotion of grass-roots and community-based approaches, these UN offices probably go beyond the definition of NGO as understood by voluntary organization representatives at the San Francisco Conference.

At this point we do not know the priority given by the various UN offices to these UN activities, nor do we know how effectively they are carried out. On the other hand, the very fact that they report that they have the intent of encompassing the seven functions listed suggests not only that practice has fulfilled Article 71 but also that the roles of NGOs have been given a far broader definition. Research is needed on the significance of the network of NGO offices in the UN system, and the potential they offer for greater citizen participation.

Table 11.2 **Issues addressed by NGO liaison offices**

Issue	City	UN office
Ageing	Vienna	Centre for Social Development & Humanitarian Affairs (CSDH)
Apartheid	New York	Centre Against Apartheid
Children	New York	UN International Children's Emergency Fund (UNICEF)
Cooperatives	Vienna	CSDH
Crime	Vienn	
Decolonization	New York	Information Unit on Decolonization
Desertification	New York	UN Sundarro-Sahelian Office (UNSO)
Development	New York	Centre for Science & Technology for Development (CSTD)
	Geneva	UN Conference on Trade and Development (UNCTAD)
	New York	UN Development Programme (UNDP)
	New York	Special Unit for Technical Co-operation among Development Countries (SUTCADC)
	New York	UN Development Fund for Women (UNIFEM)
	New York	Capital Development Fund (CDF)
Disability	Vienna	CSDH
Disaster relief	Geneva	UN Disaster Relief Coordinator (UNDRC)
	New York	UNDRC
Disarmament	New York	UN Department for Disarmament Affairs (DDA)
Emergency situations	New York	Special Emergency Programme, Special Political Questions, Regional Coop., Trust. & Decolo. (SPQRCTD)
Environment	Nairobi	UN Environment Programme (UNEP)
	New York	UNEP
	Geneva	UNEP
	Athens	UNEP Regional Office
	Bahrain	UNEP Regional Office
	Bangkok	UNEP Regional Office
	Kingston	UNEP Regional Office
	Mexico	UNEP Regional Office
	Washington, D.C.	UNEP Regional Office
Family	Vienna	CSDH

310

Table 11.2   (*continued*)

Issue	City	UN office
Food/hunger	Rome	World Food Council (WFC)
	Rome	World Food Programme (WFP)
	New York	WFP
Human rights	Geneva	Centre for Human Rights (CHR)
	New York	CHR
Human settlements	Nairobi	Habitat
	New York	Habitat
Law of the Sea	New York	Office for Ocean Affairs and Law of the Sea (LOS/OA)
Migrant workers	Vienna	CSDH
Narcotic drugs	Vienna	Division of Narcotic Drugs (DND)
Palestinian rights	New York	Division for Palestinian Rights (DPR)
Peace studies	New York	Peace Studies Unit (PSCS)
Population	New York	UN Population Fund (UNFPA)
	Geneva	UNFPA
	New York	Population Division (DIESA)
Refugees	Geneva	UN High Commissioner for Refugees (UNHCR)
	New York	UNHCR
	Vienna	UN Relief and Works Agency for Palestine Refugees (UNRWA)
	New York	UNRWA
Social development	Vienna	CSDH
Welfare policies	Vienna	CSDH

Source: Prepared from directory issued by UN Office of the Under-Secretary General, 1990, published in *Transnational Associations* no. 5 (1990), 292–302.

Non-governmental organizations in UN global conferences

Ad hoc UN global conferences have offered the opportunity for significant innovations in NGO participation in global politics. Between 1961 and 1985 the United Nations convened 147 ad hoc conferences, including Special Sessions of the General Assembly. These conferences were convened primarily to focus worldwide attention on a global problem and to cope with problems that transcend the competence of specific agencies (Willetts, 1989, pp. 35–72). The most widely publicized include those focusing on the environment, food, population, women, and the law of the sea. The first of the "mega conferences" was the 1972 UN Conference on the Human Environment in Stockholm, involving 113 states, 21 UN bodies, 19 other intergovernmental organizations (IGOs), and 298 non-governmental organizations. At the 1985 Women's Decade Review Conference in Nairobi there were 163 non-governmental organizations. In both cases additional NGOs took part without being registered as participants. The inclusion of non-governmental delegates in governmental delegations at the Stockholm environment conference is striking. The totals for all delegations were: 318 foreign office delegates (24 per cent), 777 from other government departments (59 per cent), and 203 non-governmental (15 per cent) (Willetts, 1989, pp. 52–54).

NGOs have played a role in focusing UN attention on most of the problems that have become the concern of global conferences. "In the case of the Women's Decade it was the pressure initially of NGOs rather than of states which led to the initiation of the UN activity" (Harrison, 1989, p. 243). NGOs, then, participate in preparatory meetings, which may be held at a variety of sites in order to broaden interest in the conference. At the larger global conferences it has become customary for NGOs to organize conferences that run concurrently with the inter-state conference. These NGO conferences include lectures, debates, films, and exhibitions. There are three kinds of communication between the two conferences: first, officially recognized NGOs gain access to the meetings, documents, and delegates of the inter-state conference; secondly, some of these delegates may attend events in the NGO conference; thirdly, NGOs keep their members informed about activities in both conferences and facilitate communication between the two by publishing a daily NGO newspaper, as in the case of conferences on the environment, population, food, women, human settlements, and development. These newspapers are distributed free of charge to the hotel rooms of state delegates. They are written by professional journalists and include photographs, cartoons, and editorials. "Sometimes the stories provide the delegates with their first news of what other delegations are doing. The newspapers always investigate the debate on the issue beyond the questions on the official agenda" (Willetts, 1989, p. 56).

Although officially recognized NGOs have sustained involvement in planning for ad hoc global conferences, NGO activities at these conferences provide possibilities for much wider access. At the first Women's conference in Mexico City in 1975, a small committee of CONGO organized Tribune, the parallel conference. Participants included not only NGO representatives but other interested individuals, a total of 6,000 registered participants, as well as 1,600 media people. The Tribune provided a vital arena of exchange among radical and conservative views and between first and third world participants. "Working ... 'on the creative edge of chaos' ... One enthusiastic participant called it the 'soul' of the conference." But there were complaints that the Tribune and the inter-state conference were not sufficiently related, producing a visit to the Tribune by the Conference Secretary General, where he called for "unity of purpose and cooperation in implementing whatever plan of action emerged from the official delegates" (Harrison, 1989, p. 229). Building on their Tribune experience, despite unfavourable media coverage, NGOs convened a forum at the follow-up conferences in Copenhagen (1980) and Nairobi (1985). In assessing these conferences, Harrison concludes:

Since the activity of non-governmental women's organizations as pressure groups on national governments, as publicisers and educators *vis-a-vis* the general public (and women in particular) is one of the most important instruments of reform, the stimulus and the contacts provided by the unofficial fora at the conference are clearly of great value, a value far outweighing the temporary prejudiced reporting they engender. (Harrison, 1989, p. 233)

In contrast, Groom and Guilhaudis (1989, p. 122) believe that NGOs "muffed it" at the Special Session of the General Assembly on Disarmament in 1988 (UNSSOD II), "despite spectaculars such as the demonstration by 750,000 people." In this case NGOs had the pathbreaking opportunity to address the General Assembly. But Groom and Guilhaudis conclude that "they put forward few new ideas and, for the most part, merely mimicked governments." In this case the NGOs did not develop a parallel conference, although they did publish the *Disarmament Times*. Groom and Guilhaudis also criticize Western domination of NGO activity. "Unlike in other world conferences such as development, Western NGOs found it difficult to make common cause with those from the East or the Third World." This remarkable contrast with the Women's conference raises questions about the reasons for the differences between the two. Unlike the women's conference, the disarmament conference was a special session of a main UN organ, was held at UN headquarters, and focused on questions of military power at the heart of the East–West confrontation. Perhaps these factors account for the apparent lesser success of NGOs at this disarmament conference.

NGO activities at the Fourth Session of the UN Preparatory Committee (March 1992) for the UN Conference on Environment and Development (UNCED) in Rio de Janeiro in June 1992 illuminate

313

the development of efforts by NGOs to shape the agenda for UN global conferences, to prepare materials for presentation at these conferences, and to prepare for parallel conferences. The directory of events prepared by the NGO Ad Hoc Planning Committee listed events especially for students and youth, children, women, religious groups, and indigenous peoples. Some events focused on special topics, such as bio-diversity, solar energy, trade and the environment, sustainable agriculture, alternative economic models, poverty, and the effect of the military on environment. Although most events were held in New York City, simultaneous events were held in Brazil, Chile, Mexico, the Philippines, and Geneva.

In conclusion, Groom (1989, pp. 294–295) observes that global conferences are a "step towards giving greater expression to the phrase 'We the Peoples of the United Nations'," and are "a promising step towards the enfranchisement of some relevant actors." But he notes the difficulty that NGOs have in "holistic and systemic" collaboration because of their need to maintain the support of their constituencies. Nevertheless, he sees that global conferences facilitate networking among NGOs and thereby enhance their ability to collaborate.

Human rights

Brief overviews of NGO activities focused on human rights and development will enable us to illustrate the rich diversity of citizen participation in the UN system. Following on their role in placing individual human rights in the Charter, non-governmental organizations have been the engines that have energized the states assembled to sustain the drafting of standards. The drafting in UN bodies of standards for human relationships on the planet, in numerous declarations and treaties, has been a towering achievement. Future historians concerned with the development and preservation of human potential may record this as the most significant accomplishment of the twentieth century. If human rights standards are to be implemented, NGOs have an indispensable role to play, along with a galaxy of people's movements. This is recognized in the covenants on Civil/Political and Economic/Social/Cultural rights. The preamble of each declares:

Realizing that the individual, having duties to other individuals and to the community to which he belongs, is under a responsibility to strive for

314

the promotion and observance of the rights recognized in the present Covenant ...

There is no doubt that NGOs have taken up the challenge, for "the energy, the vision, the drive, the tenacity of the international movement for human rights today lies preeminently with the NGOs" (Livezey, 1989, p. 19).

To use the words of David Forsythe, "there is a melange of non-governmental actors seeking to help implement human rights. Boundary lines are decidedly not neatly drawn within this swirling activity" (1983, p. 65). Laurie Weisberg (1990) provides a list of the seven dimensions of NGOs involved in human rights that illuminates the diversity of those involved in the movement:

(1) *Local, national, regional, international.* The geographical scope of organizations can vary with respect to the geographical scope of their mandate, and with respect to their membership and control.

(2) *Human rights specific and other interest groups.* In the "other" category, having agendas that extend beyond human rights, are churches, trade unions, labour organizations, peasant and farm-worker organizations, political parties, professional associations, youth and student organizations, women's organizations, and many others.

(3) *Broad-based and single-issue groups.* Organizations working exclusively on human rights may have a broad mandate (e.g. all civil/political rights or even the entire "World Bill of Rights") or a specific narrow mandate, such as Amnesty International's focus on political prisoners.

(4) *Differing professional perspectives.* Examples are the differing perspectives of lawyers (International Commission of Jurists), journalists (PEN), scientists, engineers, physicians, forensic scientists, and geneticists.

(5) *Mass-based and élite organizations.* "With a few exceptions, ... the overwhelming number of international, and many national human rights NGOs are still largely of the elite-type. They have been created and are run by a small group of concerned individuals, frequently from the professional or middle classes" (Weisberg, 1990, p. 19).

(6) *Ideological orientation and political independence.* Human rights organizations are distinguished from other actors in that they do not themselves seek power. They desire to keep the political process open, influencing public policy in a pro-human rights direc-

tion. But there are disagreements on what political independence means. Some believe that acceptance of government funds violates independence but others do not. Mass membership may require organizations to avoid unpopular issues, but it may provide funding independent of government.

(7) *Specialization and professionalism.* Some older organizations in particular have highly professional staffs, whereas others are run mainly by volunteers.

This overview of various dimensions of NGOs involved in human rights illuminates remarkable potential for linking organizations together into global human rights movements. There is tremendous diversity with respect to geographical scope, specificity of mission, professional perspectives, mass/élite distinctions, political independence, and professionalism/volunteer attributes. But this diversity is also a great challenge to those who are endeavouring to weave together coalitions and networks inclusive of different perspectives, interests, and scopes of concern.

Weisberg also enables us to obtain another perspective on this vast domain of actors by providing a list of seven important functions performed by NGOs in both the protection and promotion of human rights: (1) information and/or monitoring; (2) legislation; (3) stopping abuses, securing redress, and/or humanitarian assistance to victims – in effect, implementation; (4) education/conscientization; (5) solidarity; (6) delivery of services; (7) keeping open the political system for other actors (1990, pp. 23–29).

This list of functions reveals that human rights NGOs offer remarkable potential for the construction of global movements responsive to a diversity of needs. The activities of human rights NGOs range from grass-roots education/conscientization, to the drafting of national and international standards. They are working to fulfil these standards through monitoring, dissemination of information on violations, stopping abuses, expressing solidarity with those struggling against abuses, and delivering services to those suffering abuse. But this diversity of approaches also suggests that, in the formulation of global strategies for human rights fulfilment, there are bound to be disagreements on where emphasis should be placed at a specific time. Should priority be given to education/conscientization in order to expand support, or to solidarity with those already on the front lines? Should priority be given to information and/or monitoring, or should it be given to solidarity? Might the latter emphasis inhibit the ability to monitor and collect information?

Of course, there may also be disagreements about which rights should be included in a global effort, and which of those should have priority. There is still intense disagreement between those who view civil/political rights as the essential core of human rights and those who insist that economic/social/cultural rights are a part of this core. At the same time, many now see the two groups of rights as an integrated set, with the possibility for achievement of each dependent on progress in the other. Such an interdependent view is taken by Jack Donnelly and Rhoda Howard in their effort to devise a short list of 10 rights. These offer a usefully succinct overview of the field of human rights. Grouping human rights into four categories, Donnelly and Howard provide this list: survival rights (right to life, food, health care), membership rights (family rights, non-discrimination), protection rights (habeas corpus, independent judiciary), empowerment rights (education, free trade, freedom of association). Donnelly and Howard claim "methodological priority" for these rights in that they believe that "taken together they can stand as measures of performance for virtually the entire list of internationally recognized human rights" (1988, p. 215). A state that protects these 10, they believe, will be found to have protected all others. Of course, no short list would satisfy everyone. We use it only as an example of the fact that global dialogue and widespread practice are significantly breaking down earlier (and we think quite artificial) tendencies to separate the civil/political and economic/social/cultural domains. Nevertheless, when global movement and network priorities are being set, this division can still be significant.

We have obtained some insight into how a diversity of types of human rights actors link together in efforts to implement specific human rights by drawing on descriptive material for four examples: (1) the campaign against apartheid in South Africa, (2) the campaign to develop and implement a code for marketing infant formula, (3) the campaign to obtain the right to organize in a Coca-Cola bottling plant in Guatemala, and (4) the campaign by churches against the repressive practices of military rule in Latin America. All have involved actors and organizations that range from local to global, and all range across the civil/political and economic/social/cultural divide.

Based on admittedly very selective case material, we have reached seven tentative conclusions about the future potential for worldwide human rights efforts (Alger, 1990). First, although there seems to be broad agreement by many scholars and practitioners that the whole spectrum of human rights, particularly civil/political and economic/

social/cultural, consists of an integrated whole, people in local settings have difficulty in building programmes that integrate them. Secondly, non-governmental organizations have become significant participants in "conference diplomacy" focused on human rights at IGO meetings and headquarters, but the available potential for transcending state restraints in this way has not yet been fully exploited. Thirdly, based on the assumption that the spectrum of human rights is tightly linked, response to local needs may be the best strategy for beginning a human rights movement in places where specific human rights organizations may seem to be a violation of local culture. Fourthly, although divisions between those emphasizing civil/political and those emphasizing economic/social/cultural rights may be significant, issue-specific campaigns seem able to bridge this gap, as exemplified by cooperation between groups in industrialized countries and those in third world countries in the anti-apartheid, infant formula, and Coca-Cola campaigns. Fifthly, under present world conditions, legitimization by IGOs of standards for worldwide campaigns is indispensable. Sixthly, it would seem that successful human rights campaigns require a network of actors reflecting varying territories (local, national, international) involving NGOs, IGOs, and states, and also involving an array of types of NGO, such as issue-specific, churches, and unions. Seventhly, this network should not be viewed as a hierarchy, with IGOs (UN) at the top. Although it seems that IGOs may be at the top of a hierarchy for legitimization, NGOs may play key roles in promotion, and even in implementation and enforcement.

Development

From one perspective, much of the activity in the UN system over the past four decades can be viewed as a struggle over the meaning of "development." The notion of development assistance for third world countries gradually emerged out of an emphasis on relief and welfare. At first it was assumed that development meant replicating Western models, but this was eventually challenged by calls for more endogenous approaches. This in turn brought challenges to centralized national development plans and calls for small-scale local projects characterized by local autonomy and self-reliance. Pursuit of these goals leads to emphasis on local participation and empowerment, which in turn requires a supportive societal context that is compatible with grass-roots autonomy and participation.

Our point in reviewing this redefinition process is that it actually emerged out of a policy process in which grass-roots participants were increasingly involved. To some degree this was brought about by the failure of centralized approaches – by states, IGOs, and NGOs. As states, IGOs, and NGOs moved away from emphasis on industrialization and large-scale infrastructure development projects to a focus on serving "basic human needs," they became increasingly involved at the grass roots. This gradually linked more local governmental and non-governmental organizations into the policy-making process.

The development activity of NGOs can be viewed from both a third world and a first world perspective. The third world perspective focuses on the delivery of development assistance. A Norwegian scholar offers a fourfold typology: (1) federations of national development/humanitarian/human rights organizations (e.g. International Red Cross or Red Crescent, World Council of Churches), (2) international agencies run by Northern-based secretariats (e.g. Oxfam, CARE, Save the Children), (3) national third world organizations (e.g. 10,000 in Africa, with 1,600 in Kenya alone), and (4) local self-help groups, which are small, local, and informal (Egeland, 1987).

A first world perspective focuses on development education and advocacy programmes in the industrialized countries. Development education in European NGOs, initially centred on church and church-related organizations, was begun around 1970. In an initial period, "the basic image" communicated by development education was that "the development problem is all 'out there' ... caused by indigenous factors inside the low-income countries" (Lissner, 1977, p. 158; cited by Lemaresquier, 1987, p. 191). Broadening of the global development dialogue in the late 1970s spurred concern in development education for the nature of the links between first world and third world societies, and between first world and third world cities and towns. This included issues such as the impact of the international economic structure on third world poverty, the impact of global food markets on third world hunger, the transfer of technology, the role of transnational corporations, and relationships between the development policies of European national governments and the perpetuation of third world economic dependency.

Dynamic growth in NGO activity on development issues raises difficult questions for the UN system that were not foreseen by those who advocated the inclusion of provisions for NGO consultation with ECOSOC in the Charter. Expanding efforts by UN organiza-

319

tions to respond to the growth in NGO activity focused on development issues are reflected, for example, in conferences and reports of the UN Conference on Trade and Development (UNCTAD), UNDP, the International Fund for Agricultural Development (IFAD), the World Bank, and the Economic and Social Commission for Asia and the Pacific.

An UNCTAD report on a meeting on the role of non-governmental organizations in the development of the least developed countries identifies three common attributes of NGOs: autonomy, associative structure, and sensitivity to the needs and aspirations of poor communities (UNCTAD, 1990). It also recognizes the difficulties that result from the "complex set of relations between development NGOs in the South and North, governments of South and North and the United Nations system," and observes that "sustainable development processes can be achieved when these various institutions articulate and co-operate in close relationships but respecting each other's roles" (UNCTAD, 1990, p. 31). Remarkable in this report on a conference chaired by the Secretary-General of UNCTAD is recognition of the fact that development requires collaboration among an array of actors, including grass-roots groups, Northern and Southern NGOs, Northern and Southern states, and IGOs.

Another example is a record of a UNDP Governing Council meeting in 1988 in which the Director of the Division of NGOs reported on UNDP efforts to respond to the desire of the Governing Council that NGOs be involved in programmes.

Questioning the merits of "supply-driven" development, the international community had found increasing evidence that actions taken by people to help themselves led to a more viable and independent process of development. (UN Development Programme, 1989)

UNDP had found that NGOs, both indigenous and external, "had often been best able to perform that role," and also "served as a kind of laboratory" for trying out new ideas. Almost half of UNDP field offices have been involved in NGO initiatives.

There are even signs of competitiveness among UN agencies to be perceived as collaborators with NGOs. An International Fund for Agricultural Development Newsletter (December 1988) states that participants in a conference of NGOs at IFAD headquarters "recognized that IFAD is more open to cooperation with NGOs than other UN organizations." An advantage of collaboration with NGOs is indicated to be their detailed first-hand knowledge of local contexts, which facilitates the mobilization of local support for projects. As with UNDP, it is also asserted that NGOs can be employed in experiments with new approaches. Methods employed by IFAD to encourage cooperation with NGOs are a loan to the government of Zaire to encourage the establishment of NGOs, assistance to Ethiopia to set up a unit for NGOs within the Ministry of Agriculture, and a mission to Zambia to strengthen the skills of NGOs in the formulation of projects.

Perhaps the most extensive discussion of cooperation with NGOs by a UN organization is to be found in reports of the World Bank. The Bank reports that 50 of 222 projects approved by the Bank in FY 1990 had NGO involvement (World Bank, 1990). The most common form of NGO involvement is either for an NGO to receive funding for activity developed and proposed by them to a government, or for an NGO to be engaged to execute a project designed by the government. Difficulties encountered by the Bank include rivalries between public agencies and NGOs for financial resources, difficulties in dealing with "diverse and disparate NGO communities," and "inappropriate public policies toward NGOs." With respect to the latter, the Bank has "participated in discussions" that would facilitate the development of "an effective nonprofit, voluntary sector" (World Bank, 1991, p. 197). The Bank has attempted to systematize and institutionalize its work with NGOs through a booklet on how the Bank works with NGOs, staff training seminars, a three-year seminar on the role of NGOs in development, reciprocal exchange of staff between the Bank and an NGO, studies of NGO-associated projects, and efforts by resident missions to maintain Bank–NGO relations.

A very challenging approach to development emerged out of a Regional Congress of Local Authorities for Development of Human Settlements convened by the UN Economic and Social Commission for Asia and the Pacific (ESCAP), the City of Yokohama, and the UN Centre for Human Settlements (UNCHS), held in Yokohama in 1982 (Hosaka, 1992). The Congress stressed the importance of local authorities in the development of human settlements and the need for enhancing their responsibilities and capabilities. In response, the Second Congress of Local Authorities for Development of Human Settlements in Asia and the Pacific, held in Nagoya in 1987, established the Network of Local Authorities for the Management of Human Settlements, now called CITYNET. Full members of CITYNET are composed of city authorities in Asia and the Pacific (Bombay, Colombo, Hanoi, Ho Chi Minh City, Jakarta, Kandy, Kuala Lumpur, Lae, Metro Manila, Nagoya, Nanjing, Negombo, Penang, Seoul, Shangai, Surabaya, Suva, and Yokohama). Associate members include non-governmental organizations from within and outside the region and city authorities in Nancy and Lyons, France. With financial support from UNDP, and from several local authorities in developed and developing countries, CITYNET has been operating since 1988.

A final example of UN response to local needs is the proposed Local Initiative Facility for Urban Environment (LIFE) of UNDP. This initiative is a response to "a growing recognition at the global level of the role which local authorities, NGOs and CBOs [community-based organizations] play in promoting sustainable urban environment and development" (UN Development Programme, 1991). Responsive to a draft document of the UN Conference on Environment and Development (UNCED) Secretariat, "Local Authority Initiatives in Support of Agenda 21," LIFE recognizes that : (1) municipalities, NGOs, and CBOs have inadequate access to international technical cooperation resources, (2) past international cooperation in the urban sector focused on strengthening central government urban development and housing ministries but the focus should now shift to strengthening governments in cities and towns and promoting dialogue between the community and local authorities, (3) involvement of mayors is essential, (4) environmental improvement and participatory development are key components of human development (UNDP, 1991, pp. 3–4). Funding would promote exchange of experiences and innovations by CBOs and NGOs in selected countries, by joint activities of local authorities and NGOs in cities and towns, and by NGO networks, associations of cities, and concerned international agencies. Funding is to be from UNDP, bilateral donors, networks of cities in developed countries, and private foundations.

Analyses of the growing significance of NGOs (international, national, and local) in development activity, along with evidence of the responsiveness of the UN system to this growth, reveal remarkable dynamism at the grass roots, largely non-governmental but also including local government. There seems to be widespread acceptance of the fact that organizations from local to global have a role to play. Many are struggling to discern how they can be effectively linked. On the other hand, there are those, such as Sheldon Annis, who tend to de-emphasize, or even ignore, the role of global organizations. He asks: "Can small-scale development be a large-scale policy?" For Annis, significant elements in small-scale development on a large scale are: self-organizing systems of grass-roots organizations, foreign private voluntary organizations, the state and "macro" policies that affect external debt, international terms of trade, currency valuation, and import/export conditions. He emphasizes that "state policy is crucially important in determining the character and capacities of grassroots growth – and ultimately, in providing the answer to the question: ... How large can small-scale become?" (Annis, 1987, p. 133).

Two Swedish scholars see IGOs as an "expression of the logic of the state system" (Friberg and Hettne, 1988, p. 356). They begin by asking a question quite similar to that of Annis: "Can social transformation at the macro-level (national and global) be the result of micro-processes; social movements organized around very different and usually local issues? We believe so" (p. 341). But, unlike Annis, they ascribe far less importance to the state in asserting that "social transformation at the global level will be the result of the growing importance of non-state actors" (p. 356). Friberg and Hettne argue, "while the issues in the new local politics vary due to local differences, they are similar at a deeper level. Here one may speak of a tendency toward convergence" (p. 342). Noting that "there are few instruments of action at the global level and that the few that exist are controlled by elites," they opt for a "popular strategy" that "fall[s] back to the levels where ordinary men and women can act in a powerful and sustainable way, that is, in the local space where they live and work" (p. 358).

While taking a global perspective on development policies, Majid Rahnema (1986) too centres his concern on the grass roots. Similarly to Friberg and Hettne, he perceives that "many grass-roots movements have started to move ahead, indifferent to the developmental designs of national and international organizations seeking to 'develop' them." Included are networks involving university students, researchers, de-professionalized specialists, scientists, and scholars. These informal networks "not only link together the grass-roots of the South but also [are] establishing new forms of co-action between these and those of the North.... The positive results they have thus far achieved well indicate that such interactive processes have become a reality, and a serious alternative to development designs" (Rahnema, 1986, p. 43).

Because Rahnema has had considerable experience in UN development programmes, both at headquarters and in the field, the reader awaits his reflections on the appropriate role for the UN in the context of emerging transnational networks with strong local roots. But Rahnema believes that, as long as governments do not change their basic positions on development, it would be difficult to imagine that the UN system might change. While noting that "isolated yet genuine efforts have been made by some UN agencies, with a view to responding to the needs of grassroots populations," he observes that "these efforts remain exceptions to the rule" (1986, p. 45).

Rahnema sees no need for "any centralized, bureaucratically administered institution." Rather, he asks that "new ways and means are to be imagined, mainly to allow each different group to be informed, to learn about other human groups and cultures, in terms of their respective support systems." Thus he envisages the need for a "highly de-centralized, non-bureaucratic, *inter-cultural* rather than *inter-national* network of persons and groups" (1986, p. 43). He believes that this might be facilitated, "when the time comes, [by] a world network of people's assemblies, where the genuine representatives of all grass-roots movements would meet and interact freely with each other" (p. 45). This network would be supported by technical and other relevant teams capable of assisting those who seek advice from them.

Our brief survey of development organizations in the first world and the third world, and selected examples of response by UN agencies, again illuminate the remarkable responsiveness of the UN system to change in its environment. At the same time, the growth in non-governmental and local activity focused on development is significantly challenging earlier assumptions about the role of states in development. Those endeavouring to move resources from North to South, and those wishing to receive them, are struggling to create new approaches for linking non-governmental collaboration across state borders. When can the goals of both parties be simultaneously satisfied? When is the state an inevitable intervening authority between the two and when is it an anachronism? Has the inter-state system itself, and its IGO extensions, outlived its usefulness? Given the strong participatory assertions from the grass roots, is it possible that development – defined as the full development of individual human potential – can be achieved only by a highly decentralized global policy process? What kinds of global institutions, if any, would this imply? These kinds of questions emerge out of the challenges provided by creative growth in NGO development activity around the world and the remarkable responsiveness of the UN system.

Conclusion: Three alternative futures

In the past half-century, states and their inter-state system have remained at the centre of the stage in the world as represented by mainstream international relations scholarship and the world press. But at the same time, citizen groups and movements are building a parallel, and sometimes intersecting, global polity. They have fundamentally transformed the participation of citizens in the UN system, both at headquarters and in the field, and have developed their own global networks. With respect to human rights, they have played an indispensable role in UN efforts to define and implement global standards for human relations. In the case of development, they have played a key role in moving the definition of development from large-scale designs by state authorities to definitions reflective of aspirations at the grass roots. Thus, in a world that seems to be unavoidably interdependent, linked together by global enterprises for manufacturing, distribution, communication, and finance, the growing global polity created by citizens' groups seems to have an indispensable role to play. They provide avenues through which citizens from all parts of the world can help to shape the values that will set standards for these global enterprises. At the same time, these values can serve as a protection against violations by state and local governments and enterprises.

It would be appropriate to ask to what degree these citizens' organizations and movements are truly reflective of the values of most people. Many have noted that national NGOs and their international counterparts, INGOs, have often been dominated by cosmopolitan élites in national capitals and primate cities in the North. But there is no doubt that the growth of participation by local and grass-roots people in both the North and the South has made the citizen efforts that we have been describing more reflective of the global population, particularly in the South. We vitally need comprehensive assessments of the actual and potential representativeness of these efforts.

What are the possible alternative futures for citizens in the emerging global polity? We will offer three brief visions. One perspective would be to recognize that citizens have done rather well over the past 50 years with a decentralized and rather ad hoc approach. Citizen participation in the UN system has been gradually strengthened and broadened, and transnational movements outside the UN have been simultaneously developed. Why not simply encourage these citizen organizations and movements to sustain and expand their efforts?

A second approach would be to envisage the development by citizen associations of a second assembly of the UN General Assembly, as proposed by a number of scholars and others. Informally this approach has already been attempted through parallel conferences at UN global conferences. At the same time, conferences of non-governmental organizations at UN headquarters, such as CONGO in New York, are second assemblies in very embryonic form. Of course, the second assembly idea need not be confined to the General Assembly, but could be extended to the plenary bodies of specialized agencies. A systematic assessment of the performance of concurrent conferences at UN global conferences might shed some light on the advantages and disadvantages of this approach. On the one hand, second assemblies could offer citizens a more prominent place in formal decision-making. On the other hand, there would be the possibility that these assemblies would diminish the openness and spontaneity of citizen participation and create a new citizen élite alongside the inter-state élite.

Third, following the lead of Rahnema, citizens might abandon their efforts to participate in the UN system, seeing it as only a way in which they are co-opted by the state system. This vision would consist of a "highly de-centralized, non-bureaucratic, *inter-cultural* rather than *inter-national* network of persons and groups." Eventually this would be supplemented by "a network of people's assemblies, where the genuine representatives of all grass-roots movements would meet and interact freely with each other" (Rahnema, 1986, pp. 43–45). Technical and other relevant teams capable of assisting those who seek advice from them would be available. A network of people's assemblies would broaden opportunities for citizen participation and permit wider representation of the values and needs of the world's peoples. But does not the existence of an array of global problems, requiring global solutions, suggest that a global organization such as the UN system is indispensable? Will the citizen efforts urged by Rahnema be marginalized if they do not directly participate in the UN system?

Each of the three visions of the future has its appealing characteristics. It is difficult to choose one, but if we are to begin coping with an array of common global problems, we desperately need quickly to develop solutions reflective of the needs and values of the peoples of the world. Thus we are inclined to urge that all three visions be pursued at once. The decentralized approach now under way leaves open possibilities for many more people to participate. In important ways it has worked. At the same time, participation could be broadened by incorporating some of Rahnema's ideas. Stronger intercultural participation would overcome the present tendency for many NGOs to be based primarily on states. Instead of "assemblies," which tend to be parallel to UN "assemblies," a network of "people's assemblies" could be created. Expert teams could provide needed knowledge to these "assemblies," when they ask for it. In this way many more people would be participating. The most important consequence would be that many more people would be *learning*, and a broader array of perspectives would be tapped. This learning could then be applied in local, provincial, national, regional, and global governance. No global problem can be solved without simultaneous efforts that range from the local to the global.

The ferment from broadened participation and learning could contribute to the emergence of global citizen assemblies in all of the major global organizations. At first there could be experiments in developing these assemblies at UN global conferences, simply by converting existing parallel conferences into more formal institutions. As these citizen assemblies spread to organizations throughout the UN system they would at first be only advisory, as recommended by Galtung (1980, pp. 348–349). The variety of UN conferences and organizations would permit a variety of experiments in developing procedures for representation.

Perhaps the synergy from all three approaches could at last fulfil the hope expressed by the already cited citizen at the San Francisco Conference:

we are now embarking on a hope that possibly we may be able to bring into a world organization the common people of the world.

Note

1. By "citizen" we mean "a civilian as distinguished from a specialized servant of the state" (*Webster's New Collegiate Dictionary*).

References

Alger, Chadwick F. (1990) "Actual and Potential Roles for NGOs and Worldwide Movements for the Attainment of Human Rights." International Peace Research Association 25th Anniversary Conference, Groningen, Netherlands.
Annis, Sheldon (1987) "Can Small-scale Development be a Large-scale Policy? The Case of Latin America." *World Development* 15 (supplement): 129–134.

327

Chen, Samuel Shin-Tsai (1979) *The Theory and Practice of International Organization* (rev. edn). Dubuque, Iowa: Kendall/Hunt.

Donnelly, Jack, and Rhoda E. Howard (1988) "Assessing National Human Rights Performance: A Theoretical Framework." *Human Rights Quarterly* 10: 214–248.

Egeland, Jan (1987) "Discovering a First Line of Defense: Indigenous Humanitarian Organizations." *Bulletin of Peace Proposals* 18, no. 2: 111–118.

Forsythe, David (1983) *Human Rights and World Politics*. Lincoln: University of Nebraska Press.

——— (1991) *The Internationalization of Human Rights*. Lexington, Mass.: Lexington Books.

Friberg, Mats, and Bjorn Hettne (1988) "Local Mobilization and World System Politics." *International Social Science Journal* 117, 40 (August), no. 3: 341–360.

Galtung, Johan (1980) *The True Worlds*. New York: The Free Press.

Gerlach, Luther P. (1991) "Global Thinking: Local Acting: Movements to Save the Planet." *Evaluation Review* 15 (February), no. 1: 120–148.

Gordenker, Leon (1988) "The United Nations and Refugees." In: Lawrence S. Finkelstein, *Politics in the UN System*. Durham, NC: Duke University Press, pp. 274–302.

Groom, A. J. R. (1989) "Reflections on a Changing System." In: Paul Taylor and A. J. R. Groom, eds. *Global Issues in the United Nations' Framework*. London: Macmillan, pp. 285–296.

Groom, A. J. R., and J. F. Guilhaudis (1989) "UNSSODs: The Quest for Structure and Norms." In: Paul Taylor and A. J. R. Groom, eds. *Global Issues in the United Nations' Framework*. London: Macmillan, pp. 116–147.

Harrison, R. J. (1989) "Women's Rights: 1975–85." In: Paul Taylor and A. J. R Groom, eds. *Global Issues in the United Nations' Framework*. London: Macmillan, pp. 226–244.

Hegedus, Zsuzsa (1989) "Social Movements and Social Change in Self-Creative Society: New Civil Initiatives in the International Arena." *International Sociology* 4, no. 1: 19–36.

Hosaka, Mitsuhiko (1992) "Transnational Sharing of Development Experience: Two Networking Cases from Asia." Office of Human Resource Management, United Nations, New York.

Killough, T. Patrick (1991) "A Peace Made on Main Street: Private Americans Help Create the 1945 United Nations Charter." Address to The Southeastern World Affairs Institute, Black Mountain, N.C., 26 July.

Lemaresquier, Thierry (1987) "Prospects for Development Education: Some Strategic Issues Facing European NGOs." *World Development* 15 (supplement): 189–200.

Lissner, Jorgen (1977) *The Politics of Altruism: A Study of the Political Behaviour of Voluntary Development Agencies*. Geneva: Lutheran World Federation.

Livezey, Lowell W. (1989) "US Religious Organizations and the International Human Rights Movements." *Human Rights Quarterly* 11: 14–81.

Pei-Heng Chiang (1981) *Non-Governmental Organizations at the United Nations: Identity, Role, Function*. New York: Praeger.

Porter, Gareth, and Janet Welsh Brown (1991) *Global Environmental Politics*. Boulder, Colo.: Westview Press.

Rahnema, Majid (1986) "Under the Banner of Development." *Development* 1, no. 2: 37–46.

328

Robins, Dorothy B. (1971) *Experiment in Democracy: The Story of U.S. Citizen Organizations in Forging the Charter of the United Nations.* New York: Parkside Press.

Sheth, D. L. (1983) "Grass-Roots Stirrings and the Future of Politics." *Alternatives* IX (summer): 1–24.

UNCTAD (1990) "Report of the UNCTAD Meeting on the Role of Non-Governmental Organizations in the Development of the Least Developed Countries, 1989." *Transnational Associations* no. 1: 31–35.

UN Development Programme (1989) "Co-Operation with Nongovernmental Organizations and Grassroots Organizations." *Transnational Associations* no. 2: 98–100. (Excerpt from UNDP Governing Council Meeting, October 1988, DD/1988/15)

———— (1991) "Local Initiative Facility for Urban Environment." Draft prepared by Programme Development and Support Division (PDSD) in cooperation with the Division for Global and Interregional Programmes (DGIP) and Regional Bureaux, 30 December, New York.

United Nations, Office of the Under-Secretary General for Political and General Assembly Affairs and Secretariat Services (1990) "Directory of Departments and Offices of the United Nations Secretariat, United Nations Programmes, Specialized Agencies and Other Intergovernmental Organizations Dealing with Non-Governmental Organizations," New York. Published in *Transnational Associations* no. 5, 1990: 292–302.

Weisberg, Laurie (1990) "Human Rights NGOs." *Human Rights Internet* (xerox).

Willetts, Peter (1982) *Pressure Groups in the Global System: The Transnational Relations of Issue-Oriented Non-Governmental Organizations.* London: Frances Pinter.

———— (1989) "The Pattern of Conferences." In: Paul Taylor and A. J. R. Groom, eds. *Global Issues in the United Nations' Framework.* London: Macmillan.

World Bank (1990) "Cooperation between the World Bank and NGO's: Recent Progress." *Transnational Associations* no. 2: 113–118.

World Bank (1991) "Cooperation between the World Bank and NGOs." *Transnational Associations* no. 4: 197–222. (1990 Progress Report, World Bank International Economic Relations Division, External Affairs Department)

329

12

The democratization movement in Latin America: The case of Chile

Rodrigo Baño

Introduction

The contemporary analyst is rarely modest when evaluating events he has witnessed. This is all the more common as the end of the millennium approaches. For this reason it makes sense to recover an analytical perspective that, without denying the changes and redefinitions in course, situates these events within the spatial and temporal context that confers meaning on them.

In fact, the end of the Cold War as the foundation of international relations, the expansion under neo-liberal hegemony of the new economic order, or democracy as the central issue of political organization are all events that must be understood as ongoing processes rather than unexpected explosions. It is unnecessary to review the different moments of these processes to demonstrate their prior origins and continued development. Nor is it necessary to point to the mutual relations among these themes. Lastly, minimal prudence suggests acknowledging the persistent uncertainty concerning the outcome of these processes.

On the other hand, when examining the Latin American situation one should recognize the inadequacy of schemes that attempt to assess the present or future impact of these processes in the region –

or, inversely, the effect that Latin America will have upon them. This for the simple reason that these processes are embedded within trends towards globalization that no longer permit discrete spatial divisions; Latin America is part of a common process. This is not to deny the particular varieties and characteristics that this process assumes in the region, as we shall see in this paper.

Beyond the events of the Cold War – which were lived with particular intensity in Latin America – two processes are central to defining the present regional situation. They correspond to those generically specified above: political democratization and the structural reform of the economy. Naturally, the diversity of countries in the region, each with their specific structures and processes, allows us to conceive of these processes only as predominant tendencies. Nevertheless, reviewing a specific case may illustrate some of the development characteristics of these tendencies.

In this regard, Chile is an interesting case in the region. At particular moments and for specific purposes, Chile has been raised to the category of being a "model." Chile anticipated the rest of Latin America by a number of years in initiating its economic modernization and restructuring in the mid-1970s. At the same time, democratization in Chile was considerably delayed, being achieved only towards the end of the 1980s. Chile is not, nor can it be considered, an average country in the region that is representative of the majority. Rather, Chile is atypical, but it developed atypically the same central processes that the other countries are developing or attempting to develop. Given the depth of its economic restructuring and the length of its agitated process of political transition, the Chilean case has the advantage of clearly presenting particular aspects that are apparently common in Latin America.

In a few pages and with limited knowledge one cannot make great contributions to the study of processes of such magnitude. Still, perhaps I may reassert an analytical perspective that is often forgotten: that social processes and transformations are realized by social agents and do not constitute the mere result of economic, demographic, or other types of indices.[1]

Even if only in a general and approximate manner, it is useful to try to sketch out the character of the existing social configuration and to specify the actors that are significant in this context. Any rapid glance at Latin America in general, and Chile in particular, will observe the deep social changes that have occurred in recent decades. These changes have led to the appearance and disappearance of social actors and to changes in strategic positions, the articulation of interests and conflicts, as well as forms of insertion into the dynamics of the world hegemonic centres. Under these conditions, examining the characteristics of the Chilean process that roughly reveal regional Latin American tendencies appears all the more justified.

The asymmetry between economics and politics in the 1980s

For a long time, a broad consensus existed among scholars that there was a direct relation between economic development and political democracy. Especially in Latin America, the transitional theses, such as the classical argument of Gino Germani,[2] viewed economic and political development as stages that were fulfilled simultaneously.

Oddly for many, the 1980s were marked by an apparent paradox. Economically, the crisis and decline, which have been widely studied and recognized by regional organizations, led to the coining of the term "the lost decade."[3] Politically, on the other hand, the 1980s were the decade of democratization; by the end of the decade, for the first time in the region's history, virtually every country had a democratically elected government.

If one observes the preceding decades, a very different situation appears. In the period 1950–1980 there was a process of economic growth in Latin America: rates of growth of gross internal product and per capita income averaged 5.5 per cent and 2.7 per cent, respectively.[4] At the same time, political instability intensified. During the first half of the period, this was epitomized by the emergence of insurrectional movements, one of which was successful in Cuba in 1958. In the second half, especially after the 1964 military coup in Brazil, there emerged a new type of military regime, characterized as being "bureaucratic–authoritarian" owing to the institutional participation of the armed forces and their pretensions of definitively displacing democracy.[5] The Chilean coup to a large degree served as a prototype of this new authoritarianism.

Thus, there doesn't appear to be a very direct relation between the economic situation and the political situation as regards democracy. Nevertheless, this global approach obscures precisely the social action that makes possible certain political alternatives in determinate circumstances. Thus, an analysis of the political movement of the years 1950–1980[6] must take into account the context of massive mobilization, which integrated rural migrants, urbanized Latin American societies, and produced a deep transformation of the social structure in these countries. The central conflict occurred over the style of economic development and was ideologically charged, with different positions translating into alternatives for the accumulation and distribution of the social product. The respective mobilizations readily evolved into direct confrontations, accompanied by violence, such as armed insurgency and military intervention. As is known, this conflict in general took a clearly authoritarian turn, which during the 1970s extended throughout the region. The countries with the greatest democratic tradition, such as Uruguay and Chile, fell under harsh military authoritarianism. The same occurred in Argentina, Peru, and Bolivia, which thereby joined Brazil, which in 1964 inaugurated the new style. At the same time, traditional dictatorships maintained themselves or strengthened their positions in Paraguay and most of Central America. There were only a few exceptions, such as Venezuela and Costa Rica, while it became increasingly difficult to conceptualize countries like Mexico, virtually ruled by a single party, and Colombia, agitated by endemic violence, as democracies.

It should be recalled that the most common explanation of this wave of authoritarianism, particularly the new type installed in Brazil and the Southern Cone of America, was that it corresponded to a political adjustment necessary to better integrate these countries into the "new world economic order" that had been established around powerful transnational corporations. Thus, authoritarianism was seen as a type of political adaptation to an already existing economic change.

When the wave of democratization occurred in the 1980s, this explanation was rarely remembered. Nevertheless, it appears obvious that the fall of these regimes occurred during a particularly sharp economic crisis – so sharp that in 1989 the per capita product was 8.3 per cent lower than in 1980. Obviously, one cannot repeat the simple argument that explains the process of democratization in terms of the authoritarian regimes' failure to adjust political power positions to the needs of the highly internationalized new world economic order. On the contrary, it is evident that generally it is the new democracies that pursue structural transformations allowing for the insertion of the countries of the region into the new economic order.

Apparently, the thesis that the rise of the new authoritarianism in Latin America corresponded to the needs of the economy is, at least, in need of further specification if democratization is to be understood. These qualifications must recognize that the post-World War II period of economic growth generated a highly conflictual situation.

This leads us to emphasize the fundamental importance of the element of "threat" in the military resolutions that gave rise to the bureaucratic–authoritarian state. As we have maintained on other occasions,[7] these authoritarian regimes were originally defensive before a threat, real or imagined, to the prevailing social order. Although O'Donnell always recognizes the existence of this element of threat, he does not grant it primary significance; rather he emphasizes the economic explanation[8] – an explanation that is also present in the Chilean case but disappears in analyses of the democratic transition.[9] This implies the inability of these regimes later to acquire a "foundational" character and pursue a new articulation of the economy, as occurred successfully in Chile. But it is the regimes' "defensive" function that gives rise to a correlation of social forces allowing for the establishment and permanence of the regime. At the same time, once this defensive function is accomplished, democratizing movements encounter increasing possibilities for their development.

It is no accident that the most typical authoritarian regimes were installed precisely during situations of serious social agitation; for example: the Brazil of Goulart in 1964, with defiant urban and rural popular mobilization; the Argentina of radicalized Peronism, with the Montoneros and the ERP engaged in violent tactics during the mid-1970s; the Uruguay of the Tupamaros and the emergent left-wing Frente Amplio, which electorally threatened to break the traditional two-party system; the Chile that, under a Marxist government, underwent dangerous social and political polarization that explicitly threatened the existing social and economic order. More precisely, where there was threat there was a military coup, and, as O'Donnell recognizes, the harshness of the new regime was proportional to the threat.[10]

The analysis of the Latin American democratization process must take into account this defensive character of the authoritarianism. The economic crisis of the 1980s was undoubtedly a factor strongly affecting the activation of opposition movements to these regimes. None the less, not only do other circumstantial factors appear to be more determinate (such as the military defeat by the United Kingdom in the Argentine case), but Chile suffered the catastrophic effects of the 1981–1983 economic crisis without arriving at democracy. It was only once the crisis had been overcome and the economic model had been consolidated that the democratic transition arrived.

We see, then, that the democratizing movements in Latin America cannot be seen as a mere reaction to an economic crisis that the authoritarian regimes were unable to overcome. In the same manner, the breakdown of democracy did not occur because democracy maintained power positions that were incompatible with the requirements of insertion in the world economy. Nor is it correct, however, to consider the broad social mobilizations, such as those seeking democracy, as spontaneous collective actions spurred by some form of political ethics.

The social and political processes that lead to democracy are sufficiently complex as to preclude any exhaustive analysis at this point. Nevertheless, a case-study, such as that of Chile, allows us to evaluate the importance of a determinate social configuration and the articulations produced among different sectors. This appears to condition the different possible political paths, even though these courses are understood by the parties in terms of political engineering.

On the other hand, one must also consider that the growing interdependence among countries is generating conditions that globally facilitate determinate alternatives. It is undeniable that not only was there simultaneity in the authoritarian tendencies of the 1970s and democratic trends of the 1980s in Latin America, there was also a correspondence with events occurring at a more global level. But what is of interest here is the concrete form whereby a transformation is produced, since this permits us to observe the social and political forces behind the transformation, the characteristics of the process, and the expectations that reasonably can be held concerning it.

The Latin American process and the world situation

It is well known that, since their discovery and conquest right up to the present, the countries of Latin America have not enjoyed the autonomy experienced by other nations. On the contrary, with the rupture of Spanish colonial ties there followed a clear link of economic dependency with England, later followed by the United States once it displaced England.

The relations of Latin America with the United States have sharply marked the destiny of the Latin American countries, both economically and politically. Consequently, scholars of the region have always emphasized this power's role as the economically dominant and politically hegemonic centre. Studies of North American "imperialism" or analyses of Latin American situations of "dependency" are extensive, varied, and frequent. At the same time, relations with the United States are central in the definition of policies in the area. That this is unavoidable becomes evident once we recall the direct presence of the United States in these countries: from direct armed intervention to US predominance in continental organisms and alternatives, such as the Organization of American States, the Alliance for Progress of the early 1960s, or the recently launched Initiative for the Americas.

An important change in this situation occurred to the extent that European and Japanese development generated what has been termed "multipolarity." This created a diversification of economic and political centres, which in Latin America translated into greater margins of manoeuvre regarding both the economic sphere as well as the range of political alternatives. There is, thus, greater autonomy in relation to the United States. When the previously discussed wave of authoritarianism swept Latin America, this situation had a double impact, creating conditions that were often contradictory for the new non-democratic regimes.

Politically, multipolarity contributed to a certain easing of the Cold War. This displaced the threat of military confrontation as the centre of conflict, which would be replaced by the issue of human rights as the yardstick for measuring the quality of a political system. This tendency, ratified by the election of Carter to the Presidency of the United States (which raised great hopes among dissidents of the authoritarian governments), meant a resounding rejection of authorities that lacked democratic legitimation in Latin America.

Economically, on the other hand, the situation tended to favour the maintenance of the authoritarian regimes. Among other factors, the petroleum crisis increased the financial resources of the large banks holding the huge profits of the crude-exporting countries as deposits. Simultaneously, the decline in the rate of profit in some of the developed countries, particularly the United States, led transnational capital to seek the exploitation of cheap labour wherever it was available. This translated into an important flow of direct credits to the Latin American countries, the allocation of which largely ignored the nature of the prevailing political regime or human rights situation. This would later give rise to the well-known foreign debt problem. As a consequence, the transnational firms acquired a greater presence in the countries of the region. Nevertheless, the timing and conditions of this greater presence varied in the different countries since they depended on multiple factors. In the Chilean case, which we have emphasized here, the assault of the transnational firms was very strong and early, as a result of the drastic policies of privatization pursued by the military regime. These policies transferred major components of the once strong state sector of the economy into private hands.

This double condition, both political and economic, also translated into a diverse and even contradictory impact upon what could analytically be considered the external factor. On the one hand, politically and diplomatically there was a forceful rejection of the break with democracy, especially in the cases of Chile and the Southern Cone countries, owing to their traditions and proximity to European models. Even more forceful was the practically unanimous condemnation of the trampling of human rights. This rejection translated into very concrete measures: generalized granting of asylum to persecuted politicians (thereby universalizing a practice with Latin American roots), support for internal and external opposition through a constant flow of resources, assistance to the victims of violent repression or economic marginalization. Simultaneously, steps were taken towards ensuring the relative diplomatic isolation of the authoritarian regimes, and recurrent condemnations were voiced by international organisms. In Chile there were breaks in diplomatic ties, such as the Mexican example, the withdrawal of ambassadors (Italy), and constant condemnations by the United Nations, which overwhelmingly approved negative reports in its Commission on Human Rights. Amnesty International also carried out exhaustive efforts to denounce the human rights situation.

On the other hand, economic agents provided a sustained flow of financial credits that served to support the economic policies of the authoritarian governments; without these resources these governments would have had serious difficulties in surviving. In the particular case of Chile this involved not just private credits – which tend to be granted solely in view of the rate of return. Important credits were also obtained from international financial organizations, such as the World Bank, and the regime enjoyed the determined support of the International Monetary Fund. This became increasingly the case as the economic model imposed by the military regime began to consolidate towards the end of the 1970s. This international backing would be a critical base of support during the 1982–1983 crises.

This dual conditioning continued until the opposition to the military regime began to develop and there emerged within the opposition a strong left-wing insurrectional alternative. To the extent that the hardening of the regime weakened the moderate opposition's capacity to act it appeared to justify the development of the extreme opposition and its increasing recourse to tactics of direct action. This dual conditioning converged in the search for a political path to democracy.

The dangerous political polarization led to intensified efforts to seek a democratic solution. The economic interests came to view the continuation of a situation that might become uncontrollable a considerable risk to their interests. It was at this point, towards the end of 1985, that US concerns regarding a possible hardening of the military regime in order to confront the opposition led the United States to condition its support for new World Bank credits upon a political opening. As a result, the state of siege was lifted.

This cursory description of some of the external factors affecting the process of Latin American democratization (and, in particular, the Chilean case) does not pretend to ignore the fact that there are no external conditions without internal conditions. Furthermore, it could be argued that external factors ratify the internal, although limitations of space prohibit developing this point here.

Finally, one should consider the direct impact of the long process that was to culminate in the end of the Cold War. Here the reference is more strictly ideological and refers to two aspects. First, to the extent that the crisis of the so-called "real socialist" countries deepened, the magnitude of the phantom of the communist threat – the traditional ideological basis for military coups and dictatorships – dwindled. This weakened the ideological foundation of the authoritarian regimes, even though the modern "bureaucratic–authoritarian state" that emerged in the 1960s could point to visible indicators of threat to the system. Secondly, many Latin American and Chilean politicians were in exile in Europe. As a result they came into contact with a left-wing political and intellectual climate that was much more critical of the socialist experience in Eastern Europe and that was characterized by a strong democratic vocation. Likewise, those individuals who emigrated to the socialist countries found themselves faced with regimes that – except for their explicit ideological bent – often reminded them of the practices that had led them to flee into exile.

It is well known that the experience of military rule led many leftists to value democratic forms that they had previously criticized. This made them more receptive to their new European environment, strengthening the stance of those among them who already tended towards more moderate positions, while convincing others that the most developed political tendencies were to be found in this direction. These politicians played an important role in a country like Chile, which was characterized by the existence of a strong Marxist left, as they introduced elements of moderation into the agreements for a peaceful political transition towards democratic forms.

Concerning the Communist Party, the adoption of a line of direct confrontation and armed struggle arose to a large extent from contact with countries that had experienced triumphant insurrections, such as Cuba and Nicaragua. This situation contrasted with the tendencies toward *détente* and liberalization in Eastern Europe and would provoke a sharp internal crisis within the Chilean Communist Party. The control of the party apparatus by the most hard-line faction would contribute to its isolation from a left that increasingly tended towards the moderation of its proposals and actions.

The social and political mobilization in Chile

The 1973 military coup in Chile was framed within a sharp social and political conflict concerning the possibility, real or imagined, of transforming the prevailing socio-economic system and replacing it with a socialist system. The nature of the military intervention was not arbitrary; rather it involved the imposition of the interests of one of the sectors in the conflict and the vanquishing of the members of the other. Hence the armed forces' definition of the situation as a war and of their opponent as an enemy. Hence also, the highly repressive nature of the regime and the traumatic division that it produced.

The first periods of the military regime were violent and massively repressive against the partisans of Popular Unity, with every form of brutality being used, which provoked international indignation and condemnation. Social and political organizations were rapidly disarticulated to prevent any opposition. Only the Catholic Church was able to pursue efforts to limit the of repressive abuses, promoting, under very harsh conditions, the defence of human rights. Under the Church's shelter, relatives of victims of repression formed groups that became the nucleus for human rights mobilizations, which persisted throughout the military regime. Alongside these efforts and also under the umbrella of the Church, systems of economic survival were organized among the most dispossessed sectors.

Beyond these minimal defences, some political groups persevered in trying to reorganize, arduously subsisting in clandestinity. Mean-

339

while, the new regime, through a combination of political authoritarianism and increasing economic liberalism,[11] produced profound transformations in Chilean society.

The point is not to raise again the discussion over whether the regime had foundational pretensions from the outset. Regardless of whether it did possess this foundational nature or whether changes were necessary to defend itself before the threat – real or imagined – of a change of system, the fact is that transformations were produced in the economy that profoundly altered the social structure.[12] These transformations essentially involved three sectors: first, a change was produced in the entrepreneurial élites, where a sector arose linked to exports and with increased ties to foreign capital; secondly, the old middle classes tied to the state apparatus shrunk and new middle classes arose, employees of small and medium-sized businesses and the finance and commercial sectors; thirdly, the popular sectors changed drastically – the working class diminished and the urban informal sector and chronically unemployed grew. These social transformations, combined with the social disarticulation produced by proscription, persecution, and the transformation of prior social and political organizations, generated a situation of social atomization and breakdown of the channels of representation. This favoured the institutional projects that emerged within the regime once the economic model appeared to be consolidated after overcoming the 1975 shock.

In fact, lacking the foundation of democratic legitimacy that allowed the previous regime to function, the authoritarian government attempted a number of alternatives, none of which was successful. As the legitimation problem was always present, the regime persisted in two types of justifications: defence in the face of communism and economic success. Although the first was strongest initially, it always remained present and regained importance whenever the economy underwent difficulties.

This permanent legitimacy problem, which prevented the consolidation of the regime and its project, gave way to the aim of creating a protected democracy. This project was made explicit in General Pinochet's Chacarillas speech and finally took shape in the 1980 Constitution. This Constitution, the product of the legitimacy problem and internal conflicts among sectors in power, was unable to establish itself immediately as the foundational norm for political action. On the contrary, the Constitution and the plebiscite by which its approval was imposed, marked the beginning of the rearticulation of the opposition party system.

In fact, before the plebiscite was convoked in September 1980, the Christian Democratic Party had decided openly to confront the military regime and began to mobilize actively against it. For its part, the Communist Party, a few days before the plebiscite, proclaimed its confrontation with the military regime through "all forms of struggle, including acute violence."

It should be noted that the proclamation of the plebiscite and the opposition decisions occurred at a time of economic success, a time when there was talk of an "economic miracle," which was expressed in production and consumption increases. Since this same plebiscite approved the designation of General Pinochet as President of the Republic for eight more years, with provision for a possible re-election, the "Yes" victory in the plebiscite appeared to consolidate everything.

Things did not turn out this way, however. First, the 1980 plebiscite lacked even the slightest pretence of being a credible procedure, nor did it allow for minimal independent supervision. The plebiscite only confirmed the impression that power was almost absolute and that it was unnecessary to consult the citizenry. Secondly, although it was minimal, the participation that was permitted to the opposition to state its position on the plebiscite opened up some room for manoeuvre. Thirdly, the 1980 Constitution did not immediately consecrate this protected democracy; it only promised it for eight years later. As a result the plebiscite lacked any legitimating force. In summary, the 1980 Constitution, dictated during a triumphant moment for the economic model, did not fulfil the proposition of consolidating or institutionalizing the military regime, although it did clearly open up this perspective for the future.

In any case, it must be noted that the long transitional period – eight years – before the permanent articles of the Constitution were to go into effect caused uncertainty about whether the Constitution would be definitively applied or if the process would follow a different path.

On the other hand, no strong official social and political organization was created (whether because of fear of being overtaken by the demands that it might raise, or because of social groups' refusal to take part in it) and, in general, the real social organizations were controlled by elements in opposition to the regime. In this manner, an active nucleus persisted against the regime, while the mass of the population appeared depoliticized, whether owing to fear, the absence of channels of expression, or the inefficacy of political action. But this de-politicization also implied that indifference or tolerance towards the regime depended very directly upon the satisfaction of interests, which appeared to guarantee an order without other alternatives. To the extent that the military regime was unable to consolidate and institutionalize the political, social, and economic order that it had imposed coercively, there remained conflicts that lacked regular mechanisms of resolution, save for the use of force, which threatened to become arbitrary and, therefore, faced natural resistances.

Throughout the process of development of the military regime, three fundamental conflicts were always present, though in different forms and with different force: (1) within the dominant sectors in the military regime, owing to different interests and political conceptions; (2) in regard to the political regime, in terms of the alternatives of authoritarianism or democracy; and (3) in relation to substantive projects of society and economy. This last conflict was at the heart of the polarized discussion that culminated in the coup. It reappeared, although differently, once the possibility of ending the military regime emerged.

These conflicts, previously latent and of little force, exploded with the economic crisis that began in 1981 and was felt with full intensity in 1982, when real unemployment reached almost one-third of the economically active population, production fell 14 per cent, and a large number of firms went bankrupt.[13] Demonstrations of discontent overcame the fear and atomization imposed by the regime. Led by opposition union, shantytown, student, and party leaders, and nourished by the sharpening of the internal conflict, the protests expressed a decisive change in the correlation of forces, obliging the government to make concessions. On 11 May 1983, the "national protests" began. These spanned a broad range of activities: banging pots, keeping children home from school, sit-ins, honking car horns, constructing barricades, street skirmishes, etc.[14]

The government's concessions were not limited to social and economic demands. They also included a political opening intended to defuse the different conflicts. This opening appeared limited, informal, and unstable, suffering, from 1983 on, from different changes that revealed different moments, struggles and pressures, both internal as well as external.

From 1983 to 1985 and, to some degree, until 1986, the opposition to the regime – articulated politically in the Democratic Alliance (AD), led by the Christian Democrats, and the Popular Democratic Movement (MDP), led by the Communist Party – pursued a strategy of confronting the regime. Although having different means and discourses, both groups aimed for the removal of General Pinochet, his replacement by a Provisional Government, and the dictation of a new Constitution. In its organized entities the social mobilization embraced these demands, but high levels of spontaneity marked the "national protests" from the start and revealed the difficulty of politically representing a highly changed society.[15]

The strategy of overthrowing the regime gradually weakened because it lacked a clear plan outlining how the adoption of determinate courses of action would lead to the achievement of the desired goal. In terms of the parties, agreements were made at the lowest common denominator of unity among the different sectors of the opposition; but from this basis neither the Alliance nor the MDP developed consistent projects towards achieving their ends. This is clearer regarding the AD than the MDP, in which the Communist Party at least appeared to maintain a coherent line oriented towards developing an insurrectional movement, even if this alternative did not appear to be realistic. On the other hand, the lack of politicization and organization of the base hindered the realization of successive actions that could have really put the government in check; as a result the social protests turned into occasional events whose results were always unpredictable.

By combining concessions, repression, and opening in varying proportions, the regime managed to survive the strong social mobilization pretty well. It was bolstered by the recovery of the economy from 1986 on.[16]

Social and political divisions within the opposition to the military regime

Beyond the political errors committed by the opposition, underlying the failure to achieve the social mobilization's final goal were the country's social and political divisions.

As has already been noted, the application of the neo-liberal model under conditions of political authoritarianism generated deep changes in the social structure. These changes produced a sharp social division and shattered the idea of a progressive scale of social strata and social mobility. Society was split into two countries, two worlds. Here the expressions "within" and "without" clearly denote the idea of participation in or exclusion from social and cultural production. This social division, which will not be analysed here, to a large extent obliterated the idea of a national community and created differences of interests that were difficult to reconcile. Note that the first "protests" had a very broad social character, but, as the participation of popular neighbourhoods became increasingly greater, the middle classes abandoned these protests. Eventually, these were reduced to being primarily the action of the poor, popular neighbourhoods that were harshly repressed.

On the other hand, the conflict over substantive projects within the political opposition led to the inability to form a single multi-party bloc. Furthermore, to the extent that the process advanced, divisions accentuated. The right tended to lean increasingly toward the maintenance of the authoritarian regime rather than accept the possibility that the left might come to power. At the same time, an important section of the left preferred to wager on its own political alternative, even though this implied problems for ending authoritarianism in the short term. Finally, the political centre, confused and vacillating, became interested in democracy, but feared committing itself to alliances that might imply a medium-term cost to it.

These social and political divisions allowed the government to resist the pressures it faced, even those originating in the intellectual realm and, especially, from the United States. The regime also possessed considerable strength of its own, the product equally of the unity of the armed forces, particularly the Army, and the backing of important social sectors, such as national and foreign-linked business groups, as well as the warm acclaim of the economic model by the United States and the IMF.

The year 1986 marked the collapse of the opposition strategy of overthrow and the political recomposition of the regime. This transferred the conflict to the realm of defining institutions. First, however, changes in hegemony and political strategies – which would occur in 1987 – were necessary.

Left-wing political forces grouped in the Popular Democratic Movement had dubbed 1986 the "decisive year." This referred to the objective of achieving the fall of the Pinochet government that year. Political forces of the right, including the Christian Democrats, also considered 1986 to be decisive. They maintained that, if negotiations leading to a political transition out of the military regime did not occur during the year, then afterwards they would no longer be possible, given the proximity of the terms established in the constitutional itinerary of transition.

As is known, 1986 was a failure as the decisive year, particularly for the extreme left, as was clearly revealed by the discovery of arms and the failed attempt on General Pinochet. But it was not just a failure for those sectors pushing for direct action. By this point, the decline in the opposition's capacity to organize massive social mobilizations had become manifest. The social and political divisions, already referred to, were behind this decline, which was heightened by the disappointment produced by the non-success of these actions in provoking a fall of the government. The interplay of these social and political divisions would also create the conditions for the new situation that appeared to crystallize in 1987.

In fact, the predominance of a strategy of overthrow tended to favour the action and presence of the Marxist left grouped in the MDP, not only by virtue of their organization and discourse, but also because they could stimulate the disruptive mobilization of the popular sectors. The Christian Democrats, on the other hand, lacked the capacity to control these sectors and, at the same time, were cognizant of the middle classes' progressive abandonment of these types of mobilizations. The Christian Democrats had opted to deepen their line of separating themselves from any links with the Communists, and they placed particular emphasis on the problem of "forms of struggle," proclaiming their rejection of all forms of violence. Simultaneously, they put great effort into improving their position among social organizations, especially unions and student groups, while they also concentrated on those organizations most typically representative of the middle classes, such as universities and professional colleges.

The Communist Party (CP) saw its capacity for social agitation decline and tended to turn to strictly military actions. Little by little, the Manuel Rodríguez Patriotic Front (FPMR), born under the aegis of the CP, ceased being an armed group supporting popular mobilization and gained increasing autonomy as a vanguard, insurrectional nucleus. In this aspect it converged with the Left Revolutionary Movement (MIR) and other lesser groups, such as the Lautaro Youth Movement.

The clearest expression of these tactical separations and the replacement of mobilized social sectors can be seen in the two most important events of 1986: on the one hand, the arsenals and the attempt on General Pinochet, already referred to, and, on the other, the protest of 2 and 3 July. Just as the militarist tendency of the extreme left sectors can be appreciated in the first, the hegemony achieved by the Christian Democrats and the middle sectors within the social mobilization is noted in the second. The protest was called by the Assembly of Civility, an entity headed by the professional associations, and its character was eminently peaceful and passive, with very few confrontations. It also had the support of middle-class unions, such as truckers and merchants.

In any event, as we have already noted, both these alternatives failed during the "decisive year" of 1986. Whereas one failed to produce an event that might have detonated a possible insurrection, the other was unable to force some type of negotiation leading to a political solution.

For his part, General Pinochet launched a clearly triumphal challenge from the southern locality of Santa Juana in mid-1986, announcing that he "would not leave power for the pure pleasure of it," that the transition required not 8 years but 16 (8 to dictate the laws, and 8 to try them), and that he would continue the work of the regime beyond 1989. This was virtually equivalent to launching a campaign to prolong his mandate for a new eight-year term.

Later, in September 1986, using an efficient machinery based on the municipalities, General Pinochet managed to pull off a large demonstration in Santiago that promoted his leadership after the assassination attempt he suffered.

The institutional way out

From the beginning of 1987 it became clear that, alongside the developments and changes occurring within the opposition, the regime had also been changing its stance towards seeking the normalization of the political situation. The regime finally was serious about putting into effect the institutional mechanisms established in 1980. For a long time, it had not been clear that they would be applied, whether because these mechanisms might be circumvented by the opposition's efforts to end the regime or because of the government's permanent threats of imposing authoritarian continuity via a new show of force.

The regime began the year by dictating the legislation putting into motion the institutional scenario previously established. Thus, it dictated both the electoral registration law and the political party law. Despite their defects and the anomalies denounced by the opposition, these laws established relatively simple mechanisms for voter registration, as well as for the formation of recognized political parties.

These, certainly, were not laws adequate to the functioning of a normal democracy. On the contrary, this legislation bore the imprint of authoritarianism, which was evident not only in the predominance of military control in the political process, but also in other aspects of the political institutional order. Marxist political parties were excluded – in Chile, these parties represented an important sector of the population – and a sharp division between the social and the political was established through the prohibition of party political participation in social organizations and of social leaders' participation in party politics.[17]

Be that as it may, this legislation appeared to reveal the regime's intention of normalizing the political situation and of putting into effect the protected democracy established in the Constitution. It also confirmed that the 1988 plebiscite to ratify the armed forces' candidate would be held and conditions were prepared so that it would appear acceptable – the latter not only because of the desire to legitimate the continuity of the model imposed, but also to fend off increasingly strong pressure from the international community and, most directly, the United States, which feared the consequences of a dangerous polarization in Chile.

These changes confronted the opposition forces with a situation that demanded new approaches if effective action was to be taken. The failure of "the decisive year" had sunk the political forces into a process of internal discussion concerning the appropriate tactics for the new situation, in which the autonomous action of social mobilization tended to decline while the parties assumed the leadership of the opposition process. The internal discussions were also evidenced by the scarcity of demonstrations and political initiatives. Only the campaign for competitive "free elections" instead of the plebiscite remained active. However, this campaign lacked strength, as the parties were increasingly convinced of its futility. This sensation grew progressively as the term in which the plebiscite would take place approached.

This period of redefinition of political spaces and strategies also implied important divisions within parties and in some cases led to clear party splits. Simultaneously, the apparently most solid groupings declined in relevance. This occurred with both the AD and the MDP. New alliances were sought, but, in general, these never took off.

Within the right, proposed by the National Union Party, the National Renovation party was created at the beginning of the year. Together with the National Union Party, this party fused together the Independent Democratic Union (UDI) and the National Work Front (created by an ex-Pinochet minister, Onofre Jarpa). Within this new party, a sharp internal struggle developed between its different sectors: the "modernizers" drawn from the National Union, with Andrés Allamand at its head, and oriented towards creating a new right for the future political system; the "conservatives," who favoured supporting the government and standing behind the regime with General Pinochet. Confronted by the impending plebiscite proposed by the government, the conservatives predominated and imposed their position upon the right as a whole. This involved accepting the plebiscite as a valid mechanism and supporting the candidacy of General Pinochet as being the best one. Another sector of the right, the National Party, strained by the disjuncture of either entering National Renovation or allying itself with the Christian Democrats, opted to maintain its independence.

The Christian Democrats, with Gabriel Valdés' term as the president of the party over, entered into a sharp and prolonged internal discussion. Two strong, clearly defined positions appeared. The debate centred on the desirability of registering as a party and the nature of the alliances to pursue. Only in June was the contest settled in favour of Patricio Aylwin, who favoured party registration and a turn more towards the right.

Within the left, all efforts to reunite the Socialist Party (PS) failed. The PS (Nuñez) decided to accentuate its left profile by withdrawing from the Democratic Alliance and pursuing policies increasingly independent of the Christian Democrats. At the same time, the PS (Almeyda), recently strengthened and with its leader back in Chile and in jail, achieved greater autonomy from the Communist Party in its definitions of the political conjuncture.

The Communist Party bore the brunt of the failure of the decisive year and sank into deep discussions and analyses of its political strategy. Faced with the danger of increasing isolation and the continued attraction of the insurrectional perspective, the party exhibited confusion and vacillation, and voices in disagreement with the central authorities emerged.

The movements involved in direct action also faced internal problems as a result of their evaluation of the situation. This is seen clearly in July 1987, when the MIR divided into two: one military and the other political. The FPMR also split, with one sector becoming autonomous of all ties with the Communist Party.

As can be seen, even though the first half of 1987 proceeded without major mobilizations or political initiatives on the part of the parties, the parties had turned inward prior to the critical dilemma over defining positions regarding the process of institutional normalization begun by the regime.

From political opening to democratization

By the end of 1987 the regime's institutional framework had been imposed. The parties unanimously pursued electoral registration; by the end of the year nearly half of the eligible voters had been registered. Also, a significant number of political parties had registered or were in the process of doing so, with the exception of the majority of the left parties, which were institutionally proscribed. Finally, the plebiscite was accepted as a valid mechanism, and the political forces began to define their positions regarding it.

In these conditions, 1988 began as an electoral year, with political discussion centring on the necessary conditions for authenticating the validity of the plebiscite, a concern shared by the Catholic Church and the US government.

Although it is a debatable point that will be clarified only by future studies, it appears acceptable to argue that it was the massive social mobilizations of 1983, 1984, and 1985 that forced the regime towards political opening and led it to implement its own institutionality as a form of political transition. This does not imply a complete reversal, given that it was never clear that this institutionality would be applied, especially under the prevailing conditions.

Nevertheless, criticism of social mobilization was always present among the political actors, especially within sectors of the political right. This criticism would later be taken up by the Christian Democrats and other sectors of the centre, and eventually, after 1986, even by those sectors of the left closest to the centre, particularly after the discovery of arms and the failed attempt on General Pinochet's life. The criticism focused on two aspects: the ineffectiveness of mobilization for achieving the goal of removing General Pinochet, and the fact that social mobilization was manipulated by and benefited the most left-wing sectors.

This was almost irrelevant since, after 1986, there were few social mobilizations and, to the extent that they did occur, they had a different character. The mobilizations of 1987 were more sectoral, involving demands that were more corporative than political. They involved professors protesting against layoffs, students demanding more university loans, unions demanding economic gains, human rights groups demanding an end to torture, indebted home-owners demanding better repayment terms, etc.

There were only two large national mobilizations. One was a strike called for 7 October by the National Workers' Command. The other was a rally called for 19 November by the Assembly of Civility. The October strike maintained the traditional traits of the earlier protests, but, as in 1986, their peaceful and passive character was emphasized. Skirmishes were avoided, and those that did occur were sporadic and localized. The strike had less impact than the other protests, confirming the exhaustion and lack of explicit objectives of the mobilization. The turn-out for the 19 November rally was massive, although smaller than that for a similar rally held on the same site a few years earlier. The rally symbolized a rejection of the government of General Pinochet and its perpetuation in power beyond 1989, but its content appeared confused. Alongside slogans against the government and calls for free elections, some sectors also called for a "No" vote in the plebiscite to be held the following year.

Both the October protest/strike and the November rally were called by social organizations: the National Workers' Command and the Assembly of Civility, respectively. This type of convocation was indicative of the opposition's stagnation, which, as already noted, progressively intensified, particularly after mid-1986. Although moderate sectors attained greater coherence and force, the persistence of the authoritarian regime gave continued relevance to extreme positions pursuing violence.

In this context of political stagnation, these social mobilizations revealed that rejection of General Pinochet had not diminished, but that this force was not represented by any kind of unified political alternative, such as a multi-party formation, or other type of pact establishing such an alternative. Only in the course of 1988 did the centre–left political pact that would end up carrying out the transition acquire solidity.

The triumph of the democratic alternative

Towards the end of 1987 the predominance of the centrist Christian Democrats became clear, while the moderate wing of the left progressively gained strength. This deepened the isolation of the Communist Party, already deep in the throes of a long internal crisis.

On the other hand, the differences between General Pinochet, who sought to remain in power, and a sector of the armed forces that preferred to return power to civilians, were resolved by the proclamation of General Pinochet's candidacy in the plebiscite prescribed by the Constitution, but with guarantees providing for the correctness of the elections, including free access to television and the right of registered parties to place supervisors at all voting places during polling and the vote count.

On 5 October 1988, the "No" vote triumphed and a year later elections were held that were won by the centre–left coalition's candidate headed by the Christian Democrats. Although General Pinochet continues as Commander-in-Chief of the Army and institutional norms persist that will require modification to adapt them to fully democratic norms, it can be said that the transition occurred with the inauguration of the new government and the elected congress.

Six years after the economic crisis and the social protests, the transition ended up being led by the political parties. The extremist and violent tendencies of the right and the left ended up isolated, with moderation and political consensus winning out.

It is hard to specify the character of the democratizing movement or its relation with the regional movement for democratization in Latin America or with that occurring at a global level. Nevertheless, the analysis of the Chilean process appears to pose again the traditional theme of the formation of social subjects on the basis of structural positions and the social character of historical processes.

In the case reviewed, it might be said that the social conflict of the 1980s differed sharply from the conflicts of the 1960s. Clearly, it is not simply that the popular sectors had "learned" the ominous results provoked by an excess of ideological zeal. Rather, the popular sectors are no longer the same, just as the social and economically dominant actors are not the same. The social transformations referred to above broke the organizational and ideological hegemony of sectors of the organized working class. This is not only because they have diminished in number, but because the popular mass of recent migrants from the countryside are now established in the cities as a mass of permanent poor. Their social mobility is blocked and the industrial worker no longer stands as their referent. In the Chilean case, the movement against Pinochet was stronger in popular neighbourhoods than among organized workers. Although national union leaders called the protests, the unions were never able to carry off a workers' strike to spur democratization. The fight against Pinochet was more a fight of the poor than of the workers.

351

Nevertheless, unlike the "working class," which, despite its growing homogeneity, retained common elements of identification that allowed for its organization, the poor were not incorporated into modern labour and lack these common elements; generally they are atomized, without organic representation. Thus, it is not surprising that some sectors support General Pinochet's administration, forming what has been called "popular Pinochetismo." But this "popular Pinochetismo" appears to reflect the clientelism of local authorities of the military regime or unconscious adherence to the established order. In either case, this is a minority position among the "pobladores" (urban poor) according to recent electoral analyses.[18]

The poor urban popular sectors were precisely the groups of greatest activation during the protest movement, especially during the harsh economic crisis. This led the insurrectional line of the Communist Party to focus on these groups, at the expense of its until then traditional workerist position. At the same time, the middle sectors that participated in the mobilization for democracy did not make alliances with the marginal poor, as they once had with organized workers. (This coalition had formed the basis of the Popular Front governments after 1938.) On the contrary, as we have noted, they tended to differentiate their activities and mobilize only to the extent that they controlled the mobilization.

This relation among the social sectors was also apparent among the political parties until the moderate centre–left coalition gave the transition its definitive push. Here, too, we see the predominance of the middle sectors and the isolation of the marginal popular sectors. This does not imply that these popular sectors were represented by the extreme left led by the Communists; or that they supported an insurrectional line. On the contrary, their mobilization tended to be reactive – a "protest" – in the face of the deterioration in economic conditions and the repressive practices that massively affected them.

The most difficult problem facing the new democracy is precisely the problem of representation. The accusations directed at the "political class" that it has closed in on itself, ignoring substantive social problems and accepting the prevailing economic model, should consider that these facts are not solely the result of the good or bad intentions of politicians. The fact is that, in face of the enormous social transformations that have occurred, it is not easy to establish representative political parties. Furthermore, a gap has emerged between the party system – which still corresponds to its modern origins, tied to the emergence of the industrial working class[19] – and a social structure that is still not well known, but, in any case, is no longer the same.

Final remarks

Acknowledging the multiple dimensions of any process of democratic transition, here we are interested in emphasizing the social actors engaged in the tranformative movement.[20]

The Chilean experience reveals the extensive changes produced in a relatively short period of time by the application of liberal economic policies under a politically authoritarian regime. These changes are superimposed upon others that were already in progress, such as those relating to urbanization and the modernization of the productive system. In this manner, a social structure is created that is distinct from the social structure of preceding decades, and that is also not comparable to earlier stages in already developed countries. This is a division that slices within and without, separating citizens and barbarians, included and excluded, and serves as a reference for distinguishing between two countries in one: the two Chiles, the two Brazils, the two Mexicos, etc.

In the process of democratization, the excluded popular sectors played an important role by mobilizing against the military regime and by representing a threat of violent disruption, which tended to convince both external and internal powers of the desirability of a political opening and an institutional solution. In this regard, the case of Brazil, with its mobilization of popular base communities, appears very similar to that of Chile. Uruguay might be the most distant case given the permanence of a highly homogeneous social structure.

Nevertheless, democratization became possible once de-activation of these popular sectors was achieved. This de-activation occurred through the political control of the mobilizations, which led to a democratic conclusion free from sharp programmatic conflicts with the dominant economic and social powers. In other words, the popular sectors' demand for greater participation in the social product was incompatible with the interests of the dominant social and economic groups. These sectors would not accept such changes. Once popular demands are included in the project of institutional democratization this becomes unviable. Thus, the de-activation of the popular sectors was a necessary condition for the democratizing consensus.

What is possible is done, and politics is constructed on the basis of the possible; the new social structure is a direct cause of problems in respect of the formation of a community of interests, and such problems clearly hinder attempts at social organization on that basis.

Once democratization has been achieved, representation emerges as the problem. The modern party system, born to represent social sectors and their corresponding conceptions of the world, loses this character. If every party attempts to represent everything, they end up representing nothing.

From a Latin American perspective, the Chilean process exhibits many similarities with other processes of democratization – and, of course, many differences as well. But it may be worth while to note that the differences tend to correspond to differences in the transformations of the respective social structures. This claim needs to be backed by considerable analysis; nevertheless, it appears to be an interesting hypothesis.

Perhaps considerations of this type, in combination with other explanations of the global political and economic changes, might contribute to understanding problems that will probably require considerable time before they can even be clearly posed.

Notes and references

1. In Latin America there exists a long tradition of studying social subjects. Within this tradition, the works of José Medina Echevarria, Gino Germani, Alain Touraine, Fernando H. Cardoso, and Enzo Faletto stand out.
2. Gino Germani, *Política y Sociedad en una Epoca de Transición*, Buenos Aires: Editorial Paidos, 1971.
3. The term "lost decade" is found in a number of Economic Commission for Latin America documents that analyse this period. The term is made explicit in CEPAL, *Transformación Productiva con Equidad*, Santiago: CEPAL.
4. CEPAL, *Anuario Estadistico de America Latina y el Caribe*, Santiago: CEPAL, 1990.
5. Guillermo O'Donnell, "Reflexiones sobre las tendencias de cambio en el Estado Burocrático Autoritario," *Revista Mexicana de Sociología* 39 (January–March 1977): 9–59.
6. For a general view of Latin American history, see Tulio Halperin Donghi, *Historia Contemporanea de América Latina*, Madrid: Alianza Editorial. After the mid-1960s, studies tended to be increasingly focused on national cases, although ECLA's economic analyses continued to maintain a Latin American perspective.
7. Rodrigo Baño, "Ruptura hegemónica: Argentina, Brasil, y Chile en el autoritarismo defensivo," *FLACSO Documento de Trabajo* 76 (1977).
8. O'Donnell, op. cit.
9. Antonio Garretón, *El Proceso Político Chileno*, Santiago: FLACSO, 1983.
10. O'Donnell, op. cit.
11. Tomás Moulian and Pilar Vergara, "Ideologías y políticas económicas en Chile," *Revista Mexicana de Sociología* 2 (April–June 1981): 845–904.
12. Javier Martínez and Eugenio Tironi, "La jibarización de la clase obrera," *Proposiciones* 2 (January 1982), no. 5; Guillermo Campero, "Los cambios en la estructura social," *Margen, Revista de Filosofia y Letras* (March 1982): 70–79; and Javier Martínez and A. León, *Clases*

y Clasificaciones Sociales, Santiago: CED-SUR, 1987.

13. Rodrigo Baño and Manuel Canales, "De la dictadura a la democracia," in *Chile en la Década de los 80*, Madrid: CEDEAL, 1992, pp. 95–183.

14. In the press of the period there are extensive reports on the protests. Academic studies include: Vicente Espinoza, "Los pobladores en la política," in *Los Movimientos Sociales y la Lucha Democrática*, Santiago: CLACSO-ILET, 1986, pp. 31–52; *Protesta y Protagonismo Popular*, Santiago: ECO, 1983; María Eugenia Morales, "Las jornadas de protesta de los años 1983–1984," *Política* 22–23 (June 1990): 173–186.

15. Rodrigo Baño, *Lo Social y lo Político*, Santiago: FLACSO, 1985.

16. The rate of growth of GDP was 7.8% in 1980, 5.5% in 1981, -14.1% in 1982, -0.7% in 1983, 6.3% in 1984, 2.4% in 1985, 5.7% in 1986 and in 1987.

17. See, "Las críticas del grupo de los 24," *Revista APSI* (March 1981): 9–16.

18. Rodrigo Baño, "Elecciones en Chile: ¿Otra vez lo mismo o al revés?, *Revista Española de Investigaciones Sociológicas* 50 (April–June 1990): 43–60; and, by the same author, "Tendencias políticas y resultados electorales despues de viente años," *Revista Mexicana de Sociología* (1990): 59–82.

19. Umberto Cerroni, "Para una teoria del partido político," *Teoria Marxista del Partido Partido*, Buenos Aires: Cuadernos Pasado y Presente, 1971.

20. The most inspiring study within this perspective, of clearly Weberian inspiration, is Fernando Henrique Cardoso and Enzo Faletto, *Dependencia y Desarrollo en América Latina*, Mexico, D.F.: Siglo XXI Editores, 1967.

13

The transnational indigenous movement in a changing world order

Bice Maiguashca

Introduction

The role of ideas in the field of international relations has not so far been the subject of either extensive empirical research or in-depth theoretical discussion. The reason for this neglect has to do with the prominent position that the "realist" paradigm has had in this field over the last four decades. As a consequence, very few studies have been done on the recent emergence of various social movements – such as the peace movement, the feminist movement, and the ecological movement – that are questioning the normative foundations of our present world order. The purpose of this paper is to study one of these movements, the international indigenous movement, in order to show how, with no economic power and hardly any political clout, indigenous leaders have relied on the power of ideas to mobilize both their own people and non-indigenous sympathizers around their cause. The international indigenous movement, therefore, will be seen as a cultural/ideological force that has emerged on the international scene today and that has a potential role in shaping the outlines of an alternative world order.

Before I begin, some clarification of the term "indigenous peoples" is needed. According to a UN definition, these peoples are:

the existing descendants of the peoples who inhabited the present territory of a country wholly or partially at the time when persons of a different culture or ethnic origin arrived there ... overcame them and, by conquest, settlement or other means, reduced them to a non-dominant or colonial situation. (Cited in Burger, 1987, p. 6)

Perhaps the most important criterion for defining indigenous peoples, however, is the subjective dimension, that is, self-identification. In effect, indigenous peoples have chosen to emphasize this aspect when defining themselves. The World Council of Indigenous Peoples, for example, has proposed that:

Indigenous peoples are such population groups as we are, who from old-age times have inhabited the lands in which we live, who are aware of having a character of our own, ... with a language of our own and having certain essential and unique characteristics which confer upon us the strong conviction of belonging to a people, who have an identity in ourselves and should be thus regarded by others. (Cited in Burger, 1987, p. 8)

Evidence for the existence of a shared world-view that is different from that of non-indigenous peoples is the very fact that, despite their vastly dissimilar experiences and traditions, indigenous peoples all over the world have united in an international movement and, as we shall see in the course of this paper, have put forward a coherent counter-hegemonic project. If one studies the fundamental core ideas of this project – as they have been expressed both in joint declarations and in separate statements issued by various indigenous movements across the globe – one discovers that indigenous peoples, despite their differences, have adopted a strikingly similar position regarding the nature of the oppression to which they have been subjected and the means for their liberation. It is this common world-view, embodied in their counter-hegemonic project, that permits us to treat the international indigenous movement as a single phenomenon.

In this paper I will use a theoretical framework that has been formulated recently and that, unlike the "realist" paradigm, allows for the conceptualization of the role of ideas in international life. I am referring to the work of Robert Cox (1981, 1983, 1987), whose "historical-dialectical approach" seeks to integrate objective factors (socio-economic forces), subjective factors (ethical, cultural, and ideological forces), and institutional factors (organizations) into a single theoretical framework.

Cox's main unit of analysis is what he calls a "world order configuration," which emerges, develops, and declines during a particular

357

historical period. These configurations can be hegemonic or non-hegemonic. They are hegemonic when one national society gains prominence in the international system and is, thereby, able to set the parameters within which inter-state relations occur. An example of a hegemonic world order is the Pax Americana, which emerged after World War II. For Cox, any "world order configuration" is composed of three "historical structures": *modes of social relations of production, forms of state*, and *world orders*. The first, i.e. modes of social relations of production, refers to the way in which social groups organize themselves economically, politically, and culturally around the production process. The social groups themselves are referred to as "social forces" by Cox. The second historical structure, i.e. forms of state, refers to state/society complexes and concerns the relationship between civil society and the state. One example could be the liberal welfare state. As for the third historical structure, i.e. world order, it concerns a particular correlation of forces that defines certain global issues such as the East–West conflict during the Cold War period or the North–South dialogue characteristic of recent decades (Cox, 1981, p. 138).

According to Cox, each of these historical structures can be analysed from three points of view: its objective dimensions, its subjective dimensions, and its institutions. Let us now take a brief look at these three component parts.

The objective dimension of a historical structure concerns not only its economic and organizational capabilities and natural resources, but also the way in which these resources are organized into a functioning *production process*. For example, the objective dimension of Pax Americana's "world order" structure includes, among other things, the development of nuclear technology and its impact on East–West relations.

The subjective component of historical structures, on the other hand, refers to the realm of *ideas*. According to Cox, ideas can be conceived of in two ways. First, they can be seen as "intersubjective meanings," which are broadly shared notions about the nature of social relations. These commonly held beliefs serve to guide behaviour and define expectations. Although intersubjective meanings may appear to be timeless truths, in fact they are historically conditioned and change, albeit slowly, over time. When Pax Americana was at its height, for instance, the belief in deterrence as the best way to secure peace was held universally. The second way in which Cox conceives of ideas is as "collective images" of social order. These images, unlike the "intersubjective meanings," are specific to particular groups and consist of different and often opposing world-views. At the national level, unionized workers, for instance, will think differently about their lives from un-established workers and both these groups will hold world-views that are at variance with those of farmers or bureaucrats. These collective images also exist at the international level. Within the framework of Pax Americana, for example, the East–West as well as the North–South conflicts reflect the clash of different "collective images" of the international system.

The third and last component of a historical structure is *institutions*. Institutions can be seen as the convergence point for the objective and subjective factors discussed above. They have the important function of stabilizing, legitimizing, and perpetuating a particular order at the international level. During the early years of Pax Americana, for example, the United Nations and its agencies played an important role in legitimizing the dominant position of the industrialized Western nations in the new international order by providing a forum where poor nation-states and marginalized social groups were able to air their opposition to the policies of the dominant powers. Thus potentially divisive international conflicts were neutralized.

As can be seen, Cox's model offers a framework in which the role of ideas in international relations can be conceptualized. In this paper I shall analyse the international indigenous movement in Coxian terms, i.e. as a counter-hegemonic "social force" that is seeking to challenge Pax Americana's prevailing ideologies ("intersubjective meanings") and offer an alternative world-view around which a new international order can be fashioned. In the first section I will describe the global context out of which the international indigenous movement arose. In the following two sections I shall move on to focus on the development of the movement since 1975 and on the content and form of its counter-hegemonic project.

The global context of the rise of the international indigenous movement

Although indigenous peoples have been struggling against colonial forces for centuries, it was only after World War II that they began to mobilize politically in order to resist oppression. Evidence of this trend is to be found in the rise of national indigenous movements and in the proliferation of institutions aimed at supporting these national struggles. What led to the rise of an international indigenous movement? I shall answer this question by presenting the various factors that contributed to this phenomenon within the framework of Pax Americana's three historical structures.

The global expansion of capitalism: The threat of displacement

After World War II, the rapid expansion of the industrial base in the first world and the incipient development efforts on the part of third world governments created an urgent need for energy resources across the globe. In the first world this need led multinational corporations (MNCs) to explore the peripheral regions of their own countries, making the acceleration of mining the single most threatening event for indigenous peoples in industrialized countries during the last four decades (Burger, 1987, p. 178). In the United States, for example, 40 per cent of all uranium deposits and 15 per cent of surface minable coal is located on Indian reserves (ICIHI, 1987, p. 24). In the third world, hydroelectric power was generally favoured as an energy source, and dams became a core component of development strategies in Asia, Latin America, and Africa during the 1960s and beyond (ICIHI, 1987, p. 52). This again had negative consequences for indigenous peoples. In the early 1960s, for example, the Kaptai Dam in the Chittagong Hill Tracts of Bangladesh submerged 250 square miles of prime agricultural land, equal to 40 per cent of the cultivable area of the region, with the consequence that 100,000 tribal peoples, one-sixth of the total population, were displaced (ICIHI, 1987, p. 53).

This process of displacement intensified during the 1970s with the increasing globalization of production and the emergence of transnational corporations (TNCs). As opposed to MNCs, which remained as appendages of national governments, TNCs became independent entities using the international arena as their economic playground. Finding the resources and markets of their countries of origin too constraining, these corporations now sought to expand their reach to the last unexplored regions of the world (Miller, 1985, p. 140). One example of the destructive role of TNCs in the lives of indigenous peoples has taken place in Brazil where the Great Carajas Project – financed by the World Bank, Rio Tinto Zinc, ALCOA, Royal Dutch Shell, the EEC, and Japanese and US investors – is threatening to displace 10,000 Gaviao and Guayajara Indians (Burger, 1987, p. 107).

Thus, in many respects, over the past 20 years indigenous peoples the world over have become "development refugees." In effect, indigenous peoples today, unlike those who lived in an earlier period, have no alternative areas to which they can retreat. Faced with the possibility of extinction, they have been more willing than ever before to go on the offensive. Beyond this, there has also been a change in the scope of the mobilization of the indigenous peoples. The fact that today their main antagonists are transnational forces, outside the control of national governments, has made indigenous peoples realize that it is not enough to struggle at the national level and that the launching of an international movement is necessary.

The expansion of the nation-state: The threat of assimilation

Since World War II the size and jurisdiction of the state in both industrialized and underdeveloped countries have expanded at an incredible rate. In the industrialized West, indigenous peoples were incorporated into the national welfare state and this had a corrosive effect on their traditional way of life. In Canada, for example, during the 1960s all native children were subject to compulsory schooling, which resulted in a slow but thorough process of deculturation and assimilation into white society. The traditional role of the Indian elders as teachers of the Indian way of life was progressively usurped by white school teachers who taught the children to be ashamed of their race and their heritage.

As for the third world, during the 1950s and 1960s most of the newly created states concentrated their attention on establishing political centralization and fostering national integration. As a consequence, most indigenous peoples, who had enjoyed a relative degree of autonomy during the colonial period, now found themselves under the authority of local élites who were driven by the imperative of "nation-building" and who sought to consolidate their precarious hold on power through any means available to them (Burger, 1987, p. 51).

As a reaction to these assimilationist policies, we are witnessing today an ethnic revival across the globe that is challenging the legitimacy of the nation-state as a unified homogeneous political community. Within this context, indigenous peoples, along with other disaffected groups, are increasingly taking their grievances and demands to the international arena where they can appeal to international law and to the sympathy of independent experts.

361

The development of international law:
A potential resource for indigenous peoples

Until World War II, the question of human rights had always been conceived as a concern falling under national jurisdiction. The genocide of Jews during the war, however, shocked the world into the realization that the greatest violators of human rights were often governments and that the protection of these rights had to be placed under some form of international control. Despite the theoretical tensions between the imperative of national sovereignty, on the one hand, and the necessity of international control, on the other, the idea that governments should be accountable for their policies both to their own people and to the world at large was reinforced by the Nuremberg Trials of 1945 and the Tokyo Trial of 1946.

On 10 December 1948, the Universal Declaration of Human Rights was ratified by the UN General Assembly and it has since become "the moral touchstone for all claims at the international level that justice has not been done at the national level" (Rodley, 1983, p. 264). The provisions that the Declaration put forth represented fundamentally the political philosophy of Western states on the issue of human rights, a philosophy that privileges civil and political rights, such as freedom of thought and religion. These provisions received only a lukewarm response from socialist and third world countries, which argued that not enough attention had been paid to economic and social inequalities. Being in a minority position in the UN General Assembly, however, they were unable to challenge the West successfully (Cassese, 1986, pp. 297–299).

The rapid expansion of the UN membership during the mid-1960s, however, put the United States and its Western allies in a minority position within the General Assembly. The consequences of this became evident in 1966, when the International Covenant on Civil and Political Rights and the International Covenant on Economic, Social and Cultural Rights were passed. Whereas the first Covenant elaborated, once again, the rights of individuals to political and religious freedoms, reflecting the position of the West, the second Covenant put forward a new set of rights representing the recently formulated "socialist doctrine," heralded by the Soviet Union and supported by its satellite states and a majority of third world countries (Cassese, 1986, p. 303). This new doctrine gave rise to provisions declaring the right to work, to social security, to food, to education, to equal pay, to establish unions, to health care, and to an adequate standard of living. In addition, the second Covenant reiterated the right to self-determination and, for the first time, spelled out the right to non-discrimination.

The codification of these new rights presented many oppressed peoples and ethnic groups with new institutional and ideological resources with which they could legitimize their grievances and challenge the normative foundations of the present world order. We shall see later on how indigenous peoples, unable to appeal to national courts or legislatures, replete with unsympathetic bureaucrats, have turned to international law as an alternative source of legal protection. There can be no doubt that, without the development of international human rights law, the internationalization of the indigenous movement would not have occurred.

The development of the international indigenous movement: 1975–1992

The World Council of Indigenous Peoples

The launching of an international indigenous movement started in 1971 when George Manuel, a Canadian Indian, announced his intention to organize a world conference of indigenous peoples. After holding a series of organizational meetings in Guyana and Denmark – which were attended by representatives from Latin America, Scandinavia, Australia, and the United States – it was decided that the conference should be held in British Colombia, Canada. In October 1975, 52 delegates, 135 observers, 25 members of the press, and 54 staff members gathered in an old government-run school for the first international indigenous conference ever held. At the end of the four-day conference the World Council of Indigenous Peoples (WCIP) had been created, with George Manuel as its first chairman. Since then the WCIP has held six world congresses or general assemblies and in the process has become the single most important organization of the movement.

Three phases can be distinguished in the development of this institution. In the first, which lasted from 1975 to 1981, the WCIP concentrated its attention on expanding its membership, establishing itself as an international institution, and promoting the growth of regional organizations. Over a period of six years, two more general assemblies were organized (1977 and 1981). By 1981 the WCIP had also succeeded in extending its reach to include the Nordic Saami Council

363

(Scandinavia), the Coordination of Indian Peoples of Central America, the Inuit Circumpolar Conference (Arctic), the South American Indian Council, and the Ainu people of Japan.

In the second phase of its development, which started roughly in 1981 and ended in 1984, the WCIP consulted widely with local and regional indigenous organizations and, more importantly, brought their concerns together into a political project. The most important step in this process of "ideology-building" was taken in 1984 during the Fourth General Assembly held in Panama. It was here that a comprehensive and detailed declaration was produced, which enumerated 17 principles covering such issues as indigenous peoples' land rights, and cultural and political rights, including self-determination. This document has since become the manifesto of the WCIP and one of the most important declarations of the international movement. In the last section, which focuses on the indigenous counterhegemonic project, I shall discuss the main ideas of this document in more detail.

The third stage in the development of the WCIP, which started in 1984 and continues today, is characterized by an ongoing concern over the issue of membership, which until recently has been predominantly Western oriented. During the Fifth General Assembly in Peru in 1987 it was unanimously agreed that representatives from Asia should be actively incorporated into the WCIP. To this end it was decided that more attention had to be given to obtaining information about the situation of tribal peoples in this region, such as the East Timorese, the West Papuans, and the Moros peoples. This commitment has been reinforced by the WCIP's recent decision to try to have its next general assembly in India.

At this point, considering the indigenous movement's remarkable progress over the last two decades, one might ask: what strategy have its leaders adopted so far to promote their cause within the global arena? The first thing that has to be said in this connection is that one cannot really talk of a "strategy" in the sense of a single long-term course of action agreed to by all the members. Indeed, there seems to have been very little centralized planning of this type. Perhaps the best way to characterize the overall functioning of the movement is by describing it as an unstructured, decentralized network of local, national, regional, and international organizations linked to each other, either directly or indirectly, by means of advanced communications technology. It must be kept in mind that, besides the WCIP, there is a multitude of other groups, both indigenous and

364

non-indigenous, that are contributing to the movement by giving it strength and direction: for example, the International Indian Treaty Council, the Inuit Circumpolar Conference, the Indian Law Resource Centre, the Indian World Association, and the Four Directions Council. On the whole, then, we can say that the momentum of this movement comes predominantly from the activities of all these organizations at the global level as opposed to coming from one or two centralized, bureaucratized international institutions. In other words, we are dealing, fundamentally, with grass-roots movements that have gradually acquired, through networking, global dimensions.

The United Nations: The battleground of the international indigenous movement

The event that marked the beginning of direct activity on the part of indigenous peoples within the context of the United Nations was the international non-governmental organizations (NGOs) conference on Indigenous Peoples of the Americas held in Geneva in 1977. The event was organized under the auspices of the Sub-Committee on Racism, Racial Discrimination, Apartheid and Colonialism, a special NGO committee on human rights. More than 100 Indian representatives from all over the Americas, approximately 50 NGOs with consultative status at the United Nations, and 38 member countries participated in the conference (Ortiz, 1984, p. 29).

The conference drew up a number of recommendations. Perhaps the most important was the proposal to create the UN Working Group on Indigenous Populations as part of the UN Sub-Commission on the Prevention of Discrimination and the Protection of Minorities. Another proposal was that there be a second international NGO conference on indigenous peoples and their relationship to the land. Besides helping formulate these recommendations, the indigenous participants submitted a declaration of their own entitled *Draft Declaration of Principles for the Defence of the Indigenous Nations and Peoples of the Western Hemisphere*. This declaration, along with the WCIP Declaration of 1984, constitutes the core of what we have called the indigenous counter-hegemonic project.

The second international NGO conference on Indigenous Peoples and the Land was held in Geneva in 1981. Once again a recommendation was made for the establishment of a UN Working Group on Indigenous Populations, something that was implemented the year

365

after (Ortiz, 1984, p. 32). The purpose of the Working Group is two-fold: first to review national developments pertaining to the promotion and protection of indigenous human rights, and, secondly, to develop international standards concerning these rights. In terms of the second goal, the Working Group has been preparing since 1985 a draft declaration on the rights of indigenous peoples, a document that, although due to be presented to the UN General Assembly for approval in 1993, has not yet reached this forum (UN Fact Sheet No. 9, 1990, pp. 8–9).

Over the years, the Working Group has attracted a lot of attention from indigenous groups and sympathetic NGOs. In 1988 and 1989, 380–400 persons attended its sessions (UN Fact Sheet No. 9, 1990, p. 7). Moreover, a number of its recommendations have been implemented fairly quickly. In 1988, for example, the Sub-Commission on the Prevention of Discrimination and the Protection of Minorities abandoned the term "indigenous populations" in favour of "indigenous peoples." This is important since other UN bodies, such as the International Labour Organization (ILO), have strongly resisted adopting this term. In addition, the Working Group's proposal that 1993 be proclaimed an international year for indigenous peoples was approved and implemented by the UN General Assembly.

Despite its usefulness as a forum for indigenous peoples, there are a number of problems with the Working Group. It is not a court of law and, therefore, it cannot hear specific complaints with the aim of making decisions on these cases. It is, in fact, only the last link in a long bureaucratic chain of UN organizations. Any proposals made by the Working Group must go first to the Sub-Commission on the Prevention of Discrimination and the Protection of Minorities for approval, then to the Commission on Human Rights, and then to the Economic and Social Council. Once the proposal is passed at all of these three levels, it still needs to be discussed and voted on by the UN General Assembly. Given this bureaucratic bottleneck, the increasing reliance of indigenous peoples on this organization as the sole UN body in charge of protecting their rights has been a source of great concern to all interested parties. The WCIP is currently trying to address this problem by opening new venues for the international indigenous movement within the international arena in general and within the UN in particular.

Besides being part of a formidable bureaucratic maze, the Working Group does not have its own independent sources of information. It relies mainly on governmental reports, which are usually biased and which generally promote Eurocentric attitudes towards ethnic peoples. Furthermore, the predominant role of Western indigenous representatives has made it difficult for this organization to get an overall perspective on the global situation. This trend may change in the near future as more representatives from Asia are now travelling to its annual sessions.

Let us conclude by saying that the international indigenous movement, launched with the First Assembly of the WCIP in 1975, has evolved from being an almost exclusively Western struggle to one that now includes most parts of the globe. Whereas in the mid-1970s indigenous questions were an "exotic" item in international conferences and institutions, today it is difficult to find an international gathering – be that on environmental issues, colonization, labour, children, women, nuclear arms, or education – that does not incorporate indigenous representation.

The indigenous counter-hegemonic project

In this section I shall describe the indigenous counter-hegemonic project and see in what ways it challenges the ideological/normative foundations of all three "historical structures" of Pax Americana: modes of social relations of production, forms of state, and world order. What will become apparent is that the indigenous counter-hegemonic project represents an attempt not simply to reject the "modern" Western world, but in fact to appropriate certain Western liberal concepts – such as those of "development", "non-discrimination," and "self-determination" – and to redefine them in an effort to formulate a pluralistic, non-Eurocentric basis for an alternative world order.

The social relations of production: Indigenous world-view vs. capitalism and socialism

The capitalist concept of development rests on a linear evolutionary model of history in which industrialized societies are portrayed, relative to non-industrialized societies, as the final stage of development. This teleological interpretation of progress leaves no room for alternative models of development and has generated its own "expert discourse," i.e. the modernization theories of the 1950s, to legitimize itself. Economic development means industrialization, the predominance of the individual over the community, the emphasis on profit

367

over redistribution, and the importance of consumption over resource management. The overall result of this conception has been
the emergence of centralized, class-based, highly secular, homo-
centric, and expansionistic societies, in which quantitative criteria
(i.e. levels of production and consumption), rather than qualitative
criteria (i.e. degree of social satisfaction and levels of social justice),
dominate the assessment of development.

As opposed to this linear model of evolution, indigenous peoples
entertain a multi-causal, cyclical view of history. Moreover, they
have a profoundly spiritual conception of the world, which tends to
focus on the interrelatedness of all life, including man, land, animals,
and objects. Within this cosmocentric view of the world, the land
takes on a sacred quality that is absent in Western thinking, and this
spiritual bond with the earth is one of the crucial markers that distinguish indigenous societies from others. For indigenous peoples the
land is at once an economic resource and a cultural base. This fundamental interconnection between the economic and the cultural
dimensions of life sharply contrasts with the capitalist concept of
development, which is seen exclusively as an economic process. As
J. Mohawk, a Canadian Indian, explains:

Culture and economy are inseparable. A lot of people today have come to
accept the colonial definition of culture as referring to music, dress and language. But cultures are inconceivable without an economic base. Even spiritual life revolves to a considerable extent around the ways that people see
their lives supported. In the absence of culture, there can be no economy.
In the absence of economy, there is no culture. (Cited in Moody, 1988, pp.
183–184)

In general, the economies of indigenous peoples are small-scale,
non-hierarchical, based on collective or mutual labour practices, and
usually geared to the satisfaction of basic needs. As most indigenous
communities have no concept of private property, land is owned collectively and the sum total of the community's labour is redistributed
among its members according to a variety of cultural mechanisms. As
a result of this relative internal social equality, there is no incentive to
increase economic production beyond the needs of local subsistence.
This, in turn, together with the respect that indigenous peoples have
for their land, permits them to conserve their ecosystems for long-
term use.

So far we have seen how the indigenous world-view contrasts
sharply with the dominant capitalist world-view. At the same time,

however, it also differs from the socialist vision of development. The reason for this is that the premises of socialism in many ways echo those of capitalism. Both paradigms share a teleological approach to history that equates industrialization and large-scale production with economic development. Indeed, from the Marxist point of view the economic traditions of indigenous peoples are the epitome of inefficiency and backwardness.

Given the conflict between the indigenous world-view and the two predominant Western concepts of development, capitalism and socialism, what alternative economic model do indigenous peoples propose?

Their fundamental demand is that they, and not states, should have exclusive control over their lands and territories. These land rights include: surface and sub-surface soil, bodies of water, air, and the right to hunt, fish, trap, gather, and harvest (*Declaration of Principles for the Defence of the Indigenous Nations and Peoples of the Western Hemisphere*, 1977; *Declaration of Principles*, WCIP, 1984). Along with complete jurisdiction over their territories, they also seek control over the development of technology and its application: the type of technology that they are interested in promoting is low-cost, ecologically sound, labour-intensive, and easily applicable to production for local consumption (Moody, 1988, p. 184). Finally, they also want control over the production process. Keenly aware that TNCs have gone into their lands in search of non-renewable resources and have left only after these were exhausted, indigenous peoples propose a strategy of economic development based primarily on *renewable* resources. It is only by concentrating on using renewable resources and exploiting non-renewable ones with great care that humankind can provide for itself and protect the ecosystem at the same time.

What lessons can be derived from the ideas put forward by indigenous peoples? One obvious point is the need to reconsider the role of human beings in the process of economic development. The latter is portrayed by both capitalist and socialist theories as an inevitable, impersonal force that unfolds in stages according to some grand design. Indigenous peoples, on the other hand, see it as a process guided by the conscious decisions and actions of people in an effort to realize certain basic human needs. This view clearly militates against the "growth for its own sake" models and supports a more cautious and disciplined approach to economic development. A second important point has to do with the environment. Today more than ever, the indigenous peoples' plea that the environment is not simply the context in which economic development takes place, but the actual source of it, has increasing resonance and can no longer be ignored. A third relevant point has to do with the necessity to reconsider economic development in a framework that transcends the "right vs. left" ideological schism. Despite the recent dismantling of communist systems across Eastern Europe and within the Soviet Union, there is growing scepticism as to whether capitalism can provide a long-term solution to today's economic ills. The indigenous economic model, with its emphasis on renewable resource management, suggests the possibility of going beyond both the socialist and capitalist systems in order to create a self-sustaining mode of production. This new idea is gaining popularity today, particularly among environmental activists and progressive academics and administrators.

Forms of state: Indigenous world-view vs. democratic liberalism

Having examined the main ideas of indigenous peoples regarding economic development, let us now turn to their political philosophy. In this section we shall see how their world-view contrasts with the ideology of Western liberalism and how they have sought to redefine two fundamental liberal concepts – the notion of individual rights and that of non-discrimination.

Perhaps the most important single principle of the Western liberal tradition is *individualism*. Human beings are seen as fundamentally self-interested, power-seeking, and competitive. Thus, society is viewed as an aggregate of autonomous, atom-like individuals, each struggling to promote their own interests. Although not naturally social or cooperative, human beings have learned to live together for the sake of collective protection and security. As T. Qualter explains: "under liberalism the individual is antecedent to, and independent of, society, creating society and government solely for the more efficient satisfaction of the needs of atomistic beings" (Qualter, 1986, p. 221). This emphasis on the individual explains why liberal thinkers have given so much attention to the question of "individual rights," the purpose of such rights being to protect persons from the power of the state as well as from aggressive neighbours.

A second basic concept that is crucial to liberal democratic thought is that of *equality*. Two aspects of this concept are relevant to our concern. First, in the Western liberal tradition equality of opportunity is stressed over equality of condition, the latter being seen as impeding the liberty of individuals to use their abilities to accumulate wealth and property. Although liberals accept that the task of the state is to ensure that all individuals approach the "economic race" from the same starting point, they do not accept that the state should interfere with the actual race or with its outcome. The other dimension of equality has to do with non-discrimination, that is, with the principle that all citizens should receive equal treatment before the law. The premise is the idea that the similarities between human beings are greater and more significant than the differences. Individual differences, although they can be expressed in private life, should not be institutionalized in the form of differences in political, legal, social, or property rights. As T. Qualter suggests: "The egalitarian does not deny variations but does deny the extension of their significance" (Qualter, 1986, p. 110). Within this context, to grant or recognize "special rights" in any way is considered a violation of the principle of non-discrimination.

As opposed to the liberal mind-set we have just described, which puts the individual at the centre of the universe, the world-view of indigenous peoples is fundamentally cosmocentric. Moreover, they believe that human beings are social, cooperative, and consensual. Thus, the reference point is the *collective* and not the individual. The individual is seen as a repository of responsibilities rather than a claimant of rights, since the realization of the common good depends on each member of the community fulfilling their obligations to the group. The concept of individual rights per se does not exist in indigenous philosophy because the idea of protecting the individual from either an oppressive state or aggressive neighbours is not relevant to the indigenous experience (Boldt and Long, 1985, p. 166).

As for the notion of equality, it is also understood differently by indigenous peoples. Since most productive labour is done collectively, the issue of equality of opportunity is almost irrelevant to them. More important is *equality of condition*, that is, the way the products of this collective effort are redistributed among the members of the community. In the indigenous world, equality of condition is preserved, at the economic level, by a variety of cultural mechanisms that serve to redistribute wealth and resources; at the political level, by the creation of a system based on democratic participation and consensus-building; and, at the social level, by the institutionalization of mutual and reciprocal responsibilities.

So far we have highlighted the ways in which the indigenous worldview contrasts with liberal democratic ideology. In the remainder of this section we shall see in what sense indigenous peoples have attempted to reinterpret the concepts of individual rights and of non-discrimination.

With regard to the former, indigenous peoples have tended to argue against the liberal conception of rights, arguing that individual rights in and for themselves are meaningless unless accompanied by the recognition of collective rights. They go on to claim that communities as well as individuals have legitimate moral status and that the value systems of indigenous peoples emphasize the collective over the individual. Describing the position taken by the Canadian Indian leadership, Boldt and Long state:

They want to be protected as a group, not as individuals, from state violation of their human dignity and freedom ... they do assert that the doctrine of individualism and inherent inalienable rights ... is not part of their cultural heritage, serves no positive purpose for them and threatens their dignity and survival as a unique people. (Boldt and Long, 1985, pp. 172–173)

Although most indigenous leaders do recognize the potential dangers of giving preference to collective over individual rights, they tend to minimize them by arguing that a distinction must be made between the negative implications for the individual member that derive from a violation of human rights and those that derive from a mere disagreement with the group's philosophy. They point out that no society can please all its members and that every individual has the freedom to leave the community if they do not wish to submit to the majority consensus (Boldt and Long, 1985, pp. 175–176).

This emphasis on the collective dimension of social relations has not been unproblematic, however, and has posed some serious problems within indigenous communities. The increasing division between men and women in the ranks of the Canadian Indian leadership and the Canadian Indian leadership's recent refusal to ratify the Charlottetown Constitutional package provide a case in point. Arguing that native men and male-dominated organizations, such as the Assembly of First Nations, do not represent the interests of native women, the Native Women's Association of Canada (NWAC) has forcefully challenged the idea that Indian self-government must be based primarily on collective rights. They claim that native women have been subjugated to a century of patriarchal rule, institutionalized by the Indian Act of 1869, and that today they are struggling not only against an insensitive federal government, but also against the Indian male establishment created by this colonial document. They go on to argue that, until mechanisms, based on native customary practices, are set up to address gender discrimination, the Canadian Charter of Freedoms, a classic liberal, individual rights based document, must be made applicable to native communities (NWAC, 1992, p. 16). This view, however, is strongly opposed by the Assembly of First Nations, which sees the Charter as a threat to Indian philosophy and culture.

It will be some time before Canadian Indians are able to reconcile their disagreements over the issue of rights and even longer before they can institutionalize ways of addressing native women's concerns. Nevertheless, some steps towards the reconciliation of individual and collective rights have been made at the philosophical level. W. Kymlicka, a professor at the University of Toronto in Canada, has formulated an argument that seeks to justify the granting of collective rights to Canadian Indians within the liberal philosophical framework. He argues that any individual's development and self-realization depend on the range of choices offered to them by the community in which they live. Without a strong cultural community, individuals lose their sense of purpose and potential. According to Kymlicka:

Liberals should be concerned with the fate of cultural structures, not because they have some moral status of their own, but because it is only through having a rich and secure cultural structure that people can become aware, in a vivid way, of the options available to them and intelligently examine their value. (Kymlicka, 1989, p. 190)

He goes on to argue that, because the cultural structures of native Indians are being undermined by the English and French Canadians, individual members of the native communities are necessarily disadvantaged *vis-à-vis* their non-indigenous neighbours. The only way to rectify this inequality at the level of the individual is by ensuring equality at the community level, i.e. by granting Canadian Indians certain collective rights (Kymlicka, 1989, p. 198). Whether this argument will gain any purchase among the English and French élites remains to be seen.

In the same way, indigenous peoples have sought to redefine from their own vantage point the principle of non-discrimination. Whereas liberals see this principle applying to a society made up of individuals, indigenous peoples apply it to a society understood as a "multi-national" aggregate. In effect, they make a clear distinction between "minorities" or "ethnic groups," on the one hand, and "peoples" or "nations," on the other. This distinction rests on the concept of *consent* (*Statement by Indian Law Resource Centre*, 1982). In Canada, for example, the Chinese and West Indian communities are to be considered "minorities" in that they have voluntarily surrendered their separate status in order to join the Canadian national society. As "minorities" they are entitled to certain rights that allow them to preserve their cultural identity and that protect them against discriminatory actions. All these rights, however, exist within a general framework of rights and responsibilities that they have decided to adopt as their own, a decision that gives the state lawful jurisdiction over them. "Peoples" or "nations," on the other hand, like the Indian nations of Canada (Dene, Mohawk, Cree) have never agreed to be assimilated into the dominant national society. In a statement by the Indian Law Resource Centre, the case of indigenous peoples was described in the following way:

The situation is different where no voluntary incorporation of peoples has occurred and there has been no free consolidation of two peoples' political rights. A people lawlessly annexed or taken from their country by force do not thereby lose their separate voice or choice of destiny, but retain it until given an unrestrained opportunity for its existence. They do not become, by force of seizure, colonization or enslavement, a minority, but remain a people still. (*Statement by Indian Law Resource Centre*, 1982)

In short, one cannot create "minorities" by force. Indigenous peoples, therefore, remain today as they always have been: "peoples" or "nations."

We can now understand why, from the indigenous point of view, the recognition of "special rights" is not a violation of the principle of non-discrimination as the liberals contend. Individual indigenous persons who choose to assimilate into the dominant society can be seen as members of a "minority" and as such are not eligible to be granted special rights. Indigenous peoples, as "peoples," however, do not wish assimilation. On the contrary, they want to retain their collective identity. This wish is legitimate since, in a society conceived as "multi-national" in nature, all "nations" should have equal rights. By destroying this collective identity, assimilation thwarts the principle of equality among "nations" and is discriminatory in nature.

Consistent with this viewpoint, indigenous peoples have put forward their political demands as *"nations"* and not as individuals. More concretely, they argue that each indigenous nation has the right to determine the form, structure, and authority of its political institutions, i.e. the right to "*self-government*" or "*political autonomy.*" This, in turn, implies that the traditions and customs of indigenous peoples must be recognized by states as a fundamental source of law. Moreover, they demand to be entitled to participate in the political life of the state. They have repeatedly pointed out that they are willing to work with both indigenous and non-indigenous legal systems so long as they have a guarantee that, should there be a conflict between the two systems, their laws will take precedence within their own communities. In return they promise to make sure that their own political institutions and laws are in conformity with international human rights standards (*Declaration of Principles*, WCIP, 1984).

In sum, indigenous peoples are seeking to carve out a "political space" for themselves without jeopardizing their relationship with the states in which they live. Evidence of this attempt to compromise is given by their demand to participate in the social and political life of the state and by their constant reference to international law as a standard that they commit themselves to uphold. It is to international law and to its potential as a legal recourse for indigenous peoples that we shall turn next.

World order: Indigenous peoples and their challenge to international law

In an effort to put forward their counter-hegemonic project, indigenous peoples have sought to formulate it within the context of contemporary international law. This task has been fairly difficult, however, since, with the exception of the ILO Convention 169, there are no international laws that address indigenous peoples specifically. None the less, there are a number of issues that have received considerable attention at the international level and that are relevant to indigenous peoples: self-determination, racial discrimination, and genocide. In what follows I shall look at the existing international instruments regarding the concept of *self-determination* and show how indigenous peoples have attempted to appropriate and redefine it in an effort to make it more applicable to their case. By so doing they are not inventing a new concept, but rather trying to infuse new meaning into an old one and thus broaden the scope of international law. In fact discussions of concepts such as self-determination have provided them with the ideological tools to formulate their own counter-hegemonic project. As R. Falk states:

the Western role has been a contradictory one in relation to non-Western societies, both hegemonic and anti-hegemonic, transmitting as a result of its dominance the very ideas that can be reinterpreted to provide the normative foundation for resistance by those victimized. (Falk, 1990, p. 270)

Despite the fact that the concept of self-determination has been mentioned in the UN Charter, in the international human rights covenants, and in a number of other international instruments, it remains a vague, controversial notion that means different things to different people. Article 1 of both human rights covenants states that "all peoples have the right to self-determination. By virtue of that right they freely determine their political status and freely pursue their economic, social and cultural development." The ambiguity of this statement of course lies in the fact that it is far from clear who the subjects of this right are supposed to be. A number of interpretations have been used in legal argument, but only two of these have been recognized as having the status of a legal principle (Alfredsson, 1982, p. 114).

The first meaning of self-determination refers to what is called *"external self-determination"* and concerns the right of peoples to determine their own international status, including the right to independence and statehood. Within the context of political decolonization, the right to "external self-determination" has been extended to colonial peoples and territories. This interpretation is enshrined in the Declaration on the Granting of Independence to Colonial Countries and Peoples of 1960. It is important to note, however, that "external self-determination" is meant to apply only to "colonies," which have been narrowly defined as *overseas* territorial entities under foreign domination." This definition has been vigorously defended by the newly independent states of the third world in an attempt to safeguard their own territorial integrity. A Kenyan delegate at a 1963 conference summarized this view when he stated that "the principle of self-determination has relevance where foreign domination is the issue. It has no relevance where the issue is territorial disintegration by dissident citizens" (cited in Alexander and Friedlander, 1980, p. 339).

This definition of "colonies," however, presents a catch for indigenous peoples. They see themselves as "colonized" and, as such, would like the principle of self-determination to be applied to them. Yet, given the narrow definition of colonies indicated above, they do not qualify to make this claim because they live *within* the states that "colonize" them. Moreover, the fact that so far they have not been considered by international law as "peoples," but rather as "minorities," makes it even more difficult for them to argue for the right to "external self-determination." In sum, it would seem as if there were little chance for indigenous peoples to apply this concept to their own case.

A second common interpretation of self-determination is the *right of a state to its territorial integrity* (Alfredsson, 1982, p. 115). This view is limited to the instance of "captive states" and fundamentally refers to any state's right to freedom from external interference in its domestic affairs. Although this understanding of self-determination is important because it has acquired some legitimacy as being binding in international law, unfortunately it does not apply to indigenous peoples for the obvious reason that they have been unable to achieve the status of independent statehood.

As can be seen, the two prevailing interpretations of self-determination do not seem readily applicable to the case of indigenous peoples. The latter, however, have challenged them very strongly, arguing that they are outdated and Eurocentric. They point out the fact that the current concept of self-determination, which arose within the context of the European decolonization process that took place after World War II, is limited and inadequate to deal with the realities of the post-colonial world. The hasty dismantling of the colonial empires of Europe and the hectic and rather arbitrary creation of over 80 newly independent states had the effect of liberating "territories" but not "peoples." Ignoring the "multi-national" nature of their colonies and without really considering alternative options, the colonial powers sought only to reproduce the European experience through the creation of sovereign states. As a result of this myopic, Eurocentric approach, a new phase of oppression referred to as "neo-colonialism" or "internal colonialism" was institutionalized. It is this type of oppression that the indigenous peoples believe they are victims of.

Today indigenous peoples are arguing for a "second stage" of decolonization. Within the context of this new stage, they claim that self-determination can no longer be understood exclusively in terms of foreign or external domination and that the "overseas" criterion for the existence of colonialism is no longer relevant. What the world is witnessing today is "internal colonialism." Thus, the emphasis should be on the liberation of "entrapped nations" within existing sovereign states and on the establishment of constitutional arrangements between these states and the particular indigenous peoples involved. Not only would this type of self-determination reduce tensions and the ongoing legacy of civil strife in many sovereign states, it would even serve to strengthen national unity and peaceful interstate and intra-state relations.

More concretely, what form of self-determination are indigenous peoples seeking? For a general statement we could look at the *Declaration of Principles* issued in 1985 by a group of international indigenous organizations:

All indigenous nations and peoples have the right to self-determination, by the virtue of which they have the right to whatever degree of autonomy or self-government they choose. This includes the right to freely determine their political status, freely pursue their own economic, social, religious and cultural development, and determine their own membership and/or citizenship, without external interference. (*Declaration of Principles*, 1985)

As is clear from the above statement, this position is rather open-ended and flexible. Depending on the wishes of the particular indigenous group involved, there are a number of alternative ways of applying this principle. The first and most radical option would be the implementation of "external self-determination," i.e. being granted complete independence or statehood. With the notable exceptions of the East Timorese or the West Papuans, however, few indigenous peoples are demanding full statehood.

A second unlikely option would be the complete assimilation of an indigenous nation into the dominant society. In this case the people in question would become a "national minority," since the group would have exercised its right to self-determination by voluntarily consenting to merge with the state. As minorities, they would then be subject to the protection against discrimination afforded by Article 27 of both the international covenants on human rights of 1966, but they would have forfeited their right to make claims to self-determination under Article 1 of these same covenants.

The third and most commonly sought after alternative is the institutionalization of what indigenous peoples call *"internal self-determination"*. This could involve a number of different arrangements depending on the preferences of both the indigenous nation and the state involved. Basically, however, it would imply the following: free participation in the political life of the country, the right to control economic and political institutions, the right to own a territorial base, the right to control the education system, the right to engage

378

in foreign relations, and finally the right to determine one's own membership without external interference. As can be seen, "internal self-determination" is an agenda for *regional autonomy*, which, in turn, can be seen as a compromise between the right of peoples to self-determination, on the one hand, and the territorial integrity of states, on the other.

From all that has been said above about their counter-hegemonic project, it should be clear that indigenous peoples are not attempting to return to a "golden age of nativism" and are very willing to negotiate with states for an arrangement that protects the state's sovereignty while granting them freedom to determine their own way of life. In terms of development strategies, they are willing to work within either the capitalist or socialist economic models so long as they can realize sustainable development practices. With regard to their political status, they accept the notion of regional autonomy within the nation-state provided that they are recognized as separate "peoples" or "nations." Finally, when it comes to international law, they clearly state that, although existing international instruments do not protect their rights adequately, they are more than willing to respect contemporary human rights standards and to negotiate peacefully the inclusion of their own rights.

Conclusion

In the course of our account of the international indigenous movement, we have clearly seen how ideas have become powerful weapons in the hands of seemingly "powerless" social forces. Indigenous peoples have no significant economic resources of their own. Most of them exist in substandard living conditions in peripheral regions. Moreover, they have been systematically marginalized from sources of political power. Nevertheless, they have been able to launch an international movement that, while challenging the legitimacy of current economic and political strategies of nation-states and transnational corporations, has mounted a formidable defence of indigenous rights. Devoid of material power, indigenous peoples have had to rely on the force of ideas to give their movement momentum and credibility.

Moreover, ideas also played a vital role in the communication process between indigenous peoples and the dominant social forces of today's world order. Aware of the need for common conceptual parameters in their negotiations with the dominant "other," indigenous peoples have sought ways of expressing their ideas in terms of current conventional wisdom and norms. To this end, they have appropriated the language and concepts of the Western liberal discourse and turned them into political tools by giving them new meanings. Thus, the indigenous counter-hegemonic project not only provides a critique of the prevailing patterns of thought and behaviour today, but also attempts to offer an alternative ideological discourse. As Falk states:

In a fundamental sense, indigenous peoples preserve and embody alternative life-styles that may provide models, inspiration, and guidance in the essential work of world-order redesign, an undertaking now primarily associated with overcoming self-destructive tendencies in the behaviour of modern societies. (Falk, 1989, p. 205)

At this point it should be noted that the international indigenous movement is not the only voice of dissent in our changing world order. Today we are witnessing a proliferation of counter-hegemonic struggles at the global level, which, like the international indigenous movement, are challenging the normative foundations of today's international system and proposing alternative forms of social relations and organization at the national and, most particularly, at the international level. I am referring to the rise of new social movements heralding such causes as human rights, the environment, women's rights, and world peace. These new social movements, unlike the labour and agrarian movements, are not primarily class based and in fact revolve around broad, collective issues that transcend interest-group politics. In the words of R. Dalton, M. Kuechler, and W. Burklin:

A distinguishing feature of new social movements is that they lack the narrow special interest appeal to any one social grouping.... New social movements thus signify a shift from group-based political cleavages to **value** and **issue**-based cleavages that identify only communities of like-minded people. (Dalton, Kuechler, and Burklin, 1990, p. 12)

In my opinion there is a need for international relations scholars to direct their attention to these non-dominant, counter-hegemonic social forces, which are defending radically new ideological projects and which may well contribute to the reconstitution of a more pluralistic, humane world order. To carry out such studies, however, empirical research is not enough. It is also crucial to develop new theoretical models that allow for the conceptualization of the role of

380

ideas in international politics. One such paradigm is that of Robert Cox, which I have used in this paper and which, in my opinion, points to new directions in the field of international relations.

References

Primary sources

Declaration of Principles for the Defence of the Indigenous Nations and Peoples of the Western Hemisphere, 1977. (No. E/CN.4/Sub. 2/L. 684 Annex IV, 1978)

Statement by Indian Law Resource Centre to Commission on Human Rights, 38th session, agenda item 20, 24 Feb. 1982. (E/CN.4/1982/NGO/30)

Declaration of Principles adopted at the Fourth General Assembly of the World Council of Indigenous Peoples in Panama, September 1984; cited in J. Burger, *Report from the Frontier: The State of the World's Indigenous Peoples*, London: Zed Books, 1987, p. 270.

Statement by Four Directions Council to Sub-Commission on Prevention of Discrimination and Protection of Minorities, 38th session, agenda item 11, 7 Aug. 1985. (E/CN.4/Sub. 2/1985/NGO/9)

Declaration of Principles proposed by the Indian Law Resource Centre, Four Directions Council, National Aboriginal and Islander Legal Service, National Indian Youth Council, Inuit Circumpolar Conference, and the International Indian Treaty Council, 1985. Cited in J. Burger, *Report from the Frontier: The State of the World's Indigenous Peoples*, London: Zed Books, 1987, p. 271.

The Rights of Indigenous Peoples. Fact Sheet Number 9 printed by the United Nations Centre for Human Rights, May 1990.

Secondary sources

Alexander, Y., and A. Friedlander, eds. (1980) *Self-Determination: National, Regional and Global Dimensions*. Boulder, Colo.: Westview Press.

Alfredsson, G. (1982) "International Law, International Organizations and Indigenous Peoples." *Journal of International Affairs* 36, no. 1.

Boldt, M., and A. Long, eds. (1985) *The Quest for Justice: Aboriginal Peoples and Aboriginal Rights*. Toronto: Toronto University Press.

Burger, J. (1987) *Report from the Frontier: The State of the World's Indigenous Peoples*. London: Zed Books.

Cassese, A. (1986) *International Law in a Divided World*. Oxford: Clarendon Press.

Cox, R. (1981) "Social Forces, States and World Orders: Beyond International Relations Theory." *Millennium: Journal of International Studies* 10, no. 2.

——— (1983) "Gramsci, Hegemony and International Relations: An Essay in Method." *Millennium: Journal of International Studies* 12, no. 2.

——— (1987) *Production, Power, and World Order: Social Forces in the Making of History*. New York: Columbia University Press.

Dalton, R., M. Kuechler, and W. Burklin, eds. (1990) *Challenging the Political Order:*

New Social Movements in Western Democracies. New York: Oxford University Press.

Falk, R. (1989) *Revitalizing International Law*. Ames, Ia.: Iowa State University Press.

———— (1990) "Culture, Modernism, Post-Modernism." In: J. Chay, ed. *Culture and International Relations*. New York: Praeger Publishers.

ICIHI [Independent Commission on International Humanitarian Issues], Working Group on Indigenous Peoples (1987) *Indigenous Peoples: A Global Quest for Justice*. London: Zed Books.

Kymlicka, W. (1988) *Liberalism, Ethnicity, and the Law*. Toronto: University of Toronto, Faculty of Law.

———— (1989) "Liberalism, Individualism and Minority Rights." In: A. Hutchinson and I. Green, eds. *Law and Community: The End of Individualism?* Toronto: Carswell.

Miller, L. (1985) *Global Order: Values and Power in International Politics*. Boulder, Colo.: Westview Press.

Moody, R. (1988) *The Indigenous Voice: Visions and Realities*, vols. 1 and 2. London: Zed Books.

NWAC [Native Women's Association of Canada (1992) "Aboriginal Women and the Constitutional Debates: Continuing Discrimination." *Canadian Women's Studies* 12, no. 3.

Ortiz, D. R. (1984) *Indians of the Americas: Human Rights and Self-Determination*. New York: Praeger Publishers.

Qualter, T. (1986) *Conflicting Political Ideas in Liberal Democracies*. Toronto: Methuen Publications.

Rodley, N. (1983) "The Development of United Nations Activities in the Field of Human Rights and the Role of Non-Governmental Organizations." In: T. T. Gati, ed. *The US, the UN, and the Management of Global Change*. New York: New York Press.

Part IV
Change, violence, and normative order

14

Violence, resistance, and order in international relations

Raimo Väyrynen

Introduction

The world is moving towards a new international system in which the nation-state matters less and in which the relevance of civil society and the global market place is growing. This does not assure, however, that the world will necessarily be a more peaceful place. The character and magnitude of violence may change, but it may continue to plague people in new and perhaps unpredictable ways. I will explore this problem from two different perspectives.

First, I will try to define the changing nature and functions of both domestic and international violence. In this regard, a main question addressed in the paper is whether the traditional type of inter-state war is withering away and, if so, where in the international community this process starts. In the affirmative case the next problem is whether inter-state war will possibly be replaced by a non-violent system or by civil wars and other types of domestic violence. Thus, the analysis has to be expanded from inter-state violence to domestic conflicts and to the non-violent alternative. Finally, an effort is made to develop an outline for an inter-state arrangement that might possibly maintain peace and stability in Europe.

Democracy and war

In recent scholarship the thesis on the end of international war has frequently been put forward (e.g. Mueller, 1990). The argument can be supported either by pointing to statistical evidence about the declining frequency of war over time, especially among major powers, or by the specification of structural and/or value changes occurring in international relations. Particular attention has recently been paid to the spread of democratic political systems and its impact on the probability of war between states.

There is rather strong statistical evidence to support the conclusion that democratic states behave peacefully in their mutual relations. It is further specified by the finding that democratic states, even if they are declining, do not fight preventive wars but rather accommodate democratic challengers or attempt to counterbalance authoritarian challengers by forming defensive alliance systems. Only non-democratic regimes have, historically speaking, waged preventive wars regardless of the nature of the opponent.

On the other hand, democratic states have not given up aggression against non-democratic states, but have a long history of military interventions and warfare in relations with them. Thus, democracy and economic development through the market are not sufficient guarantees against military aggressions *per se*. They stem warfare only in conditions in which the international environment permits peace. Thus, it may be that peace and democracy are a part of the same political phenomenon. The perception of peacefulness by other democracies gives rise to a process of reinforcement through learning experiences (Doyle, 1986; Ray, 1989; Russett, 1990; Schweller, 1992; Starr, 1992).

According to historical evidence, in symmetrical relations democracies are dragged into wars by expanding autocracies. Once this happens they fight successfully: democracies have won 80 per cent of the 31 major wars waged since 1846. The relative peacefulness of democracies may be due to the smaller costs to society for controlling the liberal state in comparison with autocracies in which the state prevails. The dominance of the state tends to lead to expansion, whereas the strength of society makes for a more peaceful country. As democracies enjoy more legitimacy among their citizens, the nation's resources can be more effectively mobilized and utilized in political and military crises (Lake, 1992).

In accounting for the lack of war between democratic states, two broad traditions can be discerned. The Kantian thesis suggests that democratic polities develop common norms and obligations, i.e. they have a mutual political culture that prevents war. Another approach focuses on the domestic constraints due to executive selection, decision constraints, and political competition. Together they decrease the possibility that disputes escalate into warfare. The focus on decisional constraints emphasizes less the ideological and cultural differences between democracies and non-democracies and more the nature and strength of constraints that may or may not exist in these polities.

A major question in the Kantian approach is why the democratic political culture accounts for the absence of war in relations between democratic states, but permits it in their relations with other types of political systems. This suggests strongly that domestic attributes alone are inadequate in explaining the resort to violence. They may be necessary, but they are not sufficient conditions for the outbreak of war or its absence (Väyrynen, 1988, pp. 72–75).

In a more comprehensive approach, one has to consider both dyadic and systemic factors. Democracy has not prevented the waging of "wars of gain" in which smaller and weaker entities have been subjected to hegemonic control by the major powers. Democracy has permitted, in other words, imperialism and colonialism, and may even have benefited from them by relocating domestic conflicts to the world's peripheries. Democracy may have contributed, however, to the elimination of "wars of fear" in which the resort to force is motivated by the anticipated loss of prestige, wealth or security by a state (the concepts originate from Wight, 1978, pp. 138–140).

In the relations between major democratic powers, the stability produced by the balance of power is reinforced by the commonality of political values and material interests. Gains are sought by means of economic and technological competition rather than by military means. In the peripheries, these preconditions for the "democratic peace" do not obtain, but even the democracies promote their aims by "wars of gain" or sometimes by "wars of doctrine."

In other words, interventionism is not at all alien to democratic powers. Recently, their military interventions have declined in number, however, partly because of the anti-interventionary forces at work. That is why it is difficult to say whether the interventionist policies by the United States and other Western powers will continue or not in the post-Cold War circumstances (Falk, 1992). It may be that the demise of the ideological opposition has deprived the democratic powers of the impetus to use military force and the means to legitimize it.

In explaining the absence of war between major powers, such factors as nuclear deterrence, bipolarity, hegemonic management, and the spread of liberalism have been used in various combinations. According to Gaddis (1991), these safeguards of stability are, in practice, redundant and thus reinforce each other. For example, bipolarity would not have lasted without nuclear weapons, while the dissemination of nuclear weapons has largely been prevented by the desire to preserve bipolar stability.

Somewhat curiously, Gaddis states that, among these factors, the "impending 'triumph' of liberalism ... appears more likely to upset systemic stability than any other tendency now discernible on the horizon" (Gaddis, 1991, p. 50). Given the transition of international relations towards a greater and more complex interdependence, this prediction suggests a higher degree of conflict and instability in the future. In reality, the redundancy of stabilizing factors may be weakening in the 1990s, but it remains so strong that the breakdown of international systemic stability is unlikely.

What, then, are the implications of these research findings for the future of national and international violence? They seem to suggest that in Europe the probability of inter-state war will be small. Deterrence and self-deterrence meant that, even during the Cold War, the likelihood of inter-bloc war was never very high. Deterrence is still an existential fact in Europe and restrains relations between states. Now, however, it is only one factor in a larger equation as international relations in Europe are gradually built on a new basis.

Inter-state relations will be increasingly steered by common norms and interests embedded in democratic procedures and economic interdependence. This transformation means, among other things, that intra-bloc interventions of the Cold War type will wither away. This is due not only to the disappearance of the blocs, or at least of one of them, but also to a more fundamental change in the nature of international relations. Military power will matter less, and economy, technology, and culture more. Power will not disappear from the international scene, but it will change its character.

The maintenance of inter-state peace in Europe does not mean, of course, that the rest of the world will be peaceful. There is still a possibility of military interventions by major industrial powers into the world's peripheries or the occurrence of inter-state warfare in individual regions, especially in the Middle East, the Gulf, and South Asia. Thus, the use of force between states cannot be entirely excluded, but my hunch is that even then there will be less collective violence between the states than was the case in the Cold War period. This is due, in part, to the phasing out of rivalries of major powers in the underdeveloped part of the world and, in part, to the crisis of rationality in the use of violence in relations between states.

I think that, ultimately, representative democracy and equitable socio-economic development are the most effective guarantees against collective violence. There are few, if any, cases in which a stable democracy, sustaining its economic development over time, has degenerated into widespread violence and turmoil. For this to happen requires an inequitable distribution of wealth, a lack of channels for political influence, and accumulated ethnic and social hatred. All these factors were present in the Los Angeles riots in spring 1992.

Future collective violence will primarily take place within states or be associated with the breakup of multinational empires. The widespread use of force within the former Yugoslavia and organized violence in various local conflicts in the former Soviet Union testify to this point. In these areas, the possibility of an inter-state war is real. In fact, the conflicts that previously existed within the multinational entity have now assumed an inter-state dimension.

The destruction of the Muslim population in Bosnia Hercegovina by Serbian and, to a lesser degree, Croatian forces is a case in point. In the future, the promotion of Serbian hegemonic ambitions by military means in Kosovo and Macedonia may well draw states outside the former Yugoslavia – in particular Albania, Bulgaria, and Greece – into the regional conflict. The inability of the international community either to cope with the rampant destruction by Serbia and Croatia or to assist the Bosnian Muslims does not augur well for the control of violence in Kosovo and Macedonia.

In addition, there are several regions in the third world in which violence is part of the everyday reality or where peace is, at best, fragile. In order to understand this kind of violence better, one has to ponder its nature and functions, and especially the question whether it is instrumental or expressive. The answer to this question also has implications for the international opportunities for keeping violence under control.

The instrumentalism of violence

My answer to this query is that organized violence is predominantly instrumental by its nature. Political actors, and major actors in particular, have used violence to promote their goals in the existing

389

national and international structures. In order to be instrumental, violence must be controlled and directed. Charles Reynolds (1989, pp. 87–88) suggests that the notion of control has three different aspects: the specification of ends for the purposes of communication with the adversary; control over means and their technological properties; and control over the means–ends relationship. In a controlled strategy, ends must be commensurate with means and the casual escalation in the use of means must be avoided.

Not all violence is instrumental, however; conflicts no doubt have expressive features and irrational sources (North, 1990, pp. 173–178). Sometimes a problem can be solved by focusing on a critical case in search for a viable answer. Genocide may be such a critical case in the discussion on the instrumental versus expressive nature of collective violence. At the outset one has to recognize that there are several different types of genocide that tend to occur in different kinds of societies.

Although genocides obviously have their irrational traits, dominant groups resort to them surprisingly often with the most deliberate purpose of consolidating their power and eliminating the groups or nations regarded as enemies (Kuper, 1990). Genocides are seldom accidents, but are a manifestation of grim and inhumane methods of adversarial politics.

The example of genocide suggests that the problems of instrumentalism and legitimacy of violence, although interrelated, should be kept separate from each other. The interpretation of violence as instrumental does not mean its acceptance. In the instrumental perspective, two normative problems arise: how to eliminate violence in relations between individual and collective actors; and, should it erupt, how to prevent its escalation and destruction, and, if the prevention fails, how to keep the consequences below the level justified by the goals.

In Reynolds' (1989, p. 95) view, "the choice of means should not have consequences unforeseen or uncontrolled for the domestic and international environments of the actor." This conclusion, however, begs further questions on when and what kinds of goals may justify the resort to violence in social action. In Reynolds' reasoning, genocide could be acceptable if its consequences are foreseen and controlled. Such an approach is hardly tenable even in the instrumental/utilitarian tradition. The violence as such is not rejected; and the primary interest is not in how it was initiated, but in what kinds of consequences it produces. The utilitarian approach is inclined to accept

390

violence if it produces an outcome that is in the general interest, for example, by preserving national independence, by shortening the war, or by preventing greater injustices from occurring (Ellis, 1992, pp. 172–177).

Yet another task of this paper is to ascertain to what extent violence is determined by the international structures and to what degree it is fostered by actor-specific factors. The structural explanation of organized conflicts is based on the idea of a comprehensive systemic logic that fosters major and minor wars. In a dynamic mode, such a logic may combine, for instance, economic fluctuations and power transitions. Policy makers naturally make the decisions, and are responsible for their results. However, the choices of policy makers and their consequences can be significantly shaped by the system structure (Väyrynen, 1989).

In the instrumental view, wars arise from the strategies by which actors promote their own interests in contradiction to those of other actors. My vantage point is that violence can best be understood as an instrumental and goal-oriented behaviour that can be controlled by proper political arrangements. In such a conception, violence is interpreted as strategic action, i.e. as a means for social agents to defend or expand their interests in a given structural environment. The adoption of an instrumental view implies a preference for an actor-oriented rather than a structure-oriented mode of analysis. Only actors have motives, interests, and the means to pursue them. Yet the choice of such a perspective does not entirely rule out structural and institutional modes of analysis.

Violence in Angola, Iraq, Somalia, Yugoslavia, and several other places is often explained by ethnic, religious, and tribal animosities. Of course, violent behaviour always has expressive motivations that stir people's minds and help to mobilize collective movements for and against. Different identities help to divide people into categories and justify the use of force against them, not as individuals but as members of a given group. In most cases, however, the core element of violence is its instrumentalism. Violence is used, in the first place, to promote specific territorial, political, or material interests. The expansionary and plundering policies of a dominant actor are resisted by the counter-mobilization of weaker actors.

The struggle of the major powers for control of the third world has gone with the Cold War. As the grip of the system structure has weakened, ethnicity and other identity-creating and -excluding forces have a greater opportunity to manifest themselves. Behind this facade,

391

which is real enough, conflicts in the peripheries increasingly revolve around various types of entitlements such as territorial control, political power, natural resources, water, and food. Thus the focus on expressive and identity-creating factors may lead the analysis, and hence policy remedies, astray.

Somewhat paradoxically, the prevalence of instrumental aspects of conflicts also has positive consequences. Instrumental violence is presumably open to more rational control, transformation, and settlement than is expressive violence. Actors, issues, and policy choices in conflict situations can more readily be identified and subjected to resolution than can problems of identity and status. To express the matter another way: instrumental conflicts may be more tractable than expressive ones, even though both can cause a lot of damage.

The ability to resolve instrumental conflicts and to contain the violence associated with them presupposes, of course, that there are effective institutions and mechanisms that can be used for this purpose. The main problem is obviously that the interest content of instrumental violence has anchored it deeply in actors' motivations and beliefs and makes it difficult to terminate. Most, and perhaps all, conflicts thus have both subjective and objective components complicating their settlement or transformation (Northrup, 1989, pp. 59–60).

The functions of violence

Power and violence

The instrumental view of violence is closely related to the concept of power, which is a medium of attaining ends, defined in terms of interests. Sometimes the use of power is equated with the resort to violence. Force, in particular military force, is defined as the ultimate form of power. Such assertions do not make much sense, however, as they do not acknowledge the contingent nature of power (Baldwin, 1989, pp. 151–153). The effectiveness of military force is dependent on the situation in which it is applied. It would be more useful to identify the situations in which such power is effective in terms of producing desired outcomes than to elevate it single-handedly to the highest form of means to ends.

In interpreting military force as the highest form of power, attention is paid solely to manifest conflicts between actors and to their control over each other. Such a mode of analysis is flawed in that it

392

considers neither various latent forms of power and conflict nor the variety of consequences that the use of power always engenders. It is well to remember that there are multiple levels to every conflict and multiple factors at any level (Northrup, 1989, pp. 58–59).

Walter Korpi reminds us that power is embedded not only in manifest conflicts, but also in various social and economic exchanges. There are, in other words, conflicts within a cooperative relationship, especially if it is asymmetrically constructed. Then, social structure and exchange create incentives to engage in open conflict and exercise of power. Exchange may be mutually beneficial to actors, but it may also lead to discrimination and exploitation if its institutional setting is inequitable (Korpi, 1987, pp. 97–103).

This begs a broader question about the appropriate explanation of conflict behaviour. Göran Therborn (1991) has suggested in an insightful essay that human action can be explained either by actor attributes, or by the actor's cultural belonging, or by its structural location. Rational choice models, for instance, treat actors as given and attempt to explain their actions in variable social situations. Cultural and structural approaches regard the position of actors in these contexts as the principal explanatory variable.

The interpretation of actors as given and situations as variable leads easily to an economistic view that neglects cultural and structural contexts. On the other hand, the emphasis on culture and structure, i.e. the consideration of situations as given, may lead to the neglect of their variability. Obviously, composite models must be considered in conflict analysis as well – "that is, in looking at how culturally and structurally specified actors act differently in cultural and structural situations" (Therborn, 1991, p. 188).

These remarks mean that a strategic or instrumental mode of analysis and various cultural, structural, and actor-oriented approaches do not necessarily contradict each other, but can be combined. Thus, in a game-theoretic analysis, norms and rules prevailing in inter-actor relations can also be taken into consideration. For this reason it is useful to distinguish power and violence conceptually from each other. The question can then be asked how they are, respectively, associated with the strategic, cultural, and structural modes of analysis.

Hannah Arendt (1969, pp. 49–56) has given useful guidelines to how to make this distinction. She argues that power is inherent in all political relationships; it is "the essence of government." Violence, on the other hand, is instrumental and hence "always stands in need of guidance and justification through the end it pursues." The conclusion from this distinction is that "power and violence are opposites; where one rules absolutely, the other is absent." Power is thus defined positively as the human ability to act collectively for positive ends. This reasoning implies that the legitimacy of violence is impossible without its subordination to power.

The problem of legitimacy in the debate on violence is, of course, more complicated than that. At a minimum, one has to make a distinction between norms and ends. The focus on norms defines violence as illegitimate if its use hurts legal or political norms that are broadly accepted in society. The deviation from established norms is supposed to lead to punishments against the subject.

Arendt seems, in turn, to approve violence if it serves acceptable political ends and the common good. In this utilitarian perspective, violence can be judged not by any abstract criteria, but by its outcomes for a given community of people. To make this conclusion less simplistic one has to consider, for instance, the proportionality of violence, i.e. whether its amount and the destruction engendered are in a reasonable proportion to the supposed positive results. To my mind, this criterion was broken in the Gulf War by the coalition forces.

An ultimate question in exploring the legitimacy of violence is who decides about it. The answer is dependent on the relationship between the *loci* of power and the ruler's power. It is important to realize that there are always several *loci*, which results in the judgement of their relative impact and mutual relationships. Without undertaking any empirical analysis, one can observe that the ruler's power is derived from people who are the source of power in a general sense. Thus, it is up to the people, in the tradition of popular sovereignty, to decide when to withdraw their support from the ruler and thus deny the legitimacy of its actions (Sharp, 1980, pp. 27–28, 340–342). Again, the matter is not only whether certain actions by the ruler are violent or non-violent, but whether they are acceptable to the genuine *loci* of power.

The definition of power as competence endows it with an emancipatory dimension, in contradistinction to its conceptualization as control over human behaviour. This view has been advocated, among others, by Berenice A. Carroll (1972), who rejects the power-as-control approach on both normative and scientific grounds. In her view, by rejecting the cults of power and order, the world could be transformed in a more peaceful direction. Carroll lists nine types of power of the powerless, ranging from inertial and innovative to expressive and collective power. A common denominator of them all is competence – the ability to accomplish positive ends instead of resorting to the threat and use of force for negative purposes (cf. Sharp, 1980, p. 27).

A tricky issue is whether violence qualifies as an element of competence in addition to being a medium of control. Obviously, competence has to be built primarily on peaceful means, but on certain occasions it may require a resort to violence. This gives rise to a familiar problem in the peace movement; is the use of military force acceptable at all and, if it is, under what conditions? Should physical violence be accepted if it helps to remove a greater amount of structural violence, especially in circumstances in which there is no alternative channel of action to change the situation? The instrumentalist view accepts, in most conditions, a restricted amount of violence.

Power and non-violence

The idea of the "power of the powerless" is reflected in Václav Havel's thinking. In substance it differs from Carroll's analysis in that Havel stresses primarily the role of ideology rather than coercion in the exercise of power. In non-democratic systems, the prevailing ideology is part and parcel of the constitution and justification of power. Over time, however, ideology in such systems becomes distanced from the social reality. It remains as the main source of legitimacy, but its substance becomes rigid and is expressed in a ritualistic manner.

In that way totalitarianism, to use Havel's term, is based on a "public lie," which the people have no difficulty in seeing through. The "system" does not have any alternative though. The emptiness of the totalitarian ideology can be revealed only by consistently exposing it to the truth. The task of the opposition is to "live in truth" and in that way systematically to deny the totalitarian system's right to exist. Through truth, the existential threat to the official system gains moral power, spreads to the civil society (if it has been able to retain its autonomy), and ultimately leads to the collapse of totalitarianism (Havel, 1989). Similar ideas can be discerned in Aung Suu Kyi's thinking in the Burmese context and in Benigno Aquino's views in the Philippines.

Havel's guidelines for action do not solve the vexed issue of what truth is. Without trying to solve the problem myself, one may refer to Michel Foucault (1980, pp. 131–133). He has observed that each so-

395

ciety has its regime and politics of truth, which can be understood as a "system of ordered procedures for the production, regulation and distribution, circulation and operation of statements." Truth is thus linked to both the production and the effects of power. Thus, in Czechoslovakia, both the Communist government and Charter 77 had their own regimes of truth, but they differed from each other and waged a mostly silent struggle in which the opposition ideology emerged victorious.

The Havelian approach is non-violent both in principle and in practice. It does not aim to eliminate the totalitarian system by the use of force, partly because the domestic system itself may be relatively non-violent, as was the case in Czechoslovakia. At this point it may be useful to make a distinction between two types of violence. In Webster's dictionary, violence means both "severe or injurious treatment or action" and an "unfair exercise of power and force." These definitions hint at the difference between the empirical and normative aspects of violence.

Empirically, the exercise of open violence can be quite limited in non-democratic systems, while the exercise of power is unfair and can be normatively rejected in spite of the relative absence of violence. Power is used primarily by eliminating alternatives for action and thus forcing people to behave in a uniform manner. In Havel's view, there is no other option but to oppose such a totalitarian system by non-violent means. The ultimate weakness of the official system can be exposed by living meticulously in truth and by depriving it that way of its claim to legitimacy.

This view can be placed in a wider context by recalling that domination as power is composed of two elements: violence and consent. Of the two, consent can be said to be stronger as a form of power than violence, and hence it calls for more attention in resistance. Consent may be due either to passive acceptance or to enforced unanimity (Jahangir, 1989). The former meaning of consent comes close to the Gramscian conception of hegemony, which has a functional role for the social class in power – it cements the political arrangement in being and eliminates alternatives to it from public consciousness.

In the socialist societies, ideology became a form of power that was passively accepted but seldom deeply internalized by citizens. This was the niche to which Havel directed his strategy of "living in truth." Such a strategy is obviously more convenient in a system in which obedience is based on passive approval rather than the threat of force. The opposition does not need to face physical threats and to decide in fear whether to choose violent or non-violent means of resistance. The consent imposed from above can be undermined by creating a political–intellectual alternative and by consistently promoting it.

The question can be raised, however, whether in non-democratic societies the political forces in government and in opposition are usually that non-violent in their actions. In many of them, violence is often the norm and non-violence the deviation from it. Violence can be used in an anarchic fashion without any clear-cut objectives in mind. In this case it becomes an ideology, a way of life, and may be practised almost ritually. In Arendt's terms there is a complete lack of power in such a situation; violence grows out of anomie and a lack of political organization.

More often, however, violence is an instrument intended to produce desired political effects either as a means of communication or by physical destruction. In that sense, political violence is often regarded as an inevitable part of national and international relations (Townshend, 1987). There are, of course, exceptions to that rule, such as the relative absence of violence in recent East European revolutions. In the instrumental tradition, this "deviation" may be explained by the anticipated inability of violence to produce any meaningful results.

Except in Romania, this political inadequacy of violence was comprehended by the Communist Party élites. As a consequence, they resigned quite voluntarily and peacefully from power. Now the old élites are returning with economic and political vengeance to share the democratized power with the previous opposition, or even take it over. This tendency, building on people's frustration and relative deprivation, is visible, for example, in Lithuania, Slovakia, and most member states of the Commonwealth of Independent States (CIS).

The rationality of violence

The reasons for action in the rational conception of violence can be determined in two different ways: either by external observers or by the agent's own reasons. The more common choice between these alternatives favours the agent's own conception of rational behaviour (Reynolds, 1989, pp. 47–50). This choice has to be complemented, however, by consideration of the structural context.

Such a step has been taken in the historical studies of Charles Tilly.

He has placed the resort to and changes in collective action, including violent behaviour, in the context of major structural transformations of societies – the development of capitalism, industrialization, urbanization, and state-making (Tilly, 1986). Collective violence cannot, in other words, be separated from the social structures and their transformation. Power positions, inequities, and deprivations embedded in social structures foster the resort to violence to defend existing entitlements or appropriate new ones. Violence often alters, in its turn, the distribution of entitlements in society and its structural framework.

Tilly's empirical studies are primarily historical in orientation. This does not reduce their relevance for today, however. To my mind, his theoretical framework can be applied to a variety of historical circumstances, including the present ones. This is, by the way, one of the advantages of the utilitarian–rational mode of analysis. Tilly's framework of analysis can be fruitfully applied to account for the roots of violence in the Balkans, the Caucasus, and Central Asia, though in all these cases national and ethnic factors should probably gain a somewhat greater prominence.

Tilly argues that the use of violence has, as a rule, been rational, in that it has produced desired outcomes. This has been the case, in particular, with powerful groups; having other means at their disposal they prefer to avoid violence, but if they decide to use repression it usually works to their advantage. Violence pays less frequently for powerless social groups. For them the resort to violence may, however, be the only way to alter the structure of inequity (Tilly et al., 1975, pp. 280–285).

Violence invariably produces human suffering and material destruction, but it also becomes a channel for expressing grievances and opens political space that would otherwise remain closed. The prescriptions to be derived from Tilly's analysis deviate from those of Havel. Tilly's conception of rationality is predicated on the actors' positions in socio-economic structures, whereas Havel is more confident in the rationality of a "truthful" non-violent resistance.

With some hesitation, terrorist actions can be placed in Tilly's framework. They amount to communication by violence and hence manipulate the political space. As political action, terrorism is divorced from verbal politics, which has been found ineffective as a means of social influence. According to Rubenstein (1987, pp. 10–11), terrorists feel "twice betrayed," first by the ruling class resisting radical social changes, and then by the masses whose consciousness the terrorists have been unable to reach. Terrorism grows out of the feelings of cultural alienation and political impotence.

This characterization of terrorism leads, however, to its rationality being questioned if it is defined as the existence of a link between the form of action and the outcome. Terrorists resorting to violence may not have any clear-cut end result in mind. With this in mind, Charles Reynolds (1989, p. 211) has pointed out that "what might be called declaratory terrorism cannot therefore constitute a strategy designed to achieve specific goals. Its ineffectiveness in promoting revolution lies in its inability to relate means and end with any precision."

Terrorism may contribute to the collapse of government if its domestic position has been seriously weakened already. Otherwise terrorism is likely to strengthen the government's position. This conclusion is reminiscent of Lewis Coser's (1956) hypothesis, proved by subsequent empirical research, that a social system will disintegrate under external pressure if its initial cohesion has been low. In the opposite case, social cohesion will increase, because the initial consensus keeps the members of society together.

Order and rules

The utilitarian view considers violence as a means of both maintaining and changing social order, whether in the national or international context. A central issue of political theory is how the need for change and the necessity of order are balanced with each other. International order can be achieved by a structural arrangement of power, such as the balance of power, by the development of international institutions, or by the entrenchment of rules to guide inter-actor relations.

In international relations, Hedley Bull (1977), in particular, has stressed the relevance of the concept of order. Although his views on international order have been criticized (Vincent, 1990, pp. 42–49), and probably rightly so, they provide useful starting points for further analysis. The penchant for order can be traced back to the nature of social power, which is at the same time a resource and a threat. The states have an interest not only in expanding, but also in limiting their own power and especially that of their adversaries. Order is necessary, but in international relations it is always incomplete (Donelan, 1990, pp. 28–35).

The existence of order, in a benevolent sense of the word, presupposes certain common interests and a value consensus among the members of the system. Rules are general principles that require actors to behave in prescribed ways in specific situations. Order is thus maintained by common interests and rules spelling out the kind of behaviour that is acceptable to the actors involved. The rules are institutionalized in the sense that they are made, communicated, interpreted, administered, and enforced by an actor or a group of actors (Bull, 1977, pp. 53–57; see also Kratochwil, 1989).

Furthermore, a distinction can be made between three sets of rules: those distinguishing the state-based international society from alternative arrangements, the rules of coexistence, and the rules regulating cooperation between the actors. In this context, the rules of coexistence have special relevance as they restrict the use of violence in international relations. In the present international system, such rules usually recognize, though with restrictions, the use of violence by sovereign states as legitimate and usually condemn the resort to force by other actors (Bull, 1977, pp. 67–71). This is a consequence of the Weberian tradition of defining the concept of state.

A realistic view of international relations defines order in the context of the power distribution, more precisely as a function of the balance of power. It may be argued that the traditional balance of power collapsed with World War I and it has not been restored in the relations between major powers since then. The limitation of violence has been attempted either by collective security arrangements (the League of Nations and the United Nations) or by the Cold War deterrence system, which is conceptually distinct from the balance of power. These arrangements have not been able to eliminate violence altogether and may occasionally even have fuelled it, but they have also imposed constraints on the use of force.

In the conditions of the early 1990s, one can meaningfully speak of neither a balance of power nor a deterrence system. This is due to both the erosion of the state-centricity of international relations and the redistribution of power resources between states. In addition, the emerging international disorder has commonly been attributed to such factors as population explosion, spreading poverty and malnutrition, the proliferation of mass-destruction weapons, and the rise of religious fundamentalism (e.g. Lellouche, 1992). With the expansion of the political agenda of East–West relations, "European history has returned to the Europeans once again" (Szabo, 1991).

Balance-of-power politics requires the centralization of power in the hands of key policy makers. In that sense it is more of a manual than an automatic process. Nuclear deterrence continues to be an existential fact, but its political context is changing; a greater worry than the credibility of deterrence is the control of nuclear weapons, and tactical nukes in particular, as well as the prevention of their proliferation and accidental use. In addition, the problem of controlling and destroying nuclear explosives in the CIS has superseded many of the traditional nuclear issues.

For instance, the maintenance of strategic parity is not the dominant issue any more, as shown by the most recent versions of the strategic arms limitation treaty. Yet, this matter cannot be entirely wiped from the negotiating table. There are nationalist political forces in Russia that are fearful of the emergence of strategic imbalances. In the United States, there are still forces that aspire to nuclear supremacy.

In the European context, it is difficult to believe that the military balance of power or the traditional pattern of deterrence could be restored. Nor is there any "pure" collective security system in sight. That is why an intermediary solution, such as the great power concert, may be the only possibility of stemming the erosion of order. The idea of a collective European security system is not altogether dead, however.

For example, a proposal has been made to establish, building on Article 52 of the UN Charter, a regional European security council and European peace-keeping forces to transform the continent into a system of cooperative–collective security (Senghaas, 1991, pp. 315–316). In fact, the formation of peace-keeping forces is under active preparation in the context of the Conference on Security and Co-operation in Europe (CSCE). The idea was sponsored at the CSCE summit in Helsinki in July 1992, even though the peace-keeping services will probably be leased from Nato or the Western European Union rather than organized by the CSCE itself.

Concert and order

In general terms, the concert is an alternative to deeply divisive and polarized conflicts and a system to maintain order in inter-state relations. A concert is, by one definition, based on the "plurality of near-equal parties and multiplicity of intersecting lower-intensity conflicts which form the prerequisite to ... a concert" (Liska, 1990, pp. 349–350). This definition does not, however, take into account the fact that the concert is run by a relatively small group of powers that define the rules of the system. The members of the leading coalition are clearly superior to the remaining small states. In such a situation the freedom of individual states to make independent choices is curtailed. In that sense a concert limits opportunities for self-realizing policies (Miller, 1985, pp. 34–36).

The concert is based on commonly accepted rules and institutions that provide for collective action to prevent large-scale violence and the deterioration of order. In that sense the concert arrangement is conservative by its basic nature; it prefers order to autonomy, which better assures self-realization but could also give rise to instability and violence. A characteristic of the concert is its penchant for "flexible diplomatic instruments and coalitions rather than forceful military ones for resolving differences and limiting individual ambitions and gains" (Liska, 1990, p. 350).

The concert is a tool for promoting international order and can hence be defined as a pattern or a method of goal satisfaction. In this sense, the concert hints at a purposive element in the behaviour of actors. As they pursue different goals, there are also different conceptions of order (McKinlay and Little, 1986, pp. 21–22). International order is thus not necessarily a static arrangement of power relations, but a dynamic concept associated with the interests and objectives of the actors.

In the static sense, the concept of the concert is viewed as a pool of capabilities dominated by the major powers. Typically, the great powers forming a concert aim not only to maintain peace in their mutual relations, but also to advocate their interests *vis-à-vis* other members of the system. For this reason, "the middle and small powers of the world, while they stand to gain from co-operation among the great powers, also stand to lose by it." This is simply due to the fact that the "model of a great power concert ignores, where it does not actually seek to repress, the demands of weaker countries and peoples, for change" (Bull, 1977, p. 300).

The virtues of the concert arrangement are often explicated by comparing the League of Nations and the United Nations with each other. The former supposedly failed to stem international violence because its internal power relations and decision-making were too dispersed. To eliminate this deficiency, power in the United Nations system was largely concentrated in the permanent members of the Security Council, a concert.

To defend the interests of small states, a dynamic conception of concert, permitting change, must be developed. As a consequence, it would be advisable to conceptualize the basis of international order as a coalition of states managing systemic transformation and controlling violence. As observed above, the flexibility of means, including systematic consultation and coordination, is an appropriate method in accomplishing such tasks. Coordination and consultation are, in effect, preconditions for achieving and maintaining a consensus about common interests and values.

The conceptualization of order as goal satisfaction puts a premium on rules and institutions, rather than the distribution of power, as crucial approaches to building a relatively non-violent international order. The concept of a concert, both as a structural arrangement and as a form of security diplomacy, is related to collective security, while it differs from the balance of power in that the cooperative element is stronger in the concert.

According to Robert Jervis (1985), concerts have been created only in 1815–1854, 1919–1920, and 1945–1946 after major wars waged against a potential hegemon. Pretty soon concerts give way to a balance-of-power system. The transitions between these two systems are not intellectually and politically antinomical arrangements, but they occur within the tradition of political realism.

On the other hand, the emphasis on rules and institutions in the concert introduces sociological and transformative elements into it. In an international society, common rules can exist even in the absence of common government, although they may be rudimentary and unstable. Yet such rules can, especially if reciprocally observed, limit and constrain the struggle for power and the resort to violence. As a consequence, "international society, understood as an association of states in terms of common rules but without a common government, is at least a logically possible form of international order, however unstable or otherwise unsatisfactory it may turn out to be" (Nardin, 1983, pp. 39–42).

The emphasis on rules leads to the consideration of compliance and its bases in international relations. This, in turn, gives rise to their regime analysis. Oran Young, in particular, has advocated the view that rules and institutions are important constraints on the actor's behaviour. Compliance with them often becomes habitual either because of the expectation of benefits from cooperation or because of the internalization of the standard operating procedures. Then compliance with rules takes place without the fear of sanctions produced by non-compliance. Sanctions are characteristic of enforcement actions that are not common in international relations owing to the scarcity of authorized agents to compel actors to comply with the rules (Young, 1989, pp. 70–80).

Young's remarks can be connected with the Weberian analysis of rules by Onuf and Klink (1989). They distinguish three types of rules from each other. Directive rules and instruction rules are both associated with domination, the former with political and the latter with ideological domination. Both of these rules can be derived from the hierarchical nature of international relations. They may not, however, be fully applicable to the European situation, which is chosen here to illustrate the relevance of our conceptual and historical analysis. This approach could be applied, *mutatis mutantis*, to other regions of the world too.

The European situation is rather characterized by heteronomy, in which "actors think themselves to be autonomous and prudently endeavour to reduce their risks and minimize uncertainty." This can be done by commitment rules, which formalize the actors' exchange of promises on their future conduct and thus provide a basis for a long-term strategy. Commitment rules "formalize promises as duties. Corresponding to duties are rights to whatever has been promised" (Onuf and Klink, 1989, pp. 158–162).

The exchange of commitments on future conduct may be construed as a part of the grand strategy that Axelrod and Keohane (1985, p. 241) call contextual issue-linkage. This linkage means that "a given bargain is placed within the context of a more important long-term relationship in such a way that the long-term relationship affects the outcome of the particular bargaining process." This is a variant of the shadow-of-the-future argument developed in game theory to account for the predilection of egoistic actors to cooperate with each other.

The condition of anarchy adds to the risks and unpredictability in international relations. Long-term commitments to be abided by by actors and institutions are intended to reduce them. As there are definite limits to enforceable contracts in inter-state relations, other political arrangements are needed to reduce risk. For example, the relevance of trust created by rule-abiding behaviour can be mentioned. A necessary amount of trust is an important asset as it prompts other actors to engage in actions that they would otherwise have avoided (Coleman, 1990, p. 91; Young, 1989, pp. 75–76).

The notion of trust does not necessarily presuppose a departure from the rational choice framework, although it may add new elements to it. Trust can be rational if the structure of incentives and commitments is such that they encapsulate self-interests (Hardin,

1991, pp. 188–192). Trust can be treated as a means of maximizing utility under risk. James Coleman has formulated this point in the following manner: "the potential trustor must decide between not placing trust, in which case there is no change in his utility, and placing trust, in which case the expected utility relative to his current status is the potential gain times the chance of gain minus the potential loss times the chance of loss" (Coleman, 1990, p. 99).

Trust is thus predicated on expected gains but, once it is placed, an actor's vulnerability increases. This may necessitate the actor in continuing cooperation even if losses exceed gains. In addition to actors, the rational theory of trust can be applied and generalized into the analysis of institutions (Hardin, 1991, pp. 201–205).

Order and violence in Europe

Limited violence

The Kantian perspective would suggest that the spread of democratic values and systems will enhance peace and stability in Europe. The states in the region are increasingly constrained by democratic public opinion and thus shun the resort to force. The growing economic interdependence in the market strengthens common interests and makes war counter-productive. The Kantian approach suggests, in a word, that there is in Europe an evolutionary process in operation that establishes new constraints on the use of collective violence (cf. Doyle, 1986).

The idea of a civilizing process leading to a peaceful and stable Europe can be reinforced by noting that the nature of military conflict has irreversibly changed. The Clausewitzian connection between the rational use of military means and desired political consequences has been severed. This is not just because of the fear of the mass destruction to be caused by the escalation of any warlike action in Europe into the use of nuclear weapons by states possessing them. The conventional war between states is also in decline, and is suggested to be possible only in the Middle East and in Indo-Pakistani relations. Hence the traditional picture of war has become outdated (Van Creveld, 1991).

One reason for this may be that the Clausewitzian theory was designed for an entirely different society, in which the official classes rather than the people prevailed. Since the early nineteenth century, the ethical dimension of inter-state wars has become more important and so has the popular will that is mobilized, and sometimes misled, by the mass media. Instead of celebrating Clausewitz, John Keegan (1992) suggests that from the modern perspective he can be "shown to have failed as a historian, as an analyst and as a philosopher." That is why Clausewitz can be deemed "politically incorrect. It would make the world a safer place."

This judgement does not mean, however, that collective violence has disappeared. On the contrary, the demise of organized conventional war has been accompanied by the rise of limited violence. This ranges from (counter)insurgency and (counter)terrorism through ethnic and narcotics conflicts to religious and national confrontations (Klare and Kornbluh, 1988; Shultz, 1991; Van Creveld, 1991). Violence has been transformed from a largely state-controlled activity into a complex use of force by a variety actors.

A basic change concerns the roots of violence; the roots of limited intra-national conflicts are different from those of inter-state war. Inter-state war probably contains a stronger rational element embedded in rivalry for resources and other economic gains as well as political influence. Intra-national conflicts, in their turn, are more often fuelled by subjective and historical causes, such as value conflicts or incompatible power structures. Therefore, such conflicts may be more difficult to manage than politico-military confrontations between governments.

"Low-level conflicts" can be quite violent and kill thousands of people or more. In the post-war era they have occurred primarily in developing countries, but recently they have also erupted in the CSCE area. In Western Europe, Northern Ireland and the Basque country are the best-known examples. Military violence associated with the breakdown of Yugoslavia, the struggle over the future of Nagorno-Karabakh and other ethnic enclaves in the former Soviet Union, and the potential conflicts within and between the states of Eastern Central Europe all show how volatile the fringes of Europe are.

The Yugoslavian case is different again, because conflict there has expanded from sporadic fighting into a complex and destructive system of violence. It has often been described as an emotional conflict in which ethnic identities and feelings of historical grievances have led to outbursts of violence between communities. Tito's centralized rule froze the historical conflicts, but could not eliminate them.

The conclusion that ethnic and other related conflicts are by their nature expressive and irrational and hence do not lend themselves to easy management or resolution calls for some caveats, however. Even though cultural and historical factors are of obvious relevance in such conflicts, structural factors should not be dismissed either. Ethnic conflicts are embedded in social exchange relations and structures that motivate the actors involved to defend and improve their positions.

The structural aspect of conflict implies strategic, goal-oriented behaviour in which actors try to expand their relative gains. Thus the Yugoslavian violence is based, in part, on instrumental thinking. This can be easily seen in the behaviour of both Serbs and Croats, who have reached a UN-sponsored compromise in Croatia, but have expanded their turf at the expense of the hapless Muslims in Bosnia Hercegovina.

A new Concert of Europe?

An effective management of inter-state conflicts in Europe calls for the establishment of a concert of nations that has a more effective decision-making machinery than the 52-nation CSCE can provide. Europe has been moving since the late 1980s towards a concert system. Operationally, the concert is founded on consultation and co-ordination in European policy networks that have become more extensive over time. In terms of methods, the concert involves, among other things, compensations between its member states. These were arranged for the Soviet Union in 1989–1991 to save it from some of the deep embarrassment caused by its decline and dissolution.

The establishment of a concert in Europe means that a decision-making structure governed by major powers should be created. These powers probably number five: the United States, Russia, the United Kingdom, France, and Germany. The secondary powers include Italy, Spain, and the Ukraine. In addition, there should be mechanisms by which the European states can collectively deter and resist aggression (Goodby, 1991; Kupchan and Kupchan, 1991, pp. 151–160). The concert has to be benevolent in that it would not concentrate the management of Europe too heavily in the hands of a handful of powers. It should be responsive to the needs of the smaller members of the system as well and consult them frequently.

To make the decision-making system more effective, the virtual veto power, enshrined in the CSCE principle of consensus, has to be abolished. Instead, a modicum of majority principle must be introduced. The new concert of Europe must be based on the enactment

407

and strengthening of rules and institutions. Their test is in the ability to manage, transform, and settle the new manifestations of limited violence in the CSCE area. A common view is that, even in its strengthened form, the CSCE-based concert is hardly likely to become an effective agent to enforce rules. Voluntary compliance rather than enforcement will be characteristic of the future European security system. This means that deviations from rules and defection from institutions of cooperation will continue to occur. However, in a concert system, the gains from defection are smaller and the costs of non-cooperation greater than in a balance-of-power system (Jervis, 1985, pp. 64–73).

Yet the political fragility of the concert means that it can hardly effectively limit and even less eliminate subnational conflicts in the CSCE area. Its functions have to be more limited: first, to prevent the escalation of limited violence into inter-state warfare, i.e. the encapsulation of subnational conflicts, and, secondly, to limit and transform it to the extent possible. For instance, the Yugoslav conflict is hardly likely to be resolved for good, and that is why its gradual transformation is the only possibility (cf. Väyrynen, 1991). This transformation can be achieved by redefining, where possible, the issues, the actors, and their coalitions as well as structures in such a manner that they become less violence prone.

Such a conflict transformation within nations can hardly be accomplished without external political, economic, and humanitarian assistance. The Yugoslav example shows how difficult such a task is. The CSCE and the European Union (EU) have both failed to ameliorate the situation, and only the United Nations can claim partial success. An alternative to external political mediation is direct military intervention in the conflict to control and terminate violence. In the present world, such enforcement action is feasible only if a coalition of Western powers, including the United States, is formed for the task. So far the domestic constraints have been too strong to permit such a direct intervention policy.

There are many obstacles to the political effectiveness of external military interventions in situations like Yugoslavia. To overcome them there must be a strong and workable concert of powers that can act in unison to stop fighting. Such a concert could also be an effective political mediator and contribute to the transformation of conflict from outside. A benevolent concert could be more capable than the present international institutions of controlling violence without necessarily resorting to its use itself.

The concert of major powers could lend credibility to international norms and institutions by the potential of collective action. Such concert-based norms and institutions provide a cooperative base for the maintenance of international order. Cooperation between major powers helps to build on the war-preventing potential of democracy and civil society and to contain the penchant of such powers for unilateral and expansionary policies. In that way the ability of international society to deal with the instrumental aspects of conflicts between and within nations is strengthened.

References

Arendt, Hannah (1969) *On Violence.* New York: Harcourt Brace Jovanovich.

Axelrod, Robert, and Robert O. Keohane (1985) "Achieving Cooperation under Anarchy: Strategies and Institutions." *World Politics* 38, no. 1: 226–254.

Baldwin, David A. (1989) *Paradoxes of Power.* Oxford: Basil Blackwell.

Bull, Hedley (1977) *The Anarchical Society. A Study of Order in World Politics.* New York: Columbia University Press.

Carroll, Berenice A. (1972) "Peace Research: the Cult of Power." *Journal of Conflict Resolution* 16, no. 4: 582–616.

Coleman, James S. (1990) *The Foundations of Social Theory.* Cambridge, Mass.: Belknap Press.

Coser, Lewis (1956) *The Functions of Social Conflict.* Glencoe, Ill.: The Free Press.

Donelan, Michael (1990) *Elements of International Political Theory.* Oxford: Clarendon Press.

Doyle, Michael (1986) "Liberalism and World Politics." *American Political Science Review* 80, no. 4: 1151–1161.

Ellis, Anthony (1992) "Utilitarianism and International Ethics." In: Terry Nardin and David R. Mapel, eds. *Traditions of International Ethics.* Cambridge: Cambridge University Press, pp. 158–179.

Falk, Richard (1992) "Recycling Interventionism." *Journal of Peace Research* 29, no. 2: 129–134.

Foucault, Michel (1980) *Power/Knowledge. Selected Interviews and Other Writings 1972–1977.* Brighton: Harvester Press.

Gaddis, John Lewis (1991) "Great Illusions, the Long Peace, and the Future of the International System." In: Charles W. Kegley, ed. *The Long Postwar Peace. Contending Explanations and Projections.* New York: HarperCollins, pp. 25–55.

Goodby, James (1991) "Commonwealth and Concert: Organizing Principles of Post-Containment Order in Europe." *Washington Quarterly* no. 1: 71–89.

Hardin, Russell (1991) "Trusting Persons, Trusting Institutions." In: Richard J. Zeckhauser, ed. *Strategy and Choice.* Cambridge, Mass.: MIT Press, pp. 185–209.

Havel, Václav (1989) "The Power of the Powerless." In: Jan Vladislav, ed. *Living in Truth.* London: Faber & Faber, pp. 36–122.

Jahangir, B. K. (1989) "Violence and Consent in a Peasant Society." In: Daniel Miller et al., eds. *Domination and Resistance.* London: Unwin Hyman, pp. 316–324.

Jervis, Robert (1985) "From Balance to Concert. A Study of International Security Cooperation." *World Politics* 38, no. 1: 58–79.

Keegan, John (1992) "Peace by Other Means? War, Popular Opinion and the Politically Incorrect Clausewitz." *The Times Literary Supplement*, 11 December, pp. 3–4.

Klare, Michael T., and Peter Kornbluh, eds. (1988) *Low-Intensity Warfare. Counterinsurgency, Proinsurgency and Antiterrorism in the Eighties.* New York: Pantheon Books.

Korpi, Walter (1987) "Maktens isberg under ytan." In: Olof Petersson, ed. *Maktbegreppet.* Stockholm: Carlsson bokförlag, pp. 87–117.

Kratochwil, Friedrich V. (1989) *Rules, Norms and Decisions. On the Conditions of Practical and Legal Reasoning in International Relations and Domestic Affairs.* Cambridge: Cambridge University Press.

Kupchan, Charles A., and Clifford A. Kupchan (1991) "Concerts, Collective Security, and the Future of Europe." *International Security* 16, no. 1: 114–161.

Kuper, Leo (1990) "The Genocidal State: An Overview." In: Pier L. van den Berghe, ed. *State Violence and Ethnicity.* Niwot, Colo.: University Press of Colorado, pp. 19–51.

Lake, David A. (1992) "Powerful Pacifists: Democratic States and War." *American Political Science Review* 86, no. 1: 24–37.

Lellouche, Pierre (1992) *Le nouveau monde. De l'ordre de Yalta au désordre des nations.* Paris: Bernard Grasset.

Liska, George (1990) *The Ways of Power. Pattern and Meaning in World Politics.* Oxford: Basil Blackwell.

McKinlay, Richard D., and Richard Little (1986) *Global Problems and World Order.* London: Pinter.

Miller, Lynn H. (1985) *Global Order. Values and Power in International Relations.* Boulder, Colo.: Westview Press.

Morgan, T. Clifton, and Sally Howard Campbell (1991) "Domestic Structure, Decisional Constraints, and War. So Why Kant Democracies Fight?" *Journal of Conflict Resolution* 35, no. 2: 187–211.

Mueller, John (1990) *Retreat from the Doomsday: The Obsolescence of Major War.* New York: Basic Books.

Nardin, Terry (1983) *Law, Morality and the Relations of States.* Princeton, N.J.: Princeton University Press.

North, Robert C. (1990) *War, Peace, Survival. Global Politics and Conceptual Synthesis.* Boulder, Colo.: Westview Press.

Northrup, Terrell A. (1989) "The Dynamic of Identity and Social Conflict." In: Louis Kriesberg, Terrell A. Northrup, and Stuart J. Thorsson, eds. *Intractable Conflicts and their Transformation.* Syracuse, N.Y.: Syracuse University Press, pp. 55–82.

Onuf, Nicholas, and Frank L. Klink (1989) "Anarchy, Authority and Rule." *International Studies Quarterly* 33, no. 2: 149–173.

Ray, James Lee (1989) "The Abolition of Slavery and the End of International War." *International Organization* 43, no. 3: 405–440.

Reynolds, Charles (1989) *The Politics of War. A Study of Rationality of Violence in Inter-state Relations.* Hemel Hempstead: Harvester Wheatsheaf.

Rubenstein, Richard E. (1987) *Alchemists of Revolution: Terrorism in the Modern World.* New York: Basic Books.

Russett, Bruce M. (1990) *Controlling the Sword. The Democratic Governance of National Security*. Cambridge, Mass.: Harvard University Press.

Schweller, Randall L. (1992) "Domestic Structure and Preventive War. Are Democracies More Pacific?" *World Politics* 44, no. 2: 235–269.

Senghaas, Dieter (1991) "Friedliche Streitbeilegung und kollektive Sicherheit im neuen Europa." *Europa-Archiv* 46, no. 10: 311–317.

Sharp, Gene (1980) *Social Power and Political Freedom*. Boston: Porter Sargent Publishers.

Shultz, Richard H. (1991) "The Low-Intensity Conflict Environment of the 1990's." *Annals of the AAPSS* no. 517: 120–134.

Starr, Harvey (1992) "Democracy and War. Choice, Learning and Security." *Journal of Peace Research* 29, no, 2: 207–213.

Szabo, Stephen (1991) "The New Europeans: Beyond the Balance of Power." In: Nils H. Wessel, ed. *The New Europe. Revolution in East–West Relations*. New York: Academy of Political Science, pp. 26–34.

Therborn, Göran (1991) "Cultural Belonging, Structural Location and Human Action. Explanation in Sociology and Social Science." *Acta Sociologica* 34, no. 3: 177–191.

Tilly, Charles (1986) *The Contentious French: Four Centuries of Popular Struggle*. Cambridge, Mass.: Harvard University Press.

Tilly, Charles, Louise Tilly, and Richard Tilly (1975) *The Rebellious Century, 1830–1930*. Cambridge, Mass.: Harvard University Press.

Townshend, Charles (1987) "The Necessity of Political Violence." *Comparative Studies in Society and History* 29, no. 2: 314–319.

Van Creveld, Martin (1991) *The Transformation of War*. New York: Free Press.

Väyrynen, Raimo (1988) "Domestic Crises and International Wars." In: Peter Wallensteen, ed. *Peace Research. Achievements and Challenges*. Boulder, Colo.: Westview, pp. 70–102.

—— (1989) "Economic Fluctuations, Military Expenditure, and Warfare in International Relations." In: Robert K. Schaeffer, ed. *War in the World-System*. New York: Greenwood Press, pp. 109–126.

—— (1991) "To Settle or to Transform? Perspectives on the Resolution of National and International Conflicts." In Raimo Väyrynen, ed. *New Directions in Conflict Theory. Conflict Resolution and Conflict Transformation*. London: Sage, pp. 1–25.

Vincent, R. J. (1990) "Order in International Politics." In: J. B. D. Miller and R. J. Vincent, eds. *Order and Violence. Hedley Bull and International Relations*. Oxford: Clarendon Press, pp. 38–64.

Wight, Martin (1978) *Power Politics*, edited by Hedley Bull and Carsten Holbraad. Harmondsworth: Penguin.

Young, Oran R. (1989) *International Cooperation. Building Regimes for Natural Resources and the Environment*. Ithaca, N.Y.: Cornell University Press.

411

15

The United Nations and non-violence

Toshiki Mogami

Introduction

The principle of non-violence has rarely been discussed in connection with the structure and functioning of the United Nations, which is both natural and odd. It is natural because the organization is founded on the Westphalian concept of organizing the world, in which nation-states are the fundamental units[1] that wield the ultimate power in deciding on the operation of the organization; to the degree that the nation-state can be said to be an institution for war, an organization composed of those violent entities cannot be expected to become an embodiment of the principle of non-violence. It is odd if we define peace as the absence of various kinds of violence. The UN has been labelled as a peace organization from the beginning, not without reason. It was meant to be the completion of the horrific World War II, as well as the device for pre-empting another world war. Peace was there, to be symbolized in the organization. But the discourse stopped there, without elaborating on the relationship between the organization's philosophy, ends, guiding principles, and means of action, on the one hand, and the principle of non-violence, on the other: what kind of peace and in what manner would the organization pursue it?

To go further back, the theme of non-violence has virtually never occupied space in the study of international relations. Either this was because it was deemed irrelevant, since, at least according to realism, world politics is essentially the pursuit of power by nation-states, which is inseparable from the exercise of violence. Or this was possibly because the principle of non-violence has been seen as something implementable only in the individual-to-state relationship, as in the case of Mahatma Gandhi (against the United Kingdom), or of Martin Luther King, Jr. (against his own state), or of the Norwegian and some other nations' resistance (against Nazi Germany). In short, the principle is first and foremost associated with civil disobedience, and dissociated from state-to-state relationships or from an organization that comprises those states. But is it really irrelevant to a peace organization?

International organizations have been understood or explained as vehicles for the furtherance of the common interests of the participants in them. The inherent image is positive-sum, guaranteeing some benefits or gains to each. To this extent, the principle of non-violence may not distinctively manifest itself, although the hidden fact remains that peaceful cooperation through international organizations is essentially a mode of non-violence.[2] In any event, this stage unconsciously precludes the probable necessity of thinking about the application of non-violence; in so far as everybody gains, there can be no conflict theoretically, leaving little room for the application of non-violence.

A fundamental change to this idyllic picture is brought about when the organization concerned becomes truly universal, thus engulfing the near-totality of the states of the world. These members are extremely heterogeneous in their level of economic development, political and social systems, values, and domestic stability. With this overwhelming heterogeneity, the organization is now turned into a dump for troubles and disputes, and a showcase for gaps between states. Regardless of whether the organization is capable or legally competent to deal with them, it absorbs various kinds of world problems like a black hole.[3] The positive-sum conception no longer applies; instead, the organization now faces different kinds of tasks, One is to narrow the gaps, and the other is actually to solve disputes.

Narrowing the gaps may deviate from the positive-sum formula in that psychologically and subjectively it could imply, in strictly material terms, "gains" for some but "losses" for others, to the extent that the superordinate notion of "human interest" (according to

413

which the diminution of structural violence can mean "gains" for all) is not accepted: state members that are "below" the threshold will approach it upwards, whereas those well "above" the threshold will do so downwards by having to assume the material "cost" to solve the problem. The point is that this process is one of eradicating various kinds of structural violence, and that the organization is now faced with the difficult task of achieving non-violence in the broad sense of the term, i.e. the absence of violent conditions. The difficulty stems mainly from the zero-sum type of psychological impediment, seen at least at the state level, which at present is the basic unit of the possession of wealth.

The other aspect, that of dispute settlement, has equally, and more directly, to do with non-violence. The question relates to not only getting rid of those disputes, but also *how* to do so: will these disputes be resolved in a violent way or a non-violent way? Of course, tension does exist between the principle of non-violence in its pure form and the actual handling of disputes, which may require a certain coercion by virtue of the dictates of the urgency and the degree of violence of the situation. Therefore, the answer may lie somewhere in between the two extremes. However, whatever means may be employed, it remains necessary for the organization to clarify the philosophy upon which its system of security and conflict resolution is founded. This reflection seems essential at this juncture of history because what is at stake is the search for the best available modality for civilizing the world, at a time when the belief in the inevitable necessity and effectiveness of naked power may be accepted rather uncritically as a means for this civilizing. In reality, however, neither the tension nor the need to reconcile it has ever been a real problem for the UN for the simple reason that the "ideal" of collective security has been unquestionably taken for granted: violence will be countered by another violence. But is the UN inevitably destined to be an ultimate exerciser of violence? Is it consistent enough?

If the notion of peace is equated with the absence of violence, both as a state and as a process, and if the UN continues to be called a peace organization, it seems necessary conceptually to reconstruct its existence and functioning from the perspective of non-violence. This perspective could be broken down into three phases: (1) the advocacy of the principle of non-violence, which does not appear to be the essential part, since the central question is whether and how the UN as a whole can be an antithesis to violence in its activities; (2) non-violent means by which to solve conflicts; and (3) activities directed towards the realization of a non-violent state of human affairs, or efforts to eradicate structural violence. The second and third phases will be discussed below.

The dialectics of direct violence in the UN

The traumatic dialectic

The United Nations originated from a strong revulsion to the atrocious war instigated by the fascist and totalitarian states.[4] Abhorrence of violence apparently stemmed from these origins, with Article 2, paragraph 4, of the Charter as clear evidence. At the same time, however, the abhorrence did not thoroughly determine the guiding principle of the UN in such a way as to result in the total negation of violence. Rather, exactly this origin in revulsion silenced non-violence as a matter of organizational principle, circumventing its growth in and through the organization.

The dialectic that governs this constraining process can be described as follows. The "thesis" is *unit violence*, that is, the system where each state enjoys the sovereign right to resort to violence in the name of national (one-state) security.[5] *Si vis pacem, para bellum* was the dictate of reason, although the aggregate of this reason might turn out to be huge unreason. As if to verify these apprehensions, the dispersion of the units for violence has been the bedrock that unleashes a myriad of armed conflicts and even aggressions. Thus, it had to be attenuated and/or counterposed by an antithesis, one way or another.

The "antithesis" that was embossed in the UN was not non-violence but *superviolence*, which was to countervail unit violence: aggressions had to be forcefully suppressed – quite understandably, for the theme was how to repulse another Hitler. The projection of superviolence was embodied in the system of collective security, especially the designed enforcement action with a putative UN force. Once it was posited as an ideal antithesis, the world has had to agonize over the non-fulfilment of this ideal, as the force has never been established but there did not seem to exist any alternative.

Even if this "ideal" is achieved, however, where will this dialectic take us? Toward what synthesis? We pose this question not because we think that logically a dialectic must be completed with a synthesis, but because this logical discontinuance seems to suggest the transitory nature of the UN with regard to violence. What is the logical

415

defect that has rendered non-violence irrelevant to the UN security system?

To begin with, the dialectic is unexpansive owing primarily to the fact that the relationship between the thesis and the antithesis is not genuine. Both the thesis (unit violence) and the antithesis (super-violence) share the same philosophy of the *para bellum* hypothesis. The difference may lie in the fact that the former is private whereas the latter is more public in character. But it is basically a legal differ-entiation, not a qualitative one; both are commonly a violent reaction to violence.

Admittedly, the concept of collective security marked an advance-ment in the history of international security by creating the notion of public violence, which would gradually replace separate, private violence.[6] It was more than the simple revival of the just war. Mean-while, qualitatively it was an enlarged version of conventional na-tional (one-state) security in that it did not conceptually overcome the violence-versus-violence, or an eye-for-an eye formula. The pos-sible contradiction inherent in the scheme – that the UN was ex-pected to enforce the principle of non-aggression by using violence, – was hardly suspected. The dominance of the Hitlerian concept of international security was rampant here.

Now, what synthesis is expected to come out of this ungenuine set of thesis and antithesis? By inference, two hypotheses could exist. One is the eternal absence of a true synthesis, which will happen if and when the collective security system becomes successful, or at least remains trusted. This would perpetuate the primacy of collec-tivized violence, albeit more public in character, over separate and pri-vate violence. In this hypothesis, the antithesis is simply transposed to the position of synthesis, because it is the antithesis to the initial the-sis and can thus be the only true synthesis. But, as long as violence remains with us, this means the absence of a qualitatively transcen-dent synthesis. In the best case, of course, the success of the collec-tive security system may eventually help compel disarmament, result-ing in a structurally pacified world. For the time being, however, such a state of affairs looks very remote, since we have not seen the "suc-cess" of the systematized (i.e. applicable and actually applied to all similar cases) mechanism of enforcement action, despite some spo-radic demonstrations of actions resembling enforcement measures.

The second hypothesis is the emergence of an ungenuine kind of synthesis. It is the formation of alliances, which responded to the "failure" to materialize of an objectivized system of collective security. In the absence of the authoritative use of violence, states were urged to bundle their unit violences together. It was fundamentally an extension of the initial unit violence system, the only difference being that the members of alliances were now to act collectively; but the "private" nature of the use of violence remained unchanged. Ungenuine as this "synthesis" might be, it actually became the rule, and, moreover, it had been endorsed by the UN Charter, under the rubric of either "regional arrangements" or "the right of collective self-defense."[7]

Such is the result of a lack of a genuine antithesis. Accordingly, discourse on the UN has been characterized by the pathological sense of powerlessness induced by the non-existence of "teeth" in the inventory of the UN's assets. The unshaken belief in super-violence was aggrandized partly because of this non-existence. In a way, it was a strange development: few founders envisioned the UN as a superstate, but, specifically as regards the exercise of violence, the UN came to be expected to become something like one.

The situation was confounded by the Charter's virtual laissez-faire posture *vis-à-vis* armament. The contradiction was clear: the world needed the collective security system because states had not relinquished their armaments, or because the confrontation between alliances had developed to a dangerous point. Furthermore, collective security as designed by the UN Charter presupposes the armed preparedness of at least some major member states. The picture is one of a rat-race, where the root cause is left intact and only symptomatic treatment is provided. This seems to suggest that, although the perfection of the collective security system may be needed and useful at this stage of history, it is not exclusively the final answer. A peaceful world, if it is identical with a non-violent world, will have to take a step further. In order to visualize this alternative state, we need another dialectic of direct violence.

An additional trauma

Just in passing, before proceeding to the other dialectic, we would like to take a look at the by-product of the general permissiveness towards violence that permeates the UN system. It concerns national liberation movements, and the growing tendency to allow them the use of force. Although inconclusive arguments still go on about the admissibility of the use of force in them and of armed assistance to them, the majority in the General Assembly appear to have buttressed the idea. For example, the Declaration on Principles of International Law Concerning Friendly Relations and Co-operation Among States in Accordance with the Charter of the United Nations of 1970 (General Assembly Resolution 2625 (XXV)) provides that:

> Every state has the duty to refrain from any forcible action which deprives peoples ... of their right to self-determination and freedom and independence. In their actions against and resistance to such forcible action in pursuit of the exercise of their right to self-determination, such peoples are entitled to seek and to receive support in accordance with the purposes and principles of the Charter of the United Nations.

This provision is widely interpreted as granting the right to use force to national liberation movements. The resolution was followed by another one adopted in 1973, which, in reaffirming "the legitimacy of the peoples' struggle for liberation from colonial and foreign domination and alien subjugation," expressly recognized the use of "all available means, including armed struggle."[8] This right was granted to the Namibian people by yet another General Assembly resolution in 1983.[9]

It is not easy to refute this position, since the Charter recognizes even the individual and collective right of self-defence and envisions the collective use of force against international wrongdoing (then why not admit the same to the exercisers of the supreme right of self-determination?). We will not go into meticulous legal analysis of it here; instead, we would like to point out only the following.

It seems that a force has dwelt in the UN system that may encourage state and would-be state actors to vie for the legitimacy to use force – naturally so, since the basic philosophy in the system is that wrongs and evils are to be redressed or punished by force. Very roughly speaking, the UN system has in a way incited the expansion of the realm of just wars. To indicate this does not mean that wars for self-determination, as latecomers, should be excluded from that category, just as the Non-Proliferation Treaty has deprived the non-nuclear states of the chance to go nuclear. How could it be possible simply to tie the hands of the peoples suffering colonialism or neo-colonialism? The point is only that this represents another form of the relaxation in the normative restraint on the use of force,[10] and that we should be aware that something is fundamentally amiss with the present system. However understandable the use of force in the exercise of the right of self-determination may be, it cannot be denied that this has added another aporia on the route toward the non-violentization of the world.

An alternative dialectic

The other dialectic starts with a "thesis " that comprises both unit violence and superviolence on almost the same footing. As required by logic, the thesis will be confronted by an antithesis, to be sublated by a synthesis. This does not mean, it should be recalled, that the superviolence formula is meaningless or worthless, to be denied value in all respects. The attempt to collectivize violence, hence to attach a public character to the exercise of violence, could in a sense be deemed "progress." In addition, it could be said to have been the most realistic solution for an international organization for peace faced with discrete, private violences.

Yet the question remains whether making violence public was the only task that an organization for peace was historically expected to perform. Was it not charged also with the mission to make things increasingly less violent, especially the means with which the UN was to solve conflicts? Obviously, no provision to this effect can be found in the Charter, in light of which the proposition is ostensibly hypothetical. The expected mission becomes discernible only when the notion of peace (a notion that the UN is associated with) is understood in a maximal manner, and thereby elevated to the status of the overall guiding principle of the organization.

The genuine antithesis in this context is, needless to say, nonviolence. It is antithetical to both unit violence and superviolence, both private and public. It is certainly radical, but it is based on the penetrating insight pronounced by Martin Luther King, Jr. He says, first, that "the potential destructiveness of modern weapons totally rules out the possibility of war ever again achieving a negative good," and that "if mankind has a right to survive, then we must find an alternative to war and destruction."[11]

Destruction is the key word here. When, on the eve of the inception of the UN, the collective security system was conceived of, with enforcement as its core, the destructiveness of modern weapons was not fully taken into account. War was to be conducted within the confines of relative "humaneness." Nor was it clearly foreseen that those weapons would be possessed by many. The situation has drastically changed; wars were to be much more destructive and bloody than the framers of the UN imagined. Whether the violence is exercised by private actors or by a public actor, the outcome will be much the same. In this sense, collective security in the narrow sense may already be outdated.

Then what is the synthesis that should come out of this dialectic? It should be borne in mind at the outset that an international organization is not invented for the sake of logical consistency, and that the process of world politics is not logical either. Therefore it is not enough simply to avow that actors at all levels of world politics ought to respect the principle of non-violence; instead, a workable sublation has to be conceived of. At the same time, although logical consistency cannot be an aim in itself, it is important to inject reason in the development of the dialectic. What matters most is how to build a rational peace. And if it is to be rational, it has to be accomplished in the least destructive way.

Non-violentization: Some intermediate means

The conceptual core of the new dialectic is the non-violentization of the world. Logically speaking, extracting a constructive synthesis is coextensive with ridding the initial thesis of its presupposition, namely, disarming states. But the process is unlikely to be completed at a stroke. Despite past disarmament efforts and achievements, and despite the prospect that the process may be accelerated, especially with the end of the Cold War, the process appears to need more time. In the meantime, conflicts and disputes will almost inevitably occur. In the face of them, simple disapproval of unit violence would not suffice; on the other hand, simple projection of superviolence is not to be perpetuated, at least from the vista of the putative civilizing of human affairs. There is a need for a *modus vivendi* between the two: one that is operable and supplementable in the real world while being embedded in the stronghold of the penultimate principle of non-violence.

Thus the purified synthesis will be qualified to a certain extent, without undermining the substratum of non-violence. One qualification is the prevention and peaceful settlement of disputes, which, far from being a compromise on non-violence, forms part of its *modus operandi* and even reinforces it. The other is the peace-keeping operations, the need for which originates from the recognition that a minimum police force could not be dispensed with even in a more

420

non-violentized world, much less so in a world that is on its way to overcoming the negative assets of the superfluous accumulation of weaponry.

The prevention and peaceful settlement of disputes

The record of peaceful settlement of disputes and conflicts by the UN is not completely blank, there being several cases in which UN efforts turned out to be successful. Despite these intermittent successes, the system as a whole still appears unreliable. Success or failure has largely depended on the endeavours and ingenuity of the Secretary-General, who has insufficient power and resources, and on the volatile will of the parties concerned. If these conditions are not met, the disputes simply slip out of the hands of the UN.

It is strange that in the history of the UN only inadequate consideration has been given to giving substance to Chapter VI of the Charter, not to speak of the prevention of disputes, which is the stage short of that Chapter. Certainly, there are numerous cases in which either the General Assembly or the Security Council has called on the parties to halt hostilities and to start negotiations. Under that Chapter, the UN is empowered to act (and has acted) verbally, but, when it comes to acting physically, the process will be uncertain, as shown above. The obligation imposed on member states by Article 2, paragraph 3, is often ignored, and no article in Chapter VI *obligates* the UN organs to compel the parties to have recourse to effective peaceful settlement procedures. Yet, little effort has been made to rectify this inadequacy. This is in sharp contrast with the recurrently proposed activation of Chapter VII, accompanied by almost obsessive frustration with its moribundity. Indeed, as Evan Luard once commented, "Extraordinarily, after a few half-hearted attempts in its early years, the Security Council has made no more use of the procedures contained in Chapter VI than it has of those in Chapter VII."[12]

During the 1980s, however, a new orientation to substantiate Chapter VI emerged, notably out of several General Assembly resolutions and a few reports produced by the Secretary-General.[13] These seem to have reflected either the member states' loss of expectation during the period that a collective security system as designed by the Charter could be perfected, or greater recognition by them and the Secretary-General that priority should be attached to mitigating and even preventing armed conflicts rather than concentrating concern on suppressing armed conflicts only after they had taken place.

Generally speaking, these documents are intended to consolidate the states' obligation to settle disputes exclusively by peacefully means, to refer to the UN organs at an early stage of the dispute, and to make UN organs more effective for this purpose. Though far from complete, they are at least evidence of the aspiration shared by the majority of member states to make the peaceful settlement of disputes the rule, as well as not resorting to force. Whether this shift in emphasis will continue or not in the 1990s remains to be seen, particularly in view of the Security Council's readiness to impose sanctions. But even if the UN is equipped with "teeth" it will not do away with the necessity for an effective mechanism to settle disputes peacefully.

Thus the new orientation has to be sustained; but at the same time new innovations are needed, so that the previously belittled Chapter will be invigorated and organically incorporated into the security scheme of the UN, and made authoritative and workable. One idea would be statutorily to empower the Secretary-General to seek an injunction at the International Court of Justice (ICJ) over the actions of the parties to the dispute. This would involve the revision of the Charter and the ICJ Statute, and might be as difficult as the desired full acceptance by states of the Court's compulsory jurisdiction; furthermore, the parties might or might not comply with such an injunction. None the less, this is likely to pre-empt the intractability of disputes, and to nurture the sense of the rule of law, which is the minimum requirement for the meaningful operation of the system of peaceful settlement of disputes.[14]

Another noticeable trait found in the documents referred to above is increasing attention to the necessity of preventing disputes or conflicts.[15] It is surely less violent, less costly, and more efficient to forestall disputes or conflicts than to suppress them after they have broken out, but it seems to have been regarded as nothing more than an abstract dictate of reason. As such, little effort has been made to effectuate such a system of prevention. Only the annual reports of successive Secretary-Generals, in particular those of Pérez de Cuéllar, have appealed to the necessity of constructing such a system, whereby the UN would be equipped with the capability to issue an early warning.[16] The Office for the Research and Collection of Information (ORCI), set up by de Cuéllar in 1987,[17] marked part of the effort.

Abundant ideas already exist, such as the monitoring of conflict-prone areas by satellites, the establishment of local offices of the Secretary-General to provide him/her with first-hand, impartial intelligence about potential conflicts.[18] True, some of the proposed means may touch upon state sovereignty, but sovereignty is not meant to entitle any state to perpetuate a conflict-ridden world. Unless states and other national entities exercise adequate self-restraint, there will be the need and demand to bestow on the UN some supranational elements that transcend state sovereignty, to the extent that these elements help deprive the states of their liberty recklessly to resort to violence, either international or domestic.[19]

The question is how far this supranationalization of the UN can go, above all how such a development can maintain its compatibility with the principle of non-violence. Here again, tension does exist. The June 1992 report by Secretary-General Boutros Boutros-Ghali, entitled *An Agenda for Peace*,[20] attempted to take a step along this path by introducing the method of "preventive deployment" of a UN presence (most likely a UN force, though he did not clearly use this term in that context). In so far as such activity is carried out with the consent of at least one concerned party, there will not be much risk of infringing upon state sovereignty, as the Secretary-General himself emphasizes in the report; the difficulty may arise when the method is employed to intervene in a situation in which either or both of the parties asserts that the conflict is a domestic one, for example deployment of this type in Macedonia in ex-Yugoslavia. However, it is questionable if a member state can legitimately invoke the provision of Article 2, paragraph 7, of the Charter to resist this type of UN activity in cases where the exercise of its sovereignty is tantamount to unrestrained violence, atrocity, disorder, or upheaval. Then the remaining question is how far this type of activity can retain a maximum degree of non-violent character. I order to examine this question, we will have to consider the future course of peace-keeping.

Peace-keeping operations

Amidst the near irrelevance of the notion of non-violence in the setting of the UN security system, it is fortunate that the UN has invented and experienced this mode of intervention in conflicts. Contrary to evaluations in the early days, peace-keeping operations were not a mere substitute for enforcement action. They represented a profound philosophical turnabout, in that they were not meant to

423

rely on the actual exercise of violence. Maybe the turnabout was just coincidental, but the change occurred anyhow. Now the UN is endowed with a military but less violent mode of action. And, if the world continues to need some kind of police force, as it in all likelihood will, this mode appears to offer an acceptable model, provided that some conditions are met.

Where in the nexus of the UN and non-violence can peace-keeping operations be located? It goes without saying that unarmed observers are non-violent, even if they may be composed of military personnel. Peace-keeping forces, in contrast, may not be classified as strictly non-violent in so far as they are made up of armed personnel who may use weapons as need be. However, it would be inaccurate to categorize these forces among the violent modes of action for that reason alone. Rather, along the spectrum between violent (enforcement) action and non-violent action, they should be placed closer to the latter than to the former, mainly because weapons and munitions may be used only under strict conditions. As the famous epithet "soldiers without enemies" illustrates, it is not intended that they should fight a war with a wrongdoer, lawbreaker, or whatever.

The well-known principle of self-defence has been refined and reinforced as experiences accumulated. The instruction not to take any initiative in the use of force has been emphasized repeatedly. Particularly at the time of the UN Force in Cyprus (UNFICYP), the principle was not only reaffirmed but made more strict. That is, according to the Aide-mémoire of the Secretary-General concerning the operation of UNFICYP, "the principle of minimum use of force shall always be applied, and armed force will be used only when all peaceful means of persuasion have failed," and, "Should it be necessary to resort to the use of arms, advance warning will be given whenever possible."[21] In short, peace-keeping forces are ordained to be maximally non-violent.

This feature is captured and conceptually articulated by Brian Urquhart: "Peacekeeping depends on the non-use of force and on political symbolism. It is the *projection of the principle of non-violence* onto the military plane."[22] He also holds that, "A peacekeeping force should never be expected to rely on force to achieve its ends. If it finds itself forced into such a position, it will already have lost its status as a peacekeeping operation."[23] This speaks for itself.

Of course, this is a norm, and there have been derogations from it, most notably the case of the operation in the Congo (ONUC). An exception such as this, which came to the brink of an enforcement

action, should not be repeated, for the distinction between enforcement action and peace-keeping operation must be preserved. It
needs to be preserved because, precisely as it is necessary to find an
alternative to war and destruction, it is necessary to keep searching
for an alternative to a warlike, destructive mode of conflict resolution. Enforcement action, or a war conducted by the UN, would
equally be governed by the inevitable destructiveness of modern
weapons; hence its use should be limited to a minimum as a means
of last resort.

With respect to this, mention should be made of part of the Secretary-General's report quoted above, which tends to blur the distinction – his proposal to establish what he calls "peace-enforcement
units," supposedly more heavily armed than a peace-keeping force,
whose mission would be to force the disputants to abide by cease-
fire agreements or the like. Although the Secretary-General discusses this in the context of strengthening the system of peaceful settlement of disputes, this modality seems to come closer to Chapter
VII than to Chapter VI, thus rendering it plausible to name it
"Chapter VI and three-quarters" activity as compared with "Chapter VI and a half" activity, as peace-keeping operations are custom-
arily referred to. This is not to say that such a modality is bad in itself.
For example, it would be difficult to repudiate such an action by the
UN if it were directed towards effectuating humanitarian assistance,
which may be deemed bridge-building towards non-violence, i.e.
securing civilized conditions for the people in dire straits (so-called
humanitarian intervention by the UN). The point is only that the
blurring should not result in the gradual attenuation of the principle of non-violence that has by and large characterized peace-keeping
operations.

The distinction merits attention also because the possibility of
peace-keeping "sideslipping" into enforcement action was once
hinted at by Secretary-General Hammarskjöld in the nascent years
of peace-keeping: having said that a peacekeeping force could not
be stationed on the territory of a country without the consent of its
government, he stated that "[t]his does not exclude the possibility
that the Security Council could use such a Force within the wider
margins provided under Chapter VII of the United Nations Charter."[24] It is an open question how frequently such a deviation might
happen, but in any event it ought to be avoided if the UN is to adhere
to the maxim formulated by Urquhart. Here, too, Secretary-General
Boutros-Ghali's idea may border on the two types of activities; the

UN will be increasingly faced with a tension between an idealtypi-cally non-violent mode of action and a possibly less non-violent or more violent one.

In this regard, it should be noted that the decisive criterion by which to distinguish between enforcement and peace-keeping is not necessarily whether the action is enforcive, but whether it is comba-tive. The operation in the Congo was not truly enforcive, since it was begun at the request of the Congolese government, yet it was comba-tive. It was, so to speak, characterized by a *non-enforcive combative-ness*, as opposed to enforcive combativeness, which is typified by military enforcement action. On the other hand, in view of the hoped-for readiness and effectiveness of peace-keeping operations, room might well be left for something like *non-combative enforcive-ness*, as opposed, again, to combative enforciveness: as long as the operation is non-violent, it may be deployed without the consent of the parties concerned, and the collective will of the UN to start the operation will be imposed on them.[25] So-called humanitarian inter-vention, as in Somalia, constitutes a threshold case.

The difficulty with the notion of non-combative enforciveness is, of course, whether the UN can always enforce its will without any com-bat against either or both of the disputants, who may resist with force however wrong and reprehensible their deed may be either domesti-cally or internationally. In such cases, a series of tests will apply. First, the UN will be required to maintain and enhance its impartiality, ob-jectivity, and due process in the exercise of its legal power; then its moral authority and, accordingly, the legitimacy of the non-comba-tive enforciveness of its action will be upheld. Second, if either or both of the parties persist in defying even these more non-violent efforts on the part of the UN, they would cross the threshold to a more violent, combative enforciveness that might go beyond a mere police action. Such a consequence being far from desirable, things should evolve around the axis of the principle of non-violence. It should be noted, however, that the possible sequence above denotes that adherence to this principle is not exclusively up to the UN, but also demands a minimum of restraint and decency from states.

In cases where efforts to achieve complete disarmament cannot keep pace with the appearance of aggressors who are likely to devas-tate a large portion of the world, it will be tempting for the use of force beyond minimum police action by the UN to be agitated for time and again. There is nothing new about this; the principle of non-violence, to be effected by the world organization, will constantly be confronted with challenges from *Realpolitik*. But the greater challenge in an attempt to civilize the world is whether humankind can persevere in their determination to construct a condition in which that principle becomes increasingly workable. The same applies to the UN as an entity for rational peace, so it ought to be kept in mind that the projection of superviolence will be supplementary rather than primordial, short-lived rather than permanent.

It is certainly too simplistic to posit an either–or option between superviolence and non-violence. During the transitional period (though history may remain so eternally), a variety of intermediate measures will have to be worked out. Even so, we also have to be aware that the superviolence of enforcement action is neither ideal nor omnipotent. For one thing, what if the UN should keep winning one major war after another, at immense cost in terms of financial and human resources and the natural environment? Thus, military enforcement action should be the means of last resort, a deterrent to dissuade potential aggressors. For another, military enforcement action may not be usable in ambiguous cases where it is impossible to determine the perpetrator and the victim. Legally speaking, any "sanction" is premised on the possibility of judging the locus of legal responsibility; if this is not possible, it will be difficult to impose punitive sanctions. Of course, a likely *modus vivendi* in such a case would be to "punish" the side that on all available evidence could be judged *more* responsible for the situation or conflict, or both sides if both sides were held equally responsible. A case in point is the conflict in ex-Yugoslavia; whichever posture is taken by the UN, sufficient care should be taken not to aggravate the situation by simply attempting to settle the problem by force.

As to peace-keeping operations, finally, there is a caveat and a desired improvement, which will apply equally to other modes of action such as preventive deployment or the peace-enforcement unit. The caveat is that, if the Security Council is activated, as is seemingly the case with the end of the Cold War, care should be taken that peace-keeping operations do not become manipulated by the whims of the permanent members. The credibility and effectiveness of peace-keeping operations derive from their impartiality and neutrality. This tradition should not be impaired, and therefore the Security Council will be required to treat like cases alike. For instance, is it not time to consider Erskine Childers' proposal to the effect that a mechanism has to be established whereby other UN organs, specifically the General Assembly, check the lawfulness and/or appropriateness of the decisions made by the Security Council?[26] Put differently, an improved system of the rule of law within the UN seems to be necessary.

The desired improvement is, once again, to strengthen the competence of the Secretary-General, on two conditions: first, he/she has to be completely free from the influence of any member state(s); second, on the other hand, a checks-and-balances mechanism ought to be established inside the UN so that he/she does not abuse his/her power.[27] For example, would it not be desirable to endow him/her with the power to organize and dispatch at least an unarmed peace-keeping team? He/she should stand aloof from individual national interests, which fits the impartial nature of peace-keeping operations. He/she does not enjoy physical power of his/her own, to be utilized for personal geopolitical ambitions, which will add to the credibility of the UN action. In brief, it is advisable to make the most of the nature of this post, which also suits the broader aim of aligning the UN security regime with the principle of (maximum) non-violence.

The elimination of structural violence

A civilian-type UN: The enormity of the task it faces

A non-violent world needs not only a non-violent UN, but also a UN that strives to eliminate non-military forms of violence. Non-violence being originally a mode of action, the elimination of structural violence may represent non-violence only in the broader sense of the term. Nevertheless, it involves violence inflicted on the planet earth, and violence in the form of exploitation, and so on.

It should be remembered that this is precisely the field to which the UN system has directed much of its energy: decolonization, economic and social development, human rights, the environment. It is not the case that the UN was "doing nothing," as was commonly claimed. This view related only to the security field in the narrow sense, and ignores activities in other fields.

The fact is that, despite the Security Council's dormancy resulting from East–West confrontation and in the do-nothing syndrome, the organizational centre of gravity gradually shifted toward the General Assembly from the 1960s onward. But, contrary to the intention of the framers of the "Uniting for Peace" Resolution, the shift did not take place in the security field in the narrow sense. The composition of the General Assembly had been so altered that the UN could no longer be concerned about the peace/security issue alone. In its stead, development surfaced as the central issue. In other words, the shift in the organizational centre of gravity was being translated into a shift in the functional centre of gravity.

This does not mean that the UN stopped being an organization for peace. What it means is that the signification of peace went through a metamorphosis – from negative peace to positive peace. It may sound ironic in a way, for the world was not yet free from various forms of direct violence and preparation for it. Yet the underprivileged nations could not afford to wait for the prior attainment of negative peace, and thus decided to turn the world's attention to the kind of non-peace that they were experiencing on a daily basis. In face of this, the orientation of the UN had to change too, as the problems brought to it were not of a nature to be solved by the projection of superviolence.

A civilian-type UN, as one might put it, thus came to the fore. The increase in the variety of operational activities carried out by the UN system as a whole attests to this. They include famine relief, disaster relief, refugee protection, training in agriculture, the provision of primary health care, the provision of education, improvements in infrastructure, the endeavour to combat environmental degradation, and many others. Although these activities were not always successful, and they have fallen short of structural change (as was aptly criticized by Maurice Bertrand in his report[28]), their significance should not be underrated.

The non-violentization of the world has to encompass this aspect, too. The UN has to redouble its efforts, particularly when it is becoming increasingly conspicuous that the North–South problem, and for that matter the South–South problem as well, remains the principal destabilizer of world order since the end of the Cold War. Obviously, this is to say not that the UN should become the guardian of the interests of the North, which they may perceive as being threatened by the challenges from the South, but that the legitimate dissatisfaction of the underprivileged, if left unredressed, might erupt at any moment in a violent way and thus have to be responded to in a serious manner. The cause may be humanitarian at heart, yet the concern also relates to the stability of the world as a whole. This is why the civilian UN should be reinforced more than ever.

Additionally, it should be noted that the process to multiply efforts in this direction corresponded to the partial democratization of the UN system – partial in the sense that the voices of the weak came be heard, yet the imbalance between the competences of the Security Council (especially the five permanent members, the P5) and the General Assembly was left untouched. The increase in the preponderance of the General Assembly enabled this partial democratization, and encouraged the formation of organizational ideologies geared to the realization of the aspirations of the weak.[29] On the other hand, this process bred grievances among some of the developed countries, in whose eyes the process meant only excessive self-assertiveness by the developing countries. As such, the shift in the organizational centre of gravity (from the Security Council to General Assembly) also denoted a shift in the axis of main confrontation from the East–West to the North–South. Not surprisingly, the democratization was not welcomed by all, and the appeasement of this friction still poses a problem for the UN system.

Who is to steer, and how?

Now, what would the ongoing trend to strengthen the Security Council mean in this context? On the optimistic side, it could be said that its normalization is a positive thing, and that it would be fine if the Council faithfully carried through its missions entrusted to it by the Charter. On the pessimistic side, however, the "reinforcement" is likely to incur a backlash from those who fear that it might dam up the democratizing trend of the past 30 or so years and dilute the civilian UN.[30]

What will result from this is yet unknown. However, it seems that the UN is in need of a new organizational design appropriate for this new age. It still appears premature for the UN simply to felicitate "renaissance"; rather, it has to think about felicitous "re-creation." A simple atavism in organizational terms may not be enough, particularly in view of the enormity of the task facing the UN – overcoming the ever-widening economic gap, constructing a system that will allow for a more equitable redistribution of wealth, harmonizing cultural differences that could lead to antagonisms among states and nations, controlling population growth, to name only a few.

In this setting, Security Council centrism is not only undemocratic, as alleged, but also not a panacea. Apart from the disarmament issue, much of the global problématique falls outside its jurisdiction. It may be able to extinguish a fire by projecting superviolence, but the root problems could remain unsolved. Moreover, in relation to these remaining problems, it is questionable whether the five "big powers" (conventionally so called) are capable of solving them when some of the members themselves have become a nuisance to the world, whether because of their economic malaise, or their political instability, or their human rights oppression. Consequently, simple atavism seems unlikely to meet current needs.

It would be pertinent to add here a few more words about the greater than ever responsibility that the "reinforcement" of the Security Council will place on the shoulders of the permanent members. Whether undemocratic or not, this "reinforcement" could continue for some time to come. In order to strike a minimum balance between this "realistic" method and the requirements of democracy, and to augment the credibility of the UN, it will be necessary for the P5 to take the lead in constructing a better, more peaceful, more just, and more equitable world. They will have to be in the forefront of disarmament, to refrain from the use of force more than anybody else, to contribute to the development of the less privileged, as well as rectifying their own economic and political imbroglios, to contribute to the solution of resource depletion and environmental destruction, and to implement the highest standard of human rights protection. They should fulfil more of these responsibilities commensurately with the prerogatives they enjoy. Otherwise, a "reinforced" Security Council will only be a revival of the Concert of Europe.

But the question is, if the P5 states are not sufficiently motivated to move in this direction, what other organ in the UN would take on the job? Will the General Assembly, more than two-thirds of whose members belong to the South, try to revive its status as an arena in which the South voices its protest against the North's ruling of the world, thus enabling itself to nudge the Security Council in the preferred direction? And, if it does, will the South be able to become the agent of a new order while some of its countries, though apparently underprivileged for historical and/or structural reasons, are regarded by the North as causing trouble with their domestic strife, human rights abuse, or unwillingness to establish democracy despite their demand for the democratization of the UN? Or will the Secretary-General stand up to speak for the underprivileged, thus inducing effective responses from influential member states? The answer to all these is yet to be found.

The enormous task yet to be tackled by the UN is, in essence, that of civilizing the world, as was equally the case with creating a viable security system. Regrettably, however, the world is still riddled with unreason, irrationality, and lack of compassion. The perplexing problem is whether an inter-state/intergovernmental organization can really get to grips with unreason, and whether it is the most apposite tool for this purpose. We only know that the civilian, egalitarian, and compassionate UN should continue to be given a central position in its redesigning. Quick and effective responses to crises from an acknowledged and mobilized Security Council may form part of this, but not the whole. A re-created UN may need some more councils, e.g. one for human rights issues and one for the environment; rather than simply being a fire-extinguisher of last resort, the UN has to be a reliable fire-preventer and, ultimately, an eliminator of various kinds of structural violence. Yet we remain uncertain whether these institutional modifications alone can offer a tenable solution. What seems imperative is that a re-created UN should be highly responsive to the needs and aspirations of the world's populace.

To sum up, the UN is expected in the long run to both internalize and externalize non-violence: to internalize by maximally refraining from the use of violence itself, and to externalize by trying to eradicate the inhumane conditions that afflict many.

The UN as a guardian of the right to peaceful existence

The UN's ideology and identification

A UN that is both non-violentized and non-violentizing does not seem to be a mere ideal. Rather, it could be said (partly) to have emerged necessarily out of the mutations that it has undergone – one on the ideological dimension, and the other on the dimension of the UN's identification.

On the ideological dimension, the UN seems to have fluctuated from one extreme to the other with the shift in the organizational centre of gravity. As Pierre de Senarclens correctly puts it, the dominant ideology in the nascent UN was that of Anglo-Saxon liberalism and individualism. He also holds that the twin ideologies, especially the former, aimed in real terms "to project the model of Western industrial civilization onto the entire international society" and "to restore and expand the liberal economic system."[31] At the same time, the twin ideologies helped the supremacy of the notion of individual human rights to permeate the UN.

Now, with the collapse of the socialist regimes, it could be said that the economic/industrial aspect of the twin ideologies has won. But if we look back on the history of the UN, we are compelled to remember that not long after the birth of the UN these ideologies became challenged by another ideology, that of egalitarianism, which was aimed at achieving equality between states (not necessarily equality between individuals, it should be noted). This ideology, which is motivated by the theme of development, even seems to have superseded the earlier ideologies. It has seized the dominant position inside the UN, sometimes tending, in the worst case, even to belittle the rights of the individual.

Neither of the two competing ideologies has perished. Economic liberalism, or capitalism, has continued to govern the "real" world outside the UN; and egalitarianism has persisted in the normative, "imaginary" some might call it, world inside the UN. It is of little practical use to determine which of the two is flawlessly superior, each having its own advantages and disadvantages.

On the one hand, economic liberalism functions far better than a centrally planned economy; and political liberalism is surely preferable to totalitarian, oppressive regimes. Yet *laissez-faire* capitalism does not automatically lead to a humane world; freedom in economic activities is not synonymous with the freedom of humankind. In addition, it should be borne in mind that economic liberalism is not always accompanied by political liberalism. On the other hand, egalitarianism should definitely take root in the contemporary world, above all in relation to the maximization of economic well-being. But this should in no way justify the deprivation of individual human rights and fundamental freedoms, or legitimize despotism on the domestic plane.

Here we see another dialectic to be given a constructive synthesis. But the misfortune for the UN is that the competing ideologies have been treated as if they were mutually exclusive, as a result of which little effort has been made to sublate the incompatibility, which may be only superficial. But one common theme runs through: to set human beings free from oppressions, to liberate them from all kinds of misery, to guarantee the wholeness of their existence. It is, in short, the effectuation of non-violence in the wide sense.

Certainly, care has to be taken not to equate this search for a common theme with a rather simplistic universalism, which in the past has tended to impose the will and standards of the more powerful, particularly the West. Whether politically or culturally, pluralism should be the rule. On the other hand, those states (governments) that advocate pluralism on the international plane are called upon to recognize political, cultural, and ethnic pluralism on the domestic plane as well. This seems to indicate that, even after the negation of a West-inclined universalism, something incontestable will always remain. Whether we call it a new type of universalism or not, its essence is that, whatever the origins of and excuses for the detestable human conditions exemplified above, the cardinal importance of human existence should not be compromised. This fundamental goal renders irrelevant the search for ideological superiority *per se*, despite the self-righteous claim by both sides to exclusive fitness for the goal. And it is this goal that the UN should be headed for.

This point is interwoven with the mutation in the UN's identification. Whether the objective was the control of the world by the war victors, or the maintenance of international security, or the establishment of a new economic order, the basis of the UN was the nation-state system, preserving the nation-state as the basic unit. Decision-making power is virtually monopolized by *state* representatives, and decisions tend simply to concern coordination among *national* interests, with or without regard to the needs actually felt at the popular level. The shift of the location of power from the developed to the developing countries, which came about in the General Assembly and some specialized agencies, did not essentially change this situation, although it may have contributed to equality among states.

However, we have to take note of the fact that the problems that pour into the UN system are mostly existential, i.e. touch upon the human condition, which cannot be demarcated by state borders. Those problems that are transnational in nature surely require a transnationalized entity, and the real question facing the present UN system is whether it can equip itself to be such an entity.

Put differently, a *popularized* UN system is needed, which will be able to formulate the needs and aspirations existing at the popular level, and to make the most of the capabilities of non-state actors.[32] To some extent the UN system has already done this (this was referred to before as the civilian UN). The UN's identification has in fact gradually tended toward the popular level. The remaining problem is how it can acquire and enhance the autonomy that would allow it to maintain this propensity on a secure basis, and to become a truly civic UN. The Secretariat, a non-state actor, has had and will have a role to play in this process, and from this point of view it seems questionable whether the trend to constrict the size and budget of the Secretariat is appropriate.[33] Admittedly, one cannot be too optimistic about its continued straightforwardness, in view of the unwieldiness that already exists and of the danger of further bureaucratization in the future. Provided that the avoidance of such inconveniences can be assured one way or another, it is to be hoped that its competence will not be curtailed as a result of the so-called "rationalization" of this transnational, if not supranational, element. Ideal-typically conceived, international civil servants are not backed up by real power, which could well fit the image of a non-violentized and non-violentizing UN.

A note on the structural right: By way of conclusion

All the foregoing analyses seem to boil down to the right to peaceful existence of the world's citizenry. This right, often referred to as the right to peace or the right to live in peace, is tantamount to the total negation of any kind of violence: if everybody has the right to peace, everybody has the obligation of non-violence, save some lawfully controlled use of strictly limited violence for the sake of an agreed-upon order.

The problem is that the content of the right is yet to be clearly defined. Two General Assembly resolutions exist relevant to this right: one is the Declaration on the Preparation of Societies for Peace,[34] the other is a resolution entitled the Right of Peoples to Peace.[35] But, both of them simply characterize the right as being "inherent" or "sacred," and, when it comes to the content, do no more than repeat the states' obligations stipulated in the Charter (Articles 1 and 2 in particular). However, if it is a human right, it ought to be "wholly distinct from the obligation on the part of states themselves not to engage in aggression."[36] Thus, a clear definition has to be worked out. Moreover it has to be determined to what degree the right has become a positive norm of international law.

As this will entail an almost endless discussion, let us be content to say that, first, there is widespread consensus about the need for such a right in international society today. Second, being predicated on "the aspirations of all peoples,"[37] it has to mean more than the imposition of obligations on states, and should more positively define what peoples can claim. And third, the essential component of the right seems to be freedom from fear and want – in short, freedom from violence of various kinds, which should include not only freedom from being subjected to violence, but also freedom from using violence.

If we proceed along this line of thought, the right may be paraphrased as the right to the non-violentization of the world. This first imposes the obligation on every human being, every state or nation. It further entitles citizens not only to demand specific action (e.g. disarmament) or inaction (e.g. refraining from war) from their own governments, but also to claim a global condition in which violence is rendered impossible or at least not permissible. It is thus a right to a certain structure or order of the world (thence I call it a *structural right*), although it is supposedly enjoyed by separate or collective individuals.

Strange as the notion of a structural right may sound, we are here reminded of an equally strange provision in the Universal Declaration of Human Rights. Article 28 reads: "Everyone is entitled to a social and international order in which the rights and freedoms set forth in this Declaration can be fully realized." This article distinguishes itself from the other articles in that it alone refers to international order as the object of the citizens' claim. It thus endorses the validity of the notion.

It is a claim to a non-violentized world. And since the UN is bound by the dictate of this Declaration, it will be held responsible for defining its goals and fashioning its mode of action in accordance with the requirement of this Article. In this way, it could be said that a both non-violentized and non-violentizing UN is a logical conclusion, not simply an expectation. As the sole world organization, the UN is obligated to be the guardian of the right to peaceful existence. With this task yet to be realized, the UN seems to be at a critical crossroads.

Notes

1. See United Nations Charter, Article 2(1).
2. In conventional conceptualization, this could instead be termed peaceful change, which international organizations are normally expected to carry out.
3. A typical example of this is the experience of the Commission on Human Rights during the early years. Although it was not endowed with the competence to receive and examine complaints of human rights abuse from individuals, a number flowed into it. Similar phenomena are likely to continue, as long as the UN is the only multi-purpose world organization, sometimes giving the false impression that it can handle any problem that spills across state boundaries.
4. First paragraph of the Preamble to the Charter, which reads: "We the people of the United Nations determined to save succeeding generations from the scourge of war, which twice in our life time has brought untold sorrow to mankind, ..."
5. Obviously, the threat or use of force by individual states is legally prohibited by Article 2, para. 4, of the Charter. On the other hand, the right of individual or collective self-defence was reaffirmed, which runs the risk of being abused. More serious is the near laissez-faire posture of the Charter system in relation to national armaments, as will be discussed below.

6. When the "progressiveness" of the Charter system is asserted, it is basically measured against the system of the League of Nations, which gave the member states discretion in the execution of sanctions. See, for example, Inis Claude, Jr., *Swords Into Plowshares*, 4th edn., New York: Random House, 1971, pp. 262–265.

7. Articles 51 and 52 of the Charter.

8. General Assembly Resolution [GA Res.] 3070 (XXVII) of 30 December 1973.

9. GA Res. 38/36 of 1 December 1983.

10. See Richard Falk, "The Decline of International Order: Normative Regression and Geo-political Maelstrom," in: R. Falk, *The End of World Order*, New York: Holmes & Meier, 1983, pp. 167–182.

11. Martin Luther King, Jr., *Strength to Love*, New York: Harper & Row, 1963, p. 140.

12. Evan Luard, *The Blunted Sword: The Erosion of Military Power in Modern World Politics*, London: I. B. Tauris, 1988, p. 170.

13. Manila Declaration on the Peaceful Settlement of International Disputes (GA Res. 37/10 of 15 November 1982 annex); Declaration on the Enhancement of the Effectiveness of the Principle of Refraining from the Threat or Use of Force in International Relations (GA Res. 42/22 of 18 November 1987 annex); Declaration on the Prevention and Removal of Disputes and Situations Which May Threaten International Peace and Security and on the Role of the United Nations in this Field (GA Res. 43/51 of 5 December 1988 annex); Draft Rules for the Conciliation of Disputes between States (adopted by the General Assembly, 28 November 1990, UN Doc. A/45/742); Draft Handbook on the Peaceful Settlement of Disputes between States (UN Doc. A/AC.182/L.68, 12 November 1990); Declaration on Fact-Finding by the United Nations in the Field of the Maintenance of International Peace and Security (GA Res. 46/59 of 9 December 1991 annex).

14. Of course, care would have to be taken that the Secretary-General did not exceed his/her competence in an unrestrained manner. But the same care has to be taken with regard to other principal organs as well, whether the Security Council or the General Assembly. The UN being devoid of any mechanism of checks and balances, it will be necessary to devise something like the inter-organ litigation implemented in the European Union.

15. For example, Declaration on the Prevention and Removal of Disputes, op. cit.

16. *Report of the Secretary-General on the Work of the Organization*, 1982 (UN Doc. A/37/1), p. 2; 1991 (bound copy), Section V, pp. 9–11.

17. On the ORCI, see B. G. Ramcharan, *The International Law and Practice of Early Warning and Preventive Diplomacy: The Emerging Global Watch*, Dordrecht: Martinus Nijhoff, 1991, ch. 4. However, through the organizational restructuring executed by Secretary-General Boutros Boutros-Ghali on 3 March 1992, the Office was incorporated into the Department of Political Affairs (UN, ST/SGB/249, 16 March 1992).

18. For a survey of these ideas, see Thomas E. Boudreau, *Sheathing the Sword: The U.N. Secretary-General and the Prevention of International Conflict*, New York: Greenwood Press, 1991, chs. 6 and 7.

19. It should be noted, however, that if the UN ever transcends state sovereignty it will have to do so in such a way as not to give more weight to some influential member states' sovereignty than to others'. The kind of supranationality that is to be attributed to the UN should aim more at enhancing the impartiality of the organization than simply at concentrating coercive power in the organization.

20. Boutros Boutros-Ghali, *An Agenda for Peace*, United Nations, 1992.

21. Aide-mémoire of the Secretary-General concerning some questions relating to the function and operation of the United Nations Peace-Keeping Force in Cyprus, 10 April 1964 (UN Doc. S/5653), para. 19.

22. Brian E. Urquhart, *A Life in Peace and War*, New York: Harper & Row, 1987, p. 248; emphasis added.

23. Brian E. Urquhart, "Peacekeeping: A View from the Operational Center," in: Henry Wiseman, ed. *Peacekeeping: Appraisals and Proposals*, New York: Pergamon Press, 1983, p. 165.

24. Second and final report of the Secretary-General on the plan for an emergency international United Nations Force requested in Resolution 998 (ES-I), adopted by the General Assembly on 4 November 1956 (UN Doc. A/3302 of 6 November 1956), para. 9.

25. This does not imply that the will of states may be trampled on arbitrarily. Here again, the requirement of impartiality (see above, note 19) and that of a maximally non-violent character have to prevail.

26. Erskine Childers, "Gulf Crisis Lessons for the United Nations," *Bulletin of Peace Proposals* 23 (1992), no. 2: 129–138.

27. See above, note 19.

28. Joint Inspection Unit, *Some Reflections on Reform of the United Nations* (JIU/REP/85/9). 1985.

29. On this topic, see Toshiki Mogami, "The United Nations as an Unfinished Revolution," *Alternatives* XV (1990), no. 2: 177–197.

30. A reaction along these lines has already appeared. For instance, Samir Aldeeb Abu-Sahlieh asserts that the third world should consider "abandoning" the UN, which is controlled by the five permanent members of the Security Council and is thus "non-democratic" ("L'ONU et le tiers-monde," *Le Monde diplomatique*, January 1992). Though presumably an extremist view, it indicates that the third world's misgivings should by duly taken into account. See also *The Jakarta Message: A Call for Collective Action and the Democratization of International Relations*, Tenth Conference of Heads of State or Government of Non-aligned Countries, 1–6 September 1992, in which the heads "expressed concern over the tendency of some states to dominate the [Security] Council which could become an institution for the imposition of the will of the strong upon the weak" (para. 32)

31. Pierre de Senarclens, *La crise des Nations Unies*, Paris: Presses Universitaires de France, 1988, chaps. 2 and 3, esp. p. 49.

32. For this, see Chadwick Alger, "Local Individual and Community Participation in World Society," in: Roger A. Coate and Jerel A. Rosati, eds., *The Power of Human Needs in World Society*, Boulder, Colo: Lynne Rienner, 1988, pp. 101–127.

33. See the document referred to above in note 17.

34. GA Res. 33/73 of 15 December 1978.

35. GA Res 39/11 of 12 November 1984.

36. Richard Bilder, "The Individual and the Right to Peace," *Bulletin of Peace Proposals* 11 (1980), no. 4: p. 387.

37. GA Res. 39/11, op. cit.

16

The changing world order and the international legal order: The structural evolution of international law beyond the state-centric model

Georges Abi-Saab

This essay aims to examine, in a broad-brush manner, the macro-dynamics of change in the international legal order in response to changes in its environment over the last four centuries, since the structure and parameters of the present system were distilled and stabilized in the Peace of Westphalia at the end of the Wars of Religion in Europe; and more particularly since the nineteenth century, a period that had to digest first the French and the industrial revolutions, then, in our time, the rise and demise of the Bolshevik revolution, the great wave of decolonization and national liberation, as well as the ongoing "communications revolution."[1]

The initial design

The origins of the present international legal order go back to the disintegration of what Vinogradoff has called "the World State of Medieval Christendom," as a result of the Reformation and the Wars of Religion in Europe. Its traits were fixed in the Peace of Westphalia, which definitively broke away from the formally theocratic character and hierarchic structure of the existing system, invalidating once and for all the assumption – already negated in practice –

of the double allegiance of princes to Pope and Emperor, and replacing it by a new egalitarian set-up epitomized in the dictum *"cujus regio, ejus religio"* (each region follows its prince's religion).

This formula provided the basis for the coexistence of princes adhering to different versions of "truth" (i.e. with different ideologies), the Wars of Religion having shown that neither camp was in a position to impose its truth on the other. It thus recognized, in terms of the ideological conflict of the moment (to which it was supposed to provide a final and stable solution), the paramountcy of every prince in his territory and over his subjects; whence the twin legal principles, governing the new international distribution of power, of sovereignty and equality (or of the "sovereign equality" of Article 2(1) of the UN Charter).

In other words, as the legal system was meant to govern relations between antagonistic units, it had to gloss over the sources of their antagonism. It thus postulated a horizontal international structure where no hierarchy prevailed; where princes were "sovereign," both in the sense of exercising exclusive power over their territory and their subjects (internal sovereignty), and in the sense of depending on no higher authority in the international sphere (external sovereignty or independence). But in order to maintain this situation, princes had to recognize each other (i.e. to be considered) as legally equal on the international level, regardless of size, wealth, strength, form of government, religion, or ideology.

Given the main purpose of the system of making it possible for antagonistic units to coexist, it aimed – to borrow the words of David Mitrany – at keeping them "peacefully apart" rather than at bringing them "actively together." In the logic of this system, there was only one general obligation, the obligation to respect the sovereignty of others. It was an essentially passive obligation of abstention, of not trespassing on the spatial and functional confines of their sovereignty.

But if the sovereigns decided to establish or entertain relations, the system provided them with the "legal recipes" or the "how to do" formulae. In other words, to the extent that relations did take place, international law provided them with a convenient frame of reference. Indeed, the most developed chapters of classical international law fall in this category, such as the law of diplomatic and consular relations, and the law of treaties and of state responsibility.

Two important consequences flowed from this scheme of things, one relating to the representation of the new system of its rising subjects, the states, the other to the consistency and structure of the system itself. And both reflected its patently "state-centric," indeed its "state-deist," character.

In the first place, the internal logical construct of the system sketched above inexorably gave rise to the image of a "hermetic state," a black box, or a "billiard-ball" (to use Arnold Wolfers' term). Thus, in the perspective or contemplation of classical international law, states are opaque balls, whose inside we cannot see (or should feign not seeing), which are all formally equal, and which can come into contact only on the periphery or from the outside.

Obviously, this was a representation that did not completely correspond to reality even then (i.e. in the middle of the seventeenth century); much less since the industrial revolution; and even less so in our time, as we can witness in our daily lives. But it is on its basis that much of the principles and rules of international law that are still with us today have been moulded and developed.

As far as the consistency (or density) and structure of the system are concerned, states did not want to give with the left hand what they had just acquired with the right, namely their affranchisement from any and all dependence on, or submission to, a higher authority. They particularly did not want to see (re)established above them any new superior instance, whatever it might be. The new structure of international law thus had a precise and well-delimited (as well as limited) task: formally to sanction the new distribution of power in international society, i.e. to legitimize and sanction sovereignty in its newly acquired sense, without encroaching or trespassing on it.

Such a legal system, by the nature of things, could have only a very light institutional armour (in fact, none at all, except for the odd or the ad hoc occasion, with the consent of the parties), and a very light (or minimally constraining) hold over its subjects, the states, strictly proportioned to the limited task they entrusted it with. It was a system that operated through the "self-regulation" and the "self-adjustment" of the subjects themselves, rather than through its proper specialized organs.

In conclusion, two remarks are in order concerning the real social hold of this initial design, and the place of the ensuing system in the world then and now.

First, what is described above is the inner logic of the system or the manner in which it was initially articulated, in the light and as a function of the new constellation of power in the civil society it purported to regulate. But its "fit" to external social reality comprised a good part of artifice and reification. For when we speak of the centrality and all-inclusiveness or all-mightiness of the state, we are speaking of the abstract model, on the basis of abstract equality. In reality, this model eliminates from its field of vision sources of inequality and conflict of interests, and the attendant vulnerability of weak states to diktats and interventions by stronger powers, usually on the pretext of alleged violations of international law by the former, put forward and unilaterally acted upon by the latter, in the absence of autonomous organs capable of objectively verifying their veracity at the request of either party.

In the second place, it should be recalled that, at its inception, this system was not the only one contending for the status of international legal order. It had to coexist, even in Europe, with the system of Islam as well as with other existing regional systems with similar universalist pretentions. However, with time, it progressively managed to dispose of these contending systems, either by direct control, via its subjects, of large parts of the non-Western world through colonialism; or, for those communities that managed to remain formally independent (e.g. because they served as a buffer between two European empires or to avoid upsetting the European balance of power), through forced assimilation, in order to qualify as "civilized nations."

Thus, what started objectively as a regional system in the seventeenth century, ended up becoming the universal system by the end of the nineteenth century. But this universality was exclusively geographic until the post-World War II era, when the great wave of decolonization and self-assertion of the non-Western peoples of the world transformed their formal status from "objects" to "subjects" of the system.

These peoples acceded to statehood within the system and started to contest it "from the inside," striving for its development with their participation – particularly within the forum of the United Nations – to make it more "universal" in its approach as well as in the values and interests it purports to protect and promote. Thus, to understand how the system came to be what it is today, one has to start with its European origins, to the exclusion of other traditions, which indeed had no part in bringing it about, or in its subsequent evolution up to World War II, although they may now, through the participation of their former adherents in the system, influence the actual development of international law.

442

Changes in the role of the state and in its environment

What is the situation today of the system that emerged in the middle of the seventeenth century? Can we say that it is still essentially the same, in spite of the numerous transformations, additions, and excisions it has since undergone?

If we consider that it came about with a view to fulfilling a principal task or function, namely to confer legal sanction on the dominant position of the then new subjects of international relations that are the states and to provide them with an instrument allowing them to structure their interactions and order their environment, and if we remain at that level of generality and abstraction, we can say that the system has remained essentially the same. But if we go further, to examine the content of the three terms of the equation, by asking the questions "What states? What system? To order which environment?", we find that things have radically changed, at least as far as the state and the environment are concerned, while the system strives, within severe constraints, to adapt to these changes.

The state

The state has undergone spectacular mutations, moving from the *post-feudal state* of the seventeenth century to the *liberal state* of the nineteenth, to the *social state* of the twentieth. At each of these stages, ideas as well as science and technology changed. Civil society, the web of economic and social relations, also changed. And the state itself, as an institution called upon to fulfil certain functions and to play a certain role in that society, followed suit.

The post-feudal state of the seventeenth century
The state that emerged as the pivot of the new system encompassed a civil society that was still (in spite of the Renaissance, the discoveries and the *conquista*, the Reformation, and the Wars of Religion) largely hierarchic, stable, and rather static, where all social functions and activities were performed in a relatively self-sufficient, almost autarkic manner. The few activities (or actors) reaching beyond its frontiers (traders, pilgrims, wandering scholars, artists; but also soldiers, sailors, evangelists, etc.) were peripheral to the discharge of these social functions and activities. In other words, it was a society or a social process that maintained and reproduced itself largely in a closed cir-

cuit. We are not very far from the billiard-ball state that touches the others only from the outside and on the periphery.

At this juncture of the emergence and the consolidation of the state as the prime political institution, the structure of power within this society – in design if not always yet in actual fact – was absolute monarchy as a general rule. But if the power of the prince – who had become in the meantime sovereign and no longer recognized any instance above him – was absolute in theory, in that it did not suffer any horizontal division or separation of powers *à la* Montesquieu, there persisted a multitude of *corps intermédiaires* – the remnants of the feudal hierarchic set-up – who exercised, more or less autonomously, particles of power, even if they formally owed allegiance to him.

The liberal state of the nineteenth century

With the Enlightenment and the Revolution, came the liberal state; a limited state ideologically, based as it was on the theory of the social contract, whose limited power was moreover divided according to the doctrine of the separation of powers. This state, which became at the same time "the sovereign" as the oracle or the incarnation of the "popular will," was content with the role of the "night-watchman" taking charge of internal and external security, while leaving civil society to Adam Smith's "invisible hand." But it was precisely in this society that the great transformation examined below would intervene.

The social state of the twentieth century

World War I gave birth to the social state, whether in its socialist version (the state nationalizing supply, the means of production) or its welfare state one (by nationalizing demand, so to speak, according to Keynesian prescriptions). Far from the night-watchman state of olden days, or even from a "regulatory agent" type of state, channeling social flows in the manner of a traffic policeman, the social state sees itself as the Pygmalion of civil society, simultaneously its sculptor, its organizer, and its prime mover.

There is no common measure between the hold of the contemporary state on society (even in those states that consider themselves most liberal, like the United States) and that of even the most absolute of the old monarchies – not in relation to a specific individual or group of individuals, but when it comes to its role in, and impact on, the march of society in general. And this is in spite of current trends everywhere to rethink the role of (or bluntly to "roll back") the state.

It is a sprawling state, overstretched and overloaded, which strives to penetrate all the corners and recesses of society and to influence all that takes place there. But this spectacular expansion of state functions carries with it the seeds of fragility, and even vulnerability, of the modern state and its great sensitivity to its internal as well as its external environment.

The environment

By environment we refer to civil society, both internally as well as at the level of the international community. It is here that great transformations occurred.

The industrial revolution and the economic outgrowth of the state

The advent of the liberal state was accompanied (or perhaps it was even induced) by the industrial revolution, which introduced into society the means for an unprecedented intensification and extension of the economic activities of production and exchange. But, in order for these means to yield their full returns, their use had to be left to the market (*laissez-faire*), in other words, to the interaction of the economic actors, free from any interference by the state at home or abroad.

In these circumstances, the external or international dimension of economic activities becomes crucial. This is because the new techniques, by bringing this unprecedented intensification of economic activities within reach, extended the optimal scale of their operation well beyond the territorial confines of most states. They thus introduced a new categorical imperative, which progressively materialized during the nineteenth century, of an international economy on a world scale, based on an international division of labour, particularly between the producers of raw materials and those of finished goods.

THE ADJUSTMENTS OF THE LIBERAL STATE. In the face of this extension of the scope of economic activities beyond its ambit of power, the nineteenth-century liberal state tried to adapt itself in two different ways.

First, the European states extended their territorial control over the extra-European sphere through the second wave of colonialism of the nineteenth century. Parallelly, in their mutual relations (and their relations with their offshoots in the Americas, as well as with those states that remained formally independent in the extra-European sphere, such as the Ottoman Empire, Japan, China, Persia, and Siam), given the prevailing *laissez-faire* ideology, the control of economic activities beyond (and ideally even within) the territorial ambit of the state was not considered as coming within its proper functions. But two qualifications are in order here. For a start, history provides us with several examples of military intervention by Western states to "open up" certain countries like Japan to international trade and exchange; i.e. to impose on them the *jus communicationis* (the right to communicate or establish relations with them) of olden times, which was used to justify the conquest and submission of the indigenous populations of the Americas. Moreover, the self-denying ordinance of the state of origin was not unlimited. Once the economic activities of its subjects were deployed in the territory of another state, the state did come into the picture through the exercise of "diplomatic protection," i.e. of its right to protect their "vested rights," and sometimes even through "undiplomatic means" such as military intervention.

States thus gave vent to their economic conflict of interests in the guise of "colonial scrambles" (which were all but ignored by classical international law, as it was not able effectively to handle them) rather than in terms of claims of extra-territorial jurisdiction over economic activities and resources that transcended their territorial ambit of power. They thus managed to preserve the "light armour" of classical international law, in spite of the growing complexities arising from the advent and progressive integration of the international economy, which, though politically colonial, paradoxically managed to remain ideologically liberal.

THE INTERVENTION OF THE SOCIAL STATE. The social state of the twentieth century, by contrast, is by its very nature and purpose interventionist. It came about to supplement, and if need be to supplant, the "invisible hand" by correcting or compensating for its deficiencies, shortcomings, and negative side-effects as revealed in practice.

As its tendency for intervention and control spanned more and more social and economic activities, and as these activities no longer took place exclusively within the confines of the state, but were integrated in larger circuits that spanned the territories of other states as well, this inexorably led to the growing imbrication and overlap of state activities and state jurisdiction with those of other states on the international level. This situation became increasingly difficult to disentangle and legally to manage with the "light," self-regulating armour of classical international law, an armour that was starting to show signs of "fatigue" owing to "overcharge."

The technical progress of the post-World War II era
These symptoms were greatly magnified by the acceleration of technical progress in the post-World War II era, which led to the current communications revolution.

MAN'S HOLD ON NATURE. Man's hold on nature extended to limits hardly imaginable only a few decades ago.

The year 1945 marked the advent of nuclear energy, with both its threats and its possibilities and promises. It also marked, with the Truman Proclamation, the extension of man's hold to the seabed and below (always in search of new sources of energy), which was then imagined as possible to a depth of at most 100 fathoms (200 metres), whereas we are speaking now in terms of several thousand fathoms. Land drilling too has reached great depths, in search *inter alia* of geothermal energy. As to the conquest of space, it has moved in 30 years from the realm of science fiction to that of everyday reality. Some of the resources of outer space are already being exploited, like the geo-stationary orbit permitting satellite communications, while other possibilities are under exploration or in the experimental stage; not to mention the enormous possibilities (and risks) of biotechnology and of other fields of technical progress.

THE COMMUNICATIONS REVOLUTION. The field in which technical progress has had the most spectacular impact on civil society, however, is that of communications (indeed, society itself, as a web of social relations, is but a continuous process of communication). Not only have prodigious developments taken place in the traditional means of communication, particularly aviation, allowing the movement of hundreds of millions in search of work or pleasure, but it is above all the advent of mass media and the new technologies of telecommunications that has had the most revolutionary impact on civil society.

In the first place, it became possible to organize economic, scientific, or other enterprises on a world scale, and to run them as an integrated whole, in spite of the dispersal of their components all over

447

the world (which explains the great interest since the 1960s in "multinational corporations" or "transnational enterprises").

Secondly, and on a purely social level, the world has become a "global village" where messages are received at the moment of their dispatch, and we can watch "live" all that is taking place everywhere – with obviously all the attendant dangers of selectivity, manipulation, and overload that dampen sensitivity, understanding, and judgement.

Thirdly, and most significantly for our subject, these new means of communication, such as direct satellite broadcasting or transnational data flows (not to mention the circulation of audio and video cassettes), are much less amenable to state control. In any case, the state cannot participate in the new networks in order to benefit from their tremendous possibilities without running the risk of losing, at least in part, control over the flow of information circulating therein. And even if it decides to stay out of these networks, it cannot totally neutralize their effects in its territory.

The growing awareness of "limits"

This exponential explosion of technical possibilities was paradoxically accompanied, especially after the end of the 1960s (and more particularly since 1973), by an acute shock of recognition of the physical "limits to growth."

The naive scientific optimism of the nineteenth century – the myth of linear progress, of man as a rational being conquering a nature of unlimited possibilities (which went along so well with that other myth of the "invisible hand," the social version of Darwinism) – has gone out of fashion. And the threat weighs both on man and on nature, or rather on the balance between them, which is now perceived as unstable and fragile.

Man, or rather humanity, is exploding. In 1950, the world population was 2.5 billion. In 1987, it had doubled. At the end of the century it will be more than 6 billion. As far as resources are concerned, until the 1950s, introductory economics textbooks gave air and water as examples of "non-economic goods," because, though they were of great subjective utility (demand), their supply was "unlimited"! Who could use such language nowadays about these elements, not to mention energy and food resources? This growing awareness is exacerbated by the fact that these resources are unevenly distributed in space and the intensity of their consumption varies enormously between nations (a North American child's consumption of natural resources is 60 times that of his Indian counterpart).

448

Moreover, natural resources are threatened by diminution, even exhaustion, and nature itself by degradation, by Man's frantic activity in a delicately balanced ecological system that does not recognize states, boundaries, or sovereignties, and where everything depends on everything else.

All this makes for the intensification of tensions and distributional conflicts within and between states, while at the same time sharpening awareness of the common interest in reacting or facing up together to this type of global threat. Unfortunately, it was the conflictual aspect that first came into the limelight in the political evolution of the post-war international community.

The political evolution of the post-war international community

CONFIGURATIONS OF POWER. The great alliance of the "united nations," which defeated the Axis powers and was institutionalized in the UN Charter as a blueprint for the post-war international community, did not withstand the test of peace. Yesterday's allies were soon to divide into two antagonistic camps, belligerents in a war that was kept "cold" only by the spectre of a nuclear showdown; their antagonism finding an outlet mainly in the no-man's land at the periphery or between the respective fields of attraction of the two poles, the third world.

And if the recent radical changes in the former Soviet Union and Eastern Europe have put an end to this division of the world and to the Cold War, 45 years after World War II ended (and even if we set aside for the moment the uncertainties and threats arising from the rapid dissolution of the Eastern bloc and particularly the spectacular disintegration of the Soviet Union itself, without anybody being able to predict the shape of things to come), we have not yet reached "the end of history," *pace* Mr. Fukuyama. For one thing, the collapse of "real communism" does not mean that the problems to which it strove to provide an answer have vanished with it, or that the diametrically opposite answer is necessarily the right one. Moreover, what has occurred in the meantime, and is still taking place in the periphery, has profoundly marked the international community and continues to infuse it with its endemic effervescence and instability.

THE ADVENT OF THE THIRD WORLD. The emergence at the end of World War I of a state that purported to speak in the name of the working class favoured the affranchisement of this class and the advent of other varieties of the "social state" in the industrialized countries in the inter-war period. The bipolar configuration of power in the post-war era similarly favoured the decolonization movement that swept over the third world, bringing to an end the remaining colonial empires and bringing to sovereignty a large number of non-Western peoples in Asia, Africa, and the Caribbean.

This radical change in the composition of the international community was not only quantitative (by roughly tripling the number of states since 1945), although, even by itself, this quantitative change could not but affect the rules of the game in that community. Compare a soccer game between two teams of 11 with one between two teams of 33, on the same pitch: even if the newcomers do not tip the scales in the balance of power, they will affect the game by their crowding of the ground and their interference with the play of the principal actors.

But the change is basically qualitative. The newcomers are of non-Western origin and culture, and they are economically "underdeveloped," politically unstable, and consequently highly vulnerable to, and dependent on, the outside. They do not share with their former masters or the other older members of the international community either the same world vision (*Weltanschauung*) or the same material concerns, while they harbour a sense of historic injustice, and of inequality and exclusion in actual practice.

We thus find ourselves with an international community that is over-multiplied, where what dominates is no longer a single "culture" or a common vision of the world, but rather a growing heterogeneity that favours the centrifugal forces within it (despite the homogenizing effect of globalization and the attractions of the mass consumption model on a purely material level). This is not to mention the rise of nationalism and particularism everywhere, which feed into all kinds of extremisms and fundamentalisms in the face of growing material pressures, whose effects are very unevenly felt and suffered.

The system's attempts at adjustment

These profound changes in the "state" and in its "environment" have given rise to apparently contradictory trends within the system itself, in its efforts to adapt to them.

The unilateral approach: The extension of state jurisdiction and its limits

The extension of jurisdiction

States have reacted to the intensification of the activities of man and the interaction between men made possible by the most recent technical progress – and given the tendency of the state to play a growing role in all social activities – first, in the logic of the classical system, by extending their jurisdiction both in space (*ratione loci*) and into new fields of regulation (*ratione materiae*).

The extension of jurisdiction in space follows the technical possibilities for the state, starting from its land territory, to control and exploit the resources of other spaces, a range whose limits are pushed further and further all the time. The prime example is creeping state jurisdiction over the high seas. Proceeding from a traditionally narrow territorial sea, the 1958 Geneva Conventions started by recognizing a security "contiguous zone" of up to 12 miles, as well as sovereign rights – exclusively for the purposes of exploration and exploitation of mineral and sedentary fishing resources – over the continental shelf, but not over the water column above it (following, in that, the Truman Proclamation of 1945), up to a depth of 200 metres or as far as exploitation was possible beyond it (which was then considered as an absolutely moot hypothesis). The 1982 Convention on the Law of the Sea extended the outer limit of the continental shelf to a distance varying between 200 and 350 miles from the coast, while authorizing states to declare an exclusive economic zone (comprising also exclusive fishing rights) up to 200 miles.

The extended spatial jurisdiction *ratione loci* is formulated first as a functional jurisdiction for specific purposes. But states have a tendency progressively to "territorialize" (or "internalize") it, i.e. to treat the spaces covered by it to all intents and purposes as if they were part of their territory, subject only to a few exceptions or servitudes in favour of the international community (such as rights of transit, of laying cables, and of doing scientific research in the exclusive economic zone).

The extension of jurisdiction *ratione materiae* takes place internally by expanding the role and functions of the state in civil society, but is projected externally as a result of the widening scale of the economic and social processes that fall within the span of these functions. Thus, the widening state role in the national economy leads to state trading on the international level and to the multiplication of state contracts

451

with foreign concerns in carrying out its economic activities as well as to increasing state regulation of transnational activities that partly cover its territory, with unavoidable extra-territorial consequences.

The limits

THE EXTENSION *RATIONE MATERIAE* OF INTERNATIONAL CONCERN AND REGULATION. At the same time, and in the opposite direction, as a result of this very same phenomenon of the globalization of the economic and social process, we witness an increasing tendency towards "internationalization." There is growing international "interest" and "concern" in all aspects of social life considered until recently as purely "internal," but that are progressively integrated in, or at least affected – in varying degrees – by, these flows and networks transcending the state. These call in their wake for international regulation; thus progressively emptying the "domestic jurisdiction" of states of its substance. A good demonstration of this tendency can be seen in the examples given by the United States during the Versailles Peace Conference in 1919 to illustrate the new concept that it proposed to introduce in the Covenant of the League of Nations (and that ultimately figured in Article 15(8)) of "matters falling exclusively within the domestic jurisdiction of Member States." These examples were tariffs and immigration – subjects that are at present priority items on the international agenda.

The concerns of international law are no longer limited in principle to questions and activities that take place at the periphery of the territorial ambit of the state, but cover all aspects of the social process. They have shifted, in other words, from what took place on the margins to what takes place at the centre of the state, including health, population, monetary, and economic policies.

Thus, although there is an extension in state jurisdiction *ratione loci* and *ratione materiae*, at the same time new limits or servitudes attach to the powers of the state. This is occurring even within the traditional areas covered by its jurisdiction *ratione materiae* – including subjects that were considered only yesterday as being the hard core of a state's preserve, such as immigration or monetary questions – transforming state power over them from a discretionary (i.e. sovereign) jurisdiction to one bound by international law. The ambit of state jurisdiction gets wider, but the power the state exercises therein is narrowed.

THE INTENSIFICATION OF JURISDICTIONAL CONFLICTS BETWEEN STATES. We thus end up with very dense and lengthy networks of state jurisdiction that intersect, get entangled, and cannot help overlapping, as they are unilaterally interpreted and exercised by the states that claim them according to the techniques of classical international law. Again, a good example of that is the US claim to extraterritorial application of its anti-trust or strategic embargoes legislation, by attempting directly to enforce it on foreign subsidiaries of US corporations, and the counter-injunctions such attempts drew from the national courts of those subsidiaries (e.g. in the United Kingdom).

The conflicts of jurisdiction that ensue are very difficult to untangle because their technicalities frequently mask sharp distributional conflicts, e.g. over the localization and control of the economic surplus of an economic operation straddling several states. The handling of such disputes calls for a set of very sophisticated norms that would give international law a much bolder and more active role in the arbitration of the real underlying conflicts of interests and of distribution (a task from which classical international law always shied away).

In any case, this type of "dense" normative or legal regulation is very difficult, if not impossible, to implement or manage with the "light" (in fact non-existent) armour of classical international law, which leaves it to the state to interpret and exercise the jurisdiction it unilaterally claims. This leads to a conclusion in the form of a hypothesis: *to each level of normative density corresponds a certain level of institutional density allowing for the satisfactory implementation of the norms*, below which the system is unable adequately to "manage" or "implement" its normative content – a situation that would undermine its effectiveness and by the same token its credibility as a legal system.

THE LIMITS OF STATE CONTROL. Paradoxically, the all-mighty state of today (as an "ideal type"), with its wider-ranging spatial ambit and all-embracing functions, finds itself overtaken by, or relatively powerless in the face of, certain new types of activities and problems. These also reveal the limits of the traditional approach in coping with the intensification and globalization of social flows through the extension of state jurisdiction.

In the first place, at the infra-state level, the flexibility, density, and great variety of the new networks of communication make them less amenable to state control, at least to its unilaterally exercised control (e.g. if it tries to monitor or censor all communications with its territory). Faced with this situation, and if we reject the autarkic alternative, either the state has to scale down its jurisdictional pretensions to the limits of its available means of control, or, if there must be regulation and control, they have to be situated at the same scale as the activities in question, which transforms them into a global issue. This brings us to the second type of transcendence of the state and of the traditional approach of legal ordering through the exercise of unilateral state jurisdiction.

Indeed, and in the second place, as we have seen, above or beyond the state level there is a proliferation of issues of a global character, such as the diminution of resources, the degradation of the environment, and other ecological and social entropies that transcend the state taken individually, in the sense that it cannot deal with them, at least not adequately, if it acts in isolation, *uti singuli*. These problems demand international regulation and international action situated at their own level, undertaken by the states acting together (e.g. for epidemics or AIDS control, terrorism prevention, protection of the ozone layer, etc.).

The collaborative approach and its limits

Origins and evolution
Such an approach has already been followed since the nineteenth century, essentially as a response to global problems raised by the advent of the industrial revolution. Its instrumentality – the multilateral treaty – was not only a "law-making treaty" (*traité-loi*) prescribing a new type of legal regulation, but also an "organic" treaty providing for an institutional infrastructure in order to implement or "manage" this new regulation. It thus gave birth to the first generation of international organizations (river commissions, unions, bureaux, etc.). This approach, rooted in partial solidarities, was followed each time a common need or a common interest was sufficiently perceived and felt to elicit action.

But here, too, the trends are contradictory. On the one hand, this approach has taken hold, particularly in the post-World War II period, as shown by the proliferation of international organizations. These organizations cover more ground or subject-matters all the time, and have a tendency to expand their jurisdiction and powers, and more particularly to pass from sectoral (technical or specialized) questions to the central issues of international law and relations. This is witnessed in the attempts to apply this new approach in the League of Nations Covenant, and particularly in the UN Charter, to the problems of international peace and security (after all, what value, interest, or good can be more common or more paramount).

The limits

At the same time, however attractive this approach may seem at the start, it sooner or later runs into obstacles and provokes resistance and counter-currents, mainly for two reasons.

THE LIMITS OF "SOLIDARITY" AND "INTERDEPENDENCE." The first reason related to the assumption at the very basis of the "collaborative approach": that solidarity ensues from a common need or a common interest. Although certain "compulsory solidarities" are objectively forced on us, these solidarities are neither perceived in the same manner nor felt with the same intensity and urgency by all the members of the international community. In other words, they do not spontaneously and inexorably generate international cooperation. Moreover, the collaborative approach generates problems of its own that limit its progress, particularly by giving rise to conflicts over the control and the distribution of the costs and benefits of collaborative action (as was shown at the 1992 Earth Summit in Rio).

A further complicating factor is that, with the expansion and increasing heterogeneity of the international community, the problems and their possible solutions are perceived and evaluated even more diversely than before, and the distributional conflicts that underlie them are sometimes subjectively magnified out of all proportion.

STATES' RESISTANCE TO THE CENTRALIZATION OF THE SYSTEM. States have an even more imperious motive sharpening their resistance to the collaborative approach. For, as we have seen, at the very origin and basis of the present system of international law lies the radical negation by the state of any decision-making instance superior to it, its monopolization of this power being the hallmark of its sovereignty. The collaborative approach, on the other hand, implies the collective taking of decisions, which means that this power moves out of the unilateral jurisdiction of states and into that of the centralized or collective organs of international institutions. This is a loss of power that states may accept reluctantly (but always half-heartedly) for the odd occasion such as an arbitration, or eventually, on a sectoral basis, covering certain technical or specialized matters; but with much greater difficulty and resistance when we come closer to what they consider essential, i.e. questions of war and peace and what states perceive as being at the basis of their political and military power, which today is economic and technological as well. This explains the great difficulties and the mitigated results up to now of the application of this collaborative approach in the League of Nations Covenant and the UN Charter to problems of international peace and security, as well as of the efforts to apply it to conflicts over the distribution of values within the international community (except, of course, where – as in the Gulf crisis – it serves the geopolitical interests of the dominant powers, by affixing on them the seal of collective legitimization).

The present situation: A chequered map

What conclusions can be drawn from these different currents and counter-currents at work within the international legal and institutional order in its efforts to adapt to an international environment that is itself in constant change?

On the one hand, the classical, self-regulatory system of international law, operating through the unilateral action and reaction of states, is too rudimentary to deal with the increasing complexity, imbrication, and globalization of all aspects of social life, and by the same token, with their transcendence of the state (we come back here to the proposition about the necessary correspondence between the normative density and the institutional density of the system).

On the other hand, the state endeavours to preserve as much as possible of the classical system, and more particularly its prerogatives and privileged position in it, by extending its jurisdiction in order to deal with the new problems and their growing complexities. But the further it advances in this direction, the more it overstretches and dissipates itself, loses efficiency, and becomes more vulnerable, while adding to the complexity and overlap, i.e. to the very problems it is endeavouring to resolve. At the same time, the state is increasingly overtaken by the transnational flows that it can no longer manage to control, and by the global issues it cannot resolve on its own.

Obviously, the classical system of international law has reached, on very broad fronts, the stage of "absolutely diminishing returns." But the state cannot reconcile itself to the formal loss of power (which is in fact already in process) involved in moderating its pretensions as to its role in society, scaling them down to the limits of its means (though agonizing revisions in this direction are under way almost everywhere), and acquiescing in the transfer of decision-making power to the level of the global problems that call for decisions.

It is in this context that the actual assaults on the "state" of the Reaganite and Thatcherite variety can be fully understood. Capitalizing on the clear signs of fatigue and loss of control of the social state, they advocate the extreme opposite, i.e. a total "hands-off" or "self-denying ordinance" by the state from intervening in society and particularly in the economy. They thus elevate a material difficulty or inability into a legal disability. Moreover, once this incapacity of principle is decreed it is automatically transposed to international regulation as well, which may actually be the appropriate level of action for overcoming this individual material incapacity. Instead, they envisage a return to the nineteenth-century policy of leaving it to the invisible hand or the market ("marketheism"), but in fact to the naked power relations in society (in the pure tradition of social Darwinism) to find their natural equilibria. This magnifies the scale of potential future entropies such a policy is bound to produce, as it did at the time of the industrial revolution and the advent of the international economy before World War I (and as an antidote to which the social state emerged).

In the meantime, and under these diverse pressures, the system is undergoing transformation by fits and starts, in the wake of crises, shocks, and catastrophes that catalyse consciousness by demonstrating to states the necessity of this or that change. Thus, in piecemeal fashion the system is evolving, in its mechanisms as well as in its norms, through a permanent dialectic between the classical approach (well established and well known by all down to its smallest detail, but increasingly exhausted and left behind by the prodigious and immensely complex evolution of the facts and ideas of the contemporary world) and a more collaborative approach, which is dictated by the logic of the "new facts" of international life but still in search of a path and spheres of expansion in the gaps and renunciations of the classical approach as well as in the new areas calling for legal regulation.

An interim balance

The following may be a reasonably representative sample of the outcome of these attempts at adjustment by the system (reflecting its increasing awareness of the diversification and growing complexity of its environment and civil society) by way of shifts in international law from the state-centric model – Wolfgang Friedman's "international law of coexistence" – to the more collaborative approach – Friedman's "international law of cooperation."

First, as far as the *subjects* of the system are concerned, until World War II international law did no more than reflect the dominant position of the state, consecrating it as its prime and almost only subject. The rare and rather minor cases in which it exceptionally recognized a measure of legal personality to other entities involved either relics from the pre-Westphalian past such as the Holy See (until it became a state in 1929) and – for a time – the Order of Malta, or basically "imperfect copies" of the ideal type of subject (the state), such as protectorates and territories under mandate or trusteeship.

Since the late 1940s, however, international law has increasingly taken cognizance of actors or entities other than states (or variations therefrom) – beyond or outside states, like international organizations, or within and across states, like peoples and their representatives, the liberation movements. It even addresses the individual directly in certain contexts, especially human rights (but also war crimes, crimes against humanity, etc.), and strives to reach certain economic actors like multinational corporations either directly or indirectly.

It would be stretching reality too far, however, to suggest that these developments have dethroned the state as the prime subject of international law, though they may have eroded its monopoly somewhat.

Secondly, as far as *areas* of substantive expansion are concerned, the double impact of the rise of the third world and technical progress has been to push the substantive development of international law – at least on the normative level if not on that of the means of implementation – in two seemingly opposite but in fact complementary directions:

(a) Reinforcing sovereignty through the further elaboration of the principles of the Charter (Art. 2), by making explicit and articulating the implications of the "non-trespass" injunction. This was basically done through two fundamental resolutions of the General Assembly: the "Declaration of Principles of International Law Relating to Friendly Relations and Cooperation among States according to the Charter of the United Nations" (Resolution 2625 of 1970), and the "Definition of Aggression" (Resolution 3314 of 1974). But it was also pursued through recognizing the consequences of these principles in the codification of the more technical subjects of international law such as the law of treaties and state responsibility.

The total effect of these developments, though they remain squarely within the state-centric model, is enormously to increase – at least at the normative level – the visibility and the degree of specificity of the legal constraints or limits the system sets on states' freedom of action. In one respect, however, there is a great departure from the state-centric model, namely in the prodigious development of the right of self-determination. For here international law, instead of proceeding from the state as a given, reaches beyond or rather inside the state to recognize the right of a "people" already within its jurisdiction to establish its own state (or in some instances at least to a special international status within the existing state), a right that can be explained and justified only by the existence of a higher community interest or value in this regard overriding the sovereignty of the state.

(b) Strengthening the "duty to cooperate" – whose roots can also be found in the principles of the Charter and whose venue is that of the collaborative approach – by giving it an operational rendering through detailed regulations that progressively penetrate the inner preserves of the state (or what was traditionally considered as its domestic jurisdiction) in areas such as human rights, the use of national resources in so far as they affect the global environment, etc., in addition to areas falling within international relations but that had not previously been subject to regulation, such as the use of shared resources and the reorientation of certain aspects of North–South economic relations with a view to enhancing global development.

As was mentioned before, this type of regulation requires institutional or collective decision-making mechanisms and the abandonment of the unilateral action approach. But here the reticence, particularly of old industrialized states, becomes more evident as legal regulation intensifies and threatens to become constraining in these new areas or reveals more explicit "distributive justice" inclinations.

Finally (and with a view to circumventing this reticence), we are witnessing, as far as the *instruments* of law-making are concerned, a trend to get round state consent taken individually (*uti singuli*) by developing new types or species of legal instruments to penetrate the new areas (or to deal with the atypical actors) mentioned above.

These are more malleable or less constraining legal instruments (or legal commitments), whence their designation as "soft law": resolutions of universal international organization (reflecting the general will or consensus of the membership but not the individual consent of every member); codes of conduct (in economic relations based on self-restraint, particularly of atypical actors, e.g. transnational enterprise, and usually adopted in the form of a resolution); "non-binding" agreements (easier for states to conclude on controversial matters, but far from being legally insignificant, viz. the Final Act of the Helsinki Conference of 1975), etc. They are the typical instruments of the international law of cooperation – flexible tools of legal indicative planning of collective action in response to emerging global problems, needs, and values. They structure expectations and distribute roles in this desired collective action, without the aspiration of coercive enforcement, but merely on the basis of a "best effort" commitment.

All these developments, though obviously significant, do not yet cumulatively suffice to produce a "quantum leap" in the nature of the system, displacing its centre of gravity radically away from the state-centric model. For this, the "international law of cooperation" – which started in the nineteenth century as small islets in an ocean of "international law of coexistence," and coalesced into a kind of archipelago in the post-war period – will have to consolidate even further into an all-encompassing legal continent capable of imparting its character to the system as a whole, which is a conceivable but uncertain prospect.

Note

1. The essay will keep as far as possible from technical detail and debate that might baffle the layperson. Otherwise, every statement would call for the elaboration, qualification, and recapitulation of doctrinal debate, or at least very lengthy references thereto.

Further reading

No one volume in the existing literature of international law encompasses the whole range of issues covered in this essay or approaches them in the same manner (this is the ambition of my General Course in public international law, delivered in French at the Hague Academy of International Law in 1987, and which is still in the press).

By contrast, the sources of inspiration are obviously too numerous all to be cited. Suffice it to mention three books that I consider represent some of the best insights into the subject since World War II:

De Visscher, Charles. *Theory and Reality in International Law.* 3rd edn., translated by P. Corbett. Princeton, N.J.: Princeton University Press, 1960.

Friedmann, Wolfgang. *The Changing Structure of International Law.* London: Stevens, 1964.

Röling, Bert. *International Law in an Expanded World.* Amsterdam: Djambatan, 1960.

Disregarding recent textbooks and manuals, of which several (in French, English, Italian, and Spanish) are excellent, one can consult with profit, as a sample of the best current reflection in the field,

Schachter, Oscar. *International Law in Theory and Practice*, 2nd edn. Dordrecht: Nijhoff, 1991 (an expanded and updated version of his General Course at the Hague Academy of International Law in 1982).

Macdonald, R. St. J., and D. M. Johnston, eds. *The Structure and Process of International Law. Essays in Legal Philosophy, Doctrine and Theory.* Dordrecht: Nijhoff, 1986.

17

The role of the United Nations in the context of the changing world order

Maurice Bertrand

The UN is becoming more and more fashionable since the "end of the Cold War." It seems to be adapting to a new role, which in fact could be interpreted as a resurrection of the role contemplated by its Charter in 1945.

The Security Council has now recovered prestige and even some efficiency. At the beginning of 1992 the Council met for the first time at the level of heads of state, and requested a report from the Secretary-General on preventive security. The media have emphasized its role in helping to end the Iran–Iraq war, in facilitating the withdrawal of USSR from Afghanistan, and in contributing to peace in Namibia, Central America, etc. Its direct intervention in the Gulf War, concluded by the victory of the international force mobilized against the invasion of Kuwait, has been presented as the renewal of the system of "collective security" organized by Chapter VII of the Charter. And the Council is still active in monitoring its resolutions and sending warnings to governments trying to escape its control.

The peace-keeping operations are blooming, the most recent examples of Cambodia and Yugoslavia being impressive by their importance (number of Blue Helmets and supporting staff), their cost (billions of dollars), and their conception (in Cambodia, the administration of a country). The humanitarian role of the UN and the UN system is also developing at a great pace in many countries. The discussions and controversies about "the right of interference for humanitarian reasons" reveal the concern of public opinion and governments about these problems. The approval of the recent creation of a post of coordinator for humanitarian problems seems to confirm this interest. The support of public opinion in the West for the respect of human rights is also developing, thus enhancing the role of the UN in these matters.

A final touch: in February 1992 the newly appointed Secretary-General undertook a drastic reorganization of the UN Secretariat, notably reducing the number of top posts, and this operation has been appreciated by the main member states.

All these changes could give the impression that the UN is on the way to becoming a real world organization, capable of coping with the global problems of our time. This would be a wrong and naive assessment. In fact the UN is now in a phase of its history that is the result of a particular geopolitical situation; but the next phase has a great chance of being very different.

A phase in the history of the UN

The role of the UN in international relations has historically changed a great deal, depending on the geopolitical situation. Various phases can be identified:
- 1945–1946 – the phase of enthusiasm. Public opinion in the West, particularly in the United States, developed great expectations for the newly created organization.[1]
- 1946–1953 – the first Cold War phase and the Korean War, which saw the beginning of the East–West confrontation and the success of the United States in using the UN flag for its intervention in Korea.
- 1953–1960 – the phase of East–West stalemate. Owing to Lester Pearson and Dag Hammarskjöld, peace-keeping operations were invented and experimented with in the Middle East crisis and in the Congo.
- 1960–1975 – the phase of decolonization. The UN played a role in helping to legitimize liberation movements in the third world, and the newly created states began to apply in the General Assembly the collective strategy initiated in 1955 in Bandung.
- 1975–1985 – the "UN crisis." The United States, supported by the

developed countries, fought back against the majority of developing member states (the so-called 77), and against the resolutions adopted by them on the "new economic international order," and those supported by Arab states against Israel. The weapon used by the rich member states was the reduction of the UN budget and resources, and even withdrawal from specialized agencies (i.e. the ILO and Unesco), so that the UN and the UN system were in a severe financial crisis.[2]

• since 1986, a phase of renewed enthusiasm seems to have developed.

The reasons for this evolution are to be found in the ambiguous nature of the world organization and in the facility this ambiguity offers to member states for using the organization for their own national interests. The very conception of the UN in 1945 was a mixture of *Realpolitik* and rhetoric. "*Realpolitik*" was the idea of maintaining the world order established by the victors in 1945. This was called "maintenance of peace," but the project was to preserve the new balance of power and the existing privileges. The mechanisms established by Chapter VII of the Charter – the Security Council and the veto power of its five permanent members, a Military Staff Committee composed of the Chiefs of Staff of the five (Art. 47), armed forces put at the disposal of the Council by member states, (Art. 43), the maintenance of airforce contingents (Art. 45), the procedure of sanctions (Art. 41), and the use of operations by air, land, and sea forces (Art. 42) – show that the UN was conceived as a kind of military alliance, which was supposed to last for ever.

The rhetoric was the declaration in the same Charter of great principles comprising "justice and respect of international law, fundamental human rights, dignity and worth of the human person, equal rights of men and women and of nations large and small, the solution of international problems of economic, social, cultural and humanitarian character, fundamental freedom for all without distinction as to race, sex, language and religion." Even if Article 2, para. 7, did limit these commitments by forbidding the UN "to intervene in matters which are essentially within the domestic jurisdiction of any State," the hypocrisy of this discourse was that at this very moment half of Europe was abandoned to the Stalinist dictatorship, colonial empires were still maintained, and none of the signatories had any intention of fighting for the defence of human rights, particularly economic and social ones.

464

Such an organization, with no supranational power, obviously depended on a degree of consensus existing among member states, and particularly among the most powerful ones. According to the configuration of power in the world, the UN was to be used mainly as a forum for propaganda by the various ideological coalitions, East and West, North and South, and, when the possibility occurred, as an instrument for specific operations.

This is what happened during the various phases identified above. The geopolitical situation – and the variations in the perceptions of the UN role – have, of course, played an important part in this: the recent victory in World War II explained the illusory consensus of 1945–1946; the USSR's underestimation of the possibilities offered by the mechanisms of the UN facilitated their utilization by the United States in the Korean War; the growing importance and influence of the third world and the support given to decolonization by the United States and the USSR explained the negative attitude of colonial countries during the 1960s, etc.

The present phase, which began in 1986–1987 with the complete change of attitude concerning the UN by the Gorbachev government,[3] followed by the breakdown of the communist regimes in USSR and Eastern Europe, is characterized by an obvious US hegemony in the UN. The objective base of this hegemony is that, owing to the loss of the military capacity of the former USSR, the United States is now the greatest military power in the world; and it is still a great economic power.

But there are also psychological and political reasons to explain the fact that US leadership in the UN meets no opposition. The United States is the only member state to have developed a coherent conception of the UN role, which consists in the organization specializing in "collective security" under its leadership, providing "Blue Helmets" when and where necessary, providing some contribution to humanitarian activities when requested, and forgetting about practically all economic and social activities, which are considered to be the realm of the Bretton Woods institutions. The other permanent members of the Security Council follow the United States either because they have no specific notion of the UN role (like France and the United Kingdom) or because they are too weak to offer contradictory views (Russia and China). The other big powers like Germany and Japan do not seem to have specific ideas and have no permanent seat on the Council. And the "77" are mute.

This situation has permitted the United States to transform the UN according to its views. It has been in a position to use the facilities offered by the "collective security" system by activating some of its mechanisms and refusing to apply it fully. During the Gulf War, the provisions of Articles 41 and 42 were applied, but the Military Staff Committee (Art. 47) played no role, Article 43 was not used to call upon member states to provide forces, and the intervention force – which was essentially American – remained under the sole authority of the United States. The permanent members of the Security Council all concurred with US proposals or decisions without objections. And the lessons that one can draw from the experience of the Gulf War are that the collective security system has no more chance than in the past of being put fully into operation, and that it would not even be used in the same way as in the Gulf War if an aggression occurred in a place where vital US interests were not threatened.

As the big powers have a collective interest in conciliating regional and local conflicts, the US is called on to help by providing Blue Helmets in a great number of cases, as in Yugoslavia and Cambodia. But the UN is only one among several organizations (namely the Conference on Security and Cooperation in Europe (CSCE) and regional organizations) that can be used for such activities. In the present phase, the obvious advantage offered by the UN is that the organization has good previous experience in this field. But the CSCE is a candidate to replace the UN in the future for problems occurring within its zone and the United States does not seem to have specific reasons for continuing to favour the UN in the future.

The US hegemony has led to the disappearance of any role for the UN in North–South relations. The so-called North–South dialogue is already dead, but the activities of some UN departments and committees, like the UN Conference on Trade and Development, or the Centre for Transnational Corporations, or other economic and social departments, were maintaining some prospects of discussions. The Secretary-General's decision in February 1992 to apply US ideas by severely streamlining the Secretariat, particularly in the economic and social section, seems to indicate that the UN will no longer be in a position to fulfil even these modest functions.

If the US hegemony phase lasts a long time, the UN will definitely be transformed into a kind of specialized agency in charge of legitimizing the repression in the third world of activities contrary to US interests, and of organizing some peace-keeping operations, in competition with some other agencies. However, the character of the current phase is due to the beginning of the acceleration of global change that started in 1986; and global change will continue.

Global change and the next phase

The present evolution of global change already indicates that the current unipolar world will become multipolar, that new problems will occur, and that the conception of security, including military security, will be transformed.

The tendency towards multipolarity will certainly be reinforced by the rise of great economic powers – Japan, Germany, and the European Union, plus some of the important countries of the South like Brazil or India, and some day Russia will recover its strength.

The new problems will come from the enormous growth in the population of the South (another 1 billion in some 10–15 years) and from the trend towards integration of a very heterogeneous world. The popular notion of "interdependence" and clichés about the "global village" do not accurately describe the phenomenon of progressive integration of the world economy, which, in its turn, is leading to a certain social, cultural, and political integration. Every one knows that the possibility of independent national economic policies no longer exists; that transnational firms are all becoming global ones; that all national problems, whether in health, environment, or even politics, are also becoming global; that through the development of information and communication networks more and more people in the world aspire to reach – collectively or individually – the living standards of the inhabitants of the richest countries of the North; and that this is the main reason for the irresistible development of mass migration from the East to the West and from the South to the North.

The problems will consequently become different. It is likely that, owing to the pressure of population growth, growing unemployment, and political, ethnic, cultural, and religious factors, local and regional conflicts will continue to develop in the third world. But it is also likely that the countries of the North will become concerned about the very serious non-military threats (large-scale migration, environmental problems, etc.) from the South as well as military threats resulting from the development of new ideologies, integrisms, and general aggressiveness against the rich countries, combined with the spread of sophisticated missiles and nuclear and chemical weapons etc. able to reach the North.

The perceptions of these threats by the countries of the North in a multipolar world are likely to differ greatly from country to country or region to region; and the various answers that the countries of the North will define for these threats will probably continue to waver between repression and prevention. But the UN role in either of these approaches is highly likely to be very limited.

If the repressive attitude is adopted, the main difficulty will be to reach a consensus on the manner in which repression should be used and in what circumstances. In this regard, theoretically the UN "collective security" system could be applied, the concept of collective security being indeed repressive. But it is not very likely to be efficient or even to be used in the future. According to Article 39 of the Charter, "collective security" means that, if there is "any threat to peace, breach of the peace or act of aggression," the Security Council will decide the measures that should be taken in accordance with Articles 41 (economic sanctions) or 42 (action by air, sea, and land forces). Despite the words "threat to peace," this police system, with its "plans for the application of armed forces," with the assistance of the "military staff committee," is designed to work *after* an aggression has begun.

There are two types of reason for the inefficiency of "collective security." The first is that a system of this kind, which is designed for inter-state conflicts, is not able to deal with internal ones. The traditional type of dispute between states is today – despite the invasion of Kuwait – and will in the future not be frequent. The most recent security threats are not traditional: they are occurring within a single nation, as shown by too many examples – Yugoslavia, Cambodia, Afghanistan, Ethiopia, Somalia, Nicaragua, Salvador, Angola, Liberia, etc.; or they involve non-state actors such as terrorists or ethnic groups. The second type of reason depends on the UN's absence of credibility in this field: first, a real police system has never been built – the "special agreements" of Article 43 have never even begun to be drafted; second, the financial resources that would be necessary for a correct functioning have never been put at the disposal of the UN; finally, the authority of the Council, if its composition is not changed, will not be very great in a multipolar world, because of its lack of representativeness and the absence of political consensus at the world level.

If the preventive approach is adopted, the UN is not likely to be of any help in this direction. It is true that the Charter gives the Council and the Secretary-General some opportunities for preventive security: it is alluded to in the words "threat to peace" (Art. 39); the whole of Chapter VI on "pacific settlement of disputes"; the search for solutions "by negotiation, inquiry, mediation, conciliation, arbitration, judicial settlement, resort to regional agencies or arrangements, or other peaceful means" (Art. 33); "the Security Council may investigate" (Art. 34); the bringing of "any dispute" by "any member state" before the Council (Art. 35); recommendations of the Council in Articles 36, 37 and 38; and Article 99, which gives the Secretary-General the right to bring to the attention of the Council "any matter which may threaten the maintenance of international peace and security."

Despite all these provisions, and with the exception of a few rare cases during decolonization, the UN has never succeeded in preventing wars. Numerous Secretary-General's reports before 1992 drew attention to the necessity for the Council to act before any breach of the peace and not after, but these suggestions were not followed by any action, short of an imaginative new conceptual approach. In fact, preventive security is not, as diplomats sometimes believe (and the Charter confirms this interpretation), the use of diplomatic skills to convince the parties in conflict to go to the negotiating table instead of launching war. Preventive security means addressing the roots of insecurity. This is what has been done in Europe since the 1950s through two types of new approach.

The first approach was the undertaking by men like Monnet, Schumann, Adenauer, and De Gasperi of a completely new type of cooperation between countries that had been fighting wars for centuries. The problem of establishing a lasting peace was very much in the minds of these Europeans, who wanted to avoid, after World War II, the mistakes of the Treaty of Versailles of 1919 after World War I. The innovation consisted in institutionalizing serious economic cooperation. The successive establishment of a Coal and Steel Authority, Euratom, and the Treaty of Rome between the Six, its enlargement to 9 then 12 countries and its deepening through the Single Market and the Maastricht Treaty, monetary union and the progressive building of something very close to a federation have succeeded to the point where there has occurred a total elimination of the risk of war between countries like Germany, Spain, France, the United Kingdom, etc., whose rivalries had been the source of two world wars. This is a real example of a "working peace system," based not on Mitrany's functionalism but on a daring new conceptual approach of progressive integration.

The second type of a new approach has been that of the CSCE as it has developed between East and West, starting with the "Helsinki process" in 1973–1975 and becoming really effective from 1986. This represents the type of preventive security that could be effective if applied to relations between North and South. This approach relies upon:

- addressing the roots of insecurity, i.e. trying to harmonize ideas and practices on human rights and democracy and developing genuine economic cooperation;
- reducing military threats through confidence-building measures, transparency, reduction of armaments, monitoring and controlling levels of armaments on a reciprocal basis, aiming at a system of "reasonable sufficiency" in levels of armaments;
- organizing crisis-prevention efforts.

This new approach may be called "cooperative security" because it implies a totally new conception of security, built on trust and the reduction of animosities, and implying cooperation in dealing with the causes of conflict, instead of letting conflicts develop to the stage at which it is too late to prevent them. But this system has been developed only for the countries of the North. It remains limited to an intercontinental zone that includes virtually all developed countries, with the exception of Japan, Australia, and New Zealand.

The possibility of extending this CSCE type of approach to the world at large would certainly be possible and desirable, because it is far more efficient than the "collective security" system. Attempts at extension have already been undertaken, for example the project of a Conference on Security and Cooperation in the Mediterranean (CSCM), sponsored by Spain and Italy, or the idea of a CSC in Asia, as proposed some time ago by Mr. Gorbachev.

But these attempts do not seem, for the time being, to be considered very viable. One of the main arguments used by those opposed to this idea of a global extension of CSCE-type security is that the CSCE was a specific undertaking suited to East–West relations during the Cold War, and which has unexpectedly succeeded in its mission because of the disappearance of the communist regimes in the East. Consequently it would not be transferable to other types of situations. This is a sweeping ideological assertion.

The model offered by the CSCE[4] included essentially:

- negotiations organized in parallel in three "baskets": security (I), economics, science, technology, and the environment (II), and humanitarian and other fields (III);

- a very efficient system of follow-up of decisions taken by the Conferences;
- the use, in the field of security, of the notion of confidence-building measures (CBMs), i.e. reciprocal information on military activities, acceptance of verification measures, and the establishment of a linkage between the development of CBMs (since 1983 called CSBMs – confidence- and security-building measures) and a drastic reduction in armaments.

Since the Stockholm agreement of 1986, the CSBMs include (for all countries of Europe and the European part of the USSR) prior notification of exercise activities involving more than 13,000 troops and 300 battle tanks, invitation of observers from all CSCE states to all notifiable activities involving at least 17,000 troops, the exchange of annual calendars of activities forecast for the subsequent year, constraining provisions practically forbidding activities involving over 75,000 troops, and on-site inspections on the ground, from the air, or both. They greatly facilitated the negotiations on reductions in armaments concluded by the CFE (Conventional Forces in Europe) I Treaty signed in Paris in 1990 by 20 European countries, the USSR, and the United States. The "open skies" treaty signed in Helsinki in May 1992 went even further by organizing, in a zone that includes Europe, the United States, and the Community of Independent States, reciprocal inspections from the air of military installations.[5]

The transposal to the world level of these methods of negotiations and confidence building, facilitating a general reduction in armaments, could include:

- a system for identifying regions where negotiations could permit the use of the "three baskets" system and the reciprocal adoption of some CSBMs between the countries of this region;
- a larger framework of negotiations between the CSCE countries and their border states to the South (for example, between Nato countries and Mahgreb countries, or Nato countries and Latin America);
- a general agreement on control of the arms trade and arms manufacture (through measures of verification not greater than those considered for chemical arms);
- an enlargement of the Security Council in order to include all important member states and a regional representation of developing countries, and a change in its mandate so as to develop at the global level the spread of the systems mentioned above.

Such an approach is perfectly possible, and would give the UN the

471

role of establishing a new global security system that would be far more efficient and far less costly than the existing one.

However, for it to be possible for the UN to adopt such a conception of preventive security would entail a complete change in the attitude of the rich countries towards the South, because addressing the roots of insecurity in the third world would mean taking seriously the negotiations in the "basket" on economics, technology transfer, environment, and social matters, which would require an enormous financial effort to alleviate poverty. Another condition would be a complete revision of the Charter in order to change the membership of the Security Council and to replace the provisions of Chapter VII by a CSCE type of preventive security system. Such a transformation of the present attitudes of the big powers is not likely to occur in the near future.[6]

The situation is exactly the same in the field of economic and social cooperation. The North–South dialogue has stopped and there is no likelihood of a revival in this field. The decentralization of the UN system is not suited to the task of development, which requires an interdisciplinary approach and far greater resources than the ridiculously modest ones put at its disposal.[7] The great powers have created specific mechanisms, outside the UN, for dealing with global problems, and if some day they were to consider the possibility of allowing some representation of the countries of the South in these consultations, it would certainly not be done through the UN, but rather through some cautious enlargement of the membership of the Group of Seven.

This means that there is no chance of a revitalization of the UN and of the UN system, because it would entail the creation of a totally different world institution. Consequently, despite its apparent renaissance, the UN will remain one international organization among others used by the major powers to contribute to the maintenance of the "world order" they conceive as the best one, particularly in the field of security in the South. It is also likely that the UN's role will be reduced in a near future.

Conclusion

The present UN is an archaic structure that survives only because the United States finds it useful for specific purposes. But people's ideas about the type of world institution that could help to solve global problems are even more archaic.

A good example of this backward thinking is given by the report on the problems of security that the UN Secretary-General produced at the request of the Council in July 1992. The main proposal of this report is to go back to 1945, i.e. fully to activate Article 43 of the Charter, to establish and sign the "special agreements," and to put at the disposal of the Council permanent armed forces, which would be coordinated by the Staff Committee. The report admits that such an international force will never be important enough to fight against a big army equipped with sophisticated weapons, but that it would be useful for deterring lesser threats. This obviously means a repressive conception of the "collective security" at the disposal of hegemonic powers. Such a formula is not likely to be adopted, because the big powers prefer the present flexibility. But there is also no likelihood of a UN revitalization, adapting it to the needs of our time.

The real problem is not the UN's future, however. What is important is finding an answer to world problems. We are today witnessing a race between the evolution of attitudes accustomed to conceive of the international system in military terms, and the rapid development of new threats, which are no longer of a military type but are the outcome of the process of rapid integration of a heterogeneous global society, like the large-scale migrations from the South to the North that are at present destabilizing the rich and developed world. It would be a strange paradox if a society that has become capable of designing and putting into practice systems aimed at eliminating war were to disintegrate owing to its incapacity to identify the new types of threat and to set up the means of avoiding them in good time.

In order to win this race and to avoid cataclysms of the type that the history of the twentieth century offers as perfect examples (which have not been prevented because of the slow pace at which attitudes evolve), it is crucial urgently to undertake a process of maturing new concepts.

In fact this process has already begun, particularly in the field of military security, as indicated above through the CSCE, and in the field of the globalization of problems. But much remains to be done. A collective effort to update concepts in order to adapt the structures of our minds to the problems of the world today is indispensable. Such an undertaking cannot avoid dealing with the replacement of the false conception of "collective security" by a globalization of a CSCE type of preventive security, and with the establishment of a global system of economic and social cooperation that is both credible and universal.

In this regard it is not paradoxical to note that the existence of the UN, and the belief that this obsolete institution can and should play a role, is in fact a serious obstacle to the remodelling of ways of thinking.

Notes

1. Cf. Thomas M. Franck, *Nation against Nation*, Oxford: Oxford University Press, 1985, Ch. 1.
2. Cf. Pierre de Senarclens, *La crise des Nations Unies*, Paris: Presses Universitaires de France, 1988; and Victor Yves Ghebali, *La crise des Nations Unies*, Paris: Documentation Française, 1987.
3. Mikhail Gorbachev, *Realities and Guarantees for a Secure World*, Novosti Press Agency Publishing House, 1987.
4. Cf. Stefan Lehne, *The Vienna Meeting of the Conference on Security and Cooperation in Europe, 1986–1989*, Boulder, Colo.: Westview Press, Austrian Institute for International Affairs series, 1991; and V. Y. Ghebali, *La diplomatie de la détente, La CSCE 1973–1989*, Brussels: Bruylant, 1989.
5. Cf. Guirec Doniol, "Le traité 'Ciel ouvert,'" *Défense nationale* (June 1992).
6. Cf. Maurice Bertrand, "The Difficult Transformation from 'Arms Control' into a 'World Security System'" and "European Integration in a World Perspective," *International Social Science Journal*, no. 127 (February 1991) and no. 131 (February 1992).
7. Cf. Maurice Bertrand, *The Third Generation World Organisation*, Dordrecht: Martinus Nijhoff Publishers, 1989. Published in Japanese by Kokusai Shoin Co., Tokyo, 1991.

Bibliography

Bertrand, Maurice. *La stratégie suicidaire de l'Occident.* Brussels: Éditions Bruylant, 1993.

——— *L'ONU*. Paris: Éditions La Découverte, 1994.

Renninger, John, ed. *The Future Role of the United Nations in an Interdependent World.* Dordrecht: Martinus Nijhoff, 1989.

UNITAR. *The United Nations and the Maintenance of International Peace and Security.* Dordrecht: Martinus Nijhoff, 1987.

18

Democratizing, internationalizing, and globalizing

Richard A. Falk

Getting a grip on "reality"

The ending of the Cold War both concluded an era of ideological rivalry and stripped away the illusion of consensus about the shape and direction of world order. Beyond the domain of Cold War truisms that had prevailed between 1945 and 1989, there were increasingly evident analytic and explanatory difficulties: how to take conceptual account of the globalization of capital and communications; whether or not to treat the porousness of state boundaries with regard to drugs, illegal immigration, environmental degradation, unwanted ideas and threats, financial flows, and banking operations as posing a fundamentally new series of questions about the nature and effectiveness of sovereignty as the basic approach to the distribution of authority on a global basis; the extent to which generalized descriptive narratives about the economic/political/legal conditions of the peoples of the world homogenized crucial differences or illuminated vital affinities.

The position taken here is that the end of the Cold War has made it easier to focus on structural trends and counter-trends in international life and to set forth a normative critique, but that these challenges would have manifested themselves in any event. With the end of the Cold War there has emerged an irresistible disposition to debate and reflect upon the future of world order. For this reason alone George Bush's advocacy of "a new world order" during the Gulf Crisis of 1990–1991 captured headlines that sent pundits of all persuasions rushing off to their personal computers. On the one side were those who welcomed this American project as a necessary step in the direction of "hegemonic stability," giving leadership and cohesion during a turbulent time of growing geo-economic tensions. On another side were those who worried about a new exploitative, imperial order, sometimes sloganized as Pax Americana II, and what this might explicitly mean for specific regions, such as Africa, the Pacific, and Europe. And then there were those who now expected a shift of policy emphasis from geopolitics to environmental protection. As Lester Brown puts it: "The cold war that dominated international affairs for four decades and led to an unprecedented militarization of the world economy is over. With its end comes an end to the world order it spawned." Brown argues that the only foundation for hope about the future is to allow the struggle "to reverse the degradation of the planet" to "dominate world affairs for decades to come."[1] In a certain respect, these views had two misleading features in common first of all, that the shape of the future depended on the decisions of the political leaders representing the most powerful state; secondly, that the North–South axis of relations was of no particular relevance to the future of the world order in the next phase of international relations.

This chapter proceeds on a different set of assumptions. To begin with, even at the level of state action, the future will be shaped by interaction among states, with the effectiveness of United States' leadership likely to be limited in time and dependent on context. Further, since 1992 the US effort to provide a coherent vision of "the new world order" has faltered, partly by default, partly by the failure to carry off the Gulf War diplomacy in a manner that solidified Washington's claim to undisputed leadership, partly by evidences of US economic weakness and domestic restiveness, and partly by conceptualizing the future in a militarist and unipolar framework that engendered an immediate backlash at home and abroad.[2] In this regard, the shape and orientation of a new world order will emerge over the course of the next decade as an outcome of an intense political struggle among many contending actors and social forces. States will certainly play a role, with leading states exerting considerable influence, but a statist future will be modified by market forces of various kinds and by the democratizing struggles of peoples and their associations and movements in many local, national, regional, and global settings. This refocusing of inquiry gives rise to a counter-project to that of post-Cold War geopolitics: namely, the strengthening of global civil society animated by an agenda of demilitarization, democratization, equitable and sustainable development, environmental protection, cultural pluralism, human rights, and global governance.

This perspective can be summarized as follows: the main statist/ market project of the North is to sustain geopolitical stability, which in turn calls for the continuous expansion of world trade, economic growth, and the suppression of nationalist and regionalist challenges emanating from the South, by force if necessary. This project of the North is more or less challenged by several oppositional tendencies in international society, including a variety of fundamentalisms that refuse to collaborate and a range of democratizing processes that conceive of human rights and justice, not stability, as the end of politics. One major uncertainty is whether those forces supporting the strengthening of global civil society can gain sufficient influence to qualify as a genuine "counter-project," rather than merely a societal tendency, confined to the margins of policy in the North and of little relevance to the South. In this regard, the internationalization of the state, assuredly a strong tendency, can be a vehicle for promoting either emancipatory or oppressive results, and is likely historically to be perceived ambiguously and with contradictory interpretations about resisting, co-opting, and conditioning a given state on behalf of one or another project of global reform. That is, domestic and transnational forces – from society and market activity – will exert various kinds of pressure on the state, often at cross-purposes.

To develop this interpretation further, the existing world order is depicted from three complementary perspectives: the structure of the global political economy; the interplay between environmental degradation and environmentalism; the normative architecture of the planet.

The structure of the global political economy

Several characteristics of the global political economy shape the tactics and aspirations of progressive social forces: extreme hierarchy and unevenness of circumstances; acute deprivation and mass misery among the poor; erosion of autonomy at the level of the state as a consequence of the play of non-territorial capital forces.

It is notable that several recent independent analyses of global political economy invoke the imagery and language of apartheid.[3] Writing in the preface to a comprehensive and devastating critique of the global economic order, Arjun Makhijani asserts that "[t]he principal conclusion" of his book "is that the structure of the world economy is in its most essential respects like that of apartheid in South Africa – a kind of global apartheid."[4]

But it is a conclusion reached not only by third world or progressive observers in the North. Thomas Schelling, long notable as a war thinker who influenced the outlook of the United States strategic community during the formative period of the Cold War, poses for himself the question about what model of authority at a state level might "an incipient world state resemble." Schelling asks, "[i]f we were to contemplate gradually relinquishing some measure of sovereignty in order to form not a more perfect union, but a more effective legal structure, what familiar political entity might be our basis for comparison? I find my own answer stunning and depressing: South Africa."

It is worth quoting Schelling's account of the empirical underpinnings for such a radical assessment:

We live in a world that is one-fifth rich and four-fifths poor; the rich are segregated into the rich countries and the poor into the poor countries; the rich are predominantly lighter skinned and the poor darker sinned; most of the poor live in "homelands" that are physically remote, often separated by oceans and great distances from the rich.

Migration on any great scale is impermissible. There is no systematic redistribution of income. While there is ethnic strife among the well-to-do, the strife is more vicious and destructive among the poor.[5]

Schelling notes the correlation between race and poverty, as well as the refusal of the richer countries to accept "economic refugees" from the poorer. He does not extend the comparison to the use of military force: namely, the rich, light-skinned countries enjoy a decisive military superiority and engage in frequent interventionary operations against the poor, dark-skinned countries.

It is, of course, striking that even North–South military interventions in this century, and there have been more than 100 major ones, have been by the North in the South. Preserving this interventionary option undoubtedly contributes to the near hysterical reaction against third world terrorism against Northern targets and the new insistence that darker-skinned countries not be allowed to acquire nuclear weapons. In the leaked Pentagon Guidance document of 1992 it was argued as possibly necessary for the United States even to use military force to prevent North Korea, Iran, Pakistan, and India from acquiring nuclear weaponry, but no reference is made to the acquisition of such weaponry by Israel or South Africa, states with a militarist record in recent foreign policy, but governed by light-skinned élites. Double standards based on race are being extended in practice to the ultimate form of violence: nuclearism; in effect, a regime of "nuclear apartheid." Such a pattern is not explicitly or deliberately racist, but the de facto racism evident in practice contributes to the impression of a racially stratified world order.

There is one more element to be noted. Schelling, reverting to form as establishment guru, insists that the national security mandate for US policy makers to preserve "the U.S. as a free nation with our fundamental institutions and values intact ... must include what we *possess* as well as what we *appreciate*. It includes our material standard of living."[6] Such an emphasis confirms the notorious insistence by George Kennan back in 1948 within a then secret Policy Planning Staff document that the main objective of the United States in the Pacific region after World War II was to ensure that a country with only 6 per cent of the world population could continue to use 50 percent of the world's resources upon which its prosperity was based. The numbers may have changed, but the fundamental imbalances remain.[7] More recent figures reveal the same essential structure as 45 years ago. According to Daniel Kevles, "[t]he nations of the industrial north have about 24% of the world's population but use about 80% of its processed energy and mineral resources. About 33 percent of those resources are used by the United States alone, which has only about 5 percent of the world's population."[8] In effect, the Kennan/Schelling analysis implies that a principal role of military force is unabashedly committed to the perpetuation of global apartheid! No mighty invisible hand is sustaining these structures, but rather, by their own acknowledgement, the mailed fist of strategic planners in the rich countries.[9]

Without implying an inflammatory comparison with South Africa, the South Commission orients its entire report on North–South relations around a similar assessment of the intolerable character of the current structuring of the global political economy:

While most of the people of the North are affluent, most of the people in the South are poor; while the economies of the North are generally strong and

479

resilient, those of the South are mostly weak and defenceless; while the countries in the North are, by and large, in control of their destinies, those of the South are very vulnerable to external factors lacking in functional sovereignty ...

Were all humanity a single nation-state, the present North–South divide would make it an unviable, semi-feudal entity, split by internal conflicts. Its small part is advanced, prosperous, powerful; its much bigger part is under-developed, poor, powerless. A nation so divided within itself would be recognized as unstable. A world so divided within itself should likewise be recognized as inherently unstable. And the position is worsening, not improving.[10]

The South Report stresses "instability" rather than illegitimacy, possibly to communicate more easily with adherents of "the realist consensus," who are not inclined to regard normative factors as relevant determinants of international behaviour by sovereign states. Of course, under certain conditions instability flows from illegitimacy, but under other conditions instability is more likely to arise from political efforts to oppose illegitimacy.[11]

It may be wondered why such an effort has been made to substantiate the plausibility of a mere metaphor. But let us reflect upon what it is we acknowledge by this metaphor of apartheid. Even during the most divisive period of East–West tensions there was a consensus at the international level that apartheid in South Africa was morally and legally intolerable; indeed, the UN General Assembly declared that apartheid was an international crime. Sanctions were imposed to reinforce this censure, and may well have been a large part of the explanation for the dramatic repudiation of apartheid by the De Klerk leadership in the early 1990s. What has been criminalized at the global level and repudiated within South Africa is both descriptive of the global political economy in crucial respects and widely accepted as the basis of a legitimate world order, the safeguarding of which is implicitly and explicitly treated both as a central guideline for the foreign policy of the powerful and as grounds for military intervention in the South.

It hardly needs to be argued that such a manner of organizing the world economy is unacceptable to those social forces active in the work of creating a global civil society responsive to the goals earlier set forth. It also follows that the use of state power in the North to preserve such structures is an unacceptable basis upon which to establish world order, that, within the realities of "a global village," what is immoral and illegal when confined to the part is immoral and illegal when extended to the whole. Arguments of necessity and inevitability are no more appropriate here than in relation to torture or slavery. Besides, there are alternatives to global apartheid, and these possibilities are constantly being affirmed by representatives of dominant states and market forces, portraying a future freed from current miseries.

Reliance on the metaphor of apartheid is meant to be provocative, rather than fully explanatory. On a world scale, unlike in South Africa, the racist basis of the distribution of privilege and deprivation is neither formalized nor acknowledged. On the contrary, the international law of human rights, as endorsed by the white North, condemns all forms of racism. Beyond this, to stress race as the explanation of global stratification underestimates the relevance of class, gender, and imperial factors, as well as the related international division of labour based upon market forces. The élites in the North are prepared to collaborate with non-white élites if that facilitates economic gains in the South. Several Asian non-white economies, led by Japan, have broken out of a subordinated economic status as a consequence of building up a competitive edge with respect to goods and services traded in the world economy.

If these critical differences are appreciated, the global apartheid metaphor seems useful. It confronts the moral and political complacency of the North. It demands attention for certain disturbing racial features of perception and practice in recent international political behaviour. It underscores the historical associations that arise as a consequence of Black Africa remaining the poorest and most tormented region of the world. The metaphor of global apartheid, then, represents a warning as well as a provocative line of critique, suggesting the urgency of taking far more serious steps to overcome the North–South cleavage.

The race between environmentalism and environmental degradation

Thirty-five years ago there was virtually no environmental consciousness aside from elements in privileged classes eager to preserve hunting, fishing, and wilderness areas. Also, locally, throughout the industrial revolution there have been concerns about pollution of various kinds, and about the tendencies for market and government to obscure or downplay health hazards. The great Norwegian playwright,

Hendrik Ibsen, wrote a timeless play on this theme, *An Enemy of the People*, at the end of the nineteenth century.

Over the last 20 years there has been an enormous surge of environmental concern. Public attention has ebbed and flowed. An initial wave of concern in the early 1970s focused on "the limits to growth," folding the perception of environmental danger into an overall conviction that industrial civilization was not sustainable given the interplay of resource use, decay of renewable resources (air, water, soil), food supply, and population density.[12] Books written at that time had in common a multidimensional view, but tended to share the conclusion that a civilizational or even species survival crisis was imminent.

This initial mobilization of concern, well orchestrated by the Club of Rome in publicizing its famous study, *The Limits to Growth*, generated a variety of responses. Mainstream industry and academia fought back, contending that the evidence didn't support such prophecies of doom, and that continuing economic growth was indispensable if political stability were to be maintained. The third world reacted suspiciously to environmental alarmism during the 1970s, generally believing that to cut off a growth-based economy at early modernizing stages of development would deny poorer countries their best prospect of escape from the poverty trap. Governments tried, by and large, to mediate between contradictory pressures, expecting to deflect rising populist concerns about environmental quality by sponsoring the UN Conference on the Human Environment in 1972. The official intergovernmental event in Stockholm focused public concern, while leading states resolved to limit their commitments to vague rhetorical assertions and the creation of a small, innocuous bureaucratic entity (the United Nations Environment Programme, UNEP). But the media, the counter-culture of the late 1960s, and a fast-growing network of citizens' associations showed up in Stockholm to initiate a transnational environmental movement that has been expanding ever since.

The 1980s produced two significant developments: a consensus that environmental problems of long range and global scope, especially ozone depletion and global warming, required massive adjustments at a behavioural level in all countries, or else dreadful effects on health and agriculture would occur; a multi-layered environmentalist movement, which gathered real political strength and employed sophisticated and varied tactics, with industry and government eager to establish their own environmentalist credentials. Perhaps the

482

most startling conversion was "the greening of Mrs. Thatcher," expressed by way of Britain's efforts to accelerate the phase-out of chlorofluorocarbons (CFCs) as evidence accumulated that the rate of ozone depletion was faster than even "the alarmists" had earlier predicted.

If one surveys the results of these past two decades, a confusing and disturbing conclusion emerges. Environmental activism has had an extraordinary impact on mainstream politics and on state policy, including the formation of green parties in many countries and rapidly growing budgets and expanding memberships for militant environmental groups. The Brundtland Commission effectively contributed to the formation of a global consensus: the environmental crisis can be managed on behalf of sustainable development, but only if states cooperate as never before on behalf of the general planetary interest, and this will happen only if pollution is understood to encompass poverty, thus placing the economic burdens of adjustment on the richer countries and promising that third world development prospects would not be diminished by efforts at environmental protection. Despite these achievements, by virtually every indicator of environmental quality on a global basis the situation continues to deteriorate at a dangerous rate, with no signs of reversal in sight.

In June 1992, the UNCED (UN Conference on Environment and Development) took place, symbolically located in Brazil, with unprecedented fanfare (153 countries; 1,400 NGOs; 8,000 media representatives) but disappointing tangible achievements – no commitment to reduce carbon dioxide emissions, to preserve rainforests, to eliminate third world debt, or to restrict population growth and consumptive habits, and no willingness to overcome the cumbersomeness of cooperation among states through the establishment of a powerful UN Environmental Protection Agency with revenue-raising and enforcement capabilities and a democratized authority structure that would enable real influence and participation by groups representing global civil society. What was achieved at UNCED is by no means negligible: the Rio Declaration, which contained 27 principles that will provide a framework for environmental protection; a convention on climate change and another one on biodiversity, each signed by 153 countries; the adoption of Agenda 21, which, while not legally binding, is the most elaborate programme for environmental protection ever developed (comprising 40 chapters, 800 pages), and the establishment of a new body called the Sustainable Development Commission. Considerable networking among non-governmental organizations (NGOs) also occurred at Rio to sustain a citizens' global presence in relation to further efforts to promote environmental protection.[13]

At this stage, world order is adrift in relation to the environmental challenge. An impressive response has, to be sure, occurred at all levels, including the state to an extent, but it is a response that falls dangerously short of the multiple and cumulative challenge. There is no evidence that the requisite political will exists in either statist or market settings. Other priorities impinge to keep environmental adjustments at the margins of policy. The prevailing attitude remains dominated by the growth/profits/trade dynamic, possibly accentuated by a prolonged global recession. A Japanese environmental minister captured the persisting mood when he said, "I think we should be growing and growing forever. It's my personal philosophy. Quite often materials, or amounts of materials available, and the degree of happiness have a very strong correlation, so I think the more we have, the better it is."[14]

Many factors are at work, including considerations of time and political habit. Political leaders are not held accountable for adverse impacts deferred to the future; the electoral cycle is not correlated with the time-horizons of response to the most menacing dimensions of the environmental challenge; behavioural adjustment cuts directly against the grain of consumerism, the heart and soul of the capitalist ethos; the collapse of socialist alternatives, at least temporarily, generates a mood of virtual unconditional deference to market forces; even societal concerns emphasize immediate economic pressures – jobs and growth, which seem to create a trade-off between economic and environmental policy objectives; leaders of major states and their citizenry are easily diverted from the complexities and long time-horizons of the environmental challenges. Geopolitics and materialist priorities remain opiates for élites and masses.

The world order dilemma is simple to express, difficult to overcome. States are challenged as never before by global-scale problems, but lack the will to respond; the unevenness of human circumstances generates contradictory images of responsibility for causing the harm and the distribution of the burden of response. States are reluctant to facilitate coordination by establishing effective global governance mechanisms in relation to the environmental agenda. The tragedy of the commons remains tragic!

As with global apartheid, the probabilistic scenarios of environmental decay imply oppressiveness, especially in the form of shifting as much of the burden of environmental decay from North to South (relocating polluting industry – according to Lawrence Summers, the chief economist of the World Bank, "I've always thought that under-populated countries in Africa are vastly *under*-polluted;"[15] siting toxic dumps; exporting harmful pesticides and untested pharmaceuticals). More hopeful scenarios depend upon the greening of global civil society, and its capacity to overcome the modernist preoccupations of a territorially constituted system of world order.[16]

Rethinking the normative architecture of the world order

Every world order system implies a complex normative architecture, partly explicit, partly tacit. For several centuries this architecture reflected the normative dominance of Westphalia logic, which was premised upon the primacy of the sovereign, territorial state. In effect, each state was entitled to exercise supreme authority within its own boundaries, and respect the reciprocal rights of other states to do the same. Modern international law arose out of this premise of formal equality, which included the exclusive authority to participate in diplomatic relations with other states. Sovereignty was interpreted to mean that states were not subject to any legal duties other than those they had voluntarily accepted, or, according to some jurists, those founded on "natural law," which were binding independent of consent by the sovereign.

It is useful to recall that this formalized account of world order expressed a historical disposition to remove the religious affiliation of a political community from international contention. The Peace of Westphalia was, after all, a settlement of religious wars in Europe, known as the Thirty Years' War. The Westphalia approach also reflected the growing influence of secularizing trends in economic and political domains, which wanted both to centralize internal authority at the state level, and to evade the broader sorts of authority claimed and exercised by the Roman Catholic Church in feudal Europe. These secularizing trends were reinforced by developments in scientific thought, especially in the work of Galileo and Newton, reconceptualized as political theory by Thomas Hobbes.[17]

Of course, the Westphalia vision of the world was never descriptive of either normative claims or political reality, and the formulation of a world of equal sovereign states needs to be interpreted as a world order project (that is, a world to be created) and as a mystifying ideology (that is, a juridical masking of inequality).[18] The most subversive conceptual and normative challenges to Westphalian images subsequently arose from revolutionary ideas about reordering the shape of state–society and state–state relations, especially the rights of citizens, the accountability of leaders, and notions of class and racial solidarity. Some of these concerns have been incorporated into the normative framework of world order during recent decades through the developments of the international law of human rights and the adoption of the Nuremberg Principles. These subversive challenges to the core Westphalian notion of territorial supremacy have been endorsed at a formal level by governments acting on behalf of states, and thus do not in a technical sense violate the formal logic of state sovereignty, but their practical effect is to place constraints upon claims of territorial supremacy and sovereign prerogative. And what is most relevant from the perspective of this chapter is that democratizing social forces have been increasingly, if unevenly, effective in their capacity to erode statist forms of oppressive rule.[19]

In this century, the most notable shift in normative theory and practice has probably involved "the move to institutions."[20] First, the League of Nations, then the United Nations, and, last in time but most ambitious in undertaking, the European Union. As will be argued in the next section, this move was both intentionally and inevitably ambiguous, being a gesture in the direction of qualifying sovereignty by deference to an emergent organized world community and a means to extend sovereignty by restricting within the narrowest limits the autonomous role of such institutions and by structuring participation beyond the state in a manner that ensured that only states were allowed membership. Both the League and the UN were largely a response to the failures of traditional diplomacy to prevent the two world wars, and were not regarded as having any significant bearing on the scope of sovereignty except possibly in the war/peace domain. Article 2, para. 7, of the UN Charter confirms this expectation by denying the organization any right to intervene in "domestic jurisdiction" except in the context of a Chapter VII peace and security undertaking.

To a large, yet variable, degree, these institutional developments are best conceived as extensions of Westphalia logic, not as alternatives. Only states are members; the principles of sovereign equality and non-intervention are affirmed; submission of disputes to the World Court is essentially voluntary. International institutions have so far been denied independent funding and have not been permitted to develop their own peace-keeping capabilities.

Yet there is a collective identity – the organized international community – that establishes a presence and performs roles that encroach upon the claims of sovereign rights. Limiting discussion to the United Nations, there is also embodied in the UN Charter an acknowledgement that geopolitics may be more important than sovereign status with respect to the crucial undertaking of collective security. Giving leading states permanent membership and a veto in the Security Council, and confining the General Assembly to a recommendatory role, represent a deliberate choice to give dominant states the authority to decide and the capacity to block. During the Cold War this blocking dimension was continuously evident, confining the UN to the margins of the global peace and security agenda.

With the Cold War over, the Gulf War disclosed both the potentiality and the danger of an effective, unblocked Security Council, providing both apologists and critics grounds for response. The former argue that the Gulf War has finally established the credibility of collective security, the latter contend that the only thing the war established was the extent to which the UN lent its mantle of legitimacy to the geopolitical goals of the United States.

There is another aspect of normative architecture. Latent in existing international law are emancipatory ideas and commitments that await actualization. For instance, Article 28 of the Universal Declaration of Human Rights:

Everyone is entitled to a social and international order in which the rights and freedoms set forth in this Declaration can be fully realized.

Is not this norm a powerful weapon to rely upon in the struggle to expose and transform global apartheid? Such a posture is reinforced by reference to the International Convention on the Suppression and Punishment of the Crime of "Apartheid," especially Article I:

The States Parties to the present Convention declare that *apartheid* is a crime against humanity and that inhuman acts resulting from the policies and practices of apartheid ... are crimes violating the principles of international law, in particular the purposes and principles of the Charter of the United Nations and constituting a serious threat to international peace and security.[21]

Significant here is the fact that states have formally associated themselves, individually and collectively, with the legal conclusion that

487

apartheid is criminal. The distance between criminalizing the part (and by implication defining it as "the other") and acknowledging that the whole resembles the part (and is by implication embodied in "the self") is considerable. For this reason, the metaphor of global apartheid challenges the dynamics of denial that have helped world opinion to ignore correlations of wealth, class, and race on a global scale.

The normative architecture of world order has not been completely static, although the main structures of statism have remained remarkably stable and have retained their centrality. The state has tamed challenges from peace forces that were mounted in the aftermath of world wars and has even weathered the early challenge posed by the alleged incompatibility between the new weaponry of mass destruction and the retention of statist control over war-making. At this time, the most threatening challenges to the perpetuation of statism seem associated with the environmental agenda, although the most consequential may be connected with the globalization of capital and information, causing even powerful states to fail in their efforts to domesticate market forces and the dynamics of mass communication. In relation to these globalizing influences, democratic tendencies are seeking to position themselves in a range of arenas from the very local to the planetary. One aspect of this democratic positioning is associated with the emergence and empowerment of global civil society as a bearer of a hopeful and progressive vision of the future of world order.

A central question being raised at this time is whether statist responses to these new forms of challenge are sufficient, and to what extent these responses are a tribute to the growing significance of global civil society. The resilience of statism over the centuries is certainly remarkable, yet its capacity to adapt behaviourally and ideationally is being tested as never before, and not just from a single direction (world order challenges to Westphalia until the 1970s were almost exclusively motivated by fears about the recurrence of large-scale war).[22] Whether and to what extent the adaptive capabilities of the present framework of world order are sufficient will assuredly be a preoccupying drama in the closing years of this millennium and the opening decade or so of the next, but so will the normative priorities of how the burdens of adjustment are distributed between North and South. The section that follows depicts some central dimensions of this cosmo-drama, which is better understood as a manifold of distinctly experienced cosmo-dramas.[23]

The Westphalian cosmo-dramas

The intention here is to identify several settings in which the state is struggling to adapt. Reducing pressures on its claims to uphold the well-being of its citizenry increasingly requires credible control over aspects of the external setting. Often, of course, this impulse to extend control is a matter of the stronger projecting its power at the expense of the territorial supremacy of the weaker – for instance, carrying on the "drug war" in the supplying countries, while dumping toxic wastes and sub-par pharmaceuticals on those same countries. As the global realities become more integrated, the weaker inevitably hit back, desperation generating such phenomena as terrorist attacks and hordes of economic and political refugees.

What is at stake for the state are matters of legitimacy and competence, which are, of course, connected. Also, these cosmo-dramas often seem irrelevant to the circumstances of vulnerable, stateless peoples or oppressed minorities, who understandably conceive of their political emancipation as a matter of achieving full membership in the Westphalian world of territorial sovereign states with rights of full access to formal, international arenas. For the Palestinians, the Kurds, and the various "nations" of former Yugoslavia, any approximation of Westphalian statehood would be regarded as an occasion for celebration. At the same time, emancipation from ethnic oppression doesn't necessarily imply a Westphalian solution – indigenous peoples increasingly seek what is becoming known as "internal self-determination," that is, accepting the boundaries of an encompassing state but negotiating a reliable social contract that defines autonomous spheres of political activity.[24] Note that, to the extent that internal self-determination arrangements are established, the territorial supremacy of the state is relinquished, and a process of refeudalization/retribalization is initiated, reversing the geometrical neatness of modernist maps of political reality.

While acknowledging that these ethno-nationalist struggles are also challenging the primacy of the state in a variety of ways, as yet largely undiscussed, the focus here is upon the efforts by the state and states to safeguard their keystone roles in "the new world order." There are definite functional linkages with the problematic aspects of the internationalization of the state, as well as the virtual neglect of the main line of normative indictment (global apartheid). Four areas will be considered: market; nature; global governance; and information/popular culture.

489

Market

There are notable efforts by leading states, more or less deliberately, to avoid losing control over market forces. These efforts have been identified in different ways, but most characteristically by stressing the managerial task, as in the phrase "the management of interdependence." The most formalized expression of these mercantilist concerns has been the ritual of an annual economic summit bringing together the heads of state of the seven leading industrial countries in the North, the so-called Group of Seven or G7. Not much tangible policy coordination has been achieved, but these sessions do give form to the claims that the world economy as a whole is being managed by and for the light-skinned minorities in the North without voices from the statist South and without participation by representatives of global civil society.

The more substantive managerial efforts are by way of the General Agreement on Tariffs and Trade (GATT) and international financial institutions. The main objective is to facilitate trade expansion in the face of protectionist pressures that are growing more severe as the struggle sharpens for market shares among the main centres of capital and business. In the present global setting, there is no effective economic hegemon of the sort provided by the United States in the post-1945 period, and hence new mechanisms of coordination and compromise are needed to avoid unleashing a costly cycle of destructive competition resembling the cycle of the 1930s that generated both the Great Depression and the geopolitical drift that ended in strategic warfare. With the increasing complexity of the world economy and the advent of nuclear weaponry, a repetition of this earlier pattern seems totally unacceptable. Even the United States, now the lone superpower, will lose its credentials as leader if it cannot fashion effective global-scale managerial arrangements to avoid the crashing of the world economy. The Uruguay Round of GATT negotiations is taken seriously beyond its obvious substantive effects, symbolizing the degree of managerial capacity. The Trilateral Commission, an initiative of élite business in the North in the mid-1970s, seemed mainly dedicated to circumventing the inward-looking tendencies of the state so as to promote the coordinated interests of outward-looking sectors of capital – the main ideological thrust was to accord primacy to the efficiency of capital and subordinate deference to such internal priorities as welfare, environmental safety, and organized labour.

Another direction of response and adaptation involves ambitious

490

projects of regionalization. Europe has, of course, moved furthest ahead, creating a magnetic field around Brussels that draws many disparate elements toward itself. The state can conceive of this type of regionalization as a means to participate beneficially in the world economy, maximizing the advantages of a big, continental market, while minimizing the threats of competitive operations beyond the region. Yet the magnetic pull of regionalism may homogenize political economy at the state level, making franchise capitalists of us all. Sweden and Finland have been caught up in this regionalist whirlwind, finding no way to uphold their societal living standards except by eroding, and possibly abandoning, the distinctiveness of their own "models" of welfare and development. In this regard, the resilience of statism may also be its deathknell, at least in the sense that one proud claim of Westphalian sovereignty was to be the guardian of economic, political, cultural, and ideational pluralism. In many ways, the 1980s debate in the United Kingdom highlighted the tension between adapting successfully to the globalization of capital by going the way of Brussels and retaining the traditional glories of autonomous statehood at the cost of further economic slippage. The Thatcherite contention was that the Eurofeds are bent on destroying the state to save it![25]

Part of this process of regionalizing the state is to win and retain popular support. Such support is solicited, first of all, by promises of economic reward, but also by assurances that the essential aspects of Westphalian sovereignty will not be jeopardized. Further, the regional framework offers to extend the protection of human rights and to facilitate more effective forms of environmental protection, and even to enlarge democratic space – the Strasbourg dimensions of the European Union. So far, at least, regionalism in the North has turned a blind eye to the global apartheid features of the world economy, and has not pretended to offer any relief in relation to mass poverty in the South; at most, in the case of Europe it has directed its gaze eastwards in relation to Europe and the former Soviet republics or in the case of the United States (North American Free Trade Agreement) it has warily sought to include its Mexican neighbour in plans for trade expansion on a global basis.

Whether or not the European experience succeeds in mediating between statist and globalizing pressures remains to be seen, but it will exert influence elsewhere in the world either as a positive model of adaptation and compromise, or as some sort of failure either because it fails to adapt or because the autonomy of distinct countries

491

is undermined in a manner that produces some sort of populist backlash.

There is another kind of statist response to the dynamics of economic globalization. In a stimulating book, *The Work of Nations*, Robert Reich argues that traditional territorial statism will fail *functionally* because of globalizing market forces, but that what he calls "laissez-faire cosmopolitanism" will fail *normatively* because of its inability to benefit the lower four-fifths of the citizenry in even rich countries. Accordingly, Reich proposes "a third, superior position: a positive economic nationalism in which each nation's citizens take primary responsibility for enhancing the capacities of their countrymen for full and productive lives, but also work with other nations to ensure that these improvements do not come at others' expense."[26] By investing more heavily in frontier skills for successful participation in the world economy, problems of marginalization of the labour force will be minimized. In effect, educational sufficiency takes the place of disintegrating movements of organized labour. Such steps may help reduce the internalization of apartheid within richer countries – a process that is already well under way in North America and Europe, producing racial tension, widening income gaps, urban crime, drug cultures, AIDs, and proto-fascist backlashes.

At the same time, what Reich proposes seems to accept without serious questioning the background structures of global apartheid and unipolar geopolitics. It is a prescription of adaptation with particular relevance to the rich and powerful societies, which face their own serious problems from globalizing pressures.

Nature

The environmental agenda is the greatest potential threat to the viability of the state and of the realist view of world order. Responding to the varying types of environmental decay that are of regional and global scale is complicated by:

- causal factors – finding an agreed explanation for the harm and an adjustment policy;
- cognitive uncertainty – achieving a consensus about the seriousness of the threat;
- temporal dimensions – the degree of urgency, the relationship to political horizons of accountability;
- geographical exposure – the length and height of the coastline, vulnerability to flooding, latitude;

492

- financial responsibility – distributing the adjustment costs, subsidizing the South;
- behavioural impacts – regulating the acquisition and use of cars, restricting reproductive freedom.

From this partial and illustrative listing of factors, the regulatory task of proceeding by way of agreement among sovereign states – that is, voluntary patterns of cooperation and compliance – is daunting. Such complexity is more serious because of the efforts by the North to shift the effects of environmental deterioration to the South to the extent possible, perhaps symbolized by the audacity of the nuclear weapons states engaging in testing in a manner that exposed indigenous peoples of the Pacific to the highest health risks from fallout. In addition, many influential people in the South continue to regard the environmentalist approach as intended to deny their societies the material benefits of modernity.

The resilience of the state is being tested as never before.[27] In certain respects, the specific challenge of and response to ozone depletion provides support for both pessimists and optimists. Pessimists point to the continuing process of depletion, indications of increasing adverse health effects, the revelations that the rate of depletion is considerably higher than earlier feared, and that the danger is in the North as well as the South. A recent *Time* cover story bore an eerie picture of a hole burning in a normal sky with the caption, "VANISHING OZONE – THE DANGER MOVES CLOSER TO HOME."[28] Optimists point to the impressive regulatory response by way of the phase-out of the offending chemicals, the development of commercially viable substitutes that involve no encroachment on consumer uses, the negotiation of an encompassing regulatory treaty supported by all leading states and placing the burden of adjustment cost on countries in the North (the Montreal Protocol of 1986, as strengthened in 1990 and more so subsequently, as overall indications of a constructive response). However the debate is resolved, the evidence supports the view that regulatory efforts have not yet arrested the dynamics of deterioration.[29]

It would seem that the urgency and complexity of the environmental challenge call for a supranational mechanism that has political and financial independence, but only states could provide the resources and the mandate. Their reluctance to move beyond the traditional modes of diplomacy suggests the persistence of the realist mind-set, and the implied limits on regulatory effectiveness – a dependence on consensus, volunteerism, and the absence of enforcement. The envi-

493

ronmental challenge shows, then, both the resilience of statism, including its adaptive impulses, but also the gap between the problems present and the solutions provided.

From a world order perspective, the central issue raised is how further environmental deterioration will affect political behaviour. Given global apartheid, it is likely that some form of "environmental imperialism" will emerge, the rudimentary elements of which are already evident, and that "environmental refugees" will add to the planetary problems of facing human displacement. Anxiety about environmental decay is one of the main causative explanations for the emergence of a global civil society (GCS), and it is the information-disseminating and consciousness-raising activism of the transnational environmental movement that has pushed governments in the leading states as far as they have gone and that has put environmental policy on the mainstream political agenda.[30] The tactical sophistication of some GCS actors has increased impressively, exhibiting a willingness to resist militantly in certain arenas and to collaborate with governments, with international institutions, and even with multinational corporations in others. Japanese officials have called Greenpeace an organization of ecological terrorists because of its peaceful efforts to disrupt whaling on the high seas, while many governments have included Greenpeace and Cousteau Society specialists as advisers at formal meetings intended to administer the Antarctica Treaty regime.

Global governance

In market contexts, distinct corporate pressures are pushing strongly upon governments to coordinate economic policy on a transnational basis. As discussed, this leads under certain conditions to mechanisms of regional governance. Jacques Delors has been emphatic in his insistence that regional economic governance has to extend to other domains, including security and social policy, to be sustainable. In environmental contexts, GCS has generated a variety of pressures to induce a dramatic turnaround by state and business on the significance of the environmental challenge. At the same time, to the extent that regulatory claims entail enforcement authority and mechanisms to ensure autonomy, governments have been reluctant to respond; this reluctance becomes opposition when the environmental imperatives suggest huge taxes on economic operations and deep intrusions upon consumer discretion.

The political foundations for governance remain rudimentary, with renewed hopes being concentrated on strengthening the United Nations. It is notable that the UN, especially its main organs, is completely dominated by states and their formal representatives, with NGOs and GCS perspectives confined to the outer margins of proceedings. Interestingly, both world federalists and geopolitically minded leaders can perceive the UN as a vehicle for their projects. The utopian mind-set perceives the UN as embodying the elements of a nascent world government, while the realist mind-set perceives the UN, especially the Security Council, as a selectively useful framework in relation to regional conflict-resolution, large-scale North-to-South uses of force (as in the Gulf War), and, more recently, a variety of missions to bolster civic order in particular states. The UN has this dual potential, and is inherently ambiguous with respect to progressive world order values, especially in the aftermath of the Cold War.[31]

In an important respect, the UN, as a club of states, is an ideal framework for achieving structural adjustments in response to the erosion of competence at the territorial level of statist authority. In effect, states would delegate their authority outward so as to retain their overall claims to competence and legitimacy. To some extent this has already happened with regard to human rights and environmental regulation. But the retention of capabilities and discretion at the governmental level remains strongly embedded in the realist political consciousness, and is part of the reason it is so difficult for realists to cope with new de-territorializing realities of international life. The various tendencies in GCS are also disabled, however, being sceptical about intergovernmental mechanisms and finding it difficult to mount effective educational and consciousness-raising campaigns. The NGO world is also hampered by the temptations of co-optation (speaking to statist power in a muffled voice so that the powerful will pretend from time to time to listen and heed) and incrementalism (concentrating on tinkering at the margins because the more ambitious requirements for governance are off the political agenda).

There are some signs of change. The Stockholm Initiative on Global Security and Governance was a report issued on 22 April 1991 under the title *Common Responsibility in the 1990s*. It was prepared and endorsed by prominent individuals possessing high degrees of credibility as present or former participants in the formal institutions of governmental authority. Its stress on "global governance" was a definite step towards consciousness-raising about the functional need and political possibility of creating more effective regulatory authority at the global level; it was, perhaps, unduly influenced by both the recourse to and abuse of UN procedures during the Gulf crisis, being issued shortly after the cease-fire. The spirit of the Stockholm Initiative is indicated by the following: "We believe that the genuine common interest in a new global order of cooperation today is such as to rationally motivate nations to build a system of global governance."[32] Invoking "the spirit of San Francisco," the report calls for a process initiated by a global summit along the lines of Bretton Woods and San Francisco, as well as the establishment of an independent international commission on global governance along the lines of the Brandt, Brundtland, and Palme commissions.[33] Such proposals, coming from endorsers who are associated with feasible programmes of global reform, do reveal a certain receptivity by states to a second surge of institution-building, possibly correlated with the turn of the millennium. But they also reveal some dangers, that such initiatives can be diverted by geopolitical pressures and that their implementation, if it happens, will be completely insulated from democratizing forces.

From the GCS perspective, several challenges exist: to evolve ideas about global governance to offset the plans of leading states and dominant market forces; to resist where necessary, to collaborate where possible, while being wary about co-option traps and dogmatic anti-statism. In these regards, the GCS approaches in the human rights and environmental areas provide helpful models. The added difficulty with respect to governance is the absence of concrete occurrences, and the need to operate independently in large, government-controlled, bureaucracies. Several interim approaches might help:

- an emphasis on strengthening international law by concrete undertakings (accepting the compulsory jurisdiction of the World Court, a Comprehensive Test Ban);
- working toward democratizing the procedures within the United Nations itself (giving the South more adequate representation in international institutions; creating "space" for participation by representatives of GCS);
- imposing the discipline of constitutionalism on the UN system, especially the Security Council, as a counter to geopolitics (establishing a Security Council Watch that persuasively documents deviations from the Charter and that reports on "double standards" with respect to implementing Security Council decisions).

Information/popular culture

There are strong reinforcing linkages between the globalization of information/popular culture and the struggle to reshape the world order in the aftermath of the Cold War. At this stage, this dynamic of what might be called "cognitive globalization" is dominated by the United States and is image oriented. Television is the basic technology, establishing post-modern ways of knowing as well as providing the substantive content of the good life. The roles of television are multiple, and can be only hinted at here: facilitating the spread of franchise capitalism, glorifying the American lifestyle, legitimating the claims of geopolitics. These roles, in effect, are top–down expressions of the deep structures of global apartheid, despite a facade of liberal objectivity in relation to state and market.

The impacts of cognitive globalization are speculative, highly differentiated, and by no means fully discernible. One direction was evident during the initial phases of the Gulf War when CNN conveyed a carefully managed presentation of the war to the world, but another direction emerged after the war when the plight of the Iraqi Kurds spoiled the impression of "smart weapons" directed with electronic precision against military targets. Television induces passivity, but it can also serve to convey political experience. Chinese students in 1989 were inspired by the successes of "people power" in the Philippines that they had witnessed on television a few years earlier, but so apparently were the Chinese rulers, who cracked down on the demonstrators in Tiananmen Square and elsewhere. Television brings Disney World, and with it the dangers of "electropop fascism," but it also brings Madonna and others, who, despite commercialism, are mainly delivering subversive and anti-establishment messages of freedom, resistance, openness, empathy for victims, and racial equality.[34] Embodying these messages in the sinews of popular culture exerts great influence on popular attitudes in this TV age, especially given the growing distrust of moralizing politicians in many countries.

Global civil society has also depended on cognitive globalization for its growth and development, but mainly in the service of networking, relying on phone, fax, xerox, and personal computer. The greening of the imagination is the only potent challenge to the Americanized images of the market. Greenpeace has been imaginative in its appeal to visual sensibility, but its fields of operations have not challenged the structures of global apartheid and have questioned the persistence of militarism only in selective, environmentally related settings.[35] To the extent that GCS succeeds in challenging market and state it becomes "news," and plays its own role as an agency of influence on a global scale. Information/popular culture can serve the agenda of democratizing empowerment as well as operate as an instrument of disempowerment.[36] In the end, statism relies on violence in the form of militarized capabilities, whereas GCS relies upon information and conscience (that is, moral sensibility); in this complex respect, cognitive globalization is multiply contested, yielding contradictory interpretations of the future.

A concluding note

The Westphalian cosmo-dramas have been interpreted in relation to successive tidal waves of globalization. The primacy of the territorial state is being challenged as never before, making traditional realist inquiry strike even mainstream observers as increasingly archaic.[37] But the resilience of the state should not be underestimated, especially of those states capable of geopolitical ambitions on a regional and global scale. By aligning with market and other globalizing tendencies, the state may be reconceived, but not superseded, especially so long as market forces depend on militarism. To retain its ascendancy the state must also co-opt environmentalist tensions, and this probably entails strengthening existing structures of global governance, including those associated with the United Nations. Somewhat paradoxically, to retain primacy the state must give up many of its Westphalian attributes, especially those resting upon the claims and practices of territorial sovereignty.[38]

The forces of GCS are mainly oppositional, but as yet have been unable to contest the state seriously either in geopolitical settings of confrontation or with respect to the deep structures of global apartheid. During this formative period of empowerment, premised on the growth of critical social movements, the risks of co-option and demoralization are very high, and will pose a greater threat than direct oppression. For these reasons it is important for social forces that identify with global civil society to fashion their own visions of the future that can compete with the designs and visions being developed in the think-tanks of corporate, financial, media, and geopolitical élites. The advent of globalization need not be catastrophic, but its human prospects depend on struggle, resistance, and vision, which are best guided by an attuned, if diverse, embryonic global civil society.

There is some danger of demonizing state and market forces and of romanticizing an emergent global civil society. Such polarization creates an interpretation of history that is overgeneralized and simplistic. In some settings, state and market forces, especially when challenged by popular movements seeking greater economic and social justice, can serve the cause of human dignity, either by dissolving oppressive structures (the Soviet state under Gorbachev) or by overcoming the absolute depths of poverty, but usually at the cost of disturbing degrees of widening inequality. Global civil society is far from perfect. In some settings, unleashed social forces manifest regressive religious and political tendencies, as in the spread of fascist responses to foreigners, especially refugees, and in relation to societal support for capital punishment or rigid constraints on the reproductive rights of women. A nuanced appreciation of these contradictory patterns of influence will help us prepare for the challenges of a new millennium.

Notes

1. Lester Brown, "The New World Order," in: *State of the World 1991*, New York: Norton, 1991, pp. 3–20, at p. 3.
2. The key document is the 18 February 1992 draft of Defense Guidance for the Fiscal Years 1994–1999, excerpts of which were published in the *New York Times*, 8 March 1992, p. 14.
3. The idea of "global apartheid" was evidently introduced initially by Gernot Kohler as a participant in the World Order Models Project in the early 1970s, included as a selection with that title published in Richard A. Falk, Samuel S. Kim, and Saul H. Mendlovitz, eds., *Toward a Just World Order*, Boulder, Colo.: Westview, 1982, pp. 315–325, but otherwise largely ignored until recently; in the use of the terminology of apartheid, Kohler's earlier analysis is sometimes acknowledged, and at other times an author has apparently hit upon the term independently. In assessing the world economy, Susan George relies on the same metaphor: "The closest political analogy to this post-Cold War world is *apartheid*" (Susan George, "The Debt Question," Paper presented at the 90th Anniversary Nobel Jubilee Symposium, Oslo, Norway, 8 December 1991, p. 16). On the same occasion, without prior coordination, Ali Mazrui built an entire discussion of the role of race and religion in international relations around the metaphor of apartheid, ending his paper with this rhetorical question and response, "Is the twentieth century getting ready to hand over to the 21st century a new legacy of global apartheid? The trends are ominous – but let us hope they are not irreversible" (Ali Mazrui, "Global Apartheid? Race and Religion in the New World Order," pp. 19–20).
4. A Makhijani, *From Global Capitalism to Economic Justice: An Inquiry into the Elimination of Systemic Poverty, Violence and Environmental Destruction in the World Economy*, New York: Apex Press, 1992; for a shorter version of Makhijani's views see his contribution, "Global Apartheid and the Political Economy of War," in: Grace Boggs et al., *Conditions of Peace: An Inquiry*, Washington, D.C.: Expro Press, 1991, pp. 178–222.
5. This quotation and other quotes are from Schelling's contribution to a volume on security after the Cold War, edited by Graham Allison and Gregory F. Treverton, *Rethinking America's Security: Beyond Cold War to New World Order*, New York: Norton, 1992, pp. 196–210, at p. 200.
6. Ibid., p. 200.

7. PPS 23, dated 24 February 1948, classified Top Secret, and entitled "Review of Current Trends: U.S. Foreign Policy," in: Thomas H. Entzold and John Lewis Gaddis, eds., *Documents on American Policy and Strategy, 1945–1950*, New York: Columbia University Press, 1978, pp. 226–228. Kennan's exact words are worth noting: "we have about 50% of the world's wealth but only 6.3% of its population. This disparity is particularly great as between ourselves and the peoples in Asia. Our real task in the coming period is to devise a pattern of relationships which will permit us to maintain this position of disparity without positive detriment to our national security" (pp. 226–227).
8. Daniel J. Kevles, "Some Like It Hot," *New York Review of Books*, 26 March 1992, pp. 31–39, at p. 32; because such a high proportion of expected population increase is concentrated in the poor countries – estimated as in the vicinity of 95 per cent – this ratio of people to resources is likely to grow even more regressive in the years ahead.
9. With the Cold War over, controls by the West over the export of militarily sensitive technology have significantly been refocused on the South, and not only on pariah states such as Libya and North Korea. Even India and Pakistan are explicitly included among states to be concerned about, as well as of course Iran, Iraq, and China. No worry is expressed about any state in the North, despite the many uncertainties in Eastern Europe and among the states formed out of the former Soviet Union. See Asra Q. Nomani, "West Relaxes Rules on Export of Technologies," *Wall Street Journal*, 25 November 1992, p. 2.
10. See *The Challenge to the South: The Report of the South Commission*, Oxford: Oxford University Press, 1990, pp. 1–2.
11. During the UN Security Council Summit of 31 January 1991, bringing together the heads of state of Security Council members on the future of the organ, Nathan Shamuyarira, Foreign Minister of Zimbabwe, made the following comment: "A new world order that does not make a special effort to eliminate poverty and narrow disparities existing between industrialized and developing countries will not be sustainable." Quoted in materials prepared by Juan Somavia concerning the World Summit on Social Development, undated.
12. For representative literature see Edward Goldsmith et al., *Blueprint for Survival*, Boston: Houghton Mifflin, 1972; Donella H. Meadows et al., *The Limits to Growth*, New York: Universe, 1972; Robert L. Heilbroner, *An Inquiry into the Human Prospect*, New York: Norton, 1975; Richard Falk, *This Endangered Planet: Prospects and Proposals for Human Survival*, New York: Random House, 1971; Barry Commoner, *The Closing Circle*, New York: Knopf, 1971.
13. For convenient summaries of the results of the Earth Summit, see Peter M. Haas, Marc A. Levy, and Edward A. Parson, "Appraising the Earth Summit," *Environment* 34 (October 1992): 7–11, 26–33; and Haas, Levy, and Parson, "A Summary of the Major Documents Signed at the Earth Summit and the Global Forum," *Environment* 34 (October 1992): 11–16, 34–36.
14. Quoted by Kevles, op. cit., p. 32.
15. *The Economist*, 7–14 February 1992.
16. These themes are explored in Stephen Toulmin, *Cosmopolis: The Hidden Agenda of Modernity*, New York: Free Press, 1990.
17. For these influences assessed, see ibid.
18. For more detailed considerations on the emergence and structure of statism via Westphalia, see Antonio Cassese, *International Law in a Divided World*, Oxford: Oxford University Press, 1986; Lynn H. Miller, *Global Order: Values and Power in International Politics*, 2nd edn., Boulder, Colo.: Westview Press, 1990, pp. 19–72; R. A. Falk, "The Interplay of Westphalia and Charter Conceptions of the International Legal Order," in: C. E. Black and R. A. Falk, eds., *The Future of the International Legal Order*, Princeton, N.J.: Princeton University Press, vol. 1, 1969, pp. 32–70.
19. For a broad conceptual analysis that richly documents this assertion, see the numerous quality writings by David Held on this theme of the extensions of democracy, and especially his article "Democracy: From city-states to a cosmopolitan order?" in: David Held,

ed., *Prospects for Democracy*, Cambridge: Polity Press, 1993, pp. 13–52. His interpretations have influenced my thinking about the role of democratic theory within and beyond the state in many ways.

20. Cf. suggestive article by David Kennedy, "The Move to Institutions," *Cardozo Law Review* 8 (1987): 841–988.

21. International Convention on the Suppression and Punishment of the Crime of "Apartheid," see Burns H. Weston et al., eds., *Basic Documents in International Law and World Order*, 2nd rev. edn., St Paul, Minn.: West, 1990, pp. 423–425.

22. It is true that some of the more sophisticated proposals for radical restructuring included a concern for equity and human rights, but mainly as deemed necessary to gain the support of governments that were poor. See Grenville Clark and Louis B. Sohn, *World Peace Through World Law*, 3rd edn., Cambridge, Mass.: Harvard University Press, 1966.

23. The cosmo-drama in the singular is an abstraction that is experienced nowhere; what are experienced in a wide array of variations are concrete embodiments of these tensions among contending sources of authority and power; yet both the abstract, by its generalizing account of sameness, and the concrete, by its specifications of difference, inform "the reality." This formulation is indebted to R. B. J. Walker, *One World/Many Worlds*, Boulder, Colo.: Lynne Rienner, 1988; Richard Rorty, *Contingency, Irony, and Solidarity*, Cambridge: Cambridge University Press, 1989.

24. "Captive nations," including Palestine and Kurdistan, seem prepared also to accept autonomy arrangements on an interim basis, in light of their inability to attain Westphalian sovereignty.

25. Invoking, perhaps unfairly, the Viet Nam era image of the American officer who, when asked about the destruction of the village of Ben Suc responded, "We had to destroy it to save it."

26. Robert B. Reich, *The Work of Nations: Preparing Ourselves for 21st Century Capitalism*, New York: Knopf, 1991, p. 311.

27. Arguably nuclear weapons were and are a comparable test, although there is more controversy; realists contend that nuclear weapons produced "the long peace" of the Cold War and that the denuclearization of Europe would be a serious mistake. Compare here John Lewis Gaddis, "The Long Peace: Elements of Stability in the Postwar International System," *International Security* 10 (1986): 99–142, and John Mearsheimer, "Back to the Future: Instability in Europe after the Cold War," *International Security* 15 (1990): 1–56, with Robert Jay Lifton and Richard Falk, *Indefensible Weapons: The Political and Psychological Case Against Nuclearism*, 2nd updated edn., New York: Basic Books, 1992.

28. 17 February 1992, pp. 60–68; a map on p. 64 grades countries according to their degree of contribution on the basis of thousands of metric tons of CFCs and halons released annually.

29. For an account of the regulatory response, see Richard Elliot Benedick, *Ozone Diplomacy: New Direction on Safeguarding the Planet*, Cambridge, Mass.: Harvard University Press, 1991.

30. Andrew Dobson, *Green Political Thought*, London: Unwin Hyman, 1990; also Robert C. Paehlke, *Environmentalism and the Future of Progressive Politics*, New Haven, Conn.: Yale University Press, 1989.

31. During the Cold War, with exceptions, the geopolitical stalemate resulted in the marginalization of the UN in its peace and security roles; whether the ending of the Cold War will mean that peace and security will be refracted by way of a unipolar world remains to be seen; such was the evident US government hope during the Gulf crisis, but the UN is hardly mentioned in the more recent Defense Guidance document, op. cit., note 2.

32. *Common Responsibility in the 1990s*, Stockholm: Prime Minister's Office, 22 April 1991, p. 36.

33. Such a commission, under the joint chairmanship of Ingvar Carlsson and Shridath Ramphal, was established in mid-1992, with a small secretariat located in Geneva.

34. For reflections on cultural tendencies see William Irwin Thompson, *The American Replace-*

501

ment of Nature, New York: Doubleday, 1991; the phrase in the text is his, see pp. 61–62.

35. For instance, emphasizing the damage done to the environment by the tactics of both sides during the Gulf War. See Glen Plant, *Environmental Protection and the Law of War*, London: Belhaven, 1992.

36. The cassette and xerox copier played major empowering roles during the Iranian Revolution, eventually disabling the Shah's formidable military and paramilitary capabilities.

37. See James N. Rosenau, *Turbulence in World Politics: A Theory of Change and Continuity*, Princeton, N.J.: Princeton University Press, 1990.

38. Joseph A. Camilleri and Jim Falk, *The End of Sovereignty? The Politics of a Shrinking and Fragmenting World*, Hants, England: Edward Elgar, 1992.

Contributors and their main publications

Abi-Saab, Georges
Professor of International Law, Graduate Institute of International Studies, Geneva; and member of the International Criminal Tribunal for the former Yugoslavia
International Crises and the Role of Law: The United Nations Operation in the Congo 1960–1964 (Oxford: Oxford University Press, 1978)
The Concept of International Organization (Paris: UNESCO, 1982; French edition, 1981)
"Wars of National Liberation in the Geneva Conventions and Protocols," *Recueil des cours* 165 (1979), no.4

Alger, Chadwick
Mershon Professor of Political Science and Public Policy, Ohio State University
Perceiving, Understanding and Coping with World Relations in Everyday Life (New York: American Forum for Global Education, 1993)

Internationalization from Local Areas: Beyond Inter-State Relations (Tokyo: Nihon Hyoron Sha, 1987; in Japanese)
"The World Relations of Cities: Closing the Gap between Social Science Paradigms and Everyday Human Experience," *International Studies Quarterly* 34 (1990)

Baño, Rodrigo
Professor of Political Sociology, University of Chile; and Senior Researcher, Facultad Latinoamericana de Ciencias Sociales (FLACSO), Santiago
Lo social y lo político (Santiago: Ed. Ainavillo, 1985)
De Augustus a Patricios (Santiago: Ed. Amerinda, 1992)
"Estructura socioeconómica y comportamiento colectivo," co-authored with Enzo Faletto, *Revista de la CEPAL*, no. 50 (1993); English translation in *CEPAL Review*, no. 50

Bertrand, Maurice
Former member of the Joint Inspection

503

Unit of the United Nations; and former Associate Professor of International Relations, Graduate Institute of International Studies, Geneva
The Third Generation World Organization (Dordrecht: Martinus Nijhoff, 1988)
La stratégie suicidaire de l'Occident (Brussels: Bruylant, 1993)
L'ONU (Paris: La Découverte, 1994)

Briones, Leonor M.
Professor, College of Public Administration, University of the Philippines; and President, Freedom from Debt Coalition (a nationwide coalition of over 250 organizations advocating alternative strategies for solving the debt crisis)
Philippine Public Fiscal Administration (National Research Council of the Philippines, 1983)
"Privatization in the Philippines," in *Privatization and Public Enterprise: The Asia Pacific Experience*, ed. Geeta Gouri (Oxford and IBH Publishing Co. India, 1991)

Cox, Robert W.
Professor of Political Science and Social and Political Thought, York University, Toronto
Production, Power and World Order: Social Forces in the Making of History (New York: Columbia University Press, 1987)
"Social Forces, States and World Orders: Beyond International Relations Theory," *Millennium* 10 (1981), no. 2

Falk, Richard A.
Albert G. Milbank Professor of International Law and Practice, Princeton University

Published more than 20 books, of which the most recent are:
Explorations at the Edge of Time: Prospects for World Order (Philadelphia: Temple University Press, 1992)

Revolutionaries and Functionaries: The Dual Face of Terrorism (New York: Dutton, 1991)

Gill, Stephen
Professor of Political Science, York University, Toronto
The Global Political Economy, co-authored with David Law (Baltimore: Johns Hopkins University Press, 1988)
American Hegemony and the Trilateral Commission (Cambridge: Cambridge University Press, 1990)
Gramsci, Historical Materialism and International Relations, ed. (Cambridge: Cambridge University Press, 1993)

Held, David
Professor of Politics and Sociology, Open University
Models of Democracy (Cambridge: Polity Press, 1989)
Political Theory and the Modern State (Cambridge: Polity Press, 1991)
Political Theory Today, ed. (Cambridge: Polity Press, 1991)
Currently writing *The Principle of Autonomy and the Global Order: Foundations of Democracy*

Hettne, Björn
Professor of Peace and Development Studies, Gothenburg (Göteborg) University
Europe: Dimensions of Peace, ed. (London: Zed Books, 1988)
Development Theory and the Three Worlds (London: Longman, 1990)
The New Regionalism: Implications for Development and Peace (Helsinki: WIDER, 1994)

Hitti, Nassif
Special Assistant for Political and Diplomatic Affairs, Cabinet of the Secretary General, League of Arab States; and part-time Professor, American University in Cairo
Theory in International Relations (Beirut: Dar Al-Kitab Al-Arabi, 1985)

The Arab World and the Five Great Powers: A Futuristic Study (Beirut: Center for Arab Studies, 1987)
The League of Arab States: The Influence of International and Regional Factors on the Different Attempts at the Pact's Reforms (Cairo: Center for Futuristic Studies, 1992)

Kamo, Takehiko
Professor of International Politics, Faculty of Law, University of Tokyo
The Vision of International Security (Tokyo: Iwanami Shoten, 1993; in Japanese)
The European Integration (Tokyo: NHK, 1992; in Japanese)
"Changes in the Diplomatic and Strategic Environment in the South-East Asian and Pacific Regions," *Disarmament* (United Nations) XIII (1990)

McGrew, Anthony
Senior Lecturer in Government, Open University
Global Politics, co-authored with Paul Lewis (Cambridge: Polity Press, 1992)
Modernity and Its Futures, ed. (Cambridge: Polity Press, 1992)

Maiguashca, Bice
Co-editor of *Millennium: Journal of International Studies*; and Doctoral Programme in International Relations at the London School of Economics and Political Science

Mittelman, James H.
Professor and Chair, Department of Comparative and Regional Studies, School of International Service, American University
Ideology and Politics in Uganda: From Obote to Amin (Ithaca, N.Y.: Cornell University Press, 1975)
Underdevelopment and the Transition to Socialism: Mozambique and Tanzania (New York: Academic Press, 1981)
Out from Underdevelopment: Prospects for the Third World (London: Macmillan; New York: St. Martin's, 1988)

Mogami, Toshiki
Professor of International Law and Organization, International Christian University, Tokyo
The UNESCO Crisis and World Order (Tokyo: Token Pub., 1987; in Japanese)
"The United Nations System as an Unfinished Revolution," *Alternatives* XV (Spring 1990), no. 2

Sakamoto, Yoshikazu
Professor Emeritus, University of Tokyo; and Senior Research Fellow, Peace Research Institute, International Christian University, Tokyo
Strategic Doctrines and Their Alternatives (New York: Gordon & Breach, 1987)
Asia: Militarization and Regional Conflict, ed. (London: Zed Books; Tokyo: United Nations University, 1988)
International Politics in Global Perspective (Tokyo: Iwanami Shoten, 1990; in Japanese)

Strange, Susan
Professor Emeritus, London School of Economics and Political Science; and Visiting Professor, University of Warwick; Aoyama University; Johns Hopkins Center Bologna
Casino Capitalism (Oxford: Blackwell, 1986)
States and Markets: An Introduction to International Political Economy (London: Frances Pinter, 1988)
Rival States, Rival Firms: Competition for World Market Shares (Cambridge: Cambridge University Press, 1991)

Van der Pijl, Kees
Reader, Department of International Relations, Faculty of Political and Social Sciences, University of Amsterdam
The Making of an Atlantic Ruling Class (London: Verso, 1984)
The Triumph of Neoliberalism, with M.

Fennema (Santa Domingo: Ediciones de Taller, 1987; in Spanish)
"Transnational Relations and Class Strategy," ed., Special issue of *International Journal of Political Economy* 19 (Fall 1989), no. 3

Väyrynen, Raimo
Professor of Government and International Studies, and Director, Joan B. Kroc Institute for International Peace Studies, University of Notre Dame

New Directions in Conflict Theory, ed. (London: Sage, 1991)
Military Industrialization and Economic Development: Theory and Historical Case Studies (Aldershot, England: Dartmouth, 1992)

Zosa, Aileen An. R.
Director, Office of the Executive Secretary, Office of the President, Malacanang, Manila